Proceedings of the 2006

Building Technology Educators' Symposium

August 3-5, 2006

University of Maryland
School of Architecture Planning and Preservation

"A Gathering of Architectural Educators Passionate about Teaching and Technology"

Edited by:

Deborah J. Oakley, R.A., P.E., University of Maryland
Ryan E. Smith, University of Utah

Proceedings of the 2006 Building Technology Educators' Symposium

Editors / Symposium Co-Chairs
Deborah J. Oakley, R.A., P.E., University of Maryland
Ryan E. Smith, University of Utah

Copyright © 2008 retained by each individual paper author
All Rights Reserved

No part of this book may be reproduced or transmitted in any form or other by any means, electronic or mechanical, including photocopying, recording, or by any information storage and retrieval system, without permission in writing from the publisher or paper author.

A Publication of the Building Technology Educators' Society

The mission of the BTES is to promote and publish the best pedagogic practices, relevant research, scholarship, and other creative activity to facilitate student learning, advance innovation, and enhance the status of our disciplines in the profession at large.

The Building Technology Educator's Society, Inc.
c/o Department of Architecture and Interior Design
207 AAS, University of Idaho
Moscow, Idaho 83844-2451
www.BTESonline.org

An Association of Educators Passionate about Teaching Architectural Technology

Library of Congress Cataloging-in-Publication Data

Oakley, Deborah J., 1959- and Smith, Ryan E., 1976- (Editors)
Proceedings of the 2006 Building Technology Educators' Symposium /
    Deborah J. Oakley & Ryan E. Smith, Editors
p. cm.
ISBN 978-0-615-24911-7

Proceedings of the 2006 Building Technology Educators' Symposium

August 3-5, 2006
University of Maryland, School of Architecture Planning and Preservation

**Deborah J. Oakley, R.A., P.E., University of Maryland
and Ryan E. Smith, University of Utah, Editors**

Table of Contents

(Note: Papers in each section are collated in alphabetical order by author)

Introduction 1
    Deborah Oakley, University of Maryland & Ryan Smith, University of Utah

Keynote Address 5
    Edward Allen, Visiting Professor, University of Oregon & MIT

Materials and Construction

Section Introduction: Ethos of Technology – Materials and Construction 13
    Ryan Smith, University of Utah

Design-Build as Technology Coursework 15
    Jason Alread, Iowa State University

XYZ: Horizontal Vertical and Progressive Integration in the Practice Curriculum 21
    Robert Arens & James Doerfler, Cal Poly, San Luis Obispo

Updating the Miesian Curriculum 33
    Tom Brock, Illinois Institute of Technology

The Mechanisms of Surface: The Wall Section Model 45
    Jason Chandler, Florida International University

Capabilities and Limitations of Autodesk Revit in a Construction Technology Course ... 55
    Mike Christenson, University of Minnesota

Building Skins - Design Strategies for Architecture Students 63
    Ulrich Dangel, University of Texas, Austin

Hands-On: The Pedagogy of Design / Build 77
    Jori Erdman, Clemson University

Teaching Construction Details with Color 87
    Craig Griffen, Philadelphia University

Green Roof Design Workshop: A Teaching Model for Connecting Technology to Design 91
    Donald Hunsicker, Michael Fiorillo, Joshua Burdick, Laura Marrero,
    Boston Architectural College

Building [Understanding]: A Systems Approach to Building Information Modeling 105
    Christopher Livingston, Montana State University

Building Skin: Designing in Full-Scale 115
    Kathrina Simonen, California College of the Arts

Specifications and Cost in Architectural Education 121
    Ryan Smith, University of Utah

Indigenous Knowledge, Formal Knowledge, and Technology Teaching 133
    Gil Snyder, James Dicker, Marit Gamberg, University of Wisconsin, Milwaukee

Pattern in Architecture: Explorations of the Digital Modeling and Fabrication Lab 143
    Edgar Stach, University of Tennessee

The WSU Solar Decathlon – Design/Build Lessons 153
    Mat Taylor & T.Duff Bangs,, Washington State University

Ecological Aspects of Teaching of Historic Building Technology in an Architectural
Preservation Curriculum 159
    Irena Wasserman, Israel Institute of Technology

Developing an Ethos of Making 167
    Bruce Wrightsman, University of Colorado / Boulder

Why Brick? A Theoretical Basis for Designing Construction 175
    Barry Yatt, The Catholic University of America

Recycled Walls: A Materials and Methods Project 185
    Paul Zorr, Auburn University

Structures

Section Introduction 191
    Deborah Oakley, University of Maryland

"Do You Own a Hardhat and Safety Boots?": Maximizing Potential Learning
through Construction Case Studies 193
    Terri Meyer Boake, University of Waterloo

Less Is More: A Design-oriented Approach to Teaching Structures in Architecture 205
    Michele Chiuini, Ball State University

A Different Kind of Structures Problem 213
    Robert Dermody, Roger Williams University

Structural Education in Design Build Studios: Questions of Practicality
in Student Design Build Projects 219
    Phil Gallegos, University of Colorado / Boulder

Architect as Form-maker: A Fundamental Approach to Architectural Structures 225
    Dana K. Gulling, Savannah College of Art & Design

Bridging to Convergence: The Multidisciplinary Dilemma for Beginning Architecture Students 237
    Vincent Hui, University of Waterloo

Push/Pull: Bringing Technology and Design Together at Iowa State 243
    Tom Leslie, Iowa State University

Case Studies in Studio-Based Learning 251
    Bruce Lonnman, American University of Sharjah

Daylight Models, Pattern Development & Structure 263
   Kenneth S. MacKay & Shahin Vassigh, University at Buffalo,
   The State University of New York

Structural Harmony and Model Discourse 271
   Ivan Markov, The Chinese University of Hong Kong

A New Kind of Software for Teaching Structural Behavior and Design 279
   Kirk Martini, University of Virginia

Haptic Structures: The Role of Kinesthetic Experience in Structures Education 289
   Deborah Oakley, University of Maryland

Two-Way Structures: Personal Response Devices in Large-Format Structures Lectures.............. 303
   Deborah Oakley, University of Maryland

Designing Building Failures 313
   Jonathan Ochshorn, Cornell University

Seismic Web Site 327
   G. G. Schierle, University of Southern California

The Art of Structure - The Structure of Art 343
   Edgar Stach, University of Tennessee

Designing Structures: Four Exercises Integrating Fundamental Structural Issues
Into Students' Design Processes 355
   Andrea Swartz, Ball State University

Seismic Design Education in U.S. Schools of Architecture 365
   Christine Theodoropoulos, University of Oregon

Building Literacy: The Integration of Building Technology and Design
in an Architecture Curriculum.. 375
   Shahin Vassigh & Kenneth S. MacKay, University at Buffalo,
   The State University of New York

Empathic Vectors 381
   Fredrick H. Zal, Atelier Z

Introduction

Deborah Oakley, University of Maryland
Ryan Smith, University of Utah
Symposium Co-chairs

Background

In the summer of 1996, a group of architectural educators gathered in Milwaukee, Wisconsin, to share their experiences of teaching structures classes to students of architecture. Supported by an ACSA grant, noted educator and author Edward Allen spearheaded the effort and worked with the then ACSA president, Linda Sanders (herself also a structures educator), to plan and publicize the event. Held at the School of Architecture and Urban Planning at the University of Wisconsin, and working with program chair Gil Snyder, the theme of the conference was "Teaching Structural Creativity." An emphasis was placed on sharing various ways to get students involved in the decision-making process and shaping of structural systems, and included great sessions such as "Your Best 20 Minutes of Teaching." Attendees have described it as a fairly informal atmosphere with a number of excellent presentations and discussions of teaching approaches among the approximately forty participants.

While there was great enthusiasm during the event, and a subsequent discussion of forming a follow-on group occurred on the last day, in the end the outcome of the conference was mostly in the ways individual instructors applied the ideas in their own teaching and publications; no further such conferences were held nor any organization ever formed. In the words of Ed Allen, "I think it did a lot of good in freeing up the structures teaching at a few schools, but there was no big breakthrough."

Fast forward many years later. As a new tenure-track structures professor, Deborah Oakley had learned of the Milwaukee event by word of mouth and was very intrigued, particularly as it was in her area of teaching. At the last formally separate ACSA Technology Conference held in Miami Beach in 2004, discussions with Bruce Lonnman of the American University in Sharja, UAE, (who had attended the Milwaukee conference) planted the seed thought about a possible follow-on meeting. Shortly thereafter and unknown to Deborah, Ryan Smith began independently evolving similar thoughts with Edward Allen and Christine Theodoropoulos at the University of Oregon for a gathering of educators focused on materials and construction technology education.

Edward Allen reminds us of the importance of educating architectural students in form-finding versus number-crunching

Upon learning of one another's interests, it immediately seemed obvious that we should merge our efforts and plan an event that would encompass both materials and methods as well as structures education, as we see the link between these two branches of study as being so inherently strong. Our initial email solicitations with other colleagues indicated that there was sufficient pent-up interest in having such a conference that it was worthwhile pursuing. Thus began the planning for what has become this, the Building Technology Educators' Symposium.

In the years since the Milwaukee conference, there have been exciting developments in teaching structural and construction technology by numerous individuals from across the country and internationally. But, aside from the scattered individual connections made at events such as the annual ACSA Meeting, ACADIA, AIA and numerous other conferences, there has been no single gathering point to bring us together for the specific purpose of targeted discussions related to the advancement of teaching the subjects of construction materials and methods and structures. We thus learn of one another's efforts in a piecemeal and somewhat unstructured fashion, our primary exchanges occurring via the *Connector* newsletter. It is therefore the intent of the BTES to bring as many of us as possible together in one place to openly share our insights and advance the state of the art of teaching in these areas more broadly.

Development

When we began our planning for the symposium our initial concern was that interest would be somewhat moderate and few people would attend. Much to our delight, however, the request for proposals brought in an unexpectedly high number of responses and interest. With a projected attendance of nearly seventy, we are delighted that almost one third of all attendees are not even coming as presenters, but simply for the learning and sharing experience. Clearly, the need for a venue to discuss architectural technology is in great demand.

The call for proposals brought in a large number of submissions as well. With over sixty excellent abstracts received, our challenge was not in getting people to submit papers, but in deciding whom to decline. A blind peer review of the abstracts then ensued, with acceptance contingent upon the following criteria: Appropriateness to the symposium theme of building technology pedagogy in architectural education; whether the proposal had the potential to critically stimulate discussion; whether it pushed or challenged conventional pedagogy; and if it was a timely and current issue concerning teaching technology in architecture. The papers that are included in these proceedings and presented during the sessions reflect these criteria.

The University of Maryland School of Architecture, Planning and Preservation, venue for the BTES 2006

The diversity of the papers presented represents a wide range of interests and expertise among technology teaching faculty in schools of architecture. Topics that have been included in the symposium include structures and construction technology theory, technology pedagogical models, technology integrated curricular models, technology teaching tools, design-build education, building enclosures, technology education, and the current hot-button topic everywhere in our industry, Building Information Modeling (BIM).

As an emerging digital technology, Building Information Modeling has continued the discussion of the computer's role in designing and building. New materials and applications of construction provide for more efficient structures, more durable, performance based building systems, and more environmentally sensitive and responsive architecture. Simulation and performance modeling in structures and construction technology will continue to pervade the profession and therefore the role of the educator in technology becomes important in establishing a critical pedagogy. Over the three days of the symposium, discussions will ensue regarding our role as educators in technology teaching and preparation for the constantly changing climate of contemporary architectural practice. Additionally, the symposium is an excellent opportunity to find collaborators for research and teaching projects.

Looking Ahead

The overarching hope of this gathering is to work toward establishing what had been discussed those many years ago in Milwaukee: a long-term academic group interested in teaching and researching architectural technology. The Society of Building Science Educators (SBSE) has met for many years and discussed issues regarding building science in the areas of environmental controls and sustainability. Inasmuch as buildings are not isolated in their design of environmental controls, structures and construction technology as completely independent concerns, we wonder if our potential organization can join in meetings with the SBSE, or possibly become a sub-group to the established organization. We envision proceeds from the BTES being used as seed money for this work, with the potential for creation of a dedicated web site and possible establishment of the existing *Connector* newsletter as our "official" journal. The open discussion to be held on the last day of the symposium will address these questions.

We further see the need for more meetings such as the BTES that will allow for an integral mentoring process to occur between senior and junior faculty throughout the country. As educators, we are not just professional trainers, but mentors, passing between ourselves and on to students a passion for architecture and technology. In the words of Brandeis sociology professor Morrie Schwartz in *Tuesdays With Morrie*,

> *"The way you get meaning into your life is to devote yourself to creating something that gives you purpose and meaning."*

The Connector *newsletter....a possible "official" journal for a Building Technology Educator's Society?*

A final—and we trust not inconsequential—outcome of this symposium is this very collection of proceedings itself. While not a formal textbook, it nonetheless compiles in one volume (and, to the best of our knowledge, for the first time ever) a number of excellent pedagogic approaches to construction and structural technology in architecture. It is hoped that this material may be influential to other educators, particularly those new to teaching students of architecture and others (such as engineers in adjunct positions) unaccustomed to the unique educational challenges of an architectural curriculum.

We are very much looking forward to a stimulating and thought-provoking symposium, and potentially a beginning to an organization with frequent gatherings that bring technology faculty together to continue to adapt teaching pedagogy in architecture that is current, pertinent, and effective. This symposium is structured as an interactive gathering of educators passionate about teaching and architectural technology. As a member of this community of scholars and practitioners, your contributions are invited and welcome to help generate continued intellectual discourse and dissemination of the best contemporary practices in the field we love so well.

Acknowledgements

We would like to thank all of those who have offered their assistance, advice and input in planning this event. First, thanks to Edward Allen who has been a mentor to so many of us and has planted the seed with planning the first of such events 10 years ago. We would also like to thank Christine Theodoropoulos at the University of Oregon, and countless others who provided information on planning technology conferences and suggested themes and programming for the event. Additional thanks to our respective administers who have been supportive of this activity during the process of tenure track. Lastly, we would like to thank the peer reviewers who spent time in reading and commenting on the proposals; without whom the conference would not have been so rich.

Deborah Oakley, R.A., P.E. University of Maryland, Conference Co-Chair

Ryan Smith, University of Utah, Conference Co-Chair

Keynote Address: The Essence of Building Technology

Edward Allen
Visiting Professor, University of Oregon & MIT

I believe that nearly every student of architecture enters school wanting to become broadly competent in the technical areas of architecture.

They want to learn to design structures like Santiago Calatrava, to use materials and invent details like Renzo Piano, to design for energy efficiency like Malcolm Wells.

But by the end of their first year of study, we have educated that desire out of them.

By the end of their first year, they know that studio is fascinating and all-important, and that the technical courses are necessary evils that must somehow be endured.

The end result is that we graduate generation after generation of students who are not broadly competent, and whose design work suffers from a lack of understanding of the technical means by which we build. This is a disaster of major proportions for the quality of the built environment, and a personal tragedy for thousands of individuals.

Why does it happen? The simple answer is that it happens because of "The Gap."

"The Gap," that huge, bottomless gulf that separates the design studios from the technical courses in most schools of architecture.

I believe that The Gap exists because of differences in goals and language between the studios and the technical courses.

In the design studio, the goal is to create good form, and the language is shape.

In the technical courses, the goal is technical competence, and the language is math and science.

In other words, we technical teachers don't have the same goal as the design studios, and we don't speak the same language.

This often means that we communicate poorly, if at all, with the studio teachers.

Our students suffer because they get a disjointed education that fails to bring out the rich potential of building technology as an element of architectural design.

Who is to blame for this situation?

Well, let's be honest: A lot of studio teachers are technically incompetent. They show little concern for integrating technology into the studio setting. It would be easy to blame them for the Gap.

But then we must ask, "How did those studio teachers get to be this way?"

And the answer is that they got their negative attitude toward technology by taking technical courses from people like us.

If we're looking for someone to blame, we need only look in a mirror, because WE, the tech teachers, are to blame for the Gap.

Let me offer an immediate bit of evidence that this is true.

Imagine for a moment a department with no design studios or design teachers.

This department has only technical teachers, and concerns itself with structures, materials, construction, and the like.

There are no studios, and no studio teachers to badmouth the technical courses. Technology is KING.

This is a description of a typical structural engineering or civil engineering department.

Nationwide, a very large proportion of CE and structural engineering departments are faced with a life-or-death crisis.

Enrollments have diminished to the point that many of these departments can't justify their further existence. Students don't want to major in these fields because **the courses are dull**.

In a time when some of the most exciting, innovative structures of all time are being designed and built, structural engineering professors have sucked all the life out of structural design and made it a dry, unattractive option.

They're doing this by teaching only the analytical side of structural engineering, and ignoring the synthetic side. **They have no interest in getting the forms of structures right**. They teach their students to be calculators of structures, not creators of structures

Several years ago, I received a letter from a student at Swarthmore College. He was double majoring in structural engineering and studio art. He wrote:

"In the last four years, I've caught glimpses of how unbelievably interesting structural design can be, but have had very few first-hand experiences...The bridges of Calatrava, Menn, and Maillart make clear that creative decisions can be made in a structural design, but I've never had a professor who embraced these ideals. Last Fall I took a directed reading course in bridge design, but got so bogged down in the American Association of State Highway and Transportation Officials Load and Resistance Factor Design that it wasn't very enjoyable.

"Can you recommend any graduate programs in structural engineering [that would teach the DESIGN of structures]? Any ideas would be greatly appreciated."

I had to advise him to go to Switzerland or Germany. There is nothing for him in this country.

I hear the same complaints from **architecture** students around the country about their technical courses—not just structures but ALL their technical courses. In many schools of architecture, maybe the majority of them, students don't like our courses. **We have serious problems in how and what we teach.**

I think that most of our problems are caused by a lack of clarity about who we are and what we do. We've gone about our business for many years without stepping back to look objectively at what we're doing. A host of important questions have arisen, and they have gone unanswered. Questions like:

What is it that we teach, this subject area called "technology?"

What do technical courses have in common that makes them an identifiable area of the curriculum?

Is it that technical courses all employ mathematics? Or that they are all based on science?

Do we teach building science? Building engineering? Building technology? What is the difference between science and engineering and technology, anyway?

What is our purpose? Is it to furnish technical support to the design studios? Or is it perhaps to teach students what they need to know to pass the Architectural Registration Examination? Do we have a mission that is independent of the studios and the ARE?

These questions can be summed up in one big, important question: WHAT IS the ESSENCE of building technology?

What is the essence of building technology? What is most essential to our teaching? This question becomes more and more important as we are yanked in new directions by building information modeling, "green" architecture, design for the physically challenged, computer graphics, computer algorithms and simulations, computer-driven cutting machinery, and 3-D photorealistic modeling.

What is the essence of building technology? It's crucial to know the answer to this question as we are forced again and again to yield space in the curriculum to new intruders such as social factors and architectural theory. We need to know who we are, what our essential business is, and why it's important, so that we can assert ourselves and explain our mission in our schools.

I've concluded that the essence of building technology is not mathematics. It's not science. It's not engineering. It's not preparation for the Architectural Registration Exam.

These things may play important roles in our teaching of building technology, but they are not the essence.

The essence of building technology, the concern that should be the primary focus of all our courses, is GETTING THE FORM RIGHT.

Yes, you heard me right. I said that the essence of building technology is getting the form right. **Get the form right, and the rest is easy.**

Let's consider some examples that demonstrate why this is so.

Think about acoustics. What's the least expensive, most effective way to isolate a noisy room from a quiet one? It's to form the building in such a way that the two rooms are remote from one another. If they're adjacent, we can employ a whole arsenal of products and strategies to reduce noise transmission between the rooms. It will cost a bundle, and the result will never be as satisfactory as it would have been if we had formed the building so that one room was at one end of it and one at the other end. A good solution to the problem is a matter of getting the form right. **Get the form right, and the rest is easy.**

Still thinking about acoustics, the design of a theater or concert hall is above all a formal problem. Make the room a bad shape, and you're faced with poor hearing conditions and increased expense for remediation. **Get the shape of the room right, and the rest is easy and economical.**

Think about HVAC. If we want to make a building comfortable to inhabit and economical to heat and cool, the most powerful parts of the solution are formal ones: Put the building on a sheltered part of the site, orient it properly with respect to sun and wind, and get its massing right. Give it the right kinds and the right quantity of windows in the right places. Use thermal insulation and thermal mass intelligently. Plant trees in the right locations. The math and science become trivial if these formal decisions are made well. **Get the form right, and the rest is easy.**

Think about materials and methods of construction, and architectural detailing. Once again, getting the form right is important above all. Put movement joints where they are needed. Use rainscreen configurations in the wall and window details. Simplify the details to make them easier and more economical to build. All these are formal decisions. **Get the form right, and the rest is easy.**

Daylighting design is mainly about form. Window orientations, room proportions, positions and dimensions of reflecting surfaces such as light shelves, reflectances of surfaces, distances of visual tasks from windows. **Make these formal decisions right, and the rest is easy.**

And yes, structures is mainly about form. Funicular form is the key to the creation of efficient, beautiful longspan structures. Proper material and system selection, good bay layouts, and good proportioning and shaping of members are the essence of creating building framing of the more ordinary type. Good massing is a vital ingredient of seismic design with regard to reducing torsional forces and preventing pounding of one building mass upon another. Lateral force resistance is largely a matter of putting shear walls, wind trusses, and rigid connections in the right places. Mathematics? **Get the form of a structure right, and rule-of-thumb calculations done in the designer's head will be so close to final values that the serious math is largely a formality.**

All the best structural engineers have cautioned against overemphasizing mathematics in structural design. The great Swiss bridge engineer Christian Menn has written:

"Over the last fifty years engineers have paid a great deal of attention to detailed and precise mathematical calculations, especially of stresses. We realize now that reinforcement concepts, construction methods, and details such as waterproofing, drainage, joints, and bearings are even more important than 'accurate' calculations. But as attention shifts back and forth between calculations and construction, the one constant imperative is the need to give form to structure."[1]

And as my colleague and mentor Waclaw Zalewski has said to me, "A structural engineer who is preoccupied with mathematics is like a tennis player who watches the scoreboard and not the ball."

If structures is not so much about mathematics, is it science? The great structural engineer Ove Arup once wrote,

"Engineering is not science. Science studies particular events to find general laws. Engineering design makes use of these laws to solve particular problems. In this it is more closely related to art or craft; as in art, its problems are underdefined, there are many solutions, good, bad or indifferent. This is a creative activity, involving imagination, intuition and deliberate choice."[2]

Think about your own structures course. Does it involve Arup's imagination, intuition, and deliberate choice? What about Menn's reinforcement concepts, construction methods, and details? And did you notice Menn's emphasis on giving form to structure?

In the traditional structures sequence that is still taught at far too many schools of architecture, we teach students to check beam and column sizes, but we don't teach them how to make a building frame out of those beams and columns, how to provide lateral load resistance in that frame, how to detail the structure, how to integrate structure with architecture, how to create opportunities for the structure of a building to become a feature of its architecture.

In other words, we don't teach students to do the things that the best architects know how to do with building structures. We teach them instead a nonfunctional subset of the mathematics that an engineer uses to check member sizes. It makes no sense.

What does make sense in ALL technical areas is to teach students to get the form right. Creating appropriate form is the essence of building technology. But too few of us have figured this out. Driven, perhaps, by an obsolete definition of technology as having to do with math and science, we tend to teach what is mathematical about our subject, or what is scientific, rather than what is essential.

The one area of building technology that has bridged the gap is ECS, environmental control systems. Decades ago, a few inspired individuals, including Jeff Cook, Ralph Knowles, and John Reynolds, began to change the entire direction of teaching in this field. Dull, useless courses that had concentrated on sizing pipes and ducts became vibrant, active courses that concentrate on the relationship between building form, comfort, and energy flows. Students found the field fascinating and relevant. More and more of them became teachers in the field. An ECS teachers' organization, the Society of Building Science Educators, was founded to facilitate the sharing of ideas and teaching materials. You'll find throughout these teaching materials that the emphasis is on getting the form of the building right. Get the form right, and the rest is easy.

Curiously absent from our technical curricula is the subject of architectural detailing. Detailing is absolutely essential to the architect. It's our language, our sole means of turning design ideas into built reality. When working with a team of professionals on a large project, detailing is the one technical area, the ONLY technical area, in which the architect is expected to be THE expert. But only a handful of schools teach architectural detailing. We persist in teaching bits and pieces of the expertise of other professionals such as structural engineers, but we don't teach our own field of expertise, detailing. Go figure.

There are so many ways to go wrong in teaching a technical course.

One of those ways I've already mentioned: It's teaching what is mathematical about the subject, or what is scientific. Most of the important aspects of every one of our fields are neither mathematical nor scientific. They are largely formal. They are also concerned with things like craft, efficiency of assembly, and appearance.

Another way to go wrong is to slide off into the history or philosophy of a technical area, and neglect the technics themselves. It's nice to know what Heidegger said about laying bricks, but not as nice as really understanding bricklaying and how to use it in one's buildings.

Another way to go wrong is to each only what the computer can do. This is wrong so many ways that I don't know where to start, so I'll mention just two:

1. There is no direct correlation between what people have written software to do, and what really needs to be taught.

2. To teach use of a computer is more often than not to teach in a way that obscures the process.

The worst mistake one can make is to teach only what students need to know to pass the ARE. This strategy is based on the assumption that technology is irrelevant to the making of architecture, and that all we need do is to learn enough to pass the examination, after which we can forget about it. This is an inexcusable attitude.

As new tools and approaches such as BIM (Building Information Modeling) are brought to market, it is unwise to be in a hurry to restructure our technical courses around them. Getting the form right is still priority #1. By all means, we should teach BIM, but we must not lose sight of the essence of building technology as we do so.

To this point, I've been largely negative, telling you what's wrong with much of our teaching. Now I'll shift to the positive, and give you some ideas about how we can do better.

The right way to teach building technology students is to teach how to use technology to get the forms of their buildings right.

Teach them to do this in the context of design problems, either big ones they are given in studio, or smaller ones that you give in your technical class.

This is project-based learning. It has several advantages:

Students like to design. They'll generally put more effort and care into an integrated technical design project than into an abstract problem set.

Students learn that solving technical problems as part of a design process can be fun, and can contribute to the quality of the architecture.

Information and techniques learned in the context of solving a design problem stick in the mind longer and better,

1. Because the student knows why they are important, and

2. They are learned in a meaningful context, not in the abstract. This makes them more useful to the student in the long run as natural aspects of the student's personal approach to design.

Given the opportunity, students often turn out more interesting designs in their technical classes than they do in their design studios. They learn in this way that physical constraints on form can be liberating. And they get good portfolio material as a by-product.

Ideally, we would teach all of our technical courses in the design studio, because the studio is set up to teach the making of good form through project-driven learning Practically, we can do this only some of the time at best. But what we can do is offer secondary studios that are designed to teach technical content, but carry fewer credits than primary studios.

Or we can bring the studio into the classroom, as Patrick Tripeny has done at Utah, with design-relevant teaching and creative exercises given as homework.

Some of you are thinking, "Good grief, I can't cover my subject area now. How can I possibly add in all this design activity?"

To this I say, why try to cover your field? It's impossible—every field of knowledge is far too big to cover in a term. Furthermore, I've discovered that most of the technology I learned beyond the bare principles became obsolete within 10-15 years anyway.

What has served me well since graduation has been that I learned how to educate myself in each field over time.

Don't try to cover your field. It's better to seek to UNCOVER a portion of the field for your students, and teach them how to learn the rest for themselves. This should free up enough class time to engage some design projects.

To bring together the main points of what I've said, we have excavated a huge gap between our technical subjects and the architectural design studios. This has led to irreparable harm to the cause of good architecture. We have to fill this gap, and we must do it NOW.

We can fill the gap by realizing that the essence of any technical field is getting the form right.

This brings us to a crucial realization: Getting the form right is also what the traditional architectural design studios are all about.

This means that we can all be speaking the same language and sharing similar goals.

Suddenly, it's no longer the techies on one side of The Gap talking math and science, and the touchy-feely design teachers on the other side talking form. The whole faculty is now on the same solid piece of ground, talking about getting the form right.

This means that we can cooperate with the studio teachers and not work at cross purposes.

This means that our students can become better designers.

And this means that the quality of our buildings can get better and better in the years ahead.

All this can happen if we realize that building technology is not so much about math and science as it is about getting the form right.

Once you get the form right, the rest is easy.

Notes

[1] Christian Menn, quoted by David P. Billington in Robert Maillart and the Art of Reinforced Concrete. Cambridge, MIT Press, 1990, p. x.

[2] Ove Arup, Ove Arup & Partners, 1946-1986, London, Academy Editions, 1986, p.9.

Materials and Construction: Section Introduction

Ryan E. Smith
University of Utah, College of Architecture + Planning

chan-ge verb

1 to pass from one form, state, or level to another

2 to give up (something) and take something else in return

Related Words: better, improve; deteriorate, worsen

Material innovations being developed and adopted in the building industry are emerging at a dizzying pace. The architecture cultural fetish with materials is likewise unprecedented with shows like the MoMA's "Mutant Materials" and books such as T-ransmaterial by Blaine Brownell.[1] On the construction side, innovations in virtual building simulation are allowing for increased collaboration between key stakeholders in a building project. This technology, known as building information modeling or BIM, has proved to be able to create unprecedented forms and holds promise for performance based design and construction.

These technological innovations can summed up in one word - CHANGE. As Webster indicates, change can imply either an improvement or a worsening effect. Change as a result of innovation often is not a respecter of values, meaning, or ethics. In materials and construction innovation, there is a hesitancy to check change against ethics; in the name of progress. In a constantly changing building culture the academy must provide an ethical base and foster a conscience in the architecture profession.

Ethos of Technology

As change continues forward with innovative materials and information modeling practices for design and construction the role of the architect is in constant flux, one that is difficult for practitioners to understand, much less for faculty of architecture. As we will never be able to keep up with the constant change in innovation of materials and construction, educators in the academy must determine to provide primarily to students a set of core values that work to give meaning and purpose to technology in architecture.

The papers in this section deal with varying topics related to materials and construction technology teaching and research. The topics include: technology theory, integrated design, pedagogical methods, BIM and education, design/build and fabrication education, and enclosures education. Each paper is unique, timely, and considers or proposes an area of architectural education that is in need of questioning, reworking, or sustaining. The common theme in the papers, is an underlying importance to instill within students values an ethic concerning the making of buildings. This is the ideology that as educators we can pass on to students so that although architecture will be increasingly different and innovative tomorrow, it can also increasingly have an ethical dimension.

[1] Brownell, Blaine, Transmaterial: A Catalog of Materials that Redefine our Physical World, Princeton Architectural Press 2006.

Design-Build as Technology Coursework:

A hands-on approach to discovering where design, technology and community service meet.

Jason Alread, AIA, LEED AP
Iowa State University

In the spring of 2004 I was presented with a request, "Would you teach a class this summer on building technologies to the first year graduate students?" The essence of this sounds simple enough, aside from the outrageously short time frame to prepare. The key here was to get the most out of a beginning building technology course that was offered in a short time frame when no one (including myself) wanted to be in a lecture hall.

Figure 1. The Tower

Our graduate program shifted focus in 2002 with the appointment of a new director, Clare Cardinal Pett, and as a group the graduate faculty determined it was appropriate to completely overhaul the curriculum. The result was a three-pronged "new core" curriculum for the first four semesters of our three-year program. Rather than divide coursework into separate lectures, this "new core" takes advantage of our relatively small enrollment to provide integrated classwork that is entirely studio and seminar-based. While design studio remains a focal element of each semester, it is joined by equally weighted courses in culture and Sci-Tech. Most architectural students note that there is a tendency to favor studio coursework heavily over other classes, resulting in a last minute or nuisance approach to completing non-studio assignments. This is due in part to the proportionately larger number of credit hours for studio, but also to a frequent disconnect felt by students between studio work and technology courses. The shift to 5 credit hour blocks in Sci-Tech is paralleled by both Culture and Studio also being 5 credit courses. Thus we emphasize the equality of the three areas and work as equal partners in the educational process. The result is a fifteen credit-hour term divided equally into three lobes, emphasizing the interaction between the traditional 'corners' of architectural education—design, culture, and technology. To emphasize this integration, all three courses are taught in the studio, where for two weeks the students construct an operable seminar space as their first assignment. fig. 2 No separate classes are taught during this time and all graduate faculty participate to assist in the critique and assembly of this seminar 'room', which provides for group discussions, pin-ups and digital presentations.

Figure 2. The first seminar space "the birch hut"

The results of our initial design build course segments are remarkable, varied, and bring forward much reflection on how it might have been done differently with what the students subsequently learn in their first year. Because the projects are rebuilt indoors every year by variously skilled labor they tend to have a temporary characteristic that favors the quality of space more than technical skill or craft. The development of the summer course intended to address how the assembly of a project was linked to its core conceptual intentions, which required a more permanent use than the seminar space. The first two semesters of Sci-Tech address many aspects of assembly in the seminar format with examples, field trips, and laboratories, however, there is always the struggle to get to integration of a complete project. Extending this thinking into the planning of the summer technologies course, we determined that the class should connect the students to as many aspects of making a building as possible. This went beyond the normal issues of design / documentation / construction and into client relations, governmental bureaucracy, and community service. The course planning became a search for an ideal situation to bring these opportunities together. This was seen as an ideal situation for design-build, but not as a design studio.

We arrived at a project that I had begun 3 years earlier for a youth bicycling organization in Des Moines, Iowa. The original project had resulted in a bicycle motocross track at a public park in an underserved and disadvantaged part of the city. *fig.3*

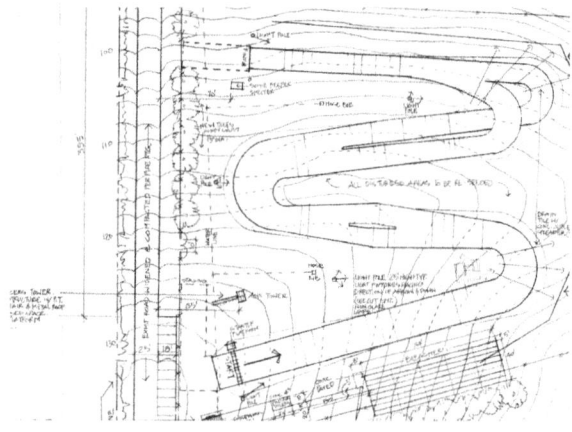

Figure 3. Site plan of the track

The track is run by the principal of the city's high school for troubled teens, a Miss Kittie Weston-Knauer. Her pedagogy rests on the ability to get kids involved in activities that they see as worthwhile. The track has been a pet project of hers for years, and at 57 years of age she is the oldest nationally ranked female bicycle motocross racer in the country. Simply put, Kitty is both tough and able to accomplish whatever she puts her mind to. Needless to say no one says no to Kitty, ever. She eventually always gets what she wants. In this case she wanted a tower, a place to announce the progress of races and an icon for the track. I was unaware of it at the time, but as soon as we approached her about the possibility of working with her group on a project we were already fully committed to building this tower. This was in April. Preliminary drawings had been done previously for the tower and the students would be asked to develop the project from schematic design through construction – the focus of the course would be less on the origin and ownership of the design and more on refinement, documentation and construction. *fig. 4*

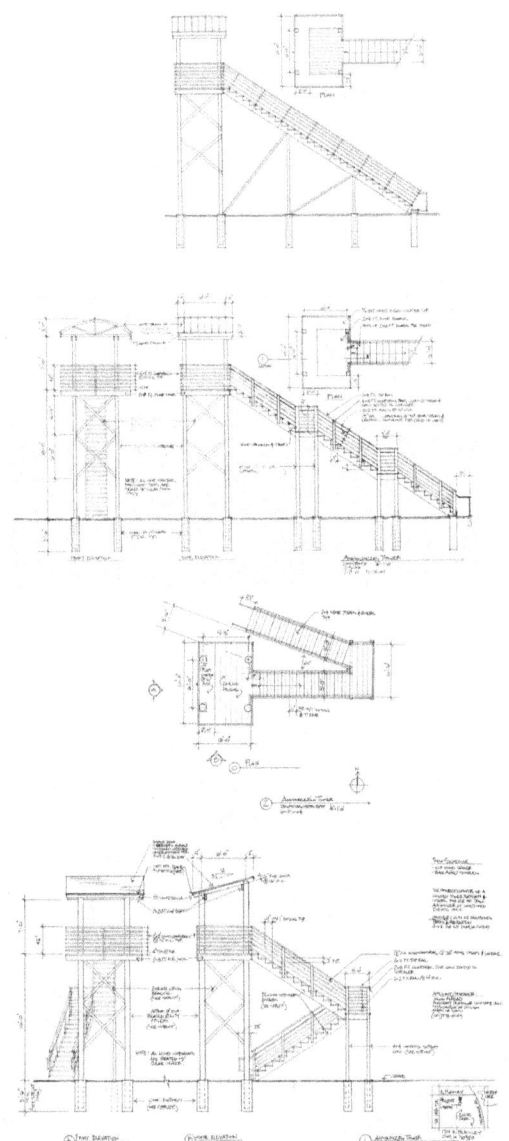

Figure 4. Preliminary and final drawings

In order to accomplish the task at hand, a coalition of people needed to be assembled. A primary concern was that we had no funding available from the university and none forthcoming. The students were enlisted in this challenge well before the class began.

We convened a design charrette with volunteers from the track and arrived at a more refined design proposal. Next we generated a parts list and began asking for donations to assist the construction. This proved to be rather effective as our cause touched on many aspects of the communities concern. We were also fortunate to have a local structural engineer donate services for the completion of the design and requirements for a building permit. Each early phase of the project was run by the students completely outside of the confines of the course – it was now late May and class wouldn't start for another month. We still had a major concern, which was how to get structural columns for a 30-foot high tower. These would be a huge expense and require heavy equipment to set in place. We would be unable to schedule a pre-application meeting at the building department until we figured out how to hold the project aloft.

Our structural engineer, sensing our anxiety about how to proceed, recommended we call a friend at the power company who might be able to find some utility poles for us. This seemed to be a potential problem due to the coal-tar creosote used as a the wood preservative, but we were assured due to the outdoor nature of the construction that it would be acceptable. An additional inducement was that they would be free. The building code official signed off on our permit with this clearly noted and we breathed a collective sigh of relief. Moments like these were a valuable part of the educational process, as certain unknown factors in construction always cause tension, possible changes and relief at positive resolution. The process at this point was going quite well. We had met with the city building official, plan and zoning department representative, user groups, and the structural engineer for very typical push and pull meetings, with the students deciding which compromises to make and which battles to take on. Additional unnecessary drawings were made, more meetings occurred, and generally the transition from drawing to structure was as friction filled, frustrating, and difficult as normal. This was part of the process I can't imagine having taught any other way, no description or case study could have illuminated how much other participants in the building process affect design.

By the first day of class we had final construction drawings, structural drawings, a building permit, most of our lumber, fasteners, all the concrete we wanted, nine anxious students, one concerned faculty, four large foundation holes, and four 40-foot long thousand pound utility poles. We arranged with the parent of a rider to bring a line servicing truck to the site after work to set the poles. The assembly of the entire tower was somewhat crude, only basic tools were used and we relied on some intuitive skills for connections. Two unintended lessons came to light as we proceeded. The first was that even though faculty may have spent significant time in construction administration and even fieldwork, architects are not necessarily good contractors. My own limited skills became apparent quickly, and it was some effort to turn these debacles of scheduling or poor planning into useful instruction. One particularly difficult case was placing foundations for a stair landing. We used an 18" diameter hand-held auger to dig foundation holes and it was very time consuming work. After digging and placing columns it was determined that the holes were in the wrong location. Losing this day of work was part of the process of checking and double checking layout, but it took some convincing to simply fill-in the holes and start over. The inclination by the architecture students was to change the design to accommodate the work done. This impulse is common in construction, but after a discussion of whether we would have allowed it if someone else was doing the work we decided to stay with the original design.

The other lesson learned was that structural consultants are much easier to negotiate with when they're being paid. Our foundation drawings indicated four 48" square foundations, four feet deep each with extensive rebar patterns. *fig.5*

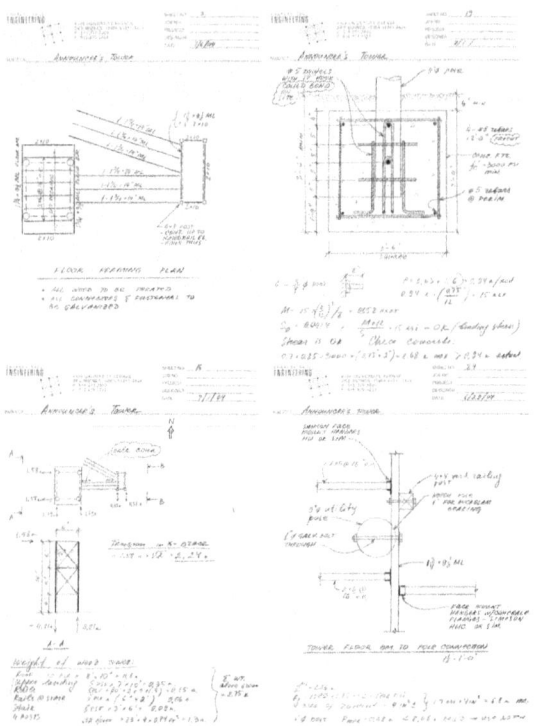

Figure 5. Structural drawings

This looked excessive on the drawings, but was unbelievably difficult to execute in the field with our 18" hand-held auger into hard clay. The engineer, however, was taking the liability for stamping the drawings on his own free time and under his insurance premium. He understandably declined to reconsider the design and we managed to construct it as drawn. Part of the teaching process required looking for ways to illuminate the give and take parts of the procedure as it happened. This is something like teaching design studio, where there is little scripted response, but more extreme as very serious problems could potentially derail the course entirely. This, of course, is what nearly happened next.

The day after the utility poles went in we tied the rebar and called for the foundation inspection. *fig.6*

Figure 6. The basic structure

Figure 7. The assembly process

The inspector arrived to tell us that utility poles were not allowed in building construction due to the restriction in using creosote wood treatment (typical of indoor construction). He recommended we switch to a different type of structure. Keep in mind that four 40-foot long poles are now erected and braced with all rebar in place. We indicated that the plan review had not thought this was a problem, but he replied that it was his call not theirs. While friction in the process was a necessary part of the pedagogical intent of the course, this was a bit extreme. A combination of the obvious difficulty this caused, some educationally valuable moments of applied field negotiation skills, woeful looks by the students and kids at the track, plus our engineer's assurances that this was overkill pushed us past the inspection. At this point we were able to concentrate on the process of craft in building the tower. *fig.7*

The community came out daily to assist in construction and the interaction was immensely gratifying. I was aware that we would not completely finish by the end of the course, and waited to see how the students would respond when the project was no longer about a grade and became truly community service. Everyone showed-up the day after class in full work gear with no questions asked. We finished our work in the first week of August. *fig.8*

Figure 8. The finished project

The tower has generated a much stronger bond between the students and the community, with both parties gaining a better appreciation for what they are capable of. Learning in relation to the technical goals of the class has been very effective and much more thorough than lecturing. Design-build appears to be better suited to teaching technology in relationship to design than it is as design studio. This comes from design authorship at the conceptual level being removed from the process, no egos are damaged or stoked at who's project it is. There has been no dissatisfaction at working as a team to solve common problems and developmental stages of the process are seen as design opportunities. Also, the hands-on collaborative process as a service project offers a much more comprehensive learning experience. There were, however, issues that make the class difficult to sustain. Finding an appropriate project with the correct time frame is extremely time consuming and unpredictable. A slight slip in the schedule can make the project unworkable. Budgetary concerns are also problematic, however, after the first success and associated press we have been able to more effectively lobby the university for funding. Overall, the trade off between the difficulties of preparing lectures versus managing a construction project might favor the predictability (and relative ease) of class time. The construction projects are immensely more challenging to teach and require excessive commitments of time for both faculty and students; however, the benefits of this model cannot be ignored. The advantages of hands-on learning have left a durable impact on subsequent work of the students, with detailing, assembly, and materiality interwoven into the conceptual underpinnings of most of the later studio projects, along with a deepened concern for the value of benefiting the community. This has ultimately met the broad learning goals of our integrated graduate program and we plan to offer this model of a summer community service design/build for the foreseeable future.

xyz: Horizontal, Vertical and Progressive Integration in the Practice Curriculum

Robert Arens and James Doerfler
California Polytechnic State University at San Luis Obispo

Unless an architect is able to listen to people and understand them, he may simply become someone who creates architecture for his own fame and self-glorification, instead of doing the real work he has to do... An architect must be a craftsman. Of course any tools will do. These days the tools might include a computer, an experimental model, and mathematics. However it is still craftsmanship – the work of someone who does not separate the work of the mind from the work of the hand. It involves a circular process that draws you from an idea to a drawing, from a drawing to an experiment, from an experiment to a construction, and from construction back to an idea again. For me this cycle is fundamental to creative work. Unfortunately, many have come to accept each of these steps as independent...(1)

Renzo Piano

Introduction

One of the toughest challenges facing educators of building technology is its successful integration into a broader architecture curriculum. How can discussions of building technology be concentrated enough to allow for the necessary focus on critical technical issues, while avoiding technology's isolation from other architectural issues? This presentation addresses how two faculty members at Cal Poly are attempting to answer this question with four new courses that are integrated horizontally, vertically and progressively within the curriculum.

Central to our our efforts is a shared interest in the merging of design and making. In the best work there is no separation between design and construction; rather they inform each other. The process of making buildings is an interactive continuum among several disciplinary strands on which every architectural curriculum is based. To define them separately denies a holistic approach to the creation of a building, whether in academia or the real world. It is our interest and goal to contribute to an inter-strand or interdisciplinary environment in which the students may glean information to inform their process, a comprehensive approach. This approach opens the content of a building technology curriculum to embrace the multifaceted nature of the architectural profession. While our concentration for our classes is building technology, we also embrace and present issues that overlap with the Design studio, History and Theory and Professional Practice areas.

Observations

We arrived at Cal Poly at the same time with the same mission: to rethink the building technology courses (traditionally referred to at Cal Poly as Practice) with an eye toward better integration of technology topics in design studio work. At Cal Poly, Practice classes address a spectrum of technology topics. These topics include sustainability, building technology, materiality, the history and theory of technology and building processes. With fresh eyes we examined the entire curriculum and considered the various approaches to its implementation. Based on our analysis we made several key observations:

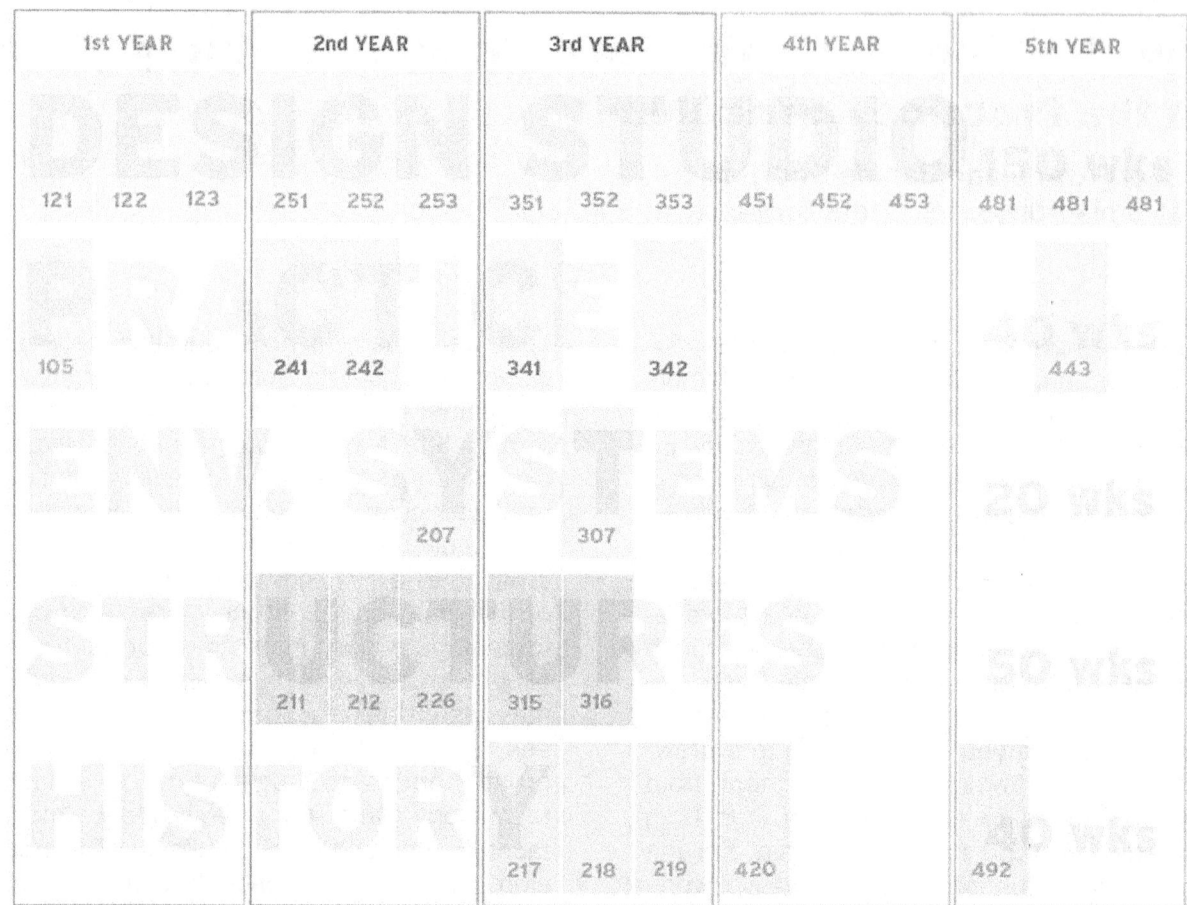

Figure 1. Overview of the major strands of Cal Poly's curriculum.

1. In terms of Design, the studios, even in fundamental years, are not highly coordinated. Objectives are achieved through highly individualized projects crafted by instructors with a wide-range of interests and backgrounds.

2. General design principles are taught well into second year with building design addressed relatively late in the curriculum, usually at the end of second year.

3. In terms of History, survey courses are taught in third year although design and technical discussions of historical precedents take place regularly in second year.

4. In terms of Practice, the present curricular model devotes considerable time to courses addressing technical issues. Although we recognize that this polytechnic model unfortunately biases technology over the humanities, it nevertheless provides ample time to focus on distinct technical topics on structures, environmental systems and construction.

5. The current format of Practice courses, i.e. two one-hour lectures and two two-hour labs per week, had great potential not only as an effective way to communicate technical topics, but also to integrate these topics into design studio. The existing

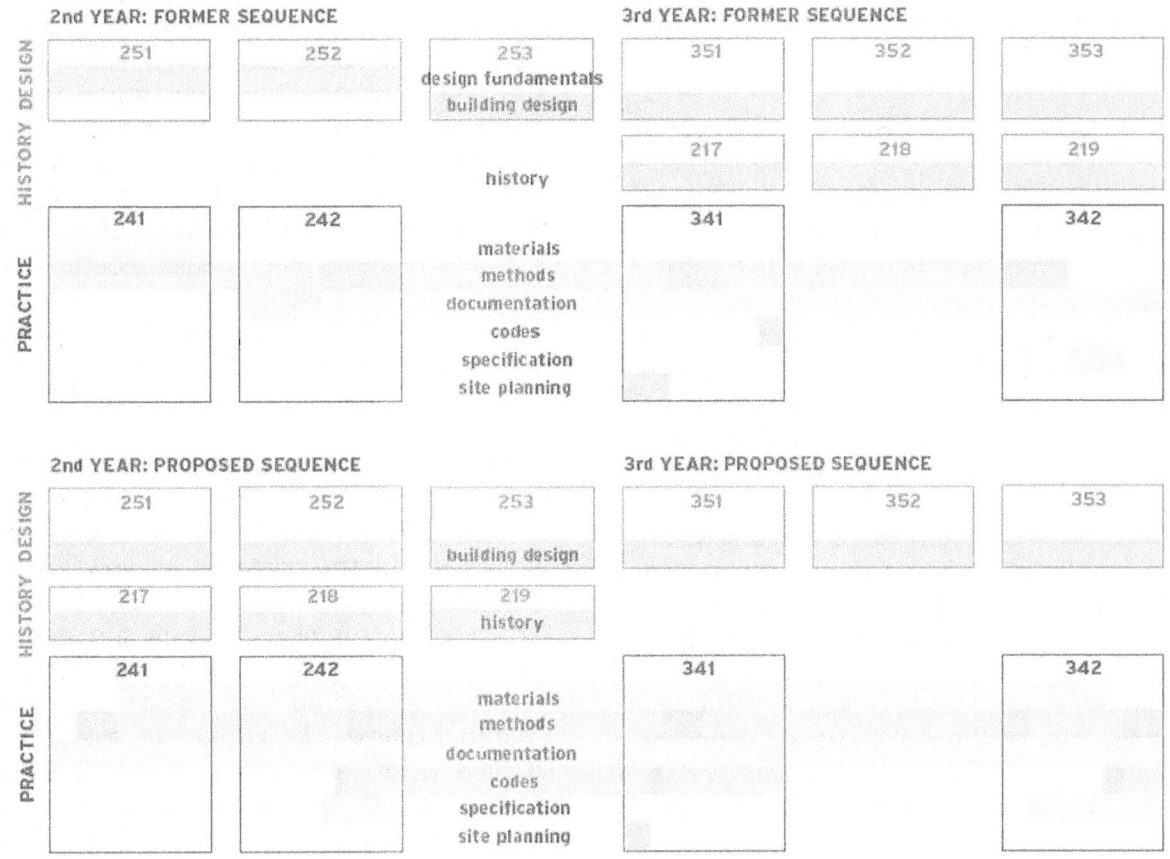

Figure 2. Horizontal and vertical integration of Practice themes.

content of the courses and coordination between the lectures, the labs and the design studios did not take full advantage of this situation.

Recommendations

Based on our observations we made several recommendations to the department's faculty regarding the sequencing of courses and their content.

1. In terms of Design, introduce basic building design issues in the first rather than third quarter of second year to allow for a more integrated relationship between practice and design.

2. In terms of History, move the three-course survey sequence to second year to allow for greater reinforcement of design, social and technical aspects of historical precedents.

3. In terms of Practice lectures, re-format the sequence to avoid isolation of topics and develop the material from general to specific across courses and between years of the curriculum. To be effective, topics need to be carefully sequenced and reinforced over the two-year period that they're taught. We recommend building in an appropriate level of overlap and reinforcement to develop a deeper understanding of technology topics by students.

4. In terms of Practice labs, develop appropriate but flexible frameworks for integration of technology into Design studios. Given the individualistic approach to Design studio at Cal Poly, we recommend that instructors be provided clear learning objectives that can be achieved through a wide range of ap-

proaches rather than highly coordinated projects.

The Practice Strategy

Practice courses at Cal Poly could previously be characterized as being segmented into basic materials and methods of construction in the quarter one, a focused discussion of Type V construction and working drawings in the quarter two, focused discussion of construction types, site planning and codes in quarter three, and focused discussion of construction systems and specifications in quarter four. This type of segmentation encouraged a disconnection between Practice and Design due to the difficulty with crafting studio projects to address narrowly focused technology topics.

Given the opportunity to rethink the Practice courses, we concluded that the themes of materials, methods, documentation, codes, specifications and site planning were sound, but the sequence in which they are introduced and discussed could be refined. With an eye towards the integration of Practice with Design we re-sequenced the six themes to align them with learning objectives and NAAB criteria for second and third year studios. We also attempted to introduce multiple themes in each course, allowing introductory or general aspects to be addressed early in the sequence and more advance or specific aspects in later courses. This dual strategy of alignment and multiplicity, we reasoned, would not only parallel the increasing complexity that occurs in the design studio sequence, but also allow an appropriate level of reiteration and reinforcement of Practice issues.

Once the six Practice themes were aligned to the approximate content of the Design studio, the content for the Practice lectures and labs could be developed. The increasing complexity of Design studio projects through second and third year made for a natural fit for the primary content. In the progression of complexity, second year Design studio begins with single cell frame construction and by third year the Design studio projects progress to multi-storey construction systems. Given our previous experience in teaching building technology and Design studios we essentially needed to make an educated guess, based on the ten-week quarter and schedule of the Design studio, the appropriate content for each of the Practice classes and devise an initial strategy to get the Design studio faculty to embrace a coordinated approach to the labs.

At the same time we began to discuss the opportunity we had to create a woven curriculum with the four Practice classes and labs. We had an interest in refining the sequential content of the courses so not only did they horizontally relate to the design studios within a given quarter, and they also vertically related to each other from one year to the next. The six themes provided a starting point from which to compare our approaches to the lecture content, aside from of the details of the content. This made for a very broad, multi-strand examination of certain aspects of building technology. By opening the structure of the Practice courses to a thematic strategy we have the opportunity to present the facts and details of "how" something is put together as is typical of building technology, and we can also discuss the "why" of the architectural decision making process.

Second Year Practice: ARCH 241 and ARCH 242

Second year is an exciting time to work with students. They are urgently ready to make architecture while at the same time completely naïve about doing so. By teaching building science at this level, each of us is responsible for introducing young, impressionable students to architectural technology. It is therefore imperative to establish a holistic method for approaching technology that prevents it from being isolated from design and other salient issues.

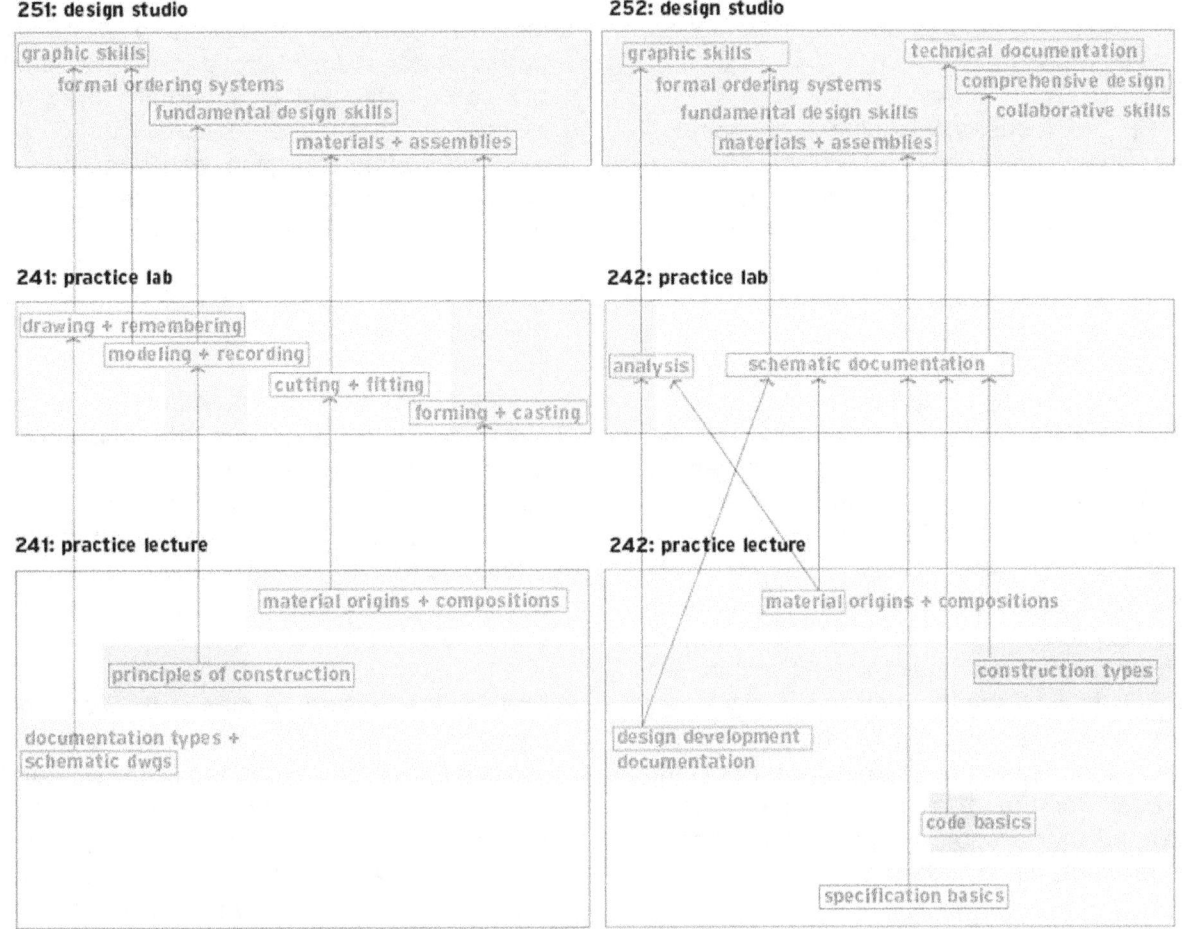

Figure 2. Progressive integation of Design and Practice themes in second-year courses.

At this stage of their development students need help translating quantitative aspects of their math and physics prerequisites into architectural issues, but is equally important to communicate these issues in qualitative terms.

The strategy for second-year Practice content is to rigorously approach materials and technical documentation, briefly introduce building codes and specifications, and build a strong, if basic understanding of construction types. Knowledge and proficiency in these areas will transfer to design studio through lab projects and will prepare students for third-year practice.

The first course, ARCH 241, focuses on the origins, composition, properties and production of materials but underpins it with discussions of documentation and principles of construction. These three themes and their sequence serve to reinforce NAAB criteria being addressed in design studio, namely graphic skills, fundamental design skills, and materials and assemblies. All three themes carry forward into the second quarter and are developed further in subsequent courses.

Lab projects in the first quarter are outlines intended to reinforce both practice and design issues and allow flexibility on the part of individual lab instructors. The emphasis is placed on processes of making that can be integrated into design projects or expanded as stand alone projects conducted in Practice Lab. The projects are Drawing and Remembering, Modeling and Recording, Cutting, Finishing and Fitting, and Sculpting, Forming and Casting.

ARCH 242 focuses on methods of construction while continuing discussions of documentation and materials begun in ARCH 241. Additionally, building codes and specifications are introduced in order to prepare students for discussions of construction systems and types. This sequence is designed to reinforce to NAAB criteria being addressed in design studio, namely graphic skills, materials and assemblies, technical documentation, and comprehensive design. All four themes carry forward and are developed further in ARCH 341.

The lab project for the second quarter is outlined as a set of design development drawings of a residential-scaled project. As in ARCH 241 the project descriptions are written to allow flexibility on the part of individual lab instructors. If an existing building is used for the main project, it is recommended that a short, graphic design analysis precede the drawing set.

ARCH 241

Although the major focus of ARCH 241 is on materials, the course begins with discussions of documentation and methods. These two themes provide both a context and a vocabulary or language with which to consider materials.

Discussions on documentation begin with an overview of the stages of architectural projects and the wide-ranging structure of design teams, intended to establish the necessity for a clear, commonly held, graphic language of construction. Schematic drawings eventually become the focus of fall quarter since they are most relevant to the level of complexity in second-year Design projects.

The lab project associated with documentation, Drawing and Remembering, can be expanded into a stand-alone exercise by lab instructors or integrated into a studio project. An example of the stand alone approach asks students to generate a small, but coordinated set of schematic drawings of their childhood home consisting of site plan, floor plan, roof plan, sections and elevations. Students are challenged to give dimensions and apply drawing conventions to a building they haven't designed, but nevertheless hold dearly in the recesses of their mind's eye.

Another precursor to materials is the discussion of the principles of construction. Issues such as strength and deformation, stability and movement, thermal transfer and insulation, water and moisture migration and, sustainability, are discussed in detail as technical factors that must be considered in the material selection process.

The lab project associated with the principles of construction, Modeling and Recording, can be expanded into a stand-alone project or related to a studio project. An example of the stand alone approach asks students to study the solar characteristics of their childhood home in its exact location. Students obtain the solar altitudes and azimuths then graphically translate this data into shade and shadow for morning and afternoon on the solstices. Shade and shadow are plotted in plan and elevation, then recorded in pen and ink.

The material taxonomies addressed in ARCH 241 are wood, stone, fired clay materials, cementitious materials, concrete and metals. Guiding the discussion of each are the composition, origins, properties and production of each material. Examples from ancient to contemporary periods are used to illustrate the evolution in production and construction methods applied to each material in response to changes in technology, sustainability economics and aesthetics.

Two lab projects are outlined to explore materials. The first, Cutting, Finishing and Fitting requires students to work directly with wood by building a functional object in full-scale. The emphasis is on the basics of woodworking: cutting, sanding, finishing and fitting the wood components by hand so as to develop a deeper personal understanding of the material before moving onto more sophisticated manipulations. One approach to this project is based on the furniture designs of Gerrit Rietveld the De Stijl architect. Students are asked to research Rietveld's Krat Series in which proposed simple, inexpensive furniture for the mass market that could be assembled at home by the average person. Students choose one of the Krat designs and reproduce it as accurately as possible; the only variation allowed being the stain used for the selected work. Although the designs are simple, the objectives are profound: building well with one's hands at full-scale to actualize something that can be tested, and enjoyed, by the user.

The second lab project, Sculpting, Forming and Casting, asks students to explore the variety of cementitious materials suitable for moving an object from a positive state to a negative state and back again. One approach to this project is based on the imaginary landscapes of Isamu Noguchi, designs he envisioned, studied in wax models and eventually cast in bronze. Students researched Noguchi and his work, chose one of the landscapes, modeled it in plasticine clay, cast a plaster mold of the maquette, then cast a final model in plaster. In this and the Rietveld project students learned valuable lessons in making and materiality that can be indirectly bridged to their Design studios. In the the process they also gained exposure to two eminent twentieth century designers whose work will appear again in their history courses.

ARCH 242

ARCH 242 focuses on basic construction methods while expanding the discussion of documentation, continuing the examination of materials, and introducing students to building codes and specifications.

Building on discussions of schematic drawings in the preceding course, ARCH 242 focuses on design development drawings. Although working drawings and specifications are briefly discussed for context, the emphasis in this course, is on those drawings situated between design phase and working drawings phase. A thorough understanding of this type of drawing, developed in lecture and reinforced in lab, will prepare students to communicate their design and technical intentions in subsequent studios.

The discussion of materials in the second quarter focuses on the taxonomies of glass, plastics, composites and coatings. As with earlier discussions, the emphasis is on the composition, origins, properties and production of each material with examples being drawn mainly from the contemporary period. When this discussion concludes, students are expected to have a basic understanding of a broad palette of architectural materials as well as an awareness of the fast pace at which new materials are entering the field in both conventional and novel ways. The CSI format is introduced as a way to classify the wide, ever expanding range of materials and their performance characteristics.

As another precursor to methods, codes are introduced and discussed. The history of codes, types of codes, governing bodies, the trend towards performance codes, and approaches to basic code analysis are briefly discussed.

When methods begin to be discussed in the middle of the course, students are required to shift from dissecting materials (necessary for a thorough understanding) to constructing components of those same materials (now possible with the knowledge of constituent parts). The components are discussed as construction types which in turn can become the tectonic vocabulary used for design projects.

The discussion of construction types is grounded with basic tectonic relationships: between form and enclosure, between enclosure and structure, between bearing wall and frame construction, and between monolithic and composite construction. Specific topics are foundation types in wood, masonry and concrete; bearing wall types in wood, masonry and concrete; frame construction types in wood, concrete and steel; bracing strategies for frames; and the roles of cladding for roofs, floors and walls are discussed.

The major lab project for the second quarter is to generate a set of design development drawings for a modest-size, residential scale building that may or may not be an original design of the student. The emphasis of this project is on communicating and co-ordinating architectural (i.e. aesthetic and technical) intentions at a minimum of four scales ranging from the scale of the site to the scale of a detail. The drawing set should include site plan, floor plans, roof plan, sections, elevations, wall sections and details. If the project is based on an existing building, it is recommended that a short design analysis precede the design documentation stage.

One approach to this project is based on *The New American House* series which presents over 100 residential designs from the years 1985-2002. The authors present sufficient information for students to extrapolate the architect's design and technical intentions. Students choose one of the houses and analyze the technical means by which design intentions were achieved. They then create an abridged but well-coordinated set of drawings that employ the appropriate graphic and organizational conventions for the design development stage. The analysis and drawings together serve as a fitting example of comprehensive design, one of the key NAAB criteria in their design studios.

Third Year Practice: ARCH 341 and ARCH 342

The increase in number and complexity of the NAAB criteria from second year to third year suggests that the nature of the lab projects must also become more complex and comprehensive. Two longer projects, one based upon independent research, the other directly related to the Design project reflect this need for a comprehensive approach.

The first third year class, ARCH 341, includes lectures which ask the students to be able to have insight into the motivations and theories of individual architects and development of building systems, and to discuss the relationship of construction and architectural theory in the 20th Century in a holistic way. The critical readings introduce a student to a broader range of concepts regarding architectural theory in regards to construction, systems and the architects motivation for deciding on a given material or construction method. The readings often stray from the topics of the lectures, but relate to an overall view of construction theory and methodology. The readings also provide a critical voice to compare to the intent of the project or where the project might be located in a continuum.

Sustainability is inherent to a contemporary design strategy. As such, it should not be an area of separate study. The inclusion of sustainability in the third year Practice course curriculum is part of the presentation of all material. Brief considerations of sustainable issues are included in the historical discussion projects as early as the Crystal Palace, in which the manufacturer leased the materials for the building with the intention to reuse the iron. The nature of prefabrication and systems being sustainable approaches to produce buildings is also discussed. The second class in third year introduces sustainable topics such as green specifications, LEED certification, double skin facades, green roofs and a ways of

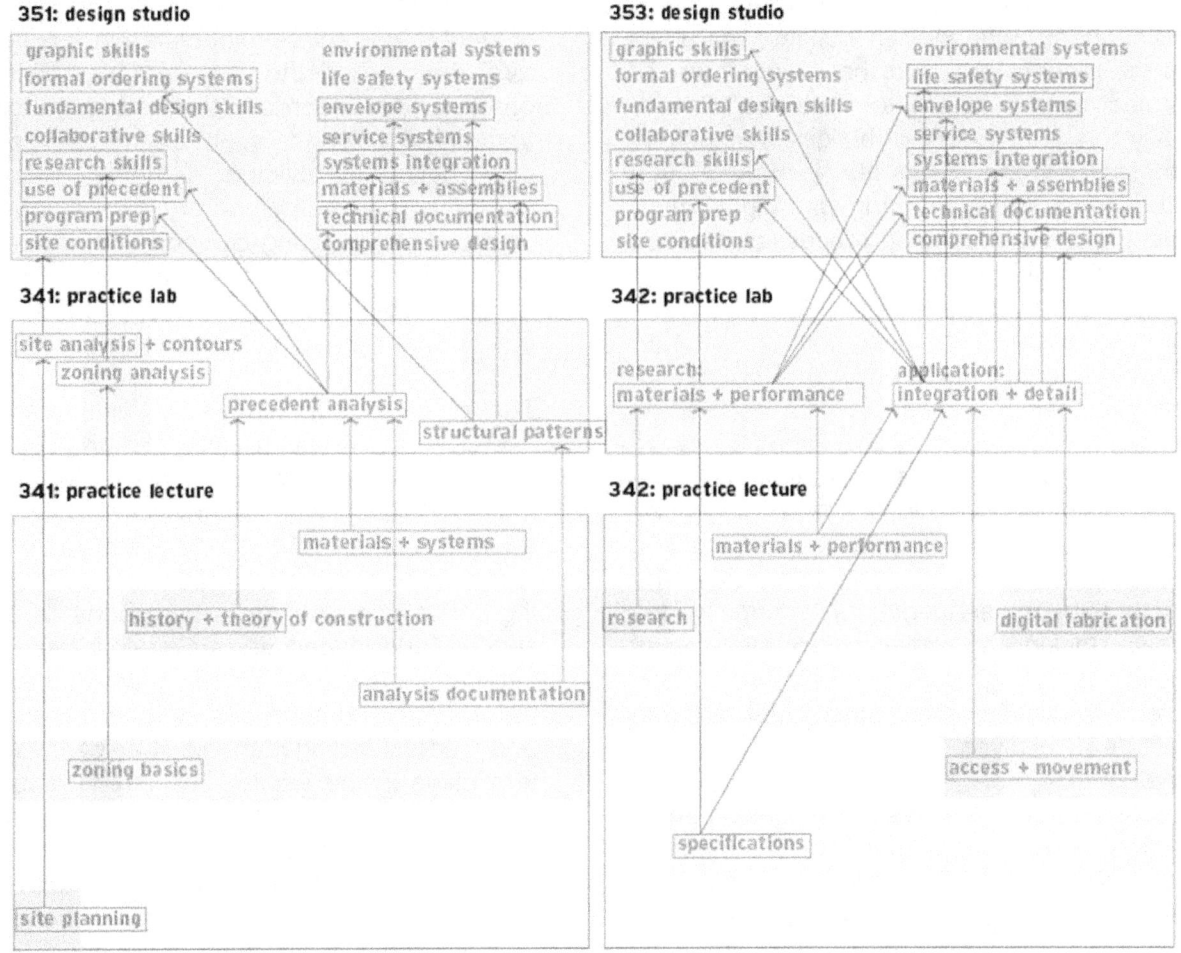

Figure 2. Progressive integation of Design and Practice themes in third-year courses.

harnessing solar energy with integral systems.

ARCH 341 focuses on the themes of methods and materials using the history of construction, material and systems, and includeds a module on site planning. Included in this class is overview of codes, with an emphasis on zoning issues relating to site planning. The lab projects elaborate on the themes of documentation and specification and reinforce and tie together many of the NAAB criteria.

ARCH 342 focuses on the themes of materials and methods with detailed presentations on the use of various materials in building envelopes. This is supported by with modules on specifications and codes, which address the necessity of research and performance in building envelopes. The lab projects engage the students in independent research as well as applying knowledge gained in the lectures and research to their Design projects. These lab projects are aimed particularly to fulfill the comprehensive NAAB criteria.

ARCH 341

The content of the lectures in the first quarter of third-year follows two streams. A historical and theoretical stream presents the development of systems and prefabricated components, changes in building materials in the modern era, and the development of project teams to create buildings. Essentially this is a history of building technology beginning in the 1840's during the Industrial Revolution and concluding with digital modeling and manufacturing processes as seen currently with the work of Frank Gehry. The analysis of systems and components in larger scale buildings also connects to the same concept presented in ARCH 242, for smaller scale buildings.

The other stream is the presentation of various building technology topics beginning with site planning, foundations, zoning and development controls, and later, after the history theory sequence of lectures winds down, looking at contemporary systems of buildings using various materials, steel, concrete etc. The concept which all of these lectures revolves around is "why?" The methodology of "why" an architect would choose to use the system is described in historical terms and then in contemporary technology terms. The student gains an understanding of the role played by the development of contemporary building materials and how these new materials influenced the development of 20th Century architectural theory.

The building typology for the third year classes is commercial or public buildings, typically three stories or higher. The complexity of construction for this scale of buildings lends itself to discussions of systems and prefabrication. The overall themes for ARCH 341 are precedent and analysis. In both the history and the technology streams the lectures present in-depth discussions of projects and buildings. A series of case studies are used to illustrate the design process, technical development, the use of new materials and construction process. This introduces students to the design and construction of complex buildings and to materiality through detailed precedent and analysis studies.

Another goal of this class is to introduce the student to current developments in architectural design and the construction industry, particularly in regards to technology transfer and digital tools in relation to fabrication and construction of building elements. This is germane to a contemporary discussion of prefabricated building components and systems. Again, precedent and analysis is used to study the changing nature of materials and construction in a contemporary setting.

The lab projects for ARCH 341 include short exercises to reinforce site design issues, zoning issues and structural patterning. The major lab project is a multi-week building analysis project. The building analysis project is an in depth examination of real buildings. The examination is by means of dissection, and inspection of systems, identifying each system as an assembly, locating the primary components of each system, and understanding the role that each system plays in the whole. The intention is to place buildings in comparison to each other and into the larger context of issues relating to current buildings as they relate to the real world. The lab instructors develop the projects during the quarter with consultation. They will be presented to the lab in the form of three-dimensional drawings and/or models, which explain the systems separately and in relation to each other. The sources of information used to develop these comparisons are professional journals, the construction documents, visits to actual buildings and interviews with people involved in the design or maintenance of the chosen examples. The intention to develop in students the tools to critically evaluate, analyze and question the built environment that surrounds them.

ARCH 342

The second third year Practice class, ARCH 342, explores the materiality of the building envelope and associated structural systems and how it relates to performance and buildability. The increase in understanding of architectural issues required by the student to choose materials appropriate for a design, provide details and performance information is linked to a design development process. The focus in this class is primarily on the building envelope. The content of the lectures includes information on building envelope performance, material performance, detailing, universal access and egress, and stair and people moving systems. Guest lecturers are also brought in for various presentations including; the Architecture Librarian to discuss research skills, an accredited LEED architect, a sales representative from Vistawall discussing curtain wall systems, and a consultant for Building Information Modeling.

The overall themes for ARCH 342 are the issues of research and performance. This is reinforced across almost all topics that are covered in lecture. Research is stressed as something that architects are required to do. And how important research of codes, materials, specifications and details is to develop a building. Linked with research is understanding the performance of these elements. Performance applies to how materials behave as well as the achievement of the life safety systems of a building. This will be reinforced through the students researching and developing their own cladding system relating to their projects in design studio.

The lab projects for ARCH 342 are intended to guide the student to develop research and detailing skills that will inform them in the design development process. The first project is structured to integrate research methods, developing specifications and performance issues of materials. The second project directly integrates with the design studio and requires both a general understanding of the performance of the project relating to codes, structure and egress, as well as a detailed understanding of the cladding system used to enclose the project. The student will design, coordinate and document the decision making process of design, details, specifications and performance of these systems in three dimensions. These projects will be coordinated with the design studio to provide an enriched learning experience across the discipline strands in the architecture program.

The goal of ARCH 342 is to help students become active and thoughtful researchers capable of managing independent investigative study.

Challenges

After completing the first year of this Practice curriculum we would like to pause and critically reflect upon the challenges that still exist in developing this coursework. While there are successes, further improvements can be made in both the lectures and the labs. The following is a summary of these thoughts:

1. The inherited Practice class structure of lecture and lab, i.e. two one-hour lectures and two two-hour labs per week, Is a positive aspect of the curriculum, which we would like to use to the best possible advantage. This structure allows for the coordination of the lab to the Design studio.

2. One of the most difficult coordination issues is the coordination of Practice lectures relating to Design. The nature of having eight to ten different studios and projects coordinated with the Practice lectures is almost insoluble.

3. We would also strengthen the integration with the Environmental Control Systems (ECS) classes. Some aspects of ECS are reinforced in the third year Practice classes, but currently these aspects are coincidental to the discussions of material performance.

4. The theme of site planning is the only theme that is also a topic. It is the exception to the thematic strategy. The importance of site planning as a topic, and the reinforcing of connections of the environmental topics covered in second year ECS is something that must be developed.

5. The coordination of projects for Practice labs will need more refinement. In place is a series of flexible projects intended to allow interpretation by Practice and Design faculty, although there is lingering reluctance to adopt them. The creation of longer projects which require research and single-session applied exercises might be more adaptable. Another possibility is to only define learning outcomes and allow instructors devise their own strategies for achieving them.

7. It is necessary to continue the development of reference materials, technology texts, critical readings and contemporary journal articles that are applicable to the lecture content.

Conclusion

Our overall strategy incorporating six Practice themes woven across four redesigned courses offers a framework on which to further develop the Practice sequence at Cal Poly. These themes are inclusive so as to remain relevant in light of new or refined content in each of our respective courses, and we already see ways they can provide potential linkages to other courses. Our hope is that this horizontal, vertical and progressive strategy for integrating Practice is more than an approach to curricular design, but also a pedagogical platform that demonstrates to our colleagues and students the possibility and the advantage of integrating design, history and technology in a holistic approach to architecture.

Notes:

[1] Renzo Piano, "Renzo Piano Building Workshop 1964/1991: In Search of Balance," *Process Architecture* (Tokyo), no.700 (1992), pp. 12.

Updating the Miesian Curriculum

Thomas E. Brock
Illinois Institute of Technology

Introduction

The College of Architecture at the Illinois Institute of Technology (IIT) has always maintained a curriculum dedicated to the idea that providing a depth of knowledge about building technology was key to educating an architect. Mies Van der Rohe's original curriculum for the college clearly showed this emphasis. This remained true even when the prevailing discourse within academia had veered away from such ideas to favor the predominance of other kinds of knowledge such as history or theory. But the times do change, as does building technology, and the College of Architecture has, in the last decade, sought to amend its curriculum to take these factors into account while maintaining Mies' legacy and the historical identity of the school.

When I was given the directorship of the Third Year Program (TYP), four years ago, this process was already underway. Since that time we have sought to clarify our goals and continually improve the program. Because of its location at the midpoint of the five year sequence of undergraduate education at IIT, the TYP is a good case-study for the program as a whole. In the pages that follow, I will attempt to situate the TYP within the overall curriculum and provide a clear picture of the five-year educational sequence. I will outline the historical curriculum as originally conceived by Ludwig Mies van der Rohe, Walter Peterhans and Ludwig Hilberseimer in 1940 and will elaborate on how the program has sought to preserve and enhance its legacy of emphasizing the understanding of materials, manufacturing, building techniques and construction practices within the studio while responding to the challenges of educating today's students with today's knowledge and today's technology.

The Curriculum Under Mies

Prior to Mies' arrival, IIT's architecture program had been a well-established school based on the Ecole des Beaux-Arts model. When he was hired by IIT in 1938, it was with the understanding that the University would accept an entirely new curriculum of Mies' design. The new curriculum borrowed heavily on the structure and content of the German Bauhaus program of education for architects (see fig. 1). Mies had directed the Bauhaus from 1930 to 1933 and placed a particular emphasis on the sequential building up of knowledge and understanding through preliminary courses and workshops before any building design was to be attempted.

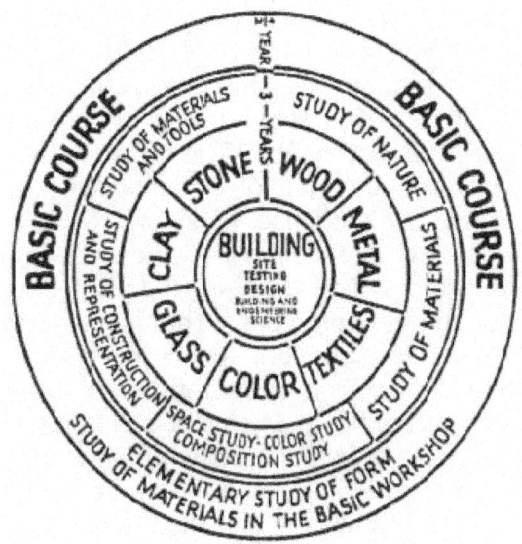

Figure 1. Diagram of the Bauhaus Curriculum

Sequence	First Year		Second Year		Third Year		Fourth Year		Fifth Year	
	First Semester	Second Semester	First Semester	Second Semester	First Semester	Second Semester	First Semester	Second Semester	First Semester	Second Semester
Architecture							Architecture I	Architecture II	Architecture III	Architecture IV
									Architect'l Practice I	Architect'l Practice II
Planning					Housing & Comm. Bldgs I	Housing & Comm. Bldgs II	City Planning I	City Planning II	Regional Planning Option (13 cr. hrs.)	Regional Planning Option (13 cr. hrs.)
Construction			Mtris & Constr. I	Mtris & Constr. II	Architectural Constr. I	Architectural Constr. II				
Visual Training			Visual Training I	Visual Training II	Visual Training III	Visual Traing IV				
Science-Engineering		Statics	Strength of Materials	Structures I - Timber	Structures II - Steel	Structures III - Concrete				
	Calculus/Analytic Geom I	Calculus/Analytic Geom II	Physics I	Physics II	Mechanical Systems	Electrical Systems				
History	History of Archtr I	History of Archtr II	Analysis of Art/Arch I	Analysis of Art/Arch II	Analysis of Art/Arch III	Analysis of Art/Arch IV				
Drawing	Life Drawing I	Life Drawing II	Life Drawing III	Life Drawing IV						
	Architectural Drawing I	Architectural Drawing II								
General Ed Program	Electives	Elective		Computer Science			Electives	Electives	Electives	Electives

Figure 2. Chart of the IIT Curriculum 1941.

The building design studios, conducted only in the final semesters of the program, were seen as the culmination of this carefully controlled sequence. In his 1938 inaugural address, Mies issues his definitive statement:

"Education must lead us from the irresponsible opinion to true responsible judgment. It must lead us from chance and arbitrariness to rational clarity and intellectual order. Therefore let us guide our students over the road of discipline from materials, through function, to creative work". [1]

With the help of two of his Bauhaus colleagues, Walter Peterhans and Ludwig Hilberseimer, also hired by IIT, Mies would refine the ideas and structure of this new curriculum and present the final form in 1941. (See figure 2). This final version expresses Mies' idea of a cumulative and culminating experience most clearly. It is organized as a series of seven overlapping sequences[2], conducted in the first four years of the program. The knowledge attained in that period is then applied in the architectural design studios in the final two years. According to Mies, "The curriculum leads naturally from the study of the means with which one builds and the purposes for which one builds into the sphere of architecture as an art." [3]

The Response to Change

The undergraduate curriculum as devised by Mies, remained essentially unchanged for 40 years, even after Mies retired from teaching in 1958. This was due in large part to the fact the most of the teaching faculty were either Mies' protégés or were educated at IIT, consequently there was little or no criticism from within and little or no interest among the teaching faculty to take part in the professional and academic discourse roiling outside Crown Hall. It wasn't until 1989, under the direction of Gene Summers, who collaborated on Mies' late projects, that the curriculum would be reconsidered. The reasons for this audit were many, but generally it was felt by Summers and his predecessor James Ingo Freed, that IIT had, in fact, grown out of touch with the times. The basic problem being that Mies' curriculum had attained a canonical status within the ranks of his followers and, over time, had degenerated into rote-learning of canonical forms, spatial and structural types, and details of construction, immune to influences from either cultural or technological change from outside. In an interview for the Art Institute of Chicago's Oral History Project, Freed comments on his Deanship at IIT,

"For twenty years I had talked to myself in my head about this. Then I went there and I tried to externalize it. Suddenly I found out

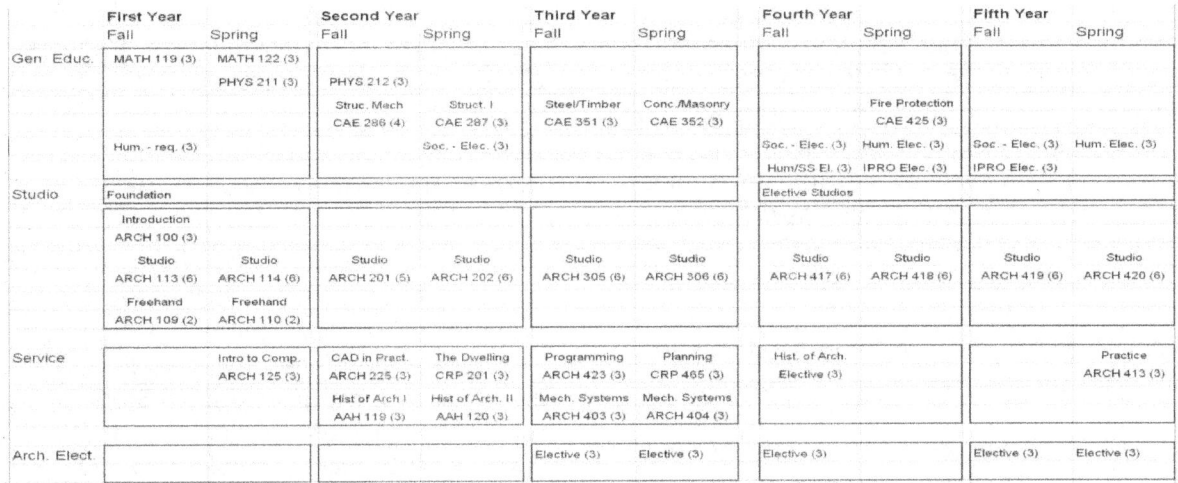

Figure 3. Chart of the IIT Curriculum 1990.

that nobody wanted to hear it. Nobody was interested in it. What they wanted me for was to take them back to the good old days. They were just in this lockhold of Mies'. Of course nobody there, which was their habit, would find fault with Mies."

The subsequent changes implemented at that time were not a complete overhaul of the program, but it is clear that the adjustments were aimed at dismantling the status quo in the hopes of eventually either transcending the Miesian influence or, at least, allowing for other, more contemporary points of view to influence the student's work. In an interview in a local Chicago magazine in 1989 entitled *"IIT architect dean may bring less Mies, more from today"*, Summers' comments on his plans,

"I hope my deviation from the normal route will teach students to know other avenues of architecture."

But the historical record also shows that at this time there was little agreement within the college about why change was needed or how to go about it.

Summers' plans also included hiring in a crop of new, young faculty, mostly educated outside of IIT, to teach in the core studios, in the hopes of breathing new life into the program. One of these was Ben Nicholson, who participated on the committee considering the reforms. Nicholson writes of that time,

"We are no longer willing to engage the pedagogical sequence leading from materials, through function, to creative work. That sequence echoed Mies' personal journey from the stone yard, to the making of programmed houses to the symphonic works.... In practical terms, the avant-garde of architecture have forged a course of action diametric to that suggested by Mies. Their first activity was to pose questions that lead to creation, their second action was to look for function, and finally to grapple with materials in the building site."

Picking up on Nicholson's characterization it suffices to say that most of the reforms implemented at that time had to do with cultural and ideological changes that had occurred outside the walls of Crown Hall, most importantly, changes in attitudes towards creative processes in architectural work and the role of "critical thinking"[4] in such processes.

The reforms implemented during Summers' tenure as Dean would affect both the overall structure of the curriculum and the content of the courses within it. In terms of the overall structure of the curriculum, the seven overlapping sequences of Mies' original Chart were abandoned (see fig. 3) and were replaced by four categories of study, which included, "General Education", "Studio", "Service" and "Architectural Electives". These were no longer seen as overlapping sequences building to crescendo with the building design studios in the final years, rather, the new structure featured a continuum of studios running through the entire five-year sequence. This continuum of studios was then subdivided into two parts, the first three years being characterized as "Foundation" Studios, and the final two as "Elective" or "Advanced" Studios. This overall structural change was implemented to allow for further changes to the content of the individual courses taught.

In the foundation studios, the first year retained its Bauhaus-style exercises in freehand drawing, technical drafting and elemental composition, but also included more investigations of spatial composition, and larger scale construction. More substantive changes occurred in the second and third years in that they were no longer characterized as a "construction sequence" although emphasis on material investigations in masonry, wood, steel and concrete remained. Additionally, the use of a wider range of potential building programs and technologies was implemented in order to challenge the students and induce them to think outside the established canons, deal with contemporary issues and research current building technologies.

The fourth and fifth year elective studios were also opened up to include a wide variety of topics to be chosen by the teaching faculty. This was seen primarily as a way of allowing the students to develop their individual interests and to allow for a modicum of specialization. At the beginning of each semester, teaching faculty within the elective studios make presentations of the projects they offer. Student can then select and rank their top three choices. Preference is given to the upperclassmen and, if necessary, a lottery is used to make the final decisions of who goes where. This has also allowed many of the existing faculty to pursue their interests within the studio and has allowed the College to engage local professionals in the curriculum.

The "Comprehensive" Year

Whereas under Mies' vision the capstone experience came at the end of the five-year program, the new model designated a capstone experience after only three years, at the end of the Foundation Studios. This was done, in part, to allow the fourth and fifth year Elective Studios to focus on specializations. But in order to meet the new National Architectural Accrediting Board (NAAB) standards the curriculum needed at least one semester to be a "comprehensive design" experience.[5] The Fourth and Fifth year studios, because of their specializations, would be too narrow in focus to qualify under the NAAB standards and so it was decided that the comprehensive design experience would come at the end of the 3rd year. The main effect of this move was to quicken the pace, and to focus the efforts of the Foundation Studios. The canonical model, with its prescriptive solutions and narrow focus, would no longer suffice if the students were to be ready for a comprehensive design experience by the end of the third year. The content of the studios preceding it would have to be richer, broader and more contemporary, and the students would have to address the design of complex buildings problems earlier in the curriculum.

When I arrived to teach in the TYP at IIT in the fall of 1999 it was at the invitation of the new Dean of the College, Donna Robertson. Robertson had picked up where Summers had left off and continued to bring fresh talent into the organization. When hired, I was told that these would be "materials-based design studios, a semester of steel and a semester of concrete", and that the projects given were at the discretion of the teaching faculty. It seemed open and straightforward enough. But once in the trenches it seemed to me that the studios did not work, or, at least, did not really deliver on the comprehensive design criteria. Although they had allowed the school to move beyond Mies', the curricular revisions implemented a decade earlier were simply not rising to the challenges of providing the students a comprehensive design experience.

Defining the Current Problems

When I was given the directorship of the TYP in 2002 it was an opportunity to correct what I perceived as the problems keeping us from achieving a comprehensive design experience for our students. The problems were many, but the key issues revolved around how well we were integrating content concerning structural technology and building science, including mechanical systems, into the course material.

The most obvious problem in the studio had to do with the sequencing of information. More often than not, we were asking the students to consider aspects of building design and construction technology before we had adequately addressed the issues in a class setting. It is important to note here that traditionally, IIT did not need a separate construction technology course as is the norm for most schools of architecture, because the traditional "construction sequence", conducted in the second and third years, covered this information through the drawing and model building exercises that were given, albeit in a narrow and canonical way. When the "construction sequence" was replaced by the building design studios, there was no separate construction technology course implemented. The studio was still seen as the place where this information would be imparted. When I arrived, a lecture series had been implemented within the studio but it was piecemeal and even tended to fizzle-out as the semester wore on and there were no definitive textbooks prescribed that would allow students to look up the information needed. Additionally, the critical information regarding building technology was not always presented in time for the students to make good use of it in their projects. There was also no real coordination between the studio coursework and the work being performed in their Structures Course and/or their Mechanical, Electrical and Plumbing (MEP) course despite the fact that the courses had intentionally been placed in the same semester to allow overlap and integration of information to occur.

These parallel courses, were, by and large, dealt with in the studio, insofar as the students were required to demonstrate knowledge of how to size beams and columns and how to calculate the loads placed on equipment. But this was often treated by students and faculty as an unfortunate obligation that one simply had to endure in order to move onto the more interesting aspects of building design.

Although the MEP course has always been taught within the College of Architecture, the Structure Course has been offered through the Department of Civil Engineering. This made its integration into the studio content doubly difficult insofar as their faculty had not been willing to coordinate efforts between the courses or participate in Studio work. Consequently, the Studio faculty had to present the structures content within the studio to insure that the students had the information when they needed it and were effectively applying it to their work. This made for redundant discussions between the courses and wasted valuble studio time.

There was also a tendency, within the studio, to simply expect too much from the students in terms of work-load. In the first few years of my experience with the course, before I was given the directorship, students were expected to finish two and sometime three building designs within a semester's time. These were not large projects, but their number prevented students from being able to adequately contemplate the work, produce and test multiple iterations of their ideas, hone in on final concept and then develop it to a level of detail, wherein which, issues of fabrication, construction and technological integration could be meaningfully discussed.

Related to this, was a lack of integration of Computer Aided Design/Drafting (CAD) and Computer Numerical Control (CNC) technology in the curriculum. This is attributable to IIT's strong tradition of emphasizing fundamental skills, hand-drafting being foremost among them, and teaching about building technology through formal drawing exercizes. As recently as three years ago, less than half of the students in the TYP produced their work with the aid of computers and computer driven technology. This had a clear effect on productivity. Those students who had the advanced skills, usually transfer students, were nearly always able to outperform their classmates in terms of project development and presentation.

Lastly, and this was likely a problem unique to IIT, student's still tended to "ape the master". This was often allowed and sometimes encouraged. This tendency was understandable on one level, they were, after all, at the school that he started and were surrounded by his work. Also, it should be recognized that, as an exercise, there is a lot to be learned by following Mies' through some of the classic design problems that he dealt with so beautifully in his built works, such as how to turn a corner with a given structural or cladding system. It is difficult to be entirely against a student who wants to "be like Mies". The problem arises when the student mindlessly copies his work in their work and fails to think in terms of contemporary practice and contemporary standards. Mies' buildings are, by today's standards, woefully inefficient in terms of energy usage. A studio filled with little Crown Halls or Berlin Museums makes it very difficult to teach any notions of sustainability with regards to material and energy usage.

The Current State of the TYP

New reforms have put us much closer to providing within the TYP a comprehensive design experience in line with the standards set by the NAAB. Just as it was with the curriculum as a whole, both structural and substantive changes were needed.

Addressing Content Delivery:

To deal with the problems surrounding the proper sequencing and delivery of construction technology information within the studio, a 24 part lecture series for each of the two semesters has been developed over the last four years. This series takes place in the first hour of studio, typically for two out of the three days per week that studio is conducted. Teaching faculty rotate through the lecture responsibility as the semester progresses. The series begins with an introduction to the principal structure material that is the subject of the semester's investigation, in our case, either steel or concrete, and includes information on the process of its manufacture as well as presentations on its structural development through history by way of case studies and examples. Once this introductory material is presented we move onto a discussion of the most common structural types, their application and a comparison of spanning capacity. The sequence then moves through discussions of building systems roughly following the construction process from the laying of foundations through interior finish work. This sequence is carefully orchestrated to coincide with the pace and progress of the studio to insure that students have taken part in a presentation and discussion of the various building systems before they are asked to consider them in the studio. In addition, all of the lecture materials are made available to the students on a course web site to allow them to revisit issues with teaching faculty whenever they feel it necessary. They can also visit an archive of student work from previous semesters on the website for examples of the level of development and quality of work expected in the studio.

In order to insure a measure of continuous improvement and up-to-date information, it is agreed that teaching faculty do not give the same lecture in consecutive semesters. They are given all of the materials from previous semesters on CD-rom and are then are challenged to make improvements to both the form and content of the lecture series. This has the added benefit of keeping the teaching faculty up to date on the technical issues important to the studio work.

At least two field trips are now conducted during the semester, one focused on manufacturing the other on construction. In programming these trips, we try to take full advantage of our privileged location here in Chicago. We have, over the years, visited the steel mills of the Indiana lakeshore, forging and casting plants within the city and structural and finish precast plants in the outlying suburbs. As most of the teaching faculty are also practicing architects, and the economy has fueled a building boom here, we have been fortunate to also have an ample supply of projects under construction for the students to tour.

Integrating the Parallel Courses:
The Structures Courses and the MEP Courses that are supposed to coincide with and support the studio are now more fully integrated both conceptually and perceptually. The structures courses are no longer taught out of the Department of Civil Engineering and the sequence of those courses has changed. Whereas traditionally, the students were given four semesters of structures focused on the resolution of equations they now take three courses, the first of which is an "intuitive introduction" to structures, offered in the last semester of the second year. This emphasizes the dynamic aspects of structures when considered as overall systems through the building and testing of models and mock-ups. The remaining two semesters, conducted during the third year, follow the emphases of steel and concrete taking place in the studios and give the student a sound mathematical competence to complement the studio work.

We continue to work with the faculty in both the Structures and MEP courses to adjust the scheduling of content to better coincide with what was being discussed in the studios. They also now require the students to actually do work on their design projects in these other courses. Students are expected to submit calculations and loading tables to their structures professors and their MEP professors require similar assignments for heating/cooling loads and the sizing of air systems. All of this material is reviewed by the studio faculty as well. Additionally, both the structures professors and the MEP faculty visit the studio for scheduled reviews of student projects, at least two times per semester. This works to blur the borders between the studio and the parallel courses. Students encounter and work with their Structures/MEP professors in the studio and Studio Professors engage the students in the integration of the Structures/MEP work into their building designs.

To again take full advantage of our setting in Chicago, we are now working on establishing a "Structures Day" and a "Mechanical Day" for each semester. The students are already reviewed twice a semester by local practicing architects invited to sit on juries at midterm and finals week. This effort will invite a dozen or so local qualified professionals, structural and mechanical engineers, to visit IIT for an afternoon of group reviews and discussions of individual projects. The day will conclude with a dinner meeting between the professionals and teaching staff to discuss the student work and, hopefully, gain insights into how to better prepare the students for professional work.

Major changes have also occurred in the CAD portions of the curriculum. We have begun to offer classes in digital graphics and modeling earlier in the curriculum. This was done to allow students more opportunities to implement the use of computers in the studios and, with faculty input, better integrate them into the design and production process. We have also implemented wireless technology throughout the 3 buildings currently occupied by the College and have expanded the range of classes being offered so that students can, if they desire, receive a minor in Computer Aided Design. Additionally, we require high proficiency in CAD from all of our teaching faculty and teach the effective use of CAD not just for production or presentation but also to aid in the design process. Although we do not require that students use CAD or CNC to complete their work in the studios all of them did in the 2005-2006 academic year.

Managing Work Load & Quality:
Rather than run a series of projects that tended to burn the students out, we now work on only one project per semester. The project is selected so as to be simple in nature, limited in scope and carefully orchestrated through regular assignments, exercises and other milestones that keep the students constantly aware of the pace and structure of the studio.

The semester is begun with an intensive one-week assignment of group-based research projects. These include relevant subjects that will be of use to the students during the design process, such as local climatic conditions, zoning and code restrictions or research pertaining to the client or site. The teams of 7 to 10 students are required to disseminate all information gathered to the rest of the studio through a verbal presentation that allows for questions and corresponding printed materials for inclusion in a project research booklet.

This research period is followed by a weekend charette in which the students are first invited to participate with faculty in a Saturday brain-storming session focused on the possibilities inherent in the site, program and structure, and then encouraged to spend their Sunday generating the first of many parti for evaluation in an in-class pinup that Monday. This is intended as a kick start for the studio and seeks to get the students quickly engaged in the core issues of the project.

The semester is divided into two periods that emulate the typical project phases of "schematic design" and "design development". By the mid-point of the semester each student is expected to have a fairly well-resolved schematic design that has accounted for some structural logic, and has effectively dealt with the program and site, including all aspects of life-safety and accessibility. After the break, the students are then engaged in a series of assignments and exercises that allow them to "re-design" their projects through architectural detailing. These exercises include large-scale sectional investigations as well as rough maquettes. This series of investigation culminates in the building of a large-scale sectional model, usually of a corner of their building.

Throughout these exercises the students are continually engaged by the faculty to reconsider the whole in terms of the detail. This method posits the notion that a single detail can "infect" an entire building design and through careful modulation, a language of form can begin to emerge. Through this method the students are allowed to see how all of their investigations, structural, mechanical and otherwise can and will inform their ideas and decisions about built form.

In the last few years we have also sought to engage "potentially real projects" for the students to work on. This started as a chance opportunity, but it so stimulated and invigorated our students that we have since then sought additional opportunities. In the years since we began working on these kinds of projects we have addressed a wide variety of building types and programs, all of which were either for "not-for-profit" organizations or private organizations that serve public interests, such as mass transit or energy usage and sustainability. The "client", usually the organization's director and their immediate department heads, works with the faculty to develop the program before the semester begins and then attends a question and answer session with the students conducted immediately before the week-end charette. They then return to take part in both the mid-term and final reviews. Ultimately, we do not expect to see any of the student work actually built and we make this clear to everyone involved. These projects are conducted for the mutual edification of both parties involved. It is our hope that when participating organizations do engage the services of a professional they are better informed as to their own needs and the possibilities that their program suggests. Thus far, these efforts have served both the students' and the "client's" interests very well and we hope to be able to continue to find organizations that we can work with in the future.

Discipline with a Sense of Purpose:
Many architectural design studios over-emphasize the importance of the open-ended, self-involved, creative thinking that is characteristic of the artist or poet, and under-emphasize the role of research in informing the design process. We have sought, in the last four years, to create within the studio a more balanced culture, in which creativity is seen as an applied act that is informed by analysis and is focused on problem-solving, and in which informed research is considered among the principal tools of the architect.

The best way we have found to keep students from simply copying work they admire or details they have found, without first understanding them and, if appropriate, adapting them to the purposes at hand, is to insist that they not only present, for instance, a wall-section, but that they also reveal their source materials and present those as well. Students are evaluated not only on the relative success or failure of the detail in question but also on the depth and breadth of the research materials informing that detail. This serves to broaden the discussion and helps the teaching faculty to understand how, if at all, a student is thinking about a given detail or design concept.

Another less direct but still effective way to insure that students are mindfully engaged in their own work is to keep them focused on issues of contemporary practice, especially ideas that contribute to the public good, such as sustainable practices in material and energy usage. Much of the discussion in studio is devoted to issues of efficiency and sustainability and the students are encouraged to evaluate proposed solutions in terms of costs and benefits. Emphasizing these kinds of issues in the TYP has virtually eliminated the tendency for some students to "ape the master" and, more importantly, it has lent a sense of urgency and importance to the work at hand.

This is also the most tangible effect of the "potentially real projects" mentioned above. Because we collaborate only with organizations that serve real and vital public needs, it tends to imbue the studios with a profound sense of purpose and the students take their own work more seriously.

A Continual "Work in Progress"

As an important historical institution, IIT's College of Architecture has had to face the realization that in contemporary civilization no set of ideas, no matter how important they were at one time, could stand for long unchanged, and that those few instances where this does happen tend to be viewed as lacking an appropriate level of healthy skepticism. As has been shown in the preceeding pages the College is making efforts to move beyond the canonical modernism that dominated Crown Hall for over forty years and bring the curriculum in touch with the spirit of the times. But there is still concern within the school that much of what Mies brought to education will be lost in the reforms and that, over time, we risk losing the school's identity altogether.

Of this, only time will tell. But I would argue that Mies' legacy is still very much intact. It remains a program dedicated to the idea that providing a depth of knowledge about material properties and building technology is key to educating an architect. It continues to strive for a level of course integration that allows students to see building design as a multi-disciplinary task that requires mastery at all levels. It continues to place an emphasis on the reasonable and efficient use of structure as a prime factor in determining built form. It remains a program that portray's design as a unique type of creative endeavor that is informed by effective research, analysis and application.
In fact, the unyielding constancy and extended duration of Mies' original curriculum at IIT could be attributable to a lack of sufficient attention to one of the central tenets of his philosophy. Mies himself pointed to the ever-changing nature of our civilization when he characterized architecture as the expression of the "will of an epoch". In his inaugural address he states,

"Just as we acquaint ourselves with materials and just as we must understand functions, we must become familiar with the psychological and spiritual factors of the day. No cultural activity is possible otherwise: for we are dependent on the spirit of our time. Therefore we must understand the motives and forces of our time and analyze their structure from three points of view: the material, the functional, and the spiritual. We must make clear in what respects our epoch differs from others and in what respects it is similar".

Mies is, of course talking about architecture here but the same notion could be applied to the curriculum of architectural education. In either case, an ongoing lack of honest re-evaluation and appropriate adjustment will eventually lead to irrelevance and obsolescence. This case-study of the Third Year Program has been offered as an example of how and why change is occurring at IIT, as a response to contemporary forces but also mindful of the philosophy and traditions from which it has descended. I believe that what has happened and continues to happen at IIT is less about completely reinventing the school, or making it more like other schools, but amounts to something more along the lines of a well-informed course correction.

References:

Carr, Rebecca. IIT Architect Dean May Bring Less Mies, More From Today. Crain's Chicago Business 31 (July 1989).

Nicholson, Ben. Renouncing Autistic Words. Published in The Presence of Mies, Detlef Mertens, Editor. Princeton Architectural Press.

Ennis, R. Critical thinking: What is it? Proceedings of the Forty-Eighth Annual Meeting of the Philosophy of Education Society Denver, Colorado, March 27-30, 1992.

Notes:

[1] Inaugural Address (1938) on the occasion of his appointment to Director of the Department of Architecture at the Amour Institute of Technology (former name of IIT, changed in 1940 when Armour merged with the Lewis Institute) by Mies Van Der Rohe.

[2] For elaboration on each sequence with the program see: Swenson, Alfred and Pao-Chi Chang. *Architectural Education at IIT*. Illinois Institute of Technology. 1980.

[3] Mies van der Rohe. *The Architecture Curriculum at IIT*. Illinois Institute of Technology, Chicago, Illinois, 1941.

[4] Because "critical thinking" has become somewhat a cliché or buzzword in academic circles, it is important to be clear on one's meaning in using the phrase. I take my definition from Ennis, 1992. *"...reasonable reflective thinking focused on deciding what to believe or do."*

[5] NAAB defines Comprehensive Design as, *"Ability to produce an architecture project informed by a comprehensive program, from schematic design through the detailed development of programmatic spaces, structural and environmental systems, life-safety provisions, wall sections, and building assemblies, as may be appropriate; and to assess the completed project with respect to the programs design criteria."*

The Mechanisms of Surface: The Wall Section Model

Jason R. Chandler, A.I.A.
Florida International University

The wall section model serves as an important tool in teaching the methods and materials of building. As a highly focused model, it requires students to explore in detail the interactions of a building's enclosure and structure. While a one to one interaction with materials is a desirable context for learning, this project focuses on the interaction of construction systems and the overview gained through architectural representation. The pedagogic intent of this model is to refocus the student's attention past the veneer of a building's exterior and connect visual concerns with the necessary mechanisms of construction.

The Class

The wall section model is a required assignment for the second of two required materials and methods classes. These classes are part of the technology sequence of a four-year undergraduate architectural curriculum.[1] Both classes are presented in lecture format. The class size is comprised of about one hundred students. The first class introduces small-scale building practices[2] while the second examines large-scale building practices.

In the second class, Edward Allen's *Fundamentals of Building Construction*[3] is used as the textbook. The structure of this book, one that organizes its explanation of building construction by material type, is used to arrange the class.

The class begins with a lecture on the primitive hut. The primate hut is presented as a distilled version of construction that accommodates shelter. The frontispiece of Laugier's *Essai sur l'architecture,* of 1775, is the first image of the class. This engraving illustrates a simple wood shelter unencumbered by decoration. This ideal is used to present other simple shelters of the twentieth century, which allows the students a focused view of a single building system. Le Corbusier's Maison Domino of 1927 is used to illustrate a simple concrete structure while Mies Van de Rohe's Farnsworth house of 1950 is used to illustrate a simple steel frame structure. Through these isolated examples, distinct materials and methods are introduced.

After the primate hut introduction, the class examines building construction by individual material types: wood, brick, stone, steel, concrete, pre-cast concrete, and glass. The Allen book offers a thorough explanation of each material type and is used to introduce a material's most prevalent quality. This study reveals the material's efficiencies found in every day construction. Simultaneously, this study of the material's standard is supplemented with a presentation of an exceptional building case study. The building case study explores a material's qualities without typical constraints and often reflects possibilities not apparent in the industry. It is in the case study that the work of mature architects is used to reveal subtle yet sophisticated understandings of a material's character. While both the building standard and its exceptional possibility are given equal presentation time, emphasis is placed on the understanding that innovation requires experience with standard building techniques.

Toward the end of the class, the lectures discuss the idea of composite structures and the role of cladding. It is in these lectures that the combination of material types is explored; specifically, the combination of different structural and material systems. Enclosure systems are highlighted as independent systems that protect the structure. In addition, the wall section becomes a tool with which to explore the complexities of present day construction. Walls are no longer monolithic assemblies, but rather expansive areas which transform from the interior to the exterior. In these walls, structure, interior and exterior cladding, insulation, electrical, plumbing and mechanical systems coexist. These lectures begin to frame the intent of the wall section model by providing a context of how these systems intermingle.

Throughout the semester, students periodically visit a building site. In the past, the class would visit building sites together with the professor, yet as class sizes grew this became untenable. The intent of this assignment is to have the students witness first hand a medium to large-scale building under construction. The building that is selected must satisfy the following requirements: it should not be past 50% completion, it must be freestanding, and it must be at least 10,000 square feet in size. The students are required to visit their site eight times during the semester and document what has occurred with a one hundred word description and photographs.

The Wall Section Model Project

The wall section model is a semester long endeavor, which involves three distinct parts: a research book, a detail drawing and a model. This is a group project; each student must select two people to work with. Both the research book and the detail drawing are meant to familiarize the students with their chosen building. These assignments require the students to gather as much information on their building as possible. Both the research book and the detail drawing are to be submitted for review at assigned dates. The students receive comments, which they can respond to by resubmitting at the end of the project. The semester is supplemented with workshops that clarify the intent of the assignments.

The students select a notable building from a predetermined list. This list is organized into five material categories: wood, brick, stone, metal, and glass. The buildings that compose this list were typically built in the mid to late twentieth century and early twenty-first century. They are medium to large-scale buildings and are often distinguished by their cladding innovations.

The Research Book

At the beginning of this project, students research their selected building. They are required to collect a wide-range of information with an emphasis placed on gathering graphic documentation. This information is then organized into a book, which explains the building's context, history and construction.

The students are asked to document in both written and graphic format the following topics:

1. Building Construction Dates: Students are required to not only determine when the building was built, but also the duration of its construction.
2. Building Site: Students draw a site plan of the building with a north arrow. They need to show the site context, any other buildings, typography and vegetation. They need to identify the building's exposures: which building walls are exposed to sun, wind and weather, and which walls are protected. They need to identify if the building is in an urban context or in a rural or suburban context.
3. Construction Challenges: The students need to determine if the site, municipal approvals, budget or time created obstacles for the builders.
4. Climate: Students record the building's longitude and latitude coordinates. They document the yearly weather cycle.
5. Cultural Setting: Students explain the culture of the area in which the building

is situated. This is a broad topic but the intent is to explore the "genius loci"[4] or "the spirit of the place." The students are required to determine what sort of cultural influences their chosen building responded to.

6. Building Historical Precedence: This topic requires the students to look past the locale of the building to broader issues of building type. They need to determine whether or not their building represents a culmination of technology used in similar buildings.
7. Client: The research book records who built the building. The client is described in terms of what their role was in determining the building's configuration, image, and budget.
8. Program: The students are required to include all plans of the building. They must also document what activities occur in those plans.
9. Circulation. The students need to describe in plan and in section the circulation through the building. They need to identify horizontal and vertical circulation elements.
10. Architect: The architect needs to be identified. In addition, the architect's other work needs to be documented. It is further required that the chosen building be considered within the architect's oeuvre. The students need to determine whether or not this is a unique building in terms of scale or technology. They need to conclude whether or not this building is indicative of the rest of the architect's work or a unique moment in the architect's production.
11. Structural Systems: It is required that the primary structural system is identified and isolated. The vertical and horizontal supports are described as well as any diagonal bracing or shear walls. Once the structural system is articulated, the students are required to determine if the enclosure system is part of the primary structure or an independent structure.
12. Climate Control: *Passive Systems:* Students analyze how, if at all, the building's configuration contributes to heating or cooling. *Mechanical Systems:* Students identify powered systems of heating and cooling.
13. Cladding Systems: The students examine how cladding controls natural light, how it protects from water intrusion, how it isolates building movements, how it weathers, how it prevents air leakage, and how it insulates the building.
14. Materials: The primary materials of the building are identified.

In addition to the preceding topics, the students need to intermix graphic information throughout the text. This information includes the following items: the architect's sketches, models, plans, sections, elevations, working drawings, wall sections, details, and building photographs.

The Detail Drawing

Once the book is finished, a selected area that represents the character of the building is drawn. This drawing is the "blueprint" for the final model (figure 1.) It typically depicts a ten-foot wide section of the full height of an exterior building edge. The full height of high-rise buildings with repetitive floor plates needs does not need to be drawn in its entirety. Instead, the building's base, a series of representative floor plates and its top are sufficient information.

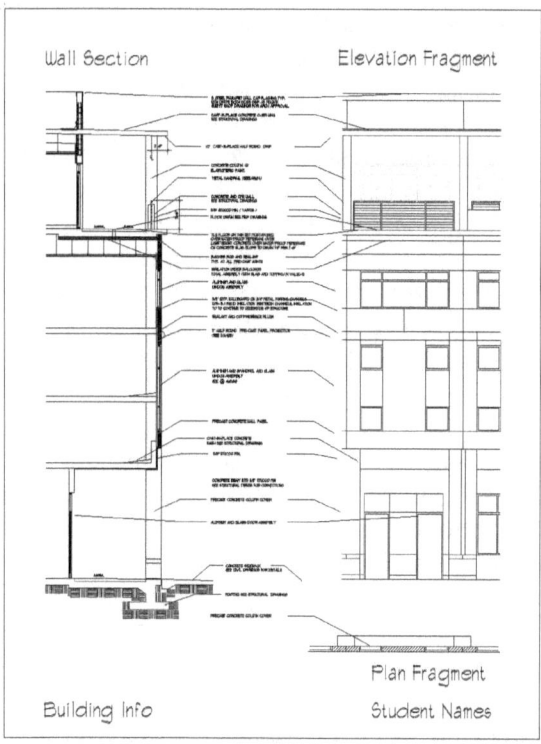

Figure 1. Detail Drawing Format

Three drawings are produced to render the selected area of the building: a wall section, a partial elevation and a partial plan. The wall section is cut at the building's edge and extends ten feet into the building. The partial elevation depicts a ten-foot wide vertical section of the façade. This elevation is often adjusted to encompass a full bay of the structure. The plan of this area is often cut at the most representative level through the building. These three drawings are then organized on one sheet and drawn at the same scale. The wall section and the elevation are aligned at the top of the page while the plan is aligned below the elevation. In addition to the drawings, text is used to label the building elements. This text is typically organized in a vertical column between the wall section and elevation.

The Model

Once the drawings are completed, the students sketch out a scheme to build their model. They determine the actual materials they will use to represent the building's materials. As this model is only a portion of the building it may not stand on its own. As a result, one of the challenges is to build a steady model. Students design a base for their model and a means to hold up the cantilevering floor edges without introducing any extraneous structure.

The ambition of these drawings is to represent the building details within the context of the full wall. Seeing the required mechanisms of a construction from the base of a building to its top allows for a comprehensive description of a building's surface. A building's surface is the result of a variety of contiguous construction events. These events exist as moments embedded in building. Any one of these details cannot be completely understood without the rest of the structure.

The scale that represents the details and a full wall section for medium to large-scale buildings without requiring too large a piece of paper is ½" = 1'-0".[5] At this scale an overview of the wall is afforded while the individual connections are depicted. A larger scale may allow for additional information but the details can become disembodied. A smaller scale may allow for a more comprehensive spatial depiction but issues of construction may dissolve.

Determining the actual materials for the model is a critical step in the model making process. The wall section model is meant to represent the building's actual construction and materials. While the use of the actual building's materials is encouraged, it is not a requirement. Instead, it is the interaction of assemblies and materials that is sought in this endeavor. Models may be made of materials not found in the building, but attention must be made to represent the building elements correctly. These elements can undergo transformation so long as their scale, proportion, texture, and relationship to other elements is accurately depicted.

The students typically work on their models for about two weeks. During this time, issues of material feasibility arise. Often a material that is found in the actual building cannot assume its role in the model. Its actual scale may be inappropriate for the model's scale. In order to simulate the material's qualities, the students select a substitute material. For example, one material that is often used in the beginning of the model building process is concrete. Students have varying degrees of success with this material and often find that their difficulties with it do not approximate its full-scale reality. Plaster is one substitute that allows the students the opportunity to experiment with a malleable material without the constraints associated with concrete. This substitution allows a freedom to explore interactions with other materials within a larger context. At the model's scale, these interactions extend past a particular material to the overall assembly.

While the models are not meant to be simulations of full-scale construction, they are challenging undertakings. They require a coordinated effort of a student team. They often are the most involved models the students have made at this point in their education. While it is the primary aim of the assignment to represent the chosen building in an accurate way, it is the precision of the model making that becomes the ultimate measure of the model's success. In the end, it is craftsmanship coupled with an understanding of interaction of building systems that distinguishes successful models.

The following are five examples of wall section models built for this class:

1. Wood Example: Shelter for Roman Archaeological Studies
   Architect: PeterZumthor
   Location: Switzerland
   Date of completion: 1986

Peter Zumthor's Shelter for Roman Archaeological Studies is an open wood and steel frame structure resting on a concrete foundation wall.[6] This model depicts the cantilever metal entry condition. While it uses wood it does not does not use metal to render the cantilever entry. Instead, painted cardboard is used (Figure 2.)

Figure 2. Student Model 2 of Peter Zumthor's Shelter for Roman Archaeological Studies

2. Stone Example:
   Dominus Winery
   Architect: Herzog and De Meuron
   Location: California
   Date of completion: 1997

Herzog and De Meuron's Dominus Winery is a concrete frame building enclosed with a gabion cladding on steel tube frame.[7] This model depicts a corner of the building (Figure 3.) The exterior is made of the actual building materials; the model uses actual stones and wire mess to represent the gabion cladding. The interior substitutes the building materials; the concrete slab is rendered with plaster and the steel tube frame is rendered with basswood. The utilization of actual stones is critical for this model. While the other materials were substituted, actual stones are necessary to reveal the gaps, which let light in through the exterior wall.

Figure 3. Student Model of Herzog and De Meuron's Dominus Winery

3. Concrete Example:
   Lloyds of London
   Architect: Richard Rogers
   Location: London
   Date of completion: 1986

Richard Roger's Lloyds of London is a pre-cast concrete frame building with stainless steel and glass cladding.[8] This model depicts a bay of the building and does not use any materials found in the actual building. Cardboard and basswood with paint are used to represent all the materials in the building (the glass is omitted.) While this uniformity of material does not represent the stark contrasts of materials found in the building, attention has been given to the size and proportion of the different building elements. In addition, the delaminated representation of the floor system begins to mimic the architect's own drawings for the building (Figure 4.)

Figure 4. Student Model of Richard Roger's Lloyds of London

4. Metal Example: Sarphatistraat Office
   Architect: Steven Holl
   Location: Amsterdam
   Date of completion: 2000

Steven Holl's Sarphatistraat Office is a steel frame building with a steel mess and glass enclosure.[9] This model depicts a section of the exterior wall and does not use any materials found in the actual building (Figure 5.) Foam core and museum board are used to depict the floor and wall structure, while a plastic mess is used to render the steel mess. While the actual materials of this model do little to mimic those found in the building, the layered and porous affect of the building's skin is represented.

Figure 5. Student model of Steven Holl's Sarphatistraat Office

Figure 6. Student Model of Peter Zumthor's Art Museum Bregenz

5. Glass Example:
   Art Museum Bregenz
   Architect: Peter Zumthor
   Location: Bregenz
   Date of completion: 1997

Peter Zumthor's Art Museum Bregenz is a concrete structure enclosed with a glass curtain. The curtain wall is composed of a series of independent glass sheets held together with a steel frame and chips.[10] This model depicts a corner of the building and does not use any materials found in the actual building (Figure 6.) The concrete structure is made of thick chipboard, the glass sheets are made of acetate and the steel frame is a combination of plastic and drywall sandpaper (Figure 7.) The concrete structure is removable allowing for a view of the curtain wall from the interior. While the original materials have been substituted, the manipulation of natural light is represented.

Figure 7. Detail of Student Model of Peter Zumthor's Art Museum Bregenz

Conclusion

The result of this study illuminates the surface of buildings. Rather than exist as paper-thin objects captured in a glossy photograph, the surface of buildings gains new depth. This depth of construction binds the entire building to its surface. While the outward expression of a building may remain a sought after effect, it can now be engaged with its means of construction. The surface of a building is a highly charged architectonic moment. As the threshold between the interior and exterior, it allows for an examination of a myriad of construction issues: the selection and use of materials, the integration of structural and mechanical systems, the use of enclosure and cladding systems, the use of glazing systems and sun control, the detailing of waterproofing and the weathering of materials. The ambitions of the wall section model reflect a dynamic moment of construction. These models serve as a vital laboratory for the understanding and making of buildings.

The architect needs to connect with the means and methods of construction, yet it must be done with the understanding of how to place these processes within the context of a complete building. The wall section model begins to anticipate the complexities of construction. It is during the making of this model, that students begin to understand how numerous construction activities are organized to produce a building.

References:

Allen, Edward. Fundamentals of Building Construction, Materials and Methods- 4th Edition. New York: John Wiley & Sons, Inc., 2002.

Ching, Francis. Building Construction Illustrated. New York: Van Nostrand Reinhold/co Wiley, 1975.

Levene, Richard and Marquez, Fernando eds. Herzog & de Meuron 1993-1997. Madrid: el croquis editorial, 1997.

Levene, Richard and Marquez, Fernando eds. Steven Holl 1998-2002. Madrid: el croquis editorial, 2002.

Russel, Frank ed. Richard Rogers + Architects, Architectural Monographs. London: St. Martins's Press, 1985.

Yoshida, Nobuyuki Ed. A+U Architecture and Urbanism. Febuary 1998 extra Edition, Peter Zumthor. Japan: A+U Publishing Co., 1998.

Notes:

[1] This four-year undergraduate degree in combination with a two-year graduate sequence forms the professionally accredited degree program at Florida International University.

[2] The required text for this class is: Ching, Francis. Building Construction Illustrated. New York: Van Nostrand Reinhold/co Wiley, 1975.

[3] Allen, Edward Fundamentals of Building Construction, Materials and Methods- 4th Edition. New York: John Wiley & Sons, Inc., 2002.

[4] This concept is framed by Colin Rowe's essay "Living with the genius loci" Koetter Kim & Associates: place/time. New York: Rizzoli International Publications, Inc.,1997. pgs 10-17.

[5] For smaller buildings three stories and under, the drawings are at a scale of 1"= 1'-0".

[6] Yoshida, Nobuyuki Ed. A+U Architecture and Urbanism, Febuary 1998 extra Edition, Peter Zumthor. Japan: A+U Publishing Co., 1998.

[7] See page 183, Levene, Richard and Marquez, Fernando eds. Herzog & de Meuron 1993-1997. Madrid: el croquis editorial, 1997.

[8] See page 130, Russel, Frank ed. Richard Rogers + Architects, Architectural Monographs. London: St. Martins's Press, 1985.

[9] See page 44, Levene, Richard and Marquez, Fernando eds. Steven Holl 1998-2002. Madrid: el croquis editorial, 2002.

[10] Yoshida, Nobuyuki Ed. A+U Architecture and Urbanism, Febuary 1998 extra Edition, Peter Zumthor. Japan: A+U Publishing Co., 1998.

Capabilities and Limitations of Autodesk Revit in a Construction Technology Course

Mike Christenson
University of Minnesota

Introduction

This paper describes the introduction of Autodesk Revit within a construction technology course, co-instructed by this paper's author, and offered to first-year professional M. Arch. students at the University of Minnesota in spring semester 2006.

Description of the Course

ARCH 5512 (Building Methods in Architecture) is a required three-credit course in the second semester of the first year of the University of Minnesota's M. Arch. professional degree program. The primary objective of the course is to elucidate connections between idea and construction, particularly as these connections are made visible through the production of large-scale detail drawings. ARCH 5512 is preceded in the first semester by ARCH 5511, which focuses on large-scale construction systems.

ARCH 5372 (Computer Methods II) is also a required course in the second semester of the first year. ARCH 5372 is a one-credit pass-fail course intended to introduce students to relationships between design and digital technology. In previous years, this course was integrated with design studio, or offered independently in a workshop format.

In spring 2006, the two courses (ARCH 5512 and ARCH 5372) were integrated into a single course with a common meeting time and place. The resulting course was co-taught by this paper's author, Mike Christenson, and by Renee Cheng, the Head of the Architecture Department at the University of Minnesota. Christenson wrote and delivered lectures based on the course text, and provided in-class instruction in Revit; Cheng wrote and delivered lectures on illustrative case studies presented at the beginning of the semester.

The combined course enrolled 50 students in spring 2006. The course met twice a week (on Wednesday and Friday mornings) for a total of approximately three contact hours per week. The typical course meeting consisted of a lecture delivered by one of the two instructors. On four occasions in the semester, this typical schedule was displaced in favor of in-class small-group reading discussions led concurrently by the three graduate assistants.

Students were advised at the beginning of the semester that they should expect to spend an average of six hours of outside-of-class work per week to receive a passing grade. The course had three graduate teaching assistants, one of whom was concurrently enrolled in an upper-level design studio engaged in the use of Autodesk Revit.

In addition to the lectures which consumed most of the semester contact hours, the course engaged several parallel tracks of instruction, including assigned readings, a site observation project conducted in groups, and an individual detailing project (which is the primary subject of this paper).

The assigned article and book-excerpt readings amplified issues relating to the construction site project and to relationships between the act of detailing and other aspects of design and construction. The construction site project required students to jointly observe progress at a local site for the duration of the semester. At the conclusion of the course, each group was required to produce and submit for evaluation a binder consisting of field reports, images, and a report tracking the fabrication and installation of a specific building element (such as a precast concrete ornament).

A series of cumulative exercises, requiring the use of Autodesk Revit, provided practical experience in applying lessons learned through lectures and readings, as well as a practical introduction to the use of the software. Spring 2006 was the first time in which this series of exercises was offered to students.

These parallel tracks of instruction were not strongly integrated throughout the semester. Rather, students were held responsible for identifying and acting upon connections between the various tracks. For example, students could bring issues introduced through case studies to bear upon the production of the final construction site project report. The final exam and an accompanying practice exam with annotated solutions were comprehensive and explicitly required students to draw upon knowledge from each of the various tracks.

The course used Edward Allen's *Architectural Detailing: Function, Constructibility, Aesthetics* as its primary text. Allen's text is not proscriptive. Rather, the text proposes that the act of detailing is (and has historically been) guided by patterns of assembly and of practice. In presenting Allen's text to the students through lectures, Christenson chose to classify the patterns in Allen's book either as "detailing patterns" which relate to the assembly of materials, or as "patterns of practice" which refer to general standards for professional operation.

Revit as a Medium

Revit is building information modeling (BIM) software produced by Autodesk. Its similarity to software such as AutoCAD or SketchUp exists in its ability to construct a simulated three-dimensional model of a building. But while AutoCAD and SketchUp stop at simulating the geometry of a building, Revit allows elements within a building model to be parametrically linked: the components of such a model are defined and characterized by adjustable parameters.

This has several implications for design and digital modeling. First, it means that in a Revit model, a change to the position or extent of a building element will automatically update other elements to which it is linked. For example, raising the roof of a building in the model will automatically increase the height of walls whose height is parametrically linked to the underside of the roof. Or, moving a wall in the model will automatically adjust the lengths of other walls whose endpoints are linked to the first wall. Similarly, changing the location of a window in an elevation view will update the appropriate plan; changing the height of a floor in a section view will update the appropriate building elevations, and so on.

Secondly, *families* of similar elements can be defined in Revit, such that changing a component within the family will automatically change instances of that family throughout the model. For example, a single family of differently-sized windows can be defined, each sharing a common trim design and mullion profile. A change at the family level to the trim design will automatically update all windows in the project based on this family, regardless of their size.

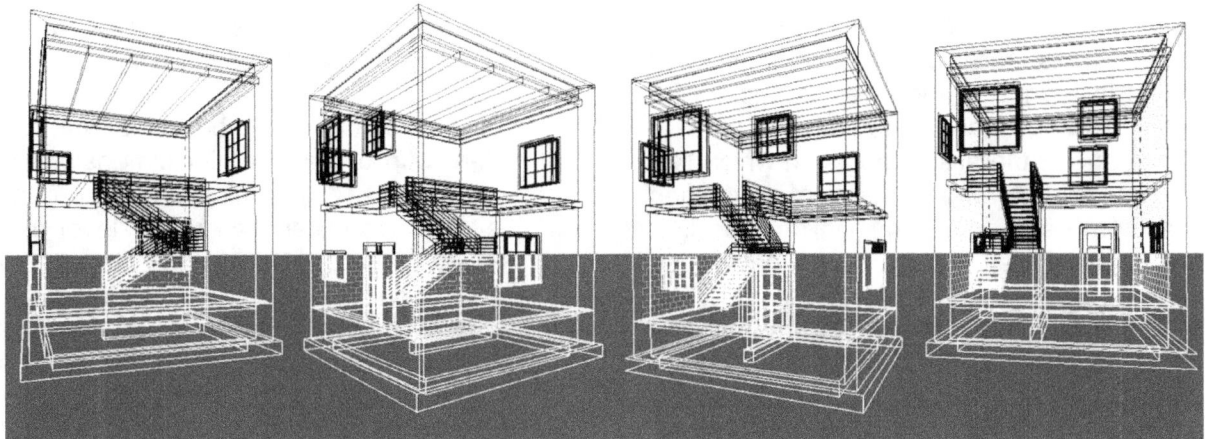

Figure 1. Completed Revit model (Student: R. Vroman).

Unlike most of the software with which incoming students were likely to be familiar (e. g. AutoCAD, Photoshop, perhaps also InDesign or Illustrator), Revit does not use layers. Instead, Revit models are organized categorically (by family and by type), and by *levels* (which correspond to datum lines within the building model, such as floor levels or window sills).

Clearly, the act of constructing a parametric building model transcends in complexity the act of constructing a three-dimensional model as in SketchUp or AutoCAD. Revit depends, as these other applications also do, upon a designer's ability to visualize and work within an on-screen simulated three-dimensional environment. But, the act of creating a parametric building model in Revit requires that a designer be able to intelligently define relationships between and within building elements. It is also true that the successful user of Revit, in addition to understanding how the software works, must understand construction technology sufficiently well in order to intelligently define such relationships.

The use of Revit in the course

Because of their experience in the prerequisite construction course taken in the immediately preceding semester, incoming students were expected to possess fundamental knowledge about typical construction assemblies. But, the students were not assumed to have any experience in digital three-dimensional modeling software (although several students did in fact have such experience, gained in undergraduate courses or in a professional workplace).

In-class Revit training consisted of two short workshops and question-answer sessions. At the first of these two workshops, students received a handout with annotated step-by-step instructions for the digital modeling of a small structure similar to the structure required for completion in class. The training was provided subject to a stated understanding that it would not lead to "mastery" of the software, but would instead provide sufficient exposure to the software to make it useful to the students in a fundamental way: that is, enough to permit each of them to construct a straightforward digital model of a small structure, and to subsequently modify the model and its associated details in response to a series of statements provided through five exercises.

The five exercises, of which the first three were grouped into a single submittal, tested the applicability of Revit to the act of modeling construction, and specifically to the act of detail production. The exercises were structured to simulate the act of producing a mini-set of construction documents for a simple rectangular building (Fig. 1), using a system with which students were generally familiar from the previous semester's course (brick veneer on CMU backup). While each student was required to construct their model in Revit, the mode of production for detail drawings was deliberately left open in all but one of the assignments, in which Revit was required for all aspects of production including detail drawings. In the assignments which left the mode of production open, most students chose to submit hybrid solutions combining printouts from their Revit model with AutoCAD printouts or precise hand drawings. Leaving open the possibility of alternating hybrid solutions with the required all-Revit submittal was intended to encourage students to confront and address the limitations and capabilities of Revit relative to traditional (or at least pre-Revit) media.

The difficulty in structuring the exercises was to conceive of content and processes which tested the students' evolving knowledge of detail patterns and their skill in applying these patterns to a simulated building design, while simultaneously focusing attention on the behavior of Revit software.

The initial exercise stated the conditions governing the entire set of exercises:

> "Beginning with initial conditions and proceeding through two successive revisions, students will test the ability of Revit to support the process of detail development.
>
> "The initial conditions define the physical limitations and general appearance of the structure. Successive revisions to these conditions simulate the scope of possible revisions which practicing architects may encounter in the production of contract documents for an actual structure. Revisions may include (but are not limited to) changes to the originally defined size or shape of the structure; changes to the originally defined materials; changes to the scope, number, and size of openings within the structure, and so on."

The initial three exercises defined the conditions of the structure to be modeled:

> "The structure shall be rectangular in plan, with overall exterior dimensions of 15'-0" x 30'-0". It shall include a ground level at grade, and an upper level at a height of 11'-0" above grade. Its exterior walls shall be insulated cavity walls, consisting of a single bearing wythe of 8" concrete masonry units (cmu) and a single wythe of brick veneer. It shall be constructed on a slab-on-grade with 12" perimeter foundation walls extending 4'-0" below grade. The upper level and roof shall be constructed of solid-core 8" precast concrete plank, bearing on the cmu walls. The overall above-grade height of the structure shall not exceed 22'-0". It shall have one standard 3'-0" x 7'-0" exterior door and a total of six windows. Each of the six windows shall be square in elevation. All of the windows shall have mullions, the pattern of which shall be common between the windows (e. g. division by mullions into thirds, or into halves, or into a nine-square). Each of the six windows shall be of a unique size. Include an internal steel stair, connecting the ground and upper levels."

Students were provided with a list of documents to be submitted with every successive exercise:

> "[O]ne floor plan of each level; four exterior elevations; two building sections (one through the stair); an exterior perspective view; and sufficient details to describe the typical corner condition, the typical wall-to-ground condition, the typical cornice condition, the typical wall-to-upper-floor condition, and a typical opening (head, jamb, and sill)."

Subsequent exercises tested Revit's applicability to construction modeling by proposing specific changes to the building model. The three primary purposes of these statements were (1) to simulate typical changes that detailers could expect during a document production phase; (2) to raise the issue of how a Revit model inherently facilitates certain kinds of changes, such as raising or lowering a floor level, or changing the location of a wall in plan; and (3) to consider the assembly of a building model as being a process of configuring separate yet contributing systems. Examples of changes required in the subsequent exercises include:

> "Omit the requirement for brick veneer at the exterior walls. Instead, provide field-assembled metal panels equal to CENTRIA Versawall."

> "Add three standard doors to the ground floor, so that there is one door on each elevation."

> "Omit two of the original windows. Instead, provide a single window, 2'-0" in height, running the length of one building elevation."

> "Revise the floor plan of the structure such that it is increased in length by 10'-0". Keep all other requirements intact."

> "In place of brick, use modular stone, nominally 4" thick by 8" tall by 12" or 16" in length."

Thus, each new exercise deliberately altered the dimensions, configurations, or materials of the structure, simultaneously provoking response, testing the applicability of learned detailing strategies, and encouraging students to question the appropriateness of the software to the situation. Students found that the appropriateness of Revit was particularly called into question at the moment of detail production.

The Act of Detail Production in Revit

Revit possesses an apparent advantage over AutoCAD relative to the act of preparing standardized construction documentation: *the automation of context*. The production of a detail drawing using AutoCAD generally requires the detailer to provide context through the use of external references, and consequently, a detailer's attention is constantly refocusing between large and small. For example, if during the production of a detail drawing, a design change should occur to the large-scale floor plan or building section, the detailer must proactively bring this context forward to test its influence on the detail; neglecting to do so runs the risk of miscoordination. Revit directly impacts this process because it automates the presence of large-scale context on the production of small-scale work. When a design change occurs to a floor plan (such as the movement of a wall) or to a building section (such as a change in the elevation of a floor level relative to grade), Revit's inherent linkages automatically bring context forward to small-scale work. Changes to small-scale components are similarly brought forward automatically to affect larger ones. In a similar spirit, Revit's built-in interference check tool automatically finds physical conflicts between systems, and numbered detail references automatically change if a drawing is moved from one sheet to another. These built-in linkages and hierarchical definitions largely reduce (though they do not eliminate) the possibility of miscoordination.

But even within this place of advantage, there exists a moment in the production of details at which the primary mode of operation shifts from the act of establishing parametric linkages and testing large-scale manipulations into the production of 2D projections. This shift in operational focus occurs at the moment in the detailing process where a "callout" (i. e. a large-scale detail drawing) is defined from a building section or floor plan. The shift occurs because *the mode of operation required when adding information to a callout view becomes practically indistinguishable from the act of tracing an external reference in an AutoCAD drawing*. Language accompanying a Revit tutorial on detailing makes this identity clear:

"In the callout view, you trace over the building model geometry, add detail components, and then complete the detail by adding break lines and text notes."[1]

Significantly, although detail components may be family-based and may embody parametric linkages, they are *view-specific*, meaning that they do not carry forward to other views. Positional changes or size changes to a detail component within a single callout view do not impact the position or size of this component within other callouts. In other words, the act of detail-to-detail coordination is operationally identical to the act of detail coordination in AutoCAD: in both cases, the detailer must expend thoughtful effort to manually update positions, configurations, hatch patterns, text-based information, and so on. Because moving 2D line drawings between AutoCAD and Revit is trivially easy, Revit's presumed advantage over AutoCAD is to some degree called into question.

As an example consider the ubiquitous bearing angle in a cmu-backup brick wall. Such a wall modeled in Revit possesses a set of descriptive properties or attributes; the same wall modeled or drawn in AutoCAD is fundamentally limited to geometry (i. e. the wall doesn't inherently possess descriptive properties). To indicate a bearing angle in a Revit callout, a detailer may elect to model the bearing angle as a component, then to extrude it around all or part of the building, and to parametrically link it to the wall. Alternatively, a 2D representation of the angle may simply be inserted as a component within the callout view. But in either case, the callout view which eventually finds its way to the construction document set is "finished" in a 2D drafting mode analogous to the use of AutoCAD (where the angle is drawn within the detail view as a simple 2D-drafted object).

Capabilities and Limitations of Revit

Seen within the primary purpose of the course, the detail assignment submittals foreground ways in which multiple tools and media can be used productively to support the act of architectural detailing. In particular, student responses to the exercises highlight Revit's success as building information management software, illustrating its ability to change information quickly at the scale of the whole building. But, the same student responses also suggest that Revit does not possess uniformly clear advantages over other media in the act of detail production. Instead, many students found that because of the ease with which 2D detail drawings can be transferred between AutoCAD and Revit, it was more efficient for them to use AutoCAD for the production of detail drawings, and Revit to support the building model and building-level changes. A limited number of students responded similarly through the use of hand-drawn details.

As discussed in the previous section, Revit possesses the capability to automate context by means of comprehensively established linkages between elements and components throughout a building model. As a consequence of the ease with which it permits changes and modifications to model elements, Revit has a strong capability to capture and hold the attention of its users. But, while clearly enhancing production, the same capability has a vaguely troubling aspect. Precisely because use of the tool focuses immediate understanding of the concrete and specific, and because changes are so easy to make, it is easy for students to come to believe that Revit models possess a sort of "truth" not available through other means. This in turn suggests that in the long term there may be

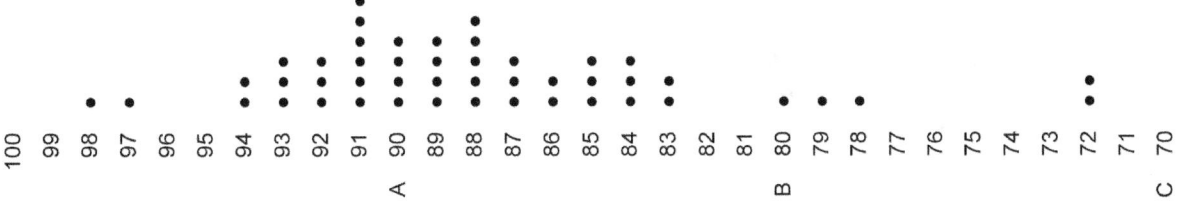

Figure 2. Chart of student performance.

a risk of students developing an overreliance on Revit at the expense of other media.

Through its multiple tracks of instruction, and particularly through the Revit assignments (which required production of content), the course implicitly raised a set of questions of recurring interest to this paper's author[2]: *what are the ways in which multiple tools and media can or should be used productively to support the act of architectural design? To what degree does the use of a particular tool or medium in a design process limit the possible outcomes?*

Conclusions and Opportunities

Student performance in the course (Fig. 2) was generally good, and student responses to the Revit assignments indicate the success of the strategy of "introduction" rather than "instruction toward mastery." There remain several opportunities for improvement in the course structure, the most obvious of which are a streamlining and integration of the multiple tracks of instruction, and expanded opportunities for Revit training.

As examples of the kind of integration between tracks which might occur in a future course offering, the construction site project could be restructured to require the students to draw details from observation, or to critique details within a provided set of drawings of the project. Or, details from the presented case studies could be made available for student critique or development based on an application of Allen's patterns.

Another approach to improved integration between multiple tracks of instruction would seek to identify commonalities between the pedagogy implied by Allen's text (instruction through patterns) and the instruction of Revit. Just as Allen posits "detail patterns" guiding the production of details, a future course could identify "Revit patterns" which guide the efficient and productive use of the software. The scale-shift discussed in an earlier section could be presented as one such pattern of use, as could the hierarchical definitions inherent in components and families.

Because students enter into the course with varying degrees of experience with three-dimensional modeling software, it would be appropriate in future course offerings to provide additional Revit training as an option to interested students. This additional training could happen in a workshop format, which could be held within class time or outside it. But, as Stephen Mamber writes:

> "[...i]f digital media courses aren't closely tied to conceptualizing the nature of the technology itself, they run the danger of becoming supervised software tutorials. .... To teach digital media, then, is to produce a new form of hybrid student who has gone beyond the parochial separations of production and theory."[3]

References:

Allen, Edward. *Architectural Detailing: Function, Constructibility, Aesthetics.* New York: Wiley, 1993.

Christenson, Mike. "Confidence in the Presence of Conflict: Digital and Analog Media in Architectural Representation", in *Pixel Pencil Progression: [Proceedings of the] 2005-2006 Design Communication Association Biannual Conference,* Bozeman, Montana: Montana State University, 2005.

Khemlani, Lachmi. "AECbytes Product Review: Autodesk Revit Building 8/8.1" (September 7, 2005). http://www.aecbytes.com/review/2005/RevitBuilding8.html

Mamber, Stephen. "Teaching Digital Media", *Cinema Journal,* Vol. 36, No. 3 (Spring, 1997), pp. 117-122.

Notes:

[1] Excerpted from Revit tutorial titled "Creating a Detail from a Building Model", included with Revit Building 8.1.

[2] Christenson, 2005.

[3] Mamber, 1997.

Building Skins – Design Strategies for Architecture Students

Ulrich Dangel
The University of Texas at Austin

Abstract

Architecture students often inadequately address and misrepresent issues of building enclosure in their design projects, revealing a general lack of understanding of the subject matter. This paper will examine how we can provide students with a set of diagramming and evaluation tools which allows them to find appropriate design solutions for building envelopes.

As educators and researchers in the field, we have a responsibility to help students realize the importance of building skins and their potential as components of sustainable low-energy architectural concepts. We should educate students on how these intelligent envelopes function, which technologies and materials are commonly used, and how they are detailed, assembled, and installed.

By employing investigation techniques that are specifically developed for a studio environment, students are encouraged to analyze building skins and their various functions. A set of criteria that includes strategies for orientation, daylighting, ventilation, shading, and insulation helps students to make decisions and allows them to integrate and apply these concepts during the earliest stages of design.

As a result, students are able to acquire a palette of drawing techniques and evaluation tools which assist them in designing building skins that adequately respond to varying climatic conditions and regional contexts. This approach to diagramming a building and its envelope has potential to greatly influence and improve sustainable design processes.

The Status Quo

During their architectural education, students are influenced considerably by the current state of the built environment and the significant changes it has undergone since the arrival of low-cost fossil fuels.

Before inexpensive energy was widely available, the efficient use of energy for heating and the principles of solar energy gain were important criteria in the design of a building and its envelope. Orientation of the building, its exposure to sun and wind, the choice of materials and the detailing of the building skin were all directly influenced by the local conditions, such as climate, topography, availability of building materials, as well as local construction knowledge and craftsmanship. Over time, this led to the evolution of a building culture which demonstrated a direct relationship between the functional criteria of a building and its external appearance, a connection that can still be found today in traditional buildings (Fig. 1). However, the arrival of inexpensive fossil fuels has inflicted a dramatic change on this building tradition, and it seems like the influence of local conditions on the design of a building and its envelope is not always a critical factor today (Fig. 2).

More recently, the continued effects of global warming and the growing realization that fossil fuel supplies are limited have led us to rethink the way we design buildings and their envelopes. These issues were first raised and addressed by Olgyay and others in the 1960s and 1970s, but it appears that many design concepts and strategies developed during that time have been forgotten. Professional practice as well as the general public have identified the need to evolve and build upon these important sustainable design principles, and the architectural education in our schools deserves continued re-examination in order to push the boundaries further.

Figure 1. Traditional architecture

Figure 2. Architecture today

Design Strategies

Students typically obtain technical knowledge in lecture-format courses, but often struggle to incorporate the acquired information into their design studio projects. Although there is a strong desire by both students and faculty to better integrate this type of material, it can be difficult to make technology readily accessible in a studio environment.

There are many strong environmental design strategies and diagramming techniques that deal with the building as a whole (e.g. "Sun, Wind, & Light" by G.Z. Brown and Mark DeKay), but there seem to be few examples that address design and performance of components, such as the building envelope, in detail. In an effort to build upon what has been taught before, a more systematic design approach for the building skin could be very useful as a different delivery system for educational purposes in the studio. The challenge is to not only engage design students, but also the design instructors. The vast amount of material can be overwhelming at times and needs to be organized and made more accessible to both. Students and instructors alike should be familiar with the concepts so that they can take the information and make it their own.

The design strategies that are subsequently explored are specifically developed for the 3rd-year integrated design studio at The University of Texas at Austin, but could be used and applied in any other studio environment. This intensive design studio integrates issues of structure and systems for the first time, and therefore is the summation of the student's design-oriented work from the previous four semesters of studios. The project completed in this studio should demonstrate broad capabilities in construction technology, climate technology, form and experiential factors, as well as sociological and humanistic design concerns.

Through personal experience, many students are unaware of the wide range of essential functions the building envelope has to fulfill, and we as instructors should put an even stronger emphasis on the fact that its performance has a significant impact on the overall energy concept of a building. While the students actively engage in the design, integration, and detailing of structure and systems, the general need for a systematic design approach regarding a building's enclosure is apparent.

In order to improve the students' design skills, a simple but effective set of strategies is being developed which will allow them to understand the influencing environmental factors and will assist them in finding appropriate design solutions.

Diagramming Approach

In a typical studio setting, we teach our students how to generate parti diagrams, site analysis diagrams, space planning diagrams, and structural diagrams. We train them to graphically represent and capture the essence of their design intentions, and how they can best use these drawings and sketches to inform their design ideas. Diagrams of this kind are a very common starting point for a designer, and most of the time they are done instinctively. However, if one considers the building's enclosure to be an important subsystem besides structure, mechanical systems, and spatial framework, obvious deficiencies in the design and diagramming process of a building can be found (Fig. 3).

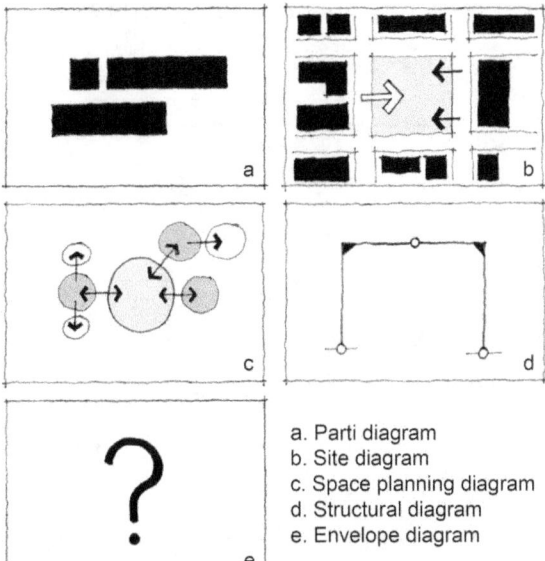

Figure 3. Design diagrams

There are many regional architectural practices and also larger international firms that employ diagramming techniques for the conceptual development of building envelopes in their projects in order to adapt them better to the climate. Similarly, the strategies initiated in this paper put an emphasis on the use of schematic drawings and sketches that can serve as a reference for the design of the building skin and its components. Diagrammatic sections and plans can be tremendously helpful in determining a building envelope's functional requirements, assembly, detailing, and material selection.

Design Process

Initially, students are introduced to the basic tasks a building and its enclosure have to perform, and important functional criteria with respect to the building envelope are discussed. Building skin typologies and fundamental principles of assembly are explored and provide the design student with the basic knowledge and vocabulary necessary for developing successful envelope concepts (Fig. 4).

Once these essential design criteria have been established, the first and most important aspect for students to consider in designing the building and its skin is the regional climate. By locating their building site, students are able to determine the applicable design climate which comes with its own set of design priorities.

Closely following these priorities, students then proceed to develop their own generic design solutions and corresponding diagrams for the problem at hand. The resulting diagrams allow them to start making basic assumptions regarding the makeup of the building envelope with respect to the specific climate zone. Students will generate a set of schematic envelope assemblies which will serve as a useful reference throughout their design process. Now that the foundation for developing and detailing the building skin has been laid, they will be able to translate these findings into workable solutions that will suit their design intent.

Starting with a more comprehensive description of the fundamental design criteria, these strategies and diagramming techniques are subsequently explored in more detail.

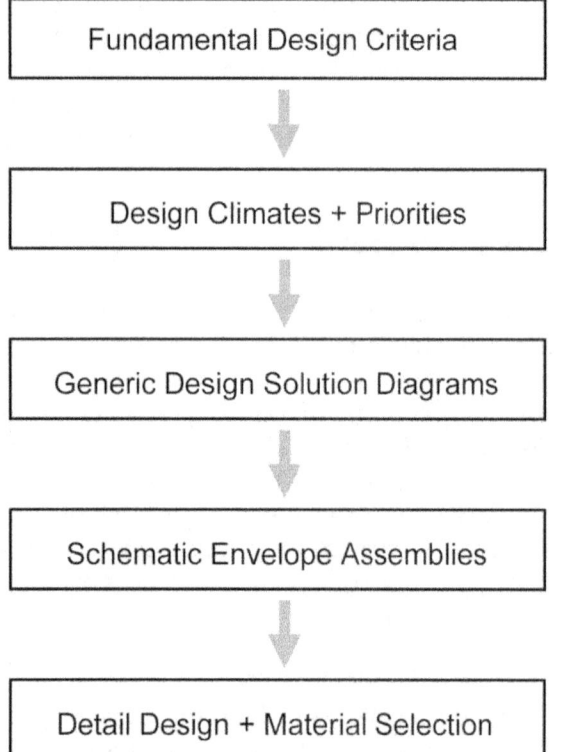

Figure 4. Design process

Comfort

The primary task of a building's enclosure is to regulate the external climate conditions in order to provide comfortable internal conditions for the occupants. Wall and roof surfaces need to respond to local climatic situations and if necessary modify their effects on the interior. The physical needs of the user are the determining factors for the design of the building envelope. These comfort factors include indoor air temperature, mean radiant temperature, air velocity, relative indoor humidity, and illuminance (Fig. 5).

All of these conditions affect the human body simultaneously, and one parameter may be adjusted to compensate for another without causing discomfort. Certain combinations of these parameters result in what most people in our society would consider comfortable conditions. Psychro-metric charts establish a relationship between air temperature and relative humidity while mean radiant temperature and air movement remain constant, and as a result these graphs are able to analyze and locate comfort zones.

However, comfort levels vary among people, and influencing factors include culture, gender, body type, clothing, and physical activity. Consequently, an individual's ability to control and regulate the comfort-related parameters by means such as operable windows, shading devices, or decentralized air-conditioning systems, has become increasingly important.

It is important to note that with the exception of relative indoor humidity, all comfort-related parameters can be directly controlled and manipulated through appropriate conception and design of the building skin. This should serve as a guiding principle for students throughout the design process.

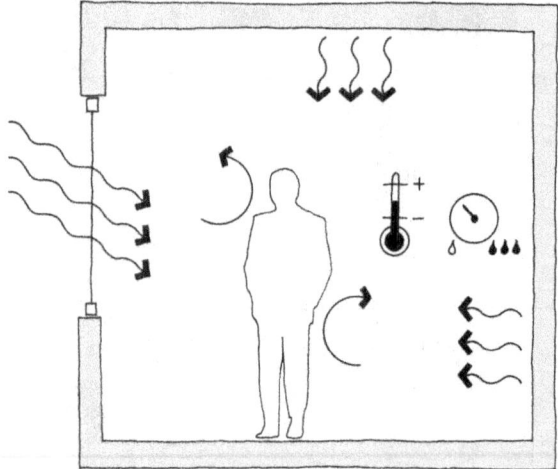

Figure 5. Comfort

Functional Criteria

Buildings today are made up of several subsystems: the load-bearing structure, the mechanical systems, the interior spatial framework, and the building envelope. The building skin is the dominant system of all subsystems and has to fulfill a wide range of essential functions. Students have to realize that the performance criteria for the roof and façade involve more than just the general protective functions of insulation and waterproofing. When developing concepts for the building envelope, they should consider the following functional criteria:

Weatherproofing
Protection from Water and Wind, Control of Water Vapor Diffusion

Daylighting
Control of Light Transmission, Visual Contact, and Transparency

Ventilation
Control of Air Flow

Insulation
Control of Heat Transfer and Solar Energy Gain

Shading
Protection from Sun, Glare Control

Soundproofing
Control of Sound and Noise Transmission

Structure
Transfer of Lateral and Gravity Loads

Safety and Security
Visual Protection, Fire Protection, Intrusion Protection, etc.

Variability and Control
Adjustability to Changing External Conditions

Aesthetic Face of the Building
Representation to the Outside

Assembly Criteria

In order for students to gain a proper understanding of the complexities involved, it is important to introduce them to the different typologies by which building envelopes can be classified. Not only will students be made familiar with fundamental design principles, but this process will also provide them with the basic knowledge and vocabulary necessary for professional practice.

Load-bearing/Non Load-bearing Building Skins

The differentiation between load-bearing and non load-bearing building envelopes results from two different historic construction principles. First, there is the method of creating simple shelters by stacking stones or tree trunks to provide protection from the elements. These load-bearing wall types are by and large bend- and compression-resistant structures and are typically made of clay, masonry, timber, and reinforced concrete. The second, equally ancient method is the construction of enclosures by means of stretching animal skins, leaves, or woven blankets over simple load-bearing structures made of sticks or poles. These types of structures can be considered the predecessors of modern curtain wall façade systems since they are the first example of separating vertical load transfer from other functions of the building envelope. While load-bearing building skins have certain limits, separating the building enclosure from the structure opens up a number of possibilities with regards to transparency, the use of materials and components, as well as the aesthetic expression of a building. Most contemporary architecture tends to separate the structure from the skin, but there are also recent developments, for example tensile structures, that go to the other extreme and explore the concept of minimal load-bearing exterior skins that combine a multitude of functions.

Single-shell/Multiple-shell Building Skins

Another important aspect for students to consider when exploring envelope designs is the fact that the external skin is made of individual shells. A shell can be defined as a material layer that is separated from other layers by an air cavity. The building envelope itself can consist of a single shell, or it can be made up of multiple shells, and it is crucial for students to distinguish between these two different concepts. The configuration of individual layers as part of the exterior wall influences its essential functions such as insulation, protection from wind and sun, and more importantly the ability to adapt to changing external climatic conditions or user requirements. In a single-shell building skin, which essentially constitutes a monolithic wall, a single building material more or less has to assume all critical functions. By dissolving a wall into individual shells, each layer can be optimized to perform a certain task as part of a whole envelope system. As a result, appropriate building materials can be selected which are tailored to carry out specific functions. A multiple-shell external wall for instance can consist of a thin, lightweight weatherproofing layer on the outside to protect against sun, wind, and rain, an insulating layer behind it to provide good thermal insulation, and a light drywall system on the inside to form the solid room enclosure and finish off the interior.

Single-layered/Multi-layered Shell Assemblies

Just as the building envelope can be made up of multiple individual shells, the shells themselves can be assembled of one or more layers which can aid considerably in improving their specific properties. A multi-layered shell consists of several layers made of the same or different building materials which are then linked to form a single solid composite assembly. A cavity wall serves as a good example where the brick veneer on the outside forms a single-layered shell while the backup wall made of studs, plywood sheeting, water barrier, and insulation can be categorized as a multi-layered shell.

Transparency/Translucency/Opacity

Lastly, the ability of the building skin to transmit solar radiation in the form of energy and light is an important factor when it comes to the overall energy concept of a building. By carefully considering the degree of radiation that is allowed to penetrate the building envelope, it is possible to regulate lighting levels, heat gain, as well as the use of solar energy. This allows for the modification and adjustment of external climate conditions in order to provide suitable and comfortable internal conditions which meet the needs of the occupants. All these different classification criteria offer numerous possibilities and design solutions for building envelope systems. Students should be aware that the correct arrangement of individual shells and layers as well as their ability to transmit light and energy is critical since it can significantly increase a building skin's performance and life span, while keeping maintenance to a minimum.

Relationship to Structure

It is important for students to realize that the relationship of the building envelope to the load-bearing structure has a significant impact on its detailing, performance, as well as appearance. In general, non load-bearing facades can be placed in several positions: in front of the structure, on the front face of the structure, in the same plane as the structure, on the rear face of the structure, or behind the structure (See Fig. 6). These geometric relationships determine the extent of envelope penetrations, the detailing of connections, and the structure's role as an expressive architectural element. The final positioning also considerably influences the building skin's performance with regards to deformations, thermal bridges, soundproofing, and weather-proofing.

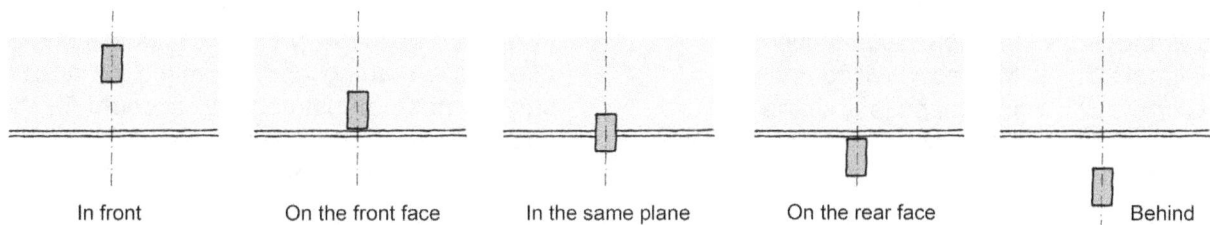

Figure 6. Building envelope in relationship to structure

Building Grids

Many students often struggle with the dimensional coordination of structure and building envelope. Building grids as three-dimensional coordinate systems are essential in establishing the position of building components as well as their relationship to each other. Often, primary structural grids are used for load-bearing elements while secondary planning grids help to locate non load-bearing components such as envelope systems. Facade and structural grids can coincide or be offset, and students should be aware that their arrangement influences the efficiency and regularity of envelope modules and as a result, the overall design and appearance of a building (Fig. 7).

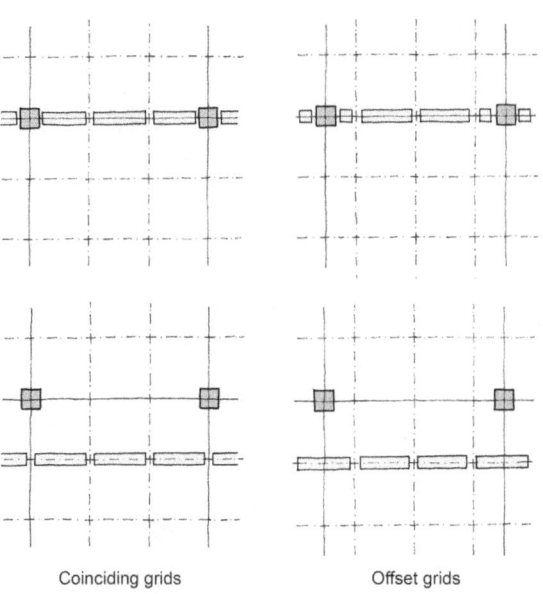

Figure 7. Building grids: coinciding and offset arrangements

Design Climates and Priorities

After establishing the preceding essential design criteria for the building envelope, the first and most important aspect for students to consider is the regional climate within which they will be working and designing. Each climate can be defined by temperature, humidity, wind speeds, and sunshine, and comes with opportunities as well as restrictions. Depending on location, different climate conditions can be advantageous or unfavorable (Fig. 8). A building has to operate within these given parameters, and maximizing the use of opportunities while minimizing the negative effects of the specific climate zone is the main goal of this design investigation.

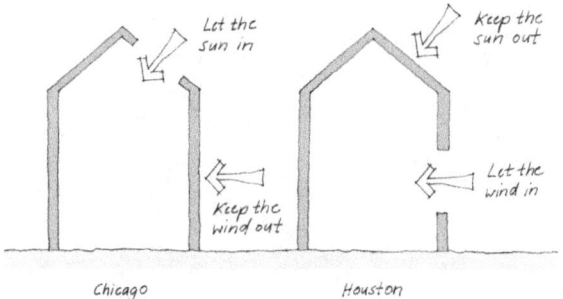

Figure 8. Design opportunities and restrictions

In the 1980s, the AIA Research Corporation established a set of design climates and priorities for the U.S. Department of Housing and Urban Development. This data is still valid today and can serve students as a useful first reference in developing design strategies for the building skin. The design climates zones can be organized in the following way (Fig. 9):

Climate	Reference City
Climate 1:	Hartford, Connecticut
Climate 2:	Madison, Wisconsin
Climate 3:	Indianapolis, Indiana
Climate 4:	Salt Lake City, Utah
Climate 5:	Ely, Nevada
Climate 6:	Medford, Oregon
Climate 7:	Fresno, California
Climate 8:	Charleston, South Carolina
Climate 9:	Little Rock, Arkansas
Climate 10:	Knoxville, Tennessee
Climate 11:	Phoenix, Arizona
Climate 12:	Midland, Texas
Climate 13:	Fort Worth, Texas
Climate 14:	New Orleans, Louisiana
Climate 15:	Houston, Texas
Climate 16:	Miami, Florida
Climate 17:	Los Angeles, California

As a first task, students are asked to locate their building site which will determine the applicable design climate zone. The selection of the design climate will automatically provide them with a specific set of design priorities. However, students have to keep in mind that these priorities should only be used as a starting point. It might be necessary to make adjustments to account for the local microclimate, especially for building sites near the border between climate zones. Closely following these priorities, students can then proceed to develop their own generic design strategies in order to modify the climate to achieve maximum energy efficiency and human comfort. To illustrate how this process works, the following example is selected and explored through the individual steps of determining possible design solutions for the building envelope.

Example: Students are asked to design a project located in Houston, Texas, which places them in climate zone 15. The AIA Research Corporation data provides them with the following design priorities:

1. Keep hot temperatures out during

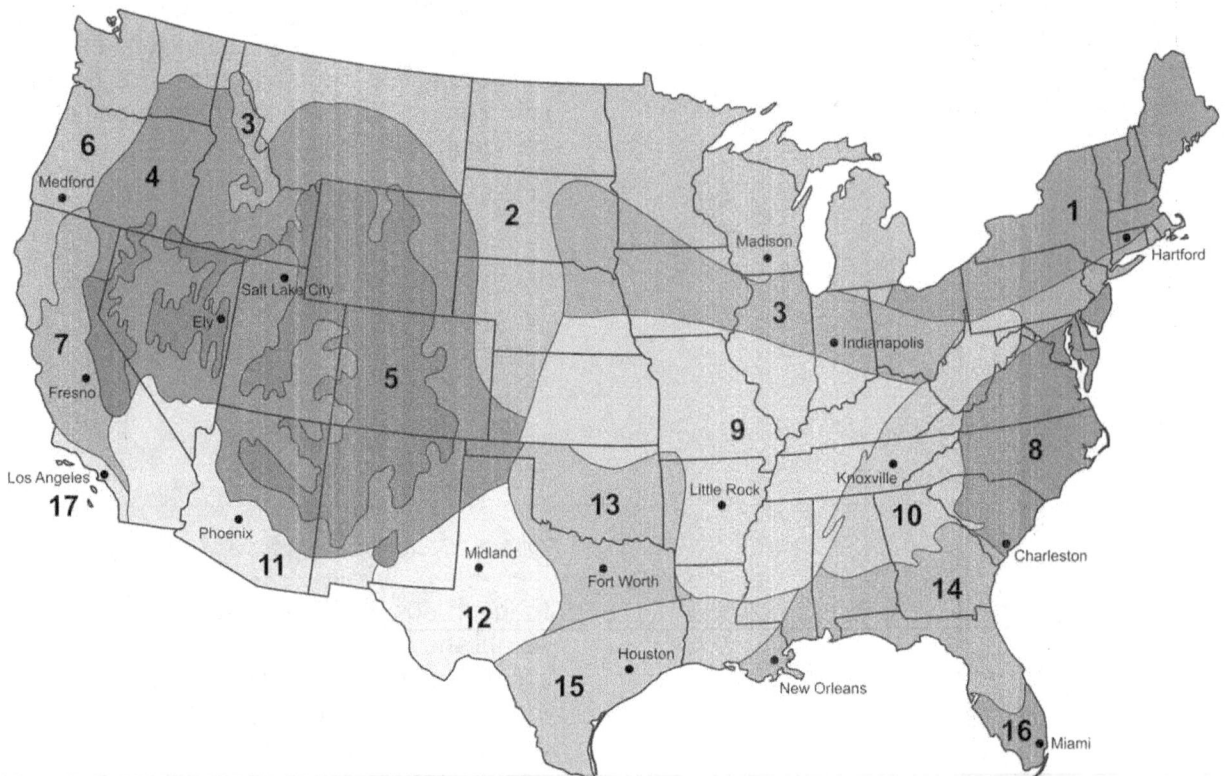

Figure 9. Design climates according to the AIA Research Corporation

the summer.

2. Allow natural ventilation to both cool and remove excess moisture in the summer.

3. Protect from the summer sun.

4. Avoid creating additional humidity during the summer.

5. Protect from the cold winter winds.

6. Let the winter sun in.

7. Keep the heat in and the cool temperatures out during the winter.

Design Solutions

As individuals or in groups, students will start to develop possible solutions for each design priority and will set up a series of diagrams taking into account orientation, ventilation, shading, daylighting, insulation, and weatherproofing. Finding appropriate answers to the design problem at hand will be a relatively simple and straightforward exercise as long as they keep the established guidelines in mind.

The following is a selection of possible design solutions and corresponding diagrams in response to the specific design priorities for Houston, Texas.

Design Priority 1: Keep hot temperatures out during the summer.

Possible Design Solutions:

a. Use compact designs to keep surface-area-to-volume ratios to a minimum (Fig. 10).

b. Site buildings into the ground to benefit from cooler temperatures.

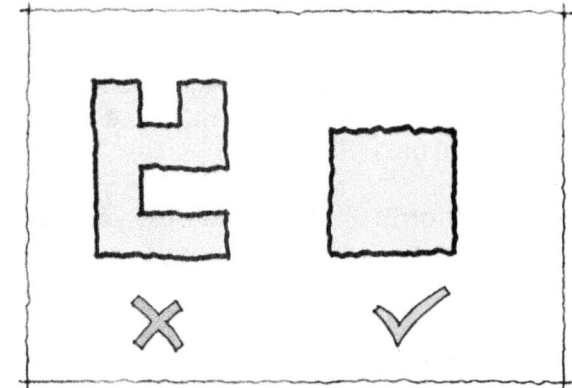

Figure 10. Design solution 1a

c. Use vegetation and shading structures to maintain cool ambient air around the building and to prevent reflection of sunlight into the windows.

d. Use sufficient insulation in the building envelope.

e. Use double glazing and movable insulation over windows to be used during the day when a space is unoccupied.

f. Isolate heat and moisture producing rooms (kitchen, laundries, etc.) from the rest of the house.

g. Zone buildings so that certain spaces are cooled only when occu-

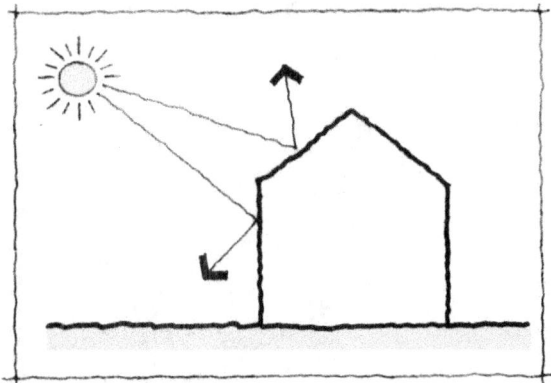

Figure 11. Design solution 1h

pied.

h. Use light-colored or highly reflective building surfaces to minimize solar heat gain (Fig. 11).

Design Priority 2: Allow natural ventilation to both cool and remove excess moisture in the summer.

Possible Design Solutions:

a. Keep enough distance between structures to allow for maximum air movement around and through the building.

b. Orient buildings to capture the prevailing winds (Fig. 12).

c. Elevate the main occupied floor to avoid the high humidity found near the ground and to take advantage of higher wind velocities.

d. Maximize cross ventilation by using large openings on both the windward and leeward sides of the building.

e. Use open floor plans for cross ventilation. Use high and low openings to benefit from the stack effect.

f. Use double roofs to allow the wind to extract the hot air collecting between the two roof surfaces (Fig. 13).

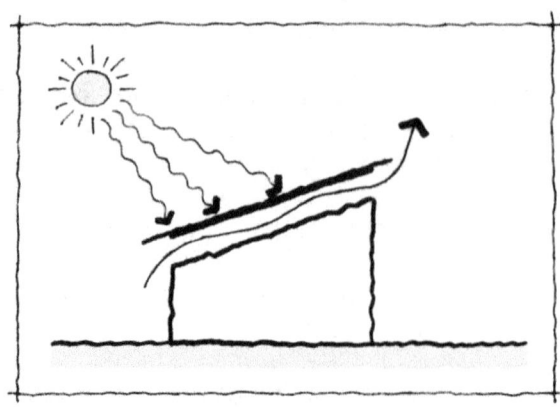

Figure 13. Design solution 2f

g. Use double-height spaces for vertical air movement and to benefit from stratification.

h. Induce ventilation through solar chimneys on calm days or in areas with no summer winds (Fig. 14).

i. Use roof openings to vent both attic spaces as well as the whole building.

Design Priority 3: Protect from the summer sun.

Possible Design Solutions:

a. Orient the short sides of the building to the east and west and avoid windows on these facades if possible (Fig. 15).

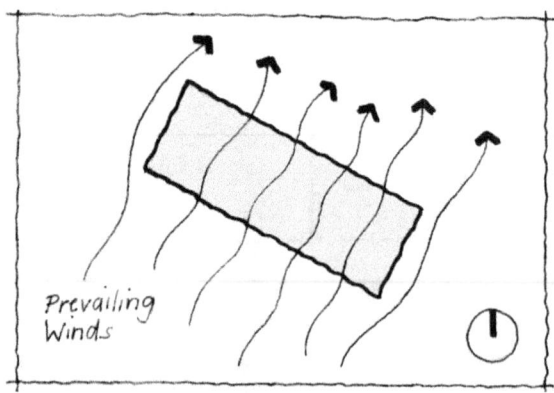

Figure 12. Design solution 2b

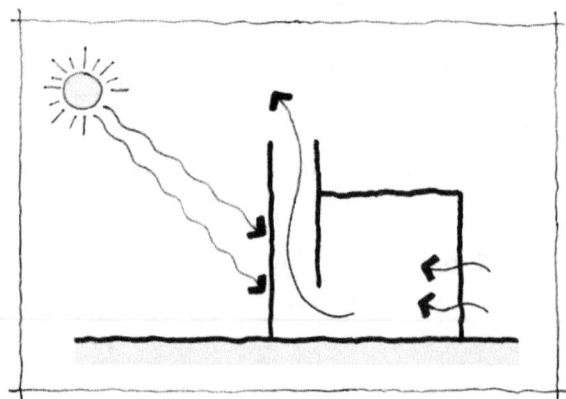

Figure 14. Design solution 2h

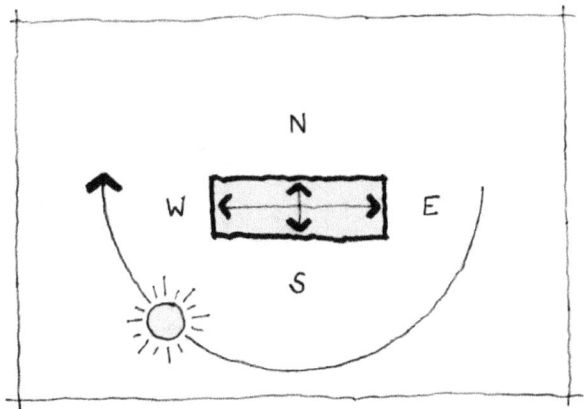

Figure 15. Design solution 3a

b. Use the shape of the building to provide shade for itself (e.g. cantilever floors, balconies, court-yards)

c. Use exterior shading devices on all windows.

d. Protect exterior wall surfaces, especially the west façade, from the sun with porch and trellis systems (Fig. 16).

e. Use movable shading devices that can retract to benefit from full sun penetration in the winter.

f. Use open rather than solid shading devices to avoid trapping hot air in front of windows.

g. Use light-colored or highly reflective building surfaces to minimize solar heat gain, especially on the roof and the west façade.

h. Use planting to shade the building. Evergreen trees are best used on the east, west, and north sides. Deciduous plants are most appropriate to provide shading for the southeast, the southwest, and the roof.

Design Priority 4: Avoid creating additional humidity during the summer.

Possible Design Solutions:

a. Ventilate kitchens, baths, and other moisture-producing spaces to the outside in order to remove excess moisture.

Design Priority 5: Protect from the cold winter winds.

Possible Design Solutions:

a. Use compact designs to minimize surface area exposure to the wind.

b. Place utility spaces such as garages and storage rooms on the windward side to protect occupied spaces from cold winter winds.

c. Minimize openings on the side facing the wind (Fig. 17).

Figure 16. Design solution 3d

Figure 17. Design solution 5c

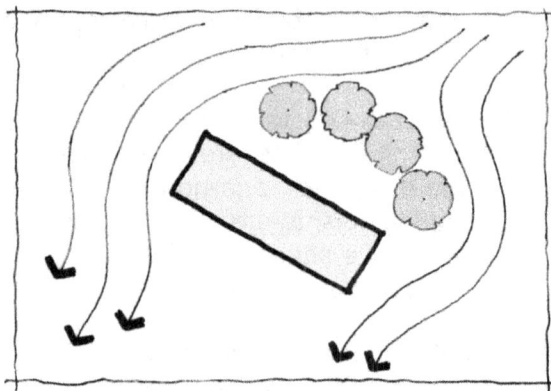

Figure 18. Design solution 5e

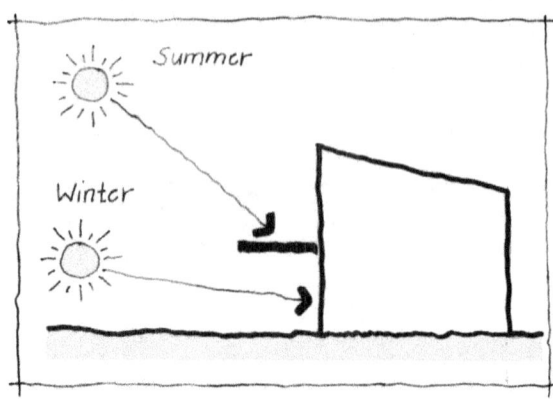

Figure 19. Design solution 6d

    d. Use tight construction and high-quality windows and doors to reduce winter infiltration.

    e. Plant or build barriers against the wind (Fig. 18).

Design Priority 6: Let the winter sun in.

Possible Design Solutions:

    a. Arrange spaces that profit the most from solar heat gain along the south elevation. Spaces that benefit the least such as utility spaces should be located along the north elevation.

    b. Use south-facing windows and clerestories.

    c. Use open floor plans to allow the sun and sun-warmed air to penetrate throughout the building.

    d. Use overhangs or shading devices that provide summer shade but admit the winter sun (Fig. 19).

    e. Use direct solar gain for effective passive heating.

    f. Plant deciduous trees which allow the winter sun to reach the building envelope while blocking the summer sun.

Design Priority 7: Keep the heat in and the cool temperatures out during the winter.

Possible Design Solutions:

    a. Use compact designs to minimize surface-area-to-volume ratios.

    b. Minimize window areas on all orientations except south.

    c. Use sufficient insulation in walls, roofs, and around slab edges.

    d. Use double or triple glazing, low-e coatings, and movable insulation.

    e. Insulation should be continuous to prevent thermal bridges (Fig. 20).

    f. Arrange buffer spaces with lower temperature requirements such as utility rooms along the north facade.

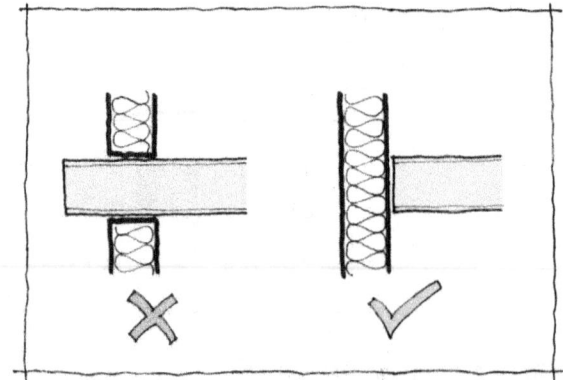

Figure 20. Design solution 7e

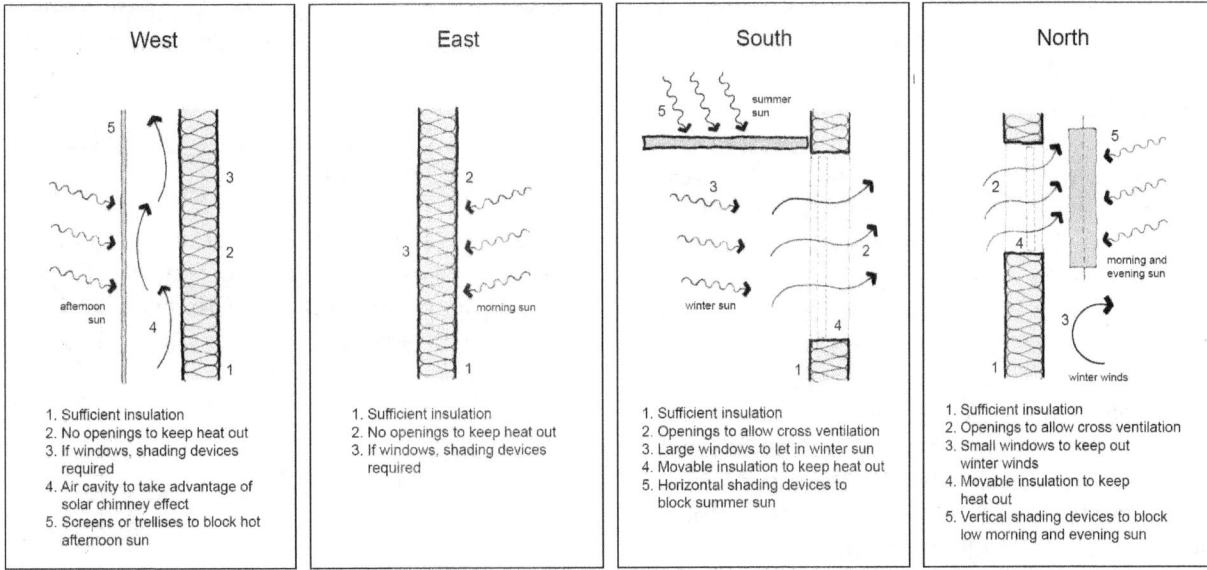

Figure 21. Schematic Envelope Assemblies

Schematic Envelope Assemblies

The design principles resulting from the previous exercise allow students to start making basic assumptions regarding the composition of the building's enclosure. Since the diagrams were conceived in isolation from each other and might even contradict at times, students have to be careful in the selection, combination, and prioritization of design solutions. Paying close attention to the microclimate, site-specific issues, and surface orientation, they will be able to develop generic wall sections for every façade of their design project (Fig. 21).

Students can start to establish basic interrelationships of the individual layers that make up the building envelope, even without taking materiality and detailing into consideration at this point. These diagrams will include exploring the placement of windows and doors, ventilation openings, shading devices, insulation layers, thermal storage mass, air cavities, and waterproofing membranes. Students will be in a position to start addressing light and energy transmission through the building skin by investigating different degrees of transparency, translucency, and opacity. Most importantly, they will be able to determine the role each individual layer plays within the assembly, as well as the function and performance of the wall component as a whole.

The establishment of generic wall sections concludes the pre-design of the building envelope. The conceived set of diagrams will serve as a useful guideline and reference throughout the students' design process, and will assist them in generating strong design ideas that are in keeping with the regional climate requirements.

Detail Design and Material Selection

Now that the basis for developing the building and its envelope in detail has been established, the next task is to synthesize the collected design information. The detailed buildup for the building's skin can be developed, thicknesses and precise relationships of the individual layers can be determined, suitable materials for the specific design climate can be selected, and the integration with other systems can be coordinated. All these decisions have a significant impact on the architectural expression and external appearance of the building, and students should ensure they translate their findings into feasible solutions that are in keeping with their initial design intent.

Conclusion

Architecture students are in need of a systematic design approach with regards to a building's skin. By establishing essential design criteria, the strategies presented in this paper can inform the design and detailing process of the building envelope and allow for a better integration of technical issues into the studio setting. A set of carefully considered diagrams can formulate and illustrate important design priorities which will provide students with a better understanding of the subject matter.

As part of a comprehensive architectural education, it is our responsibility as instructors to provide students with the necessary design tools. Not only will these strategies introduce them to the vocabulary they require to efficiently communicate with engineers and façade planners, but more importantly, it will allow them to find appropriate design solutions for building envelopes that adequately respond to varying climatic conditions and regional contexts.

References:

Allen, Edward. How Buildings Work. New York: Oxford University Press, 2005.

Brock, Linda. Designing the Exterior Wall. Hoboken, NJ: John Wiley & Sons, 2005.

Brown, G. Z., and Mark DeKay. Sun, Wind & Light. New York: John Wiley & Sons, 2001.

Herzog, Thomas, Roland Krippner, and Werner Lang. Facade Construction Manual. Boston, MA: Birkhäuser, 2004.

Lechner, Norbert. Heating, Cooling, Lighting. New York: John Wiley & Sons, 2001.

Olgyay, Victor. Design with Climate. Princeton, NJ: Princeton University Press, 1963.

Schittich, Christian. Building Skins. Boston, MA: Birkhäuser, 2001.

The AIA Research Corporation. Regional Guidelines for Building Passive Energy Conserving Homes. Washington, D.C.: US Government Printing Office, 1980.

Hands-On: The Pedagogy of Design/Build

Jori Erdman, RA
Clemson University

Given the prevalence of design-build projects executed in architecture schools across the US, it is clear that the education of architects has expanded its role to embrace the acquisition of full-scale, hands-on knowledge of building. This is can be seen as a largely technological subject, for it is technology that allows us to interact with the environment through the making of artifacts. As the quantity design/build explorations continues to increase, we must ask ourselves how they relate to the pedagogy of our discipline and how these endeavors might be further embedded and enhanced through the re-thinking of traditional pedagogical models that divide architectural education into categories of design, representation, history and theory, technology and professional practice.

In addition to more fully developing an account of the current state of design/build programs, this proposal will present a pedagogical model that responds to the desire for students to engage in these types of projects as part of a more involved and thorough educational system. While there is not one clear objective in the variety of projects identified as design/build, it is clear that both students and educators alike find full-scale investigations to be of value in architectural education and therefore we are compelled to examine the pedagogical implications.

Introduction

The current state of most design/build programs is that they exist as isolated experiences within the educational framework, without the sequential attention paid to other topics. Most often these types of experiences are adopted by the studio teacher as a way to explore a variety of issues, depending on the individual interests of a critic, including: community design/public service projects, purely design-based installations, materials based investigations, and most recently, explorations of the possibilities of digitally driven processes as a method of production. However, I know of no programs that seek to define the role of design/build within their curricula as a topic worthy of the iterative, sequential development we find in other identified content areas.

With technological questioning as the core of design/build pedagogy, technology courses, particularly those focused on materials and methods, are the most obvious place to begin introducing students to the exigencies of full-scale construction related to materials and processes. Alongside the typical lectures on the properties and uses each material, students can simultaneously engage in laboratory exercises that develop their sensibilities about the other aspects of the materials and the ways in which they are used in the built environment. This core knowledge and skill base will allow students a much more sophisticated response in their advanced studio projects and a heightened appreciation of the history of building production. Educational theory supports the heightened potential for knowledge acquisition with the introduction of this type of hands-on exercise.

Figure 1. Image from http://www.ucls.uchicago.edu/photo_album/1900s/images/playhouse.jpg the John Dewey archive at the University of Chicago.

Pedagogy of Hands-on: Dewey and others

Pedagogy simply means the art or science of teaching. The term is commonly used to refer to the strategies and values held by certain individuals or institutions that are reflected in the ways that schools operate. Through curricular structure and content, teaching methods, and even class size, pedagogical aims are executed. Pedagogy is an umbrella term that implies a deliberate and thoughtful approach to the ways in which knowledge and skills are imparted to students.

John Dewey is probably the most well-known philosopher/educator to expound the virtues of hands-on educational experiences as pedagogy. Throughout his career he promoted this concept and executed it through the University Elementary School founded by Dewey at the University of Chicago. Although Dewey's focus was primarily on K-12 education, his work and writings about the virtues of hands-on learning can be extended to higher education.

Dewey believed deeply that there was a scientifically provable connection in the mind between acting and knowing that provided for a significantly heightened ability to acquire knowledge through hands-on experiences. His writings provide many examples of his experiments and experiences to support this assertion. In a superficial analysis, it might seem that Dewey was an advocate for a very basic type of vocational training rather than a more enlightened approach to the growth of intellect. In fact, Dewey believed that the hands-on approach actually opened the doors for more a more enlightened perspective on the world at large as well as the task at hand as illustrated in the passage below from his book The School and Society:

> The discussion of the Iron Age supplied a demand for the construction of a smelting oven made out of clay, and of considerable size. As the children did not get their drafts right at first, the mouth of the furnace not being in proper relation to the vent, as to size and position, instruction in the principles of combustion, the nature of drafts and of fuel, was required. Yet the instruction was not given ready-made; it was first needed, and then arrived at experimentally. Then the children took some material, such as copper, and went through a series of experiments, fusing it, working it into objects; and the same experiments were made with lead and other metals. This work has been also a continuous course in geography, since the children have had to imagine and work out the various physical conditions necessary to the different forms of social life implied. What would be the physical conditions appropriate to pastoral life? to the beginning of agriculture? to fishing? What would be the natural method of exchange between these peoples? Having worked out such points in conversation, they have afterward represented them in maps and sand-molding. Thus they have gained ideas of the various forms of the configuration of the earth, and at the same time have seen them in their relation to human activity-, so that they are not simply external facts, but are fused and welded with social conceptions regarding the life and progress of humanity. The result, to my mind, justifies completely the conviction that children, in a year of such work (of five hours a week altogether), get indefinitely more acquaintance with facts of science, geography, and anthropology than they get where information is the professed end and object, where they are simply set to learning facts in fixed lessons. As to discipline, they get more training of attention, more power of interpretation, of drawing inferences, of acute observation and continuous reflection, than if they were put to working out arbitrary problems simply for the sake of discipline (Dewey, 63-65).

In this example, the students are not just receiving a skills based education, or vocational training, but are actually gaining knowledge about a variety of topics which can be supplemented by the more abstract lessons of in-class teaching. I would not argue for a fully hands-on based education, particularly at the university level, but rather a look at the benefits of more fully incorporating this type of learning in our current system. The studio as it exists is often touted as a great integrator for many different topical areas due to the breath of complexities in solved any architectural problem, even if only on paper. However, as evidenced by the Dewey example, there are clearly increased learning opportunities when hands-on exercises are strategically included in an architectural curriculum.

History of Hands-on Architectural Education

Booker T. Washington established one of the most notable design-build programs when he decided that he could combine a learning opportunity for students with a need for buildings at the Tuskegee Institute. In this decade's long experiment, students constructed over 40 buildings on the campus and also began a very successful enterprise of brick-making at the Institute. Washington based his concept for

Figure 2. Image from Up from Slavery: An Autobiography by Booker T. Washington of student constructed building.

vocational training on the model of the Hampton Institute founded by General Samuel Chapman Armstrong. The General founded the Hampton Institute in Virginia as a center of higher learning and vocational training for African Americans and Native Americans following the end of the Civil War. Booker T. Washington attended the Hampton Institute and later taught there before being hired to establish the Tuskegee Institute.

Washington had a fairly practical rationale for the use of students in construction of the buildings on the Institute grounds: he was driven both by a need for the buildings and by the need of students for income to support their education. As he stated in Up from Slavery: An Autobiography, "Many of the students, also, were able to remain in school but a few weeks at a time, because they had so little money with which to pay their board. Thus another object which made it desirable to get an industrial system started was in order to make it available as a means of helping the students to earn money enough so that they might be able to remain in school during the nine months' session of the school year"(138).

The students at Tuskegee were paid for their labor on the buildings while at the same time instructors used the construction as an opportunity to train and teach students. While the system was not without its critics, it certainly accomplished both goals and is not unlike many work-study programs in practice today. "As soon as the plans were drawn for the new building, the students began digging out the earth where the foundations were to be laid, working after the regular classes were over. They had not fully outgrown the idea that it was hardly the proper thing for them to use their hands, since they had come there, as one of them expressed it, 'to be educated, and not to work.' Gradually, though, I noted with satisfaction that a sentiment in favour of work was gaining ground" (Washington 143).

Washington continued to pursue this type of education for his students, echoing the values expressed by Dewey when he says, "My plan was not to teach them to work in the old way, but to show them how to make the forces of nature - air, water, steam, electricity, horse-power - assist them in their labour" (Washington 148). In this way, the seemingly simple tasks involved in constructing basic structures, became lessons about much larger and broader concepts. The value in this pedagogical model was not so much in the labor itself but in its potential to educate, assuming there is a teacher involved who encourages students to see the larger issues, as well as a curricular structure that supports the overall system and understanding.

In the intervening years since the last group of students completed a building project at the Tuskegee Institute, there was a long period of inactivity for hands-on projects. Anecdotal evidence suggests that many schools incorporated hands-on experiences in piecemeal fashion as opportunities presented themselves but these projects never became part of the agenda of any one school. There is very little in the way of notable activity at schools until 1967 when Charles Moore began the building project at Yale University which continues today. Several more enduring programs have been initiated in last 15 years such as the Rural Studio by Auburn University and ARCH 804 by the University of Kansas.[1] However, almost every school in the US now sponsors such programs, albeit sporatic and individualized.

The Rural Studio at Auburn University is probably the most well-known and received of all the current design-build programs. This program began in 1993 under the guidance of Auburn University School of Architecture Professors, Samuel Mockbee and D.K. Ruth. The first projects executed by the Studio were houses for families in the community of Mason's Bend, Alabama. As conceived of by Mockbee and Ruth, second year architecture students would spend a year designing and building a home for a family. The program quickly expanded to include thesis projects for graduating students and added programmatic typologies for community buildings.

Figure 3. Author's visit to Rural Studio Project Spring 2002.

In its current incarnation, the Rural Studio consists of three programs: the second year program; the thesis program and the outreach program. While it would seemingly have great impact on the overall structure and content of the curriculum, there is little evidence that this is the case. The stated mission and objective of the Studio is to engage students with community in the service of a greater good. While certainly this is laudable and has some educational value, the educational benefits of this type of program do not seem to be fully explored by Auburn.[2]

Literature Review

William Carpenter, in his 1997 book, <u>Learning by Building: Design and Construction in Architectural Education</u> gives an overview of design-build programs at some institutions. Some of them no longer exist as presented in his text. Carpenter focuses on the learning benefits as they relate to design and a students understanding of the complexities of project execution. He discusses the notion of craft as related to the full-scale construction of projects and also spends some energy on a discussion of the good that such projects can do in the community. His basic suggestion for curricular change, however, remains rooted in the sense that these types of projects are studio projects and should focus on craft and form-making as the major learning opportunity.

Carpenter's book also neglects to incorporate a serious critique of design-build as pedagogy; instead he relies to a great extent on the self-reported successes of each program. Many of the programs are driven by the particular interests of a given faculty member and suffer from a lack of wholesale buy-in from a faculty. There is little evidence of the success of these programs, other than some anecdotal evidence of student's satisfaction with the experience of participating in the programs.

Ernest Boyer and Lee Mitgang's special report titled, <u>Building Community: A New Future for Architecture Education and Practice</u> published in 1996 makes some mention of design-build programs but does not focus on this mode of teaching in particular. However, the report does make two important assertions that have bearing on this paper. The first assertion is a call for a "connected curriculum," in which critical thinking plays a large part in the students success. They discuss a curricular model that is both broad but also where courses with the discipline relate strongly to one another. The second assertion is their call for "service to the nation." In this chapter Boyer and Mitgang challenge schools of architecture to take on models of engagement and the generation of new knowledge, thus becoming better participants in the world and in education.

The observations outlined above relate to the questions of design-build pedagogy both directly and indirectly. The "connected curriculum" concept emphasizes the importance of inter-relating course work for educational gain. Thus, design-build programs that exist as an isolated experience within a curriculum fail to achieve their maximum potential for learning. The service challenge is one that many, but not all, design-build programs attempt to address by doing community projects and low-income housing projects. The report has been extremely influential over the past decade as schools of architecture try to meet the challenges posed by Mitgang and Boyer, but much work still needs to be done to fully integrate the hands-on experience into an architectural education.

One thing that should be noted is that with the term hands-on projects, I am referring to projects that involve students in projects that have full-scale material implications. This is to be distinguished from projects that involve architectural students with projects that make use of representational skills, often at great benefit to a community or individual. Hands-on projects can include temporary installations, or permanent constructions such as houses. These projects may be conducted in service to community or simply for their own sake. They may be entirely hand crafted or in today's world, may make use of digital processes. In any case, the value is derived from the student's interaction with real materials and full-scale construction. This type of hands-on experience can allow the student, in the words of John Dewey, "more training of attention, more power of interpretation, of drawing inferences, of acute observation and continuous reflection." These are powerful tools in a changing world and a profession that will certainly see as radical transformation in our student's lives as it has in ours.

Curriculum

Figure 4. Students working on construction project.

The majority of architectural education programs in the United States are predicated on distinctions among five major components of the discipline and profession: 1. Design, 2. History/ Theory, 3. Technology, 4. Graphics, and 5. Professional Awareness. While design, in the form of studios, includes the possibility of incorporating the other components in various ways, these are almost always supplemented by lectures and seminars in those content areas as well. In the best programs, the reverse is also true; each of the topical areas of history/theory, technology, graphics and professional awareness also include related design content. The integration of content through iteration in other classes is a well-documented, successful pedagogical strategy for architectural education.

The pedagogy of hands-on gives a school the opportunity to focus on full-scale making as a fundamental part of the architectural eduction. The distinctive attributes of a design-build focused curriculum include collaboration, stewardship, craft, and professionalism. The primary goal of a hand-on curriculum is the acquisition of knowledge about materials and construction but could also include lessons in community service, delivery methods, budgeting, culture, history, etc. The underlining philosophy of hands-on is that architecture as practice and discipline contributes to the making of the built environment and that the education of an architect must prepare students think and respond constructively.

While I have not yet found a program that fully focuses on a hands-on approach to architectural education as I am proposing, in executing projects and courses at two different schools, I have developed my own thoughts about how a curriculum could work. Although these courses and projects were not part of an integrated curriculum, I offer my experiences as an example of how a curriculum could begin to incorporate a pedagogy of hands-on.

To that end and for the purposes of this paper, I would ask how can design-build programs, which are primarily the focus of studio projects, be strengthened and elevated by the inclusion of relevant content and skills-building through other course work. It seems like a natural fit for technology courses to begin to underwrite a design-build curriculum. Materials and methods classes are inherently focused on many of the same issues that would support a design-build curriculum. By incorporating hands-on exercises as part of the content in these classes, students can build a body of skills and knowledge that could later be implemented in the execution of their own designs.

Foundations courses could begin the process of teaching students to think through full-scale exercises. At Drury University, where I taught from 1997-2000, they had a course titled "Construction Principles" that was required in the second year of a five year program. The course was intended to fulfill what would typically be called Materials and Methods. The textbook for the course was Edward Allen's Fundamentals of Building Construction and was supplemented with readings from Frank Ching's Building Construction Illustrated. I was scheduled to co-teach the course with the School's Woodshop Supervisor, who had previously had a long career as a contractor. The course was scheduled to include 2 hours of lecture and 2 hours of laboratory each week.

Figure 5. Students working on a detail by Tadao Ando.

Our approach to the course was to focus on the primary methods of construction while also instilling in the students a sense of history and the role of building and culture within the built environment. We followed the curricular model outlined by Ed Allen but also included readings on tectonics by Kenneth Frampton, Marco Frascari, and others. We supplemented the abstract lessons in the lectures and readings with hands-on experiments in the laboratory such as framing a stud-wall when we talked about wood-frame and laying a brick wall when we discussed masonry. We also made site visits to construction sites when available.

In the second half of the semester, we challenged the students work in teams to study the methods and philosophies employed in the construction of 20th century masterworks. Their studies included research through texts, drawings, photographs and finally, the construction of a full-scale replica detail from a building. These details were installed at the entry to the School of Architecture as models for all to study but the primary educational lessons came to those students who were involved in the construction.

A significant part of the value of this course can be derived simply from the title, Construction Principles. A focus on principles shifted our mindset from simple rote knowledge to a quest for deeper understanding of the underlying forces at work in construction. Instead of teaching students only about brick construction, we tried to get them to understand the principles of stacking parts to create a whole. In that lesson we looked at the entire history of the constructed world for examples and cultural and environmental contributors to the development of the building method as used today. As part of an integrated hands-on curriculum, this course would be a key component in teaching students the value of technology in their thinking and making as they proceed to upper level courses.

Figure 6. Graduate students studying a detail.

In a graduate level design-build project that I was part of at Clemson University, we took another approach to hands-on construction when we worked with a local community. For this project, we required the students to not only take our studio, but also a seminar that could focus on issues related to culture and construction in the classroom. The project was not as focused on tectonic potential but more on cultural readings of place and construction. I would argue that the project would have been much stronger if the students had come to the studio prepared to think about problems from a tectonic base rather than simply as a formal problem. But it did teach me the value of an integrated curriculum where other courses can contribute to a greater understanding of the complexity of a design/build project.

Figure 5. Graduate students in seminar.

Conclusion

The pedagogy of design/build has to be considered by any school wishing to be identified in that way. The value of hands-on experiences are clear, whether we are looking at John Dewey's examples, or our own lives. The problem with current projects is that they lack the rigor expected of other courses because they have not been fully integrated into a curriculum. By focusing on a curriculum that seeks to engage students through this model of learning, schools can elevate the status of these types of projects from one-off, formally based exercises, into highly sophisticated lessons that contribute to the base of knowledge, not just for the students themselves, but for the discipline and society.

References

Boyer, Ernest L. and Lee D. Mitgang. Building Community: A New Future for Architecture Education and Practice. Princeton, New Jersey: The Carnegie Foundation for the Advancement of Teaching, 1996.

Carpenter, William J., AIA. Learning by Building: Design and Construction in Architectural Education. New York: Van Nostrand Reinhold, 1997.

Dewey, John. "Chapter 1: The School and Social Progress." The School and Society. Chicago: University of Chicago Press, 1907.

http://www.cadc.auburn.edu/

http://www.cadc.auburn.edu/designbuild/index.htm

http://www.cadc.auburn.edu/soa/

http://www.ruralstudio.com/

Notes:

[1] The Yestermorrow School in Vermont has been teaching a Design-Build curriculum since 1980. While this program is very successful, this study is intended to focus on accredited schools of architecture that incorporate aspects of design-build, therefore I have left out a discussion of this school.

[2] Within the College of Architecture, Design and Construction at Auburn, there is a new program called a of Design-Build Masters degree begun in 2005. This program seems to echo the initial directives of the Rural Studio but is not part of the program. The curriculum is not highly articulated and like the Yestermorrow School, does not give an accredited architecture degree.

Teaching Construction Details with Color

Craig Griffen
Philadelphia University

Color in Technical Drawing

A technical drawing mainly differs from a design drawing in the fact that it conveys greater detail of the physical relationships between various materials and their methods of assembly. Communicating this precise information often results, by necessity, in rote working drawings that can be understood by the contractors who must build the design. Traditionally, technical drawings have been 'black and white' line drawings because of the necessity for low-cost blueprint reproductions. But the main purpose of any architectural drawing, whether design or technical, is to communicate the design intentions to the reader. Therefore, new digital methods of graphic reproduction create a new potential for technical drawings that can better communicate these intentions, especially as a teaching tool in academia.

The two-dimensional nature of working drawings is efficient in specifying exact dimensional relationships between materials but it flatness can make it difficult to distinguish what is drawn in section versus what is drawn in elevation. Students, who typically have little experience with working drawings, often have a hard time reading them. A variety of line weights can help create spatial depth but is still limiting in a black and white format. Computer drafting can make line weight even harder to understand as thickness is replaced by color on the screen. While a standard set of colors that tries to match heavier lines to advancing colors and lighter lines to receding colors can help imply thickness, students read colors differently. Some see red as an advancing color and some see it as receding. Therefore they often create their own line weight-to-color assignments that make it even more difficult to read their work. Plotting the drawings is the only way to test the legibility and students are reluctant to stop and take the time to print. They *think* they understand what they are drawing even if others don't. This reluctance to print presents problems since colored lines on a black monitor screen are the reverse image of the final drawing with "black" lines on white paper. So a paradox of drawing on the computer is that while it has the potential for amazing graphics in a short period of time, the interface between screen image and paper image is more disconnected than drawing by hand. It takes practice, imagination and a lot of trial and error plotting to be able to visualize the final drawing from a screen image.

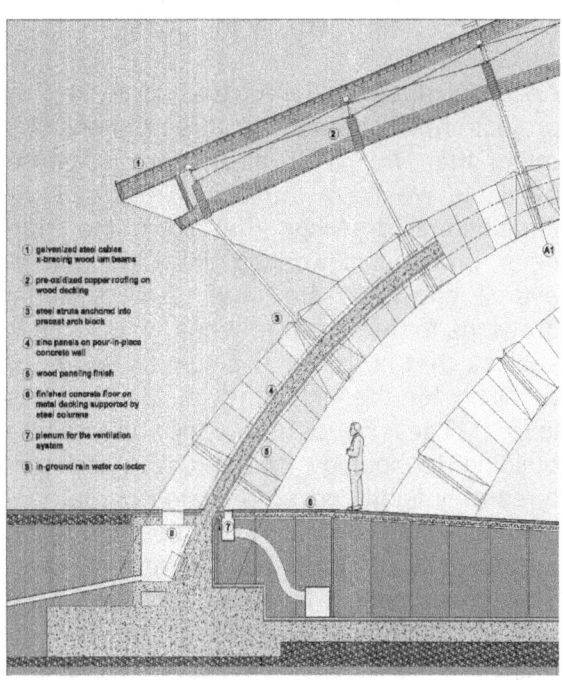

Fig. 1 Wall Section of Padre Pio Church (Ben Liddick)

In terms of rendering patterns in black and white, material designations and symbols help distinguish between materials cut in section or shown in elevation as well as identify the materials themselves. However not all symbols are universally accepted and while some help distinguish a material as different from what is next to it, they don't always specifically identify it. (i.e. glass, metal panel and even an open void can look the same in elevation) New methods of color reproduction can be helpful to more clearly identify materials. The computer provides us with the ability to quickly add tone, color, texture, shading, etc. to explain and enhance the reading of a drawing. Another key aspect of computer drawing is of course speed. In the days of hand drawing it could take hours to apply tone films or hand stipple. Therefore it rarely justified the expense. Now a 2-second click of the mouse can render any size area and allow for multiple testing of different patterns to find the best result. The time versus cost factor is now mostly irrelevant. Therefore the use of color, texture and shading in technical drawings has applications for students who are just learning about construction by being able to easily and clearly identify the parts.

An initial question I had was whether this project should be done in three dimensions rather that two. With all the new software available we have the ability to create 3-dimensional drawings that solve the 'flatness' problem of working drawings. However I chose to stay with 2-dimensional drawings for two main reasons. First, this is a class that is teaching students issues of detailing for the first time, at least at this level. They have had prior introductory building technology courses, but the lectures only lightly covered issues of material assembly and too much of it seemed to be forgotten by the time they get to this class. Therefore I feel it is easier for the novice student to approach detailing from two dimensions first. The second reason is that even though we have digital technology available to produce 3-dimensional drawings, the vast majority of firms today are still producing mostly 2-dimnesional details. The reasons for this may be inertia, people stay with working methods they are familiar with; or it may be for clear communication, all trades including engineers, consultants and contractors understand this format. Regardless of the reason it is the most common language for communicating detailed construction information and needs to be understood by students. In the future, as technology advances and becomes more common, this approach will need to be adapted or discarded.

Fig. 2 Detail of Beyler Museum (Kevin Hollenbeck)

Procedure

The course in which we study technical drawing is a fourth-year construction documentation class that utilizes AutoCAD as the primary program for investigation. (While this program may not be the best, its popularity in the profession still necessitates its use, for now) When I started teaching the class this past year, I significantly changed its focus. Before, the class concentrated more on the creation of a set of working drawings on the computer. All aspects of a set of drawings were taught from schedules to stair sections. I noticed that many students already know some of the basics of working drawings from working in offices where they will also acquire many firm-specific techniques while working as interns. On top of this I found a severe lack of understanding of construction techniques. As I felt the understanding of detailing more important to students than creating door schedules, I changed the emphasis from a computer-drafting course to a course on construction detailing and documentation using CAD.

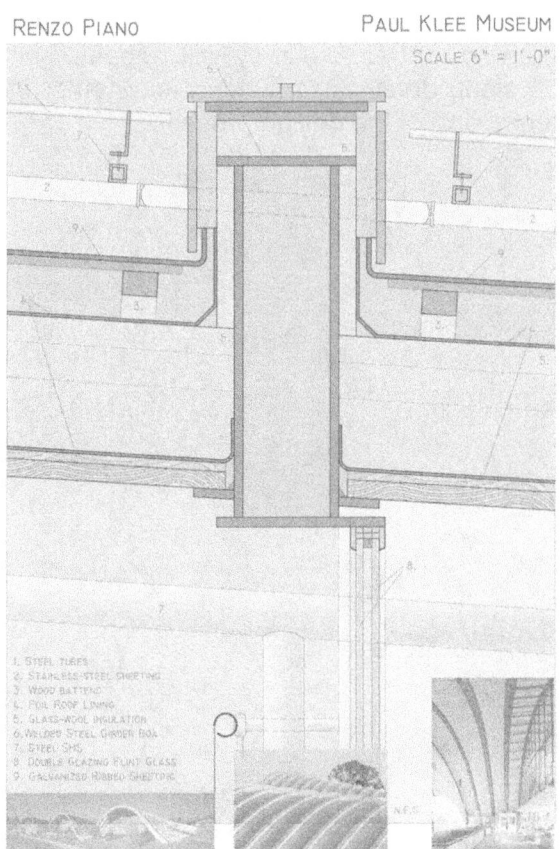

Fig. 3 Detail of Paul Klee Museum, Nicole Sandruck

The course is taken concurrently with a fourth-year design studio in tectonics that I also teach. The first exercise of the studio is a six-week design project for a small-scale building that uses structural steel as its main support system. When the design portion of that project is complete, it is moved into the detailing class to be developed in technical detail for the remaining 9 weeks of the semester. By the end of the semester the students (as well as I) have spent the entire time on a single project, thereby producing a well-developed building design. While they were designing their studio project for the first 6 weeks, I needed a good project for the documentation course to prepare them to detail their own work later. Therefore the first project in the documentation class investigates the materials and methods of assembly of a prominent existing building. It then demonstrates how rendering can describe the building's materiality and add a sense of three-dimensional space. This project also allows for those less knowledgeable of AutoCAD to catch up with the more advanced.

The students choose a building from a short list (this semester all were by Renzo Piano) and are required to document a detail and a wall section from it. Since wall sections of a student's own design are rather rudimentary at this time, detailing an existing building helps focus on learning about drawing and construction techniques of a master. Buildings I select should meet certain criteria to facilitate success. They must have adequate documentation in drawings and photographs, be of a low to medium height, and have a rich diversity of materials. Students first draw a detail of the building as a line drawing in AutoCAD to learn about construction materials and techniques as well as drawing standards. They must scale the published drawings and convert them into measured drawings in CAD. This is the first step in understanding the scale issues of real materials. When the drawing is well developed, it is exported into Adobe Photoshop and/or Illustrator to be rendered. These programs allow for more rendering options than AutoCAD. After an in-class review of the most useful commands of these programs, they add color, texture and shading to describe the materials used in the construction. They then add critical written text and dimensions to convey the scale and physical relationships between systems. If they have rendered the materials well they should not have to add many written notes as the drawing should speak for itself. They then repeat this process for a wall section of the same building. This is why a shorter building is preferred so that the printed scale can be as large as possible. From the detail they expand outward to show it in its context within the building envelope. Starting with the detail establishes the multiple layers of construction used. Expanding the detail into a section reveals the scale. A major benefit to adding color is that the student must learn the exact identity of each material in the wall section to render it correctly. With line drawings, a mysterious empty space in a wall could be read as the side of a beam, an air space or insulation. In a colored rendering it must be positively identified to drawn correctly so they student must be diligent in their study.

At the end of this first project, they have gained a better understanding of the construction sequence, the distinction between structure and envelope materials and some basic ideas about assembly details. They can then carry this acquired knowledge into the detailing of their own design for the rest of the semester.

Whether or not graphic reproduction techniques will ever become fast and cheap enough to use color in the profession, this technique still can prove useful as a teaching tool to help students understand the complexities of construction. The additional process of adding color can transform, in the student's eyes, what they perceive as a potentially dry working drawing into a *design* drawing. Therefore they will hopefully understand detailing for what it is, another integral part of the design process.

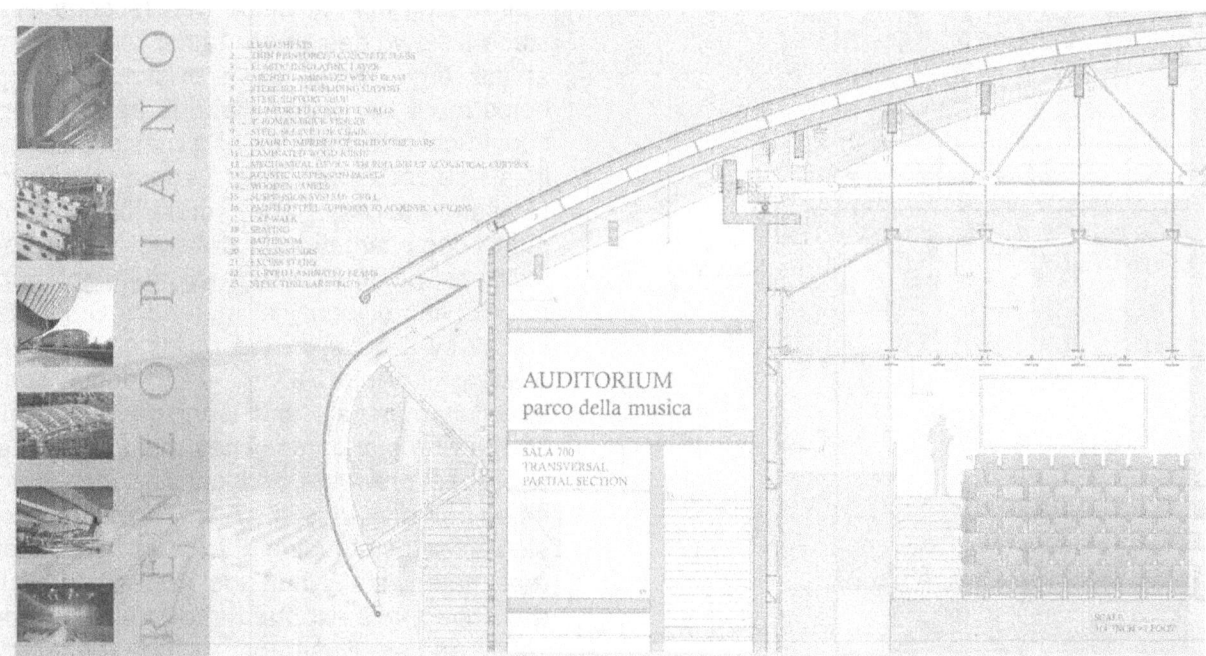

Fig. 4 Wall Section of Auditorium Building (Victoria Weaver)

Green Roof Design Workshop
A Teaching Model for Connecting Technology to Design

Donald Hunsicker, Director, Design Studies Program
Michael Fiorillo, Green Roof Workshop Instructor
Joshua Burdick, Green Roof Workshop B. Arch Student
Laura Marrero, Green Roof Workshop B. Arch Student

Boston Architectural College

Introduction
Donald Hunsicker

As architects, we know that architectural design and building technology become an integrated whole in the buildings we build. As educators, we know that architectural education typically segregates, rather than integrates, design and building technology.

At the Boston Architectural College, one method by which we attempt to bridge the divide between design and building technology is through what we call *concurrent learning*.

Our *concurrent learning* curriculum consists of two components – the academic component and the practice component. The academic or traditional classroom learning component happens from 4 p.m. to 10 p.m. During the workday hours, our students are engaged in what we call the practice component. Our students are typically employed in full-time, salaried positions in design firms. This full-time employment – or practice component of the curriculum – is integral to the students' education. In order to graduate in the architecture, landscape architecture or interior design professional degree programs, students must earn approximately one third of their total credits through experiential/practice learning and they must advance to positions involving project supervision and oversight within their respective disciplines.

Despite integrating practice and academic study in our concurrent curriculum, we have achieved limited success in integrating building technology into the design curriculum. Our capstone design projects for both graduate and undergraduate students do emphasize and require design solutions that integrate the engineering disciplines and appropriate building technologies. At the introductory and advanced studio levels, however, there is limited integration of building technology into design problems and no structured collaboration between our design studio faculty and our building technology faculty.

The Green Roof Design Workshop was one step toward closing this gap between our design and technology curricula.

Green Roof Design Workshop: Where It Fits in the BAC Curriculum

Design workshops at the BAC are part of the advanced sequence of design courses. This sequence is typically taken during the fourth or fifth year of what is normally a seven year undergraduate program.

In this sequence, students are required to complete four design studios and one design workshop. In a studio, students design a building. In a design workshop, students may design a component of a building, investigate a landscape, a design methodology, or a building type, or study some element of building technology.

Workshops give students the opportunity to explore an idea that contributes to their understanding of design but does not necessarily result in a building design. The inherent structure and substance of the design workshop at the BAC allows for flexibility in terms of approach, content, and scale of project.

BAC students, who have reached this level of the academic curriculum, typically have at least two to three years of full time employment experience in a design office. They have a working knowledge of design development, contract drawings, detailing, and some level of understanding of construction means and methods. In addition, some have begun to supervise other team members in the execution of project work.

Our design workshops, therefore, are intended for students who are advanced academically and are well past entry level positions in a design firm.

Green Roof Design Workshop: Course Goals

The Green Roof Design Workshop specifically came about as a result of a groundswell of student interest in sustainable design, the need for a new roof on our building, and the desire among certain members of our faculty and staff to integrate technology and design.

Michael Fiorillo, the workshop instructor, worked closely with Karen Nelson, the Director of Advanced Architectural Studios, and me to plan the course, establish the course goals, and develop the course syllabus.[1]

We set several fundamental goals for the workshop. One goal was, of course, to provide students the opportunity to develop their design skills.

In addition, Michael wanted to focus on the need for research into, and the use of, building technology in reaching design responses. The intent was to foster a connection between the studio design area *and* the building technology curriculum.

Developing a deeper understanding of sustainable design and how to integrate sustainable methodologies into building design was a goal inherent in the subject matter of the workshop.

As an institution, we emphasize experiential learning, and we always want to "connect" the students' academic learning, and in particular their design studio learning, with their practice experience. Some, but not all, of our students have contact with their firms' clients. Because the BAC is, indeed, planning the installation of a green roof we saw the opportunity to introduce a "client" into the studio setting. Our Facilities Director, Art Byers, was invited to participate in the workshop. His concerns and point of view would give the students a perspective they would not normally see in a design studio. (Figures 1 and 2 show our building and the roof plan.)

While the students did not have to meet a budget, and while they were given free rein to propose and design whatever it was they felt was appropriate, we wanted them to hear firsthand about the institution's concerns for such a project from the facilities director. We also wanted to give the students the opportunity to "educate the client" to the possibilities a project like this might present.

Finally, we wanted to foster collaboration among the students. Design and project implementation is a collaborative effort involving the ideas, insights and work of many people. A designer, no matter how extraordinary or visionary his or her concept might be, must be able to work with others to implement that concept. We wanted this design workshop to stress how designers can and should work together.

Figure 1. Boston Architectural College – 320 Newbury Street

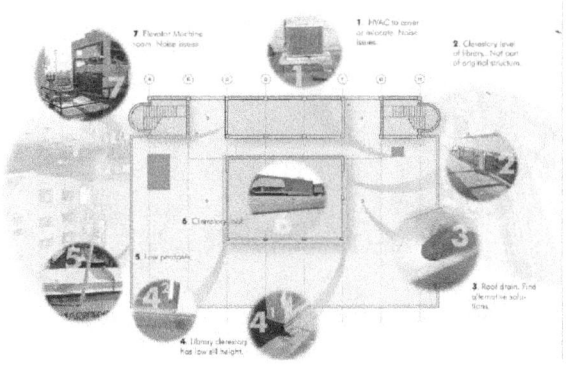

Figure 2. Student site analysis: roof plan and existing conditions (Aaron Margolis)

The next sections of this paper offer reflections on the course from the instructor's perspective and from the perspective of two students. Each was asked to evaluate candidly the opportunities and challenges the course offered.

The Instructor's Perspective
Michael Fiorillo

I served as the instructor of the Green Roof Design Workshop at the BAC this past fall and spring. Teaching this workshop has given me some insight into how building technology might be integrated into a design course.

The class size was limited to eight students, and we met for three hours a week for sixteen weeks. Students were expected to work approximately six hours a week outside class on their projects.[2]

The Green Roof Workshop employed four design teaching strategies. While these strategies were simple, I found them to be effective.
1. The first strategy was to create a course that focused equally on technology and design. I refer to this focus as a "hybrid" course.
2. The second strategy was to introduce the technical content of the course primarily through the students' own self-directed and collaborative research.
3. The third strategy was to have the BAC's Director of Facilities serve as the client for the workshop and to provide information to the students both about the existing conditions and the institution's plans for the roof.
4. The fourth strategy was to integrate an exceptional and experienced practitioner into the class both as a source of information and as a regular critic who was familiar with green roofs as a type of landscape.

The Green Roof Workshop was organized so that students spent the first seven weeks of the course researching green roof technology, the context and history of green roofs, conventional roofing technology, and the advantages, disadvantages and costs of green roofs. Students investigated specific green roof products that are available on the market. They looked at green roof precedents and garden design typologies. They also researched related sustainable topics such as living walls, solar collection, and living machines.

In each class meeting during these first seven weeks, the students presented their research to their classmates. In effect, they had to learn enough about their subject matter to teach that topic effectively.

At the end of this seven week period, the students spent two weeks analyzing the site – i.e., the roof of the building. They visited the roof, built a model, and reviewed the existing building plans. They analyzed the roof environment including ambient noise, solar orientation, and wind conditions as well as explored, albeit in an abbreviated fashion, other considerations such as handicapped access to the roof, the roof edge condition and related code requirements, and allowable modifications to the building façade in an historic district. (Figures 3 through 5 are examples of the roof analyses the students conducted.)

The students also met with the client, the College's Director of Facilities, to discuss his ideas about how the roof might be used, his concerns about on-going maintenance, and his knowledge of the rooftop mechanical equipment.

The final seven weeks of the workshop were dedicated to an accelerated design phase. The students were urged first to take up this design problem from an experiential and program-based point of view, and then during the final weeks to address materials selection, construction details, and planting strategies. (Figures 6 through 8 and 9 through 11 are some of the final design boards that Laura Marrero and Joshua Burdick presented.[3] These illustrate how these students studied and applied their knowledge of conventional construction details and their green roof technology research in developing their green roof designs.)

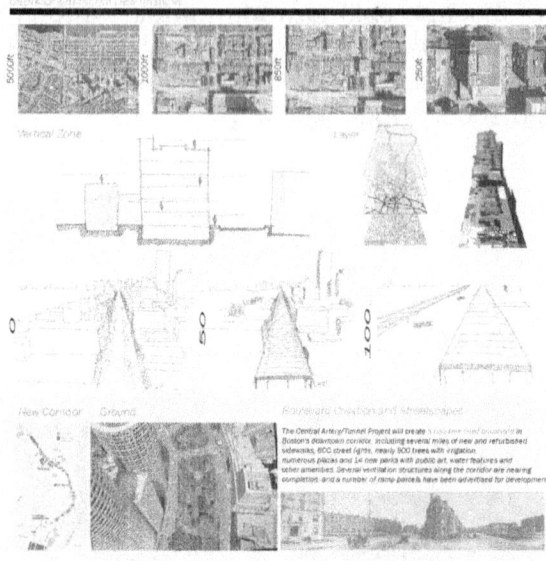

Figure 3. Student site analysis (Jung Hoon Choi)

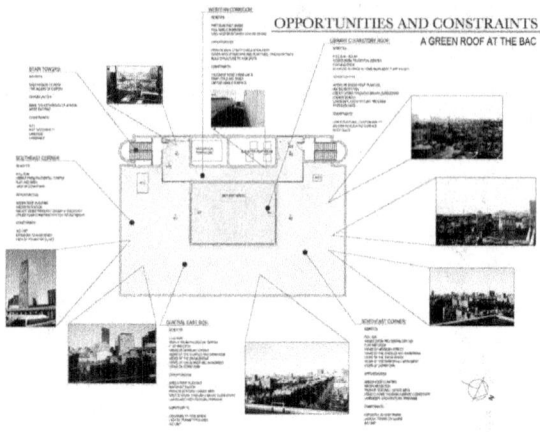

Figure 4. Student site analysis (Joshua Burdick)

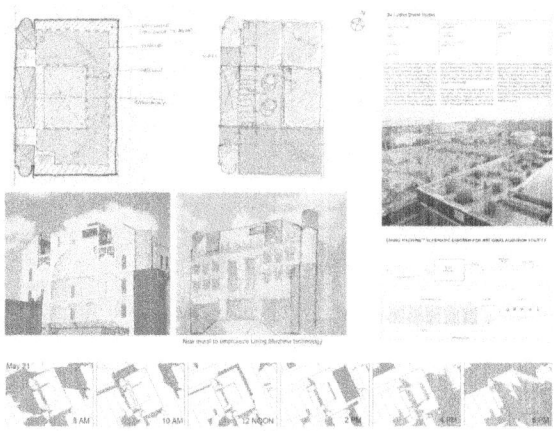

Figure 5. Student site analysis (Oliver Klein)

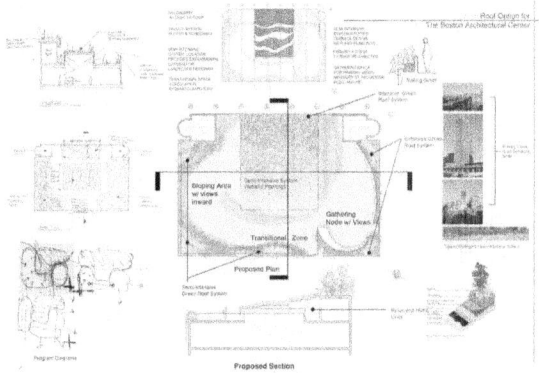

Figure 6. Design presentation (Laura Marrero)

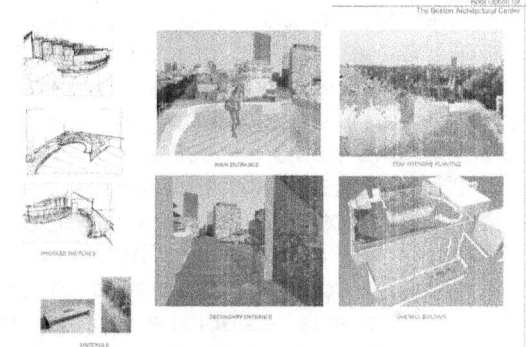

Figure 7. Design presentation (Laura Marrero)

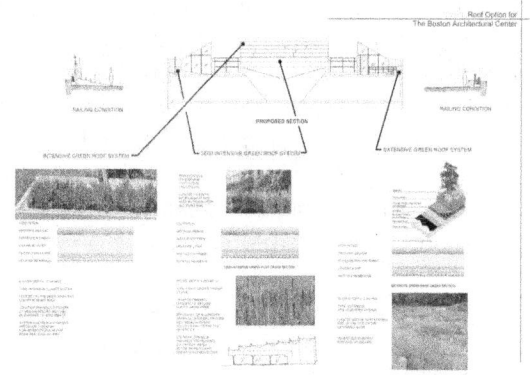

Figure 8. Design presentation (Laura Marrero)

It is critical to recognize and emphasize the course schedule and nature of the BAC studio and workshop settings. Unlike traditional schools, BAC students do not meet for extended periods of time in their studio setting. Their contact time, both with their fellow students and with the instructor, is limited to three hours per week. Hence, the actual instructor/student contact time during the research, site analysis, and the design phases of the workshop was quite abbreviated. For students to successfully complete the technology research, the site analysis, and the project design within this limited time frame, they must enter the course with a developed set of design tools and sensibilities as well as technical skills. Even with the abilities that many advanced BAC students have, they would find this to be a difficult course. It would not work in our introductory or foundation design classes.

The "Hybrid" Strategy: Challenge and Opportunity

During the two semesters I taught this course, I found that this hybrid technology / design course posed two particular challenges. The first challenge resulted from the very nature of dividing the course into the technology research portion and the design portion. This structure limited both the technical and design topics in their scope.

The hybrid nature of the course, by necessity, restricts the amount of research a student can carry out, and it holds the size of the design project to a smaller scale. Broader research topics would be difficult to cover adequately in one-half semester, and more complex design problems would require more time to explore satisfactorily.

The second, and more significant challenge, however, was to structure the seven week design phase so that students could apply the technologies researched to their designs and bring those designs to a gratifying level of resolution.

The course emphasized and encouraged the students to approach designing a green roof, not simply as an implementation of technology, but as a design problem. Because the time allowed to design the green roof was short, a number of students had difficulty balancing the various elements required by the project.

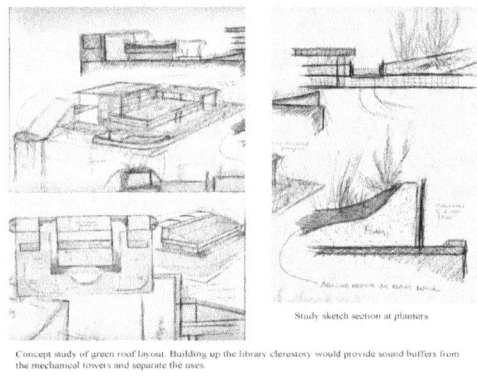

Figure 9. Design presentation (Joshua Burdick)

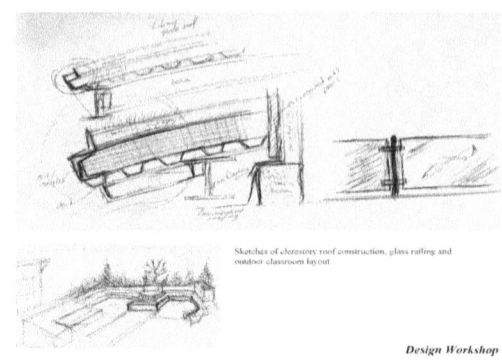

Figure 10. Design presentation (Joshua Burdick)

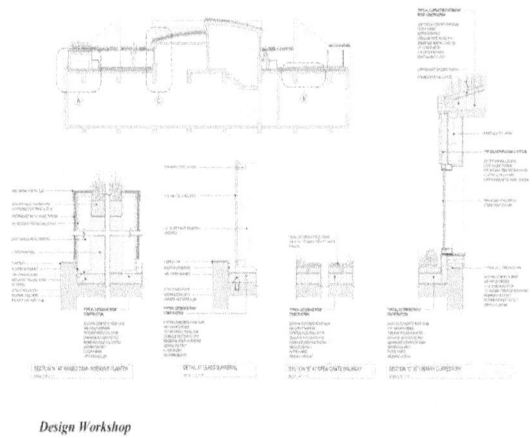

Figure 11. Design presentation (Joshua Burdick)

These elements included the existing conditions of the roof and the programs that the students developed for themselves. There are the various pieces of mechanical equipment one would expect to find on any roof. There is also a large clerestory in the center of the roof that juts above eye level and hems in the roof space. The structural capacity of the roof was likewise a consideration. Students established programs such as creating a living laboratory for landscape architecture students and creating student gathering and resting spaces which our facility needs.

Students naturally struggled with these competing and conflicting elements. Given the abbreviated design period, I found that it was necessary to provide more guidance than I had initially thought would be necessary to help the students make progress with their designs each week.

While the course structure presented these challenges, it offered the advantage of closely connecting the acquisition of technical knowledge to the design process. In the professional world, this connection is strong and consistent. In school, the design and technical curricula are usually dealt with separately. In the Green Roof Workshop, the "nitty-gritty" of the different roof types and systems became a primary part of the design parameters that the students faced. In that sense, the technology provided design opportunities for the students to employ. In developing their green roof designs, the students developed their own relationships with the technical knowledge gained in the first half of the class. The opportunity to build a technological understanding and to develop design responses directly related to that understanding is not common in school. This hybrid course gave students the chance to implement a design process not often implemented outside of professional practice.

Student Directed Research: Challenge and Opportunity

The second strategy employed in the course was student-directed research. Each week during the research phase, the students investigated two topics associated with green roofs and developed materials on those topics. Typically, I assigned one topic and the students would select the second topic. Each student was then required to present and share that information with the class. (Figures 12 through 14 are examples of the topics students researched and presented to the class.)

This strategy is useful for a range of technical topics, but it is particularly suited to emerging issues, such as green roofs, for which there is not yet an accepted curriculum and for which the technical knowledge base is still in flux. In addition to their in-class presentations, the students pooled their research through an on-line website where they provided each other with digital versions of their presentation material and research bibliographies. This "database" allowed them to pick up on each other's research and further it, as their interests dictated.

The student-directed research in this instance was highly successful; however, at least part of this success was the result of the students' enthusiasm for the topic. Student interest in green roofs (and all sustainable issues) is presently strong, and I did not have a problem with student interest. If students are less interested in the topic, there is the real possibility that the research will be less rigorous and less well-presented. Less favored topics might exacerbate this potential problem.

Another concern that arises from the student-directed research is that the range of the technical content is partly dependent on the student interest. As a result, there is the real possibility there will be "holes" in the research and the material presented. This was not a problem in the Green Roof Workshop because of the students' high interest level. They were willing and able to identify the most important topics and research them regardless of how "dry" they seemed; however, without this level of enthusiasm for the research, some important topics might not be taken up by the class.

Figure 12. Student research: green roof components (Jonathan Scamman)

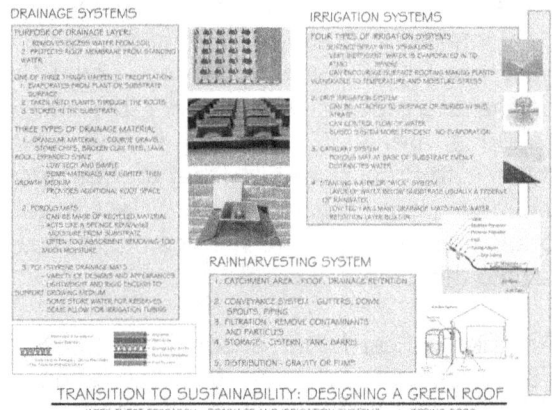

Figure 13. Student research: drainage and irrigation systems (Jonathan Scamman)

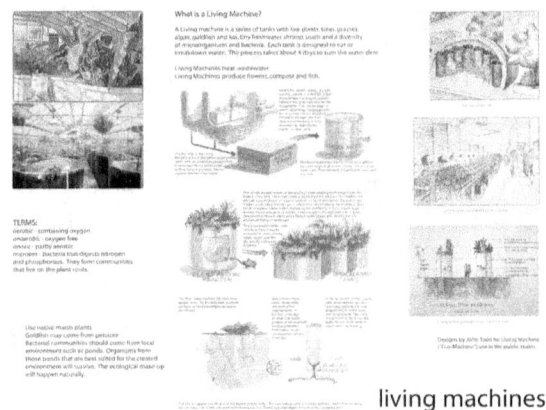

Figure 14. Student research: living machines (Amanda Russell)

The advantages of this student-directed research, however, are worth the risk of the challenges described above. One advantage is that students have the opportunity to present their research at each class meeting. This hones their presentation and public speaking skills. It also makes them realize that they must learn the material thoroughly in order to teach it to someone else. By being exposed to each other's research from week to week, the students realized that they had a responsibility to their peers to present good information, and they were spurred on by the better quality work of others.

Because the research topics were generally chosen by the students, they had a strong sense of ownership of their work and more enthusiasm for and commitment to researching the topic. By pooling the interests of the whole group, a wide range of topics were brought to the class presentations.

The most significant advantage that this student-directed research model offered, however, was that it taught the students research skills associated with design problems. The connection between research and design is more and more important in contemporary practice. However, research skills are generally not emphasized in design classes. The strategy of allowing students to decide what they researched encouraged them to develop tools they will need to educate themselves about any topic that might affect the project they do in the future.

Finally, this strategy developed into a highly collaborative effort that allowed the students to share their research and information. While I had always intended that this research component would foster collaboration among the students, I was pleased to see the extent to which the students did in fact depend upon each other to provide information and the extent to which they did learn from each other's efforts. While each student, in the end, designed his or her own project, all of the students used the information other students provided in developing those individual designs.

The Client in the Design Workshop: Challenge and Opportunity

One goal of the workshop was to introduce a level of reality to the project, not only by using the BAC's own building and its own project as the design problem, but by introducing the voice of a "real" client into the studio setting. While the workshop allowed and encouraged the students to think creatively and to explore freely as wide a range of design possibilities as they wished, we did want the students to have the opportunity to hear and learn what a client's concerns would be for a project like this.

The risk of introducing a facilities director into a design studio is the potential for a clash of cultures. A facilities director/client, who only saw the difficulties of implementing a new technology or who would not entertain different and even fanciful design ideas, could certainly have a negative impact on the students' vision and hamper their creatively.

The BAC is fortunate to have a facilities director who was a model "client" for this type of student design effort. While our facilities director was candid and straightforward about his concerns regarding the realities of implementing, paying for and eventually maintaining a green roof, he is an enthusiastic proponent of greening our building. He also supports wholeheartedly the educational value and necessity of the creative design experience students must have in school. As a result, his participation in the design reviews was always constructive and encouraging.

In addition, he came away from the workshops in both semesters seeing possibilities for the project that he had not previously envisioned.

For those students who are not exposed to clients in their design practices, this was an opportunity at least to experience, if not resolve, conflicting client desires in their designs. Students were able to deal directly with the facilities director and learn about his concerns and priorities.

The Practitioner: Challenge and Opportunity

The last strategy we employed was the integration of a designer, experienced in green roofs, into several facets of the course. An experienced professional who has expertise in an emerging topic is not easy to find. But to find an experienced professional, who has this expertise and who is willing to volunteer her time to participate in an evening class, is even more difficult. While finding that professional was a challenge, it provided perhaps the most extraordinary opportunity of the course.

We were particularly fortunate that Laura Solano, a design principal at Michael Van Valkenburgh Associates, Landscape Architects, participated in the workshop. Ms. Solano brought to the class not only design and landscape expertise, but also substantial experience in roof gardens, terrace gardens, and green roofs.

After the students completed the research and analysis phases and as they were beginning their design phase, Ms. Solano presented a green roof project that her office had recently completed.[4] The project was similar to the BAC's roof in many respects. It was enlightening for the students to see how her office had approached the same types of design challenges that they themselves were facing and to learn how her office was able to turn those challenges into a stunningly successful design. The exposure to the MVVA design process gave the students confidence in their own convictions about their projects and opened up a range of possibilities they might not have considered otherwise.

Ms. Solano also attended both the mid-term and final reviews and developed a strong rapport with the students and their work. Her critiques of the student design work offered them an extraordinary level of professional insight.

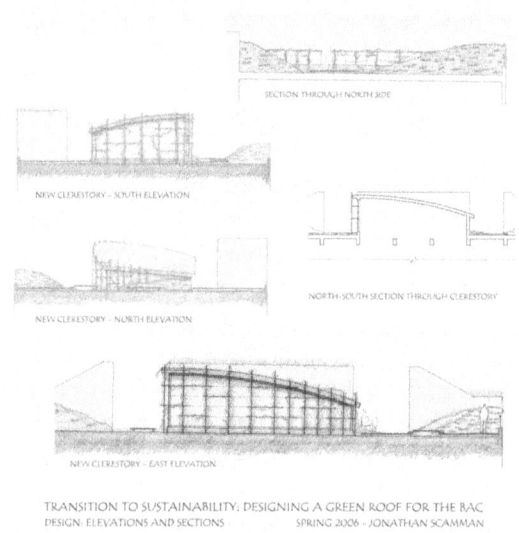

Figure 15. Design presentation (Jonathan Scamman)

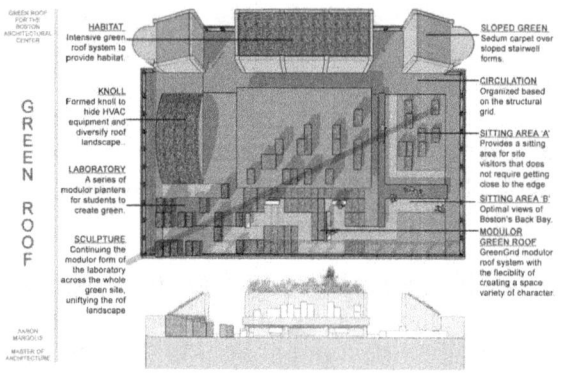

Figure 16. Design presentation (Aaron Margolis)

(Figures 15 through 18 are examples of the work done by other students in the workshop.)

Conclusion

In the end, I thought the students' experiences with the Green Roof Workshop were positive and beneficial, and that the strategies employed were successful. Nevertheless, the course was not without legitimate problems. The most significant problem was that several students did not achieve a level of design completion that they themselves found satisfying. For other students, I felt that additional time would have afforded them the opportunity to achieve a more successful design. More experience on my part to keep the students always forging ahead would have helped to alleviate this, but taking up a design problem of this complexity in a studio setting for seven weeks would be a challenge for any instructor.

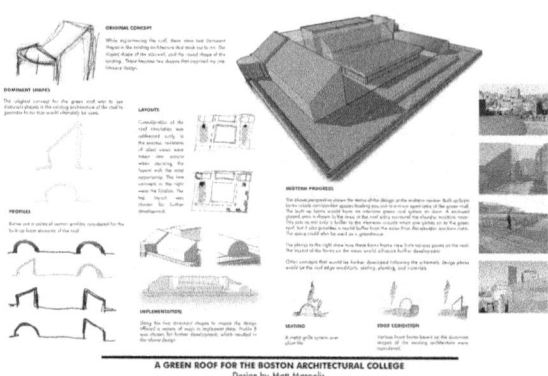

Figure 17. Design presentation (Matt Margolis)

Figure 18. Design presentation (Matt Margolis)

Despite this reservation, I believe that the class, as it was taught, did provide the students with training and practice in skills that are not usually emphasized in design school curricula. These are the knowledge and experience of interfacing technology with design and the role of research as a fundamental tool for contemporary design practice. In my opinion, the opportunity to develop these skills counterbalanced the limited design time.

A Student's Perspective
Joshua Burdick

At the BAC, my design classes have focused primarily on building analysis, program and schematic design while technical classes have focused on building systems and drafting techniques.

My employment as a designer in an architectural firm has provided the opportunity to become familiar with building technologies and utilize those technologies in real projects. In particular, I have experience with building systems, components of building envelopes, and construction details.

While both my academic and practice experiences have fostered my education, my employment experience has always been much more technical and real-life oriented, while the classroom learning has been more design and theory based. The Green Roof Design Workshop was one course that combined both the technical and theoretical aspects of a project.

The Green Roof Workshop course description stated that students would be exposed to the technology of green roof systems in the context of a design for a 'real' project at the BAC. The BAC facilities department would be the project client. I was excited to enroll in this class, and I looked forward to a class that explored new materials and technologies and applied them to a real project with a real client.

The sixteen week class was broken up into two sections, nine weeks of research and analysis and seven weeks of design and exploration. The small class size of eight students enhanced the research portion of the class. Each student was responsible for multiple research projects. Existing site analysis, precedent studies of existing green roof systems, and an extensive investigation of green roof technologies were researched by the students. We also had access to the original drawings and details of the BAC building, which allowed us to understand the constraints the existing building imposed on us.

During the first half of the course, each student presented his or her research and analysis in each class. In the end, the class had a substantive compilation of information that we all shared. This collective body of student research enabled us to benefit from each other's work and helped to inform and inspire us regarding the possibilities for the green roof design. Each of our final projects reflected the information gathered by and shared among all of us.

During the first few weeks of the class, we were introduced to Art Byers, the facilities director for the BAC. Mr. Byers conducted a tour of the roof and gave us background information about the roof structure. He also explained the school's intentions for the roof and asked the students about the possibilities we saw that the roof might have to offer. It was exciting to have a real representative for a real project, and this made the design project that much more interesting to pursue.

After touring the roof, it became apparent that the BAC roof was an untapped resource for both students and faculty. The roof could be turned into a great space that offered unparalleled views of downtown Boston, Boston's historic Back Bay, and Cambridge. The project parameters were expansive but not overwhelming. As we conducted our research and precedent studies, we were able to see the many design opportunities the roof offered.

Half-way through the semester, Laura Solano visited our workshop. Ms. Solano presented her office's design for the green roof at the American Society of Landscape Architects in Washington, D.C.

Her presentation illustrated all of the basic components of a green roof structure we had previously researched while showing a final design that was both economically feasible and visually attractive. The roof design was a beautiful transformation of a standard black, flat roof to a wonderful outdoor garden and terrace space.

The Van Valkenburgh design made it clear that green roofs did not have to be just flat, open expanses of short vegetation over a membrane roof. We saw how the creative use of rigid insulation could add topography to a level roof and create a surrounding that resulted in a more interesting space. We saw how the use of different plants could provide architectural-like elements such as walls and roofs while providing the benefits of rainwater retention, reduction of heat island effect, and additional building insulation.

Ms. Solano's presentation gave us a terrific starting point for our own designs. The students in the workshop produced a wide range of designs using different green roof technologies, building materials and plantings. Several students incorporated alternative energy recovery systems such as solar technologies into their designs.

I feel this workshop was a very successful class and exposed me to technologies I usually become familiar with only in my work setting. Researching the materials and precedents for the green roof allowed for collaborative discussions and brainstorming about the different materials and allowed ideas to flow freely. The research presentations were informative and the precedent studies provided inspiration for our designs.

The reality of the project was a positive aspect of the class. Being able to visit the "site" was helpful, and having a project in which real materials were chosen required us to give careful consideration to those choices. The designs we developed were all influenced by the confines of the existing conditions and requirements of the materials we selected.

Being able to present our design to Mr. Byers as a client gave us experience in the art of explaining design intentions to someone not familiar with the design field. It was rewarding to see his enthusiasm grow as each student presented his or her design.

Another way I think this workshop was successful was in the exploration of landscaping and the influence it can have on a building design. All of the students' designs used to some extent hardscaping and typical architectural elements, but the designs focused primarily on the landscape features. As a student who has studied horticulture and landscape design, I think it was beneficial for those students who have not worked with landscaping to experience the effect plants can have on an otherwise empty site. Laura Solano's presentation of the green roof at the ASLA was a perfect example demonstrating the multiple uses of vegetation and how plants can transform a space.

The only way I think the workshop could have been improved would be to allow more class time. My workshop met for only one and one-half hours per week for the semester.[5] The quantity of information gathered was almost overwhelming to digest in such a short class period. The majority of work was done outside of class, and I think it would have been more successful if there were more class time to research, discuss and finally design.

In conclusion, the green roof workshop was perhaps one of the most informative and rewarding class I have taken. This workshop allowed for an in-depth exploration of green roof materials and technologies and combined that exploration with a traditional studio design project. This combination resulted in a comprehensive and realistic green roof proposal.

A Student's Perspective
Laura Marrero

My experience at the Boston Architectural College has been wide-ranging and challenging. The BAC's program structure is unique: academics and practice go hand-in-hand. As a student and a practitioner, I learn more from and can offer more in both settings.

The BAC environment is different from a traditional college. I quickly realized when I enrolled in the school six years ago, that as an eighteen-year old, straight out of high school, I was an exception at the BAC. The school's community consists mainly of mature, adult students. Instructors are likewise different from the teachers in traditional schools. They are not full-time professors. They are practicing professionals, who bring real world knowledge and experience into the classroom.

The Green Roof Design Workshop speaks to the BAC method. Initially, the design problem was what interested me the most – to design a green roof for the BAC's existing building. But I learned as the class developed that the technical aspects of a green roof would be given equal weight in the course.

The structure of the class allowed for a positive learning experience through a collaborative student effort. The class included the methodology of a small scale thesis project. The workshop syllabus incorporated both in-depth research of green roof system technologies and our own design of a green roof.

The research portion of the class was successful because it consisted of individual research in a collaborative setting. We shared our research through in-class presentations. Our precedent studies of existing green roofs, along with the exploration of options for materials, plantings, irrigation, etc., provided a foundation of information and knowledge about green roofs that greatly influenced the nature of our designs.

During the course, we were introduced to Art Byers, Director of Facilities at the BAC. Mr. Byers acted as the "client" for the project. He made us think about factors like:
- cost-effectiveness and budget considerations
- details of retro-fitting an existing roof
- structural integrity of an existing roof
- green roof design that offers a practical use for the institution.

Our "site visit" to the roof was instructive. We had the opportunity to see first-hand the extensive views of Boston and Cambridge, observe existing conditions, and take field measurements. This site visit inspired many of our design concepts and programmatic considerations for the green roof design.

During our design process, Laura Solano, a professional landscape architect with experience in green roof design and construction, was introduced to the class. The case study that Ms. Solano presented gave us a working example of how a green roof project, which was similar to the BAC roof, could use green roof technology in a cost-effective way to create a spatially exciting and habitable space.

There is one final aspect of this course that should be mentioned. This course generated broad interest within the BAC. Other faculty and members of the BAC's green roof committee wanted to see what the students in the workshop were designing. This interest was a motivating force for us. Through this design workshop, we had the opportunity to experience design in a realistic environment, and this made us part of a valuable community effort.

Notes:

[1] Pat Loheed, Director, Landscape Architecture, and Jeff Stein, Director, Architecture, supported and contributed to the course planning and instruction.

[2] In the fall semester, the Green Roof Design Workshop met for 1½ hours per week. It became apparent that by increasing the class time to 3 hours per week, we could improve the quality of the course substantially. The additional time compelled students to delve more deeply into their research because their class presentation time was longer. The additional class time also allowed for more wide-ranging discussions and inquiry into both the technical and the design topics.

[3] Ms. Marrero's and Mr. Burdick's evaluations of the workshop are part of this paper.

[4] Ms. Solano presented the green roof design for the American Society of Landscape Architects in Washington, D.C. For more information about this project, visit www.mvvainc.com (click on "Projects," then "Gardens," and then "ASLA Green Roof") and www.ASLA.org (navigate to the ASLA Green Roof Webpage and the ASLA Green Roof Webcam).

[5] Josh Burdick completed the workshop during the fall semester. As noted above, the spring semester workshop was expanded to a three hour class period.

Building [Understanding]: A Systems Approach to Building Information Modeling [BIM]

Christopher Livingston
Montana State University

"The idea that science can, and should, be run according to fixed and universal rules, is both unrealistic and pernicious."[1]

Architecture in practice is a combination of both skill and calculated chance. The growing complexity of building sciences, myriad technologies as well as insatiable material development has continued to challenge the skill of architects, in many cases forcing specialization or mediocrity. In addition, the external forces impacting architecture; social, political, economic and spatial, continue to increase at a similar rate. We live in an increasingly 'connected' world; an open system of flows and exchanges.

This paper stems from a reaction to the prevalent view that architectural education is largely executed within an academic bubble, cut off from the world of practice. This view conditions many to believe this hermetic environment is in fact the way the profession functions: 'I design and it gets built'. This paper is based on the work completed in a course entitled 'Advanced Building Systems' taught at the Montana State University School of Architecture during the fall semester of 2005, attempting to dispel this view. The course utilized current building information modeling [BIM] techniques, seminar readings as well as the ideas of general systems theory to analyze and evaluate landmark architecture through the case study method. The course proposed that a thorough understanding of both the internal and external factors influencing architecture would allow students a more realistic analysis of building and its mutable role in society today.

Building Information Modeling

Building information modeling [BIM] continues to gain widespread attention with the promise of streamlining the design and construction process.[2] BIM, the process of constructing a single 3-D building in virtual space which integrates all of the major building systems, allows the architect and their consultants to share better information with each other and with the contractor. These models, drawn by the various consultants and compiled as a single document, also have the ability to be used for quantity surveys, site studies of shadow and sunlight as well as visual time lines for the construction process. As a result, more information is discovered earlier in the design process, errors and omissions are discovered earlier, reducing questions and costly change orders as well as reducing the construction time, cost of construction and increasing the value to the owner. Much of the excitement in BIM has come from the contracting world as aspects of documentation and the construction process is where, at least initially, BIM appears to exhibit the greatest value.

As BIM is gaining acceptance in practice, it is also gaining popularity in architectural education as a design and presentation tool. Three-dimensional modeling has replaced conventional 2-D drawing and the ability to show structural, mechanical and enclosure systems, has revolutionized the presentation of design projects.

Figure 1. Gallatin Valley Food Bank [BIM] by Ed Murray

The use of BIM in this way allows students a more thorough understanding of the complexity of design and integration as systems are coordinated together to form a holistic design solution. But while the use of BIM would appear to expand the limits of design, it is my contention that students view the presentation of both design and construction documents as a closed system, distinct from the ideas that generated the design; in other words, once the documentation is complete, the project and related systems achieve a state of equilibrium where the final design work is in essence *'complete'*, with no further input or output. While this may be true for student design work, the actual world of building is based on open systems; a continuous flow of materials that achieve not equilibrium but a continuous steady state.[3] These open systems are contingent upon many diverse systems interacting with one another to produce desired or undesired results. Many of these systems are not related to physical building but impact the building process nonetheless. This is space that is *'produced'* as Henri Lefebvre describes in The Production of Space. Utilizing nature as a resource, space is the product '...of an activity which involves the economic and technical realms but which extends well beyond them, for these are also political products, and strategic spaces. The term 'strategy' connotes a great variety of products and actions: it combines peace with war, the arms trade with deterrence in the event of crisis, and the use of resources from *peripheral* spaces with the use of riches from industrial, urban, state-dominated centres."[4] With this description, Lefebvre illustrates the far reaching effects that dictate spatial production. Global economics, a-spatial activities and political will, through the use of 'labour, technology, knowledge, property, institutions and the state'[5], all have an impact on spatial production and thus influence, in large part, the built environment. These diverse systems in many respects are paramount to the built environment and therefore impact society in profound ways. I believe it is an understanding of these systems that begins to expand the boundaries of design and sheds light on architecture's complex relationship with society. To expand upon the systems that impact architecture, it may be useful to examine the tenets of the general systems movement during the 1950's.

General Systems Theory

Figure 2. GST founders, source: www.isss.org

In 1954, a group of men conceived of a research society devoted to the understanding of complex systems through interdisciplinary inquiry.[6] A year later the group would form the Society for General Systems Research and based on the work of Ludwig von Bertalanffy almost two decades before, would assume a radical position with regard to the structure of scientific research; they would openly question the scientific method and the mechanistic world-view based on the writings of Descartes some 330 years before. This radical position would be based on the thought that the scientific method could no longer thoroughly explain certain complex phenomena found in research fields including biology and the social and behavioral sciences. They believed that a more holistic view was required that would essentially reverse the traditional logic of reductionist thinking; the breaking down of a whole into it's smallest pieces to explain the dynamics of the system, and begin to look at the dynamics of the whole to understand the properties of it's constituent parts.[7] This would revive the Aristotelian argument that the whole was more than the sum of the parts. They would have many admirers and detractors over the years.

In what may be considered the systems theory manifesto entitled, "General Systems Theory: The Skeleton of Science", author Kenneth Boulding placed systems thinking 'between the specific that has no meaning and the general that has no content'[8]. General systems theory was not intended to be a 'theory of everything' like the quest for a unified field theory in physics but instead sought an "optimum degree of generality"[9] which would link theoretical models in different areas of study thus filling in the gaps that existed between research fields. In the minds of these systems thinkers this would solve the crisis in science due to specialization that did not allow for an analysis of the wholeness of any discipline to be seen and understood. "Specialization has outrun Trade, communication between the disciples becomes increasingly difficult, and the Republic of Learning is breaking up into isolated subcultures with only tenuous lines of communication between them – a situation which threatens intellectual civil war."[10] Boulding felt that with increased specialization there would be less communication between various branches of science and thus stagnate the growth of knowledge. Within the wholeness that would emanate from systems theory, a renewed sense of interdisciplinary learning would appear. Fields such as social psychology and cultural geography, as hybrid disciplines, owe their origins to the concept of systems theory and the foundations of a holistic worldview.

The position of the systems theorists at mid-century has been forwarded by thinkers including Fritjof Capra, who see the world as an interconnected 'whole'. This world, again, is more dependant on the 'dynamics of the whole, defining the properties of the parts' and not the properties of the parts explaining the whole. For Capra, whose book *The Turning Point* became the genesis for the systems theory movie, *Mindwalk*, interconnectedness [or systems thinking] is used to explain all of life, from physics to economics to biomedical and related human health issues:

"To associate a particular illness with a definite part of the body is, of course, very useful in many cases. But modern scientific medicine has overemphasized the reductionist approach and has developed its specialized disciplines to a point where doctors are often no longer able to view illness as a disturbance of the whole organism, nor to treat it as such. What they tend to do is to treat a particular organ or tissue, and this is generally done without taking the rest of the body into account, let alone considering the psychological and social aspects of the patient's illness."[11]

This current fascination with systems theory has resulted in hundreds of books on the subject in a wide array of disciplines. While widespread acceptance of systems theory is far from a reality, we can see the effects of systems thinking in many fields of study, including, to a certain degree, architecture.

Architecture in practice has always had to negotiate systems thinking as a necessity of material integration. With the introduction of building materials comes the responsibility of integration in Vitruvian terms; firmness (how does the integration work?), commodity (how does the integration respond to economics, repair, etc.?) and delight (how does the integration work visually?). Examples of integration over time, utilized in academic settings, include Kahn's 'served and servant' space as well as the work of many British 'high tech' architects and illustrate a need for integration which BIM has and will continue to respond to with time. The following description of the Advanced Building Systems course is intended to address these issues as well as expand the traditional boundaries of architectural investigation to areas of study that impact the way we see building.

Course overview

While architecture has become increasingly specialized, working in scientific reductionism to isolate smaller and smaller systems and parts of the whole, the application of General Systems Theory, in contrast, works towards a holistic view to understand the myriad interactions and implications that ultimately influence the 'whole' architectural product.

This holistic view frames the basis for the course described below, Advanced Building Systems, a four hundred level course taught in conjunction with professional practice and a comprehensive design studio. The goal of this Advanced Building Systems course was to encourage students to evaluate case study buildings in the context of architecture as an open system; a flow of input and output between the building organization and its environment. This research was conducted utilizing three tools of inquiry, first, the investigation of landmark buildings through the use of building information modeling. Second, the use of the case study method as an investigative tool to encourage the students to better understand the complex decision-making that is inherent to the architectural process. Finally, general systems theory was employed in the form of seminar readings to instigate or provoke discussion of systems outside the realm of building that could be utilized for a comprehensive investigation of their particular case study buildings.

Tools of Inquiry

The creation of a building information model [BIM] for a selected landmark building was completed by the students, in teams of two. Over the course of the semester the students created a series of building information models depicting four of the five primary systems: structure, envelope, mechanical, and either the interior or site for their particular case study buildings.[12] Each information model was presented in 24x36 board format with pertinent written and graphic information. All four individual models were successively integrated to form a master 3-D model in the same way a master building information model would have to coordinate all systems in an office environment. In addition to the building information models, the students also had to analyze each of the primary systems with six performance mandates: building integrity, air quality and visual, thermal, acoustic and spatial performance.[13] The use of the mandates required the students to fully analyze all of the major building systems together, utilizing some of the systems in a secondary and tertiary fashion to connect the system in question to the particular mandate. As an example, one would have to consider the mechanical and envelope systems when describing air quality as a performance mandate of the structural system. This allowed for a more thorough investigation by the students forcing them to synthesize various information sources and make evaluations based on that information.

The students were encouraged to select any well documented landmark building for case study research and were also asked to initially create a comprehensive bibliography, ensuring that necessary project information, both written and pictorial was available. For case study research, the students utilized the *Development Checklist for the study and practice of Case Studies in Architecture*[14] prepared by the AIA and the Large Firm Roundtable. Almost all of the projects selected limited the students to case study information gathered through printed sources with no client or architect correspondence. This placed a premium on gathering thorough bibliographic information so a full case could be constructed and cross-referenced for accuracy. The *Development Checklist*, specifically the sections related to project abstract and project perspectives and analysis, provided questions regarding each project that challenged the students to evaluate areas including measures of success, financial implications and special resources required. As important as the physical systems integrated into the buildings are the decisions that make these system choices possible. Logistics, technological limitations and design constraints are only a part of the overall process of building. Throughout the semester, students were continually asked to investigate their case studies within this holistic open system approach.

The weekly seminars were centered on a group of readings intended to expand the notions of architecture and building. They were also meant to represent the General Systems Theory portion of the course to provoke a greater sense of the external forces surrounding architectural production. Readings including, the production of space on a global scale, control, hyper-reality and representational questions of material and systems are a few of the topics covered during the semester.[15] The readings were issued on a weekly basis and discussed in class. Questions were issued at the beginning of each class and then discussed in a seminar format.

Each team of students produced four 24x36 presentation boards for each case study building with accompanying text. The boards were graded on the overall presentation, thoroughness of research and completeness of the BIM. One shortfall of the course was that case study information discovered through the seminar readings, information the students found to be external of the physical building systems, was not found uniformly by all teams. Additionally, the information found was somewhat superficial and not achieving the depth of inquiry necessary to fully understand the issues surrounding spatial production in Lefebvrian terms. This may have been due to factors including project selection not lending itself well to these types of discoveries or the particular perspective each respective student team. Additionally, this level of investigation may not have been realistic within the course structure and expectations. In many instances the students discovered the information as part of their research, as opposed to seeking out these larger issues framing their projects. This was in many ways the most exciting aspect of the case studies, witnessing the students uncover findings on their own and presenting them to the class, dispelling many myths regarding design, academia and practice.

As a teaching and learning model, the three aspects of the course allowed the students the opportunity to analyze particular case study buildings from a systems perspective, not limited to just the building but to include larger external issues that influence or dictate how buildings comes into being. As a final analysis, the students were issued a blue book final to present an essay that culminated their findings over the semester. The essay was a response to Michael Benedikt's introduction to the Center 10 publication entitled, *Value*, where he contemplates that our physical environment must not be valued due to our built environment becoming increasingly more commodified and devalued, subject to short term investment and resale.[16] The student responded favorably to the opportunity of an essay final, one student writing, "It is time for architects to embrace the scientific approach used by other industries to develop and utilize new materials which will improve the manner of living experienced by the general public."[17]

Case Studies

What follows are examples of the student's case study projects and their findings.

[**British Pavilion**, Seville expo]- The British Pavilion at the Seville exposition in 1992 by Nicholas Grimshaw and Partners is an intriguing case study from the aspects of sustainability as well as the projects fabrication, delivery and assembly methods. As a study in sustainability the building is a collection of passive energy and climate moderating systems working together to temper the scorching heat of Seville. Fabric shading devices, a water cooled curtainwall and trombe wall created from water filled shipping containers were employed to create a tempered environment inside the pavilion while photovoltaic panels created energy from the sun for electrical pumps and other necessary items.

Figure 3. Image from British Pavilion presentation. Students: Doug Halsey and Scott Macbeth

As a study in energy conservation and sustainable technologies, the building is a virtual cornucopia of interrelated systems working in concert to create a pavilion that was both innovative and comfortable for thousands of visitors.

Equally important to the sustainable issues is the fabrication, delivery and assembly of the building as a study in the logistics of global architecture. The building, produced in Britain, was constructed almost entirely of prefabricated parts, transported to Seville and assembled on site. With the building being produced in Britain, the logistics pertaining to international shipping routes, container sizes as well as trucking to the site became critical to the design of the project. It could be argued that these criteria were the primary design constraints imposed on the project, occupying the talents of both the designers and fabricators:

"...These too would have been fabricated in Britain and shipped in containers, probably via the nearby port of Cadiz. The more distant port of Santander on the north coast offered more flexible handling facilities, however, and after checking the road route via Madrid for possible bottlenecks, the designers and fabricators decided that it was feasible to transport much larger components, up to 24 metres long and weighing up to 7.5 tonnes."[18]

In addition to the travel logistics, the building is also a study in prefabrication and the use of related technologies, in this case yacht sail and rigging design. The students realized this during the initial case study research and were able to look at the design of the pavilion through the lens of fabrication and transportation, similar to Grimshaw's office, in their documentation of the systems.

[Milwaukee Art Museum]- The Milwaukee Art Museum completed in 2002 by Santiago Calatrava has become a landmark and destination museum for the City of Milwaukee. The building is best identified by its distinctive curvilinear skeletal form with prominent mobile brise-soleil 'wing' shading devices.

The students had assumed that the winged brise-soleil shading device was in fact that, a shading device, and had reserved this item to be included in their mechanical system analysis. They were surprised to conclude that in fact the shading device was nothing more than 'signage' for the museum.

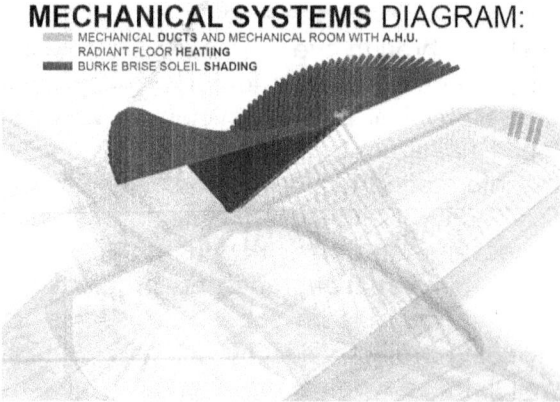

Figure 4. Image from Milwaukee Art Museum presentation. Students: Lance Hayes and Josh Vernon

"It is most intriguing that the most captivating elements, the mobile wings, are in fact not an integrally important component to any of the systems. Paraphrasing Charles Loomis, facilities engineer at the museum- there have been many speculations as to the operation and functionality of the brise-soleil, but in fact, it is really just a tourist attraction."[19]

This is part of the landmark status that museums have gained over the past few years. Museums in many ways have become destination points for economic gain. This global phenomena is best expressed by David Harvey in his article, *The Invisible Political Economy of Architectural Production*, discussing explorative economic success similar to '...the Cargo Cultists of Papua New Guinea, who seek to lure passing aircraft to earth by building imitation landing strips in the vague hope that some might land.'[20]

[**Blur,** Swiss expo]- The 'Blur' project, one of the pavilions for the Swiss exposition in 2002 by Diller & Scofidio creates a case study in the variability of the environmental systems employed, in this case fog, as well as in the unpredictability of the capitalist system at large. Constructed on the shore of lake Neuchatel, this temporary structure was equipped with a state of the art fog system and other technologic innovations that created a pavilion that became much more than the sum of its parts.

One such move was in the areas of marketing and advertising. The project was accompanied by a massive marketing blitz that resulted in the image of the 'blur' on vodka bottles, candy bars, packets of sugar, stamps, phone cards and even lottery tickets throughout Switzerland.

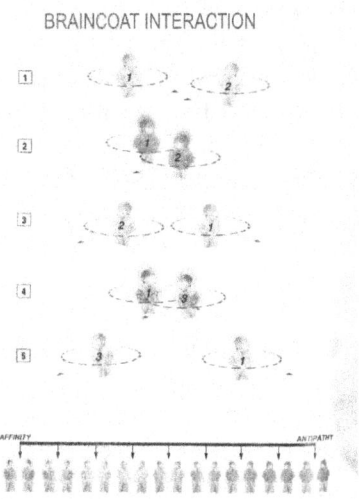

Figure 5. Image from 'Blur' presentation. Students: Eric Druse and Jim Howeth

Another intriguing aspects of the Blur project, and tied to aspects of capitalism, was the 'braincoat' raincoat. The 'braincoats' were technologically enhanced raincoats that incorporated smart systems to store personal data of each individual wearer for 'communication' while in the cloud. Utilizing tracking and location technologies, the coats were able to compare personal data between individuals that came into proximity and light up or produce sounds to react to the degree of attraction found between each individual's personal data. Sadly, the 'braincoat' was never to be utilized due to lack of funding by a corporate sponsor. In this case the students were able to see how design is subject to the fickle world of corporate finance and economics. Financial systems, unrelated to architecture, in this case substantially impacted the desired effect of the architectural experience and while capitalism was able to exploit the branding of 'blur' as a national icon, it was unable to ensure one of the more intriguing aspects of the project.

Conclusions

In summation, the building information models, presented in a system by system format, gave the students an opportunity to analyze the material and building systems that were utilized in each project. It also made them more aware, through the construction of the models, of the interrelation and interdependency of each major system to the building as a whole. The performance mandates enhanced the level of investigation between the various systems allowing for in depth synthesis and evaluation that could not have been possible with a more conventional case study analysis. Finally, I believe the reading and seminar discussions stimulated an additional level of investigation into each project with an understanding of the logic and decision-making processes that occurred before, during and after the initial design and on into the construction process.

Notes

[1] Paul Feyerabend, *Against Method*, (London: Verso, 1975): 295.

[2] [BIM] related articles have regularly appeared in *Architectural Record* since 2004, the most recent being: Larry Flynn, "Getting on Board with Building Information Modeling: Using 3-D modeling to integrate the design and construction process", *Architectural Record*, (April 2006): 163-167.

[3] L. von Bertalanffy, "The Theory of Open Systems in Physics and Biology", from F. E. Emery, editor, *Systems Thinking*, (England: Penguin Books, 1969): 71.

[4] Henri Lefebvre, Translated by Donald Nicholson-Smith, *The Production of Space*, (Oxford, UK and Cambridge, MA: Blackwell, 1992): 84.

[5] Ibid., 85.

[6] The principal members of the Society for General Systems Research were Ludwig von Bertalanffy, Kenneth Boulding, Ralph Gerard, James G. Miller and Anatol Rapoport. See The International Society for the Systems Science, www.isss.org.

[7] Ervin Laszlo, editor, *The Relevance of General Systems Theory: Papers Presented to Ludwig von Bertalanffy on His Seventieth Birthday*, (New York: George Brasiller, 1972): 5.

[8] Kenneth E. Boulding, "General Systems Theory-The Skeleton of Science", *Management Science*, 2/3 (April 1956): 197.

[9] Ibid., 198.

[10] Ibid., 198.

[11] Fritof Capra, *The Turning Point, Science, Society and the Rising Culture*, (New York: Simon & Schuster, 1982): 157.

[12] These are the generally recognized 'major' systems categories. See Leonard R. Bachman, *Integrated Buildings: The Systems Basis of Architecture*, (New Jersey: Wiley, 2003) and Richard D. Rush, editor, *The Building Systems Integration Handbook*, (New York: John Wiley & Sons, Inc., 1986).

[13] See Richard D. Rush, editor, *The Building Systems Integration Handbook*, (New York: John Wiley & Sons, Inc., 1986). This is the same mandate list sans the matrix connectivity.

[14] AIA, *Case Studies in the Study and Practice of Architecture, Development Checklist and Submission Guidelines*, (AIA: New York, 2001).

[15] A partial list of readings includes, David Harvey, "The Invisible Political Economy of Architectural Production", from *The Invisible in Architecture*, O. Bouman and R. van Tourn, editors, (London: Academy Editions, 1994): 420-427., Colin Davies, "Introduction: High Tech-A tentative definition", from *High Tech Architecture*, (New York: Rizzoli Press, 1988): 6-21., Margaret Crawford, "The World in a Shopping Mall", from *Variations on a Theme Park, The New American City and the End of Public Space*, Michael Sorkin, editor, (New York: Hill and Wang, 1992): ., Michel Foucault, "Panopticism", from *Discipline & Punish*, (New York: Vintage Books, 1995): 195-228., Albert Borgmann, "Hypermodernism", from *Crossing the Postmodern Divide*, (Chicago: University of Chicago Press, 1992): 82-97.

[16] Michael Benedikt, "Introduction" from *Center 10/Value*, Michael Benedikt, editor, (Austin, TX: University of Texas Press, 1997).

[17] Student, Corwin Dormire final essay, fall 2005: 13.

[18] Colin Davies, *British Pavillion, Seville Exposition 1992: Nicholas Grimshaw and Partners*, (London: Phaidon Press Ltd., 1992)

[19] Milwaukee Art Museum case study. Students: Lance Hayes and Josh Vernon.

[20] David Harvey, "The Invisible Political Economy of Architectural Production", from *The Invisible in Architecture*, O. Bouman and R. van Tourn, editors, (London: Academy Editions, 1994): 426.

Building Skin: Designing in Full-Scale

Kathrina Simonen
California College of the Arts

Designing the Detail

Architecture students in an advanced design studio at the California College of the Arts analyzed the performance and created full-scale detail models of cladding systems proposed for the San Francisco Academy of Sciences Building in San Francisco, (then still under design), by Renzo Piano's Building Workshop. This exercise set the stage for a dynamic studio, focusing on performative building skins, in which the students were actively engaged in the resolution of their own design proposals to the level of the detail: first through the re-design of the facade system for Morphosis's San Francisco Federal Building and second through the design of a pavilion adjacent to Herzog and deMeuron's deYoung Museum in San Francisco's Golden Gate Park.

Figure 1. Students presenting models and drawings

Working with the project architects from the offices of the Building Workshop (Brett Terpeluk), Morphosis (Tim Christ) and Herzog and deMeuron (Christopher Haas), we configured the studio to take advantage of the three exemplary buildings by these firms in design or construction in San Francisco. Over the course of the semester, students studied the design and detailing philosophies of the three offices in particular looking at the differing approach to detailing the building skin.

Figure 2. Sectional model

The primary intent of the full scale modeling exercise was three-fold: to demonstrate the benefit of studying designs at full-scale, to provide students the opportunity to translate abstract two-dimensional construction drawings to three-dimensional form and to provide a framework to teach the technical performance and construction issues relevant to building envelope design. Becoming 'experts' on how one facade system was resolved, both technically and aesthetically, helped the students understand how their designs would be manifested in full-scale details and become critically engaged in the creation of details that support primary design intent.

Figure 3: Digital model and exploded axonometric of operable window system

Process

Given access to design development drawings for the San Francisco Academy of Sciences Building, students were asked to first analyze a facade system and then refine the details to address issues of aesthetics, constructability, and performance in the creation of full-scale models of portions of the building. Interestingly, this building has at least five distinct types of exterior skin, which permitted groups of two to three students to work on unique systems, with each student developing a portion of that system at full-scale. This created an atmosphere of collective learning. In addition, the exercise highlighted the differences and similarities of different systems, providing a rich pool of models for discussion.

The students were required to extrapolate and interpret Piano's design intent in the resolution of the details. Through lectures, discussions and critiques with Piano's architectural team, and independent research into the history of the Building Workshop, students were able to appreciate the architect's design philosophy and understand the performance intents for the complex façade systems of this building.

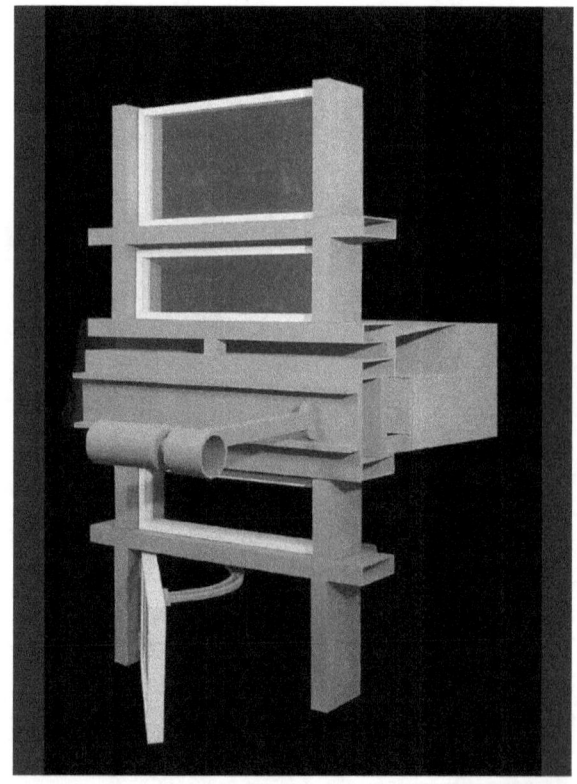

Figure 4: Full scale operable window model

The Building Workshop's tradition of finely articulated and often custom fabricated building components made the study of their details at full scale particularly appropriate. The office has a tradition of designing in full scale--both prototypes for custom fabrication of components and mock-ups of building assemblies--to evaluate design integration. Seeing photographs of the office's model shop, detail studies and building components helped the students recognize how the modeling effort is integrated within a broader design practice. Understanding this design culture gave the exercise professional relevance as students could see how the exercise could benefit the design documentation and the resulting built product.

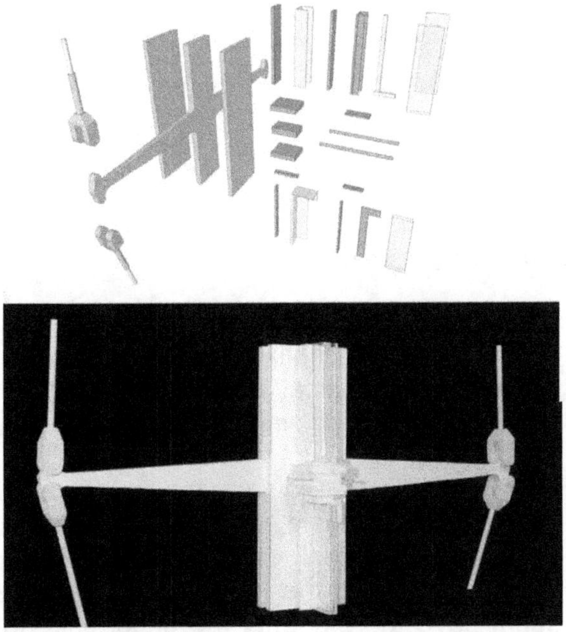

and to create full-scale fabrication/assembly drawings. During this component, the faculty presented examples of methods to visually describe building performance and instruction on the conventions of construction drawing notation.

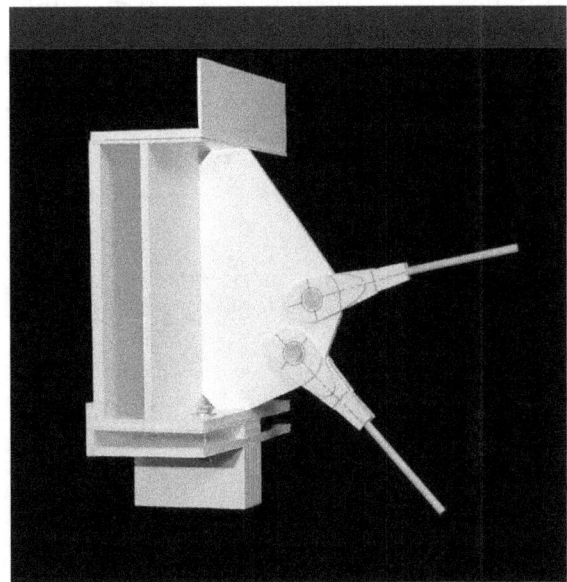

Figure 6: Roof connection detail model

Figure 5: Exploded axonometric and model of custom steel façade system

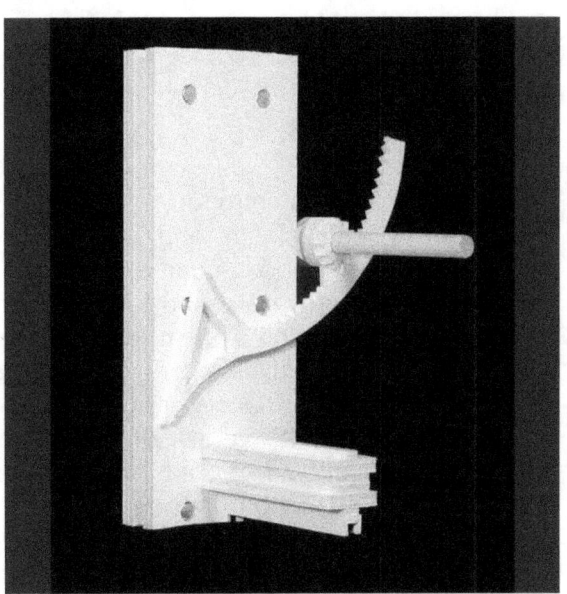

Figure 7: Custom operable façade model

We asked students to select a region of intersection between horizontal and vertical components of the building so that they would study more than the sectional information presented in a typical construction detail. Initially students analyzed the skin systems to establish performance objectives

As the assignment was designed to study detailing and design intent rather than construction process, we required the students to model geometry of assembly components and material translucency rather than use actual materials. Thus students created models of inexpensive and easy to manipulate materials. The geometry and assembly of the components inherently addressed issues of material and construction (expansion joints, cast steel vs. built up steel plates, slotted holes for building movement and construction tolerance etc) and thus the physical
conditions of actual construction and finished product became integral to the discussion, even if the materials were not replicated. We intentionally focused the students' effort towards gaining understanding rather than manipulating or representing materials. Restricting the color palate to gray-scale helped to simplify the project and to create elegant results.

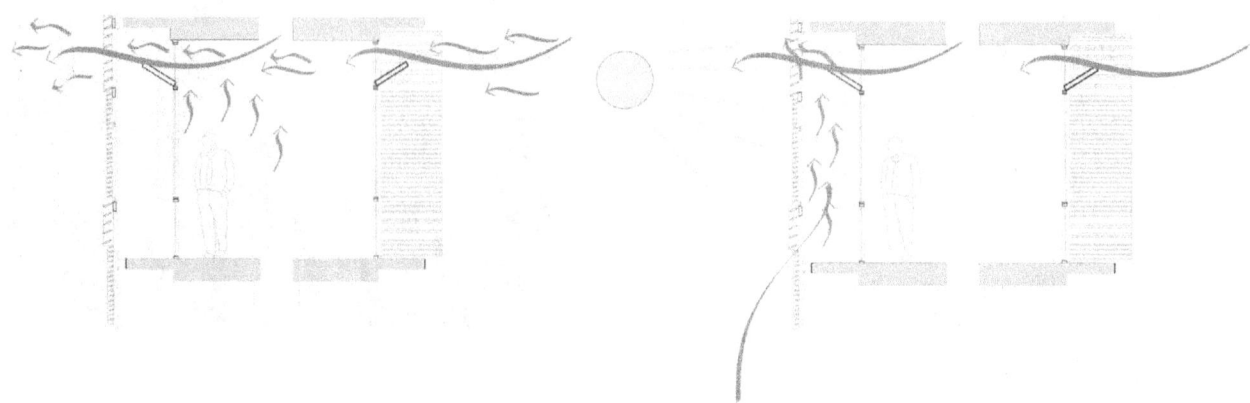

Figure 8: Thermal performance study of student design of Federal Building re-skin

Design Translations

The success of this introductory exercise translated to enthusiasm and successful detail exploration in the second exercise, in which the students were asked to conceive of an alternate cladding system for the San Francisco Federal Building by Morphosis. The primary performance requirements (shading and natural ventilation) of this building's non-structural cladding system were to be met within the framework of the (then nearly complete) primary concrete structure. The students were able to tour LA, the Morphosis office and the construction site as well as study construction and fabrication drawings of the skin as designed. Morphosis's use of 3D prints to version their designs as well as large scale physical models to study complex internal space and custom fixtures reinforced the value of the physical even when much of the design occurred within the digital realm.

The final project required the students to design a freestanding cafe pavilion adjacent to the Herzog and deMeuron's deYoung Museum. Touring the nearly complete museum gave the students the opportunity to study a dramatically different approach to treating the building skins as surfaces, solids and translucencies with smooth transitions rather than tectonic assemblies and discuss the design, detailing and construction implications of these decisions. The objective of the final exercise was to give students the freedom to establish design intent and translate this to the design of a full-scale detail for this proposal. Although introduction of the third firm was quite effective in advancing the discussion, the objectives of the studio would have been better served by continuing to develop the designs of the second project. Even within the fairly constrained design problem, students had developed individual design direction that could have benefited from having more time to develop.

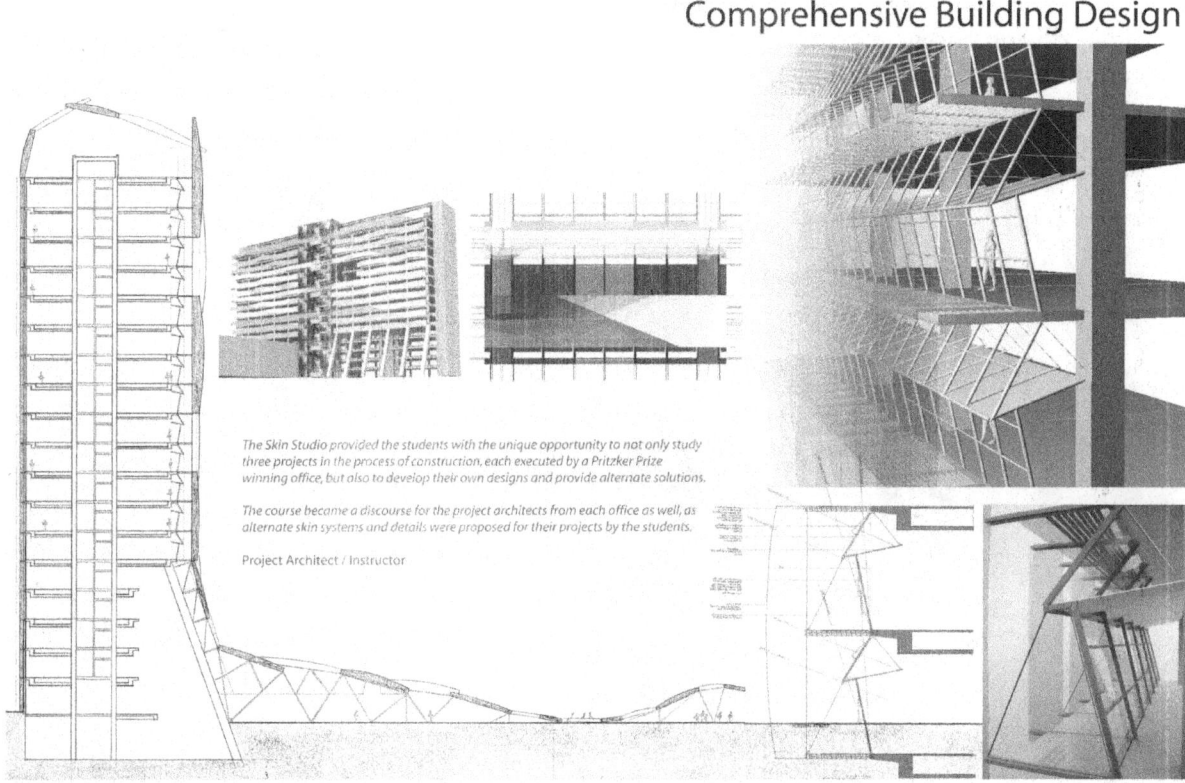

Figure 9: Student proposals for the Federal Building re-skin

Conclusions

The preliminary modeling exercise was effective in getting the students engaged quickly with designing towards the 1:1 finished construction. The problem had significant knowns (knowledge to be obtained) and unknowns (problems to be solved) which ensured it would be both instructive and creative. Although the students initially perceived this aas an analytic exercise, they quickly shifted to seeing this as a design problem, becoming engaged in the challenge of integrating performance, construction and aesthetic objectives.

Developing the details of a Building Workshop design was particularly didactic as full-scale exploration is typical of the office in practice. This façade system was an ideal model for students new to designing at the scale of the detail since detail is critical to articulating the architectural vision and essential to the character of Piano's architecture.

Having the opportunity to study exemplary and diverse projects and firms helped to develop students' understanding of construction detailing as a design process. It emphasized that, rather than look for 'correct' or 'standard' solutions, they should be looking for solutions that support the overall design intent. This recognition helped to emphasize the importance of articulating a clear design intent that can be effectively communicated to the typically large and diverse teams that must work together to create a finished building.

Credits:

This studio was part of a series of Sponsored Advanced Studios at the California College of the Arts conceived of by Rodolphe el Khoury, chair and coordinated by Neal Schwartz, Associate Professor. These studios were awarded a NCARB prize in 2006.

Figure 10: Students presenting with their models

The pedagogical value of building at full scale clearly transcends the specifics of the specific firms and buildings. The students pride in their work and confident ability to apply their newfound technical knowledge in their own design work was a compelling argument towards future variants of this exercise. Although a similar full-scale modeling exercise could be translated into a seminar, we found that integrating the technical learning within the studio helped invigorate the studio with the dynamic mix of technique, research and innovation that is representative of an integrative practice.

Specifications and Cost in Architecture Education

Ryan E. Smith
University of Utah

Introduction

The National Architecture Accreditation Board (NAAB) outlines 34 performance criteria that must be evidenced by students in architecture programs. According to the 2005 procedures for accreditation, NAAB Student Performance Criterion 25 *Construction Cost Control* reads, "Understanding of the fundamentals of building cost, life-cycle cost, and construction estimating". Criterion 26 *Technical Documentation reads*, "Ability to make technically precise drawings and write outline specifications for a proposed design". While necessary to be an accredited program granting professional degrees to future practicing architects, building/facilities cost, cost estimating and specifications are difficult criteria to fulfill and often challenging to locate by visiting accreditation teams.[1] Because of this it is unclear as to what degree architecture students learn costing issues in construction/facilities management and an ability to write an outline specification.

Recent discrete surveys by Christine Theodoropoulos and David Thaddeus concerning architecture education have revealed that one of the primary reasons for absent technical information in curricula is due to the lack of teaching materials available to faculty for instruction.[2] In an effort to fill a missing gap and provide materials to teach cost and specifications, the author is developing a education module supported by Architectural Computing (ARCOM), publisher of MASTERSPEC, the industry standard for specifications. Additional key stakeholders participating in the project include: RS Means, industry standard for construction costing, Association of Collegiate Schools of Architecture (ACSA), and the Construction Specifications Institute (CSI).

This paper will present background research that has been prepared for the aforementioned education module in an effort to receive feedback from symposium participants regarding the theory, and method of development of such a module. The paper will: explain the NAAB process including visiting team selection and student performance criteria development as a precursor to why and how specifications and costing are considered necessary for accreditation; evaluate the role of architects in specification development and cost assessment to justify the need for such a module; review current teaching resources and methods; and finally suggest the direction of a specification and costing teaching tool that the author is developing with a industry partners.

Understanding NAAB

In order to understand the intention and validity of the student performance criteria in establishing the accreditation of architecture programs, a background of NAAB's operations must be understood. The National Architectural Accreditation Board is the sole agency authorized to accredit U.S. professional degree programs in architecture. There are currently 114 schools offering NAAB accredited professional programs in architecture, leading to the Doctor of Architecture, Master of Architecture or Bachelor of Architecture degree. A NAAB accredited degree is required by most states in order for interns to prepare for licensure and take the Architectural Registration Exam (ARE).

The standards and procedures for accreditation of a professional program in the U.S. by NAAB are developed by the Executive Committee in collaboration with representatives of collateral organizations including: ACSA, American Institute of Architects (AIA), National Council of Architectural Registration Boards (NCARB), American Institute of Architects Students (AIAS) and the public. The collateral group constitutes the NAAB Board of Directors. (Figure 1) In addition to the 34 criteria discussed, NAAB also requires 12 conditions to ensure that accredited programs produce graduates who are "competent in a range of intellectual, spatial, technical, and interpersonal skills; understand the historical, sociocultural, and environmental context of architecture; are able to solve architectural design problems, including the integration of technical systems and health and safety requirements; and comprehend architects' roles and responsibilities in society." [3]

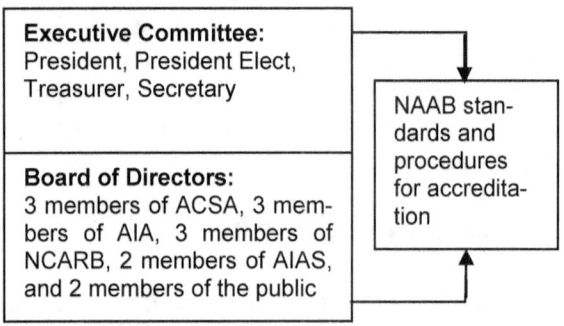

Figure 1: NAAB Standards and Procedures decision makers. Members of the Executive Committee are drawn from the Board of Directors and represent at least one each of the ACSA, AIA, and NCARB.

Changes, edits, or additions to procedures and criteria are instigated by any of the collateral organizations and/or special interest groups. These changes are discussed and voted upon once every three years at the NAAB Accreditation Review Conference (previously called the NAAB Validation Conference) where the Executive Committee, the NAAB Board, invited additional representatives of the collateral organizations and other individuals from lobbying interest groups meet. The next NAAB Accreditation Review Conference is to be held in 2009 with proposals for addendum being accepted in the summer of 2008. [4]

Sharon Matthews, Executive Director of NAAB indicates that the changes that led to criteria 25 and 26 dealing with cost and specifications came from a holistic reworking of the technical criteria for accreditation and not from a specific interest group organization representative/board member. These changes were made at the 2003 Accreditation Review Conference and were implemented in 2004, effective to accreditation criteria starting spring 2005 accreditation visit reviews. The criteria are much more specific than the previous set of criteria from 2002 regarding technical standards. Another change that occurred from the 2002 to the 2005 version of student criteria was the abandonment of the term "Awareness" in describing the extent to which students are required to demonstrate learning. Instead, only the terms "Understanding" and "Ability" are used to determine student performance evidenced in the student work. [5]

"Understanding", according to NAAB, refers to the "assimilation and comprehension of information. Students can correctly paraphrase or summarize information without necessarily being able to relate it to another material or see its fullest implications." Therefore, according to NAAB criteria 25, students must demonstrate that they comprehend the fundamentals of cost, life-cycle cost, and estimating. "Ability" according to NAAB refers to the "skill in relating specific information to the accomplishment of the tasks. Students can correctly select the information that is appropriate to a situation and apply it to the solution of specific problems." This definition then indicates that according to criteria 26, students must have skill in writing outline specifications for a design proposal. [6]

Although the criteria must be met for a program to maintain or initially obtain accreditation, the manner in which it is met is not specified nor is the method of determination of met criteria by visiting teams members entirely scripted. The criteria are then guidelines to evaluate a curriculum for balance in all areas of architecture and ensure that students are obtaining a well rounded education. Additionally, NAAB visiting teams encourage schools to develop curriculum and coursework that supports an overall pedagogical identity, suggesting that each architecture program have its own unique method for teaching specifications and costing, deciding in what format, location in the curriculum, etc. the topics occur. [7]

In order to ensure that programs maintain a high standard of education, accreditation assessment visiting teams are assembled from the collateral groups and flown to a school's location to evaluate the program and determine accreditation continuance. NAAB avoids a conflict of interest and makes every effort to confirm that team members and all observers have the qualities to represent a balance and diversity of views about the education of architecture.[8] Although collateral representatives work to maintain objectivity, individuals from specific organizations, foster attitudes that are naturally more of interest to the organization for which they represent. For example, NCARB Health and Safety Welfare (HSW) requirements for the Internship Development Program (IDP) and the ARE tend to sway the opinion of its representative toward the technical areas of professional practice, including the topics of specifications and cost. Although this subjectivity can be viewed an undesirable, it is also a positive idiosyncrasy as it ensures that a wide range of topics and teaching are being advocated within a visiting team and therefore are being expected within a program curriculum. [9]

NAAB is empowered with the ability to place criteria meeting deficient schools on a three year probation with a return visit for evaluation. After the 3 years, if the items of concern are not met, a school may be stripped of its accreditation. Schools that pass accreditation are given a 6 year term. A probationary period is not uncommon even among reputable and deeply seeded school of architecture. [10]

For schools of architecture, fulfilling NAAB criteria and meeting pedagogical goals is often difficult to reconcile. The short time allotment for architectural education (5-6 years) coupled with an intensive post graduation professional internship requirement (3 years minimum) in preparation for taking the Architectural Registration Exam, persuades many academics to view certain NAAB student performance criteria as exhaustive, unrealistic, and not pertinent to the purpose of architectural education. Many think that some criteria are better suited for the professional internship period following graduation. The question whether or not it specifications and cost is appropriate for academics is even more controversial. However, if the role of the architect can be defined with regard to specifications and cost in a project's life-cycle, then a validation of the NAAB criteria 25 and 26 is justified as a precursor to the actual activities of architects within practice.

Role of the Architect

Role in Specifications

Specifications have changed over the course of building history in the U.S., however, the basic notion of the designer communicating intention through specifications has remained ever-present. (Rosen vii) As design and construction becomes more complex due to new and technically innovative materials, form making possibilities, and advanced construction methods and systems, architects have a greater responsibility to understand the role of specifications in the process of building. Often the idealized practice model that is presented to students is Frank O. Gehry Associates (FOGA). It is noted that although Gehry has not produced specifications for the most recent projects in his office, his interest in specifications is obvious and integral to the design decision making process in the studio. At the 50th Annual CSI Convention in Las Vegas in late March 2006 Gehry, along with colleague Dennis Shelden, discussed building information modeling and the difficulty, yet necessity of the role of specifications in that process. The "4 Cs" of specifications from CSI describe communication being clear, concise, complete and correct are a concern for any design, especially geometrically and spatially complex design/construction projects such as the Disney Concert Hall.[11] As building information modeling becomes more ubiquitous in architectural unique and standard practices, the role of specification understanding and control will be paramount (Figure 2)

Figure 2: Walt Disney Concert Hall, Los Angeles, CA.

With regards to all kinds of practice therefore; what is the role of the architect with respect to specification writing and development? When making design decisions with respect to specs, architects must make certain choices that determine the direction of construction including: functional performance, aesthetic result, legal issues, economics, and sustainability. (Allen 12) This decision making process however does not happen systematically or thoughtfully and often specifications in practice are thrown together in a haphazard and ad-hoc manner borrowing from previous projects within a firm and piecemeal a less than desirable or accurate description of building materials and systems.[12] It is paramount therefore that students of architecture understand specifications and are able to begin developing specifications in perspective of the design decision making process in order to communicate effectively with building contractors later down the road.

Rosen and Regener in <u>Construction Specification Writing</u> present a thorough guide to specification writing for architects and engineers. They discuss that in order to be prepared for specification writing architects must understand the role of specifications in the design and construction process as an integral part to communicating design intention in tandem with drawings. "Most conditions of the Contract recognize the significance of construction specifications and refer to the Specifications as part of the Contract Documents, with importance equivalent to that of the Drawings." Rosen and Regener therefore argue that the architect should be just as skilled at preparing specs as in preparing drawings, although much of our education in the academy and internship in firms is focused on graphic representation. The importance of specifications is increased by the fact that legal issues arising with respect to construction litigation are resolved by attorneys who's limitation to understanding information relies on 8.5x11 pieces of paper. Specifications inevitably become the significant determining factor in construction legal disputes. (1-3)

Role in Costing

Architects and issues of cost have been the point of discussion and debate among the AIA for many years. <u>The AIA Handbook of Professional Practice</u> reads, "The liability crisis of the 1980's pushed architects further from job site responsibilities and pressed new risks on contractors". (170) Owners sought after a way in which to manage cost and therefore the role of the construction manager was born. An 1844 document of specifications and costs for a building illustrates the responsibility and control the architect had over the budget (Figure 3). Today, projects are built quicker, involve many more stakeholders, and entail more risk that those over 150 or much less, 20 years ago.

The concern among architects regarding cost involves maintaining too much responsibility or risk over control project budgeting during project life-cycle. To deal with risk the AIA has started a Risk Management Committee and adjoining website called "AIA Trust"[13] that aids professionals in resolving issues of risk, insurance, etc. Since the then, ironically, the 1997 edition of the American Institute of Architects Standard Form of Agreement between Owner and Architect (AIA B141-1997) was developed and has fundamentally changed the role of the Architect regarding responsibility for controlling construction costs by placing more charge on the architect to ensure that costs are not overrun during the preliminary and later stages of a projects progression. (Zambito) This change to the AIA B141 however makes sense in a time when digital modeling for schedule and costing potentially allow design teams to test simulation scenarios for owners in order to anticipate cost overruns. The advent of building information modeling again will demand that architects understand more holistically the role of cost in project preliminary and later phases of construction and on into facilities management.

The design/bid/build contract structure in the U.S. puts architects and engineers at an adversarial relationship with builders. The transfer of information happens at the signing of the agreement between architect and owner and contractor owner respectively. In order for the efficiencies of design and construction to take place a reworking of contract structures is necessary to suggest a more collaborative, less conflict inducing process for construction that will lead to reduced RFI and change orders and thereby reduce the inefficiencies and cost. Although contracts are being reworked by the AIA, much of this can be mitigated in short-term through the quality and precision of specifications. Therefore, the architects' role must be one of integrated understating of specs and cost.

With respect to construction cost, the AIA Handbook states that the architect's role entails: providing within the budget limitations, an appropriate use of resources and value for the money, optimize longer-term life cycle costs, and to provide to the owner relevant cost information related to design decisions. Cost estimating for construction is generally done by single-unit rate methods such as area or volume, elemental methods such as assemblies or systems, and/or quantity survey methods. For the purpose of instructing students of architecture however, a basic understanding of what is involved in contractor estimating including time and materials, and life-cycle cost issues is appropriate. (349)

NAAB criteria justification

In summary, the NAAB criteria for specifications indicate that students should demonstrate an "Ability" to write outline specifications for a design proposal is consistent with the expectation of practicing architects to write specifications for a design project. An introduction to what specifications entail, their role, and how to begin to write them is then important in preparation for an office environmental to continue the process of learning how to actually write and craft an effective and complete specification. Likewise the NAAB criteria for cost indicates that students should demonstrate an 'Understanding' of building cost, cost estimating and life-cycle cost. This criterion is consistent with the expectation in practice from architects to participate in preliminary cost estimating. Often architects are not directly involved in construction pricing, however need to understand the methods of determining cost in order to read estimates and inform the client in design decision making process.

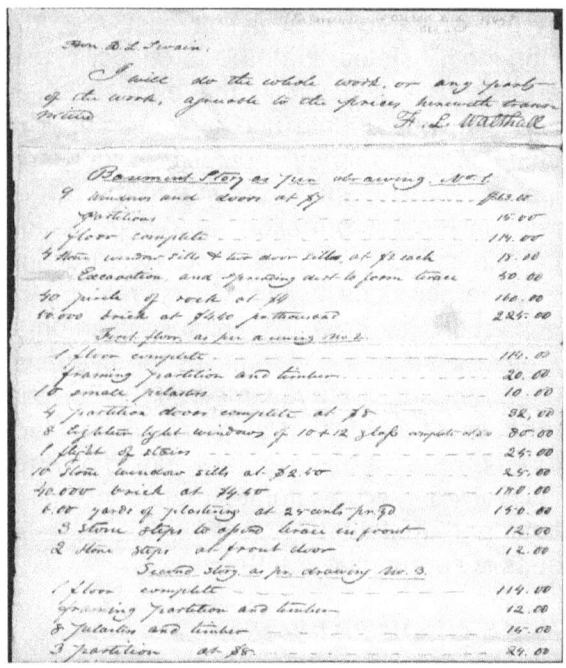

Figure 3: List of building specifications and costs compiled by Alexander J. Davis for David L. Swain, 1844. Used with permission of The University Library, The University of North Carolina at Chapel Hill

Teaching Resources

Various resources exist for teaching specifications and costing, however, each resource is specific to an audience, without a cohesive resource existing for instructing students on a variety of levels regarding these technical topics. Resources exist from both education and industry. In this section an overview of the available materials will be discussed for their potential contribution to teaching specifications and cost in architectural education.

Specification Resources

A host of specification formats called classifications have been developed to organize information in a building project. The industry standard for specification formatting in the U.S. and Canada is MasterFormat, introduced in 1963 by CSI and CSC (Construction Specifications Canada). MASTERSPEC is based on MasterFormat 1995 classification system and was developed by the AIA. MASTERSPEC is published by ARCOM.[14] MasterFormat 1995 is organized into 16 primary divisions that correspond with manufacturers' technical cataloging and filing system. Its new 2004 edition, MasterFormat is further articulated into 50 classifications. MasterFormat is organized by construction trades to provide a combination of products and methods. "The main purpose...is to organize the project manual, reference keynotes, and detailed cost estimates." (CSI PRM 5.28) Both SectionFormat and PageFormat are sub-organizational levels also developed by CSI to work within the larger overarching Project Manual under the MasterFormat classification system.

UniFormat (NISTR 6389), first introduced in 1998 by the CSI and ASTM organizes construction information by elements, systems, and assemblies. The systems are therefore characterized by use or function and not by specific product. UniFormat is then used for "performance specifying and preliminary cost estimating." (CSI PRM 5.28) The most recent edition is called UniFormat II and expands it use over additional phases of a building project's life cycle including: planning, programming, design, construction, and operations. (NISTR 6389)

Most recently developed, OmniClass Construction Classification Systems (OCCS) incorporates both MasterFormat and UniFormat as a broad brush organization tool throughout the life of a project. Under OmniClass hierarchies of formats exist, with Uniformat providing early stage specification information, MasterFormat providing project specific construction documentation and life-cycle information, and Section/PageFormat used to organize sections in more detail. (Figure 4)

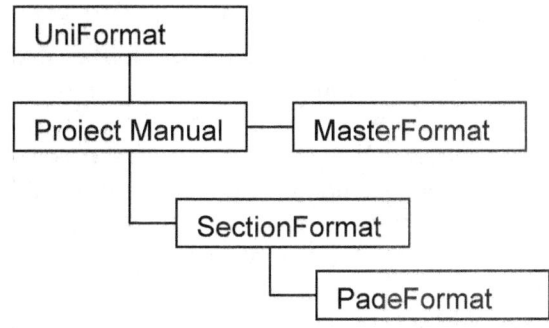

Figure 4: OmniClass Construction Classification System (OCCS)

The outlines of classification systems are readily available, but full extended versions are available at a premium. Students generally are taught in programs a combination of UniFormat and MasterFormat, learning elements, systems, and assemblies that determine the schematic of a building design and the materials and manufacturing for construction trades.

An example is the text Fundamentals of Building Construction: Materials and Methods by Edward Allen which provides an overview of MasterFormat but introduces the information in a combination of both Uniformat and MasterFormat, sometimes covering topics with respect to material or manufacturer while other times describing systems and assemblies. Nearly every chapter in Allen's textbook provides the major MasterFormat designations for the topic of the chapter(s) so that students may reference MasterFormat and technical literature for more information. (12) (Figure 5)

Construction Specifications Writing, by Rosen and Regener, discussed in an earlier section, is an excellent resource for teaching specification writing. The text is its fifth edition and continues to be updated to present the principles and procedures for specification writing for design professionals. Valuable sections for instruction include Chapter 1 – 7 which discuss the purpose of specifications, the relationship of drawings to specs, format of specifications, types of specifications, and specification writing principles. (pg. 1-53) The last chapter of the text, Chapter 21 introduces the concepts of outline and short form specifications which lends itself to architectural instruction (pg. 187)

C.S.I / C.S.C.

MasterFormat Section Numbers for Sitecast Concrete Framing Systems

3300	CAST-IN-PLACE CONCRETE
3310	Structural Concrete
03345	Concrete Finishing
03350	Concrete Finishes
03365	Post-Tensioned Concrete
03370	Concrete Curing
03430	Structural Precast Concrete - Site
03470	Tilt-Up Precast Concrete - Site

Figure 5: MasterFormat classification for Chapter 14, Sitecast Concrete Framing Systems in Fundamentals of Building Construction, pg. 555.

Costing Resources

The AIA Architect's Handbook of Professional Practice Thirteenth Edition (student edition) provides information for professional practice courses regarding specifications in construction agreements, construction documents, and coordination with drawings. With respect to costing, the text covers the factors affecting building cost, life cycle analysis of cost, cost estimation principles, and the availability of estimation software. The handbook therefore focuses on the role of the architect in specification writing and cost estimation/life cycle costs. Because it is developed by the AIA, the textbook reviews in depth MASTERSPEC and explains its functionality and advantages in project specifications through the use of SPECWARE, a parametric specification program for automating the writing of specifications. Although the text offers much information with respect to specifications and costing in relation to professional practice, it is simply a shortened version of the handbook for practitioners and does not offer any exercises or information on the activity of specification writing and/or cost estimation. (ix)

Costing information is constantly in flux. RS Means, an industry leader is a North American construction cost estimation data source that began with a single print publication in 1943 and has since grown to provide a range of construction estimating services.[15] For architects RS Means provides texts and software to estimate costs per square foot and assemblies estimating. A new product "CostWorks" utilizes a parametric system to evaluate costs. Other industry providers offer costing software and texts as well, including ACE Guide to Construction Costs; however these resources tend to be too detailed for the purposes of practicing architects, must less students of architecture.

The Construction Specification Institute Professional Development Team and its subgroup, the Academic Affairs Program Committee, oversee educational chapters. The committee claims to build bridges between academia and the profession.[16] Currently their method of support is by way of information to chapters in many higher education institutions. These chapters can primarily be found in community colleges or the engineering/construction management departments at universities. Future programs have been discussed to include research initiatives to universities and potential teaching resources via the CSI website.[17]

The CSI Project Resource Manual (previously the CSI Manual of Practice) publishes a student edition that is available at reduced cost. The information however within the text is identical to the professional edition. The manual is organized into eight modules that reflect CSI's "Facility Life Cycle" (1.5) Under each module, specifications and cost are discussed, however the manual is geared towards practice and treats the topics exhaustively. Jefferey Callahan, Professor of Construction Management at the University of Alaska discussed in his presentation at the CSI Convention in April of 2005 that the CSI PRM it is so inclusive and comprehensive in its approach, the manual covers all the necessary aspects of both costing and specifications for architectural education and serves as a excellent source of information. However, the material is hidden within sections and chapters dealing with concurrent issues in professional practice and project delivery, making it inaccessible to students of architecture. Additionally, similar to the concerns of the AIA Handbook of Practice, the manual does not offer any exercises or information on the activity of specification writing and/or cost estimation. The CSI Project Resource Manual is an excellent resource with a wealth of information in order to teach not only costing and specifications, but professional practice and construction documents. In order for the resource literature to enter into the classroom however, faculty must understand the content of such texts and critically develop lecture material, exercises, etc. in order for students to internalize and learn the information. (Callahan 5)

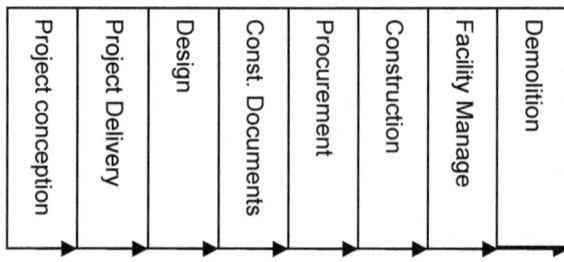

Figure 6: CSI Project Resource Manual, modules of "Facility Life Cycle", Section 1.5

Pedagogical Models

Few models of implementing costing and specifications exist within architectural education. Of the models discovered, the most common location for specification and cost information to occur is within professional practice courses and second in Materials and Methods courses. Within these classes one primary pedagogical models has been explored: design based integrated learning.

At Montana State University Professor Christopher Livingston teaches a comprehensive architectural project that incorporates specifications and cost. The specification assignment involves first creating a comprehensive list of materials/assemblies to be utilized on the design project in the studio. The students organize the materials and systems by MASTERSPEC outline divisions and sections, and then create an outline specification. Livingston indicated that critical to the assignment is the inclusion of example outline specifications for students' reference during the exercise.

Cost estimating was also performed during the assignment utilizing RS Means data through an elemental method for the materials/systems in the outline specification. The experience was reported successful by students and Professor Livingston because students had invested interest as it was their design project they were specifying. Another factor in the students' success with the assignment is scale of the design project kept to a small, manageable chapel of 1300 square feet.[18]

Another example of teaching specifications and cost is from Matthew Boomhower, Professor at Woodbury University. The material is presented in a professional practice course. Boomhower's course includes required reading from The CSI Project Resource Manual and the AIA Handbook of Professional Practice. Discussion in class involves topics related to the readings with specific learning outcomes focused on NAAB criteria involving cost and specifications.[19]

Education Module

The impetuous for developing a cost and specification module for architectural education was instigated by Ted Smith and Christopher Bushnell of Salt Lake based ARCOM, publisher of MASTERSPEC. Smith and Bushnell, the past and current president of ARCOM approached the author with interest in providing a response to NAAB technical criteria 25 and 26. In consulting with ARCOM it became apparent that in order to prepare properly for the module development, a process of gathering background information became necessary. This paper represents this background research. From this study, a suggested direction will be proposed in this section and orally presented in a plenary session at the Building Technology Educators' Symposium in order to receive feedback from colleagues and end users of the proposed module.

Before proposing a direction for development of the education module, below is a summary of the research findings presented in this paper by topic heading:

1- *NAAB* has established criteria for understanding cost and having ability to write outline specifications. The criteria did not come from a specific source but from the board as a whole representing collateral organizations. Each program of architecture is encouraged to implement coursework that is consistent with the pedagogical goals of the institution.

2- The *role of the architect* in these activities within practice is consistent with NAAB criteria: architects must have an ability to write specifications and an understanding of cost in a design project.

3- Various *resources* exist for teaching specs and cost; however they are fragmented and buried within concurrent topics. If one could however pull the information from these resources in a useable format, it would be of great value to architecture education. The resources also fail to offer exercises for learning specs and cost.

4- Few *pedagogical models* of teaching cost and specs in schools of architecture exist. The examples that have been located suggest a design-based integrated project direction for the teaching of specs and cost.

To respond to the research findings, the proposal for the education module dealing with cost and specifications is envisioned as a website with four sections: literature resources, lecture slides for instructors, macros enabled interactive parametric, and classroom specific exercises. (Figure 7)

The first section of the website is proposed as an information source that links literary resources and acts as a "reader" to support the instruction in specifications and building cost. The literature resources have been evaluated in this paper (CSI PRM, AIA Handbook, Construction Specifications Writing, Fundamentals of Building Construction) and serve as the basis for the information, however would be reformatted to be more accessible and specific to the topics of specifications and cost.

In the second section, lecture slides are proposed to be available for download to accompany the resources in section one and to provide presentation materials for the instructor regarding cost and specifications.

The third section is proposed to provide access to outline specification information from ARCOM MASTERSPEC and costing data from RS Means. The format would be macros based parametric interactive for student to input data and test scenarios of specifications against cost to evaluate the impacts of design decisions.

The fourth section involves boiler plate exercises to support both specifications and cost. The exercises are essentially design-based projects that take any size building and can run it through the macros interactive parametric on the website to write an outline specification and test the systems against cost. The purpose of the exercises are to work to develop *ability* for specification writing by filling out an outline spec for materials and systems, and foster *understanding* for cost, testing case scenarios for the given materials.

Materials and Methods instructors might utilize the web materials for a week of instruction and assignments, or for a specific study of a system or material discussed in class that student can practice specifying and/or costing. Professional Practice courses could potentially also utilize the website for an activity related to the design studio where students test their design projects against cost scenarios. In addition, structures and environmental controls classes could use this website to evaluate structural systems and alternative heating/cooling systems within the context of specification and cost. For the case study method utilized in many architectural schools, student could research the specifications of a specific built project and perform schematic cost estimation. As a web-based module, students could potentially utilize the ARCOM and RS Means parametric for an unlimited types of projects in the studio and understand how cost and specification are determining factors in the process of design.

The module is conceptually therefore, flexible enough to allow for this to occur in any class dealing with the topics and be utilized to accept diverse pedagogical methods.

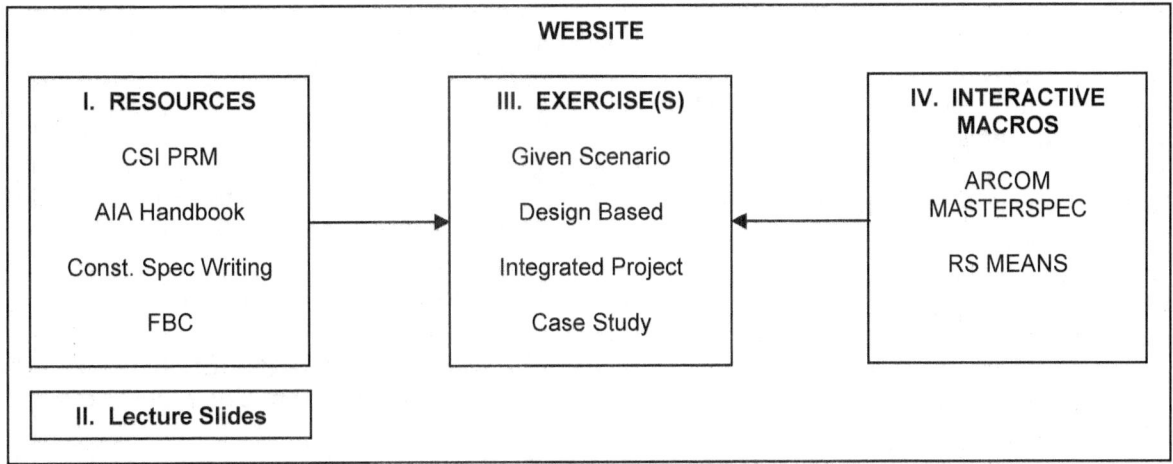

Figure 7: Specification and Cost Module Conceptual Website Organization

References

Architects Contractors Engineers Guild To Construction Costs 2006, Design and Construction Resources, Vol XXXVII, Copyright 2005

Charette, Robert P. & Marshall, Harold E., Uniformat II Elemental Classification for Building Specifications, Cost Estimating, and Cost Analysis, U.S. Department of Commerce, Technology Administration, Brown, National Institute of Standards and Technology, NISTIR 6389. October 1999.

The Project Resource Manual CSI Manual of Practice 5th Edition, The Construction Specifications Institute, McGraw Hill 2005.

The Architect's Handbook of Professional Practice Thirteenth Edition, The American Institute of Architects, John Wiley and Sons, Inc. 2002

Rosen, Harold J. & Regener, John R., Construction Specifications Writing Principles and Procedures Fifth Edition, M.D. Morris Ed. John Wiley and sons, Inc. 2005.

Allen, Edward & Iano, Joseph, Fundamentals of Building Construction Materials and Methods Fourth Edition, John Wiley and Sons 2004.

Callahan, Jeffrey C., "Using the CSI Project Resource Manual – CSI Manual of Practice in College Curriculum", Construction Specifications Institute Convention, April 23, 2005.

Hall, Dennis J., Understanding "CSI Format" Construction Specifications Institute New Digest, August 2004.

NAAB Procedures for Accreditation for Professional Degree Programs in Architecture 2005 Edition, The National Architectural Accrediting Board, www.naab.org.

Zambito, Victoria, "Role of Architect in Controlling Construction Costs", redvector.com, September 19, 2000, July 30, 2002 Update.

Notes

[1] Interview with William Miller, FAIA & NAAB visiting team leader, June 2006.

[2] AISC Survey of NAAB programs, David Thaddeus 2005 & NSF Seismic Survey of Architecture Programs, Christine Theodoropooulos & Ryan Smith 2005. Both surveys indicate that nearly half of technology instructors in NAAB programs are in their first five years of teaching and are therefore most in need of teaching materials.

[3] National Architectural Accreditation Board Website: www.naab.org

[4] Sutton, Sharon A., "Visiting Team Member Selection and Preparation", NAAB Newsletter, www.naab.org NAAB News Section 3.

[5] Phone interview with Sharon Matthews, Executive Director of NAAB. July 2006.

[6] "Condition Changes", NAAB News, www.naab.org

[7] Phone interview with Sharon Matthews, Executive Director of NAAB. July 2006.

[8] National Architectural Accreditation Board Procedures for Accreditation 2005, Section 5.3.4

[9] Interview with William Miller, FAIA & NAAB visiting team leader, June 2006.

[10] National Architectural Accreditation Board Procedures for Accreditation 2005, Section 5.3.4

[11] The Construction Specifications Institute Website: www.csinet.org

[12] This is the method by which I was introduced and most interns in my expierence are introduced to specification writing during professional internship.

[13] www.theaiatrust.com

[14] www.arcomnet.com

[15] www.rsmeans.com

[16] CSI Academic Affairs Program, Chair Gregory W. Sprinkel, FCSI, CDT Sprinkel & Associates – Salt Lake City, UT 801-972-8753, gsdiv7@xmission.com

[17] Interview with Gregory Sprinkel, CSI Academic Affairs Program Chair, July 2006.

[18] Montana State University, Arch 440 - Comprehensive Architectural Project, Summer 2006, Professor Christopher Livingston

[19] Woodbury University, AR 450 Course Syllabus, Professional Practice 3: Documents and Project Administration, Professor Matthew Boomhower

Acknowledgements

I would like to thank Ted Smith and Christopher Bushnell of ARCOM for their funding support and vision in initiating this project, Bob Ghair of RS Means for their willingness to provide access to data, Stephen Screiber and the ACSA for information on professors research backgrounds, Sharon Matthews at NAAB for her answering of questions and patience, and Bill Miller for his insight into the NAAB process.

Indigenous Knowledge, Formal Knowledge, and Technology Teaching

Gil Snyder, James Dicker, Marit Gamberg
University of Wisconsin-Milwaukee

"At this point in history, it is for us to think clearly, for us to discover a way out, for us, in a tumultuous time when events take place beyond human control, to regain the path and discover again the scale which will halt the chaos, strike down the disproportions in our world from which all misery stems. Here folklore presents us with a poetic goal, that of bestowing the benefits of sensitivity, the expression of a creative instinct on the land" (Le Corbusier 61).

Introduction

The concept of Indigenous Knowledge refers to a body of knowledge that belongs to a culture and a people. It describes local systems and practices passed down through generations of close interaction with the natural environment. This knowledge forms "part of a cultural complex that encompasses language, naming and classification systems, ways of using resources, rituals, spirituality and a worldview." Contemporary teaching practices in architectural education are predicated on western-based systems of Formal Knowledge. These practices are defined as formal "because it tends to be supported by written documents, rules and regulations, and technological infrastructure."

As teachers we are constantly in search of methods to enhance our students' ability to critically assess technology, especially as it relates to first principles. Since indigenous knowledge is based on local solutions that are very context-specific, these systems and remedies are founded on first principles derived from experiential trial and error. They are often very effective solutions that contribute significantly to sustainable development and resource management in architecture. By introducing the concept of indigenous knowledge into technology teaching and marrying it to the development of modern solutions to issues in technology, the classroom is enriched.

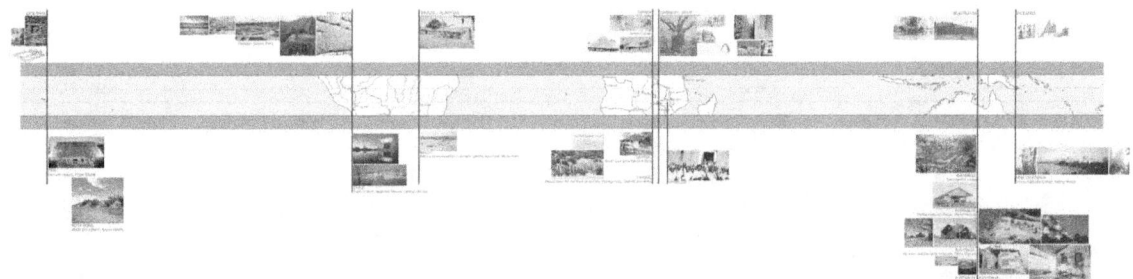

Figure 1: 13 degree line of latitude

Figure 2: long house and Marika Alderton house

This paper will focus on three examples of the analysis of indigenous technical knowledge in building and the appropriation of that knowledge for use in a modern context. The first two models come from the fertile architectural practices of a solo practitioner, Glenn Murcutt, and a relentlessly collaborative one, Renzo Piano Building Workshop. Interestingly, these two Pritzker laureates, so often characterized as master builders, are born in the same year: 1936. Two different buildings for two different cultural contexts produced by two different office cultures are examined.

The third project examined is "Mpumulo," a health center and shelter for battered women in Malawi, Africa. This project has been undertaken by a collaborative team of architects, nurses, and students, and includes this paper's presenters. The work of Mpumulo explicitly excavates the indigenous knowledge tradition to develop modern detailing systems appropriate for the culture and the place. Drawing from categories established by Murcutt and Piano, self-conscious detailing strategies derived from local practices, systems and materials are joined with modern techniques to create hybrid solutions sympathetic to environmental sustainability and cultural sensitivity. The focus of the presentation will be on how we synthesized the raw data collection for this project based on the precedent strategies of Murcutt and Piano to formulate our own technology strategies. These new strategies for Malawi will be exemplified with an explication of the major detailing and supporting technology systems we employed. Finally, the categories and techniques employed are catalogued with a particular emphasis on employment of this detailing approach as a model for classroom instruction.

The two projects by the recognized architects have been selected for close study not only for the quality of thinking and design they represent, but much more prosaically, for their proximity to the 13 degree southern line of latitude, ten degrees above the Tropic of Capricorn.

In preliminary research undertaken for the Mpumulo project, there was a distinct poverty of information on architecture and its traditions in Malawi. To broaden the field of discovery, the 13 degree line of latitude running around the earth was used to Analysis of each of the two precedents, along with the subsequent architectural design that results from synthesizing the identify other environmental locations similar to those found in Malawi.

aboriginal long house, with the predetermined intention for it to serve as a model prototype for a contemporary aboriginal housing solution. This "machine for inhabiting the landscape," as Murcutt describes it, embodies a cultural critique of the original European settlement that rationalized the displacement of Aboriginal populations based on their apparent lack of production of building stock. This supported the perception of illegitimate land occupation and was confirmed in a declaration of terra nullius and invasion against the Aboriginal peoples (Dovey 90).

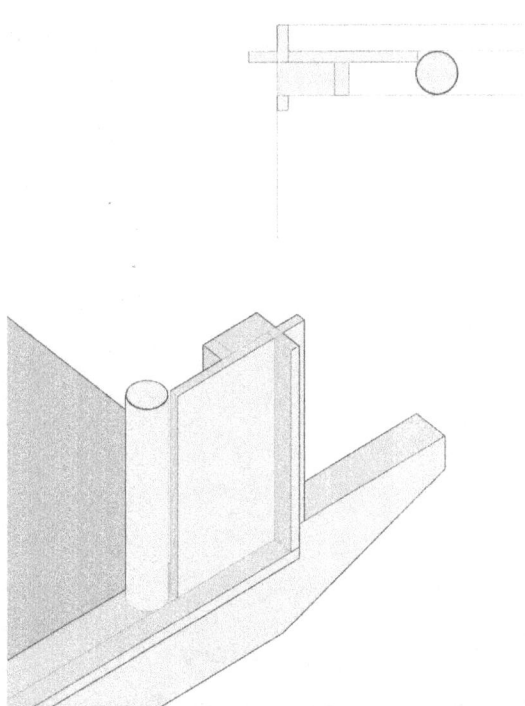

Figure 4: Re-entrant Corner Detail: Marika Alderton

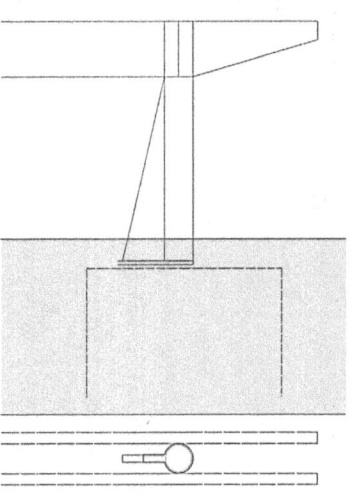

Figure 5: Meeting the Ground: Marika Alderton

90 Percent/10 Percent

In a 1992 interview, Glenn Murcutt remarks, "understanding a place is understanding 90 percent of what you've got to achieve. And then you've got the 10 percent of understanding the culture, and how that culture works in that place" (Melhuish 40). While his work is redolent with that sentiment, the house Murcutt designed for the Aboriginal artist Banduk Marika and her English partner Mark Alderton in the Northern Territory of Australia serves as a concise distillation of strategies and details. It is conceptualized as a transformation of the traditional

In direct contrast to the aggressive impact this invasion policy fomented, the Marika Alderton house is often compared to "a plant because the walls open and close like petals and leaves" while at the same time it invokes the Aboriginal proverb that counsels modest engagement with local ecology. Architectural critic Kim Dovey uses the language of the myth, to note, "it is as if these 'leaves of iron' had fallen from the eucalypt trees to 'touch the earth lightly'" (Dovey 91). Since the climate hovers in the 25 degrees centigrade range, ventilation is required for cooling and comfort. The operable wall panels serve to provide a controllable enclosure surface to accommodate wind and solar forces.

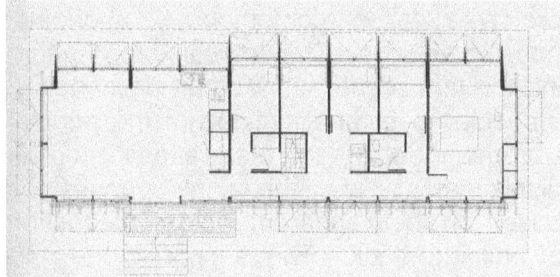

Figure 6: Plan Marika Alderton House

Exemplary details abound in this project. These are tied both to the rigors of production, and the demands of nature and culture. The project was fabricated off-site by two builders from the yacht industry to very precise tolerances. Careful calibration of components was critical to assembly once imported to the site.

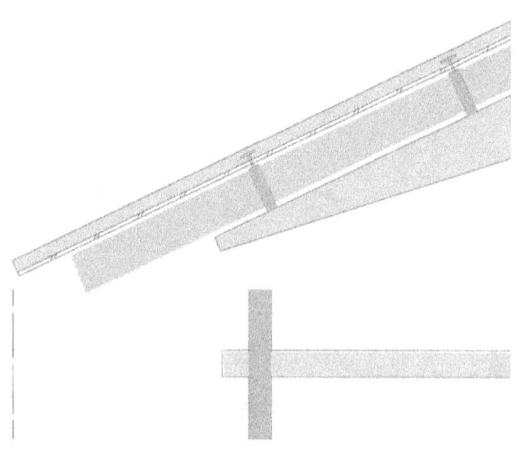

Figure 7: Meeting the Sky: Marika Alderton House

Notable in the detail composition is the lifting of the house from the landscape plane on hollow circular steel tube columns with tapered steel stiffener plates that support a primary wood beam and deck floor structure. This response to prevailing winds is supported with a double roof tied to roof ventilators. Each component of the roof system is expressed as an element. The re-entrant corner detail reveals the logic of prefabrication, while the structural plan logic is completely integrated with the sun shading strategy.

Figure 8: horizontal zones

Finding the Right Cutlery

The second precedent is the Tjibaou Cultural Center in New Caledonia by Renzo Piano Building Workshop that seeks to "address the exploitation of the currents of air and the difficulties of finding a way of expressing the tradition of the pacific in modern language." Piano reminds us in describing his initial approach to the Tjibaou Cultural Center competition that "When we say "culture," we usually mean our own: a fine soup blended from Leonardo da Vinci and Freud, Kant and Darwin, Louis XIV and Don Quixote. In the Pacific it is not just the recipe that is different, but the ingredients as well. We can approach their soup with detachment, bringing our own cutlery. Or we can try to understand how it was born, why it has gone in certain directions, what philosophy of life has shaped it." (174)

Figure 9: Model of Tjibaou Cultural Centre

Jean Marie Tjibaou Cultural Center is located in Noumea, New Caledonia. This facility serves as a resource documenting the origins of the Karnak people of New Caledonia and the South Pacific. The centre is named for Jean-Marie Tjibaou who died in 1989 fighting the French colonial government. It is designed as a series of huts in a linear composition that vary in size according to their function. Larger huts contain major program elements in "Great Houses" or "cases" in French. The design of these huts is the locus of reflection on the indigenous traditions and explicitly references the Karnak people of New Caledonia who have a strong connection to the landscape. These rooms are shaped to take advantage of the trade winds blowing over the site. While their shape is derived from modern wind tunnel testing, their method of enclosure draws inspiration from dried plant materials used in indigenous housing. Piano removes the thatch from the traditional *cases*, and replaces it with cross bracing battens of iroko wood, while the traditional wall posts are replaced with a system of glulam iroko forming upright structural ribs (Lindley 103).

Figure 10: Tjibaou Cultural Centre

These huts are made from carefully developed combinations of wood and metal. Cast steel connectors join horizontal steel braces to pairs of glulam arches forming the exterior wall system. This primary structure frame structure is infilled with wither wood or glass panels with varying degrees of opacity. The glazed panels are either fixed or operable using a jalousie type blade system. The wood panels are made from wood which is either solid or perforated depending on its location in the skin, and it's conformance with the thermal characteristics of the assembly.

Figure 11: Model of Tjibaou Cultural Centre

Site and Program

To test the knowledge gained from evaluation of the two precedents, the Mpumulo project is developed. The site for the Mpumulo project is located in Blantyre, the main economic center of Malawi, at the eastern edge of its suburban agglomeration. The site itself is a former garbage dump scheduled for remediation by the City of Blantyre, and masterplanned for a mix of detached housing and institutional uses. Matching the economic insecurity of the region, the project compound is required from the outset to be contained within its on security wall.

The program for the health center includes screening rooms for infectious and non-infectious disease. One-room houses are provided for the residents, along with bathroom facilities. Both an indoor and outdoor kitchen forms a communal center. Community oriented features include a vocational training room dedicated to fair trade production, a chapel, and intake rooms.

Figure 12: Residents of Mpumulo

Mpumulo

"Mpumulo" is from the Chichewa language and means "relief." It is also expressive of the need to address the culturally embedded abuse of women that is epidemic in Africa. Developing strategies for addressing situations of abuse is a paramount concern in all parts of the world. While these strategies vary in focus and form, they all require innovative and aggressive thinking in their development. This is particularly evident in social structures where the order of economic life is in transition from an existing localized mode to one influenced by global forces. This is the case in Malawi, an impoverished African nation, struggling to improve its global status, while addressing a series of intractable social and physical problems. Malawi is one of the poorest populations in the world, numbering 13,014,000 with an annual GNP of $170 per capita. The region's low life expectancy of 40 is further exacerbated by the spread of AIDS where HIV prevalence is 14.2% of the population and 900,000 are living with AIDS.

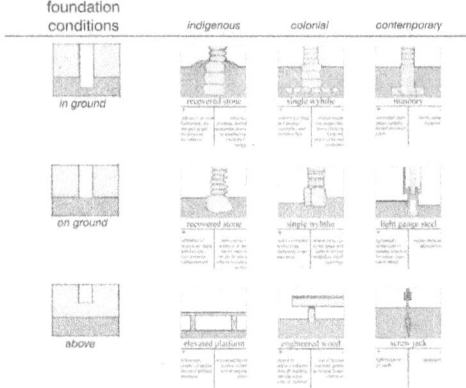

Figure 13: analysis

Methodology and Invention

Access to information on Malawi is sparse and difficult to obtain. While examples of indigenous building strategies exist, they have been supplanted with construction techniques from the nineteenth century colonial settlement period. These building patterns in turn have been updated to conform to contemporary standards of "modern' construction technique, drawn more from an international, progressive stylistic impulse than from the vicissitudes of climate and place. Materials selection and system configuration match those found even in Milwaukee, Wisconsin, despite the large cultural and environmental gap that exists between Malawi and Milwaukee.

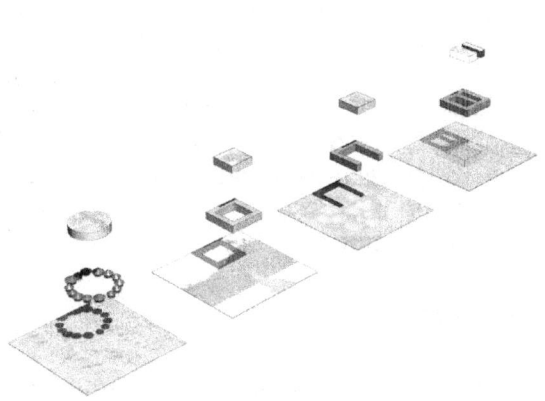

Figure 14: indigenous/modern courtyard analysis

By directing our gaze at the Australian and New Caledonian projects, we deduced a set of categories around construction and around environmental sustainability. These categories were buttressed by the specific solutions developed in these two projects. Next we had our students focus their attention on Malawian architecture, to privilege critical thinking for our students in an arena of investigation where they are more likely to seek uncritical imitation. The intention was to turn the lens of investigation towards indigenous, non-western solution types, and then use that primary knowledge as the basis for developing workable modern techniques that can achieve the same ends. Preliminary research and investigation with our students has generated a majority of solutions that are a hybrid system of indigenous and formal knowledge that requires deep understanding of technical performance in order to accomplish. This approach also serves the important function of emphasizing the production, transmission and utilization of indigenous knowledge and technology, while broadening the perspective our students take in developing their research.

Evaluating Malawian Tectonics and Form

The influence of the colonial period on the form and material character of architecture in Malawi is dominant. The preponderant building material for combined enclosure and bearing wall systems is hand-fabricated brick generally produced at the construction site. Corrugated steel decking is used as the roof spanning configuration, and this is tempered at the interior with acoustical hung ceiling and plaster rendering of the walls. Indigenous architecture employs wood extensively. This is manifest in woven vertical enclosures similar to Piano's Tjibaou Cultural Center, and the use of reeds for thatch on roofs. However, that natural resource is no longer readily available as it has been virtually exhausted for household fuel. Contemporary architecture adds both sitecast and small-module precast concrete to the use of brick, as well as floor-to-floor metal and glass walls. The accommodation of environmental conditions is not a primary design concern in contemporary buildings, but when addressed is handled with brick vents in vertical walls and increased wall mass.

To draw this panoply of time and type into a comprehensible order, a matrix of materials, structure, and enclosure types serves as a resource for developing pure and hybrid detailing solutions to a variety of conditions. To stand in for the lack of primary resources related to Malawian architecture, students researched indigenous architectural solutions throughout sub Saharan Africa with a focus on locations that matched the climatic conditions of Malawi.

Simultaneously with systematic analysis of building technique in Malawi, a formal architectural solution to the Women's Shelter and Health Clinic was developed. Designed to serve residents who have migrated from non-urban communities, this was based on a close reading of indigenous assemblages in rural areas, along with examination of the most widespread current housing stock in cities. Traditional housing is organized around a centralized primary open space, with varied smaller open spaces providing a service function. All compounds, even traditional ones, are surrounded by a continuous wall, employed in traditional housing to contain animals. Modern housing consists of single prismatic blocks constructed from brick and organized in compounds.

This was re-interpreted in the Mpumulo project design with a single and double courtyard system. The design is predicated on a series of supporting walls that provide both structure and enclosure. These walls were evaluated for construction value using a variety of materials including wood, metal, and brick. Coupled with materials selection for enclosure is the strategy for primary structure: frame or wall.

Malawi is located in a sub-tropical zone along a narrow elongated plateau with rolling plains, rounded hills, and some mountains. The land varies in height from a low at the Shire River of 100 feet to the highest point on Mount Mlanje of 10,000 feet above sea level. The climate is characterized by a rainy season lasting six months from November to May, while the dry season occurs during the remaining six months of the year from May to November. Control of groundwater during the rainy season is a significant factor in the project detailing. Modern houses provide concrete trenches to control water run-off from roof overhangs.

Exploitation of natural ventilation is reflected in the use of the courtyard system for planning, and the introduction of ventilating zones in the roofs and walls

Conclusion

This international project allows us to identify the contributions architecture can make in addressing the larger culture issues in a world increasingly characterized by the interconnection of peoples and their economic and social lives. Architecture is an integral part of a globalizing world culture. Working with students to develop physical and operational design models in school that mesh with culture and place has become a necessary part of their education. Nowhere is that more evident than when we are investigating construction systems and materials use. The projects presented make the case that connection to modern production techniques does not preclude tectonic strategies in architecture that ennoble the difference of place, while still reflecting the transformation of technique and assembly at every stage of our lives in a modern world.

References:

Bensa, Alban. "Entre Deux Mondes." L'Architecture d'Aujourd'hui 308 (1996): 44-57.

Crouch, Dora, and June Johnson. Traditions in Architecture: Africa, America, Asia, and Oceania. New York: Oxford University Press, 2001.

Cuno, James and Martha Thorne. Zero Gravity: The Art Institute, Renzo Piano, and Building for a New Century. Chicago: The Art Institute, 2005.

Dill, H., R. Ludwig, A. Kathewera, and J. Mwenelupembe. "A lithofacies terrain model for the Blantyre Region: Implications for the interpretation of palaeosavanna depositional systems and for environmental geology and economic geology in southern Malawi." Journal of African Earth Sciences 41 (2005): 341-393.

Dovey, Kim. "Architecture for the Aborigines." Architecture Australia 85.4 (1996): 90-96.

Findley, L. "Piano Nobile." Architecture 87.10 (1998): 96-105.

Fromonot, Francoise. Glenn Murcutt: Buildings + Projects 1962-2003. New York: Thames & Hudson, 2005.

Lang, Werner. "Is it all "just" façade? The functional, energetic and structural aspects of the building skin." Building Skins: Concepts, Layers, Materials. Ed. Christian Schittich. Basel: Birkhauser 2001.

Le Corbusier. Le Corbusier Talks with Students from the Schools of Architecture. Trans. Pierre Chase. New York: Princeton Architectural Press, 1999.

Melhuish, Clare. Marika-Alderton House and Kakadu Landscape Intepretation Centre (with Troppo Architects), Northern Territory, Australia." Architectural Design 66 (1996): 40-45.

Piano, Renzo. The Renzo Piano Logbook. London: Thames and Hudson, 1997.

Varanda, Fernando. "2004 On Site Review Report: Women's Centre, Rufisque, Senegal." ArchNet. 12 June 2006 <http://archnet.org/library/sites/one-site.tcl?site_id=8218>.

Pattern In Architecture: Explorations of the Digital Modeling and Fabrication Lab

Edgar Stach
University of Tennessee

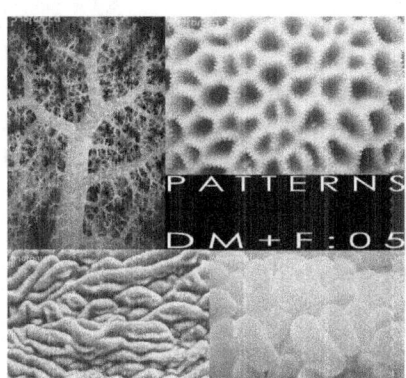

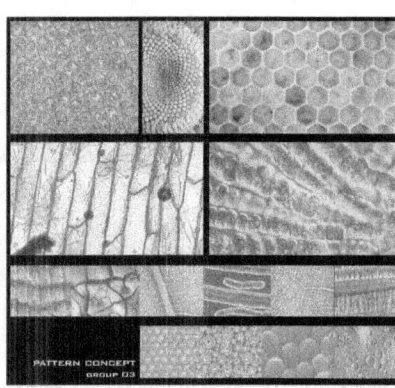

DM+F Lab

To what extent can digital manufacturing methods inform the creation of architecture? What is the effect of architectural systems inspired by nature to be translated and produced using computer controlled machines? To explore these possibilities became the basis for the Digital Modeling and Fabrication Lab.

The DM+F Lab was created to introduce students to advanced computer modeling techniques using Alias Maya 6 and manufacturing techniques. The lab instructed students on designing and manufacturing architectural surfaces and the modeling and manipulation of nurbs surfaces for output to digital manufacturing devices. Research, fabrication and assembly procedures centered on digital fabrication using 2d laser cutter and computer numerically controlled (CNC) production processes, in varies scales. The course attempted to teach at various levels between 'how to' considerations of learning hardware and software, while exploring a deeper understanding of the technological implications on design and digital fabrication

The semester broke down into two critical phases: Project 1: the design and production of an object based on fluid dynamics using 3D software, the laser cutter and a technique similar to stereo lithography. Project 2: The exploration and the creation of an architectural panel system based on this pattern using 3D software, the

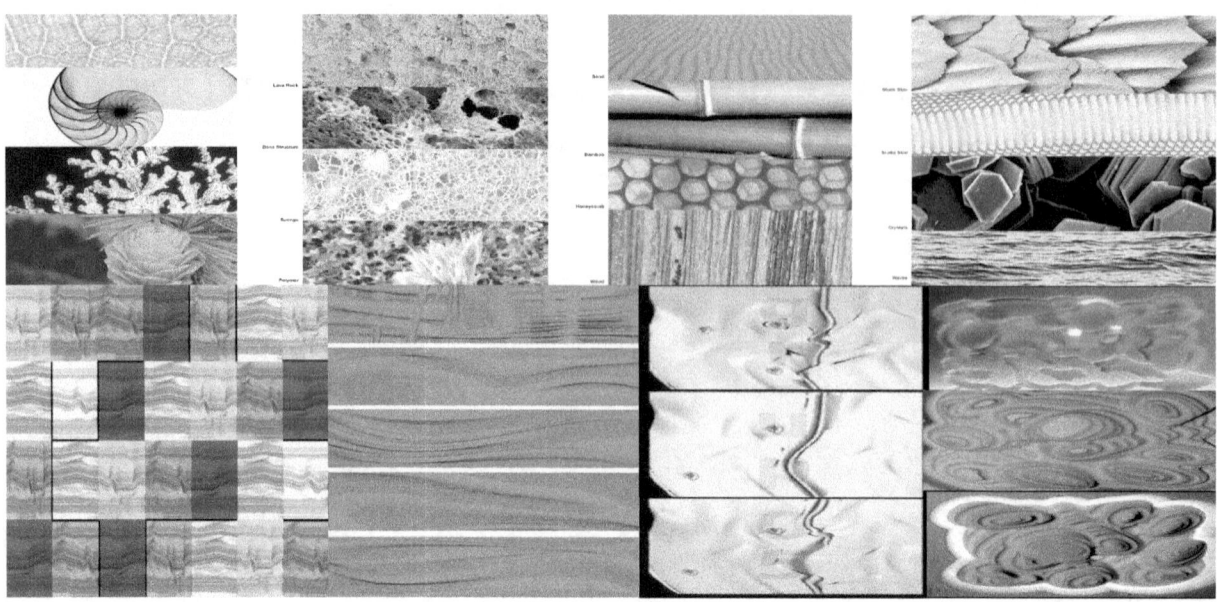

CNC milling machine, and material exploration.

Each project would then be broken down into three sections:(1) the introduction of Maya 6.5 software, Autocad 2005, and Mastercam Mill software, (2) the exploration of the design problem (3) execution of the design via application of the new software to the 2D laser cutter and CNC machine.

The main objective of the DM+F Lab became how to use this new digital software to explore how different typologies of pattern could be applied to architecture, and then produce prototypes using the computer controlled machines. Students began by investigating patterns found in nature, mathematically defined patterns, patterns created through physical changes, and patterns found in nano structures. Students in the lab examined pattern mathematically, physically, and algorithmically to better understand how they could be translated into digital modeling software.

After intense investigation of patterns through digital modeling and experimenting with the laser cutter and CNC machines, students in the DM+F Lab used their results to create a panel system with architectural applications. A variety of applications were explored, including lighting, shading, structure, and industrial applications. Scale issues for indoor and outdoor panels and the challenge of creation a seamless repeating pattern became critical issues in student designs. The panels themselves were to be designed with the production method as a driving factor, therefore showing the relevance of these new technologies to architecture. The ability of the CNC technology to create the final product or to generate a mold for mass production was often a driving force in many explorations. The work of The University of Delft became an important reference for students in the Lab, because of their work on the "subject of materializing 'blob' architecture" in the face of the many technical challenges posed. The DM+F Lab therefore made an effort to apply these

Pattern In Architecture: Explorations of the Digital Modeling and Fabrication Lab

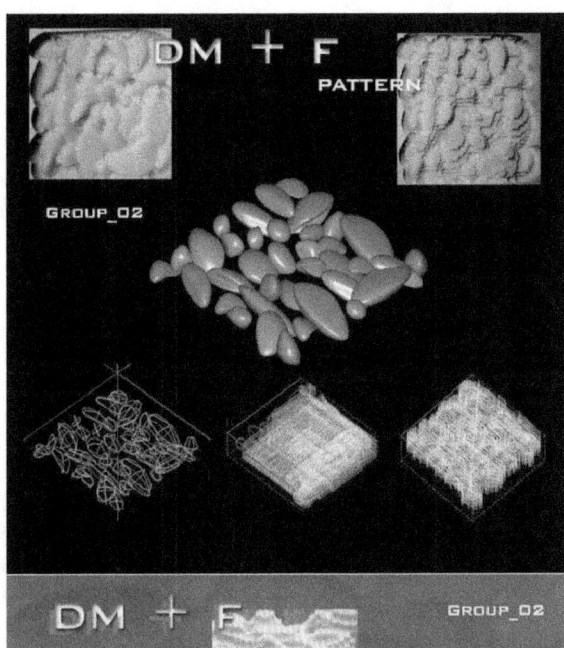

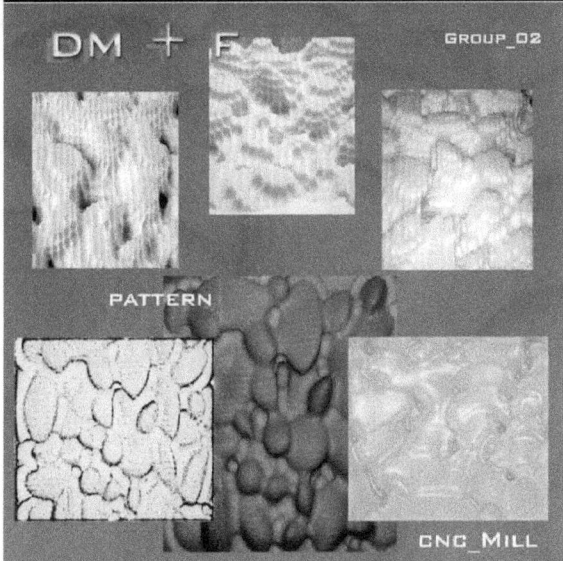

technologies in a way that was grounded in reality, creating an architectural panel system via direct interface between designer, computer, and machine.

Object Based on Fluid Dynamics

Design Objective and Production Method

The first exploration began by proposing a design for a small flower vase, no larger than 10 by 10 inches. Focusing on structures fluid dynamics and liquid flow, students in the DM+F Lab used Maya Alias software to create digital models and renderings. To create a final prototype, the 3D model was sliced into layers, imported into Autocad, and cut using a laser cutter. The fabrication process is similar to stereo lithography, where thin layers are laminated to form the complete object. Students of the DM+F Lab created non-working prototypes using basswood, chipboard, foam core board, and Plexiglas. The objective of the exploration became not only to explore the use of nature systems to design a flower vase, but also to design a flower vase using digital software expressly to be made using the laser cutter. The prototypes produced therefore investigate and express the actual process of their fabrication as well as the design objectives.

"Ice Block" flower vase

In one specific example, the life processes of a plant became a diagram in the form of a flower vase (fig 2b). Using Maya Alias software, the prototype was specifically designed to be constructed of .08" layers of clear Lexan laminated together (fig 2c). The functioning part of the flower vase exists only as the negative space subtracted from a block of "ice". The exterior of the vase is a hard rectangular block with organic voids undulating inside. Three long bulbous shapes hover inside the block of ice, growing upwards until they breach the surface like seedlings reaching for sunlight. Here, the negative spaces become protrusions on the top of the block, which is depress half an inch to form a pan to accept water. When the pan is filled, water slowly seeps into sixty-four small holes organized in a grid. As these tubules penetrate the ice

block, they quickly abandon the rigid grid organization and find their way to the distended bulb space where the flower resides. The vase shows the cycle of watering, sprouting, and growth in a three dimensional diagram that the user interacts with. The hard exterior shape and grid pattern contrast the wild organic growth contained within. The interior surface becomes the exterior surface only when the growth cycle is complete, when the plant bursts through the surface, distorting it at the same time.

Architectural Panel System

Project Description
Next the Digital Modeling and Fabrication Lab began exploring patterns of different types as generators for an architectural panel system. Students looked at patterns such as sand dunes, atomic structures, Fibonacci numbers sets, river stones, cellular structures, and physical processes. Emphasis was put on structure, form, and how these patterns are created in nature instead of visual aesthetics alone. Prototypes were created with two inch polycarbonate foam using a CNC milling machine. Later, an architectural panel system would be designed by each group based on the pattern explored. Application and panel size were determined by the students as well as the proposed material for the project. Prototypes and ½"=1' models were created on the CNC using a variety of materials, such as rubber, wood, MDF board, plastic, and Plexiglas. Once again, students in the DM+F Lab were encouraged to design specifically for the fabrication process. The capabilities of the CNC informed much of the final design.

Octopus Suckers
One group focused on the random pattern of suckers found on the underside of octopus tentacles (fig 3c). These soft forms move in an almost liquid way, behaving independently and as a group as the octopus searches for prey. The appearance and movement of the suckers was examined and translated into Maya software (fig 3d).

The goal became to explore the application of this pattern of soft shapes to an interactive architectural panel system that speaks of movement and tactility. The application of these panels in a public space such as a subway tunnel, airport, or along a sidewalk would allow for the highest possible interaction (fig 3e).

The final design proposed a system of sixteen 4'x 8' panels oriented vertically. The panels are non-repetitive and organized in a row. While the design process began by investigating patterns found in nature, the undulating motion created by the octopus suckers became the motivational factor of the design. To emphasize this point, the random arrangement and differing scales of the suckers as they appear in nature was abandoned in favor of a standard size, 3" diameter, and a rigid grid arrangement. Here, the soft shape of the sucker is severely abstracted into a ring shape that is embedded into the panel surface. The sucker grid interacts with the panel surface as it ripples and swells in and three dimensional wave forms. As a result of this interaction, large sections of the sucker grid are swallowed by the wave and disappear. Fiber optic lights inside each sucker respond to motion across the wall surface via tiny motion sensors. The swelling and dimming of individual light creates an ambient effect that animates the solid wave surface of the panels. By changing intensity, color, and duration, the fiber optic lights respond to passersby as if engaging them in a conversation. A single person walking in front of the panels might see their own silhouette illuminate and walk next to them in real time. A runner might leave a comet-like tail on the wall as they pass. A crowd of people in front of the wall might see the entire wall swell and dim and change colors in response.

Conclusion

The use of new digital modeling software and computer controlled production methods allow for a new type of interface between design and production. The digital model created by the designer can be sent directly to the laser cutter or CNC mill and created with extreme accuracy. The development of software for both design and production facilitate this link and allows for rapid protoyping. The computer controlled machine can be used to create the final product or to create molds for the mass production of the design. Therefore, the connection between the designer's mouse and the CNC cutter is immediate and personal. The architect or designer must now design with the production method in mind, to utilize the capabilities of the machine for the best result. The machine gives immediate and honest feedback to the designer, proving or disproving the feasibility of the design. The link created between the human mind and computer controlled fabrication methods will allow for the realization of architecture acknowledges its own design and creation.

The use of pattern as ornament in architecture has long been a subject for debate. The explorations of the Digital Modeling and Fabrication Lab work shows that pattern could be used to generate systems with functional applications. These panel systems would become part of an architectural language of display, lighting, or acoustic paneling. Most importantly, the work of the DM+F Lab made statements about human interaction. While the final product would be designed for and created by a machine, the design itself would be created by and for a human being. This influenced not only the scale of the wall panel systems, but proposed materials, production methods, and placement of the design.

The work of the DM+F lab shows that a connection can be made between new digital software, computer controlled fabrication, and new applications of pattern in architecture. The new tools allow architects to consider surfaces in a new way, while the application of function to panel systems allow for people to interact with architecture on a more intimate scale.

References

www.arch.utk.edu/dmf

http://www.e-panelite.com/

greg lynn/form::http://wwww.glform.com

http://www.thurlowsmall.com/

un studio::http://www.unstudio.com/
blob.tudelf.nc

cca::http://cca.qc.ca/

cooper hewitt::http://ndm.si.edu/

max protetch gallery::http://www.maxprotech.com

http://www.nai.nl/

Venice biennale::http://www.labiennale.org/

techno/isel::http://wwww.techno-isel.com

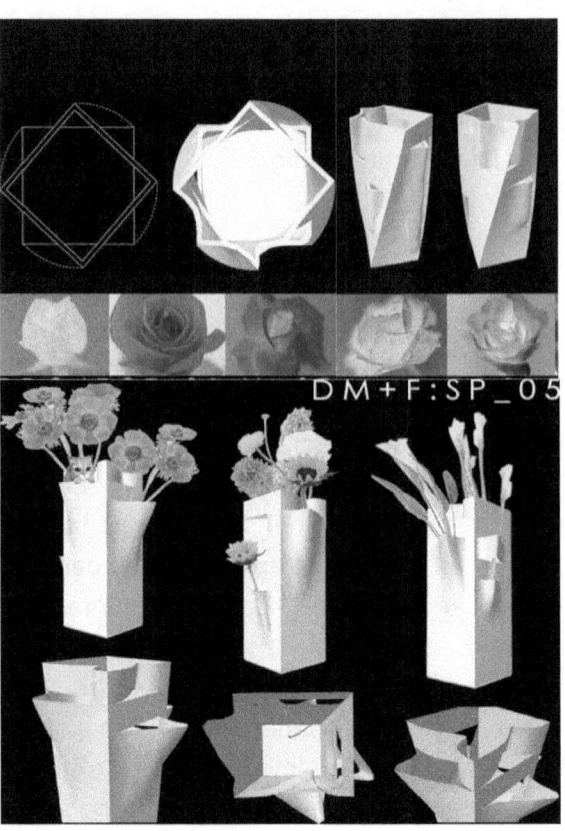

fig 2a   Maya model of a flower vase based on the organization of rose pedals

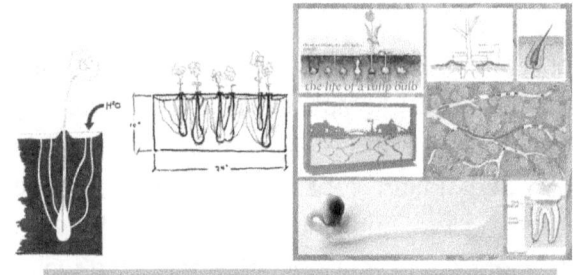

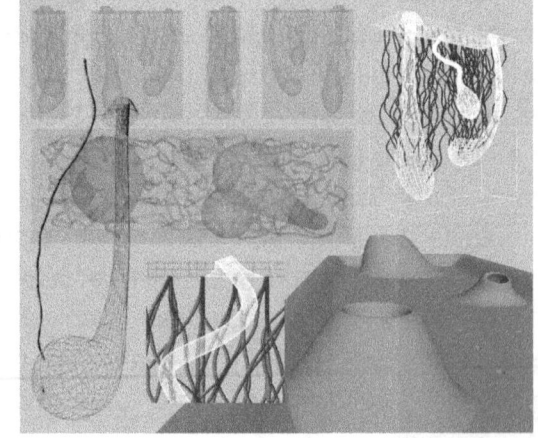

fig 2b   Initial concept sketches, images, and Maya model

Pattern In Architecture: Explorations of the Digital Modeling and Fabrication Lab

fig 2c   Prototype of "ice block" flower vase created using laser cutter

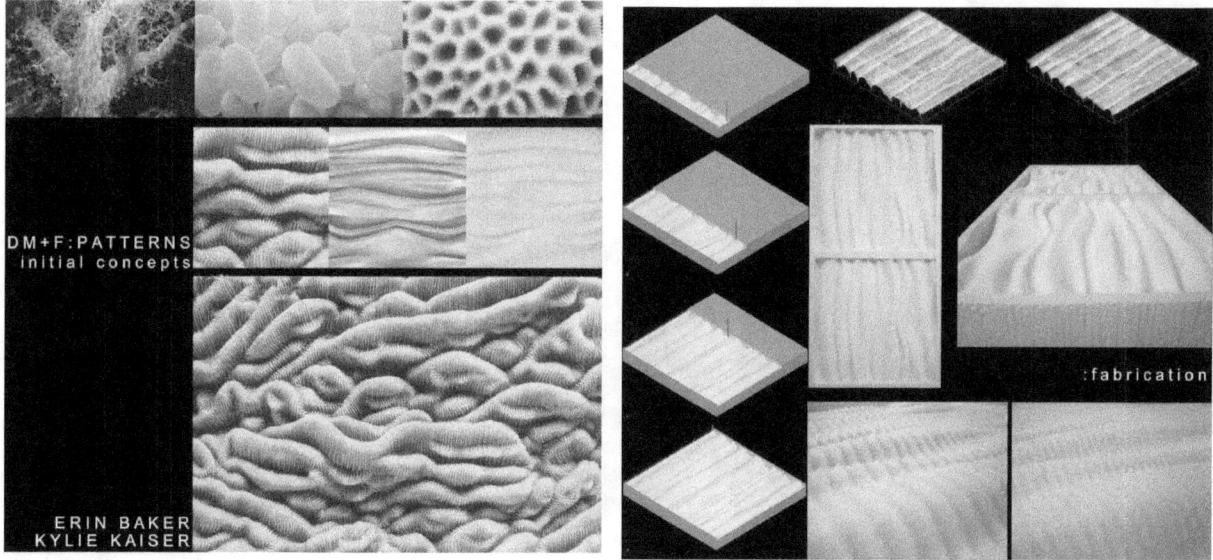

fig 3a   Pattern found in coral and images of panel prototype created on the CNC out of foam

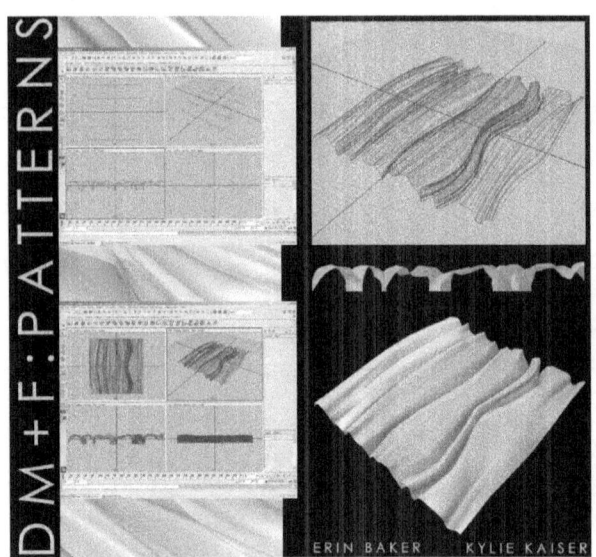 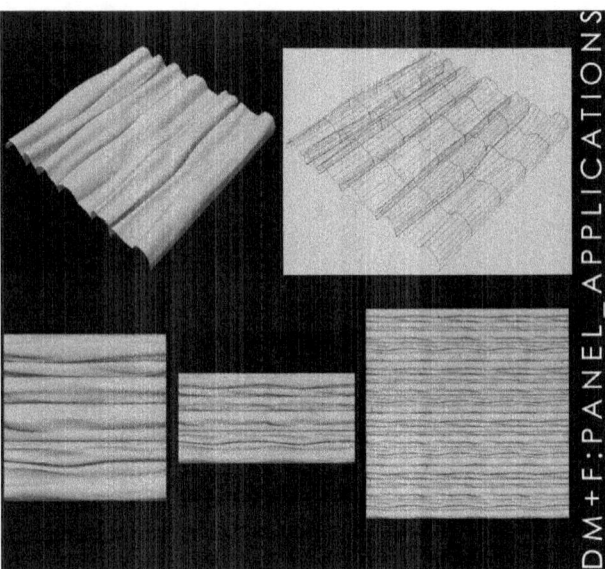

fig 3b   Images of Maya model of panel based on coral pattern

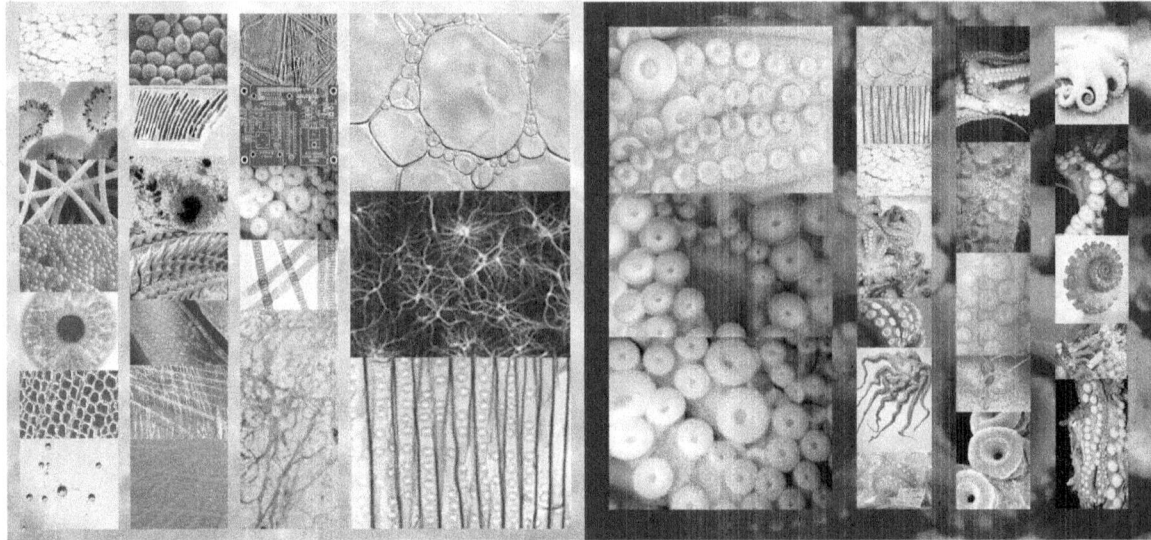

fig 3c   Images of organic patterns and specifically octopus suckers

Pattern In Architecture: Explorations of the Digital Modeling and Fabrication Lab

fig 3d   Images of Maya model, CNC router, tool paths generated by Mastercam, and a rendering of full scale wall panel.

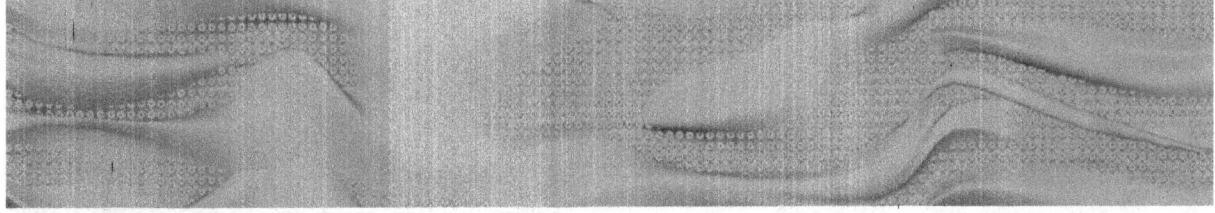

fig 3e   Image of entire wall panel system

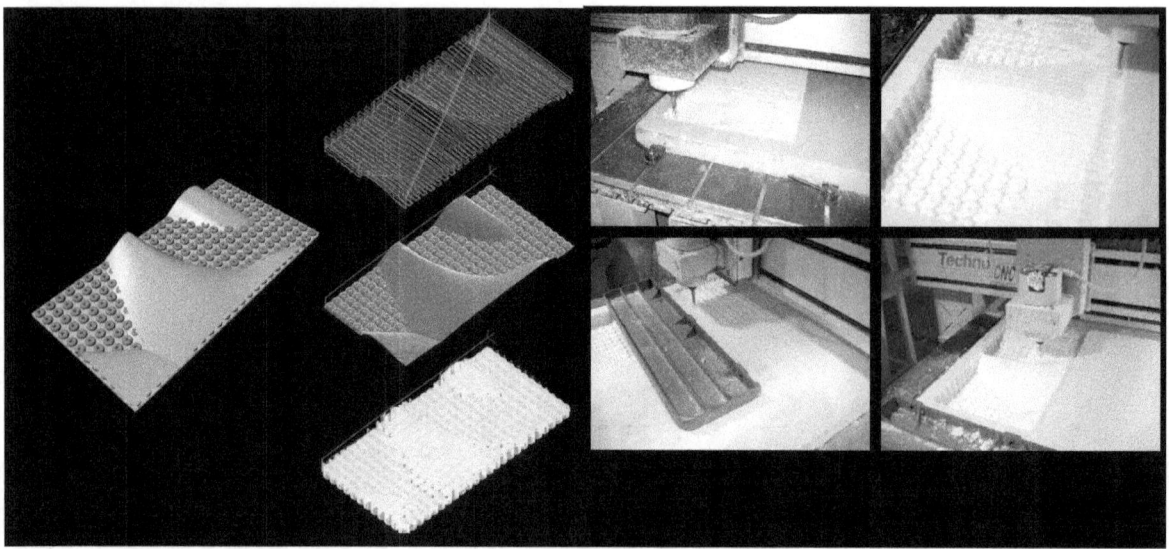

fig 3f   Tool paths in Mastercam and CNC carving prototypes out of foam

fig 4a   Application of panels systems explored in the DM+F Lab

The WSU Solar Decathlon – Design/Build Lessons

Mat Taylor, Assistant Professor, and
T. Duff Bangs, Graduate Student
Washington State University

Introduction and Overview

The Solar Decathlon project, sponsored by the US Department of Energy, is an incredibly effective tool with which to teach the lessons and details of Design/Build. In this age of more interdisciplinary building methods, the contest teaches lessons that few (if any) coursework can effectively deliver. Students who participate in the project grow practically and academically, and for those who participate fully, are quite literally transformed.

The contest asks student teams to design, build and deliver a small, solar-powered home to the National Mall in Washington DC. The home must be entirely powered by the sun and can use no fossil fuels. The 2005 contest began with a grant of $5,000 and the rest was left up to the teams.

This paper examines the lessons learned in the project delivered by Washington State University in 2005. Discussed herein are pieces of the project that distinctly enabled students and a few possible improvements to the project that could inform the DOE and, perhaps, make a better demonstration for the wider goals of solar energy and renewables in general. This paper is presented in two parts: *Lessons learned* and *Suggestions*.

PART ONE: LESSONS LEARNED

The following sections describe design decisions and ideas that were followed from which the WSU teams learned valuable lessons. A brief description precedes the "lessons" and it is hoped that the lessons can inform future Decathlon teams.

Moving from Diagram to Design

Schools of architecture and design tend to encourage students to only get to (what the authors feel) is a *schematic design*. Design development and construction phases, the lengthiest part of the building process, are rarely pursued in design studios. It makes sense. Unless a project is very modest in size or complexity, or unless a project spans over a few semesters or terms, the design lessons pursued in design education have little to do with detail and even less to do with production/construction documents.

Because design students are accustomed to stopping at an early design phase, design/build projects push students to untested ground. They are simply not experienced in getting to a detail level, so getting them there is a difficult task. Figures One and Two show the WSU team's first massing diagram and initial floor plan.

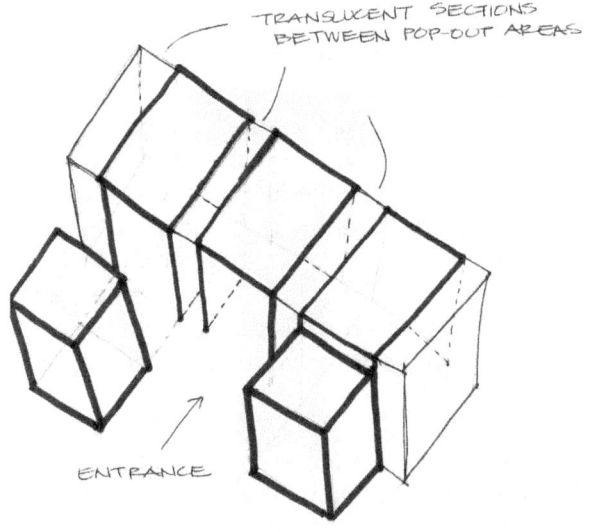

Figure 1. An early massing diagram

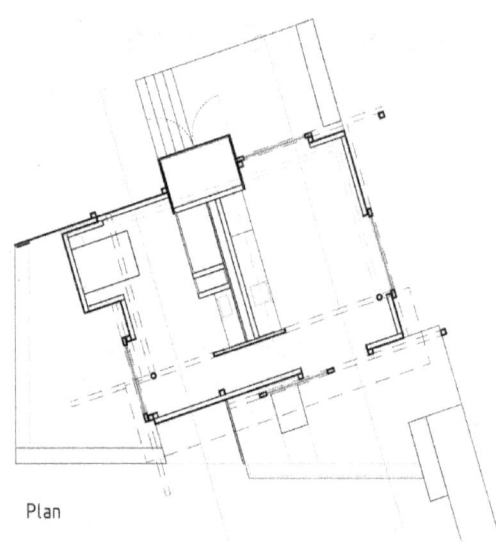

Figure 2. The first real floor plan

The process that led from the diagram to the initial design took over one year. There was quite a bit education that happened in the intervening months (systems, solar technology, etc.), but the reality of actually having to build what was designed made the students overly cautious and, in a sense, a bit timid.

Lesson One: Spend a short but intense time in pre-design and early schematic design and encourage the team to move quickly to a mature design.

A Team with Ownership

The WSU team was initially comprised of architecture and construction management students only. As the design progressed, more disciplines were added, including electrical engineering, civil engineering and interior design. The core team emerged quickly, but they didn't understand their role until the team had a sound plan for a project structure.

The Team advisor (co-author) took a "Taoist" approach to team management. The project belonged to the students, so any decisions and any work that needed to be done was coordinated, managed and done by the students on the team. The advisor's role was only to enable students and to help out with College logistics.

The approach worked remarkably well. When the project had a deliverable, the students were self-motivated and self led. When materials were needed, the team was not led but rather enabled. When products were not delivered, a student was responsible. When things arrived, then the students were equally responsible and fully rewarded. The students owned the project.

On a volunteer basis, little got done. If credits or courses (grades) were tied to the project, then things got accomplished. On the engineering side, senior projects were solicited to move the design forward. In the design disciplines, studio work and elective courses were used to ensure that work got completed. Without the tie to academic performance, there were few incentives for students to complete what was needed.

Lesson Two: Tie the project to academic requirements and credits to ensure that students have ownership and responsibility.

The Multidisciplinary Design Team

As modern design/build projects would suggest, all disciplines were involved at a schematic design level from the start. The team worked together rather awkwardly at first, but soon found that working together produced a more sound design.

The process produced very smart students. After the first two years of the project, the team had engineers who could intelligently discuss building form and design intent, architecture students who could speak to the advantages of heat pumps and the concepts of refrigeration, and interior design students who could speak technically about photovoltaics and solar hot water. It was a beautiful thing to witness.

Lesson Three: Involve all disciplines in all aspects of design and development.

Schematic Design to Materials

Moving to design development and an in-depth understanding of materials was constrained only by the donations available. The team was blessed with very giving donors, but the donations available basically created a "kit of parts" for the team to use in design. Despite any limitations to design freedom, the constraints turned out to be quite freeing. Once donors were in place, the team was limited to the materials given. The suppliers and donors forced the team to use specific materials and in turn enlisted a host of experts and consultants.

The fundraising task was daunting at first, but the students quickly adjusted. Rather than working from a design/bid/build approach, the students pursued designs based on what was available. Once the design was in place, at least in a schematic sense, the students on the team went about getting building materials. The answer was not always what they wanted, but it was amazing to see the design adapt to the availability of products.

Budget was another factor in design. Donations were key in getting the home built, but unless the material was free (or at very low cost), the team could not use it. The students had to choose where to put the scarce amount of money received from fundraising, a wonderful and useful learning opportunity.

Lesson Four: Start fundraising and product donation requests early and create a dedicated team for the tasks.

The Crux: Design Development

The key turning point in the project came after schematic design review from the project sponsors. The US Department of Energy returned comments to the team and, more or less, scared them into action. It was clear in the DOE assessment that the team was way behind, so efforts were started to get moving.

The overall design concept revolved around an eight-by-eight-by-twenty-foot shipping container, the core and service module of the home. Once it was delivered, the team found new motivation to start the "build" part of the project. The students contacted a local framing company and acquired steel framing members (and a willing installer) to get the project going.

Once framing got going, the team looked to the next step, the floor and wall structure, albeit a bit late to have timely delivery. Again, delays were a wonderful learning opportunity for the students. The team got so busy modifying the container that they forgot the next step. They very quickly learned to look ahead. Figure Three shows the shipping container core and the first layout of the main structure.

Figure 3. The shipping container and initial structure

Systems and Appliances

Since the team understood the value of "looking ahead," the systems and appliances for the home arrived on time and almost fully donated. This step of the project was perhaps the smoothest part of the entire undertaking. With good leadership and a very well integrated group of dedicated students, the systems arrived on time and on schedule. Installation of the systems, like the rest of the project, was all performed by the student team members.

Lesson Five: *The contest is all about systems – start thinking, planning and designing early and get the products as soon as prudent.*

Renewable Energy Systems

By contest mandate, each home must be completely stand-alone from an energy standpoint. The WSU team designed and sized the photovoltaic and hot water systems for optimal performance, a design that is, in hindsight, a bad idea. Both systems were designed for three days of foul weather; unfortunately, the home ended up having to endure eight days of rain and deeply overcast skies. To make matters worse, the team decided to start the competition with the battery bank at 75% charge, a strategy they hoped would help ensure a positive energy balance by contest end. After two days of competition, the batteries were down to half charge.

Lesson Six: *Design for the "worst of the worst" case and over-design systems so that the team can guarantee to compete.*

Donated Parts and Systems

Because of budget constraints, the WSU team could not buy the photovoltaics (and balance of system components) outright. A deal was set up with a Washington State utility where, once the contest was over, the utility would maintain ownership of the electrical energy system and the home would become a shared demonstration facility with WSU.

The arrangement seemed like a good idea as it saved the team from spending about $42,000 in all. Looking back at the contest, the arrangement actually took away some competitive advantage. While other teams could "ride" their battery banks until near depletion, the WSU team had to ensure that the batteries survived the contest. Although the team showed a positive energy balance at the end of the contest, the other contests suffered greatly.

Other systems, such as donated appliances and materials, worked out extremely well. In some cases, the team received used systems, an idea that should have been examined more closely. Some of the used systems in the home did not work as well as they should and, again, reduced the team's capacity to compete.

Lesson Seven: *Ensure that the team has complete control and ownership of the lifetime of the critical systems of the project.*

Commissioning and Start-up

This is perhaps where the WSU team was the most lacking and least prepared. The final integration and finish-out of the home took as long as expected, but some of the critical systems (batteries, the custom refrigerator and the solar hot water system) incurred several weeks of delayed delivery. The team had to wait so long to integrate all of the systems that the entire home was not commissioned until it was erected on the National Mall.

Luckily, most of systems worked as hoped. Two systems, however, did not perform as expected. The hot water system had a number of fouled tubes and the refrigerator, a custom "holding plate" design, never worked well. As a result, the team did not compete in the hot water or refrigeration contests.

Lesson Eight: *Leave no less than one month to start up, commission and test the home as an integrated whole.*

The eight lessons described above are only a hint at the wonderful experience gained by the entire WSU team. This *post mortum* look at the contest will hopefully serve to inform any University team entering the Solar Decathlon in future years and may inform design/build projects in general.

The following section gives hints and suggestions to make the Solar Decathlon a better competition.

Figure 4. The Solar Decathlon Project Completed on the WSU Campus

PART TWO: SUGGESTIONS

The following sections describe ideas and requirements that are problematic in the success of renewable and sustainable technologies as they are portrayed by the Solar Decathlon contest. A brief description precedes the "suggestions." In future contests, it is hoped that these issues will be discussed and the contest modified to better represent the direction of renewable and sustainable technologies.

Stand-alone versus Community

The stand-alone requirement conspires with the need to compete to produce systems that are grossly oversized. The budget impacts alone are tremendous, but there is a larger issue: portrayal of solar technologies to the public. With such large systems on very small homes, the public sees that solar systems dominate the budget and the architecture of the homes. It is, frankly, detrimental to solar acceptance to showcase such tremendously large and expensive systems. The WSU team found themselves apologetically explaining the need for so many batteries and so many PV panels. When visitors asked how much the system would cost, the team again had to qualify the high cost and size, and WSU had one of the smallest systems on the Mall.

In the wider argument, and in accordance with current industry thinking, a better approach would be to have a *community* of solar buildings. The logistics may be difficult, but the reality would better show the grid-tie approach to renewable energy.

Suggestion One: *Tie the homes together in a community "mini-grid" and show the public that solar works in a cooperative way.*

Running It Into the Ground

To effectively compete in the 2005 contest, due to the extremely uncooperative weather, teams had to deplete their battery banks and, in many cases, "kill" thousands of dollars worth of system components. As stated earlier, the WSU team did not have the luxury of being able to destroy their batteries, and as such, could not compete on a level with other teams. There must be an allowance for not sending the wrong message by wasting resources.

Suggestion Two: *Make the contest require a functioning home before and after the contest.*

The Further the Better

Contest Ten, called "Getting Around," asked the teams to drive an electric car and charge it from the home energy system. The contest awarded more points to the teams that drove the furthest each day. From a transportation viewpoint, and from an ecological viewpoint, this is the wrong message to send. Imposing a cap on miles driven per day would be a better way to convey sustainable transportation. A distance cap would also help reduce system size, system cost and, again, send a better message to the public.

Suggestion Three: *Change the contest to reflect a more conservative example of driving or eliminate the contest entirely.*

Way Too Much Money

The WSU initial budget was estimated at approximately $130,000. The project ended up costing about $60,000, most of which covering lodging, travel and transport. The bulk of the project was donated. The estimated construction cost based on no donations, with labor and transport included, is estimated at $200,000.

In conversations with the public, the retail cost of the WSU home seemed reasonable. Other teams had (literally) ten times the budget, some teams spending well over one million dollars for project delivery. This is perhaps the most dangerous portrayal of the contest. Despite the fact that the homes are "cutting edge" and prototypical in nature, it is completely inappropriate to display homes that cost well over one thousand dollars per square foot. In a sense, this precedent shows that brute force and nearly unlimited resources make solar energy viable. It is the wrong message to send. Having no budget cap or having little reward for cost performance also discriminates against smaller or less well-funded schools.

Suggestion Four: *Include a budget cap or some other mechanism to help ensure that schools are rewarded for cost performance.*

Even More Money

One of the biggest expenses in the project was getting the home from Pullman to DC. WSU and San Luis Obispo, for example, had to move their homes a total of roughly 6,000 miles. East coast schools, such as Maryland and Virginia Tech, had only a few dozen miles to move. Perhaps a program could be put in place to level the costs.

Conclusions

The Solar Decathlon Contest is, in the mind of the WSU team's faculty advisor, THE most profound teaching and learning tool available to Universities. The concept is sound, has very far-reaching effects on the public, and has the opportunity to drastically increase public awareness and acceptance of a more sustainable way to live.

From the student perspective, the contest gives opportunities to experience "real life" design/build projects and truly valuable interdisciplinary teamwork. Of the ten key students on the WSU team, ALL TEN have received job offers based on their Decathlon experience. This is enough to prove the contest's validity.

Should the contest change in the subtle ways given, perhaps it would become a bit more fair. Further, should the contest emphasize design elegance rather than "brute force" design, it is hoped that the contest will send a more meaningful message to the public.

Ecological Aspects in Teaching Historic Building Technologies in an Architectural Preservation Curriculum

Dr. Irena (Rina) Wasserman
National Building Research Institute, Faculty of Civil Engineering,
Technion – Israel Institute of Technology

Introduction

The study of historical construction poses a number of very significant challenges to the architect. Difficulties stem not only from the need to model complex geometries, materials and actions, but also from the significance of history and the need for linking the structural analysis with the historical events (1). Disconnecting analysis of historical construction from history may yield results in contraction with reality.

Natural materials have been used in construction for many centuries, but only now are their qualities being fully understood and utilized, to the benefit of buildings, people and nature. An examination of the physical properties of historic building materials, their deterioration mechanisms, and strategies for assessing conditions, conserving and rehabilitating historic resources should be done in connection with the climate situation (i.e. global climate changes, high air pollution levels, changes in building materials manufacturing, etc.). Therefore, the interconnections between historical construction technologies and historical ecology could bring a great deal in planning strategies for sustainable preservation, restoration and renovation of historic buildings.

Scientists and managers alike are increasingly using environmental history as a "base datum" for understanding and managing ecosystems (2). The buildings around us represent an important link to our living history. They are an integral part of the particular ecosystems and, therefore, completely affected by the actual ecological alterations. Use of history enables determining the range and variability of ecological processes in different historic epochs and their interaction with the development of building technologies.

Connection between global climate changes and architectural heritage

Since 1995, world conservation-policymakers have faced a completely new challenge: how to ensure sustainability of historic architectural legacy subjected to combination of dangers caused by global climate changes and man-made hazards; such hazards as salinity, moisture, acidity, air pollution, bio-deterioration, earthquakes, fire loss, etc. Generally it might be suggested that:

- The durability of historic building materials, such as stones, mortars and stuccos depends on weathering conditions.

- Global climate changes related to increased levels of solar radiation, rainfalls and floods are particularly dangerous for the integrity of architectural heritage, causing accelerated deterioration.

- The preservation and conservation of architectural heritage is essential for the protection of legacy resources for future generations, as for a sustainable tourism industry (3).

- If we are to do anything to reduce or prevent loss of our heritage in the new climatic conditions, we must firstly to study the possible implications of climate changes on the historic architectural heritage and then to develop harmless conservation techniques sustainable in conditions of global climate changes.

- This approach is especially important for the Mediterranean region, incl. Israel, in view of extreme high temperature events in summer and severe rainfalls in winter, which have become frequent in Mediterranean in past thirty years (4). Although the total rain precipitation in the European Mediterranean climate has decreased, global climate warming has caused severe rainfalls and increased salinity of the environment.

- This scenario will continue, according to Inter-governmental Panel of Climate Change, in the next 100 years (5). Thus, a risk of elevated pollutant precipitation on the historic fabrics is continuously increasing, causing accelerated deterioration and disintegration of materials.

- Architectural conservation practitioners now face a new challenge of revealing and defining the possible limits or risks of the common conservation practices in conditions of global climate changes. The new harmless conservation methods have to be developed for sustainable preservation of architectural heritage which will be now continuously exposed to the new environmental conditions and hazards.

State-of-the-Art of research on environmental implications on architectural heritage

Environmental factors crucially impact the sustainability of cultural heritage. Most research on the long-term performance of cultural heritage has been carried out on the vulnerability of cultural patrimony to natural and man-made hazards. In May 1996, the IVth European Conference of Ministers responsible for cultural heritage, held in Helsinki, discussed for the first time the threat for cultural heritage by global climate change (6). The necessity of long-term risk-prevention policies which take into account global climate changes has been recognized by conservation decision-makers. Despite this consciousness, scientific research on this topic in relation to cultural heritage is still scarce. A few pioneer works were carried out in the 90s of the 20th century by Maltese scientists (7-9). Nevertheless, increased strength of winter rainfalls becomes more and more frequent in Eastern Mediterranean, incl. Israel. According to scenarios of Mediterranean climate, incl. Israel, for the 21st century, the risk of flooding will increase substantially in coastal areas.

The above mentioned natural disasters could be extremely harmful for the performance of air-exposed historic fabrics, for example: stones, mortars, stuccos, mosaics, wood, metal, etc. Accelerated weathering and deterioration of ancient and historic stone-like materials in a polluted urban environment have received enormous attention in the past two decades (7-14).

However, the architectural conservators are still lacking the fundamental knowledge of ecological processes in the past. Nevertheless, reference conditions may be used, along with current condition assessments, social and economic considerations, for understanding the character of ancient and historic construction methods and for setting achievable and sustainable management of architectural legacy.

Ecological applications in studying historic construction technologies

It should be emphasized that the climatic alterations are not the only factor affecting the development of construction technologies. Implications of political, economic, social and cultural circumstances on the construction technologies used at different historic epochs have been profoundly investigated by humanity disciplines.

However, the implementation of natural variations or reference conditions derived from historical ecology to understanding the development of historic construction technologies is still lacked. The course "Historical rendering and conservation of historical renders" was developed by author within the frameworks of M.Arch. Programme in Architectural Conservation, Faculty of Architecture, Technion, Israel. The main philosophy of the course is to connect the reference climatic conditions with the changes in the construction technologies used during the different historic epochs.

The timeline of binding materials proposed in (15) was accomplished by author, and the historic ecological processes were compared with the data about the construction technologies during the different historic epochs.

Changing ancient building technologies upon global climate alteration

~ 9,000 BP (before present)

The archeological remains of the ancient floor from around 7,000 BC was found in 1985 when a concrete floor was uncovered during the construction of a road at Yiftah El in Galilee, Israel (16). This concrete archetype was consisted of a lime concrete. Lime was apparently produced by calcinations of the local clay soils with high calcium content. Quicklime obtained from this clay soil when combined with water and sand forms a «slime» - mortar which coming into contact with the carbon dioxide of the atmosphere becomes stiffer and renders a solid compound. If this mortar is mixed with stones, it bonds-sticks together the stones and forms a type of concrete. It should be emphasized that the calcination of clays with high content of calcium leads to formation of feebly hydraulic lime which is more durable in wet climate then ordinary air lime.

Between 8,000 and 5000 BC the Mediterranean climate apparently became wetter and warmer (17-19). Common knowledge is that the wet and warm climate is favorable for binders with hydraulic properties and is-negative for mortars based on air lime undurable in these conditions. Application of blended binder described above in a wet climate made a great deal in formation of durable archeo-concrete successfully performed during following 9,000 years.

~ 8,500 BP

A village of trapezoidal houses from around 6,500 BC was found in Lepenski Vir, Serbia. Lepenski Vir stands out upon the map of prehistoric Europe: for its methodically planned architecture and for its diverse sculptures (20). Alike Yiftah El, there was found kind of floor made of a mixture of lime with stones. However, this lime is pure air lime, which is durable in dry climate and deteriorated in wet conditions. The last researches of paleoenvironment in Europe revealed the abrupt climate event between 8,600 and 8200 years ago. This brought generally cold and <u>dry</u> conditions to broad northern-hemisphere regions (21-22). Therefore, application of air lime in mortar was a technology compatible with a particular environment around 8,500 BP. This compatibility seems to be not a least factor for the impressive durability of lime mortar in Structures in Lepensky Vir.

~ 5,000 BP

"And they made their lives bitter with hard bondage, in morter, and in brick, and in all manner of service in the field: all their service, wherein they made them serve, [was] with rigor" (23). The Egyptians began the first to use mud mixed with straw to bind dried bricks (24). Morter or mud earth is a special mixture formed of a clayey solid component, a liquid component (water) and an organic components and bitumen that mainly forms during the maturation period. The strength of earth bricks is a function of moisture content. Too high moisture content leads to liquefaction of bricks, whereas too low water content would cause their disintegration. The climate of ancient Egypt was extremely hot and dry (25). Mud earth was an excellent binder completely compatible with the local climate conditions. Bitumen and organic components seem to keep optimal moisture content in mud earth. Thus, over-drying of earth and disintegrating of bricks might be prevented. Furthermore, dry conditions are essential for polymerization of bitumen and some mineral oils. Therefore, dry hot weather promoted developing an optimal composite structure and strength gain of bricks. Use of gypsum mortar was also very abundant in ancient Egypt. The dry and hot weather might be very favorable for performance of gypsum plasters kept till our days. Gypsum was also placed in between the carefully squared stone blocks were not actually used as joints, but mainly as lubricant agent in order to accurately arrange stone blocks on the structure (24). It is obvious that in ancient Egypt, like in the previous two cases, the ecological factors had a strong impact on the applied construction technology. The compatibility of sun-dried bricks and gypsum with the particular hot and dry weather promoted the long-time performance of these building materials at that epoch.

~ 4,000 BP

The next example of environmental impacts on construction technology is an erection of Ningirsu´s temple in Babylonian around 2,140 BC. Gudea, ruler of Sumerian city Lagash, dreamed that the god Ningirsu wanted a new temple. Gudea decided to build the temple in accordance with the god's prescriptions. Sumerian texts describe the construction as follows: "He (*Gudea – auth.*) poured clear water into the ... brick mould. He prepared the excavated earth for making ... the brick, and hoed honey, ghee[1] and precious oil into it. He worked ambergris[2] and essences from all kinds of trees into the paste... Gudea placed the clay into the brick mould and acted exactly as prescribed; bringing the first brick of the house into existence in it, while all the bystanders sprinkled oil or cedar perfume. He shook the brick mould and left the brick to dry. He looked at the ...... with satisfaction. He anointed it with cypress essence and ambergris" (26). Gudea's actions look like a cult ritual. However, analysis of this text and applying the relevant ecological data about the reference climate in ancient Mesopotamia make possible following assumptions and conclusions:

- Constant inundation by an ameliorating climate around 3,200 BC promoted accumulation of bio-organic mass in the soil (27).

- However, in ancient Mesopotamia, mistreatment of water with no adequate drainage resulted in high salinity of soils (28). Usually salinity of soils resulted in high alkali and calcium content.

- At 2200 B.C. a marked increase in aridity and wind circulation occurred in Mesopotamia (29).

- High content of calcium and bio-organic compounds in the soils promotes chemical reaction between calcium hydroxide and silica.

Therefore, such soils are highly appropriate for adobe construction.

- Honey, a bio-organic compound, is enriched in enzymes which catalyze formation of colloid silica (30). A content of organic acids and sacharides is very high in honey. These compounds are capable to increase the surface of calcium hydroxide and to inhibit its setting (31-32). Thus, honey might improve the earth workability allowing sufficient time for brick pouring.Furthermore, honey enzymes might accelerated puzzolanic reactions in the earth brick and its strengthening and stabilizing (33).

- Expected effects of ghee[1], oil and ambergris[2] as bio-organic substances on lime-containing earth could be, as following: air-entrainment; improved workability; water retention to allow better setting of calcium hydroxide; preventing over-drying; air entrainment and water repellence to prevent moisture damage.

- Tree essences contain various carboxylic acids (i.e., oxalic acid) Oxalic acid acts as a very good binder for free calcium ions presenting in earth because of the formation of an insoluble protective film of calcium oxalate, which also shows the thermal stability and long-term durability.

Generally, it could be suggested that all bio-organic compounds added by Gudea to earth had improve its quality, making the soil appropriate for adobe construction and improving durability of earth bricks in the arid climate of Mesopotamia around 4,000 BP.

~ 3,000 BP- 500 AD

The Greeks were the first who broadly used hydraulic lime mortars. These mortars were much harder than later Roman mortars and water-proofed. The Romans used pozzolanic limes, i.e.: broken brick aggregate embedded in a mixture of lime putty with brick dust or volcanic ash from Pozzuoli, Italy near Mt. Vesuvius. Vitruvius and Pliny the Elder were the first who described in details the lime-mortar technology and the use of puzzolanic admixtures (34-35). The climate in Ancient Greece, from around 2,000 BC to 500 BC was wet and cool with strong rains and floods (36). There are evidences of general warming of climate during Rome Classical Period, from 500 BC to 500 AC. However, a climate was still very wet and rainy from the 5th century BC, to the 3rd century BC (37). Therefore, use of pozzolanic admixtures during these two historic periods was compatible with the environmental conditions. Obtained mortars were water proofed and highly durable in wet environment. Furthermore, the wet environment was highly essential for enhancing the chemical reactions between lime and puzzolanic admixtures. It should be emphasized that the most famous Roman structures preserved today[3] were built between 312 BC and 312 AC, therefore during the wet climate phase. Since the second half of the 3rd century AC the climate in Roman Empire became very hot and dry. Taking in account modern knowledge of cementitious materials it could be easily understood that the use of pozzolanic limes in the hot and dry climate might be completely insufficient without any special wet curing for accelerating the pozzolanic reaction. Thus, declination of the use of puzzolanic limes during the late Roman and Byzantine periods could be related to very hot and dry climate unfavorable for development and completion of puzzolanic reaction.

Another sample of changes in masonry technology is use of burnt bricks and bitumen in Babylonia around 300 BC: "Semiramis ... built Babylon and constructed round the city a wall of burnt brick; bitumen, a substance which everywhere oozes from the ground in those parts, being spread between the bricks instead of mortar" (38). Recent researches on historical ecology have revealed that the climate in Near East was relatively cool and rainy from around 8th century BC to around 1st century BC (39). Therefore, use of sun-dried earth bricks was completely impossible in this climate. On contrary, the burnt bricks laid with joints pointed by bitumen were completely waterproved and highly durable in the wet climate.

Conclusion

Ancient construction technologies are of a great interest for architects and civil engineers. The archeological evidences and historic documents describing these technologies are numerous. The recent researches on environmental history have provided specialists with data on climate circumstances through the different historic periods. An evaluation of construction technologies in interconnection with the environmental situation during the erection of different ancient structures has been carried out in this study. A strict correlation between the compatibility of the different ancient construction technologies with the particular climate conditions has been established.

The implementation of construction technologies compatible with the particular climatic conditions was a most essential factor for the long-term performance of the different ancient structures. However, this fact does not mean that all ancient construction technologies were excellent. Numerous collapses of buildings in Ancient Rome were described in details by Vitruvius and Pliny (34-35). Nevertheless, the structures built compatible with the particular climatic conditions had better performance for a long-time period, sometimes for millennia.

References:

1. Roca, P. Considerations of the significance of history for the structural analysis of ancient construction. Structural Analysis of Historical Constructions – Modena, Lourenco & Roca (eds), © 2005, Taylor & Francis Group, London.

2. Swetnam, Thomas W., Allen, Craig D., Betancourt, Julio, I. Applied historical ecology: using the past to manage for the future. Ecological Applications, 9(4), 1999, pp. 1189-1206

3. International Cultural Tourism Charter (Managing Tourism at Places of Heritage Significance", Adopted by the International Counsel on Monuments and Sites, ICOMOS at the 12th General Assembly in Mexico, October 1999

4. Climate Change: Israel National Report. Prepared by Guy Pe'er and Uriel N. Safriel. The United Nations Framework Convention on Climate Change Impact, Vulnerability and Adaptation, October 2000

5. Climate Change: Synthesis Report, Watson, R.T. and the Core Writing Team (Eds.), IPCC, Geneva, Switzerland, 184 p. (Available on-line http://www.grida.no/climate/ipcc_tar/vol1 4/index.htm)

6. Resolution No. 2: The cultural heritage as a factor of sustainable development. IVth European Conference of the Minuisters responsible for the Cultural Heritage, Helsinki, 30-31 May 1996

7. Cassar, JA., Bonnici, A., Schembri, P.J., Ventura, F., Preliminary report on the relationship between climate and conservation within the Hal Saflieni Hypogeum in Malta. Actes Journees Internationales d'Etude sur la Conservation de l'Art Rupestre. Dordogne, Perigord, France, 20-23 Août 1990, pp. 155-162

8. Cassar, JA., Torfs, K., Van Grieken, R., Environmental effects on deterioration of monuments: case study of the church of Sta. Marija taí Cwerra, Malta. Proceedings, European Commission Research Workshop: Origin, Mechanisms and Effects of Salt on Degradation of Monumentsin Marine and Continental Environments.25-27 March, 1996, Bari, Italy. Protection and Conservation of the European Cultural Heritage Research Report No. 4, pp. 441-452

9. Cassar, JA., Torfs, K., Van Grieken, R., Monitoring of environmental parameters to explain stone deterioration: church of Sta. Marija taí Cwerra, Malta . 8th International Congress on the Deterioration and Conservation of Stone, 30.9 – 4.10. 1996, Berlin, Germany, Vol. 1, pp. 265 – 271

10. Winkler, E.M., Problems in the deterioration of stone. Conservation of Historic Stone Buildings and Monuments. Commission on Engineering and Technical Systems, US National Academy of Science, Engineering and Medicine, 1982

11. Torraca, G., Air pollution and the conservation of building materials, Durability of Building Materials, 5, pp. 383 – 392

12. Del Monte, M., Stone monument decay and air pollution. Stone Materials in Monuments: Diagnosis and Conservation, 1991, pp.101-110. Crete: Comunita delle Univarsita Mediterranee, Scuola Univarsitaria Conservazione dei Monumenti

13. Price, C.A., Stone Conservation. An Overview of Current Research, The Getty Conservation Institute, The J. Paul Getty Trust, Santa Monica, USA

14. Moropoulou, A., Koui, M., Kourteli, Ch., Theoulakis, P., Avdelidis, N.P., Integrated methodology for measuring and monitoring salt decay in the Mediaeval City of Rhodes porous stone. Mediterranean Archaelogy and Archaeometry, V. 1,No. 1, pp. 57 – 68

15. Auburn, Historical Timeline of Concrete, AU BSC 314, Auburn University, http://www.auburn.edu/academic/architecture/bsc/classes/bsc314/timeline/timeline.htm, June 2000.

16. Brown, Gordon E., Analysis and History of Cement, Gordon E. Brown Associates, Keswick, Ontario, 1996, 259 pages.

17. Bar-Matthews, M., Ayalon, A., Kaufman, A. Late Quaternary paleoclimate in the eastern Mediterranean region from stable isotope analysis of speleothems at Soreq cave, Israel, Quaternary Research 47 (2) (1997) 155–168.

18. Frumkin, A., Magaritz, M., Carmi, I., Zak, I. The Holocene climatic record of the salt caves of Mount Sedom, Israel. The Holocene 1 (3) (1991) 191–200.

19. Kislev, Mordechai E., Hartmann, Anat, Galili, Ehud, Archaeobotanical and archaeoentomological evidence from a well at Atlit-Yam indicates colder, more humid climate on the Israeli coast during the PPNC period, Journal of Archaeological Science 31 (2004), 1301–1310

20. Marler, Joan, The Body of Woman as Sacred Metaphor. In Il Mito e il Culto della Grande Dea: Transiti, Metamorfosi, Permanenze, 2003, pp. 9-24. Edited by M. Panza and M. T. Ganzerla. Bologna: Associazione Armonie.

21. Alley, Richard B., Ágústsdóttir, Anna Maria, The 8k event: cause and consequences of a major Holocene abrupt climate change, Quaternary Science Reviews 24, 2005, pp. 1123–1149

22. Feurdean, Angelica, Palaeoenvironment in North-Western Romania during the last 15 000 years. PhD Thesis, Stockholm University, Department of Physical

Geography and Quaternary Geology, 2004

23. Bible, Genesis 11:3, Blue Letter Bible. http://www.blueletterbible.org/index.html

24. Moropoulou, A., Bakolas, A., Anagnostopoulou, S., Composite materials in ancient structures. Cement & Concrete Composites 27 (2005) pp. 295–300

25. Kuper, Rudolph, After 5000 BC: Human palaeontology and prehistory: the Libyan desert in transition. C. R. Palevol 5 (2006) 409–419

26. The Electronic Text Corpus of Sumerian Literature. University of Oxford. http://www-etcsl.orient.ox.ac.uk/

27. Brooks, Nick, Cultural responses to aridity in the Middle Holocene and increased social complexity. Quaternary International 151 (2006), pp. 29–49

28. Pasternak, D., Combating poverty with plants. In: D. Pasternak and A. Schlissel, Editors, Combating Desertification with Plants, Kluwer Academic/Plenum Publishers, New York (2001), pp. 17–30

29. Weiss, H., Wetterstrom, H.A., Senior, L. Meador, R., Guichard, F., Curnow, A. The genesis and collapse of the third millennium north Mesopotamia civilization, Science 261 (No. 5124) (1993), pp. 995–1004

30. Bouligand, Yves, General Palaeontology (Palaeobiochemistry): The renewal of ideas about biomineralisations. C. R. Palevol 3 (2004) pp. 617–628

31. Garci Juenger, Maria C., Jennings, Hamlin M. New insights into the effects of sugar on the hydration and microstructure of cement pastes. Cement and Concrete Research, V. 32, Issue 3, 2002, pp. 393-399

32. Chandra, S., Eklund, L., Villarreal, R. R. Use of Cactus in Mortars and Concrete. Cement and Concrete Research, V. 28, Issue 1, 1998, pp 41-51

33. Preliminary Laboratory Investigation of a Commercial Enzyme Solution as a Soil Stabilizer. University of Minnesota, Center for Transportation Studies. http://rip.trb.org/browse/dproject.asp?n=8691

34. Vitruvius The Ten Books on Architecture. Translated by Morris Hicky Morgan, in 1914, edited by Tom Turner in 2000

35. Pliny the Elder, Natural History:Book 36-37.

36. Lespez, L., Geomorphic responses to long-term land use changes in Eastern Macedonia (Greece), CATENA, V. 51, Issues 3-4, 2003, pp. 181-208

37. Reale, O., Dirmeyer, P., Modeling the effects of vegetation on Mediterranean climate during the Roman Classical Period. Part I: Climate history and model sensitivity. Global and Planetary Change, V. 25, No. 3-4, 2000, pp. 163-184

38. Justin, Epitome of Pompeius Trogus (1886), pp. 1-90. Preface, Books 1-10

39. Neumann, J., Parpola, S., Climate changes and the Eleventh-tenth century eclipse of Assyria and Babylonia. Journal of Near East Studies, Vol. 46, No. 3, 1987, pp.161-182

Notes:

[1] Ghee - clarified butter or pure butter fat
[2] Ambergris - waxy substance, a form of excrement of sperm whales
[3] Appian Way; Roman Baths of Caracalla, Basilica of Maxentius, Coliseum and Pantheon in Rome, Pont du Gard aqueduct in South France

Developing an Ethos of Making

Bruce Wrightsman
College of Architecture and Planning, University of Colorado

In his early observations of architecture, Richard Rodgers underscored the architect's value through directing instruments for building, and inventing new tools that expand our opportunities for creation. By embracing emerging technologies and materials, Rodgers advocated a fundamental shift in the role of design, led by the architect, which would control the means of production (from office to site). This is achieved through built forms that are a manifestation of how an object is constructed. This core architectural value directs my own pedagogical interest in an "ethos of making," which critically explores the tectonic relationship of technology with technique and materials. Where architectural form becomes a manifestation through its material connection.

As an educator, this "ethos of making" is explored through design/build projects engaging real materials in real scale and through seminar/studio projects, which create design proposals and installations. Each project addresses how "materials and processes" can be explored through multiple operations; formal, spatial and programmatic.

Influences

Growing up in the Midwest, I was introduced to the work of Nebraska architect, Neil Astle. His work could be defined as a *Gesamtkunstwerk* or synthesis of the arts[1], where architecture is shaped principally through its inherit material attributes. In the design of his own house, Astle explored the material potential of wood, through investigating technique as part of the expression of formal logic. To do this, Astle reinterpreted traditional wood framing and its inherit relationship of material to structure. Knowing he would be building the house with limited labor, as well as limited availability of material and equipment, Astle used new construction logic from which to build. He devised a method using a 'nailed scantling technique' that is based upon 2x2 cedar scantlings nailed to each other on both the inside and outside of the wall, forming an interlocking structure [image 1]. The successive layers where then rotated in the opposite direction with the lengths of the scantling left random, thus engaging the walls, floors and roofs planes together.

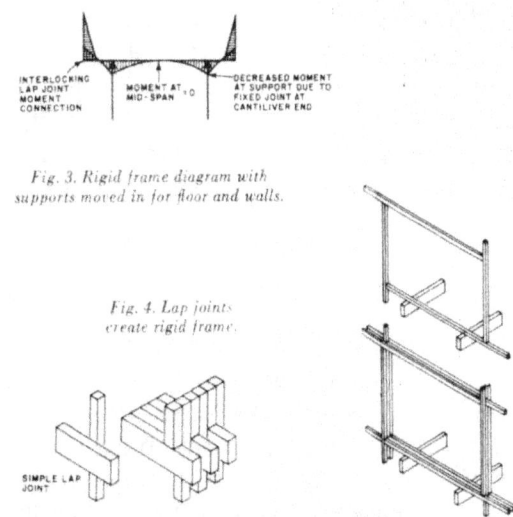

Image 1 – Nailed Scantling Technique

The interlocking connection creates a rigid connection and reduces the moment forces within the system. The overlapping ends were trimmed and used in other parts of the construction. The rigid frame eliminated the need for plates, stiffeners and corner bracing and reduced the material waste to less than 2%. Through the design of his own house, Astle captured an opportunity to explore wood's material potential through investigating building technique as part of the expression of building form. Astle's strategy of design has greatly influenced my own architectural ideas towards an "Ethos of Making."

As a practicing architect, I've learned how site constraints and labor issues often drive design decisions. Gaining a better understanding of material properties and building methods can lead to a transformation of design at the building site. The work of Japanese architect Kimura Hiroaki exhibits a strong understanding of the physical properties of sheet steel and its potential as a factory-produced material to be used as a monocoque (single-shell) system. Because of tight site constraints common in many Japanese cities, Hiroaki's goal was to discover a new method for on-site fabrication, which he found by understanding the off-site production potential of steel sheets. Steel sheets are lightweight, easily disassembled into shippable units and bolt together to create a unitary façade[2]. Similar to the fabrication techniques for airplanes and large ships the joints are welded together to form a seamless surface.

Research

Material innovation in architecture can come from a strong understanding of material properties. Hiroaki explored the high-strength property of steel because its potential lies in its manufacturing flexibility to be cut and rolled into many shapes that compose more complex forms. This knowledge directed Hiroaki to redefine the surface/structure relationship of his architecture. Understanding the manufacturing potential of the steel sheet allowed Hiroaki to change the entire construct for residential construction as well as his design approach. For my research interests, this presents a lucid understanding of the design potential of composite materials and emerging construction technology for architecture.

My research at the University of Texas in Austin investigated composite materials and alternative building systems. Part of the research focus was to re-address building principles through investigating techniques and tools used in other industries outside of architecture, such as airplane and boat manufacturing. By researching other industries, I discovered that, by in-large, composite materials were the catalyst in changing the material structure and the ethos of making for those industries.

Boat construction has witnessed a transformation from traditional wood construction in the late 18th century, to copper sheathing over the wood to improve performance[3]. This was the beginning of composite assembly technology, whose principles still drive the manufacturing industry. In fiberglass composite boat construction, the predominant manufacturing process is the wet lay-up process in which a liquid resin is applied over a mold while fiber reinforcing is placed on top. To better understand the design and fabrication process of the composite system, I visited the manufacturing facility of Cobalt Boats in Neodesha, Kansas. Cobalt Boats has been manufacturing boats for over 30 years and is respected within the boating industry. Cobalt's design process begins with a rendering that is then used to build a full-scale wood mock-up of the primary deck and hull components. A wood mock-up is sent to Janicki Industries in Sedro-Woolley, WA, which digitizes the mock-up to create a 3-dimensional graphic model. This information is then transferred to a 5-axis CNC-routing machine, which fabricates complex composite molds and plugs from foam. This methodology forms a prototype design operation in which molds can be quickly created from various materials such as wood, plastic or foam. Current boat fabrication technology, like that at Cobalt boats, uses a woven process of fiberglass sheets placed in successive layers between resin binders. Workers at Cobalt Boats employ rollers to impregnate the fiber in resin, while squeezing out the excess resin to create a uniform distribution of the resin throughout the surface. The composite is allowed to cure for three or more days, and then, a balsa or honeycomb foam core material is adhered to the fiberglass, creating a sandwich panel structure. The foam plug is later thrown away and the first fiberglass shell becomes a physical template that is referred to as "master 1." [image below] This fiberglass shell template is then used to make other hulls of the same profile, a process referred to as "tooling," in which the process of making one object (tool) is used to determine the shape of another[4]. This methodology and the technology used is seen in many applications of product design and presents a flexible and efficient option for utilizing composite materials without sacrificing the creative potential that architectural components often require.

Master 1 shell

While researching boat manufacturing, I discovered similarities and distinctions between the methodology for boat construction and traditional building construction. One similarity is the dependence on hand-labor for craft and building performance. The primary reason for this low-tech, manually driven process in boat construction is that much of the machinery used is unable to adequately control the often-unpredictable behavior of fiber and woven materials. Manual application can more easily control fiber orientation. For architecture however, the key difference is that buildings are primarily component driven; i.e., they are the summation of diverse parts that comprise

them. In contrast, boat manufacturing has largely been transformed by minimizing the whole structure into two primary components, the deck and hull. These components would be comparable in scale with a small architectural space. Fiber-composite materials have a superior weight-to-strength ratio over traditional homogeneous materials. The layered assembly of fiberglass components allows for large, lightweight, complex forms to be manufactured within tight tolerances and fabrication requirements. These tolerances meet and in some case exceed those found in traditional building practices.

The research goal was to allow potentials within the material investigation to define the working parameters both intellectually and physically. The design project used to test this research was a 'true' material investigation. I physically explored the potential of fiberglass as a material along with the hand lay-up process, like that used in the fiberglass boat industry, and created composite samples from which to test multiple design and fabrication criteria. Comprehension of the material's construction process was critical to designing a composite material system that could address multiple issues of lightweight building construction.

In the wake of Hurricane Katrina in 2005, a concern for those left homeless and those who have been displaced by disasters has become more dominant theme in the media as well as the average American home. It has spawned new debates and created a new fervor for finding solutions to transitional and permanent shelter for those affected. This research chose the transitional shelter typology as the means to develop a fiber-composite building system. Examining the design and manufacturing methodology of fiberglass boats discovered material and fabrication flexibility that could be applied to a composite building system. The design goal was to create a kit-of-parts system that served multiple physical conditions, existed completely or partially off the grid and was not solely dependent upon a specific site.

Material Experiments

The first series of material experiments investigated a built-up methodology, which used fiberglass. The samples began as flat mock-ups using an embedded network of tubes incorporated within the material layers that were then oriented in different configurations in order to understand the resin/fiberglass lay-up process and the relationship of an embedded system within a fiberglass matrix. [*Sample 1*] The research investigated how the lamination process could include a second material as part of the assembly while expanding the role of the material component. The tube system evolved into a two-shell composite that joined to form a single shell with a contiguous flat inner surface. An outer surface with bevels created hollow slots that could serve as a potential distribution system for water or electricity. [*Sample 2*] This sample began to address more successfully the potential of a multi-functioning skin and led to additional experimentations with surface and form.

Designing the shell volume from the perspective of multiple surfaces changed how the build-up process would direct the design thinking. A CNC-router was used to rout multiple surfaces out of foam that would be used as a mold to conduct the resin/fiberglass castings. The CNC machine creates a seamless link from the virtual to the physical understanding of a design and allows for more iterative work. In one case, a folded form surface [*Sample 3*] was cast with the intent of analyzing form through overlapping planes and 'kinks' that could provide stiffness to the structure and test its potential for longer span elements, such as a roof.

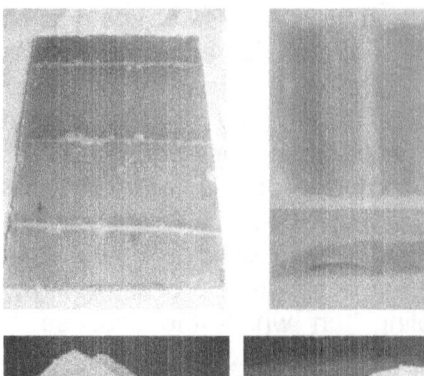

 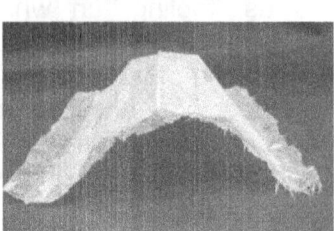

Samples 1 & 2, top
Sample 3 - Folded Form, bottom

Learning through the material process

The material experiments conducted were intended to work at multiple scales. It was through working with the fiberglass material that I began to understand the multiple scales of deformation within the fiberglass material. Surface and form have both micro properties of structural strength, yet also macro properties of program and service integration. This became paramount in helping to further develop a fiberglass system of shell components. Following the material experiments, the design for a fiber-composite building system using a kit-of-parts began to develop. This building system could be fabricated off-site (at a boat manufacturing facility like Cobalt Boats), then shipped to various locations and installed on a raised structure or steel chassis system, not unlike that used for manufactured housing. Joined together, the parts formed a small Single Occupancy Room (SRO) unit that could be used for multiple temporary housing needs.

A benefit of this type of building system, over other transitional housing options, is its design flexibility and its ability to manufacture building systems based upon specific needs, budget concerns and time constraints. A manufacturing facility like Cobalt Boats manufactures as many as 50 boats per week. A new material system like the one explored could be accomplished using the same methodology, tools and workforce.

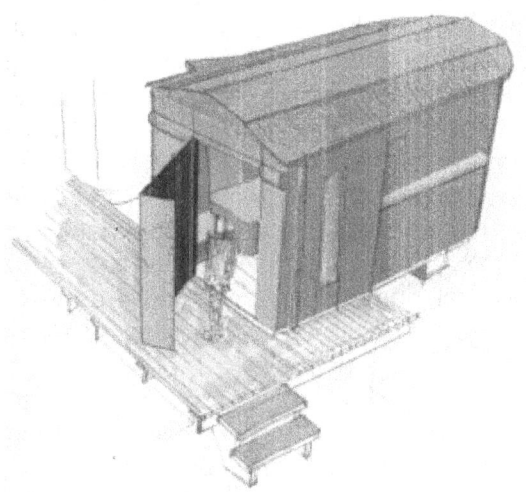

Image of fiber-composite SRO unit

Design + Build

Architecture is a dynamic and synthetic process; this material and methodology research engages the craft of architecture at the level of material awareness. This approach to understand design as a physical act of making has progressed into a pedagogical approach encompassing design + build projects, small and large-scale installations, methods of operation and the tools used.

Currently at the University of Colorado, I am working with Assistant Professor Michael Hughes on TrailerWrap; an innovative, community design + build project that allows students to physically engage issues of sustainable and affordable design within the context of a traditional urban trailer park. The project explores the potential of affordable housing through the adaptive reuse of an old and inefficient mobile home.

While often overlooked, the mobile home represents an important but under appreciated housing typology in the United States, because it serves a wide range of citizens. However, poor construction techniques and use of materials have proven to be major flaws in mobile home design. In response to common misconceptions related to mobile homes, the TrailerWrap project provides a simple and affordable solution that improves both the spatial quality and energy efficiency, which is typically lacking in conventional manufactured housing.

The pedagogical objective of TrailerWrap is to be a laboratory for teaching and learning. Students develop an ethos of making through a physical engagement of materials and methods. As a design + build project, the key challenge for students is working with a set of limitations that rarely if ever are addressed in a typical design studio. Instead of being viewed as obstacles these traditional boundaries of building codes, budget constraints and the physical honesty of construction have presented some unique design decisions on material selection, detailing and construction techniques. Learning through building, I believe heightens a student's knowledge of architecture as a craft, a practice sculpted through material engagement.

At the site, the interface between materials and building trades are problematic. This interface between components can in fact become a design element in itself. The concept of a well-designed and fabricated building component became a driving force in the TrailerWrap's design process and has directed the strategy for its construction.

The project began in the Fall 2005 semester in Assistant Professor Hughes' Design Studio with the re-design of an existing chassis system that integrated a new building structure and infill wall system. TrailerWrap's innovation lies in its reconstitution of an existing building typology vetted through new materials and building techniques.

Construction began in February and is continuing through the summer with a new group of students. The construction has involved both steel fabrication and wood frame construction so that students could engage various building techniques. As part of the design project, students also built full-scale mock-ups of key building components to further their ethos of making and deepen their understanding of craft. As part of the learning experience, the University of Colorado-Boulder facilities management staff is available to provide assistance on trades such as electrical wiring and plumbing. We plan to have the construction completed at the end of Summer 2006.

TrailerWrap project under construction

Kinetic exploration

Furthering my pedagogical objectives, I have also developed a graduate-level seminar that investigated the working methodologies of multiple design disciplines. As part of the seminar, students researched and presented theoretical positions, and methodologies used from a variety of design practitioners such as artists, writers, filmmakers, product designers, and emerging architectural practices. Learning from these theoretical positions, the students developed design strategies along with methods of working that later were tested through two projects. The goal and ultimate result of the seminar was about understanding design as a physical act of making.

The first project explored text and composition by re-envisioning the book as a relationship of text, image and reader. Each student selected a book from which to "re-text" and re-fabricate as a made object. The page was to be viewed as a potential architectural space from which to create a new physical narrative; students then re-envisioned the operation of a book as a container of that narrative. The second project explored the "kinetic object." The objective was to understand movement and dynamics as an operation of the object, a value that pertains to architecture as well. This design methodology develops an ethos of making by emphasizing the relationship of material to process, working iteratively to determine how they (material and technique) lead to form. Working through the material/technique connection, students investigated various forms of kinetic phenomena. The kinetic paradigm took many forms of shape, scale and material connection. The kinetic objects, once made, operated on multiple levels of movement and explored multiple forms of transformation.

This summer, I expanded upon the kinetic paradigm in a studio that focused on the design of temporal spaces for the urban nomad. The urban nomad is without a permanent domicile or place. Nomads move about our cities, finding leftover and residual spaces in the city from which they construct personal interventions and additions to the urban fabric. These modifications, although only temporary, create new spatial identities within their context. The spatial conditions of nomadic lifestyles were explored through two divergent forms: the technological or urban worker and non-technological nomad of the homeless individual. The studio used the dynamic social space of the nomad as praxis from which to explore the transportable and adaptable space paradigm and how it can respond to multiple urban conditions.

Kinetic Object – Ethos of Making seminar
Project by Will Babbington

Le Corbusier described the work of Carlo Scarpa, with his fetish for materials and details, as evolving around the joint. The joint is treated with a tectonic attentiveness that Corb would term "the joint as the generator."[5] Similarly for this studio, the kinetic, or dynamic operation at the joint was to become the generator for innovation. Students researched kinetic movement and transportable structures then tested various kinetic strategies through large and small-scale mock-ups and prototypes to better understand how the dynamics of their strategies can create multiple spatial conditions. It is critical to understand kinetic paradigms such as folding, hinging, nesting, expansion and contraction and how these kinetic operations can lead to various spatial and formal transformations of design. This became prime in defining the relationship of materiality and methods of making. Investigating materiality, whether rigid or flexible, heavy or light, forced students to further test how their strategies changed or necessitated modifications when the substance of materiality became imbedded in their physical form. Operating on the level of a machine that is able to be controlled, these spatial devices allows students to manipulate kinetic phenomena to better engage how architecture is manipulated through the use of space, surface and materiality, and how it directly affects the audience. The goal is to change the way students think spatially and materially. Their work will result in constructed large-scale nomadic spaces that will be adaptable to three different urban conditions. These will have the ability to be transported to various sites and re-deployed in their new spatial configuration. Successful projects will be the urban interventions that demonstrated their spatial potential and how well they operate within their urban context.

Ethos of Making

Aesthetic language is largely determined by the fabrication techniques and materials used[6]. However in architectural education design aesthetics often do not critically address the tectonic relationship, instead relying steadfast on a formal aesthetic language that is separate from a material/structure language. To understand craft of a made object is to understand the knowledge of materials and methods and to reveal what is latent within the process of making that object. Whether created by artist, architect or builder, the result should merge the work of the mind with the work of the hand. It is through this connection that an ethos of making is both defined and developed.

I have been engaged in architecture for over 12 years as a practitioner, through design/build practices and as an educator. Through these experiences, I have gained both an understanding and a deep questioning of normative building practices. These beliefs have directed my architectural interest towards an ethos of making and how that can inform us as designers in areas of materials and technology. My goal as an educator is to present a culture of learning in which students investigate architecture as a critical instrument in a complex meshwork of form and material, translated through an understanding of its making (tectonics).

In the attitude of Richard Rodgers, I have tried to foster an ethos of making through teaching that is developed through design/build projects and both small and large-scale prototyping; projects intended to bring together the mind and the hand. Classes are meant to challenge a student's understanding of materiality as a holistic relationship of material with form, process and detail. I believe such thinking will expand an architectural student's design decisions and provide avenues for exploration that will only augment their architectural education and future positions as practicing architects.

References:

[1] Mallgrave, Harry Francis and Herrmann, Wolfgang, Gottfried Semper: The Four Elements of Architecture and Other Writings. p. 1.

[2] Hiroaki, Kumura, Steel Sheet House, p. 73.

[3] Gordon, J.E., The New Science of Strong Materials or Why You Don't Fall Through the Floor, p. 152.

[4] Burns, Marshall, PhD. Automated Fabrication: Improving Productivity in Manufacturing, p. 136.

[5] Frampton, Kenneth. Studies in Tectonic Culture: The Poetics of Construction in Nineteenth and Twentieth Century Architecture, p. 307.

[6] Lim, CJ. Devices: a manual of architectural + spatial machines, p. 008.

Why Brick? A Theoretical Basis for Designing Construction

Barry D. Yatt, FAIA, NCARB, CSI
School of Architecture and Planning, The Catholic University of America

Have you ever felt like Lucy Riccardo in the old *I Love Lucy* show when the assembly line of candies just overran her ability to package them, and she finally just gave up any attempt to manage? That's how I feel sometimes when I open the most recent architecture magazine or profession website or manufacturer mailing and am reminded, once again of the pace at which new construction products are hitting the market. I can't keep up.

But I have to keep up. That's my job as an architect even if I didn't also need to somehow teach it to architecture students. For my clients' sake and my students' sake, I need to stay abreast of new products. But how? It seems that the fourteen headings (or folders or bins or boxes if you prefer) that MasterFormat allocates to architectural data overflowed a long time ago. Each of those fourteen headings has tens of thousands of entries. I can't image how my students avoid being overwhelmed. Maybe it's time to declare a time out and look for some meaningful way to get organized.

The Need

No theoretical basis currently exists for construction detailing. The subject is learned as a series of facts with little or no overarching or unifying framework. The term "architectural theory" is always assumed to refer to the theory of aesthetics, never of construction technology. That's because there has never been a theory of technology. The best organizing strategies we've been able to come up with to date are MasterFormat[1] and Uniformat II[2], both of which can be used to categorize materials or details, but neither of which can serve as a framework for understanding the universe of architectural forms, assemblies, subassemblies, materials, treatments, and products, and how all of them relate to one another. Still, almost every book on construction design and every course taught is organized using one of these very limited forms of organization.

As a result, even the best technical students say they don't know which material to use for their studio projects or how to put them together. Students attribute their confusion to the approach of "means and methods" courses, which rarely consider materials from a design perspective. And how many people have ever found the answers to their detailing questions in *Architectural Graphic Standards*? The problem isn't only faced by students; interns and practicing architects deal with it also. **They don't want information, they want guidance.**

So about four years ago the author set out to devise a new approach, a system of thinking, a logic tree, to guide students, interns, and practitioners when trying to make decisions about component selection or use at any level. While still evolving, the system is now fairly complete. It has already been used as the organizing strategy for a course syllabus and for the draft of a textbook (which has already been used very successfully with students). Software is also being developed based on it that designers can use to guide them when making such decisions. This paper will describe the concept underlying and key features of an effective logic tree, and suggest ways to use it to help students finally "get it".

Architects Don't Design Space

Space is always there, even without architects and even without builders. What architects design are spaces — defined parcels of space. But even spaces aren't what get built. The only way to make spaces is by designing and building "solids", the horizontal and vertical planes, the walls, floors, and roofs that enclose and define space. So while architects may start off designing spaces, in the end, they must design solids, since it is only through the design of those solids that the intended spaces come to exist.

But all too often, architects have little interest in designing solids. That's a problem, since they're the only ones with the educations and licenses to do it. Perhaps if the topic wasn't so inscrutable, they'd have more interest. Architects manage to appreciate "architectural theory" as it relates to aesthetics. It brings order. Yet somehow they don't even seem to notice that there's no theory for the design of solids. Perhaps the number of architects interested in the design of solids is insufficient to develop the needed theories. Perhaps the funding, infrastructure and incentive for such research is insufficient. But without a rational underlying theory, it's difficult to raise the quality of solids design. Perhaps it's time to develop one.

Good architects might begin to develop a theory with a look at the problem. Problems occur on many levels. To start, there's no method to the way information related to construction detailing is managed, the way architects learn to design details, the way manufacturers disseminate or update information related to detailing, the way contractors present alternative approaches to detailing, the way architects evaluate proposed substitutions, or the way property managers use information to maintain the construction of their projects. In addition, the ongoing trend toward architects being asked to do more and more with less and less is showing no signs of abatement. Architects comment on how frustrating it is to try to find the answers to their technical design questions, on the overwhelming nature of the information they deal with—its range, scope, and inconsistency—on the technical nature of that information, and on the sometimes frustrating lack of technical content in technical information.

But Do These Issues Constitute A Problem?

People have been building since civilization began. Surely the system must be working as is. Well, it is. But what worked under yesterday's expectations of efficiency is becomingly increasingly unacceptable. In these days of ultra fast, error free, and cheap, it is critical that the design professions, construction industry, and real estate business work more efficiently.

This issue has surely been raised before. Architects have traditionally learned to design solids. What guided them? Perhaps the best-known model for technical design was Louis Kahn's dictum to "ask a brick what it wants to be." This attitude works where a material has already been selected. If the building *must* be brick, then brick should be asked what it wants. But who or what says that a project must be brick? Should material determine form, or should form determine material? Maybe Kahn should have asked "What material is most appropriate for the part of the project I'm designing?" Because then he would have answered "It depends on what role that part plays in the project." And that matter can't be resolved solely by a look at materials.

So, one need look beyond Kahn. What else is there? One might say that there is a kind of theory represented by the standards currently used in the current industry. These include MasterFormat® and Uniformat II®, the National CAD Standard and SectionFormat®, and industry Standards such as those written by ASTM, ANSI, UL, and others.

But none of these classification, ordering, or formatting systems are able to provide guidance. They organize the elements of construction according to what or where they are, not what they do. But design decisions must be based doing—on performance. So, existing systems will never be able to serve as an organizational framework for decision-making.

What Effect Does this Have on Us?

Practicing architects and students of architecture say that they don't want to do technical design. Even those who start out with a real interest in technical design are often talked out of it by graduation. We can do better on this issue, but doing so requires a cultural shift in architectural education and practice. That won't happen overnight. And those architects and builders who know a lot about materials may still not be able to choose.

In addition, those in the industry have trouble internalizing information without a context in which to consider it. They have no cataloguing or searching system beyond the memory of the office's older staffers. And they find the details in detailing books to be of limited applicability to real projects.

So what do they do? Many architects collect "clipped" details until their employees stop thinking. Then they ban such details, working from scratch until work efficiency plummets. Then they start to clip again. It's a tough cycle. They commonly have a tough time evaluating substitutions that are suggested after the reasons for the initial decision have been forgotten.

Ultimately, as a result of this lack of a theory of detailing, time is wasted by architects, and especially interns and designers, trying to figure out how best to design details. More time is wasted by manufacturers and contractors re-designing poorly detailed construction during the shop-drawing process. Claims arise from poorly designed details.

Further, design professionals increasingly turn to "delegated design" to transfer some of the responsibilities they're incapable of meeting. But manufacturers aren't always able to accept those responsibilities because either they don't have knowledge of the products made by other manufacturers being used in a detail, or they don't have the requisite skill or license.

And one could fairly easily argue that the profession and industry suffer from a sense of general confusion and lethargy as a result of having no clear method to their madness.

Yet these factors are getting worse. The demand is growing for well-designed buildings. The complexity of technical design is increasing but compensation is not. Increased use of CAD makes it easier than ever to grab and insert inappropriate details that are insufficiently considered. More and more new products are being introduced as options. Software is moving more toward BIM, three-dimensional Building Information Modeling, which absolutely requires some form of informational organization to work effectively. It's time that a theory be developed.

Approaching a Solution

A coordinated, unified way of thinking about technical design is needed to guide decisions, one that can be navigated easily, but that doesn't make decisions for design professionals, and that can be used by everyone in the construction industry who is involved in deciding what gets built, or that is affected by that decision. That includes developers, architects, builders, property managers, manufacturers, distributors.

A logic tree is needed that fits the way technical designers commonly make decisions. But there is no consensus on how they do that, and method may depend on the particular issues of each project. Still, it's possible, and perhaps even likely, that there are just a few ways we could agree on as effective for organizing technical design information.

For example, information related to decisions could be organized from macro to micro: What forms should be used in the project? What assemblies should be used in the forms? What subassemblies should be used in the assemblies? What materials should be used in the subassemblies? What treatments should be used on the materials?

Such a logic tree could help designers, builders, distributors, manufacturers, and property managers appropriately find, evaluate, and apply information related to construction even when they haven't yet decided what they're looking for.

And there's no law that says that such a logic tree would only work when navigated linearly from one end to the other. It's possible that it would serve just as effectively in reverse, or even when started from the middle and then navigated outward in either direction. Books organized using the Dewey Decimal system are easily located wherever they are, simply because the order in which they are arranged makes them navigable.

The utility of and justification for a logic tree seems so obvious. But it doesn't already exist for possibly several reasons. The computer technology necessary to take full advantage of such a logic tree has only recent become feasible. There is no real research infrastructure in the US to support this kind of project. (Maybe this is something that the BTES can look into.) And most of the designers that could develop it are likely either be too busy with their practices or lack interest in technical design.

The Potential Impact

But if it did exist, one could do a lot with it. A theory such as the one described could have potential impacts on many levels and in many areas.

One could potentially automate the logic tree as software, do graphic "what if" analyses while evaluating substitutions or alternatives, compile performance assessments of various combinations of subassemblies, implement factory-to-shop-to-site-to-placement inventory control, and facilitate post-construction property management

In architectural education, it could help students understand how each component used in construction is related to every other component. It could help bring detailing into the design studio, the heart of architectural education where technical design rarely appears.

On architectural practice, it could enable senior designers to more directly control technical decisions. It could maximize the effectiveness of a limited number of senior technical designers. It could avoid the need to "offshore" the required detailing services.

On contracting, it could help coordinate information generated by construction management and contract administration. And it could help with inventory control on construction sites.

On manufacturing, it could let manufacturers better help architects improve the quality of their technical designs. And it could help architects direct the manufacturing process by linking detail design with computerized fabrication.

If it's time to develop such a theoretical basis for designing construction, where and how does one start? Does a theoretical basis for designing construction exist? It appears that it does, at least in theory. Nobody's ever gone looking for one, so none has ever been codified.

Creating a Theoretical Basis

But since the design professions and construction industries need one, the sooner one is developed the better. Awareness must be deepened and a dialog must be opened. Development of a theory must be pursued.

The author has been working on developing a theoretical basis for detail design for several years, and has some discoveries to share. To start with a look at the basics, note the following:

- Any theoretical basis must have a logic structure. Logic structures are inherently hierarchical or vertically differentiated. When there are too many alternatives at a given level of organization, that level is subdivided. This aids navigation.

- Elements organized by such structures are related by their position within the structure. Such structures put best alternatives to any given selection on adjacent and nearby branches of their logic trees. By contrast, searches such as those conducted by Internet search engines include no logic structures, no hierarchies, and thus depend completely on word or parameter searches. Every search starts over from scratch, ignoring whatever insights were gained from previous searches.

  Of course, we already have at least two construction logic structures in common use—MasterFormat and Uniformat. But neither is sufficiently hierarchical. Once past the first level of organization, their ability to organize is quickly exhausted. We need a system that has no more than a half dozen headings at each level but that has many levels if we are to maintain our sense of orientation within the vast universe of construction.

- The hierarchy in any theoretical basis must be organized in a macro-to-micro way that puts strategic design decisions ahead of tactical ones.

- Any terms or labels used for the headings must be "baggage-free", so they don't imply unintended meanings. This rules out such terms as "slab" or "block" since they imply not only a geometry but also a specific system or material

- Multiple portals to the organizing scheme must be available. Different people think in different ways, and individual people may need to think differently for different tasks. So while a single method of organizing elements may be required to avoid ambiguity, several "skins" must be provided for it to make it accessible to any reasonable designer in any reasonable context.

- It must have the openness and flexibility to accommodate future developments in the construction markets and sciences. In addition, it must be able to contain all of the millions of elements that it needs to classify. The scope is enormous.

- It must have the openness and flexibility to be compatible with existing ap-

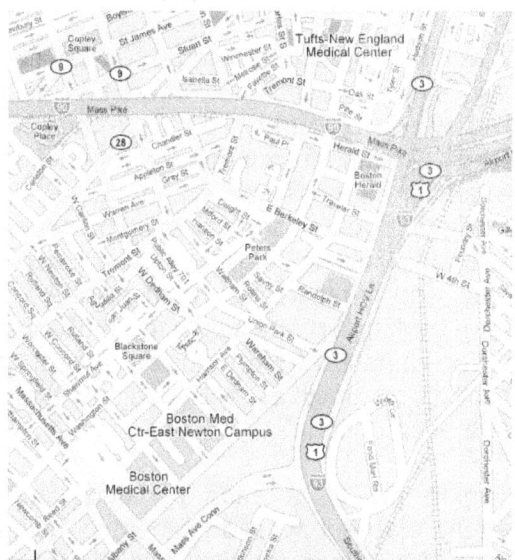

Logic trees are like roadmaps. When you know you're in the neighborhood, or know which artery your destination is near, it's a lot easier to find the place you seek.

proaches to documents production and contract administration while accommodating new and future developments, such as Building Information Modeling (BIM), the National CAD Standard (NCS), the ability to work with data organized by the latest editions of MasterFormat/OCCS or Uniformat.

Since the author's theory is still in development, the patents are still pending, and the costs of developing it are being borne by private industry (since there really is no funding infrastructure for basic architectural research), it can't yet be discussed in its full depth, or fully published here. But some additional elaboration may be appropriate.

Specifics

Consider first an analogy. Think about children's books whose pages are split into thirds. You've all probably seen them. A toddler can explore such possibilities as an alligator-headed, cat-torsoed, cow-legged creature, or one that is cow-headed, alligator-torsoed, and cat-legged. All that's known for sure is that every creature must have a head, torso, and legs. But each of those elements can be swapped out and substituted for other elements, so long as they are all similarly formatted. The formatting is critical to enabling them to match up where page segments meet.

In this scenario, a child could come up with 6 different animals from the options offered. Per the table below:

	Head	Torso	Legs
Animal 1	Alligator	Cat	Cow
Animal 2	Alligator	Cow	Cat
Animal 3	Cat	Cow	Alligator
Animal 4	Cat	Alligator	Cow
Animal 5	Cow	Cat	Alligator
Animal 6	Cow	Alligator	Cat

When designing details, what if an architect could swap alternative wall assemblies, floor-ceiling assemblies, and roof assemblies? Is it so far-fetched? Every detail needs all of those elements, the same as every animal in the children's book needs a head, torso and legs. Some are incompatible combinations, but such incompatibilities could either be learned or disallowed by the rules of the system.

Need such a system stop at this level of complexity? If it did, it would be of very limited use to an architect. So to continue with the previous analogy, what if the child was able to swap beyond the scale of head-torso-leg? Imagine if the little book allowed them to customize the head by itself, using the nose of a dog, the eyes of a fish, the ears of a lion, and the skin of a turtle. For one thing, the little book wouldn't be so little anymore. Yes, it starts to get complex, but think of the possibilities!

How does this apply to detail design? What if, instead of choosing from among a limited number of complete wall assembly options, an architect could customize a wall assembly from multiple surface, support, separation, and systems subassemblies?

What if the architect could go further, swapping at the subassembly level just as the child swapped to make a custom head? Instead of picking from a number of packaged separation subassembly alternatives, one could put together one's own combination of thermal, acoustic, vapor, and air separations. And what if one could go even further—cooking up one's own thermal separation combination from a custom mix of convective, conductive, and radiant thermal separation options?

Imagine also that each particular subassembly element was documented using a single consistent format. A designer who chose metal studs for a support subassembly, and then decided instead to use concrete block could simply swap the text related to that support subassembly option within the specification, and swap the image of it within the construction detail.

How big a system is needed to make this work? A universe of three swappable animal alternatives gave us six (6) possible creatures. But he number climb astronomically. If instead of three, we had ten alternatives, we could arrange them in 3.6 million (3 x 10^6) different sequences. Fifty alternatives could be arranged 3×10^{64} different ways. That's thirty billion billion billion billion billion billion billion different ways—from only fifty elements. Compare that with the eight or ten alternatives for each type of detail, composed of fixed combinations of elements, offered by the usual books on detailing. Customize them at your own peril!

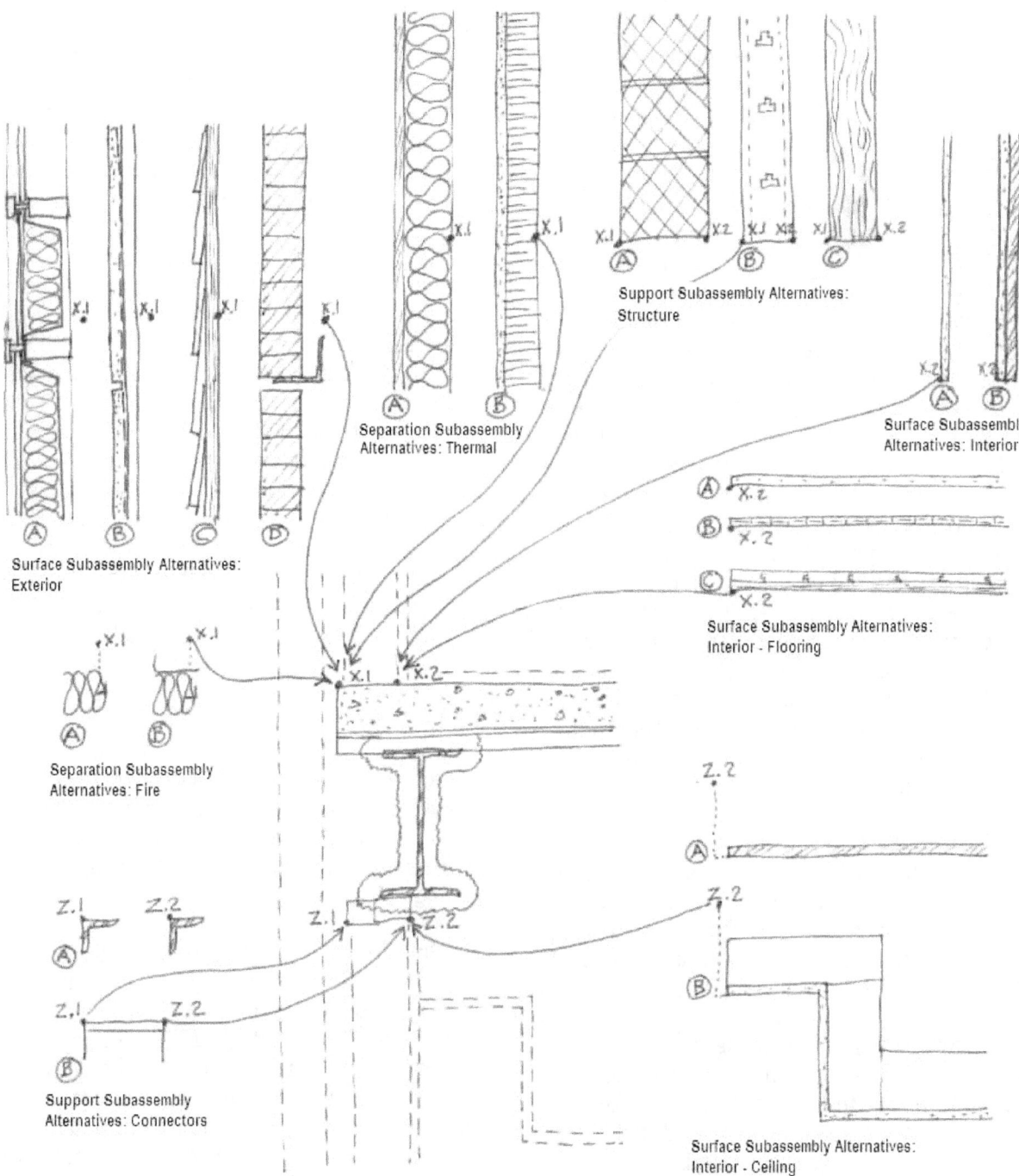

The idea of such a theory is very simple. And yes, the scope is huge. But the possibilities are virtually infinite. They would certainly impose no practical limits on design. So we must proceed to develop a practical, applicable, tool from this idea. But it will be a challenge to develop both a classification system and a formatting system that each have the needed complexity but also the needed clarity. The author, after four years, is currently on the seventy-fourth major revision of his classification scheme. But it's getting close.

Conclusion

Think of how much easier it would be to teach construction design (what we traditionally mislabel as "means and methods of construction"—we're not teaching construction management, after all) if we first explored the characteristics of the different construction details. What are the design considerations for a spandrel detail and how do they differ from those for a parapet detail? Once students understood that, we could talk about the connection alternatives from which the details are composed, and then the assembly alternatives that are connected at the connections, and then the subassembly alternatives from which the assemblies are composed, eventually getting all the way down to exploring the different treatments that could be used for the different materials from which one could make the different subcomponents of each of the subassemblies.

It's a lot to learn. But that's always been the case. What changes in this scenario is that finally both students and practitioners would be provided a flexible yet rational organizational structure to guide their leaning of, and eventual use of, that information.

Perhaps the points raised here will serve to stimulate discussion and get people thinking not only about the value and need for the kind of theory discussed here and the role it could play in the schools and profession, but also about the need for architectural research and the funding infrastructure that would support it.

Lucy Riccardo would appreciate it.

Notes:

[1] MasterFormat was first published by CSI in 1963. It organizes elements of construction by the products from which they are built. It becomes useful primarily after products have been selected. The system groups products in multiple ways with no particular consistency. For example, some products are grouped by material (05: Metals), some are grouped by form (04: Masonry) and still others by function (09: Finishes). So a concrete paver used outdoors would be classified for its location under division 2 (sitework), one used indoors would be classified for its use under division 9 (finishes), a concrete floor slab would be classified for its material under division 3 (concrete), a concrete block wall would be classified for the fact that it is installed by stacking, under division 4 (masonry), while a concrete countertop would be classified under division 11 (equipment) or division 12 (furnishings) for the fact that it is fabricated off-site. Its recent expansion into the OCCS (Omniclass Construction Classification System) adds categories, so is perhaps better articulated, but carries no changes in basic functionality.

Students whose coursework or texts are organized by MasterFormat tend to know all about products but remain confused about where and when they are appropriate as design responses.

[2] UniFormat was first published by CSI, ASTM, and others in 1998, to aid in the earlier stages of design before products have been selected. It organizes elements of construction by where they are located within the project (enclosing walls, substructure, etc.). While location sometimes translates to function or use, and therefore to selection criteria, it doesn't necessarily.

While Uniformat is certainly more context-based than MasterFormat, and can be far more useful to a designer, it has little to no depth. Once a construction element is classified by location, there's no system of sub-classification to further organize it, or to further guide a designer trying to figure out which elements are most appropriate for a given application.

Recycled Walls - A Materials & Methods Project

Paul A. Zorr, AIA
School of Architecture - Auburn University

Abstract

An understanding of Materials and Methods of Construction should incubate within the mind of the student thoughtful feelings about design. How better to accomplish this goal than to apply Edward Allen's Principles of construction to a "Hands On " Construction Project.

This paper on Recycled Walls attempts to bridge the gap between Lecturing about Technology and the Technology of Making.

We live in a world of Consumption and Waste. Basic raw materials have been become depleted or have been found toxic to human health. We are challenged by technology to economically produce acceptable alternatives. Our response to this dilemma will be presented in this paper.

I chose to look at interior walls of our buildings. The pedagogy behind this project could have just as well been applied to roofing, flooring, exterior cladding, or any other construction system used in a building. The study of interior walls produced valuable lessons for future projects.

It became apparent to the students that a list of criteria was essential to evaluate and refine their work. The list included the following criteria: Inventive, Aesthetic, Interactive, Economical, Feasible, Tactile, Durable, Sustainable, and finally recycled.

Working "Full Size" was critical to the success of the project. Gathering materials from salvage yards, land fills, and the immediate world around was only part of the solution. It was the experimenting with the means of assembly that presented novel and creative insights.

The students were confronted with the opportunity to look at old problems with fresh eyes. Their creative results illustrated an understanding of the issues, problems, and solutions related to Design and Construction.

This paper and presentation of Recycled Walls will narrate a path of discovery in words and images.

Introduction

Teaching Materials and Methods of Construction within the context of an Architectural design curriculum presents opportunities and challenges to the instructor. In my opinion, the subject matter should be an integral part of the design studio. Unfortunately this is not always possible because of the interest, expertise, or priority of the faculty. In defense of offering specific courses on the subject, the school or department is assured that each student has received uniform instruction on the subject.

With that thought in mind, let me argue for the best way to teach and have the students retain and apply this knowledge.

First, a world-class textbook is essential to provide the foundation and reference point for discussion and further understanding. Edward Allen's "Fundamentals of Building Construction Materials and Methods with drawings by Joseph Iano" provides the student with the "Construction Bible".

Second, one needs the means for students to read, apply, and understand construction information. I use a three-part approach to achieving these three objectives.

The **first part** is to quiz the students on the content of each chapter. Rather than having them memorize facts and figures, I have them answer in an essay response to a hypothetical situation. Always applying their knowledge. The **second part** is at the end of the semester in the form of a comprehensive final exam. Patterned after the NCARB Architectural Registration Examination the students have a good measurement of what they need to know to become registered Architects.

The **third or final part**, which is the subject of this paper, is an applied "Hands-On" built construction project.

The Recycled Walls Project

Before I begin in detail about this project, let me provide some background information. I have always felt strongly that Making and a Hands-On experience is critical to the education of an Architect. The Rural Studio at Auburn University has put these efforts on a world stage. It was only natural for Materials and Methods add to those efforts.

Finding the right project took many tries to achieve success. I tried small concrete pours where students explored texture, color, and finish. I tried Constructions joining three different materials to explore fasteners and expression of material. These were all fun projects but they did not seriously connect back to issues of technology and construction.

My next attempt was to construct "Mockups" of traditional Wall, Floor, and Ceiling Details. I knew I was on to something with that project. The students used the tools, materials, and techniques as illustrated in the book to apply what they learned but the projects lacked invention and expression.

The Pedagogy of the Project

Rather than trying to use the project to cover the entire book, I chose to limit the project to the design and construction of traditional interior wall finishes. This focus on just one element of construction allowed the class the freedom to explore with some limits. The intention was to use recycled, salvaged and/or a limited amount of manufactured materials.

The final presentation requirements were to fit a two-foot by two-foot size for both model and drawing and a maximum weight of two hundred pounds. I asked them to consider both the technical and aesthetical issues as they developed their final solution.

Each team of two students was asked to list the design criteria that would be used to judge their results. Also required from each team was a breakdown of the cost of the materials used and documentation of the process used to make the Wall.

The Recycled Walls Examples

They had two weeks to construct and present their design for review. The following are some examples of their work.

Figure 1. Arachne's Web Recycled Wall

This wall finish used white Women's panty hose tights and dowel rods to creative this innovative wall finish.

Figure 2. Drum Sticks Recycled Wall

This wall used recycled drum sticks and scrap Polygal polycarbonate plastic sheets to offer privacy while allowing light to filter into a room beyond.

Figure 4. Recycled Studio Trash Wall

This wall used some of the tons of trash that is generated in a design studio. The innovation of this solution was the way it was assembled and tactile surface texture.

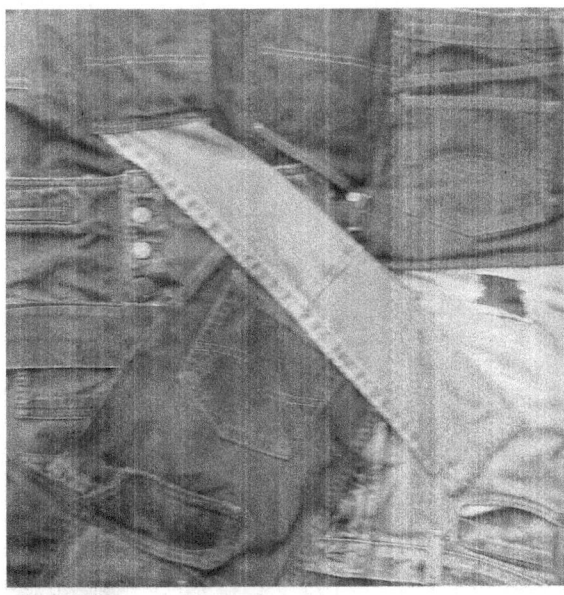

Figure 3. Recycled Blue Jeans Wall

This wall used old Blue Jeans, Starch, and hot glue to create soft comfortable Country look and feel.

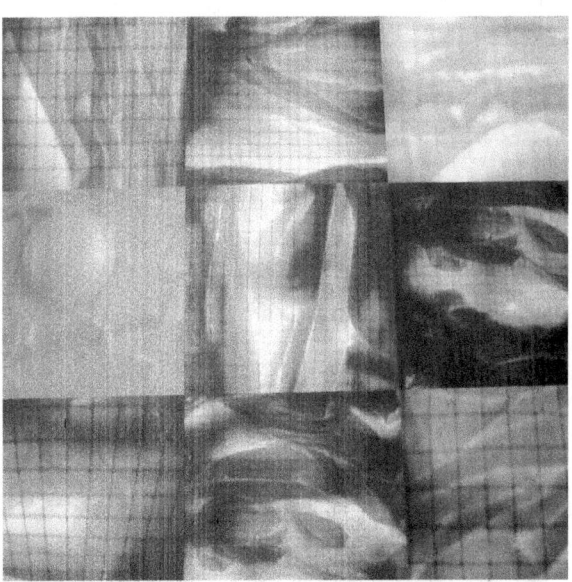

Figure 5. Recycled Tee Shirts Wall

This wall was the most creative when it recycled promotional tee shirts. Using chicken wire, mini Christmas lights, and hardware cloth the assembly came alive.

More Recycled Walls Examples

Figure 6. Recycled Screen and re-bar Wall

This wall used recycled window screen and re-bar to create a semi-transparent divider with a magical flow of space.

Figure 8. Recycled Dowell rods Wall

This wall was unique in its use of dowel rods. This wall becomes interactive by moving each rod in or out to create infinite patterns.

Figure 7. Recycled Old Magazines Wall

This wall using old magazines created art as a wall. The fragments of color and text were sealed between plastic films to allow the wall to be illuminated from behind.

Figure 9. Recycled Drywall and Steel Cable Wall

This wall looked at a new way of installing drywall. Using steel cable and adjustable fastener from off the shelf components, this wall design appeared to float in space.

Conclusions

The project "Recycled Walls" generated the following conclusions:

First, that the teaching of Materials and Methods of Construction demands innovation and application to achieve the learning objectives. Without this important emphasis, our profession will find itself in the hands of others.

Second, instilling a curiosity about the built world and a passion to make it better will educate the designer to become a better Architect. Excitement was generated by this project. The work became a gallery show for the entire school to see. It was also on exhibition at Auburn University's Earth Day Celebration.

Third, working the project full scale and using real material removed any abstraction from the work. I am a strong believer in the detail of construction. Refinement and final design decisions take place full size.

Fourth, using recycled materials was topical to current issues of Sustainability and Building Green Architecture. We must look critically at the ways we build. We have wasted long enough.

Fifth, the pedagogy of the project has application to other building systems. For example, the exterior cladding of a building could be used for a similar investigation. The criteria for evaluation would be different but I would expect innovative and a creative result.

Sixth, finally we must find ways to reinforce the traditional methods of teaching this important subject matter. Our students today have more distractions and demands on their time. We must find new ways to deliver the information and have it retained.

Acknowledgements

I wish to acknowledge and thank my students from my Fall Semester 2005 Materials and Methods II class whose work illustrates this paper. They are as follows:

Sara Agnew, Philip Amthor, Joey Aplin, Kevin Barnes, Cayce Bean, Brad Bell, Harrison Boyd, John Braxtan, John Brennon, Becca Broome, Emily Bullard, Ashley Campbell, Skip Carleton, Sam Chandler, Elizabeth Clayton, Samantha Coffey, Ryan Coleman, John Daley, Danielle Dratch, Betsey Ferrell, Shannon Gibson, Jennifer Givins, Marilyn Gassell, Whitney, Hall, Jenny Hammock, Jennifer Hammer, Jason Holland, Samantha Huntley, Simon Hurst, Kevin Kempke, Adam Kent, Audrey King, Billy Maffett, Rebecca Marshall, John Marusich, Walter Mason, Matt Murphy, Raven Parmer, Adam Pearce, Rand Pinson, Richard Pitts, Joe Rasnick, Ryan Rohe, Melissa Rouse, Thomas Russell, Brian Shirk, Katie Simpson, Leslie Simpson, Kendal Smith, Hong Sol, David Stone, Raleigh Sullivan, Nicholas Thomas, Joey Tudisco, Anthony Vu, Steven Wall, Daniel Wicke, Billy Wilson, Dominique Witt-Bass, Adam Woodward, and Jessie Zenor.

References:

Allen, Edward. <u>Fundamentals of Building Construction Materials and Methods</u>. New York / Chichester / Weinheim / Brisbane / Singapore / Toronto, : John Willey & Sons. Inc. Publishers, 1999.

Structures Sessions Papers: Introduction

Deborah Oakley
University of Maryland, School of Architecture, Planning and Preservation

Historically it seems that structures class has gotten a bad rap in architectural education. Not to prejudice those truly great programs with rich traditions of structures teaching, but more often than not the relationship of structures to design studio is one of conflict versus cooperation, of a necessary servitude—or even worse, a necessary evil—instead of collaboration. But must structures be the lonely stepchild? Do students have to be bored to tears with technology, and need we drive out from them the burning desire to design great structures that shape and inform architecture at the most elemental tectonic level?

Growing numbers of educators strongly believe quite the contrary and see the relationship in terms of potential opportunity versus confrontation. Models of practice in offices the likes of Foster, Piano and Calatrava on the grand scale, and Miller/Hull, Cutler Anderson, Kieran Timberlake and many others on the small scale portend the possibilities of what we can really do.

It is a little discussed truism that we actually have considerable latitude for how structures is taught in an architectural curriculum. For accredited schools, the most stringent guideline comes in the form of Criterion eighteen of the National Architectural Accreditation Board, entitled *Structural Systems.*" In one succinct paragraph, this criterion reads "*Understanding of* principles of structural behavior in withstanding gravity and lateral forces and the evolution, range, and appropriate application of contemporary structural systems."

This leaves wide latitude for implementation, with pedagogic approaches including coursework integrated into studio, innovative hands-on approaches, and applications using modern computer technology among others. Nowhere in that paragraph does the NAAB *dictate* we must drill students on shear and moment diagrams to the exclusion of broad considerations of appropriate systems selection. In fact it *emphasizes* the importance of fundamental principles. Recognition of our educational mission is therefore also recognition of the basic difference in the needs of students taking architectural structures classes versus their peers in comparable engineering programs. Students of architecture need more to learn *how engineers think* than to *think like engineers.*

The papers in this section represent a diverse body of approaches that address these and many other pedagogic questions. They reflect a depth of research on a variety of topics including the use of computers in conjunction with structures teaching, structures integrated studio models, hands-on projects and lab type work, the role of construction observation, and the need for improved education relative to seismic load conditions. In addition, structures as *design* in its own right is a path of enquiry worthy of study.

In this we see ourselves continuing the legacy of the likes of Mario Salvadori and other inspirational leaders who find structure as one of, if not the, singularly essential aspect of making architecture. We owe our profession and the next generation nothing less.

"Do You Own a Hardhat and Safety Boots?": Maximizing Potential Learning through Construction Case Studies

Terri Meyer Boake
School of Architecture, University of Waterloo

Introduction

The developing tectonic culture of architecture, as expressed in the effective use of materials in design and construction, requires that the designer have a high level of expertise in the development of structural and cladding systems as well as details. It takes a great deal of innovative teaching and "tools", to bring architectural students to a level of expression in the technical aspects of design that is reflective of a good knowledge base in the requirements of the material, as well as inspired thinking when it comes to the actual detailing of the material, its construction and connections. Basic construction teaching must be followed by exposure to high quality case studies that address the full range of design, fabrication and construction concerns. Such learning is more easily developed if highly detailed case studies are available to reference.

The Nodding Off Factor + Credibility

In an ideal world, most professors would like to own a "Magic School Bus™", and transport their students (and themselves for that matter!) for live visits of all of the buildings and projects that form the basis for their teaching. There is truly nothing that can effectively replace the direct experience of a space or a construction site. Although I can cite no hard statistical evidence to back up this point, empirical evidence would indicate that the "nodding off in class" factor seems more prevalent when instructors are speaking to "pictures from books" as opposed to images taken during a personal experience with a space or building. Credibility is also at stake when using the images of "others". If the sum total of the professor's learning and experience is derived from the same books to which the students have access, there may be nothing substantive that can be added to the discussion. Such can parallel the classic problems encountered with teaching from a text. If the professor only uses the text, many students skip classes as they find nothing extra is offered.

A very renowned Architectural historian was presenting at our University several years back. Having long used his text in one of my courses, I was keen to hear him present in person. The talk drew from examples in his most recent book. The images presented in the talk were the same black and white images that were included in the book. It soon came to be apparent that the author had never visited the subject buildings, and was also relying on stock photographs, taken by others. Not only did the experience leave me feeling skeptical about the authority behind the research, but it also revealed an increased distancing from the source material by referring to the work of this author. Rather than citing work that was immediate, that work was an additional step away from any direct experience with the actual architecture. Where this might be acceptable when speaking in terms of theory, form and planning, it does fall short of describing issues of construction process and tactile aspects of structural materiality.

Difficulties in Obtaining Live Construction Information

Unfortunately, whether the teaching of building technology is grounded in its beginnings in history and theory, or based upon current examples, it is fairly safe to predict that the majority of lectures on the subject make extensive use of images of buildings. Since our audience is North American, and much of the early material and structural innovation in Western Architecture occurred in Europe during the 18th and 19th centuries, distance also removes both us and our students from direct experiential access of historically significant structural and material examples. The work of Pier Luigi Nervi, for instance, was a critical influence on subsequent North American efforts in innovative use of cantilevered and plastic concrete shaped in buildings.

For lack of travel budget, I had included historic construction images of Nervi's Palazzo dello Sport in the EUR from the first offering of a lecture on the origins of innovative concrete construction, delivered in 1985. Twenty years later, I finally had an opportunity to experience the building and it was so much more inspirational than I was ever able to convey in a lecture based upon book images.

New architectural movements also tend to emanate from Europe or the Pacific Rim, and this also causes distance issues. Most innovation in the realm of double façade construction, for instance, has happened in Europe, with few North American examples to be found. The corporate culture of the United States and Canada has tended to limit highly innovative and ground breaking projects. Norman Foster's Swiss Re, Wembley Stadium and Greater London Authority projects[1] may all have their unique construction and performance problems, but from a purely academic perspective, these can be some of the more beneficial lessons for our students. What can be learned from the World Trade Center project, which could have been an exciting and innovative tower project, is that politics overrides. The final building will likely have little to do with any of the original design or technical inspirations behind the winning scheme.

Extensive site visits to either actual buildings or construction sites are not common and often difficult to fit within the time and financial constraints of most technical courses that are typically relegated to supporting roles within the curriculum. Many schools are not located close to significant buildings or construction projects. Although students of architecture and engineering should be encouraged to own safety boots and a hardhat to make site visits possible, many do not. Classes of 70+ students are logistically difficult to handle on a construction site tour as site conditions are often dangerous and congested. Noise is also a factor, making discussion difficult to hear.

Figure 1. Palazzo dello Sport, Pier Luigi Nervi, under construction 1956 and complete (image taken 2005).

Additionally, most published images of notable buildings focus on the completed work and fail to document the construction process. This is particularly true of historic examples. Even current projects that tend to have more images available as a result of Monograph, periodical and internet based publication (legitimate and independent "blogs"), continue to fail in searches for construction images. If the particular project is not showcasing a highly expressed or exposed structural or cladding system, teaching and learning must rely on educated guesswork.

This tendency may be changing in light of more widespread adoption of BIM (Building Information Modeling) on high profile projects. Daniel Libeskind's Denver Art Museum has come in on time and on budget as a result of extensive use of computer modeling and integrated consultant efforts. Such success on a high profile project has resulted in a proliferation of interesting technical information.[3] This was also evident in publications on the Disney Concert Hall by Frank Gehry. Frenetic steel has a tendency to be more widely photographed. A movie of the construction of the Disney Concert Hall was made. Personal sites about more controversial buildings, such as those by firms such as Gehry and Libeskind, are beginning to proliferate. When researching projects for lectures, such passionate interests can yield valuable resources and construction progress images. Such a site can be found for Gehry's Disney Concert Hall, which includes an extensive site of exposed steel framing images as well as installation of the complex cladding system.[4]

Construction Sites as Impermanent Resources

Construction projects are themselves ever changing and "impermanent". Architectural historian William Dendy, published a book in 1978 entitled "Lost Toronto". Its purpose was to document the many historic buildings that formed the foundation of the City of Toronto, that were demolished to make way for modern progress. Such photographic documentation provides the primary memory for preserving the time and place of building, once the people and their physical remembrances are gone. Completed buildings are not the only architectural artifacts that are evidence of the design and culture of a city. So too can be the construction sites, as they exist as indicators of the spirit, vitality or simple growth of any period. As with any temporal event, effort is required to make multiple and sequential visits to construction sites in order to both document and experience the phases of the project.

The increasing use of "webcams" to track construction progress of significant buildings is evidence on a growing cultural interest in the construction process as a significant event or state. Webcams can be found on many current projects and can be a source of sequential construction images, although somewhat lacking in enlargeable detail.[5]

Figure 2. The ROM Webcam: December 2004, December 2005, May 2006 [2]

Figure 3. ROM steel under construction and the rendering of the completed building.[6] The steel will be, for the most part, concealed beneath gypsum board.

Architecturally Exposed Structural Steel (AESS) and some heavy timber framing provide a permanent viewing and learning opportunity for students of Architecture and Engineering. The connections are highly visible, often exquisitely detailed, and extend the basic principles of connections from the rudimentary to the creative. In the case of AESS applications, much of the construction and erection process can be imagined by an "educated mind", given its permanently exposed state. In the case of structural steel or timber construction that is to be clad, this is no longer the case. The construction process becomes a temporal event. Not only is examination of the structure, materiality of the building and connections permanently concealed from view, but in many cases, once gypsum board is installed, even the idea or rationale behind the structural system is no longer evident. In some instances it is not possible to discern whether a steel or concrete frame system has been used.

The Limitations of Textbooks

Available building construction textbooks (Allen, Ching, et al) tend to focus on preparing students to design and detail relatively standard buildings with typical details. By virtue of the need to address all materials, and appeal to a wide geographic audience, textbooks on building construction also tend to sidestep various climatic, building envelope and thermal issues. Texts might provide a good base for subsequent development with respect to structural systems, but limiting use does compromise effective teaching of cladding systems as thermal insulation and moisture approaches vary so much with climate and geographic location.

With such a vast field of investigation and the potential complexity required via the addition of some contemporary buildings, this deference to standardized detailing is not surprising. Students, however, tend to design few buildings that can rely on the typical level of detailing that is addressed in most textbooks. If building construction and technology courses are intended to prepare students to handle more complex architectural design projects, constructed in a wide range of geographic and environmental locations, such as those in the Comprehensive Building Design Studio, they need to be exposed to a higher level of detailing, coupled with climatic responsive design standards and real building references. Supplementary case studies are essential to address local climate, building code and detailing issues.

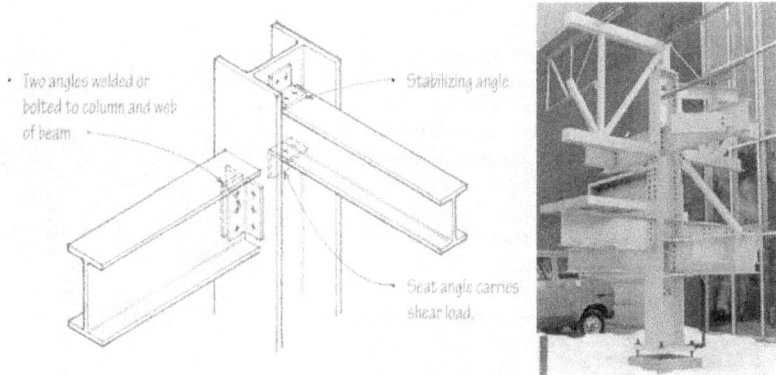

Figure 4 (left) and Figure 5 (right). Excerpt from Francis Ching's "Building Construction Illustrated".[7], CISC Member donated Teaching Aid installation at the University of Alberta

The steel teaching aid pictured above is intended to expose students to full scale mock-ups of the full range of standard steel connections. Such devices are helpful in assisting students in the understanding of the scale of real building materials. It does take significant academic extension and exploration to adapt the same technical details to Libeskind and Gehry-like connections. Relating standard textbook information to more complex real projects is critical in empowering students to develop such expertise within their own design tools. An element of a construction case study can focus on issues like the design and generation of connections and details, showing how they simultaneously are similar to the text details, and how they vary or modify the status-quo to achieve particular project requirements.

The tubular connection below can be seen to be similar to the diagram, yet modified to incorporate round tubular members rather than WF sections. Discussion can be enlarged to address issues of transportation, limitations of geometry, numbers of connections to be made on each assembled piece, and potential (and real) difficulties arising during construction.

A study of the actual erection sequence on such projects is capable of providing a greater insight into the issues associated with transportation, staging, erection and accuracy of fit, than would be the case for more standard construction that would have less demanding geometrical complications. Such was the case for the installation of a large truss at the Leslie Dan School of Pharmacy in Toronto. A 50 tonne full storey

Figure 6 (left) and Figures 7 & 8 (center and right). Double Detail from Ching of a type of tube to WF connection; Detail of tube to tube connection with plate on the Leslie Dan School of Pharmacy by Norman Foster; Crane lifting pod segment for placement

Figure 10. Leslie Dan School of Pharmacy, University of Toronto, Norman Foster – erection of a 50 tonne steel truss at the fifth floor level.

truss was erected at the fifth floor level of the building, atop a leggy concrete atrium. The truss was ultimately used to suspend a "pod – classroom" within the atrium space below. The truss required precision alignment in a vertical slip joint at one end, a beam connection at one-third down the length, and alignment atop a column at the end point. Complex structures require great precision in fabrication, erection and alignment, as well as skilled ironworkers working at some risk to install large steel pieces. The study of such processes can highlight to the students the need for accuracy and constructability of details and connections. Students often have the mistaken impression that connections have a good deal of "play" in their fit – when the opposite is actually the case. Lack of precision can compound dimensional discrepancies that can ultimately mean unnecessary refitting of elements on site. Or in the worst instance, complete replacement parts that require special re-fabrication that cause construction delays.

Although I have been using Edward Allen's "Fundamentals of Building Construction" as my course text since I saw it introduced at the very first ACSA Technology Conference in the early 1980s, it is necessary to take students beyond the basics of connections, as addressed in this and numerous other building construction source texts, and expose them to the potential "play" that lies in detailing. If you comprehend the basics, *the fun lies in really detailing the structure*. Case studies are an excellent way to tie basic construction teaching to an elevated presentation of architectural design. Real buildings can show students how to take the principle ideas of connections and begin to create expression in their structures and buildings.

Cultivating a Culture of Project Documentation

It is essential, therefore, to cultivate a *culture of project documentation* that strives to create a permanent record of the construction process for a wide and ever growing range of buildings. It is only through this type of imagery, that students will be able to "see", and subsequently "learn" about the technical realities and potentialities of material choices throughout the design and construction process. *If construction is not documented, this part of the history of architecture is forever lost.*

For the interest of architectural educators such documentation needs to be stored in or through an accessible place or medium or database. Such material is not likely to attract hard copy investors. Runs of architectural books tend to be limited and as a consequence, very expensive.

One of the great benefits in the creation of an interested network of Building Technology Educators – and one that might derive some inspiration from the Society of Building Science Educators[8] – is the basic notion that teaching resources are best if shared. One of the limiting factors to the collection of case study information lies in "access" to pertinent buildings and projects. We as a group, can create a network of resources to enable education that can step outside and augment our local examples. They may be "someone else's images", but they may have better technological and construction information than can otherwise be found. The use of the internet can be seen as a critical forum for information sharing and publication. In the spirit of SBSE, I maintain a very large database of images, including both finished and construction shots that are freely available to other educators.[9]

Do you own a hardhat and safety boots? And a camera?...

This is not a rhetorical question. Having taught building technology for over 20 years, and attended countless conferences and site tours, it is not uncommon to see more cameras at a wedding, than in the hands of architectural professors on a site tour. If these professors are not taking photographs, then they may not be visibly incorporating their own experiences of construction and architecture into their lectures;

i.e. relying on the "classic" finished images available in texts and Google[10]. If those of us who teach construction technology to future architects, are not interested enough in finding out more about how more complex buildings are constructed, then who can we count on to gather and document this essential information? With digital photography, even contractors are more thoroughly documenting the construction process. These images, however, are not taken for publication purposes and may not necessarily focus on issues that are of interest to those of us in education. Documentation must be elevated to "photography" in order to engage students who tend to be a highly critical and easily bored audience.

Additionally, the inclusion of video footage, can increase the information and interactivity of the lecture material. Real time footage of steel erection processes, for instance, gives students a better understanding of the strategy, cooperation, time and "weight" involved. Video clips can also stress sequencing and access issues, as well as explain the range of construction aids that is necessary. Staging areas on the site for materials delivery, site access and crane operation, are all important to enabling an effective construction process.

Dissecting Case Studies

Since beginning to create and teach courses in building construction in the mid-

Figure 11. BCE Place, construction and finished images. Excerpted from SSEF Case Studies CD-ROM Volume 1

1980s, I have actively been collecting images for use in my lectures. Initial time and budget constraints created a reliance on the "images from books" that can be problematic. Time has allowed many of these to be replaced in whole or in part with images of personal experiences of buildings and construction.

In 1995 I attended the first meeting of the Steel Structures Education Foundation, and viewed a presentation by Wayne Baigent who was the steel fabricator involved with the construction of the BCE Place Galleria designed by Santiago Calatrava. When the SSEF queried the educators present to respond to the presentation, the opinion was unanimous that all wanted access to the fabrication and erection process images. This has led to the creation of three educational CD-ROMs, funded by SSEF, that focus on the fabrication and construction of significant steel buildings.

The first CD looked at the construction of Caltrava's Galleria in Toronto, as well as the Vancouver International Airport by Architectura. The photographic data used for these projects was based upon construction images taken by the fabricators and erectors, with supplementary finished stills and video clips by myself during site visits. The second CD (due for release in Fall 2006) examined the Vancouver Skytrain Stations. Again the construction photographs were supplied by the steel fabricators and erectors, with supplementary finished stills and video clips taken by myself. All of these projects used Architecturally Exposed Structural Steel, and limited exposed heavy timber framing. Detailing was still very evident even after the buildings were complete.

The current CD-ROM project, "Stars + Steel", highlights the construction of three recent/ongoing Toronto projects whose use of AESS is extremely limited. The Addition to the Ontario College of Art and Design by Will Alsop, The Leslie Dan School of Pharmacy by Sir Norman Foster, and the Addition to the Royal Ontario Museum by Studio Libeskind primarily use non-exposed structural steel systems. Each of these projects exhibits extremely innovative steel framing systems and construction techniques to erect the steel. In all cases, the majority of the steel will be clad in a fire protective system that forever hides it from view. The *mission* of this CD-ROM raises the notion of case study "documentation" to the point of preserving the vitality and "knowledge of" the steel structure, and its construction, before it is forever hidden and essentially lost. Although quite dissimilar from the demolition that was causal to "Lost Toronto", the effect is quite similar. The vitality of the construction and the understanding of the steel structure and its erection process vanishes forever once the construction is complete. There is a greater sense of urgency to capture these projects as case studies, than projects whose making is less concealed.

The above images were taken by the constructor of the process of raising 90' tall steel legs in place to support a building. Site access was limited due to the narrow surrounding streets. As an "event" it must have been exhilarating to watch. After the fact, supposition of the erection process is not clear.

The focus of this paper/ discussion/ brainstorming session intends to look at the development and subsequent *sharing* of construction case studies.

Ingredients of an Effective Construction Case Study

Thorough case studies are not easily found. The majority of glossy publications normally include only images of the recently finished building, and rarely any construction images or connection details. If in the final instance, the structure has been left exposed, such finished images can be useful when discussing the building. In the case of concealed structure, finished images give no useful information with which to address construction and detail related concerns.

Figure 12: Erection sequence for HSS legs on OCAD project. Photos: PCL Construction.

The type of structural material or system might not even be readily apparent.

Creating good case studies "from scratch" that can address the wide range of issues related to the teaching of structural design from an architectural viewpoint, requires not only dedication, but also "being in the right place at the right time". Access to construction sites is not always available, nor necessarily, is the time to make repeated visits to obtain sequence shots. Student field trips are difficult to arrange (although excellent opportunities for learning), and rely on a certain degree of serendipity – hence giving students in subsequent years an uneven chance of touring through a "good" building. Although constructors are required to document the construction process, these images are in many cases taken for legal protection, and most constructors are not willing to share or publicly distribute their images for the same reasons. Fabricators can also be guarded due to production "secrets" (particularly in the case of challenging and highly competitive AESS work) – or simply don't take an interest in documenting the process.

For a case study to be truly useful, it must come close to addressing the entire design and construction process. In this way, as an educational tool, it can be used to bridge the gaps that currently exist between teaching areas in most schools of architecture. A *thorough* case study requires:

- knowledge of the design intentions of the architect
- why was this structural or cladding system chosen?
- access to design sketches, models, computer renderings
- detail drawings that show the relationship between the structure and the skin
- connection development from an engineer's or fabricator's viewpoint
- fabrication images
- transportation images
- erection sequence images
- video footage, if possible, that can explain the actual erection process
- completed images

The final case study must be presented or available in a form that can be easily adapted to the specific course with respect to style of teaching/learning, amount of time available to address issues and the experience level of the students. Usefulness also unfortunately is dependent upon the technologies available at varying schools: from slide projectors, to DVD, to Powerpoint™ or video. Based upon conversations with professors of architecture, the *least* easily used format seems to be video, particularly if the run time exceeds the amount of time available. The most useful formats would be sets of digital images or slides, if accompanied by a "script or narrative" that explains the project, and CD-ROM or DVD format presentations that allow the instructor to select portions of a case study for use if time or subject area does not permit the inclusion of the full case study. Image based data that can be accessed via the internet for either download or direct use is helpful as it increases the ease and immediacy of access. With every case study presentation, the "a-ha!" factor is important. There needs to be some key, unusual, value adding information that is not otherwise, or easily available. Anecdotal information is always helpful. This is usually only obtained through personal interaction with the people and project/site itself.

Other questions to be asked when preparing a construction case study:

1. What are the necessary attributes that elevates a building to warrant documentation?
2. Are there different types of case studies?
3. Primary ingredients/checklist for this case study to include?
4. Types of documentation: drawings, photographs and video.
5. How much material is *enough*? Do all require equal development?
6. Involving students in documentation.
7. Exploring the use of multimedia.
8. Next steps – are we doing enough with case studies?
9. How to maximize the learning potential of materials.
10. Logistical difficulties: site access, legal issues.

The Nodding Off Factor Revisited

In the end sleep deprivation can and will govern, and all efforts of instructors to provide a meaningful, interactive presentation based upon unique personal experiences, images and video footage will still fail. But ultimately, through the fog, students will realize that they missed something important – something that cannot be caught up after class or through reference to the notes of "others".

References:

Allen, Edward and Joseph Iano. Fundamentals of Building Construction: Materials and Methods. New York: John Wiley, 2004.

Boake, Terri Meyer. "Ordering Chaos: Computerism vs. Humanism" – ACSA Annual Meeting 2006
http://www.architecture.uwaterloo.ca:16080/faulty_projects/terri/pdf/boake_chaos_colour.pdf

Ching, Francis D. K.. Building Construction Illustrated. New York: Van Nostrand Reinhold, 1975.

Personal Image Gallery:
http://www.architecture.uwaterloo.ca/faculty_projects/terri/gallery.html

Steel Structures Education Foundation CD-ROMs:
http://www.ssef.ca/cdrom.html

Steel Structures Education Foundation Case Study Gallery:
http://www.ssef.ca/cdrom.html

Steel: Fun is in the Details – Case Study Gallery:
http://www.architecture.uwaterloo.ca/faculty_projects/terri/steel.html

Notes:

[1] The Swiss Re building was sealed in April 2005 after a window fell out of its frame and crashed to the ground. Wembley Stadium is behind schedule due to strikes. GLA has

been in the news due to issues of interior environmental quality and a green building that is not living up to its performance expectations.

http://www.bdonline.co.uk/story.asp?storyType=80&sectioncode=448&storyCode=3050737

[2] Renaissance ROM Webcam:
http://www.rom.on.ca/renaissance/hyatt.php

[3] Article in Engineering Record News, May 2006.

http://enr.ecnext.com/comsite5/bin/comsite5.pl?page=enr_document&item_id=0271-27583&format_id=XML

[4] "Frank Gehry Disney Concert Hall: A Construction Diary", by Paul Viapiano

http://home.pacbell.net/viapiano/gehry/gehryindex.html

[5] Denver Art Museum webcam:
http://www.mortenson.com/index.php?t=projects/denver_art_museum_expansion_webcam

[6] Image of completed building taken from ROM Website: http://www.rom.on.ca

[7] Ching. p. 4.18

[8] Society of Building Science Educators website: http://www.sbse.org/

[9] Terri Boake website and Image Gallery:
http://www.architecture.uwaterloo.ca/faculty_projects/terri/

[10] Googling for images, for instance, "Falling Water", normally yields a high percentage of repeat hits of almost exactly the same image, from the same vantage point, seeming to infer that there is really only one view of any building.

Less Is More: A Design-oriented Approach to Teaching Structures in Architecture

Michele Chiuini
Department of Architecture, Ball State University

Introduction

We are all familiar with the main issues that haunt structures courses in architecture schools:
- students struggle to understand statics and with applying mathematical procedures to solve structural problems;
- there is inadequate time to teach statically indeterminate structures and other systems that are a bit more complex than simple beams and columns;
- there is a perceived separation between design disciplines and structures courses.

The design studio is normally the focus of architecture students, and structural design is seen as something so different conceptually, that it is left out of their design process altogether. As Richard Bender put it: "The classical sequence of presenting statics, strength of materials, analysis and 'design' may represent a logical progression of information. However, divorced as it usually is from involvement with the total process of design, this sequence has resulted in architectural graduates who have no understanding of the basic principles involved, cannot apply them, nor retain for a significant period after graduation the basic core of material encountered."[1]

One way to make structural systems part of the "intuitive" design vocabulary of architecture students is to remove structures from the abstract realm of mathematics and bring it into the context of building design[2].

Like in any design field, structural design is not a precise science: instead, it is an art that requires initial assumptions based on experience. Students should understand that decisions on the structural system often have to go through several iterations before a precise solution if finalized. There are similarities and differences with the architectural design methodology, but there is a strong interrelationship with the building design process in terms of selection and configuration, and certainly in the architectural use of structures. The initial steps of structural design go hand in hand with architectural decisions, and they are the most interesting and potentially creative. There are two approaches to bring this structural creativity into the studio: one is to make structural design an integral part of the studio problem statement. The second, which is equally important, is to introduce a degree of "realism" into the structures courses by teaching around a building design project. The "structures project" has some resemblance to Edward Allen's "second studio" idea[3], with emphasis on system selection and configuration, but also on the understanding of structural materials, connections and member sizes. The understanding of the structural behavior of systems, which is obviously important for system selection purposes, can be significantly facilitated by the use of structural analysis software, allowing the students to understand the behavior of complex systems and test alternative configurations in order to refine their design solution.

The structures project: emphasis on integrated design

Since 2001, the "structures project" has been a feature of the structural design sequence I have been teaching, covering steel, wood, and concrete systems. It is now part of the fourth year structures course, in a revised curriculum, which includes concrete, wood and masonry.

In the structures project, students are asked first to configure a system in the context of a basic architectural brief. Then each primary element of the system is analyzed, members are sized and connections designed. Typically the brief requires the structure to be exposed, so that member shapes and connections became architectural design problems. Over the years, the structural systems designed have been mainly steel and wood long span, and steel and concrete multistory frames (Fig. 1). In both cases the system can be statically determinate or indeterminate. In the steel structures course, both long span and multistory frames were statically determinate; in the following course the project work has included a concrete rigid frame, providing the opportunity for comparisons with a steel system. The introduction of statically indeterminate systems has been the major innovation in the course content (versus methodology), and it has been made possible by the use of engineering software.

This approach addresses one of the somewhat surprising student attitudes: the idea that in a structures course they are not designers any longer, but only formula solvers. There is a frame of mind in the student sitting in front of his/her structures assignment (which would deserve some psychological attention), that makes the students forget how to draw and design, or think that, because it's not studio work, their drawings can be sloppy. It has been a constant effort in my course to make the students sketch (Fig. 2) as they think about the structural problem, versus jumping straight into the formulas. Students are also asked to submit structural drawings with the same graphic quality (and probably more precision) that they would adopt for a studio project.

Having the type of system as a given (e.g. a concrete braced frame), there are two

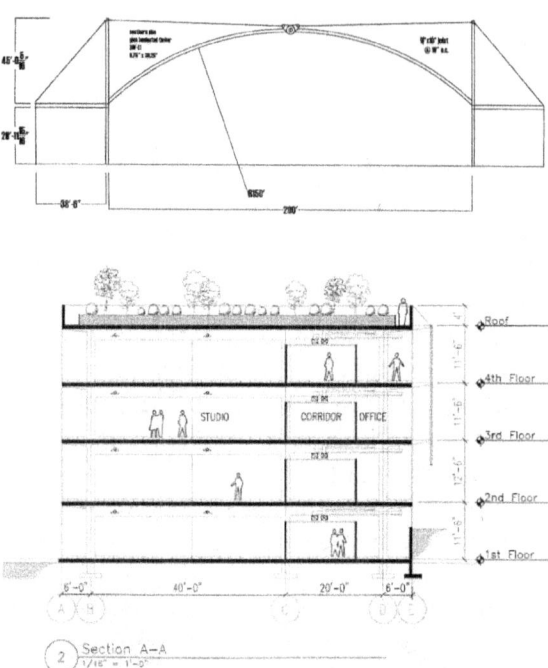

Figure 1. Types of structures project: long span system and multistory frame

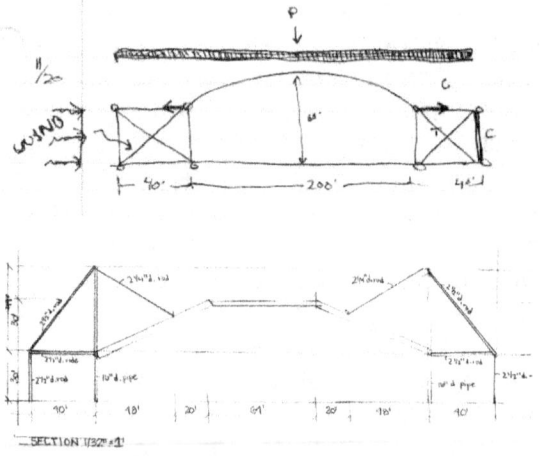

Figure 2. Preliminary sketches for selection and configuration of a long span system

things students are asked to address as they first approach the design of a structural system: the configuration and the construction. Both have to do with loads and with the understanding of how loads are transferred to other structural members as they travel down to the foundations.

Loads seem to be one of the hardest things for students to figure out, but is this also one of the most important aspects of structural design: statics calculations can be perfect, but if the loads are wrong the results will be wrong. Making decisions about construction and sketching a wall or roof section helps the students to understand how loads are supported, and allows them to relate better to building technology and architectural design (Fig. 3). One could say that an understanding of structural design is not complete when divorced from knowledge concerning materials and methods of construction[4].

The design process for the projects is paralleled by the introduction of related topics in the lecture course. In the case of a steel long span system, for instance, the first members to be designed are the roof joists, so the course deals at that point with simple bending members. The design and the course material then proceed with the design of beams, columns, tension members (suspension or bracing), and finally connections (welds, pins, bolts,

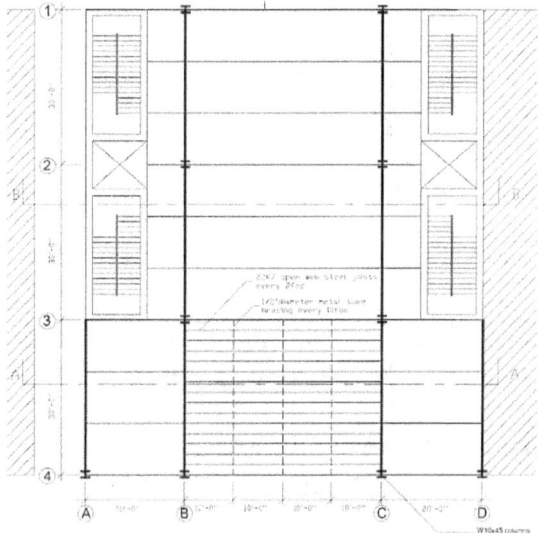

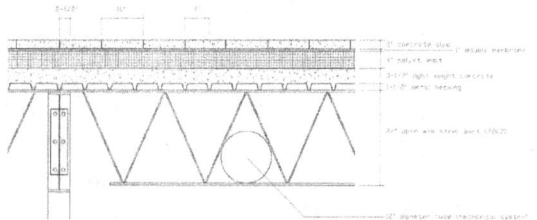

Figure 4. Steel frame configuration and construction detail

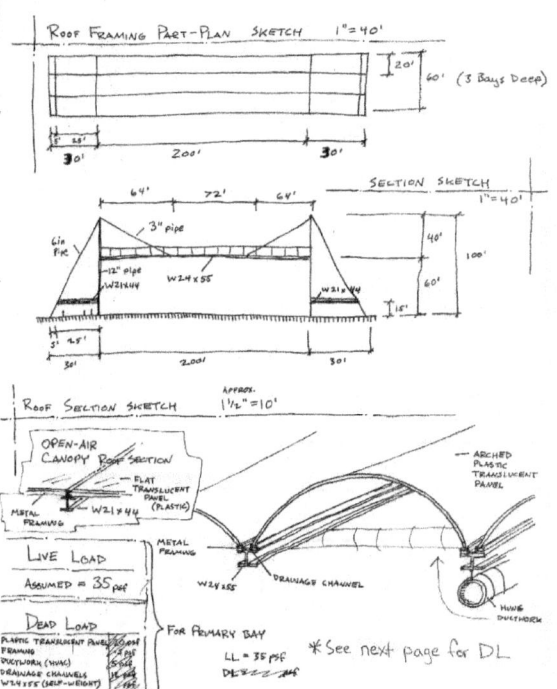

Figure 3. Preliminary sketches for load calculations: long span frame

plates) (Fig. 4). As mentioned before, the students are asked to look at the details of the structure as aspects of architectural design, and therefore the solutions must be elegant and well presented.

The design of a steel staircase is one of the opportunities to engage in some structural/architectural details (Fig. 5). It is probably the first time students are made to think about the components of a staircase as structural systems: the stringers, the

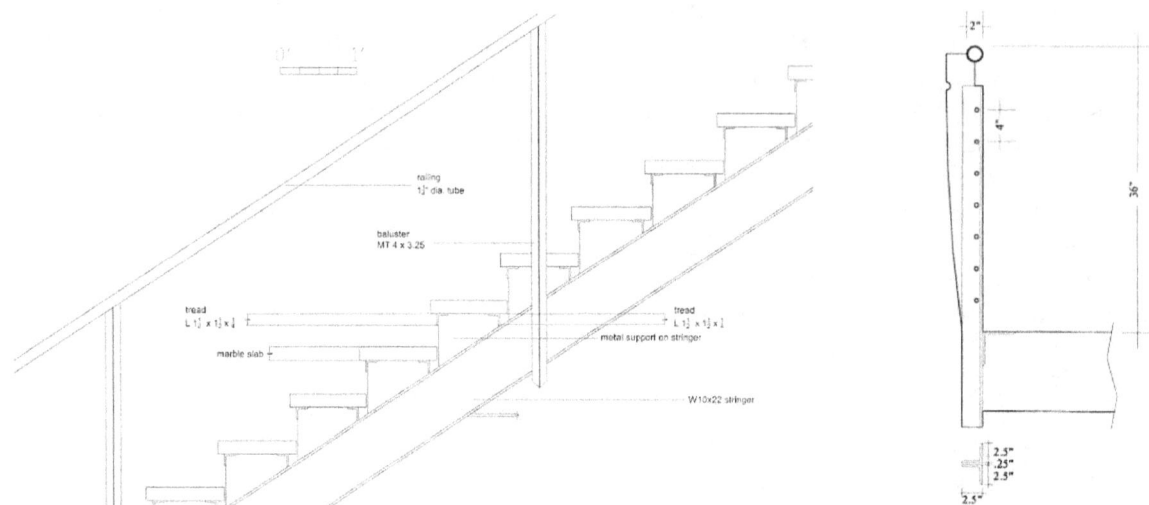

Figure 5. Steel staircase design and detail of railing

treads, the railings, and the mountings, each subject to code requirements.

Structural analysis software: emphasis on "systems"

In the current upper level course (ARCH 418 Structural Systems 3), the concrete frame project is a way to introduce statically indeterminate systems (Fig. 6). Using a design project to discuss this topic helps the students to ground it into something concrete (pun unintended). The behavior of rigid frames is explained visually with a series of *Multiframe*[5] workshops, starting with simple systems like portal frames and continuous beams. The first two or three weeks of the project are spent configuring the system, calculating the loads on the beams, and analyzing the frame to obtain the moment and shear diagrams with alternate loads (Fig. 7).

Students then, as in the projects described before, design the main structural members (beams, columns, footings, and others) including the steel reinforcement. One of the primary issues is to make students understand the concept of continuity of the frame, reflected in the way the steel bars are placed at the columns (Fig. 8).

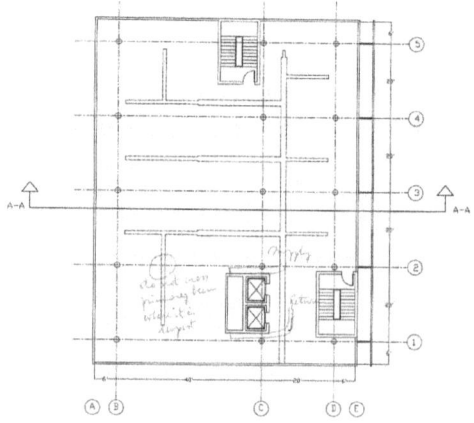

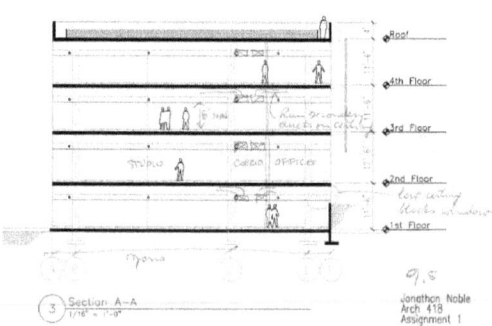

Figure 6. Configuration of concrete frame: integration of circulation, stairs and ductwork in plan and section

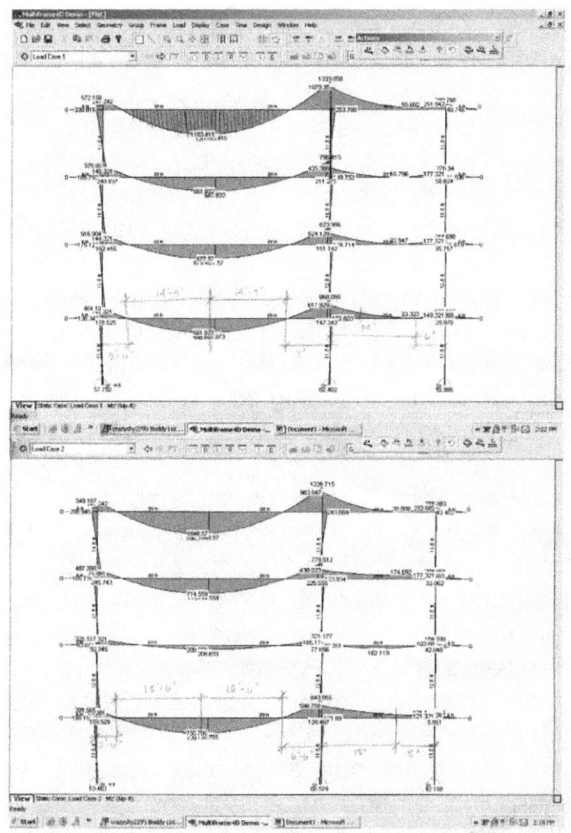

Figure 7. Moment diagrams for full live loads and alternate live loads on beams

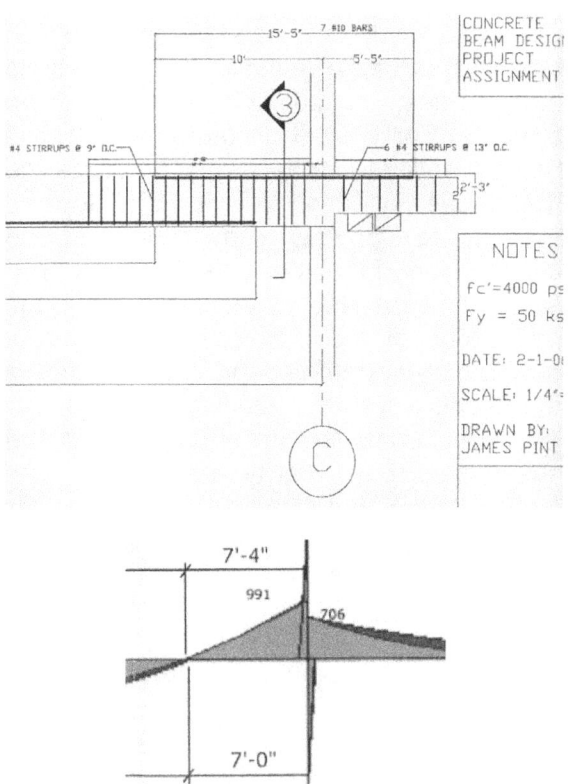

Figure 8. Detail of concrete beam design and corresponding detail of M diagram envelope: beam depth is changed according to M change to accommodate HVAC ducts

The design of the shear walls is one of the major issues in terms of integrated design, and inevitably revisions of the floor plan are necessary at that point (Fig. 9). The design method for the shear walls is kept simple and does not require the use of the computer, but it is an opportunity to discuss the frame behavior under lateral loads without shear walls, which can be easily done with *Multiframe*.

There seems to be some degree of consensus that the main objective of structures courses should be the understanding of structural behavior. A 1995 survey[6] indicated that the two primary objectives of structures courses were the qualitative and intuitive understanding of the behavior of building systems, and the quantitative (mathematically based) analysis skills.

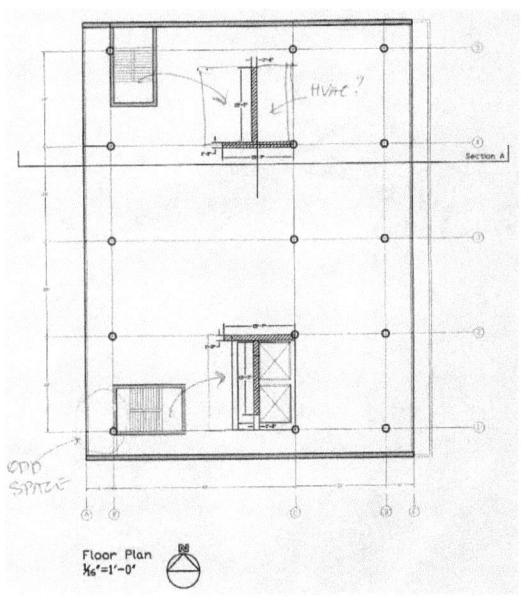

Figure 9. Revisions on the floor plan due to location and sizing of shear walls

Computer analysis is used in the course to teach about other systems, such as arches and domes, in addition to suspension systems. For a steel system, the software has the ability to calculate and visualize the deflections, offering an additional tool to study the optimal configuration and combination of member sizes (Fig. 10). The students can also understand how the deflections of the long span beams in a suspension system depend on the behavior of the entire system, including the deflection of the columns and the elongation of the suspension rods. This type of holistic view of the system would be very problematic for students if approached with the traditional tools and methods.

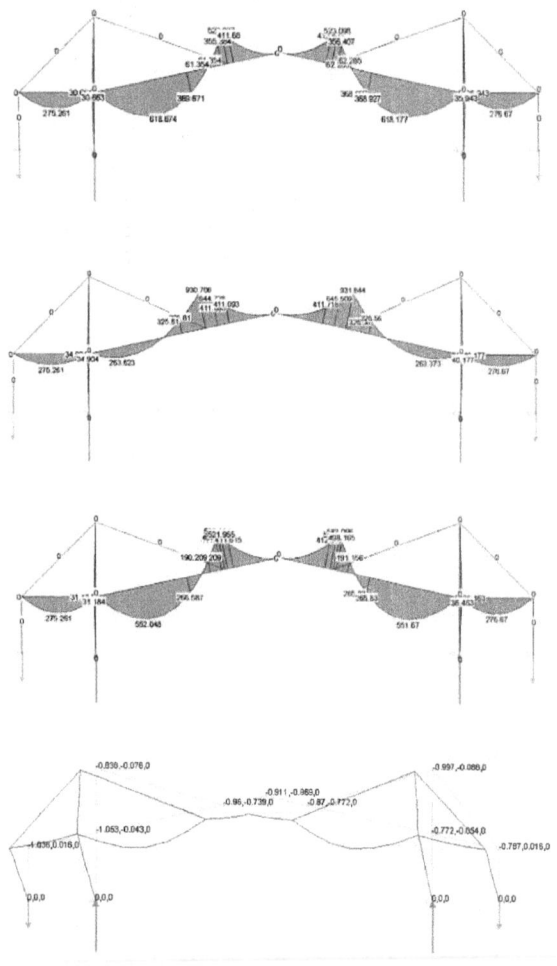

Figure 10. Tests of alternative configurations with the same load using the M diagram
Deflection diagram of long span steel system

One of the possible criticisms of using computer software to solve problems of statics is the "black box syndrome": the computer analysis produces results the students have to use blindly, without understanding how they are worked out. In order to accept the computer as a valid pedagogical tool, we first must ensure that the students are introduced to statics and have a basic understanding of internal forces and deflections. After all, we accept similar methodologies in studio: perspectives, for instance, are today generated by computer (and are much more sophisticated than what students could do by hand). This is acceptable because the students are first taught the principles and methods of perspective drawing. In fact we understand three-dimensional digital modeling as a different, more potent tool than conventional perspectives to investigate complex issues like light and movement in space. Similarly, computer modeling of structural systems can be a heuristic device to test ideas that could have hardly been understandable by an undergraduate architecture student before. The way students (and I'd say professionals) calculate structures is, after all, full of "black boxes": from deflection diagrams to code formulas for which we rely on ACI, AISC, AITC, and other professional institutions. We can accept these "black boxes" in our design process because we understand the principles that lay behind, and know when those formulas are applicable. In an architecture course, students can use structural software to go a step further. The use of the software is not just to produce design solutions, but to understand more - and with less effort - about structural systems and the structural design process.

Conclusions

Of the three innovations introduced in our structures courses, two are about method - the project and the computer analysis - and one is about content - statically indeterminate systems. The methodology has allowed to enrich the course content and to reach the two primary objectives:

1) enable the students to see structures as part of the design disciplines, and part of the architectural design process;
2) enable the students to learn about complex structures previously considered to be beyond their ability but, at the same time, very common in practice (such as rigid frames).

Before I introduced the use of computer analysis, we had four structural design courses, and there was not even the mention of statically indeterminate systems. Students would graduate without any conceptual understanding of rigid frames or continuous beams. Now we have reduced the structures sequence to three courses, and yet students are able to discuss a multistory concrete frame and even design the structural details.

Not all calculations are done by the computer: students are asked to go through the sizing procedures the traditional way (code formulas, pocket calculators, pen and paper). However, the most complex statics calculations are relegated to machines, as Leibniz was trying to do by inventing a mechanical calculator in the seventeenth century[7]. Because the course is not really about statics but about design of structural systems, students can focus on the understanding of principles and processes of structural design. This helps the students to see the mathematical calculations not as an end to themselves but a design tool.

This experimentation is addressing a number of pedagogical issues and leaves some open questions:

- The attempt to reach the studio from the Structural Systems course should be mirrored by the same effort in studio so that, at least at some points, the two courses can hold hands together. The problem, however, is that in a fourth-year studio the architectural design work is likely to require very complex structural solutions; in addition, it is practically impossible for one structures instructor to follow the individual work of six or seven different studio sections with a total of over eighty students.

- There should be a more systematic exploration of engineering software and its appropriateness for the classroom, eventually resulting in writing structural software packets for educational use; the applications should not be limited to statics[8] but could also deal with databases, graphic representation, and integration with architectural CADD software.

- We should eventually find a way to assess the integration of structural knowledge and architectural design in the studio work of the same or following semester.

In my experience, the teaching of structures as a design discipline can be eventually more effective than teaching technology in a studio, with technology "support" courses. A structural design course using design projects can provide the necessary degree of "rigor and depth required for effective integration [of technology in the design process]"[9]. At the same time, the design studio is an excellent teaching method to follow, because it works based on the principle that students truly understand only what they discover for themselves[10]. The same discovery approach could be used in teaching structures; the reason this does not happen in conventional courses is because of the mathematical complexity of structural analysis once we go beyond the most basic systems. The software effectively allows using an empirical method to explore structural behavior, by testing alternative configurations and comparing force diagrams and deflections. It is easy to demonstrate how in statically indeterminate systems the relative rigidity of members alters the distribution of internal forces. This approach is similar to testing physical models, which can give a measure of the stability of a certain configuration or of their strength as visualized by deformations. However, computer modeling gives much more information with much less demand on time and resources compared to physical models.

Both the project and the use of Multiframe have been extremely well received by students, as evidenced by evaluations during the course (with specifically targeted questions) as well as the semester-end evaluations, and this can be a first (but only partial) measure of effectiveness. The results of this methodology can be summarized by paraphrasing the famous sentence by Mies van der Rohe: "less is more," or less time can be devoted to toil on statics and calculations, while the students acquire more knowledge about structural design and more understanding of how it is relevant to architecture.

Notes:

[1] Quoted by R. Gary Black and Stephen Duff in: "A model for teaching structures: finite element analysis in architectural education." 1994: *Journal of Architectural Education*, Vol. 48 No. 1, 38.

[2] This topic has been amply discussed by James Ambrose, *Teaching Structures*. 1994: New York, distributed by Wiley (unpublished manuscript).

[3] Edward Allen. "Second Studio: A Model for Technical Teaching." *Journal of Architectural Education,* Vol. 51 No. 2 (November 1997). See also Ryan Smith in note (4).

[4] This is paraphrasing a statement by Ryan E. Smith in his article "Bridging Structures, Construction and Studio" in *Connector*, Vol. XIII No. 1 (Spring 2004). The objective of the technology course described in this article is to make students discover the logic of space organization intrinsic to a construction system, reversing the common design process, which goes from space requirements to construction system.

[5] S.B. Haley, P.E. "Graphic magic's Multiframe 2D & 3D." In *Modern Steel Construction*, May 1992, p. 14. The decision on this application was actually based on a presentation by Spiro Pollalis from Harvard University at the ACSA Annual Meeting, 1992 and on a personal conversation with him.

[6] Faoro, Daniel. "ACSA Structures Curriculum survey."1994: North Dakota State University (unpublished). Results indicated that the two primary objectives of structures courses were the qualitative and intuitive understanding of the behavior of building systems, and the quantitative (mathematically based) analysis skills (Question 11). Question 13a was a review of software specific to structures courses.

[7] "For it is unworthy of excellent men to lose hours like slaves in the labor of calculations which could be safely relegated to anyone else if machines were used."

Gottfried W. Leibniz, *De Progressione Dyadica, Pars I*, (MS, 15 March 1679), published in facsimile (with German translation) in Erich Hochstetter and Hermann-Josef Greve, eds., *Herrn von Leibniz' Rechnung mit Null und Einz* (Berlin: Siemens Aktiengesellschaft, 1966), pp. 46-47. English translation by Verena Huber-Dyson, 1995. An interesting discussion of this idea by George B. Dyson can be found at The Reality Club, www.edge.org.

[8] The use of computers can go beyond statics and include a database of systems and methods. See for instance Vassigh, Shahin. "Teaching Structures with Computer-based Media." In *Connector*, Vol. IX No. 2 (Fall 2000), 8-9.

[9] G. Goetz Schierle. "The Pedagogy of Architectural Technology," in *Journal of Architectural Education,* Vol. 51 No. 2 (November 1997). This is effectively Allen's opinion when he states the need of a separate "technology studio" (note 3).

[10] Bowser, Wayland. "Reforming design education." *Journal of Architectural Education,* Vol. 37 No. 2, 12.

A Different Kind of Structures Problem

Robert J. Dermody
Roger Williams University

Introduction

Structures courses in many architecture programs have long relied on analytical, calculation based problem sets as their primary pedagogy. However, this approach is both unrealistic and does a disservice to students. Abstract problem sets do not accurately represent the limited role that calculations play in developing efficient, exciting forms for building structures. They also incorrectly reinforce the notion that structural design is all about number crunching. Students, who are challenged in studio courses to create beautiful spaces in response to practical programs on real sites, are often forced to manipulate select formulae for abstract examples in structures class. In an effort to refocus the content of structures courses on form finding, students are challenged with Structural Design Exercises. These active learning exercises require students to "design" a small building on a local site. "Design" solutions in this case include both architectural drawings and the corresponding structural calculations. It is evident by students' thoughtful questions and successful presentations that teaching structures as design by using structural design exercises has many benefits. This paper will explain the structural design exercises and describe both experiences administering these assignments and students' experiences completing them. Typical questions asked by students and some of the challenges they encounter will also be discussed.

Background

An informal review of structures courses offered in architecture programs across the U.S. reveals that many schools require between 2 and 4 "structures" courses. The most common topics covered include statics, strength of materials, wood, steel and concrete[1]. When a curriculum is organized in this fashion it is quite common to rely on traditional textbooks (often engineering) and "problem set" style homework assignments as the main pedagogy. However, calculations such as the sizing of discrete structural members play hardly any role in determining the form of a building structure. The architect's role in structural design occurs early in the process during schematic and design development phases. In fact, any required calculations are typically done by the structural engineering consultant, and they are performed after the primary design phases, during construction document preparation. Therefore, teaching architecture students how to select and configure structural systems would more closely mimic real world design processes and could potentially improve their studio design projects. While the underlying theory of mechanics and basic calculation techniques are quite useful, it is never too early to teach structural concepts within the context of design. This is especially important in the advanced courses of wood, steel, and concrete design. One of the challenges of any structures course is to relate it to the rest of the curriculum, most obviously, design studio.. By treating structures as design, architecture students will gain a better appreciation of the implications of spatial design on the corresponding structural system requirements.

The Problem with Problem Sets

The main drawback to traditional problem set style homework assignments is their abstract nature. Problems from the back of a textbook chapter tend to narrowly focus on only one specific aspect of structural calculations at a time. Finding reactions on beams, constructing shear and moment diagrams, or analyzing trusses are certainly useful skills. However, these types of problems are too often performed on isolated elements devoid of any architectural or structural context. Also, the analysis of discrete members is limited to one specific, arbitrary loading condition. When the loading information is given in a problem statement, a very important analytical step is already done, and the effect of structural configuration on tributary areas and load paths is missed. This is another major shortcoming of repetitive problem sets. as an investigation of loads and loading conditions is fundamental to any structural design problem. Careful modeling of the loads and a clear understanding of the load paths is crucial.[2] A critical aspect of structural design is the interdependent relationship between the configuration of structural systems and the resulting load paths. Loading patterns directly affect the subsequent selection and sizing of members within the system. Furthermore, the manipulation of select formulae is almost useless in design studio. Specific calculation skills learned in structures classes are of little use to students' for their studio projects due to the vast difference in scales at which students work in the two types of classes. Learning to select and configure appropriate materials and structural systems to accommodate *and* enhance architectural programs is much more valuable to architecture students in their studio courses. Teaching structures as design is a way to bridge this gap between form finding and the requisite calculations needed only to confirm member sizes.

A Different Kind of Problem

Structural design exercises are a dynamic, interactive way to teach structures as design. This style of assignment offers several advantages over traditional problem sets, which are often completed individually. The primary benefit of the design exercise format is the active learning processes these assignments promote. Unlike typical homework assignments, the exercises emphasize an iterative, integrated design process. Students work in teams of two and are required to meet often with the instructor as they develop their solutions and come up with questions. The problems are done in short phases with preliminary due dates of partial submissions closely mimicking the traditional schematic design, design development and construction document phases. Typical assignment durations range from 2 to 4 weeks. The problem statements are easily adapted to different levels of student or course topic, but seem to work best at the advanced levels for the typical wood, steel and concrete design classes. Design exercises also provide an opportunity for students to use concepts they have learned in introductory structures courses.[3] Design exercises allow students to see the relationship between the spatial layout of an architectural design and the requisite supporting structure. This relationship is manifest directly in the analysis of the loads and loading patterns on the structures. Using structural design exercises recreates a studio style problem even in a lecture course setting. A typical structural design exercise problem statement begins with a statement of objectives as follows:

> To use the concepts from structures sequence classes on load tracing, tributary areas, allowable stress design, deflection, beam design, and lateral stability etc., to design a small wood frame structure.

The specific task of the assignment is stated as follows:

In teams of two, design a 1000SF, one-story, wood-framed structure to be supported on a flat, slab-on-grade foundation to contain three spaces; a small office / information desk, a display / seating area, and a restroom. Strive to create a building in which architecture and structure are blended to enhance the program, and inspire delight. Roofs may be flat, sloped, curved or multi-level. Spaces within the building should relate both visually and spatially to the framing of the structure. Include lateral stability elements, such as shear walls, and/or diagonal bracing. (Be sure to show these in plan.) The pavilion must be universally accessible and may be partially or fully enclosed.

A detailed list of submittal requirements is also provided in the problem statement: (figs. 2-4).

> Please submit all work on 11 x 17 sheets, using as many as needed. Computer OR hand drawings are acceptable. All drawings must be done to a scale noted on the drawing.
>
> 1. A clear, concise written description of your design, and an explanation of the structure....1 page max.
>
> 2. Free-hand conceptual sketches.
>
> 3. Two primary elevations.
>
> 4. Basic framing plan, showing configuration, size, and orientation of all members.
>
> 5. Lateral stability system diagrams; in plan and elevation/section. (See *Allen*.)
>
> 6. A critical building cross-section.
>
> 7. Large scale section through "roof" structure.
>
> 8. A typical wall section showing relationship between enclosure and structure.
>
> 9. State load assumptions.... (dead load, live load, snow Load, wind load)
>
> 10. Design calculations for typ. joist.
>
> 11. Design calculations for a typical beam and/or girder.
>
> 12. Design calculations for column with maximum load; check axial comp. stress and slenderness ratio.
>
> 13. 2 or 3 critical details of *different* connections/joints/supports; in plan, section, elevation, & (exploded) axon.
>
> 14. Properly cite all references used.
>
> 15. Carefully compose all of the above information into a professional presentation. Also, please submit an electronic copy on a clearly labeled CD. Keep a copy for your records.

Most of the class periods during the span of the assignment are devoted to in-class consultations with the instructor. These are an important part of the structural design exercise experience. Unlike helping students solve specific problems from a textbook, these meetings are much more interactive. They permit quick feedback and further engage students in the design process. The "back and forth" discussion during consultations closely mimics real world design processes. A note about consultations appears in the assignment handout:

> Regular consultations/meetings with the professor are required as part of this assignment. These meetings are to foster development of your project. These may occur during class or during office hours. You are expected to prepare appropriate documentation / questions for each class or office

meeting. A minimum of 3 or 4 consultations is suggested. Consider all aspects of this project as a professional design exercise.

Results and Experiences:

Students quickly adapt to the more "open-ended" style of these assignments after a short adjustment period. One of the early stumbling blocks for students is to understand that they have control over their solution to the problem. It is not governed by simple formulae. Since they are used to having most, if not all, of the given parameters stated in a problem, they often have difficulty in stating their own assumptions about their structure or loads. The first consultation requires a preliminary submission of conceptual sketches and site analysis documentation. (fig.1) This information is usually enough to begin a dialogue with the students regarding basic structural systems and load paths. Subsequent discussions cover the students' assumptions regarding load magnitudes and patterns. A major breakthrough typically occurs when students begin to analyze the structure needed for their conceptual designs. Most of the major revisions occur soon after this point. Students quickly realize that they must make sense of their architectural designs in order to design the corresponding structure. It is interesting to note that most students begin by sketching how they want the building/structure to look without differentiating what is the "structure" and what is the "architecture". The students quickly realize the interdependent relationship of form and structure. They also see the influence of structural layout on member sizing, but as part of the overall design process, not as an isolated, abstract problem. Long spans have larger tributary areas, which beget larger loads and therefore require deeper supporting structural members. Calculations are therefore only used at the end of the design process to verify the efficiency of their layout of the framing system. Impromptu or mini lectures can be given to the whole class when appropriate questions arise during consultations with individual teams. Students' early questions often concern how to progress from their original conceptual sketches to selecting and configuring appropriate structural system. This is the heart of the matter that these problems directly address. It is all about design. Later in the project students often have questions regarding lateral loads and their resisting systems, as this is typically a new topic. However, the students ask because they want to know how to stabilize their buildings not because they after the answer to a specific problem. The design of a small building is an ideal way to present this three-dimensional topic. They also begin to ask more specific and thoughtful questions as new challenges arise during the project. Some students even admit to enjoying structures class!

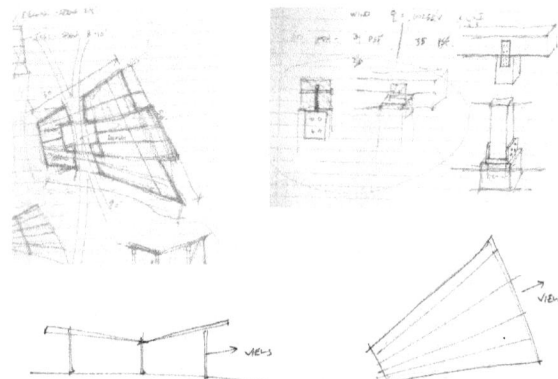

Figure 1. Conceptual Sketches by Stephanie Dillon and Dan Herchenrother, Spring 2006.

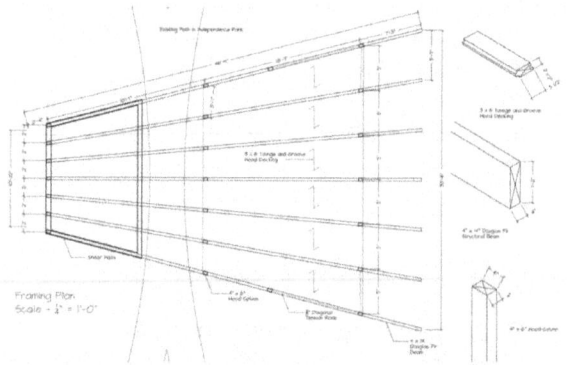

Figure 2. Framing plan by Stephanie Dillon and Dan Herchenrother, Spring 2006.

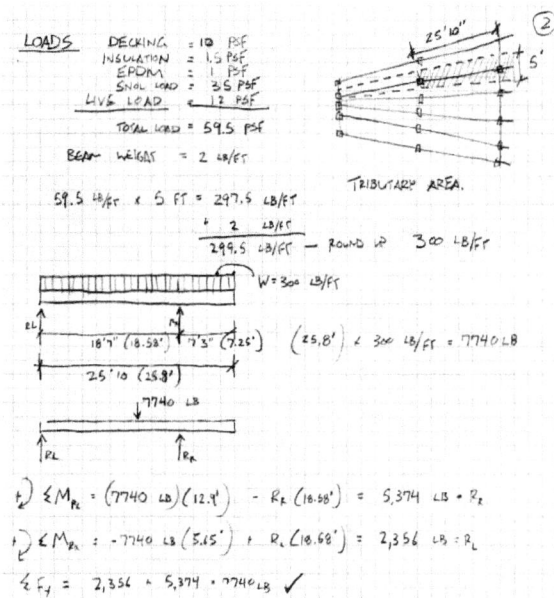

Figure 3. Calculations by Stephanie Dillon and Dan Herchenrother, Spring 2006.

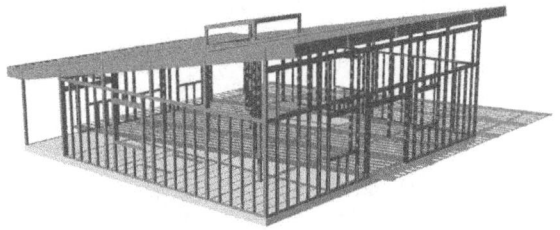

Figure 4. Axon by Molly Salafia and Josh Roth, Spring 2006.

Conclusions:

Teaching structures as design through structural design exercises has proven to be a successful way to actively engage students in an active learning environment. By refocusing structures courses on form finding and only using specific structural calculations to check and confirm schematic designs, architecture students realize the role calculations play in the overall design process. It is apparent, after several semesters of assigning structural design exercises that students gain a better understanding of the role that structural design can play in creating great architecture.

Notes:

1. These observations are based on my own teaching experiences, informal research of architecture program websites, as well as through discussions with colleagues at various institutions.

2. For a clear discussion of the importance of load paths see: Taly Narendra, "Continuous Load Paths." *Structural Engineer* Nov. 2003: 36-42.

3. To date, I have only assigned structural design exercises to students who have already taken statics and strength of materials courses. However, given the fruitful discussions with student teams and the positive feedback received from students during these assignments it is evident that teaching structural concepts as design should work at introductory levels as well.

Acknowledgements:

The first versions of the structural design exercises were born out of many informative and inspiring conversations with Edward Allen. He has also been kind enough, on several occasions, to participate in informal reviews of student's projects based on theses exercises. For all his help, I am deeply indebted. I would also like to thank the numerous students and teaching assistants that have greatly influenced the development of these exercises.

Structural Education in Design Build Studios:

Questions of Practicality in Student Design Build Projects

Phillip Gallegos
University of Colorado

Pedagogical Context

"Science and technology may change fast enough for the media, but built architecture and urbanism are typically too slow, complicated, and expensive. Although the build environment is becoming less permanent, it is still society's biggest investment and one its longest-lived artifacts." [1]

In the world of practice and the marketplace of ideas, speed of delivery is valued above all else. The market place of architectural practice began to deal with the need for fast-tracked project delivery and it has evolved into design-build under pressure from the construction industry. Design-build has grown partially in response for speed of project delivery. One of the current trends developing in the design-build environment is the integration of disciplines, technologies, the trades, and management as a baseline team for the delivery of architectural and engineering projects in the built environment.

Yet, the act of construction and the *individual* skill sets and technical knowledge base required to produce fast tracked, fully integrated, on time, under budget and efficient buildings or structures remain the same. Principles of structures have not changed, only the speed of engagement of basic principles. The manner and important primacy of calculation is viewed differently in the delivery of projects.

Thus, what has changed significantly is the viewpoint; the way design professionals are utilizing the basic skill sets of structural analysis environmental controls and construction techniques. Schools of architecture have begun to emulate the marketplace, with experiments in design, materials, form-making, and fabrication techniques applied in design-build studios, activities, and fabrications.

Critical questions arise regarding structural technologies in educational curricula. What is the role of traditional structural technologies? How do we deal with traditional, basic structural calculations in education when they are under pressure for speedy delivery of answers? While analysis techniques such as statics, mechanics, structural analysis, and material design can be computed at ever-faster rates, in the world of integrated delivery of design-build services, what are the lessons for the educational enterprises?

Once the foundational structural principles are presented to students, a number of possibilities exist to imbue meaning, understanding and purpose to structural principles.

Pedagogical Responses

Typical educational responses to impart meaning to structural calculations can be categorized in several major areas.

First, in recognition of the world of rapid media, virtual evidence of calculated structural forms and materials can be modeled. Several programs currently exist and continue to be developed in which spans, heights, and composite structural systems can be both viewed, and calculated by students. Textbook publishers have supported the exploration of virtual representation in structural calculation of components and assemblies. Wire frame representations are omni present in structural education.

Second, in response to the environment that favors speed and accuracy, digital fabrication has also emerged from the virtual world with multiple experiments in materials, assemblies, and reconfiguration of built components for architecture students to explore. A wide variety of studio activity currently exists that require full-scale fabrication precisely calculated for exploration of forms as structurally important design experiments. Fabrication issues deal with the full-scale problem of materials, joint calculation, and assemblies, even if it only fits in one room.

Third, in the traditional of the Beaux Arts and Modernist movements, real modeling of structural behavior to explore basic principles continues to be a requirement for many first year students, as well as capstone experiences. Many schools still utilize full-scale sections, scaled models, or components that can be tested in simulation of structural conditions, joints, and maerials.

Fourth, the emergence of design-build studios in schools, as in professional practice, has required the integration of multiple building technologies with management and professional systems. Structural technology and material systems have taken on an increased importance since school projects at full scale are often shells or portions of buildings that explore building forms. Shells and material forms seem to be a favorite since they can be highly expressive and open to form manipulation.

All four of these approaches of structural principles have the advantage of immediate application of basic calculation and understanding at some level for students. Each process can be significant for students with a diversity of learning styles. Design-build studios and construction activities have their own advantage for educational goals and embedding learned structural behaviors.

University of Colorado Design Build History

At the University of Colorado, as at many schools of architecture, a 15-year design-build program has built numerous student designed projects in the summer semester. The program began as an outgrowth of the structures coursework. Structures coursework presented traditional exercise problems to be solved. However, students did not know how to set up the analysis of a problem. The first exercises engaged 15 years ago were the requirements for students to design a small artifact and then provide an analysis. When a community approached the class to build one of the artifacts, the design-build program was born.

The program that began as a structural design exercise became a full-fledged construction program. The program, of necessity, was required to integrate structural and building technologies into a design-build competition and, later, the studio. The resultant construction program dealt with a microcosm of the entire building process with a heavy emphasis on structurally significant form and materials.

Of necessity, the design-build program deals with multiple facets of the building beyond structural technologies including estimating, scheduling, negotiations, contracts, insurance, risk management, project management, and communications. Yet, given the nature of the original program focus on structures, structural technology crosses all the disciplines. In the context of design and construction, structural technologies, i.e., statics, structural analysis, and material design react in a fluid process with materials, insurance, contracts, costs, and construction efficiencies. Since the program is in a school of architecture, of course, the primary driver of exploration is design intent, design investigation, and even some theoretical debate, While it is tempting to create a design environment in which structural determinism and material essentially predominates all activities, the truth is that all facets of design, analysis and construction compete for central attention at any point. Taken in that context, structural technologies become as important as material selection and form.

The lessons of recent design build activity has pointed to delivery systems in which all parts of design are simultaneously important, central, and, yet paradoxically, subordinate to the goal of collaborative efforts and processes that require considerations of efficiencies and aesthetics. Structural technology has been required to occupy the role of prime importance and simultaneously secondary role. Design-build activity has provided legitimacy of structural technology in the minds of students since they are mandated to a hierarchy of priorities in response to design intent.

Three Comparison Projects

The current student design-build studio has produced external classrooms and some shade structures in public parks for local communities. Students are required to work in teams and prepare competitive design alternatives to the communities

The three chronicled student projects for comparison are:

- Denver Fairmount Elementary School Outdoor Classroom, 2001

- Lyons Colorado Park Community Stage, 2004

- Montrose Colorado Cerise Community Park Entrance Shelter, 2005

Figure 1. Fairview Elementary, Denver, 2001

Figure 2. Lyons Park Community Stage, 2004

Denver Farimount Elementary School was designed as an outdoor sun dial with double sided roof and strategically placed roof openings designed to cast sunlight on the ground plane. Given the requirement for control of sunlight, the object was designed as a fixed benchmark in space placed upon a base of columns.

The studio design team conducted a full classroom discussion on the implication of wind. The intuitive discussion and scaled model investigations revealed problems with torsion loads at the base. The studio divided the problem into straight beam calculations, the steel arch, and the torsion load problem. One student, a former aerodynamic engineer, led the group exploration of torsion load. During a site visit to the new Mile High Stadium, which was being constructed under a design–build program, a similar condition was observed. The group, with encouragement, decided to add additional struts at the column connection and strengthened the concrete column. The aeronautical engineer, Bob Dawson, led the group in an exercise in which he simulated the torsion wind loads. Details were selected and designed. One requirement of the class placed by the instructor was for redundancy in structural design. This was due to the relatively low construction skill level of students.

<u>Lyons Community Stage</u> presented another problem for student designers. The cantilever proposed for the stage cover had to be spanned with steel. Driven by the requirement to incorporate donated limestone slab, the winning design team responded by cantilevering over the large slabs. The resultant cantilever was not great but presented problems students had not encountered in previous structures coursework.

The design team was required to provide a team response in which the foundation, the compression struts and tension panels were all combined to extend the cantilever. The instructor set up the calculations and the response team was required to generate beam sizes independently of each other. All answerers were compared and reported to the class. Another group was assigned to verify the calculation. Needless to say, the foundation required significant sizing due to overturning moments.

At least half of the class did not participate in the calculation exercise and simply accepted the reported results. However, upon

Figure 3. Montrose Colorado Park Pavilion

installation of the large foundation base, students not engaged in the calculation asked about the possibility for reduction of foundation size. In the resultant on site discussion, the design team refused to reduce the size of the footing but still reexamined the calculations. Pumping action of the soil condition compounded all of the discussion.

The lessons learned by the lead team and the student non-structural questions was profound experience for the students. The entire construct could be represented as one large force diagram which was comprehended by most. It is clear that lessons are passed from student to student upon completion of each project. There seems to be a lore and mystique about the need to solve physical structural problems. However, each session seems to end with the possibilities and potential not realized by each session. Since the emphasis is on structures, each class seems to inspire the next to experiment further than the previous group.

Montrose, Colorado Park Pavilion was one such experiment that grew from the knowledge that the previous year had produced full-scale physical results that could be expanded. The winning design team proposed a very large span with curved steel elements. When confronted by budget, fabrication, and span problems, the group researched, altered and reconsidered assumptions in order to achieve their design intent.

The excessive span condition caused the students to transform the curved roof into an open shading device. Thus, there were no live loads to carry such as snow. The eccentric connection forced the group to increase the column size and reduce its height in order to achieve stability from torsion loading. The increased column size also facilitated connections requirements. The curved steel form, which required reshaping in the directions perpendicular to the X-X axis of the section caused them to research and find a manufacturer who could accomplished it within the budget. Fully half of the cost of the project was in the rolled steel. In addition, the rolled steel was not as accurate as required for construction and students had to review calculation in the field for the final assembly.

Conclusions

Design-build activity in the marketplace has responded to requirements for tight budgets, speedy delivery of projects, and central managerial control. Design-build activities in schools of architecture have often been implemented in order to teach, experiment with materials and forms, and create a critical dialogue between design and construction.

Design-build studios do not seem appropriate for teaching primary structural principles such as vector analysis, moment or shear diagrams. If this knowledge base is not present to some degree in students, the dialogue cannot identify significant and critical design choices. Design-build studios or competitions do foster significant dialogue between calculation, as a basis for understanding construction problems, and the latitude for change in the field. In studio activity or the market place, speed of decisions, accuracy of information, and efficiency of construction means are paramount. It is clear that structures can be a group consensus based upon individual preparations and ordering of the problem sets.

Speed of calculation does not guarantee accuracy of construction or efficiencies. In a fluid decision making environment of construction, rapid answers with acceptable variations on material response is required in order to make decisions. In the final analysis, students do not yet have all the experiences that may tell them what the acceptable range for variations in construction may be possible. Many structures courses, my included, are very linear and sometimes give the impression that all calculation and resultant details are linear, logical and without many alternatives.

In order to make field decisions, architects and builders must be use experience gained from many works to make rapid and critical decisions that will guarantee structural safety. Without a full-scale project such as those in design-build education, students cannot enter the profession with confidence to take leadership positions in the construction industry. The best result of the design-build studio activity is to understand the integrated decision making implications of the project as a whole. Equally important is an appreciation of the simultaneously importance and subordinate role of structure and materials. Structural principles must be honored to insure safety, but design can guide the selection of the range of possible physical responses. These are all things the practicing profession and instructors are acutely aware, but students gain a deeply embedded understanding when the also must respond in a guided, yet urgent fashion during the design-build construction phase.

References:

Ambrose, James. Building Structures. New York: John Wiley and Sons, 1993.

Notes:

[1] Douglas Kelbaugh, "Seven Fallacies in Architectural Culture," *Journal of Architectural Education*, 2004, p. 68.

Architect as Form-maker: A Fundamental Approach to Architectural Structures

Dana K. Gulling
Professor, Savannah College of Art Design

Introduction

The profession of architecture began as the practice of all things relating to building and building construction, including materials, structure, design, program, clients, and code. There was no differentiation between the architect, the engineer, the surveyor, and the contractor; as Vitruvius indicated in his treatise they were all one and the same. In Kiernan and Timberlake's book, Refabricating Architecture, they define the idealized architect as one of master builder. A master builder combines the role of architect, builder, engineer, and scientist. Kiernan and Timberlake point out that until the recent few hundred years, most buildings were designed and erected by master builders (29).

Because of a dramatic increase in available materials, building components, electrical and plumbing systems, and environmental controls there are too many components for today's architect and so they are no longer master builders. As Kieran and Timberlake point out, "Most buildings are no longer simple vessels, shells formed around a use, but machines of enormous complexity, coursed through by numerous systems that control the environment of its interior and connect it to the external world" (29). It is this complexity of the profession that has lead the architect to relinquish primary control of the art and science of building. We are no longer the master builder, testing and controlling all aspects of the design. Instead we have relegated ourselves to the only aspect we feel adequately capable to control—the building's appearance.

Unlike the earlier days of the master builder and a more simplified building process, architects cannot be responsible for all aspects of construction. Architects need to delegate the work and responsibility of designing our complex buildings by utilizing the expertise of engineers, contractors, and product specialists in order to design the specifics of their systems. Architects should not however, rely on those consultants to integrate their systems into the building design. Instead, the architect should be able to utilize fundamental concepts from these areas for the overall building design. It is these concepts that affect the architectural form of the building. The architect should not be the marginalized role of aesthetician, but should be the building's form-maker. Not only does the building's aesthetics affect building form, but so too do the environmental, structural, and tectonic systems. Because of this we need to bring the responsibility for the fundamentals of those areas back into the architectural profession.

In order for the architect's role to shift into one of form-maker, we need to alter the teaching of our architectural students. The typical pedagogy of the past has been to pressure architecture students into understanding and calculating all aspects of the building through their support classes. In Environmental Controls, Building Technology, Acoustics and Lighting, and Structures, we tell the students that they will be liable for their consultants' decisions. This fear of liability is perpetuated by academia by the professors we typically hire to teach those technology classes. For an environmental controls class the department may hire an engineer or someone with a building science degree and often structural engineers teach the structures classes. These professors are very qualified to teach the subject matter and may spend a great deal of the class time on a in depth study and quantitative analysis of the problems, without relating the issues to the qualitative nature of the architect as form-maker. In the end these professors are amazed and frustrated by the lack of enthusiasm that their students have for their class, finding themselves in a constant battle with the studio course workloads. To help combat what is seen as student apathy, the professors insist that their class information is inherent to the student's success as an architect and without it they will not succeed. What academia does not promote is that by understanding the technology fundamentals, without an in-depth knowledge of the subject, one can still be a successful architect.

The architect as form-maker reinforces the education of the architect as one of problem-solver. The architect is required to quickly assess problems from a variety of trades and come up with a design solution that best addresses those trades along with his or her architectural agenda. To broaden the education of the architect not only as a designer or technological manager, we need to bridge into the area of problem solving. We need to bring the concepts from our architectural support classes by engaging them with the design process. Historically the support classes, especially environmental controls and structures, have focused on the quantitative aspects of the topic without addressing some of the more qualitative practices. By combining both the quantitative and qualitative, we can utilize concepts from the support courses to teach our students a more integrated design process.

Quantitative and Qualitative Approaches

In order to imbue our architecture students with the ideal of the architect as form-maker, we need our technology support courses to engage the students through the design process. By illustrating the courses' connection to the architectural design process, we will cease battling with the studio workloads and begin engaging our students by demonstrating the link between technology and design. Technology should not something that is applied to a building once the design has been completed, but instead should affect the shape, expression, and organization of the overall form. This understanding of architect as form-maker will lead us away from the focus of the technology support courses from a quantitative class to one that also focuses on the qualitative concepts.

It is the quantitative aspects of our courses that specifically size our building components; however, in practice, it is rare that the specific size of any component has a major impact on the architectural form. During the early design phases, sizing ducts to handle the acceptable CFM or finding the correct section modulus of a beam have little relevance to either the architectural student or the architect. For the early phases, it is the concepts from these courses that affect the building form and thus the design process. Later, as the building's design progresses, the specifics of those trades can have an impact on the building's dimensions and because of that, architecture students need the fundamental language and tools of the consultants in order to work with them to finalize the building.

For most programs, the battle between the technology support courses and the studio's design focus is most clearly exemplified by the structures sequence. Historically, this course has been math-based in its focus and those students who are less skilled in advanced math find themselves struggling with the quantitative content, lost in the information, and thus disconnected from the subject's fundamentals. As educators, our failure is this disconnect. In the end it is often these frustrated students who ask, "Why are we learning this? Isn't this why we hire structural engineers?" Students need to know that although they may have difficulty with their calculations, they can still design using a building's structural fundamentals, creating buildings that are tectonic, logically organized, and structurally coordinated. These structural fundamentals are not the responsibility of the engineer, but are the responsibility of the form-maker.

It is difficult to find one textbook that properly mixes the required amount of quantitative study, analysis, and problem solving with an engaging amount of qualitative or fundamental work for many of the architectural support courses. Usually, the quantitative texts are written by engineers, who attempt to thin the material for the architecture students. For our structures classes, we use books titled with the phrases "Simplified Engineering" and "Elementary Structures"[1]. These texts tend to be quantitatively focused, statically solving structures and sizing the members. They also tend to have less of a relation to the architect's role in structural design, but are instead more focuses on the engineer's interrelationship with the architect. Finally, these texts often utilize the abstracted free-body diagram, or FBD, for developing solutions rather than the architectural reality of the structure.

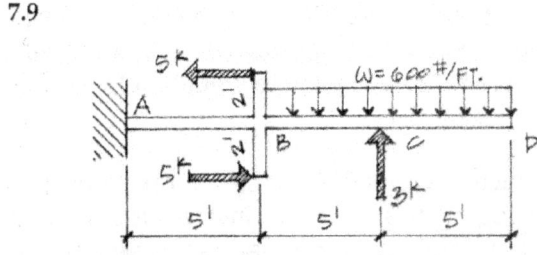

Figure 1. Free-Body Diagram problem, typical in architectural structures classes (Onouye, 372).

Schodek, in his textbook titled Structures, states that the FBD "shows the complete system of applied and reactive forces acting on a body" (42). The FBD is an abstraction designed to reduce the structural components into isolated elements in order to make mathematical computations easier. Oftentimes, in order to teach the mathematics, the FBD's of the given problem are too complex, demonstrating a particular loading that would be rare in the reality of building design. See Figure 1. The FBD is the first step for structural designers to find the loads, stresses, and strains on structural members, but often the FBD is the only presentation of a problem and thus is the only exposure that students have with the required computations. They no longer understand the FBD as a necessary abstraction that is created to find the solution, but understand it as the problem itself. This is not to say that the FBD is at fault for this lack of connection; it is a powerful tool, stripping a structural problem down to its essential elements. However, we need students to also learn to relate the FBD to the structure and the architectural design.

Almost all of the quantitatively focused structures texts tend to focus on the breaking down of their information into easily digestible chunks for the students. For beams, FBD's are used to find the beam's reactions. If given a particular loading on a beam and its reactions, students are asked to draw the beam's shear and moment diagrams. If given a maximum moment, students are asked to find the beam's maximum bending stress. The texts and the homework problems are often presented in this step-by-step process, building the learning of one task upon the other. At the same time, in order to alleviate our assessment of our students, we tend to test the student's learning though a breakdown of the problem into easily regurgitated pieces. Our assessment for the minimum standards of the architectural profession, the Architecture Review Exam (A.R.E.), also is an illustration of this piecemeal approach. According to the Ballast's Guide to the A.R.E. "For the structural portions of the exam, extensive complete calculations of a structural problem are usually not required.... Instead, you should expect to do portions of a calculation in order to answer a question." (xii). Because of this, students find it difficult to understand how each of these steps relates to the overall solution for the building's structural components and the overall building design.

Despite the quantitative approach of many structure textbooks, there are structures books written by architects that are much more qualitative in nature. These texts tend to demonstrate the inherent link between architecture, structures and design, using existing architectural buildings to demonstrate their structural concepts. These books have titles such as "Shaping Structures" and "Understanding Structures"[2]. Focusing less on the mathematical computations, these texts illustrate clear structural principles by discussing structural concepts. These books use either existing buildings to teach the structural concepts (supported by limited mathematical work) or they discuss the design of a few simple buildings through potential structural systems and detailing.

Although these texts do cover a great deal of the subject's concepts they also use mathematics to support those concepts. The books limit the use of the FBD. Instead of relying on mathematics for solving reactions and force components, they use the less precise and often confusing graphic approach. These textbooks often also focus on the building statics, while devoting little attention to material strengths, designing structural members or testing connections. Because of these shortcomings these texts provide good companion material for the course sequence, but often do not provide enough information to be the sole course's textbook.

Lessening structure's quantitative approach for one inclusive of its qualitative aspects better demonstrates to the students their role in the architectural profession. Architects tend to spend little of their career completing calculations for their designed buildings and instead often employ a structural engineer. This may be due in part to building designs leading to an increase in structural complexity, a fear of liability, or the prolific availability of sizing charts for fabricated members.

Conversely, focusing solely on structure's qualitative issues instead of the quantitative components will not teach the subject's fundamentals either. Through the mathematical equations, students can predict how building or building components will behave and can help them in the structural material and size selection process. The concepts of the equations can answer questions such as "Should you raise or lower a column's slenderness ratio to carry more load?" or "Do you need to select a beam with a higher or lower section modulus?" It is the combination of quantitative and qualitative approaches that is the subject's fundamentals.

Teaching both quantitatively and qualitatively encourages a variety of student strengths. Students who find it easy to complete the mathematical computations should also understand the descriptive subject matter and those students who excel at the descriptive aspects should use those aspects to better understand the mathematical components. The A.R.E. study guides and exam also reinforce studying the subject's fundamentals. The study advice offered in the Ballast's Guide states, "You are generally better off reviewing the concepts of all the divisions of the test than becoming an overnight expert in one area." (xiii). The exam's intent is to test the beginning architect's ability to select what is needed to solve a problem rather than the solution of the problem itself.

I have developed my structures course by engaging the students in the fundamentals and reinforcing the ideal of the architect as form-maker. I teach the second structures course of a three-course sequence. This is a materials structure course focusing on the design of wood and steel beams, columns, and connections. As part of the class, I teach vertical load tracing and review other statics work, including shear and bending diagrams. For this course, I have developed two student projects. The first project is a structural research project. Completed early in the quarter, it is the analysis of an existing architecturally and structurally significant building. The students are required to research the building, study its structure, and create a diagrammatic structural model that is a tectonic representation of the original building. Through this project students conceptualize the load path for the building, abstract material properties and joinery, understand potential structural weaknesses, and hypothesize structural improvements. The second project, which starts at the middle of the quarter and is due on the last day of class, is a structural design project. Here the students are asked to architecturally and structurally design a building. Architecturally, the design project is fairly simple and is required to use steel as its structural material. The focus for this project and the most difficult aspects for the students to master is not the actual sizing of the beams, columns, connections, and foundations, but instead is the iterative process of architecturally designing a building with its structural system.

Structural Research Project

In pairs, students are asked to research the building's structural systems, focusing on either the entire structure or a significant structural component, and present their findings to the class. The student presentations may contain an architectural overview of the project, with the majority of the presentation on the building's structure. A variety of issues can be addressed such as materials, loading conditions, construction sequencing, structural failure, and/or structural uniqueness. The buildings researched for this project are fairly complex and would require an engineer to fully design the building's structural members.

Figure 2. Tommy Nickoloff and Katie Walker's testing of the Brooklyn Bridge by John Roebling. Still image from video

The list of potential buildings is organized around structural typologies and covers a large historic range, allowing the class to have an exposure to a variety of structures. Because this project occurs at the beginning of the quarter, the focus for the students is less on the quantitative tools that they will learn as the quarter progresses, and instead focuses on the qualitative information such as material properties and structural shapes discussed in the first few classes.

It is a requirement that the construction of the model is consistent with the building's construction. For example, if the building uses a post and beam system, where the columns are separate from the beams, the students are not to build that bay out of a continuous material such as chipboard; or if the building's structure is concrete, a con-

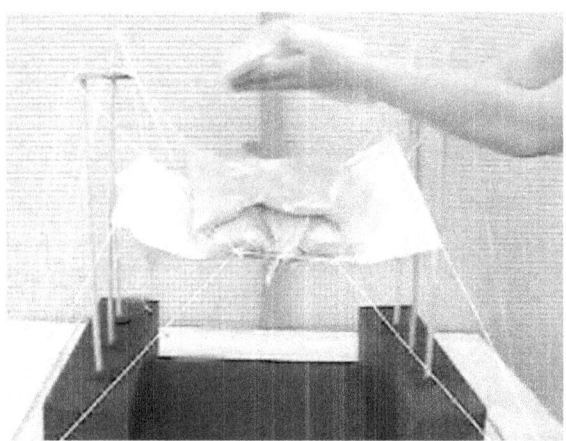

Figure 3. Joe Feys and Caitlin Hill's testing of the Denver International Airport. Still image from video.

tinuous or cast material should be used. Recording the testing process with a video camera, the students are asked to load the project similarly to the actual loading of the building. Because of some building's shapes and because of potentially complex loads, loading the model is a creative task for many projects. If the model does not break, additional or under-designed loading types are applied until destroyed. (An example on an under-designed loading would be adding a lateral load to a post and beam structure.) Teams are to note where structural failures and extreme deflections occur, and to provide potential solutions to ward against future failures.

Through this project students learn how building form dictates structure, but also how the structure informs the building's shape. Tommy Nickoloff and Katie Walker's study of the Brooklyn Bridge illustrates this. See *Figure 2*. The existing structure uses a combination of suspension and cable stays to support the bridge deck. Similar to the cable anchoring of the actual bridge, Nickoloff and Walker provided diagonal support at the end of the model to resolve the lateral and vertical forces exerted by the main cables. As the cables were tightened, a bending stress was produced on the deck, causing a camber in the structure. It was this prestressed camber that counteracted the added live load during the testing process, thus resulting in a lowered bending stress for the deck and ultimately a higher load for the structure.

Students are also required to think dynamically in order to solve the problem of applying complex loads or loads to a complexly

Figure 4. Lauren Mollica and Peter Adams' testing of the Olympic Games Tent by Gunter Behnisch. Still images from video. Shown are 30 mph wind, 50 mph wind, and final failure due to uplift.

shaped structure. To test vertical live loads caused by snow on the roof of the Denver International Airport, Joe Fey and Caitlin Hill used bags of sand. *See Figure 3.* The sand acted similarly to the snow, by settling into the valleys of the structure while placing less of a load on the roof peaks. Post-failure discussion concluded that the building's design for a non-symmetrical tensile roof form resulted in uneven lateral loads on the masts, thus introducing a bending stress. Instead of changing the iconic form of the building by re-orienting the masts to bisect the roof's angle, the students suggested that the mast's moment of inertia should be increased to reduce bending stress. Students also noted that the central masts carried a larger load than the exterior masts because of their larger tributary areas.

Lauren Mollica and Peter Adams also studied a tensile structure though their analysis of the Olympic Games Tent in Munich, Germany. *See Figure 4.* They tested their diagrammatic model in heavy wind conditions, by placing it on the cab roof of a pickup truck and driving with an ever-increasing speed. They hypothesized that the tension members' connection at the base would fail. In their model they had glued the tension members into the base, protecting those members from uplift; however they had hooked the tension cables into the top of the compression mast, thereby not protecting the connection—and ultimately the structure—from uplift forces, causing final failure.

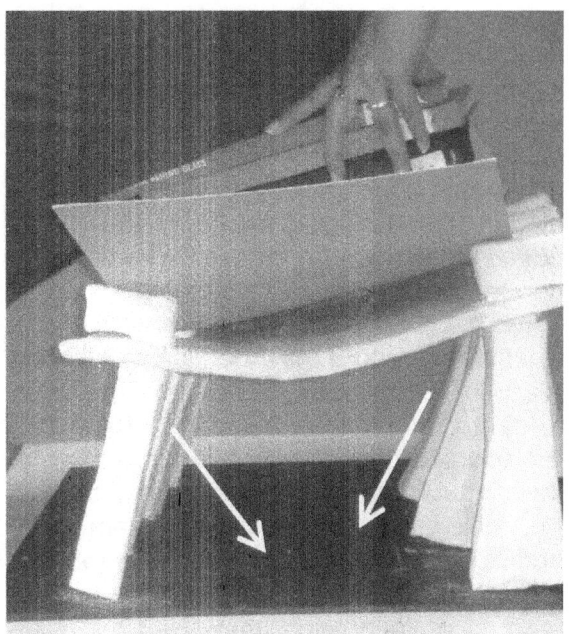

Figure 5. DJ Benn and Sonia Carias's testing of the Dulles International Airport. Resistive compression forces in the roof prevent the building's columns from collapsing inward.

Through their diagrammatic models, students are also asked to indicate actual building material properties by the selection of proper model materials and abstracted joints. Abstracting materials requires that the student understand the actual structural material properties and connection strengths while conceptualizing those materials and joints used for the model construction. For some students it is difficult to separate the finish material from the properties of the structural materials. In the diagrammatic model constructed by DJ Benn and Sonia Carias of Dulles International

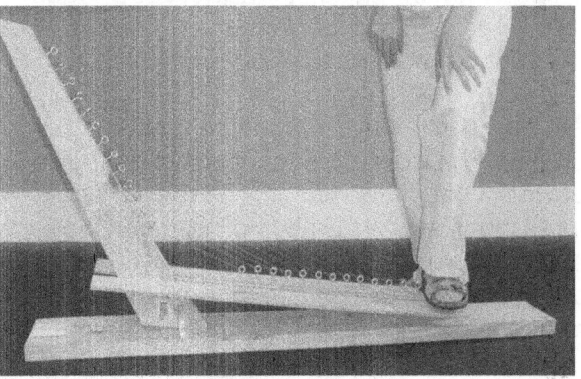

Figure 6. Brian Green and Stacy Sheridan Alamillo Bridge by Santiago Calatrava. Failure for testing occurred at the pin connection of the mast.

Airport, they utilized plaster-of-Paris to represent the terminal's concrete roof. *See Figure 5*. This model's material represented the finish of the concrete of the roof, but failed to represent the tensile nature of the actual roof structure's steel cables. Because of this, the deflected shape of the model during testing was an unrealistic representation of the building.

Brian Green and Stacy Sheridan studied the Alamillo Bridge, by Santiago Calatrava. They constructed an elaborate model that represented the compression member of the singular mast, the tension members of the cable stays, and the central beam of the bridge deck. *See Figure 6*. To abstract the assumed pin connection of the singular mast to its foundation, they used two steel L-brackets screwed to both sides of the mast. For loading, Green and Sheridan chose to stand on the free end, adding a great deal of live load at a distance far from its support; thus creating a large moment at the joint. Because of the correct abstraction of the joint as an assumed pin connection, the structure quickly failed at this joint. The class discussed the typical loading issues for this bridge through the model's failure. The compressive mast and its weight resist the bridge loads, but as is typical with most bridges there is a very high dead load relative to a proportionally low live load. Because of this, an engineer can predict the majority of loading that the structure will experience and thus design the mast with a pin connection to resist the bridge's vertical loads. It is only when the live loads become proportionately higher than the dead loads that a resistant moment must be created at the joint for the structure to remain stable.

As demonstrated through the student examples, this structural research project is a powerful teaching tool for teaching structures qualitatively. It should be noted however, that the project does have some drawbacks. Because these are diagrammatic models, they neither depict the actual building structure nor the actual potential for building failures. Teams that diagram and test buildings selected by earlier teams will find that their model will not fail in the same manner. The diagrammatic model is merely an abstraction of the structure and so the model testing is only indicative of potential structural weaknesses for that building type. The focus for this project is qualitative in nature, and does not allow for any quantitative testing. This is partially due to the aforementioned abstraction of structure and building materials but can also be attributed to the square-cube effect. Simply put, the allowable stress of a member is based on the cross-sectional area of that member and the units of measurement is squared whereas the weight of the scalable model is a function of density and volume and is expressed in cubic units. Because of the square-cube effect, there is not a linear relationship between strength of the model relative to its scale.

Many of the researched buildings for this project would have required an engineer to fully resolve the building's structural components and systems. However, this project demonstrates that the architect, by understanding the architectural form, its relationship to the structure, and the applied loads, can discover the building's structural fundamentals and can easily understand a building's potential structural strengths, weaknesses, and failures.

Structural Design Project

The second of the two projects is introduced in the middle of the quarter and is completed on the last day of class as a cumulative assessment of the students' learning. This project teaches more of the subject's fundamentals—both the quantitative and qualitative tools learned throughout the quarter. Even though students have to trace the loads and size structural members and connections to complete this project, its focus is not on their quantitative solutions, as

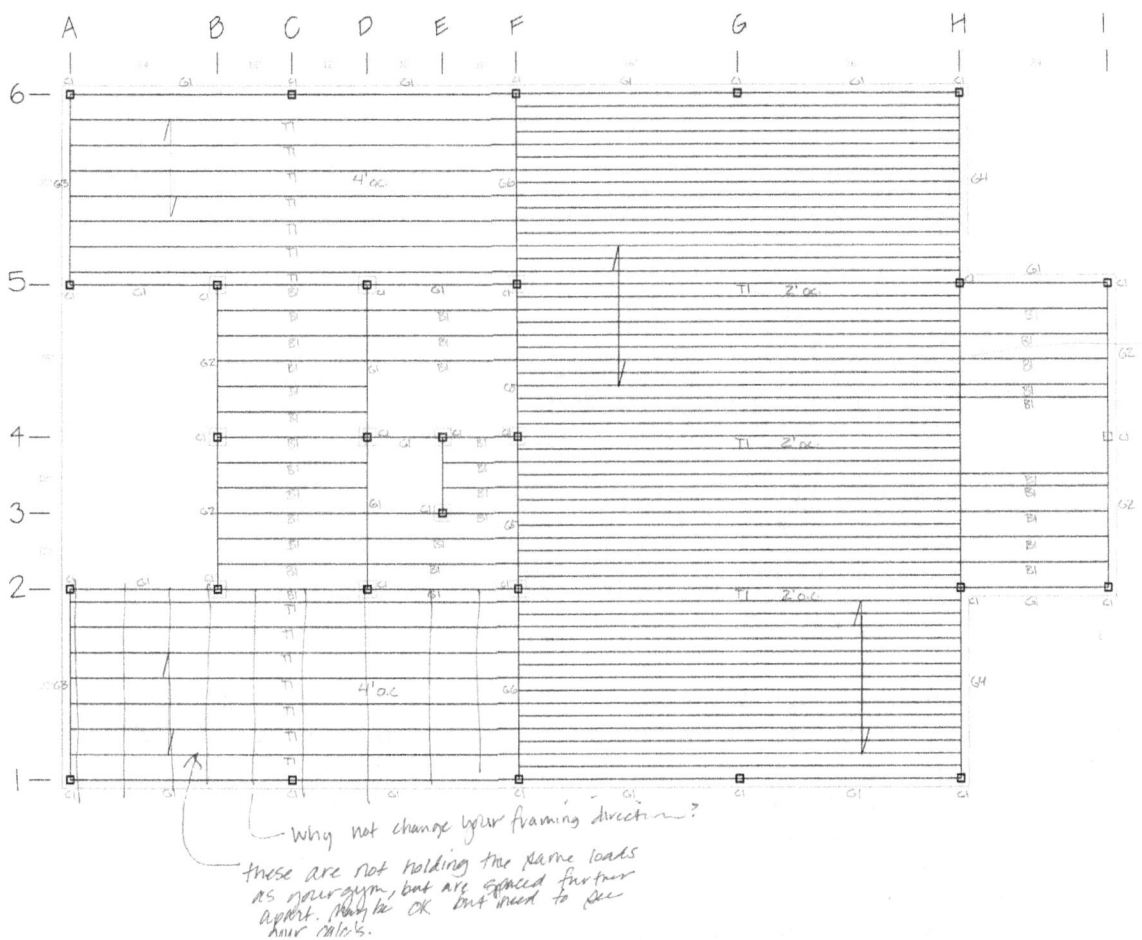

Figure 7. A Structural Design Project completed by Nicolas Loeper and Ryan Meres, showing their first floor structural plan for a small YMCA. Comments on the drawing are by the author.

they are provided with the American Institute of Steel Construction (AISC) Manual charts and graphs that reduce their arithmetic to a minimum. Instead, this project links the structures class to the design process and teaches students that decisions cannot be made structurally that do not affect the architecture and vice versa.

This project's description calls for a fictional building design set in Goshen, New York. The project is architecturally fairly simple—usually an office building or a small YMCA. Both buildings use rolled sections for their horizontal spanning members, with the YMCA also using long-span joists over the gymnasium and swimming pool. A non-composite steel decking with a topping slab is to span between the beams and/ or joists.

Rolled sections are used for the columns, and bolts and clip angles are used for the standard connections. Holes in the floor structure must be provided for two fire-stairs and an elevator. Depending upon the building assigned, four or six Trane HVAC units are to be placed on the roof. Cut-sheets are provided to the students for load and size reference. Geotechnical information for the site is also provided to size the foundations. Various supporting charts are given to them, including: weights of elements of building construction (for dead loads), building code requirements for uniform live loads, minimum roof live loads, soil bearing capacities, and excerpts from the Vulcraft catalog to specify the required decking and steel joists.

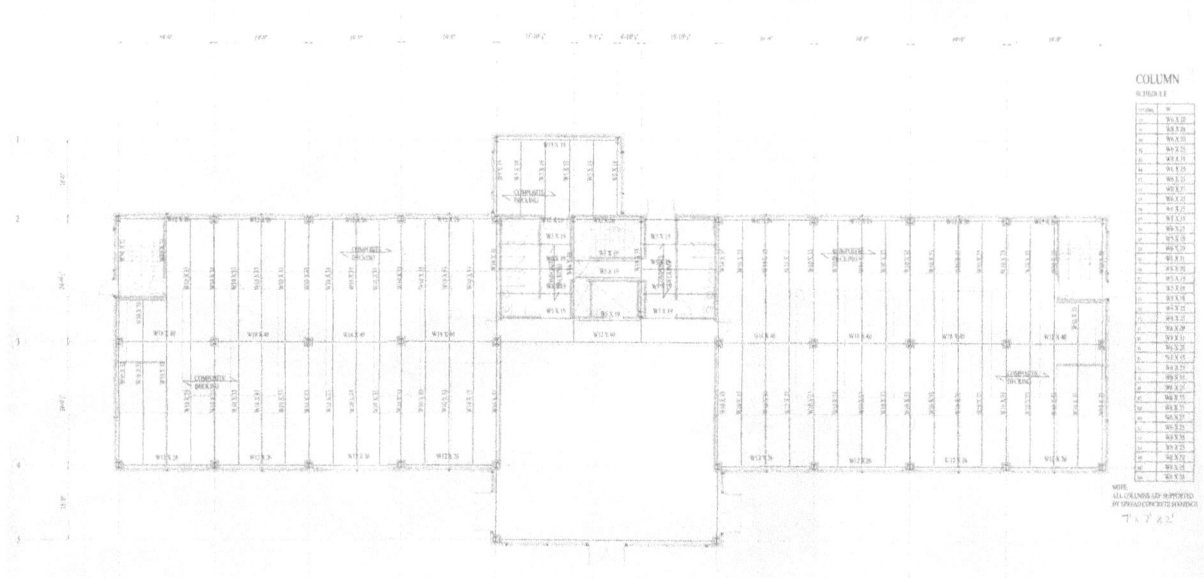

Figure 8. Joshua Younger's first floor structural plan for an office building.

Students are required to design a building that meets the criteria established by the program, the applicable codes and, that once built, would be structural sound. They are to determine all of the loads on the structural members—including, but not limited to: decking, beams, girders, columns, foundation and connections. Because this is a structures course, students are asked to focus on the structure for the building, rather than the architecture. However, it is important that they demonstrate that the structure has been coordinated with the architectural plan and that coordination is illustrated in both plan and section.

As part of the final presentation, students are to provide a foundation, architectural and structural floor plans; one elevation, to denote exterior finish materials; and a transverse section, to indicate floor-to-floor heights. Dimensions, direction of decking and joists, and a structural grid must also be included. Students are not required to size every structural member for their building, but are asked to focus their efforts on the members that carry the largest loads.

Through this project, students learn to create a structural grid, and coordinate that grid with the building's architectural plan. Often, because it is something with which they are very familiar, the students begin with the architectural plan and then attempt to organize the structural bays around their architectural plans. For the first pass, the students usually place columns within a majority of the interior walls, wherever they may be located, creating a very complicated structural grid and a very inefficient structural organization. *See Figure 7.* Here, because of the designed joist orientation, very deep joists are required to span the seventy-two feet from grid line A to grid line F. Simply re-orienting the joists to span the thirty feet between lines 1 and 2, and 5 and 6 would have allowed for joists with much less depth. Also, the students restricted their horizontal members to a four foot module over the building's support spaces. When the building dimensions were in conflict with their established structural module, they simply introduced another beam, essentially doubling the structure. This can be seen in Figure 7 along grid lines 2 and 5.

To combat organizational issues early, we have an interim student pin-up to review their initial designs. Students are encouraged to reorganize their architectural plans

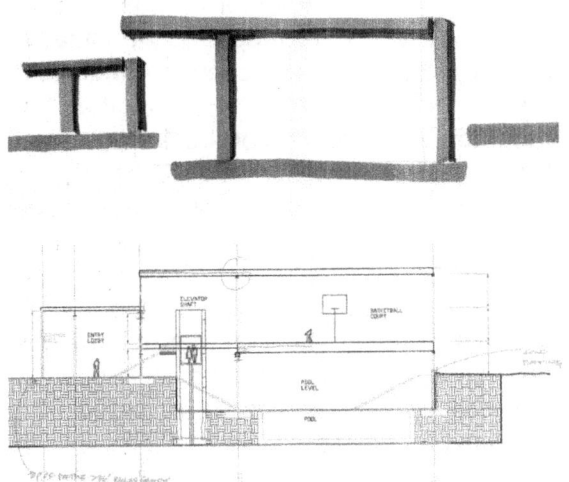

Figure 9. Tommy Nickoloff and DJ Benn's concept sketch and building section for a YMCA. Comments on the drawing are by the author

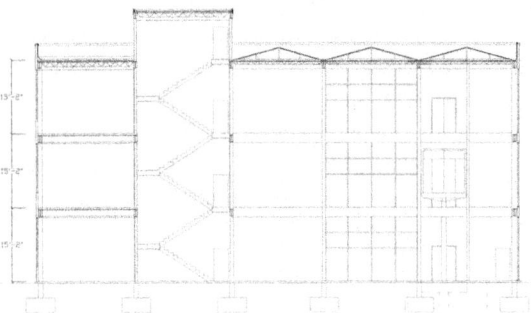

Figure 10. Peter Adams and Porter Wincuinas' building section through the manufactured skylights over their central atrium.

so that there is a consistency in plan for the beam, girders, and columns, reducing the required calculations. This iterative process of the building design is one of the most difficult aspects for the students to master and often they are amazed that the sizing of the members took the least amount of effort, whereas most of their energies are concentrated on the integration of the building's design and its structural clarity. See Figure 8.

Sometimes for the students, the structural concept may actually lead the design process. See Figure 9. For the design of a small YMCA, DJ Benn and Tommy Nickoloff, designed their building using beams with a single overhang. The overhang reduced the maximum moment of the beam, allowing for a smaller section modulus than that of a simply supported beam. Not only did this concept inform the quantitative analysis of their design though the selection of the steel sections, but also helped drive the organization of their building's design through section.

Because of the project's description is fairly loose, students are allowed and encouraged to explore different aspects to their design and calculations. Wanting to use a skylight over their central atrium, Peter Adams and Porter Wincuinas researched skylights manufactures and included the cut sheets and estimated dead loads in their calculations. See Figure 10. Because it is outside the scope of this class, students typically use the easier Method 1 from the Uniform Building Code to calculate the building's snow loads[3]. Occasionally students will investigate more precise methods for calculating a building's snow loads. Josh Younger, in his design for an office building specifically researched how to calculate the snow load requirements for Goshen, NY, by researching New York States' building code.

Conclusion

These two projects focus on the teaching of the fundamentals for an architectural structures course, rather than concentrate on the traditionally quantitative aspects of the course. Through the structural research project student learn problem solving skills filtered though the creation of a diagrammatic structural model. Students are asked to apply complex loading to potentially complex shapes, abstract building material and connection properties, and analyze potential solutions for the structure's failure, presenting their findings to their fellow classmates. During the second half of the quarter, students are asked to complete a structural design project. Typically, the building is fairly simple architecturally in order for the students to focus on the building's structural solution. By designing the building's architectural and structural plans, they are able to understand the interrelationship between these two disciplines. At the same time, the students size all of the building's beams, girders, columns, connections, and footings, bringing together all of their quantitative skills that they learned throughout the quarter. Because of this project's loose description, it is as much as the students make of it. For some students, the structural organization leads the overall concept for the building's form and for others, they complete additional research for some of the calculations. Both of these projects encourage the students to think outside of the box in a class that is typically concerned with how one keeps the box up.

To teach the fundamentals for this structures course, I have integrated quantitative and qualitative approaches through the creation of these projects. I feel that this fundamental approach can be applied to all of the architectural support courses. By understanding the fundamentals and integrating them into design, architects can retake the leadership position in the design process. This will establish the architect as the form-maker; one who can provide a comprehensive aesthetic solution to a building while still allows consultants to perform the specifics of their tasks.

References:

Ballast, David Kent, AIA. Architecture Exam Review: Ballast's Guide to the A.R.E. Volumne 1, "Structural Topics". Belmont, CA: Professional Publications, Inc. 1992.

Kieran, Stephen and James Timberlake. Refabricating Architecture. New York: McGraw-Hill Companies, Inc., 2004.

Onouye, Barry with Kevin Kane. Statics and Strength of Materials for Architecture and Building Construction. Upper Saddle River, NJ: Prentice Hall, 2002.

Schodek, Daniel L. Structures. Upper Saddle River, New Jersey: Prentice-Hall, Inc. 2001.

Notes:

[1] Ambrose, James. SIMPLIFIED ENGINEERING for Architects and Builders. (emphasis in the title). New York: John Wiley & Sons, 2000. and Shaeffer, R.E. Elementary Structures for Architects and Builders. Englewood Cliffs, New Jersey: Prentice Hall, 1988

[2] Zalewski, Waclaw and Edward Allen. Shaping Structures: Statics. New York: John Wiley & Sons, Inc., 1998. Moore, Fuller. Understanding Structures. Boston: WCB/ McGraw-Hill, 1999.

[3] Although it is no longer the nation's primary code, the Uniform Building Code's charts are used in the majority of structures text books and the A.R.E. still relies on this code for a majority of its questions. I do tell students that we can use these charts to learn the process of referencing charts rather than learning the information that the chart provides.

Bridging to Convergence: The Multidisciplinary Dilemma for Beginning Architecture Students

Vincent Hui
University of Waterloo

"...Desire to borrow tools and techniques from elsewhere can only be satisfied effectively when we fracture inviolable discipline boundaries, a change requiring a significant cultural shift."

-Mark Burry[1]

Every good designer has realized that an idea alone, no matter how potent or innovative it may be, is unable to develop into a successful project without both an understanding of the design's dynamics, and ultimately the ability to express the design to others. It is at the intersection of these facets that first year design students often face their greatest obstacle. Neither familiar with how the idea may be brought to reality, nor skilled in the proper conventions of articulation, these students become overwhelmed. Yet specifically in architecture, the traditional pedagogic paradigm for the synergy of these elements has relied on experience, exposure, and development over time.

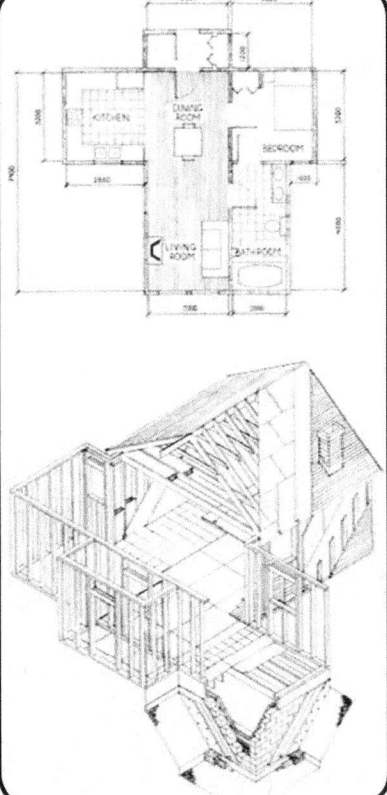

Figure 1: A sampling of projects from a typical first year architecture program that do not directly integrate with each other. (From left to right) A design studio investigation in architectonic form, a residential building construction exercise, and a digital case study model introduce discrete facets of an architectural education.[2]

Worse still, many academics and professionals alike lament the "compartmentalization" of knowledge that has plagued design education over the past two decades, still hoping to see a more holistic and integrated perspective.[3] A change in design pedagogy is required. Rather than see Design as autonomous and "above" the other courses they take, first year design students must approach Design as an intersection and culmination of all courses in their prescribed curriculum. Recent modifications to the first year program at our school of architecture have brought about a paradigm shift, integrating multiple facets (design, technical construction, and digital design and presentation knowledge) to be considered simultaneously rather than autonomously. This paper will discuss how a coordinated, integrated approach to architectural design for beginning students was implemented by following a specific joint project that epitomized the process.

The motivation behind this divergence from traditional design pedagogies comes from the desire to integrate a wider spectrum of tools, knowledge, and techniques to assist first year students in realizing a higher level of design excellence. Far too often first year design students are only able to develop their work to an underdeveloped state due to unfamiliarity with a certain production practices and often also because of a lack of an adequate foundation in proper expression and technology. The two courses taught in the first year program which this paper investigates are building construction and digital visual communication. Though traditionally segregated from design studio, these courses were coordinated to supplement the students' design process. The annual Steel Structures Education Foundation (SSEF) student design competition provided an excellent opportunity to instigate, and subsequently illustrate the success of this pedagogical shift.

The SSEF competition embraces the ideals of an integrative design process whereby students draw on knowledge in structures, fabrication, and materiality in exploring their conceptual design.[4] Students were required to design a single span pedestrian bridge that not only met aesthetic objectives and expression, but also had to exhibit proper building construction knowledge and steel detailing. To cater to these design objectives, pertinent courses were coordinated to ensure students would design with technical as well as execution considerations. The bridge was not simply a design exercise; rather it was the convergence of several disciplines.

The first aspect of the project students had to face was the design itself. Unlike many early formative design projects adopted in design studio courses (such as explorations in patterns, light, or massing), the SSEF bridge required students to address a function as well as a form. Students conceptualized their designs in sketches and quick models. One previous exercise in their parallel design studio required students to suspend the weight of a large ball steel bearing using thin wooden dowels, thread, and glue. Many students learned (with a resounding crash) that the laws of physics can be the harshest design critics. Rather than immediately focusing on traditional fundamental aspects of architectural design studio such as scale or functional programming, it was invaluable for students to begin experimenting with how structures work in a design context. Far too often is this neglected at an introductory level and perpetuated into the industry.[5] By intersecting knowledge from other "non-design" courses with their SSEF designs, students would ideally come to understand the curriculum as intact rather than in disparate elements.

The building construction course covers a wide spectrum of material ranging from masonry to building code with an inclination towards residential construction practice. Despite this, many students in the past have neglected to apply such knowledge in their residential design studio projects and were met with severe criticism. Within the coordinated building construction course, a deep

investigation into steel detailing, construction techniques, and modern precedents were stressed over traditionally discussed topics such as material overlapping with other courses (the historical development of metal in architecture) and overly technical aspects
(engineering specifications). Emphasis on the nature of steel including its modularity of fabrication, rapid erection procedures, strength of components, and the opportunity for architectural expression, encouraged students to consider these aspects for their entries into the SSEF bridge competition. Clearly a focus was put on integrating the knowledge to the students' designs rather than "learning in a vacuum". Traditionally a large problem many first year design students face in design (both in studio and in the industry) is the credulous optimism with which their designs begin, only to have it dashed by the realities of technical details.[7]

If one of the largest problems facing first year design students, specifically in architecture, is the jarring leap they must take when leaving academia for entry into the industry, then the adoption of an integrated interdisciplinary teaching approach is absolutely critical.

The digital communication and design course was coordinated with the students' design process and building construction course. Conventionally similar courses instruct students on the use of computers as a tool for expressing a resolved design (whether one of their own or as a case study) through two and three-dimensional representation at varying degrees of photo-realism. However the true power of computing is its potential as a design tool. Despite the shift of industry and pioneering academics to do so, most design schools fail to capitalize on this ability.[8] Perhaps out

Figure 2: Students investigate aspects of form and function in a pragmatic structure design exercise.[6]

of fear that students will become restricted in their early design process or seduced by imagery over substance, computer use has been a divisive issue among many design instructors. For decades advocates of CAD have bewailed the fact that it has been relegated to generate imagery alone because many traditional instructors refuse computer use on such a premise.[10] Within this course not only was there instruction on traditional means of CAD (computer aided/assisted design), rendering, and photo manipulation, but also a focus on the potential of iterative component design. Students could develop their relatively primitive structural investigations at a higher level in CAD and articulate the finer details and assembly of connections without physically constructing them. The introduction of CAD has often been referred to as "one of the most radical shifts in architectural history concerning their immense formal and procedural implications".[11] The digital realm also afforded students the ability to constantly update, experiment, and alter their designs through the use of parametric tools. In addition to designing their work in CAD, the quick visualization with OpenGL rendering enabled students to view their details in real-time, from all angles. In doing so, students could critically see how their bridge detailing worked (or did not work) and appreciate the process of assembly by rotating and zooming in to parts of their model. With the ability to generate a finer rendered output with Quicktime VRML's, students were able to not only visualize the massing and form of their design but also investigate different qualities of materiality and lighting traditionally very difficult to translate with conventional studio techniques.

This process opened up the potential for students to use digital media in a multitude

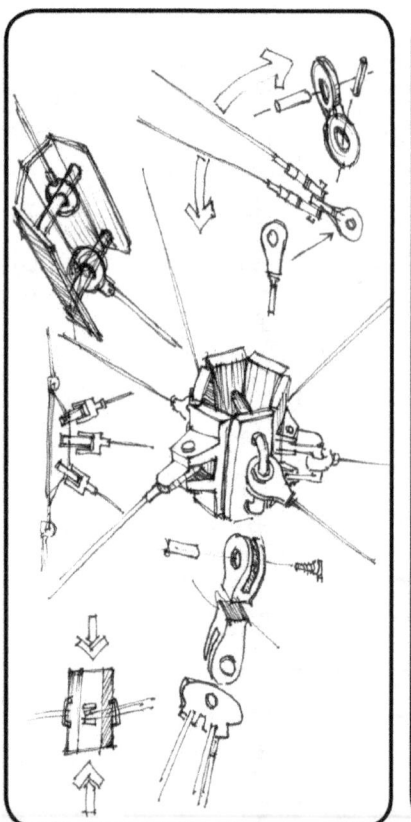
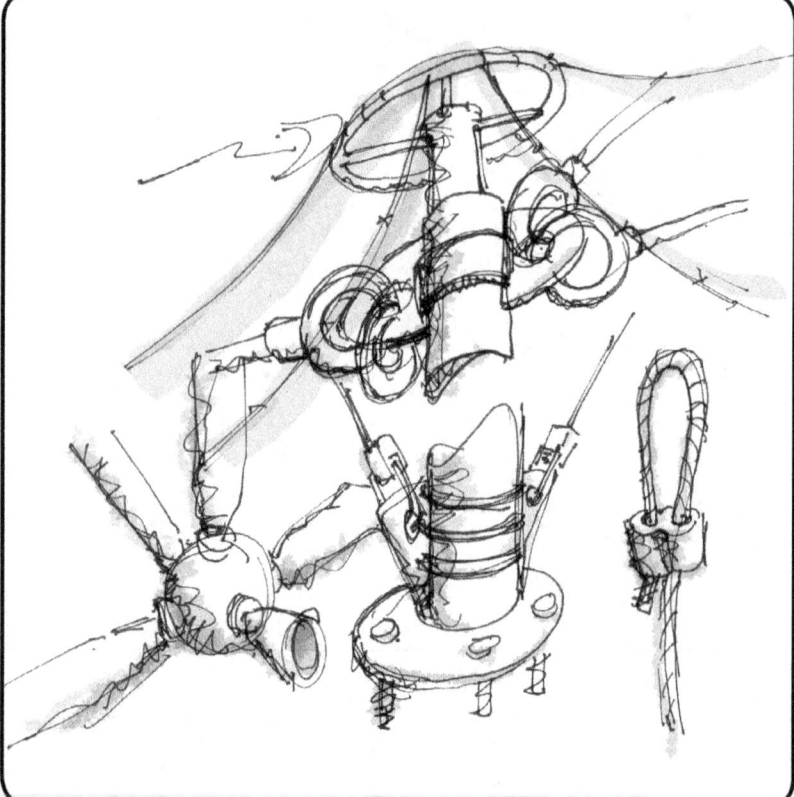

Figure 3: Emphasis on detailing and properties of steel in building construction courses fostered a higher degree of creative comfort for Beginning Design students in their design process.[9]

of design applications from conceptualization to presentation. Furthermore, rather than learning basic commands in various applications, students were able to use these skills in preparing their final presentation. As the SSEF competition required submissions of the design in context, students readily used their knowledge in digital photo montaging to situate their projects in a specific location and activity. Layout and presentation boards were generated for the SSEF entries with applications students had learned in the digital visual communication course.

Ultimately the coordinated integrated design approach proved to be a remarkable success where the class had achieved the highest overall averages in both building construction and digital visual communication in years – as a direct result of the high quality of the integrated approach as reflected in this, their final term project. The higher volume of output and quality of work were all clearly a result of students' avid interest in what they were studying. The students understood the significance the multiple intersections their design endeavors had made with knowledge from other courses. The convergence of knowledge proved to be both an academic and competitive success. The national competition has steadily seen an increase in participants and though official registration into the competition was not mandated from any course, nearly all the students involved in the integrated design curriculum chose to enter the official competition. When the bridge designs were juried for this national competition, half of the top eight entries were Beginning Design students from this program whose projects were the direct result of the integrated coursework. The other finalists were predominantly 3rd year and higher students. Some of these first year students' projects are to be published in an upcoming CAD

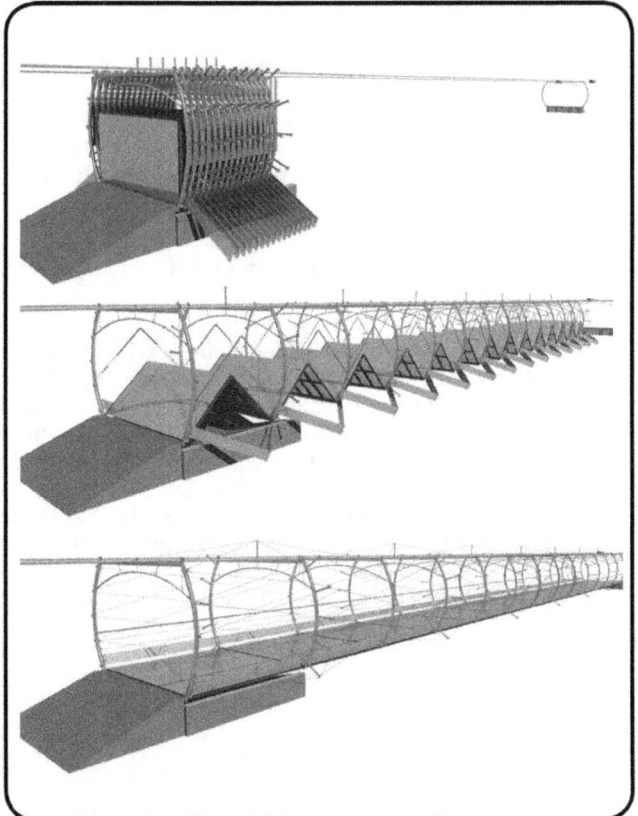

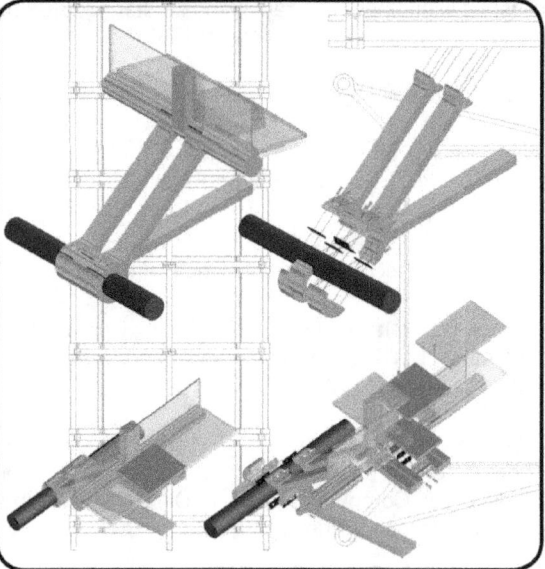

Figure 4: Modifications to the digital visual communication curriculum focused on the use of computing as a tool for design rather than simply representation.[12]

journal.[13] The coordinated, integrated design curriculum was a resounding success. Building upon the successes of the past 2005 SSEF results, the students entered in the 2006 SSEF once again competed against, and beat out several upper year students from other universities and colleges.

In this modification of traditional architectural design pedagogies, first year design students were simultaneously taught design principles, building construction, and architectural media in an integrated format. Only through coordination between building construction and architectural media courses was the success of the students' designs possible. Whereas within traditional pedagogical systems that tended to compartmentalize curriculum, students would often be exposed to indirect material in other courses, this integrated design approach strived to coordinate information on visualization and presentation techniques and technical construction knowledge with the design and detailing as a central point of focus. This exemplifies the paradigm many design academics and practitioners have been calling for - "the falling boundaries razed by a partnership" which are the underpinnings for the development of this approach.[14] In this instance the boundaries between design and other coursework were broken by a bridge.

Notes:

[1] Burry, Mark, "Digitally Sponsored Convergence of Design Education, Research and Practice." In: Martens, Bob and Brown, André (Eds). Computer Aided Architectural Design: Futures 2005. (Dordrecht: Springer, 2005)

[2] Figure 1 Images (left to right) courtesy of Christina Karney, Terry Sin, and Ted Teng.

[3] Jackson, Barry, "Total Studio: Interdisciplinary Collaborative Design for Engineering and Architecture." In: Young, B., Katsanisi, C., Tidafi, T., and Richard, R. (Eds). Technology In Transition: Mastering the Impacts. (Washington: ACSA Press, 1999)

[4] SSEF website: http://www.ssef.ca

[5] Trebilcock, Peter and Lawson, Mark, Architectural Design in Steel. (London: Spoon Press, 2004)

[6] Figure 2 Images (left to right) courtesy of Alan Macdiarmid, Coco Keyu Xiong, and Renee Kuenle.

[7] Brookes, Alan. J. and Grech, Chris, Connections: Studies in Building Assembly. (Oxford: Butterworth-Heinemann Ltd, 1992)

[8] Seebohm, Thomas, and Van Wyk, In: Seebohm, Thomas, and Van Wyk, Skip (Eds), Digital Design Studios: Do Computers Make A Difference?. (Albuquerque: Universal Printing, 1998)

[9] Figure 3 Images (left to right) courtesy of Gloria Lei and Xiao Wang.

[10] Madrazo, Leandro, "Computers and Architectural Design: Going Beyond the Tool." In: Seebohm, Thomas, and Van Wyk, Skip (Eds), Digital Design Studios: Do Computers Make A Difference?. (Albuquerque: Universal Printing, 1998)

[11] Kocaturk, Tuba and Veltkamp, Martijn, "Interdisciplinary Knowledge Modeling for Free-Form Design – An Educational Experiment." In: Martens, Bob and Brown, André (Eds). Computer Aided Architectural Design: Futures 2005. (Dordrecht: Springer, 2005)

[12] Figure 4 Images (left to right) courtesy of David Schellingerhoudt, Jamie Usas, Bradley Paddock, and Richard D'Alessandro.

[13] Of the eight merited entries in the 2005 SSEF competition, the top three were upper year students while the remaining were all students from the coordinated design approach class. In the 2006 SSEF under the same conditions, one of the entries garnered second place while three other entries merited citations. Several of the entries are to be published in the 2005-6 issue of InFormZ under the Joint Study Program.

[14] Dollens, Dennis, D•2•A (Digital to Analog). (Santa Fe: Sites Books, 2001)

Push/Pull: Bringing Technology and Design Together at Iowa State

Thomas Leslie, AIA
Iowa State University

Introduction

Current architecture curricula generally make mention of the need to integrate technology and design coursework. After a generation in which representation pushed technology aside in design studios, practitioners, students, and faculty today recognize—hopefully—that the problems we face in building today demand a more fully comprehensive approach to resource efficiency and building performance. At the same time, we have a new set of tools—both materials and design processes—that should make this sort of design engineering easier.

Iowa State has, like most other schools, looked carefully at how we might encourage students to take a more integrative approach, to see technology as a vital element in not only getting things done, but also in conceiving designs. Circumstances have pushed us toward two apparently unique solutions, both of which have given us insight into the links between design and technology courses, and the learning styles they require and suggest. These two curricular innovations have led to demonstrable changes in our department's culture; technology has been mainstreamed as both a subdiscipline and as a conceptual center for much of our teaching at the graduate and undergraduate level.

The unique circumstances involved both faculty hiring and NAAB-led changes in our department's offerings. Major changes to the faculty and departmental administration in 2000 introduced new personnel, several of whom had come from practice seeking mid-career moves. This gave us—almost by accident—a group of so-called 'utility infielders' who could move easily between design and technology courses, where their expertise lay, and history and theory courses, where their research agendas were heading. At the same time, we had two major curricular changes—the introduction of a dedicated Comprehensive Design semester to our B.Arch. program, as per NAAB standards, and the complete overhaul of our M.Arch. program, based on a desire to reconstitute the program to focus on what we call 'critical practice'. Blending new requirements with an existing urban design studio led to a uniquely productive approach in the former case, while in the latter an opportunity to re-think the traditional 'tech' curriculum from first principles led to what we believe is a profound improvement on technology pedagogy, one that accommodates the wide variety of learning styles found in a first professional degree program such as ours.

In both cases, there are lessons to be learned from the admittedly young results. By 'pushing' technology out of the lecture hall and into the design studio in the graduate program, and by 'pulling' it into studio in our Comprehensive Design semester, students report an amplified appreciation for these linkages and overlaps, and that their understanding of architecture as an inherently interdisciplinary practice has been nurtured by these experiences.

PUSH—Graduate SCI-TECH

In 2003 an ad hoc group of faculty was charged with reviving what had become a moribund graduate program. We took this opportunity to rebuild, from scratch, a program that would be both pragmatic and idealistic, and we focused on a model that could connect practice with society, culture, and the environment as our three primary issues of focus. However, we were concerned that these issues be addressed throughout the curriculum, and not in sub-disciplinary 'silos.' Therefore, particularly in the initial two years of the three-year program, we proposed a tripod structure. Rather than repeating the common format of a massively credited studio with a large number of smaller, less credit-intensive classes, we proposed three courses with equal credit hours—a five-credit design studio, a five credit Seminar, and a five credit science and technology course. This last course, dubbed SCI-TECH, was charged not only with delivering the requisite NAAB-mandated technology work, but also with drawing connections between that work, the other two classes, and the primary themes of the program.

Because our program is a first professional degree, our pedagogy for SCI-TECH had to be flexible. Our students have a wide variety of backgrounds, from jazz musician to psychiatric nurse, and from civil engineer to neurosurgeon. We therefore had to find ways to appeal to a number of different learning styles, to a range of mathematical abilities, and to a range, frankly, of interest levels in more technical material. Jason Alread and I were given responsibility for developing this coursework, but it has been productively and consistently challenged by the other members of the faculty, and the result is, we believe, a unique and successful delivery strategy.

Fundamentally, SCI-TECH can be described as a spiral ramp. We move between four basic areas—human factors, structural design, environmental response, and materials. Each of these are revisited in the four-course sequence, and we have intentionally layered these themes so that, for instance, materials-based course modules on steel and concrete can occur near those on beam design, and those on aluminum near curtain walls. Throughout, we emphasize socially and environmentally responsible practice. Materials coursework constantly emphasizes issues of embodied energy, for example, while building codes are discussed in the context of ethics versus efficiency. Coursework is also tied to the other two major course elements—anthropometric design, or design for people, is paired with a studio project to redesign the working or meeting space, while a summary of structural design topics includes a history of Chicago School architecture designed to tie into a field trip in that term's history and culture-based seminar. This emphasis on the interconnectedness of the four technical themes amongst themselves, and to the curriculum's other two areas of study, enables students to understand the fluid roles of technique and performance.

Day-to-day, SCI-TECH is structured to appeal to varying learning styles and mathematical abilities. We typically organize themes into one-week modules, making them interchangeable as the course structure evolves. Mondays are typically devoted to pure lecture setups, although the small size of our classes—12 to 16 students, makes even these feel more like seminars. Students are encouraged to raise issues and to ask questions during the lectures, and this size enables a comfort level with discussion that has led to a much more free-flowing dialogue between faculty and students, and often amongst students themselves. Wednesdays are generally dedicated to either case studies or examples, connecting the historical and theoretical emphasis of the Monday classes to real-world situations. Here, we take advantage of SmartBoard technology that permits the integration of written and graphic information. Multi-page displays enable us to go through examples in great depth, or to quickly copy base information for use in related examples. During our week on Moment of Inertia, for example, one of the most challenging structural concepts to absorb, we calculate I for various depths, widths, and thicknesses of material, adjusting a set of basic, shared dimensions with each example. SmartBoard enables us to go back and forth between pages, comparing the results for small variations in dimensional conditions.

On Fridays, students engage the topic to hand with a 'laboratory' session, where we physically test the basic principles that we've covered during the week in an intuitive, hands-on fashion. Sometimes this involves a field trip—to a local water tower fabrication shop during the steel classes, for instance—but the signature experiences of the sequence are definitely those where we test principles of architectural science using scaled-down situations. To emphasize the role of moisture on human comfort, for example, the students build a 'swamp cooler' with a wet towel and a fan, experiencing the cooling effect of the evaporating moisture. During structural design weeks, we illustrate

Fig. 2. "Laboratory testing" of a cardboard beam shape using Sweet's Catalogues.

complex theoretical ideas by building beams, columns, and frames out of chipboard and basswood. We then test these for various aspects of structural sufficiency using both scientific weights and, for larger assemblies, donated Sweet's catalogues. We keep an intentionally light tone during these labs, with students naming their constructions and keeping 'score' to see which teams can build the strongest, the lightest, and the best looking test subjects. These labs are consistently noted by students in end-of-course evaluations as the course sessions that really 'brought home' the abstract theoretical material we've covered earlier in the week.

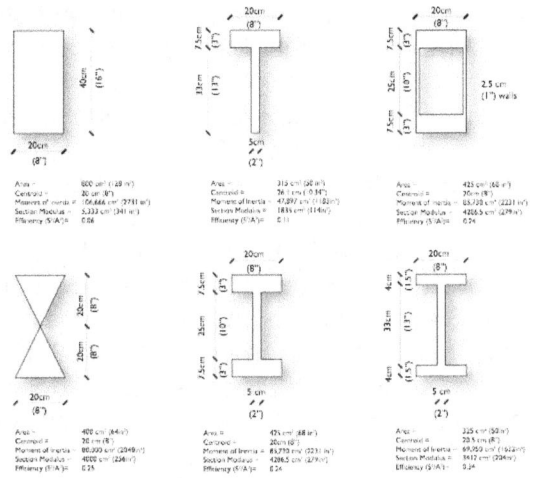

Fig. 1. Smartboard "index" summary of structural shapes. Common parameters are used to emphasize the importance of sectional location in figuring Moment of Inertia.

As important as the course logistics, our working relationship with studio instructors has allowed students to put SCI-TECH coursework into 'play' right away. Even in the first semester, studio coursework is tuned to allow students to explore issues of anthropomorphics, circulation, and elementary solar design. Later studios add requirements for structural design, environmental response, and code compliance as these issues come up in SCI-TECH, and the two instructors are regularly included on project reviews to help bring technical issues into the mainstream of design coursework.

Fig. 3. SCI-TECH problem solving using Smartboard.

The approach we have adopted for SCI-TECH has formed the basis for a new textbook, to be published this Fall by Elsevier/Architectural Press, entitled Design-Tech: Building Science for Architects. This book will be organized as both a stand-alone textbook, and as a studio reference, with material organized to match the typical pace of a studio project—covering in turn site and program analysis, circulation, structural design, environmental response, and detailing. Throughout, our emphasis is that of the SCI-TECH sequence, seeing technology's connections to design, to history, and to social factors as primary issues in connecting the 'how' of building with broader questions of 'why'.

Pull—The Montreal Project

By happy coincidence, we have adopted precisely the opposite strategy in our undergraduate program. Where SCI-TECH 'pushes' technology out of the classroom and into studio, our comprehensive design studio 'pulls' technology into student design work by means of a structured approach that relates technical issues to socio-cultural and aesthetic values, that provides a 'scaffold' to ensure that students address these issues at appropriate times during the semester, and that uses an intentionally difficult program and a provocative site to bring these issues to the forefront.

In 2001, after feedback from our last NAAB accreditation visit, we recognized the need to create a dedicated Comprehensive Design project. We initially looked at three options: a dedicated 'tech' studio, revising the requirements for what was then our fifth year Diploma Project, and reconfiguring our technology course sequence to include space for a purely 'tech' driven project.

For various reasons, none of these options appealed to our desire for a truly integrative experience. In particular, we reacted against the idea of Comprehensive Design being shuttered away in our tech sequence, and against the idea that our largely theoretically-based Diploma Project might have a few desultory requirements tacked on. Instead, we looked at the possibility of radically expanding our existing fourth year studio. What is now the 'Montreal Project' began as an urban design studio that focused on sites in complex urban environments with diverse cultural influences; New Orleans and Montreal were cities chosen for their unique manifestations of urban forms that showed the influence of French design and planning. Looking at this existing studio, Matt Fisher and I wondered whether we could make "Comprehensive Design" truly comprehensive, requiring students to respond to technical issues not in isolation, but within the mix of urban, civic, representational and contextual concerns that the Montreal project had provided. We realized that this could give us an opportunity to talk about technology in context, to see the links, for example, between façade strategies and climatically-based building traditions, between structure and street-front 'patterning,' between internal circulation and urban pedestrian routes. Working with a hybrid faculty team—half of them veterans of the urban design studio, the other half more technology-based—we expanded the existing program for a digital research laboratory with new requirements dealing explicitly with life safety, structure, enclosure and environmental response. Other aspects of the earlier studio remained; students were required to respond in meaningful ways to the immediate urban context and to larger issues of identity and culture that are embedded in the character of Montreal. That first group responded enthusiastically to the challenge, leading us to further expand the requirements for the program, and to begin to develop additional coursework that would further 'pull' these issues into the studio.

The result was a workshop course dedicated to supporting the notion of 'integrated design' in the studio. This course is an optional 3-credit class that can be taken in conjunction with the design studio. We cover six major topics in a sequence that parallels what we believe students should be focusing on at various stages in their semester-long design projects' evolution: Program Analysis, Site Analysis, Circulation, Structure, Environment, and Cladding. For each segment, we offer 'refresher' classes that emphasize practical applications, we take students through a handful of case studies that show not only how these elements are 'solved,' but also how they can inform and influence design, and we invite students to present their own design projects, offering group critiques in smaller settings. Students are required to submit three 'client binders' throughout the semester showing how each of these six themes are incorporated in their design work, with an emphasis on graphic and textual explanation. These binders are also typically used during studio reviews, and the diagramming exercises they incorporate have proven to be valuable tools not only for presentation, but also for refining designs throughout the semester.

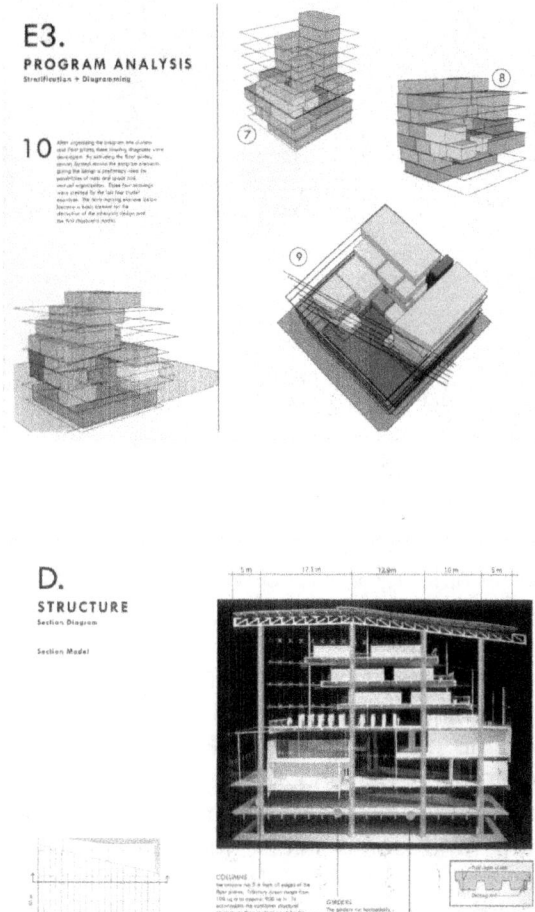

Fig. 4. Pages from 'client binder' submitted for the Montreal studio's 'scaffold' class. Alissa MacInnes.

In studio, the Montreal Project has evolved into a flagship semester for our program. We have changed the site roughly every other year, and have modified and altered the program to both clarify the structural issues we want students to grapple with, and to emphasize the civic nature of the studio. Currently, the program is for a 'Mediatheque' incorporating long-span cinema spaces, multiple levels of heavily loaded book stacks, light-sensitive digital media spaces, and significant public areas that must relate meaningfully to the dense surroundings. Beneath all of this, the program asks for just enough parking to efficiently cover the site, forcing students to balance

Fig. 5. 1:200 site model, Mediatheque du Montreal project. Tonia Sorenson & Kristin Jensen.

the complexity upstairs with the need for a regular grid below.

All of this technical work, however, must be seen within the context of Montreal. We take the group there about five weeks into the term—long enough that students will have made preliminary studies into the program, and some initial guesses as to its massing on the site. We spend four days in Montreal, documenting the site, but also experiencing the city's unique architectural heritage, its rich mixture of cultures and languages, and its intense nightlife. Almost invariably, students' projects are profoundly influenced by the experience of seeing Montreal first hand, and the diagrammatic 'solutions' to the program very quickly take on real meaning after the trip, as students try to balance those objective needs with the very understandable desire for their schemes to acknowledge and support the vibrant city life they've seen.

The Montreal Project has evolved its own unique studio culture, which supports its foundational ideals of integration. In particular, the project has become a predominantly collaborative one, with students pairing up for the semester. This is helpful given the intensive requirements that we've developed, including ones for large 1:50 section models, but interestingly it has also led to students recognizing the inherent

Fig. 6. 1:50 detail model, Mediatheque du Montreal. Jason De Vries & Ben Foth.

benefits to discussion and debate within the design team. Very often, students will pair up based not on similar skill sets or values, but on conscientiously different ones; a 'tech-head' will often seek out a skilled designer and vice versa. Needless to say, these are often the most rewarding and most successful collaborations. This sense of interdisciplinary collaboration extends to the faculty; our backgrounds range from practice to history and theory, and we conscientiously employ one another's expertise as guest reviewers, lecturers in the workshop course, and tour guides in Montreal. Likewise, we make sure to arrange midterm and final reviews with juries composed of various backgrounds and interests, drawing on professionals from Chicago, Des Moines, Minneapolis and Kansas City, but also library directors from campus and nearby cities, historians, theorists, and even philosophers. Students know that they must respond to the multitude of interests and values that these groups represent, and

Fig. 7. The field trip to Montreal includes walking tours of significant precedents in integrated design

typically respond with projects that demonstrate their agility as designers alongside their mastery of technical issues.

Student assessment takes place on an individual basis with studio instructors, but we have also instituted a group walk-through after reviews to discuss, as a faculty, the semester's projects and ways in which the studio might improve either logistically or pedagogically. This allows us to learn from one another's experiments in scheduling, review requirements, or in-class exercises. Feedback from students via the University's evaluation process is typically supplemented by written questionnaires. In general, we have been consistently surprised at our students' enthusiasm for the challenge level of the project—most report that the studio is not only the hardest one they've had, but also that they feel the project is their strongest work to date. Numerical feedback in the fifteen categories measured by Iowa State has been higher than collegiate and University averages by an average of 10%. Perhaps more importantly, recent graduates tend to report that the Montreal project most closely resembles the holistic thinking that is required in practice.

Conclusions and Future Experimentation

We believe our two-fold experience in linking technology and design may hold important lessons for pedagogy in both areas. In particular, we have been impressed by how positively students have reacted to coursework that conscientiously demonstrates how technology can be applied to—and how it can inform—architectural design. Our experience in SCI-TECH has suggested that the depth of traditional technology curricula can be productively shifted towards an emphasis on breadth. Such a re-focusing reflects both the wide availability of expertise in engineering and construction to the profession today, and the discipline's own shift toward more holistic, integrative roles. Amongst students, this has obvious benefits for those whose own interests and skill sets are more design- than tech-oriented, however we have also found that students with backgrounds in engineering and physics enjoy and are challenged by the need to connect what might be familiar knowledge to design situations. Likewise, we have found in the Montreal project that design studios can productively incorporate rigorous technical requirements if students are supported in their efforts by a thoughtful course structure, assistive 'scaffold' classwork, and instructors who are both knowledgeable and persistent in challenging projects to constantly focus on broad integration and detailed development.

As these courses continue to evolve and change, we anticipate several ongoing experiments to refine and improve them. SCI-TECH is just now undergoing a major overhaul to try to better connect various course units. Students have pointed out that constant shifts in emphasis can be confusing rather than integrative, and we have thus attempted to re-organize the offerings in larger groups of about 5-6 weeks, instead of 3-4. Likewise we are attempting to use more laboratory and field trip sessions, as students consistently report that these are the most useful elements in terms of understanding real-world applications and developing intuitive appreciations for how theoretical information can connect with design work. The Montreal project, meanwhile, is due for a programmatic overhaul, as the Mediatheque problem is now familiar to incoming students each year. We have discussed the possibility of changing to a long-span problem, or to a similar institutional problem but with a different program. We are also re-designing the 'scaffold' course to incorporate a broader mix of studio faculty, in response to suggestions from students that the course is too tightly annexed to individual studio professors' schedules, in particular.

These refinements are, however, ultimately tactical, and we continue to believe in the pedagogical strategies for both SCI-TECH and the Montreal project. Both elements have helped bring technology into the mainstream of our graduate and undergraduate programs, and both have demonstrated convincingly that technology might be best discussed as an adjunct or partner to design studios, where conceptual and pragmatic information can be tested and applied right away. Moving from the lecture hall to the studio and the laboratory table has been an important element in Iowa State's curriculum. We believe it has the potential to serve as a model for other programs interested in transitioning from traditional modes of technology coursework to ones that might better serve students whose mid-career point will be somewhere around 2030, when integration, sustainability, and high performance will have moved beyond buzzwords and will, instead, be crucial aspects of everyday practice.

Case Studies in Studio-based Learning

Bruce Lonnman
American University of Sharjah

Introduction

Precedent research in design has a long history in studio teaching and is sometimes used as a first assignment to jump-start a design project and provide students with some basic knowledge and visual references pertaining to the problem. In the study of structure, precedent or case study research can be extended as a methodology encompassing a wide range of activities including structural behavior model studies, hypothetical transformations of structural assemblies, visual analyses of form, as well as the use of quantitative analysis to understand or verify structural design assumptions. In fact, the use of carefully selected, well-documented case studies can support the active-learning environment of the design studio in a number of useful ways that focus on building structure and its relationship to other design considerations.

Active Learning in Design Education

Active learning is a term that has come to describe the unique approach to design education that architecture schools have long embraced. The studio setting, which is key to this approach, is part lab, part classroom. Sometimes it simulates a design office, while at other times it is a place for tutorial exchange. More often it is akin to a workshop. It operates under a different premise than a typical classroom. It is a place where learning occurs in the context of problem solving and the making of things (or of the making of representations of things to be built). In Donald Schon's terminology, the studio "is a kind of practicum, a virtual world that represents the real world of practice but is relatively free of the pressures, distractions, and risks of the latter" (Schon, 17).

Mark Gelernter provides insight into the nature of studio-based education and how it differs from the conventional university model typified by the lecture hall and based on a positivist view of objective knowledge and the scientific method. Positivism viewed education as a passive activity, one in which the primary goal was transmitting to students the objective facts discovered through empirical research. Architectural education on the other hand has been shaped by alternative theories of learning (e.g. John Dewey and Jean Piaget) that emphasize the active role of the individual in constructing a "self knowledge" based on perceived usefulness (Gelernter, 284). The differences between these two forms of education is striking and helps to explain the difficulty students encounter adjusting between studio courses and the various non-studio classes that generally follow the positivist, lecture-based model of passive learning.

In a design studio, learning is instigated and directed by a problem, normally a building design project. Students are challenged to create a solution that addresses many separate and sometimes conflicting issues. Fundamental to this process is the generation of a hypothesis. A hypothesis in architecture is a design proposal, a three-dimensional form that is tested for its suitability in meeting the conditions of the problem. These conditions range from objective facts such as area requirements of the brief or conformance with the laws of gravity, to more subjective criteria related to expression and aesthetic character.

This aspect of the design process involves a kind of visual speculation that is guided by experience and knowledge. Obviously, with practice and the acquisition of knowledge one becomes better at generating workable design alternatives. The paradox for the design student, however, is that to learn how to design it must be attempted and generally the student lacks the requisite knowledge and skill needed to create an acceptable design proposal. This usually leads to frustration and immobility. To overcome this impasse a student needs to be coached through the process. The design critic fulfills this role either by example or through directed actions (e.g. "create a simple massing model of the major volumes"). A second form of design aid is through the introduction of specific knowledge that can provide resource material to serve as a point of departure. This might be in the form of a particular design precedent or a set of typological components (e.g. various long span structural systems) relevant to the problem.

Despite the advantage that knowledge or 'content' might seem to offer in assisting the design process, many studio critics resist this approach. Some maintain a traditional view that studio focus exclusively on the synthetic aspect of design and assume that relevant knowledge is obtained in non-studio courses. In this approach a student working on a design project and faced with the need to select and configure a structural system would rely on the knowledge gained in a separate course on structures or building technology. The timing of such a course as well as the relevance of the course content typically do not match the studio requirements. Objective knowledge or facts learned in a passive context and not applied to problem solving are quickly forgotten. Also the constant revision and shifting of curriculums as well as the migration of studio teachers between levels further erodes the possibility of establishing coordination and continuity.

On the other hand, a design curriculum that adopts the studio-based learning model exclusively must carefully outline the sequence and content of studios to insure that a minimum level of skill, knowledge, and conceptual understanding required for professional competency (e.g. the topics identified by NAAB) is provided to all students. Studio projects would need to be designed to meet learning objectives across the curriculum and sequenced accordingly. The difficulty of implementing such a scheme probably makes a total studio curriculum unachievable. On a limited scale, Ed Allen's description of a second and parallel studio for technical teaching is an experiment in incorporating technical content into a design studio setting (Allen). Despite the advantages of this approach, it is improbable that any program would devote the manpower resources required to convert large lecture class teaching to the relatively inefficient studio-based model. However the lessons pointed out in Allen's essay can be incorporated into large, non-studio classes with certain adjustments and compromises. The essential point is that a design problem creates the need for specific knowledge to develop and test a design, and that this interaction of knowledge acquisition and application enhances learning.

Figure 1. The studio as a place of active learning.

The Case Study: Content for Design Studio

A well chosen, carefully documented case study supports the design process by providing useful knowledge specific to the design problem at the time when it is most needed. If a case study is made by students in the context of a design problem they are working on, it takes on a role much different than a research assignment in a non-design oriented course. The value of knowledge gained in the exercise becomes clear as students make the connection between a hypothetical design project and an actual built design. Most important, the exercise of making the case study is a valuable teaching opportunity that provides the design instructor a chance to discuss the relevance and relationship of specific issues (e.g. building technology) to the design problem at hand. In addition, a rigorous examination of a built work will inform an understanding of the design process itself. learning.

The Tectonic Case Study: Integrating Technology and Design

The following is a description of a case study exercise used in a mid-level architectural design studio focused on building technology, specifically structure and envelope.[1] Emphasis on exposed well-detailed structures, materials, and their expression led to the assignment being called the Tectonic Case Study. Although the technical aspects of the case study project are highlighted, documentation and analysis of the building design is not restricted to these issues.

In the first phase of the assignment students form teams and select a case study from a list of available choices. The list is composed of contemporary built works that have certain characteristics coinciding with topics explored in studio design project. These include:

1) medium to long-span roof design.
2) repetitive structural bay system.
3) structural framing and assembly.
4) natural lighting and/or passive environmental design features.

Additionally each case study must have excellent documentation such as detailed plans and building sections, extensive views, development drawings of key details, etc. The availability of documentation is the first issue considered. Books, journals and other publications containing information are reserved. In some cases construction document sets are used. The last criterion is that the case study should be an exemplary building design. Typically the availability of documentation through monographs and high quality journals ensures that selected projects are all recognized for their design excellence.

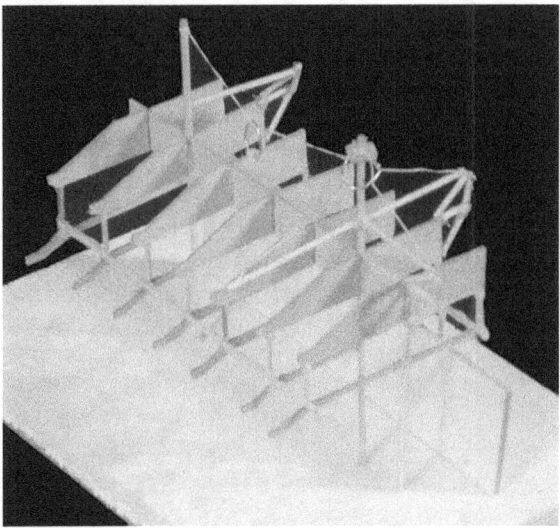

Figure 2. Study model (Moundstand Lords Cricket Stadium, Michael Hopkins Architects.) Golsa Naghizadeh and Sanez Malek.

With resources at hand in the studio, the actual exploration of the case study begins. Precedent analysis requires certain skills that develop with practice and guidance. There are many techniques for investigating a precedent, yet perhaps the most valuable is asking the right questions. In studio, discussions between the team members and the instructor follow a format similar to a design critique. Verbal reasoning is supplemented by visual thinking in the form of freehand drawing and sketch models. At this stage it is important that the instructor actively participate in the process by demonstrating from experience how a designer uses drawing as a tool for exploration and discovery. It is worthwhile to emphasize that the same technique of analytical drawing is used in the design process to visualize, test, and explore potential design solutions whether at the scale of a parti or a construction detail. In either case freehand drawing should strive to be proportionally accurate and clearly legible.

During an interview recorded on camera the architect Santiago Calatrava provided a vivid demonstration of his drawing skill (Adda). At one point in the film, Calatrava visually explains the structural system of the soaring entrance hall of his Satolas TGV Station in a series of freehand sketches that accurately describe the curvature and proportions of the enclosure and structural armature. Throughout his career Calatrava has often revealed his skill in drawing. A study of his design drawings shows that the proportions and profiles of his preliminary structural design sketches are generally very close to those of the final engineered structures.

Figure 3. Study model (Hall 4, Hannover Exhibition. von Gerken, Marg, & Partners. Engr: Jorg Schlaich) Abeer Khatid and Engi Gaber.

Throughout the first exploratory phase students are encouraged to create simple, diagrammatic models of a structural bay of the project. Extremely basic and reductive in detail, these quickly constructed sketch models are a necessary first step in visualizing the three-dimensional form of the structural system. Often they provide clues into the behavior of the system, especially with regard to stability. Complementing these physical models are three-dimensional drawings that articulate the structure and enclosure systems. These begin as freehand drawings and are then refined into layered computer-drafted digital models.

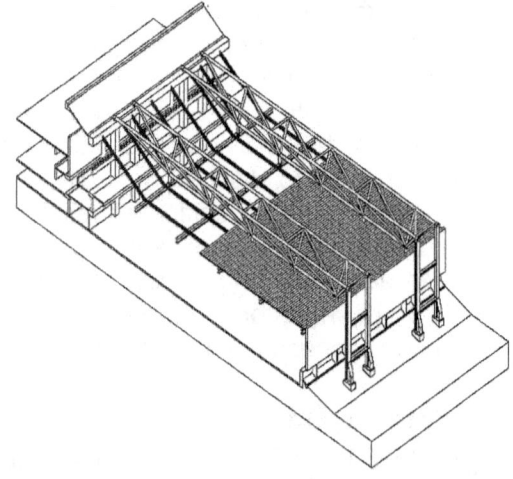

Figure 4. Cutaway Axon (Exeter Academy Athletic Facilities, Kallman, McKinnell & Wood. Engr. Wm. Lemessurier) Julie Macar and Waleed Hashim.

A period of about two weeks is needed to meet with all the case study groups twice and uncover most of the building's mysteries. Most of the basic structural issues such as framing, load path, means for ensuring lateral stability, and so forth are discussed and diagrammed. Likewise questions about the building envelope and other systems are addressed. What is the position of the envelope relative to the structure? What does it consist of and how is it assembled? How does the design control air temperature? Although conversations of this type tend to be lengthy (and not very time efficient), the dialog is one of the most effective ways to motivate students and connect building technology with design. Often students from other teams drop in and out of the discussion and pick up on comments that apply equally to their case study research.

At this stage each team begins the design and construction of a detailed physical model of a single structural bay depicting structure and envelope. In a real sense this becomes a design project as many details of the model, such as the depiction of connections or the fabrication of formally complex elements has to be studied and an appropriate strategy for making it needs to be explored. In some cases the fabrication of a component will require a specially designed secondary device either to support or guide the shaping of the piece. This is a concept we tend to stress; that something might have to be designed in order to make something else.

Figure 5. Forming trusses. (Fuhlsbuttel Air Terminal, von Geran, Marg, & Partners) Pooja Satish and Reeny Thomas.

Generally the models are constructed of high-density particle board (MDF) in part due to the precision of cutting that is possible. In some cases soldered metal tubing, Plexiglas, and other materials are used. The connection to the woodshop and the introduction of hand tool and machine shop practices is a conscious decision to extend the means of exploration available to students and further emphasize the value of learning by making. The size of a model is determined by the scale, either 1:50 or 1:100 depending on the building's span. A typical project with a 90 m span will produce a model of about a meter in length at a scale of 1:100. Building a scale model of this size and using materials that require fabrication with small tolerances and proper joinery is analogous in many ways to a real construction project. Numerous issues confronted in the model design and its construction are not intrinsically different from those that are routinely encountered on the job site.

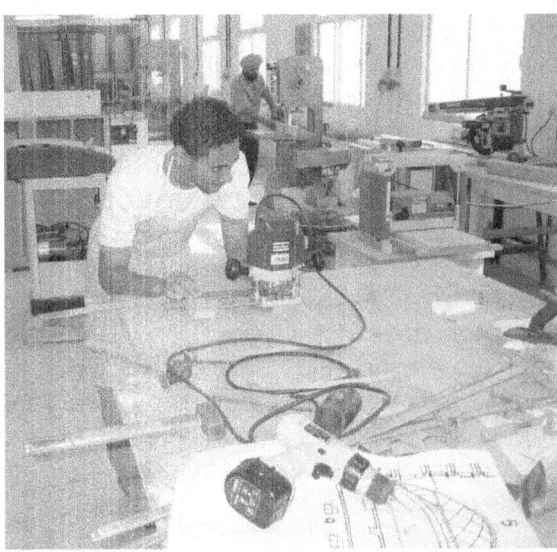

Figure 6. The woodshop is an extension of the design studio. (Fabricating arches for the glass roof of the New Parliamentary Building, Michael Hopkins Architects) Tariq Nour.

The Structural Transformation Diagram

The *structural transformation diagram* is a tool that helps students understand the concept of structural efficiency. Although most of the case studies have structural systems that are fairly legible, nearly all of the projects have some interesting innovation or sophisticated handling of the load path that can be seen as an improvement over a more conventional design. To begin a conversation about the design features that result in an efficient, highly refined structure, the student team attempts something like the equivalent of reverse engineering. The structural transformation diagram is an imagined process of enhancement beginning with the most basic form of the structural span and by stages, transforms it into the actual structure of the case study.

A typical example is the diagram created for the Exeter Academy Sports Facility, an elegant gymnasium center designed in the seventies by the firm of Kallmann Mckinnell and Woods. Beginning with a basic four column frame that defines the bay, successive structural improvements involve transformation to a subdivided framing system with deep edge beams, replacement of the deep beams with open web trusses, displacement of the trusses to the top side of the roof, transformation into 3-D trusses, and finally, transformation of the single column support into paired columns supporting each upper chord member of the truss. The number of "improvement" stages and the specific order is an aspect of the design of the diagram. Although the invented transformation does not intend to represent the original engineering design process, in some cases it may approximate it. The real value of the exercise develops out of the discussion regarding the structural logic of each successive design improvement.

Structural Behavior Performance Model

Another parallel activity in the case study assignment involves an exercise in verification of structural behavior. Termed the structural behavior performance model, each team of students identifies a structural behavior associated with their case study and designs a simple performance model that will visually demonstrate the assumed action. The choice of behavior can range from conditions of member stability to proving the efficiency of a member section.

To enhance the visualization of the behavior for demonstration purposes, soft flexible materials such as polystyrene foam and cardboard are used in the model. Joints are simulated by various means (pins, nuts and bolts, wire, etc.) and loads are placed or hung on the model. The use of polystyrene

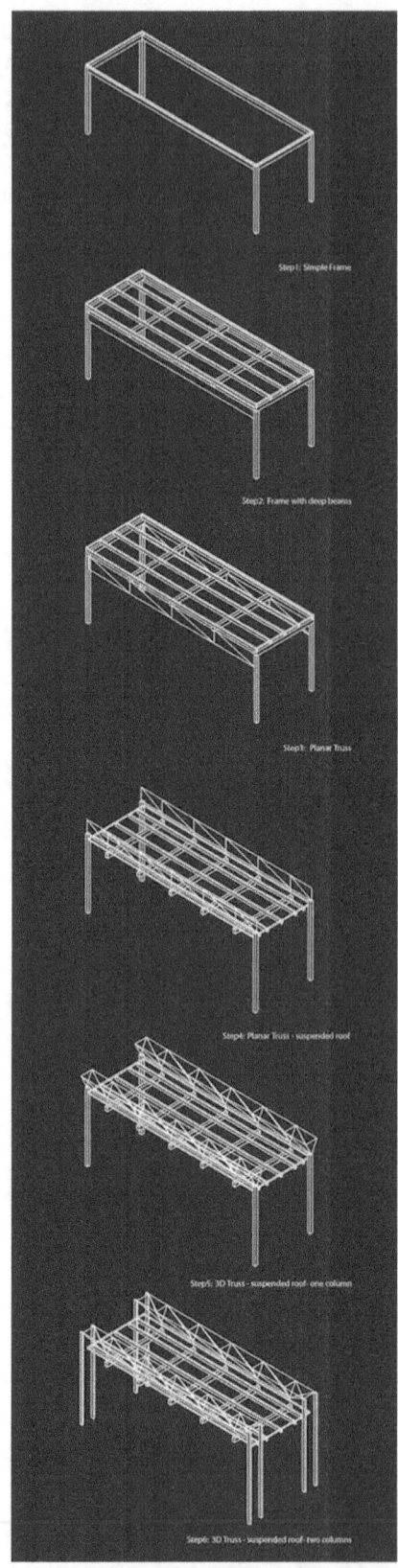

Figure 7. Structural Transformation Diagram. (Exeter Academy Athletic Facilities) J. Macar & W. Hashim

foam (PSF) enables large deflections to occur with small weights.[2] It is also a material that has thickness and comes in large sheets (insulation), can be shaped easily with a hotwire, and is economical.

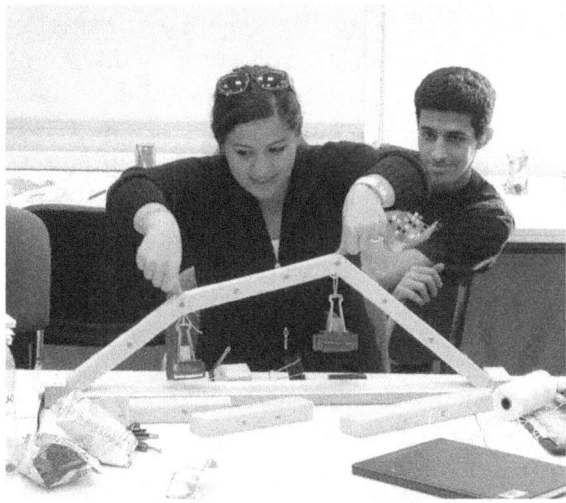

Figure 8. Testing a structural PSF behavioral model. Mona Ganjineh and Barrak Al-Babtain.

There is no real need to make the structural behavior model look like the structure of the case study that it represents. Only that it has the correct characteristics so that the behavior can be tested. In some cases several models are constructed so that one parameter can be modified to test the effect on the behavior. For example, three identical trusses except for the proportions of the panels can be made to test an assumption about how trusses resist shear force. Upon testing it becomes clear how panel proportions (and the inclination of the diagonal member) directly influence the shear capacity of the truss.

This type of active participation in designing the test, constructing the model and the test setup, and finally testing the structure in front of the class causes this assignment to be the most popular project of the semester. The testing requires good communication skills on the part of the instructor if the lessons about structure are to be absorbed by the class as a whole. Students generally become overly concerned with the breakage and need to be reminded of the structural principles that resulted in the failure. Outlining structural relationships on the screen, asking the class to make predictions, and taking measurements and plotting results are some of the ways to focus students' attention on the learning how structures behave. Including questions about the tests on a quiz is also effective!

Documentation of the Case Study

Following the completion of the wood "Tectonic Model", the major finished product of the assignment, each team prepares a set of posters (A2 or approximately 18in x 24in) summarizing the research on the case study. Documentation of the case study building includes views, selected published drawings as well as new drawings prepared by the team. New constructed drawings vary with each project but are created to dissect the building in three dimensions and describe the systems analytically using cutaway sections, transparent volumetrics, pulled apart axons, and layered digital models. Some rendered computer models are created to clarify systems. Representational renderings are discouraged unless they serve to illustrate the tectonic qualities of the design. Often the rendered view of a complex joint explains the logic of the design and the artistry of its production.

Perhaps even more important than the model, the documentation of each case study contributes to a digital precedent research document that is distributed to each member of the studio. This visual reference material provides specific examples with detailed analyses that are specific to the functional and formal characteristics of the new design project the studio will begin work on.

Conclusion

Case study or precedent research is a standard method for introducing knowledge or *content* into design studio education. The case study assignment provides a frame for creating a foundation of knowledge appropriate to the task at hand. The task may be a design problem with greater focus on a limited range of issues. In the example referred to here, an emphasis is placed on building technology, specifically structural span, envelope, and passive environmental controls. Consequently, the Tectonic Case Study targets these issues and identifies a broad selection of contemporary buildings notable as exemplary works that artfully address technical questions and provide innovative design solutions.

Figure 9. Final Model of a Case Study. (Lyons-Satolas TGV Station, S. Calatrava) Laila Barakeh & Tagoug El-Hag.

In conclusion it is observed that students develop a passionate attachment to an in-depth research project focused on an exemplary building of the student's choice. Whether the project is presented as a studio-based case study exercise or a term project in a structures lecture course has implications on the timing, schedule, and the form of teacher-student interaction. In either format, however, the commitment and intensity of interest on the part of the student confirms case study learning as an excellent pedagogical method for teaching structures.

References:

Allen, Edward. "Second Studio: A Model for Technical Teaching." Journal of Architectural Education 51.2 (1997): 92-95.

Gelernter, Mark. "Reviving Higher Education: Lessons from the Architectural Studio." Proceedings of the Annual Meeting of the ACSA (199?): 282-285.

Satolas – TGV: un monument a la campagne. Prod./Dir. Catherine Adda. Films d'ici: La Sept Arte, Paris, 1998.

Schon, Donald A. "Toward a Marriage of Artistry and Applied Science in the Architectural Design Studio." Journal of Architectural Education 41.4 (1988): 16-24.

Notes:

[1] This case study assignment is given at the beginning of the semester in a third year design studio class at AUS. Third Year Level has approximately 32 students divided into two sections taught by separate instructors. However, the syllabus of both studios is identical allowing students and faculty to work and teach across sections. The assignment lasts approximately five weeks and is followed by an eight week design project that addresses similar issues.

[2] The author is indebted to Richard Kellogg, now Emeritus Professor of Architecture at the University of Arkansas for the inspiration of creating simple test models from polystyrene foam. His research on psf model demonstrations was presented at the first Structural Teachers Conference in Milwaukee, WI, in July,1996.

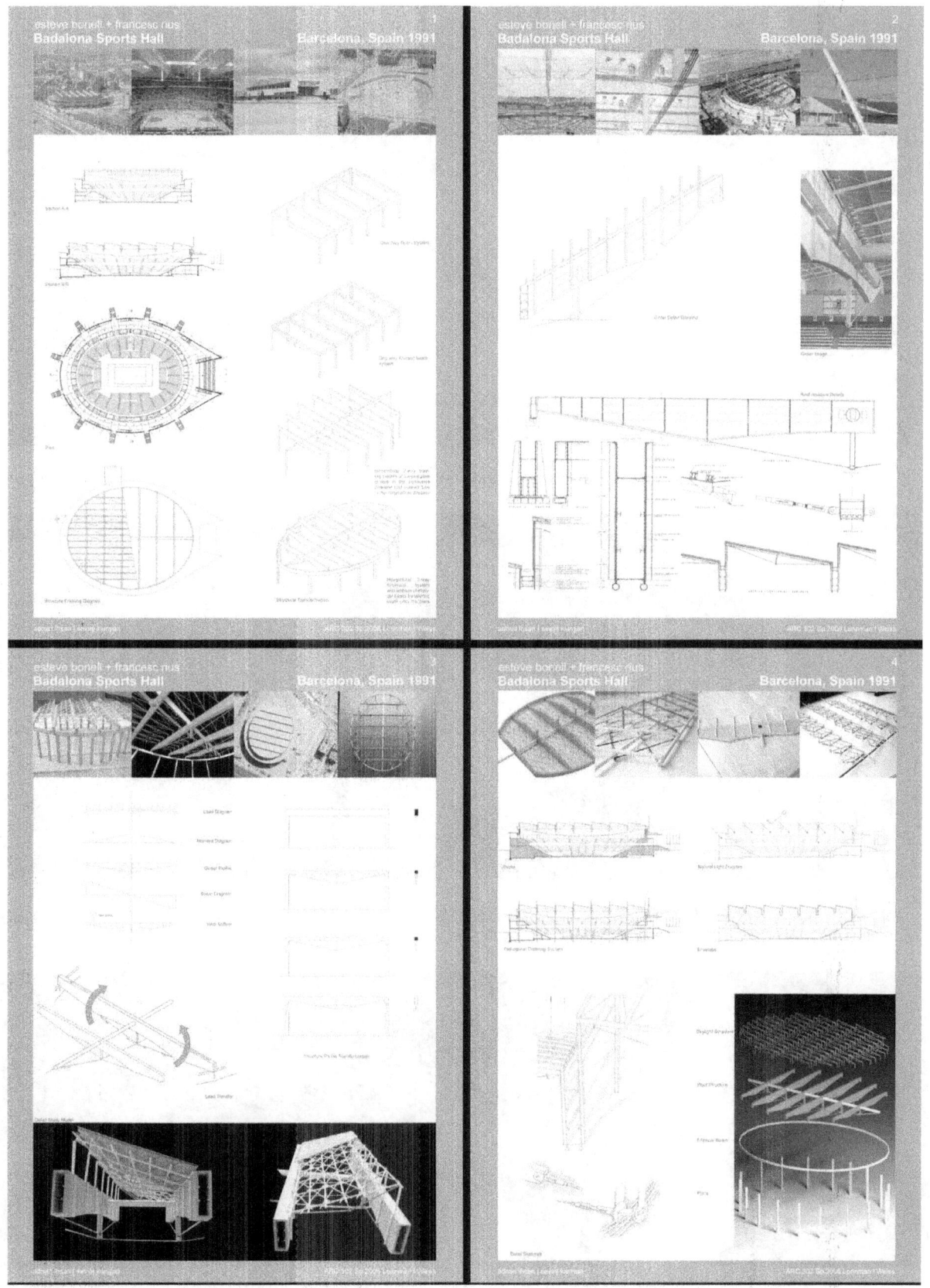

Figure 10. Example of a Case Study Documentation. (Badalona Sports Hall, E. Bonell & F. Rius) Adnan Ul Haq & Sevinj Kianyan.

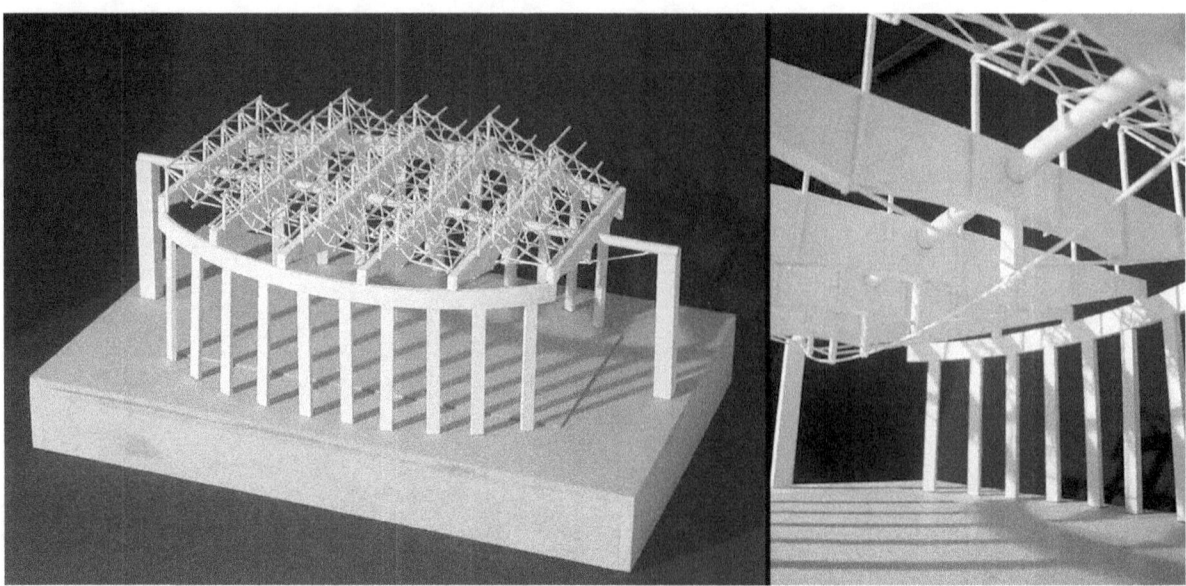

Figure 11. Case Study Final Model. (Badalona Sports Hall, E. Bonell & F. Rius) Adnan Ul Haq & Sevinj Kianyan.

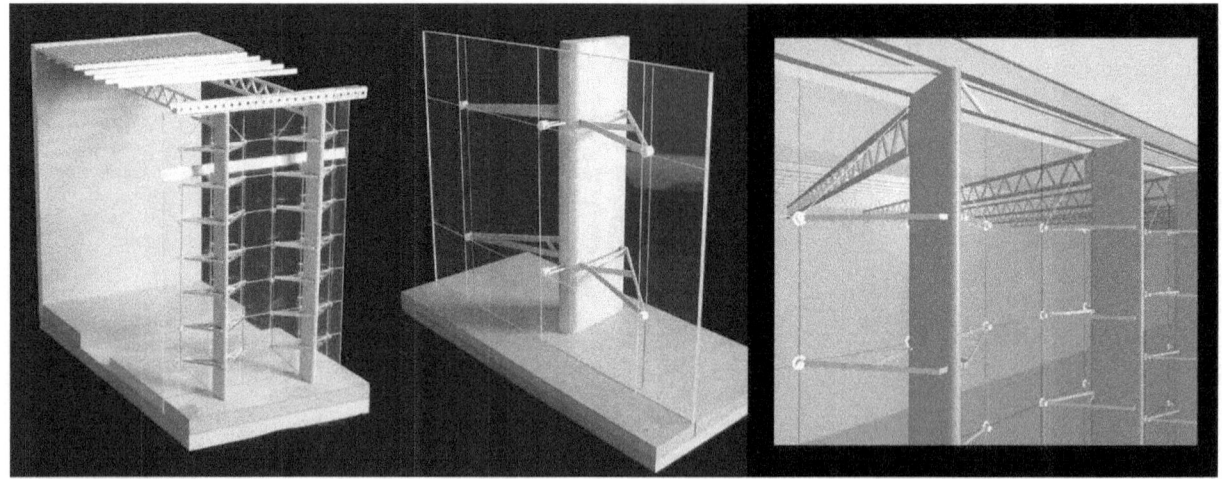

Figure 12. Case Study Final Models: Structural Bay, Detail Model, & Digital Model. (Financial Times Printing Facility, Nicolas Grimshaw & Partners) Nour Asayed, Borzoo Mehrzad, Arash Ravari, & Sina Trama.

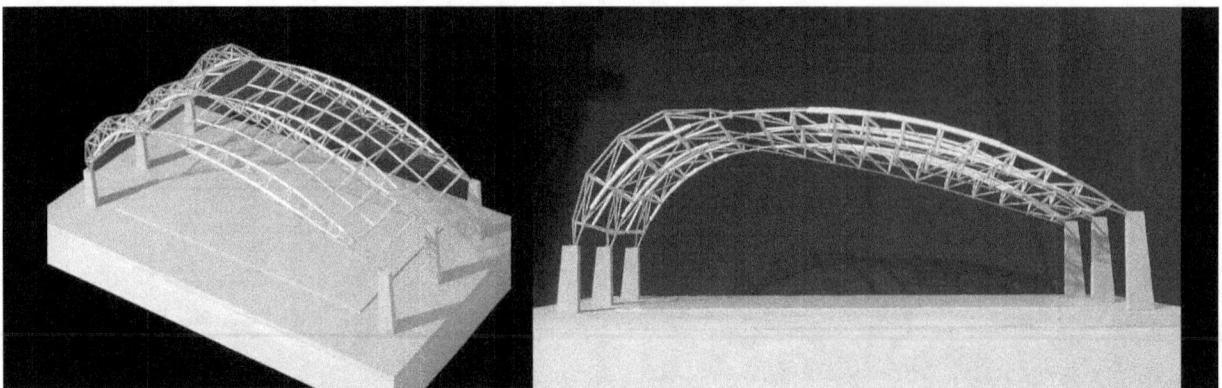

Figure 13. Case Study Final Model. (Waterloo Rail Station, Nicolas Grimshaw & Partners) Sawsan Al-Qasimi & Amar Kalo.

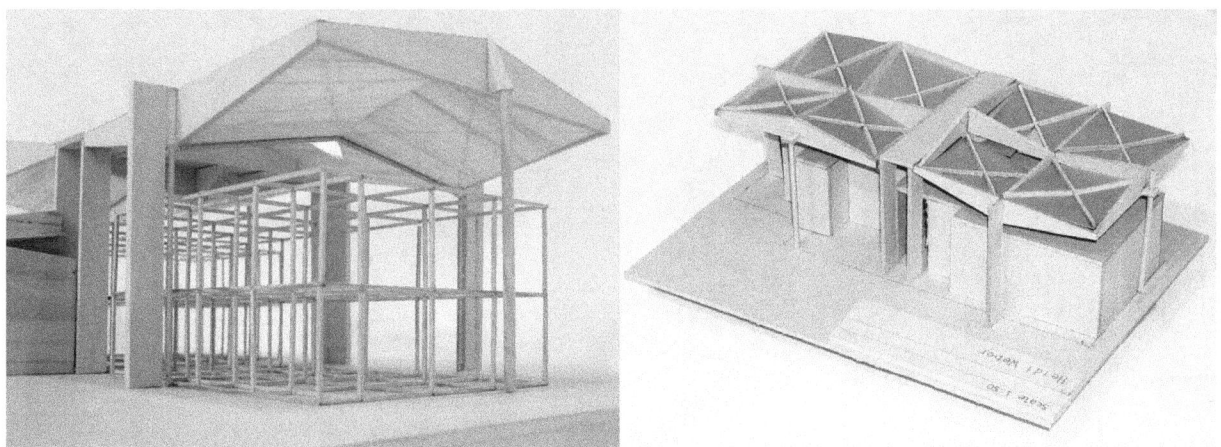

Figure 14. Case Study Final and Study Model. (Zurich Pavilion, Le Corbusier) Nasreen Tamimi & Amina Ahmadi.

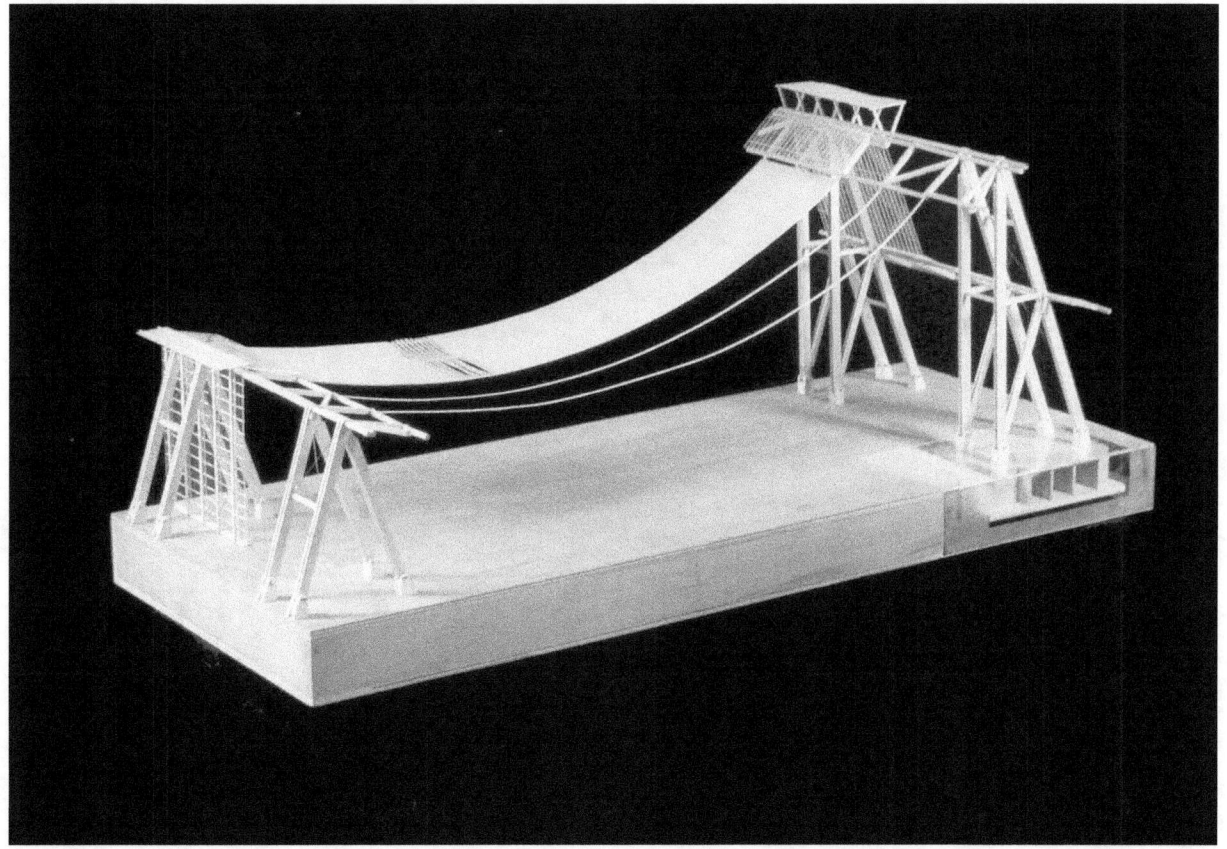

Figure 15. Case Study Final Model. (Hall 26 Hanover Expo, Thomas Herzog & Partner) Nemat El-Suloh & Zaki Ajjawi

Daylight Models, Pattern Development & Structure

Kenneth S. MacKay, AIA
Shahin Vassigh
Department of Architecture - University at Buffalo - State University of New York

Figure 1. Pattern developed into Water Tower

Abstract

In *The Reflective Practitioner*, Donald Schön concluded that the "technical rationality" whereby professionals passively incorporate new technologies should be tempered by a more reflective approach which focuses on 'problem setting', rather than merely 'problem solving'. This paper presents the results of collaboration over two years between an undergraduate architectural design studio and a structures course. The goal of this collaboration was to integrate a structural system into a building where the main interior space was generated with a primary focus on daylight or the three-dimensional projection of a pattern. This approach was intended to emphasize the conflict between the standardized structural solution and the architectural implication of the students' original design. This studio was unique in that students used daylight models to study complex relationships between the light source and the interior surfaces which defined the space and the effects of light filtered through a three-dimensional construction. The use of large-scale physical models to study daylight is not new, but they have been generally limited to building science courses. The goal of this project was to help students to understand the mutability and interrelationship of architectural space and structural design, rather than imposing *integration* on the design process.

The Reflective Practitioner

In the February 2001 *Journal of Architectural Education* devoted to "Technical and Place", Kenneth Frampton, one of the most astute writers over the past three decades on the relationship of architectural technology to culture, provided an introduction essay; *Technoscience and Environmental Culture*.[1] Frampton opens the article with a quotation by R.L. Rutsky stating that "the consequences of techno-cultural processes are not inevitable" because "in this realm, nothing is inherently stable, secure guaranteed"[2]. The article attempts to come to terms with the role and responsibility of the architect in this "unstable field of continually fluctuating data and mediatic images", which he refers to as the 'technological sublime'[3]. As one solution to these problems, Frampton proposes the "place-form" which has been one of his preferred solutions since he first wrote on critical regionalism nearly a quarter of a century ago.[4] In this article, the 'place-form' takes on a socio-political dimension by contrast with the "productform". The term "productform" derives from the "Swiss architect Max Bill, who employed it to refer to industrial design elements, which are determined by constraints of production rather than by ergonomic or functional considerations".[5] What is interesting in this context is the way in which Frampton is able to relate this to the political; by noting "the way in which such a technological 'value-laden' sensibility comes to be gradually incorporated into the everyday culture may be suggested by citing the way in which placeconscious, sociocultural benefits come to be incorporated into building legislation".[6] In other words, the site-specific place-form, in contrast to the leveling of sites for development is an act of resistance against "the homogenizing tendency of universal consumerist technology has the potential to become an exemplary work eventually influencing building legislation". It is not clear that this advocating of the place-form is more effective than the avante garde approach which he later criticizes as 'the continual attempts made by the profession, ever since these 1960's, to legitimize its practice in terms of technological fetishism'.[7]

The significant question raised by "Technoscience and Environmental Culture" emerges in the final section subtitled "Reflective Practice" in which Frampton asks the following; "...what should be the ethical role of the architect in the face of the technological sublime...?"[8] Although Frampton provides neither a clear definition nor bibliographic references as to the source of the term 'technological sublime'[9], it is clear that the 'technological sublime' is not restricted to mediated images, but encompasses the broad spectrum of the problems presented by human development. Acknowledging that architects 'are only responsible for less than 10 percent of the build environment',[10] Frampton proposies that there are 'two choices facing the profession and schools of architecture'.[11] The first, an approach the profession seems increasingly to adopt, is to embrace the technique of the spectacular. Frampton sees this approach represented by architects seeking plastic visual effects derived from digital processes and the use of high-tech materials. The second choice which represents "a more objective and ethically responsible alternative" is to "maintain a distance from the technoscience whirlwind without denying the potential capacity of advanced technology and the unavoidable effects of its influence".[12] Frampton acknowledges that this second approach is based on concepts first proposed by Donald Schön in his 1983 book; *The Reflective Practitioner: How Professionals Think in Action.*

The Reflective Practitioner was one of the most prominent and important studies of professional practice published in the 1980s. The original study focused on what Schön believed was a problematic dichotomy between scientific theory and the application of scientific theory to practice. As a sociologist responding to the increasing skepticism of 'professional expertise' by the general public, Schön studied several professions to uncover what he believed was the underlying difference between 'theory' and 'practice'. The problem he saw, shared by all the professions, consisted of the application of scientific theory and technique in instrumental problem solving, which he termed 'technical rationality'.[13] In his view, technical rationality had imposed upon professional practice an unreflective process of problem 'solving'. Problems of choice or decision were inappropriately solved through the selection of available means, which resulted in pre-established ends. Schön believed that the 'problem solving' application of technical rationality often lead professionals to define the specific problem in terms of the available scientific theory or technique. Through this emphasis on problem solving, professionals were ignoring the process of problem 'setting'. In other words, the process by which they predefined the decision to be made, the ends to be achieved, and the means which may be chosen, based on technical rationalism rather than an appropriate response to real needs. As he conducted his research, Schön concluded that, "increasingly we have become aware of the importance to actual practice of phenomena-complexity, uncertainty, instability, uniqueness and value-conflict which do not fit the model of technical rationality."[14] In real-world practice, according to Schön, problems do not present themselves to the practitioner as givens. The unique solution required in professional practice must be constructed from the materials of problematic situations which are puzzling, troubling, and uncertain. For Schön, professionals were increasingly coming to see 'problem setting' as central to practice. In order to convert a problematic situation to a problem, a practitioner must do a certain kind of work to make sense of an uncertain situation that initially makes no sense. Even though "problem setting" is not itself a technical problem, Schön developed the concept that "problem setting" was an activity necessary for technical problem solving. Its importance can best be summarized by his statement that "when we set the problem, we select what we will treat as the 'things' of the situation, we set the boundaries of our attention to it, and we impose upon it a coherence which allows us to say what is wrong and in what direction the situation needs to be changed. Problem setting is a process in which, interactively, we 'name' the things to which we will attend and 'frame the context in which we will attend to them'".[15]

The significance for architectural education of *The Reflective Practitioner* lies in Schön's assertion that "technical rationalism" had become the primary justification and description of professional knowledge.[16] Schön believed that this resulted in a division of labor between those who were theory-oriented and those who were practice-oriented. The result of this was that "researchers are supposed to provide the basic and applied science from which to derive techniques for diagnosing and solving the problems of practice. Practitioners are supposed to furnish researchers with problems for study and with tests of the utility of research results".[17] This division was also reflected in the 'normative curricula of professional education and the institutionalized relations of research and practice'.[18]. His review of curricula within the various professional schools found that the basic and applied sciences were taught first and comprised the primary educational experience. The skills required of real-world problems of practice were placed at the end of the curriculum sequence. For Schön, this order of curricula reflected the model of "technical rationality" and reinforcing a belief that 'real knowledge lies in the theories and techniques of basic and applied science', and 'skills are the ambiguous, secondary kind of knowledge'.[19]

For Frampton, Schön's 'Reflective Practice' is important in that in that it provides two interrelated levels at which reflection-in-action needs to take place. The first is the relationship between the architect and the client, in which the client should participate actively in the design discourse along with the architect and the various technical consultants. The second level is the civic responsibility of architects to relate their designs to the larger general principles which shape their resolution, thereby engaging the 'body-politic' in the formation of environmental policy. For Frampton, Schön's reflection-in-action when put in practice becomes democracy-in-action, providing a guide for the ethical role of the architect in society.

The Implications for Teaching

It has been nearly a quarter of a century since Schön wrote 'the Reflective Practitioner'. It is debatable whether many of Schön's underlying assumptions still apply to all of the professions he studied. It is also debatable whether *The Reflective Practitioner* can provide the basis for an ethical approach to architecture as applied in Kenneth Frampton's article. It is also debatable whether any specific design methodology can be asserted as more or less ethical as any other methodology. Despite this, *The Reflective Practitioner* made a significant contribution to the study of the professions and Frampton's reference to this is especially relevant in light of the increased awareness of the responsibility for sustainability. In light of this (and beyond the scope of this paper) there would be value in revisiting *The Reflective Practitioner* with regard to three significant issues. The first issue is the relevance of "refection-in-action" to current professional practice. Much of Schön's argument is based on a dichotomy between 'theory' and 'practice' which may or may not still apply. For Schön, the "reflection-in-action" of the practitioner provided an antidote to isolated theory, however, a survey of the American landscape leads one to question if the current dilemma is not between 'theory' and 'practice' but the thoughtless repetition of standardized solutions by many practitioners. Second, Schön's study was remarkably broad in its scope, which often lead to general conclusions which are assumed to apply across very diverse professional fields. Although there have been several excellent studies which focus specifically on the professional practice of architecture, none have addressed the topic of "refection-in-action" within the field of architecture. The third issue, related to the second, is that Schön's working definition of "reflection" is often hard to pin down. Within the fields of philosophy and critical theory, 'reflection' has a very specific meaning about which volumes have been written. In re-reading *The Reflective Practitioner,* it is not clear that what he observed and described did not fall into more sociological descriptions such as 'creativity' and 'non-linear thinking'.

Despite these shortcomings, Schön's *The Reflective Practitioner* highlights the problem of assuming that technological solutions, especially solutions developed in engineering disciplines, can simply be incorporated or smoothly integrated into the architectural design process. For Schön, what made the practicing professional an interesting study were the 'puzzling, troubling, uncertain and problematic situations in which they were placed'. With regards to pedagogy, this might mean the development of projects which initially lead students in one direction so that they might have to later struggle with the technological implications of their initial decisions. It is with type of 'critical resistance' that the following projects were developed.

Studio Pedagogy

Over the past four fall semesters, the faculty of the Junior Year has developed a series of projects which begin by having students generate a particular space, focusing on the unique spatial conditions produced through such tools as large-scale daylight models. These individual spaces are then multiplied and/or incorporated into a larger complex building program. This approach has been developed based on an agreement that the

Figure 2. Canopy for Farmers' Market

introduction of a complex building program presents a unique dilemma. Broadly stated, when faced with a complex program, students often move away from a unique generative and transformational process, and instead, begin to rely on normative assumptions about how a particular program (in this

Figure 3. Pattern projected into three-dimensions

case a hotel) should 'look like' or be organized. Restated as a pedagogical question, it would be how to introduce a building with complex programmatic requirements which builds upon the foundation of design fundamentals and exploration introduced in previous semesters while questioning normative assumptions. During the fall Junior Year, students are also enrolled in the required structures class which focuses on steel construction. As a requirement of the structures class, students are required to develop a framing plan for the final building project designed in the studio. In addition, students are required to detail several structural connections. The work and projects presented here are from the fall 2004 and fall 2005 studios.

The first project of the fall 2004 studio was a canopy for a farmers' market (Fig 2). Students selected a two-dimensional pattern and built a three-dimensional projection of this pattern (Fig 3). Students then studied the structural possibilities presented by this projection, how this construction filtered daylight (Fig 4), and the material implications of weather-protection. The second project of the semester was a 30-room hotel located on a riverfront site overlooking downtown Pittsburgh. Drawing from the tradition of designing through empirical knowledge established in the first two years of the program, this project was intended to encourage students to draw inspiration from personal experience. This experience is intentionally mutated by the distance and distortion that can be attributed to reliance on memory. The documentation of a window that is significant to each student lays the foundation for the project. A narrative written about the window is used as a generative tool for the analysis and transformation of that window. The narrative and the window are intended to generate a framework that controls the design development of the building, in this case a hotel, conceptually, formally, and tectonically. In this process the students were asked to use

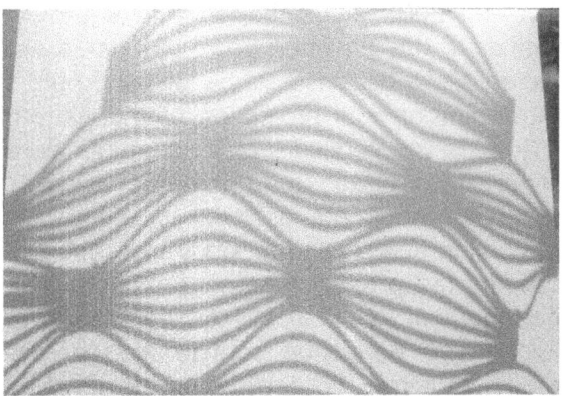

Figure 4. Shadow study of three dimensional pattern

language to see their windows anew. They used the narrative to guide their eyes in a re-reading of the drawing of their window. Issues emerging from the narratives lead to the alteration of the form and function of the window. The conventional use of a window is challenged by the emerging structures that sometimes function in ways contrary to it. Conditions of window as a viewing mechanism, a light source, a break in the boundary between exterior and interior, etc are challenged and pushed to extremes.

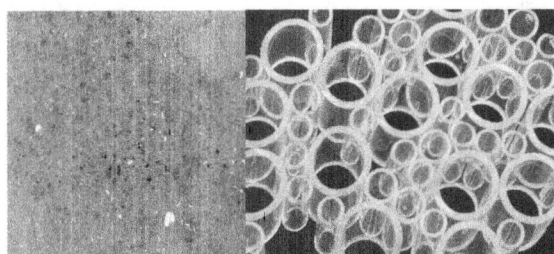

Figure 5. Pattern and model developed from pattern

The interaction of public and private space, circulation, site orientation, relationships of interior and exterior, and other decisions made during the design of the hotel are measured against the guidelines laid out by the narrative and the transformed window. The work documented here, represents ways in which the window transformations develop significant ideas that challenge the building program.

The fall 2005 studio began with a project similar to the previous year. Students selected a two-dimensional pattern and built a three-dimensional projection of the pattern (*Fig 4*). In the second project, students were required to attach their three-dimensional projection horizontal onto the top edge of a projection screen and to study the shadows cast by the projection in natural light. The pedagogical intent of this project was twofold. The horizontal configuration of the model required that the model be attached to and cantilevered from the projections surface; which required the three-dimensional pattern to accommodate the forces placed on it. In addition, since the final presentation for this project was limited to a photographic image which included only the shadow, not the construction itself, students' attention was drawn to the solid-void configuration of the model. In the third project, students further developed the structure of their pattern transformation as a wall system. Students were asked to consider the primary, secondary, and tertiary structural members which might need to be added to the pattern to ensure the system's vertical stability. As additional material was added to the construction, students were to consider how this material would relate to the original At the final presentation for this project, the structural stability of these 12" X 18" models were tested by placing a high-velocity fan 10' away from the model. For the fourth project, each studio group (15 students) constructed a large scale model (1/2" = 1'-0") of Diefendorf Hall, a late-modern classroom building designed by Edward Durrell Stone which is located across the quad from Crosby Hall, the building which houses the architecture studios. The assignment was to replace the existing screen wall with a new wall which further developed the three-dimensional pattern from the previous projects. The new screen wall was to be structurally self-supporting pattern. and to have as few connections to the existing building as possible. The primary consideration of the new screen was the modulation of light entering the existing classrooms and the mediation of both inte-

Figure 6. Screen wall derived from pattern

rior and exterior views through the wall (*Fig 6*). In the next major project, *Containment*, students were required to construct a container or a series of containers/bladders that held one gallon of water. The intent of this project was to expand upon the three-dimensional pattern construction to include volume and weight. Students were provided a triangular site on the campus adjacent to the power plant and the old gymnasium. Students were to expand on their explorations of 'containment' to develop a 'water tower' which would both hold and display water. The final presentation requirements included a scale model which held one gallon of water, and a series of photo-collages which juxtaposed the project onto the existing site. The above projects were completed within the first half of the semester. The remainder of the semester was devoted to a complex building program; and aquatic enter located on a site adjacent to the university campus.

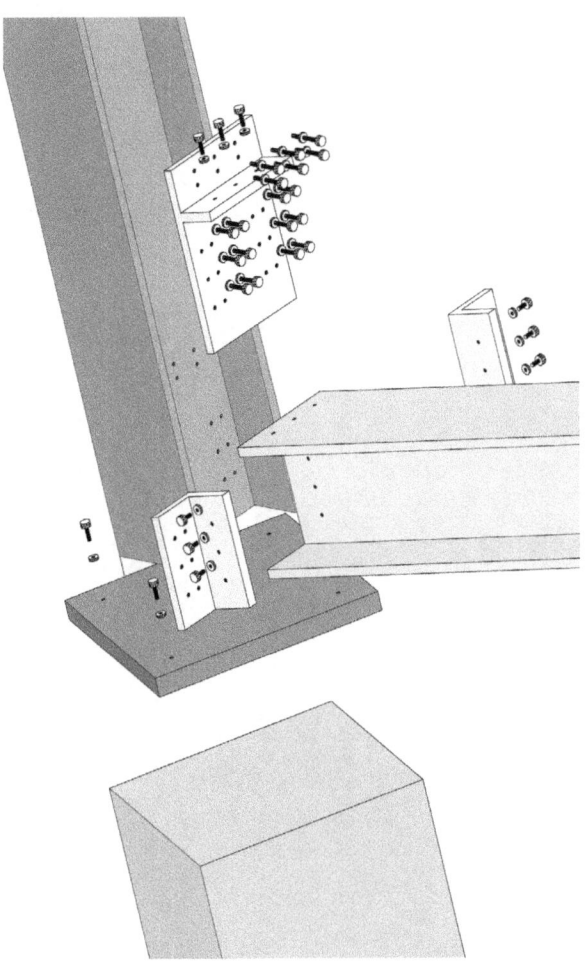

Figure 7. Detail at column base

Notes:

[1] Frampton, Kenneth. "Technoscience and Environmental Culture: A Provisional Critique." Journal of Architectural Education 54(2001): 123-129.

[2] Ibid, pg. 123.

[3] Ibid, pg. 123.

[4] Frampton, Kenneth. "Towards a Critical Regionalism: Six Points for an Architecture of Resistance." In Foster, Hal. The Anti-aesthetic: Essays on Postmodern Culture. Port Townsend, WA: Bay Press, 1983.

[5] Frampton, Kenneth, JAE, pg. 126.

[6] Ibid, pg. 127.

[7] Ibid, pg. 128. Frampton appears to be using the word 'avant-garde' in its more general, popular definition rather than the precise definition used in the field of art. Burger, Peter. Theory of the Avant-Garde. Minneapolis: University of Minnesota Press, 1984.

[8] Ibid, pg. 128.

[9] Most references to the technological sublime refer to: Marx, Leo. The Machine in the Garden; Technology and the Pastoral Ideal in America. New York: Oxford Press, 1964. However, Frampton's use of the phrase is similar to the concept of 'blockage' or the 'sublime terror' experienced when faced with an overwhelming amount of information as described by: Hertz, Neil. The End of the Line: Essays on Psychoanalysis and the Sublime. New York: Columbia University Press, 1985.

[10] Frampton, Kenneth, JAE, pg. 128.

[11] Ibid, pg. 128.

[12] Ibid, pg. 128.

[13] Schon, Donald. The Reflective Practitioner: How Professionals Think in Action. New York: Basic Books, 1983. pg. 21.

[14] Ibid, pg. 40.

[15] Ibid, pg. 40.

[16] Ibid, pg. 26.

[17] Ibid, pg. 26.

[18] Ibid, pg. 26.

[19] Ibid, pg. 30.

Figures:

Fig 1: Laura Karnath

Fig. 2: Maciej Kaczynski

Fig. 3: Maciej Kaczynski

Fig. 4: Maciej Kaczynski

Fig. 5: Laura Karnath

Fig. 6: Laura Karnath

Fig. 7: Yee Man Wong

Structural Harmony and Model Discourse

Ivan Markov
The Chinese University of Hong Kong

Abstract

The two disciplines of architecture and engineering have departed in recent history and it is the growing need to bridge this gap on which primarily architectural curricula will have to focus on. This paper outlines why there is a need for integration and where it may happen, and explore examples of how it can evolve.

Workshops of physical models, from The Chinese University of Hong Kong and Syracuse University, are used to demonstrate the various approaches. These models are of indispensable value to design studios but are also essential to the visualization of basic structural principles. Important differences between small-scale and large-scale models are addressed in this paper. New rapid prototype technologies are capable of building models with embedded structural properties.

Introduction

Is it a brick or a bridge? It may well be a little brick bridge, comprising a structure and a material that illustrate well the indispensable relationship between architecture and engineering. A little bridge needs structural and architectural attention to emerge in an attractive and pleasing form. Masonry is superior in compression; thus, an arch might be a natural form. Brick is part of the masonry family and is a truly dual-purpose material, capable of carrying complex loads and articulating architecture. It allows for endlessly creative and pleasing architecture through combinations of unit shapes, texture, and color. There is no other material that serves both architects and engineers at the same time, which could well be the reason why brick as the first manmade material has survived and is still widely used in contemporary design.

Typically, buildings with small spans are predominantly designed by architects, followed by engineering designers. Bridges and large-span structures are areas in which engineers generally take the lead. Steel and concrete are usually the materials of choice for larger buildings, while glass and masonry are typical choices for cladding and building expression, and wood, amongst other materials, is the choice for openings and interior design.

This is the general pattern of design for the majority of common building types. For innovative and nonconforming architecture, there is a need for a nonconformist approach. Architects and engineers need to join together in the early stage of preliminary design, as outstanding architecture frequently emerges from outstanding collaboration. This paper focuses on modes through which we can cultivate this collaboration, in the educational process of future architects.

Cultivation of Creative Architecture

The first question is why do we need to cultivate collaboration between architects and engineers? In the past, they were one profession, but with evolving complexity, it split into more professions, never reintegrating subsequently. Architecture as an art may lead to the creation of fascinating forms. Computer parametric programs can generate shapes that were hard to explore just a few years ago. However, creating something new and extraordinary may lead to the creation of "useless" forms. The imagination and intent of architects may never be realized if they don't stand-up. No matter how great an idea is, it has to be feasible, economic, and safe. There are no "great" architects without the work that promoted their recognition in the first place. In other words, paper can take anything but reality cannot, and structure is a check on reality. Not much has changed since the 1st BC Vitruvious perception of architecture as "beautiful, convenient, and solid." The "solid" stands for structure and is an integral part of all architecture.

Unfortunately, in the US, due to lack of support from studios, technology is mostly considered as an area that supports architecture curricula and not an integral part of it. Yet today, creative built pieces of architecture demonstrate the opposite, perhaps because most of the world's leading architects are not educated in the US. Imminent drive of new technologies may modify approach to architecture.

The second question is where to cultivate this collaboration. Structural engineering curricula offers a rather deep understanding of the subject and quickly submerges into areas such as material properties, structural analyses, foundation, fracture mechanics, reliability, and so on. Experts for each of these areas rarely are the experts for the entire field of structural engineering. The curricula faces its own challenges concerning integration. Architects seek just a tiny fraction of integral engineering knowledge; thus, the architecture curricula is a more logical area through which to respond to the needs of the discipline.

The third question is what structural topics are essential if future architects are to provoke fruitful collaboration between cross-disciplines. Some topics are unavoidable, such as the selection of structural systems and understanding their behavior, strengths, and weaknesses. The systems are combinations of individual structural elements, the approximate sizes and shapes of which may be decided using the rule-of-thumb, preliminary calculations, or intuition. Connections between the structural elements are essential to the performance of the elements, and to the system as whole. The system needs to efficiently sustain gravity and lateral loads and convey them to the foundation. Material selection is based on the specifics of material properties and the specifics of the system. All of these selections have to blend with architectural intention, construction efficacy, and safe structure, as the consequences of structural failure are far more costly than the consequences of architectural failure.

These topics are commonly fragmented. Architectural design is a rather complex task of many simultaneous aspects. The integration of structure and architecture and intention of using structure to enhance architectural design are generally the least covered issues in studio design yet they are what architects will certainly need to consider in their practice. This does not come as surprise, as first, neither engineers nor architects are educated in how to teach this integration. They are good in repeating the methods that they were taught during their own educational process, and so the opportunity to excel is missed. Today, examples of sparkling architecture are produced through practices in which the benefits of close collaboration between the two disciplines are fully recognized.

The fourth question is how to bring structure into the process of architectural design. This is a controversial issue, one with many challenges. Who is most suitable to teach the subject? What are plausible ways of doing it? How is it blended with architectural design? Structures as engineering subject require special attention in the implementation of architectural curricula. Unfortunately, in reality structure is given the least attention due to the lack of focus from the faculty body as whole, though this may well be the only place where students of architecture may have to apply some quantitative skills architects should have. Engineers are used to analytical learning, they learn principles that are applicable to any engineering design, and they have more of a knowledge-based approach. On the other hand, architects are better trained in the visual, they are focused on learning from precedents and they take more concept-based approach.

For architecture to take full advantage of structures, it is of the utmost importance that the faculty teaching structures fully understands the engineering aspect of structure as well as the architectural needs. Unfortunately, such a profile does not come ready-made in any curricula. Whoever enters this area of teaching has to have additional education and an adjustment period. Usually, the teachers are self-taught with regard to how to motivate the students for the subject, how to convey the knowledge, how to make the subject interesting and meaningful, and how to collaborate with the design studio faculty. If the subject is marginalized and taught by a faculty with blurred knowledge of the area, it may be rather confusing and the opportunity for enhancing architectural design may be missed.

Structure Courses and Thematic Studios

The main focus of the structure courses at The Chinese University of Hong Kong (CUHK) is to explain external loads such as gravity and the lateral and efficient architecture needed to transfer them to the ground. Structure responds to external forces through the development of the internal forces of structural elements. Understanding the concept of decomposition of internal forces is crucial to the creative design of structures. There can be no meaningful discussion about structure if internal forces such as tension, compression, shear, and moment are not understood. It would be similar to teaching architecture without understanding space, function, environment, or relationships.

Elements respond to internal forces through deformation. Through the visual presentation of various deform patterns, students can appreciate the importance of internal forces. Physical models are used to visualize the presence of internal forces to better understand their effects. Figure 1 shows teaching models used to demonstrate the concepts of axial, shear, and moment respectively.

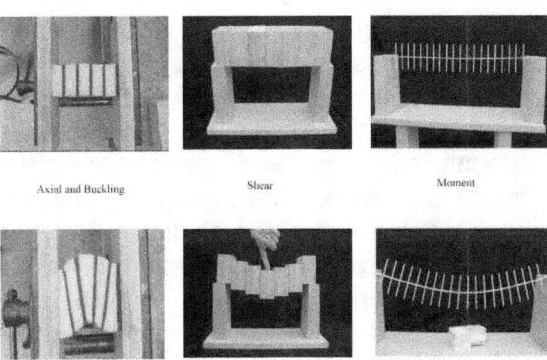

Figure 1. Visualization of axial, shear, and moment force

As shown in Figure 1, axial force acts perpendicularly at a cross section and tends to extend or contract the element. Buckling is a phenomena associated with compression as opposed to bending, as often confused. Shear force acts parallel at a cross section and tends to slice the element. Moment force rotates at a cross section and tends to bend the element. As the result, deformation is proportional to the magnitude of the internal force.

Once the presence of internal forces is well understood, the next step is to study their distribution throughout structural systems. It is important to emphasize that the distribution of internal forces is directly related to the selection and type of structural system, the size and shape of the individual elements, and the method and amount of material used in their connections.

One way to blend subject courses and design studios is to have curricula of thematic studios. For example, at the Chinese University of Hong Kong structures are offered as required courses and are tested in thematic studio environments. The thematic studios are habitation, urbanization, tectonics, and technics. Each studio has three sections. Students have to take all four studios but may select the sequence themselves. Students from various years working together create a dynamic design studio environment.

Of the four thematic studios, the technics studio is the one associated with the creation of buildings as it explores natural forces such as gravity, wind, light, air, thermal, and sound. This is the place where, for example, material, structure, and fabrication, steer design exploration. Two projects are assigned per semester: the studio project and the school project. The studio project is structured to incorporate the study of specific issues as common theme to the entire studio. This is followed by the school project, which integrates the issues in a final design exercise.

The technics studio relies on physical modeling and digital tools as means of exploration. While physical models may well serve the purpose, it is important to be aware of their limitations within the studio setting. What students make is not the end product but rather a materialized stage of the process. Models are of utmost value when it comes to understanding space and special relationships, and are also indispensable in understanding structure, behavior, and relationships among structural elements. Yet there is large discrepancy between the actual structural performance of full-scale buildings and the structural performance of the models. The discrepancy comes from the scale factor, when the properties of the materials and sizes of the elements are not properly scaled. As a result, models are substantially oversized and stronger.

To address this issue in the studio, two workshops were carried out. A recipient of the Gold Medal from the British Institute of Engineers, Tony Hant, was invited to inspire and challenge the students.

In the first workshop, students were asked to make a paper bridge. The bridge was to span 11 inches and be freely supported on the sides. The students could use four sheets of A4 paper and glue, but the glue could not be used as additional reinforcement. The bridge was to carry a point load at its center and the goal was to construct a bridge that carried the largest load.

It was pleasing to see students explore different shapes and forms of paper to develop a firmer bridge. Entertaining ideas emerged, yet important lessons were also learnt. Some of the paper bridges are shown in Figure 2.

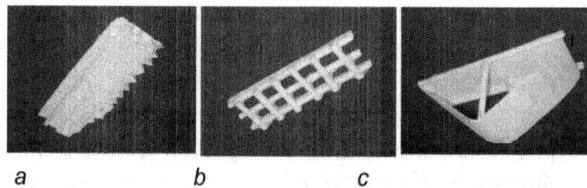

a   b   c

Figure 2. Paper bridges models

The model shown in Figure 2a explores the idea of depth. Paper itself is very thin and if used as a horizontal plane cannot take substantial loads. Yet it does have certain strengths if crafted in bundles of vertical sheets that resemble beams or the waffle slabs system. A similar idea is carried forward by the model shown in Figure 2b, for which paper is bundled in tubular forms to create a grid of horizontal beams. The tubular shape is favorable, as it prevents buckling. Here the elements are stronger and the bridge is stiffer. In both examples, the bridges were designed as beams ignoring weak material bending strength.

The model in Figure 2c capitalizes on dominant paper properties. Paper is rather strong in tension but extremely week to buckling in compression. The load was hung from the center of the bridge and transferred by a single sheet of paper to the upper plane, where tubular beams acted in compression. Horizontal mid-bracing helps to decreases the buckling length of the compressive cord. It is interesting to note that vertical bars actually decrease the capacity of the bridge due to additional mid span bending of the compressive cord. Surprisingly enough, the bridge took about 8 lb in weight. The overall shape of the bridge is efficient and resembles a moment diagram for a mid point loaded beam.

In the second workshop, students were asked to design and build a real bridge. The bridge was to span a 9 feet gap, and only natural material, such as bamboo, wood, rope, and cotton, could be used. Students worked in groups and once finished, a "volunteer" member of the group had to walk over the bridge. If the bridge sustained the load, it remained in the competition, and the lightest bridge among those was the overall winner.

 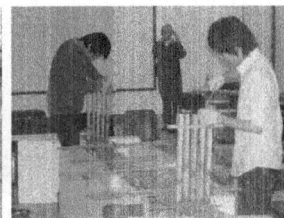

Figure 3. Construction of real bridges using bamboo, wood, and rope

Figure 3 shows the students assembling bridges using bamboo and wood as the core materials. The importance of connection was recognized from an early stage, and it become clear that with the use of rope, the fixed connection capable of transferring moments between elements could be realized only through parallel layout of the elements. Two members were stronger than one member if forced to deform together, and members were bundled up with rope.

A variety of design strategies were explored. Figure 4a shows a hybrid wood and bamboo bridge, the design of which was based on the concept of space truss. It worked well since with the rope it was easy to create hinge joints. The top and bottom cords were curved to resemble the shape of a moment diagram of a uniformly-loaded simply supported beam. The top cord had two members, to provide a platform for walking, but also to improve the buckling capacity of the bamboo members in compression. Surprise came at the very end when it was realized that two pinned supports could not provide torsional stability of the bridge. Issues of torsion are often overlooked in studio projects.

a   b

Figure 4. Space Truss Concept Bridge and Hesitant Beam Bridge

The bridge in Figure 4b is an example of an unsuccessful attempt at increasing the depth of the structure by suspending the deck from the top cord. The two top cords acted as independent beams and could not carry the bending.

Figure 5b shows an astonishing solution, based on a modified cable-stayed bridge concept; that is, the bridge length was restricted to 9 ft. That created a problem for anchoring the tie-back cables. The students resolved the issue by extending the column's height and using tie-down cables instead. Ultimately a solution hardly seen before resulted in the best performing bridge. Because of a large shear force, an important detail was the hinge between the beams and columns, constructed by drilling columns and inserting a bamboo stick across the holes.

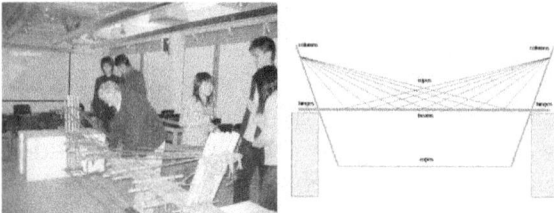

Figure 5. Ingenious Rope-Stated Bridge in Self-Equilibrium

By doing the workshops, students were exposed to hands-on learning experience of how to discover forms and shapes that will stand up. These types of exercises allow for better understanding of how loads are carried by structures, what are the challenges, and how we can respond to them. It is essential that these exercises be properly utilized, in order to provide maximum benefits to students. They need to fully demonstrate and explain certain structural concepts and not to become self-serving exercises.

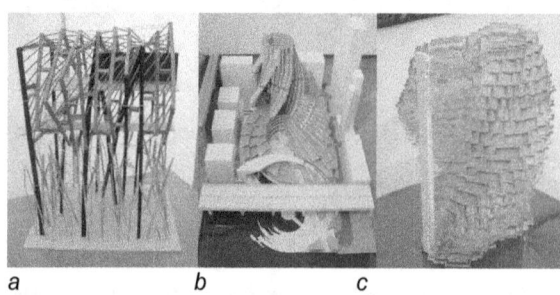

a b c

Figure 6. Samples of Studio Projects

The theme of the recent technics studio was "A Place of Transport." Material, structure, and fabrication played critical roles in creating a space with sentiments of motion, purpose, and excitement. Year two engaged in the exploration of weather bus-stop shelters and year three the exploration of subway train stations and the remodeling of existing platforms. Master students were involved with the building of a habitable bridge connecting the city and the waterfront ferry. Figure 6 shows some typical models.

Figure 6a shows a model of subway platforms carried by two set of frames, with wood used as the primary material. Mainframes hold together the entire structure, while smaller sub-frames are incrementally rotated to create a dynamic space, and the rotational force is controlled by a set of cables spanning between the main frames. The concept of the proposed structural system is appealing and attractive. Figures 6b and 6c show a thesis project that deals with Hong Kong's high-rise, high-density environment. A mega structure concept is investigated for which lattice shear walls or double spiral forms are used to increase stability. Wood and polymers were selected as the material of representation.

New technologies allow for the creation of advanced methods for making models directly from digital data. The sandy plaster type of material enables production of models of quality and accuracy far superior to that of classical physical models. Therefore, visualization and exploration of structure by rapid prototype models is elevated to a new level.

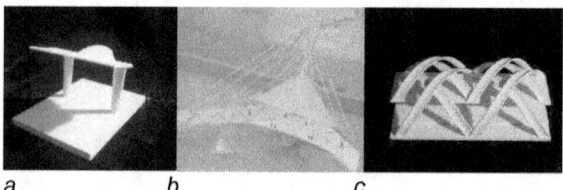

a b c

Figure 7. Rapid Prototype 3D Models

Figure 7a shows a rapid prototype model of a bus stop shelter. A folded plate concept in longitudinal direction, combined with a spherical shell in transverse direction, was used to create the carrying capacity of the roof. The columns are tapered towards the roof, and more material at the top of the columns was required to collect the moments from the roof. Inclined columns reduce gravity moments at the support. The fragility of the model best illustrates the critical points in the structure. Figure 7b shows a habitable bridge concept where the cable-stayed idea is used to hold space truss, which in turn supports the platform. Split inclined columns respond well to the bi-directional bridge space pattern.

Figure 7c demonstrates the full advantage of new technology. A sophisticated three-pin arch system is explored, in which the center pin is in the form of an upper platform. A double-curved lamella approach creates exuberant structure. The arch cross-section is u-shaped to increase the strength by increasing the moment of inertia.

The fragility of the models in all three examples reveals the potential fragility of structure itself. This would have be rather difficult were it not impossible to achieve using widely used wood models.

The Controversy of Masonry

A plain masonry building is complex structural assembly and potentially rewarding architectural material. Steel is a homogeneous material in which the properties of tension and compression are equal. Concrete is a heterogeneous material, superior in compression but in need of additional materials, such as steel bars, to take tension. The structural complexity of masonry comes from complex wall assembly and the additional layer of mortar joints, not present in steel or concrete.

Masonry falls between the professions of architecture and engineering. It encloses space and provides load bearing. That dual role led to the current situation; that is, that masonry is considered in some schools of architecture and in some schools of engineering but unfortunately not as cross-disciplinary course. There are vast numbers of curricula in which masonry is not sufficiently covered, as it is assumption that it will be covered by the other discipline.

A structural engineer teaching in architectural curricula has the opportunity to bridge the gap. An elective masonry course at Syracuse University is developed with a balanced architectural-engineering approach. The course brings together educators, designers, contractors, producers, and officials to share their experience with students.

Field trips to factories and construction sites are common, yet the most attractive components of the course are hands-on sessions and a model competition. Students work with trowels and build mockup masonry details with the help of experienced journeymen. For the final project, they work in groups, first to design and then to build masonry details such as an arch, a wall with an opening, a corner wall, a column, or sculpture as shown in Figure 8. The models are built on campus so they can be seen by the wider university community. Bricks, blocks, stone, and tiles are donated by local producers.

Figure 8. Masonry Model Competition

Last year students' projects were inspired by and thematically allied to the existing sculpture "Six Curved Walls" by acclaimed artist LeWitt that is located on campus. One of the main benefits of these masonry details is that they are the full scale models assembled from the real size units with intact structural properties.

The course, which is one of the largest masonry elective courses in the US, was very well received by students. Masonry is explored not only in terms of its conventional role of building material but also as an material of expression, for example, in practice a little brick bridge has attributes of both structure and architecture.

Summary

The disciplines of architecture and engineering departed from each other in the last century. There is currently a growing realization of the importance of bridging the gap between them. It is more reasonable to expect of architectural curricula to be modified in order to serve the needs of architecture than engineering curricula.

The paper explains why there is a need to integrate structure and architecture, where that need may be addressed, and what are the most important issues that architects need to know, and it presents an example of how this integration can be carried out.

Physical models are of indispensable value in design studios to understand special relationships but they are also central to explain basic structural principles. The important differences between small-scale, large-scale and full-scale models are addressed. New rapid prototype technology models offer embedded structural features.

A New Kind of Software for Teaching Structural Behavior and Design

Kirk Martini
University of Virginia

Introduction

Structural analysis software has now been commonplace in teaching architectural structures for many years. The advantages in visualization and indeterminate analysis are widely recognized and accepted.

The most widely used analysis programs are intended for commercial engineering design: programs such as RISA (RISA Technologies) and Multiframe (Formation Design Systems). The great majority share two key characteristics:

1. **Interaction**: These programs are based on a three-stage model of interaction: 1) model the structure, 2) analyze, and 3) interpret results.

2. **Theory**: Most programs are limited to linear elastic theory. Even those that model aspects of non-linear behavior are still based on the direct stiffness method, which mathematically requires that the stiffness matrix be invertable. Physically, this means that the structure must be stable.

Experience has shown that a wide range of useful teaching can be done despite the limitations imposed by these characteristics.

This paper describes a program, called *Arcade*, which takes a different approach to the user interface and to the underlying theory to create a new kind of structural analysis program, which enables new modes of teaching with analysis software.

The interaction model and the computation methods of Arcade are both derived from computer games. For the interface, this means that the analysis and interpretation stages are merged, making it possible to interact with a model while an analysis is in progress. It is possible to make changes to the model and then see the effects instantly, the way that a game player sees a game respond to input from a controller.

Accordingly, Arcade's computation method is one widely used in computer games to model the physics of moving objects with greater visual realism. The method is commonly called a *physics engine* or *particle system* (Hecker; Witkin). This method makes it possible to model non-linear large-displacement phenomena such as the changing shape of a hanging cable, or the buckling of a frame (Martini 2006).

The program was developed by the author and has been used in architecture courses at the University of Virginia (U.Va.) and Yale University, as well as engineering courses at U.Va. The following discussion describes examples and experiences in using Arcade in an introductory structures course for architecture students.

Elementary Statics Examples

It is widely accepted that students should learn statics before they begin working with structural analysis software (Black and Duff), based on the reasoning that without a knowledge of statics, students will be unable to understand what the program is doing.

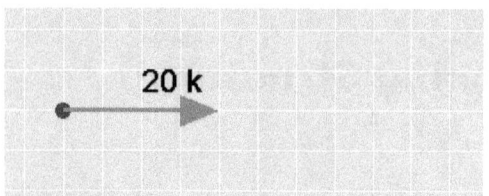

Model of particle with force, before the simulation begins.

Stop-motion rendering of the simulation, showing the response of the particle to the force.

Figure 1. Simple particle mass with force.

Experience with Arcade has shown that it can be used to teach statics from the first day, because of the program's basis in the fundamental physics of $F=ma$. Figure 1 shows an Arcade example that is used in a lecture demonstration. The upper part of the figure shows the basic model: a single particle of mass with a force applied. The lower part of the figure shows a stop-motion rendering of the animated motion when the simulation is run, the particle accelerates in the direction of the force.

This primitive example illustrates some fundamental characteristics of a program:

- **Dynamic simulation**: The program models all phenomena as dynamic events unfolding over time.

- **Particle masses**: A structure is modeled as a collection of particle masses. The dynamic computation is done by stepping through time and solving $F=ma$ for each motion degree of freedom of each particle.

A structural framework is modeled by connecting particle masses with springs, in the form of elements similar to those used in conventional analysis.

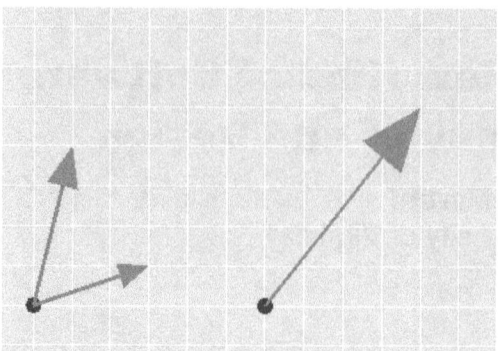

Model of two particles with different force systems.

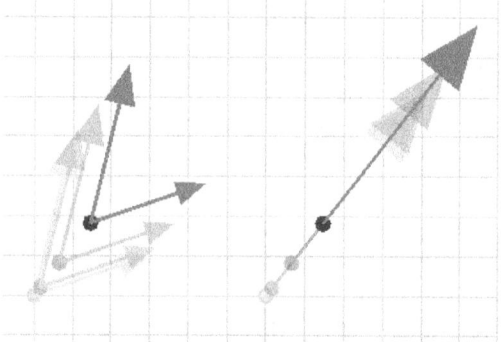

Stop-motion rendering of the simulation, showing the response of the particles to the forces.

Figure 2. Two particles with equivalent systems.

Figure 2 shows another example from this series, this one illustrating the parallelogram rule.

The upper part of the figure shows the initial model. By counting squares of the background grid, it can be demonstrated that the single force on the right is on the diagonal of a parallelogram formed by the two forces on the left. When the simulation is run, the animation shows that the two particles move in exactly the same way.

Of course, $F=ma$ and the parallelogram rule are usually not among the most elusive concepts for architecture students, so it is reasonable to question the value of these demonstrations. The answer is that it enables a different perspective on force systems, shifting greater emphasis on thinking about how the particles will behave, with less emphasis on the values of the vectors. An example of this shift is shown in figure 3, with another slide from this series.

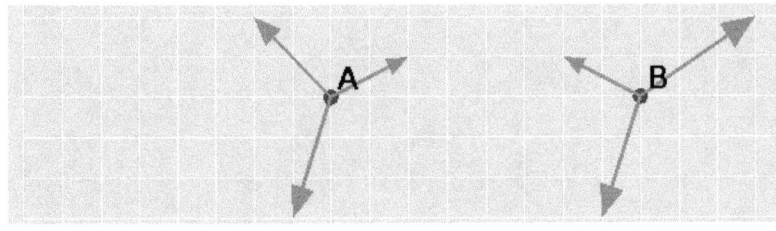

Two particles with different force systems. One is in equilibrium and one is not.

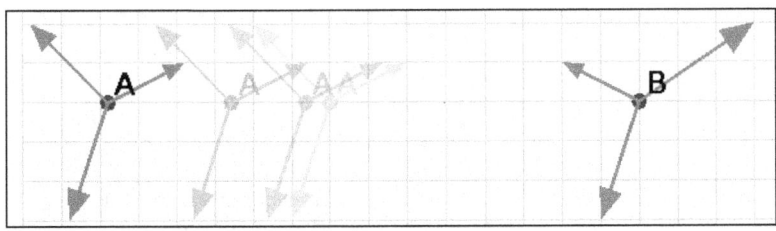

Stop-motion rendering of the simulation. Particle A has an imbalance of horizontal force components, while particle B is in equilibrium.

Figure 3. Predicting which particle will move, and in what direction.

The upper part of the figure shows two particles. With this slide on the screen, students are put the following question:

> *One of these particles will move when the forces are applied, while the other will remain stationary. Determine the one that moves. If you do that, then describe how it will move*

Students are given a few minutes to discuss the problem in pairs, and most pairs correctly identify that the forces on particle A are unbalanced and will move the particle to the left. Students use the technique of counting grid squares to check the balance of horizontal and vertical components. The grid counting technique is of course not practical for more complex problems, but is effective in a lecture setting because it allows the discussion to focus on concepts of force balance rather than details of vector component calculation. More important, students are focusing on a question of physical behavior (How will the particles move?) rather than on one of mathematical properties (What are the vector resultants?).

Figure 4 shows an extension of this approach to the statics of bodies. In this homework problem, students begin with an Arcade model where a body is represented by particle masses connected by stiff beam elements. The force system is configured so that the horizontal and vertical components balance, but the body rotates under the action of the forces, as shown in the right part of the figure. Students are given the task of adding exactly two forces to the figure which put the body in equilibrium. The correct answer is any two forces that produce a counterclockwise couple of 800 kip-feet (the grid in the figure has a module of 10 feet).

As with the particle examples, this problem places the emphasis on the physical behavior rather than mathematical properties, although both must be understood. Free body diagrams are often a difficult concept for both architecture and engineering students, in part because students have little life experience dealing with free floating bodies with forces applied. The author has found that a group that has been taught statics with Arcade becomes quite quick to answer correctly when presented a free body with unbalanced forces and asked the question "how would this move?"; this is probably because these students have seen a dozen or more examples of free bodies moving under unbalanced forces and most begin to develop intuition based on that experience.

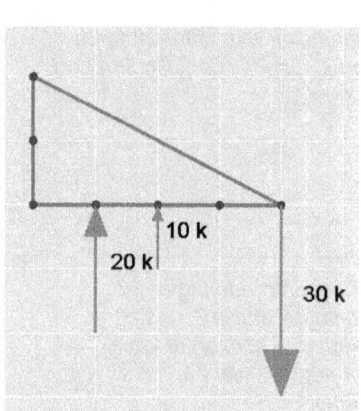

Body with rotationally unbalanced force system.

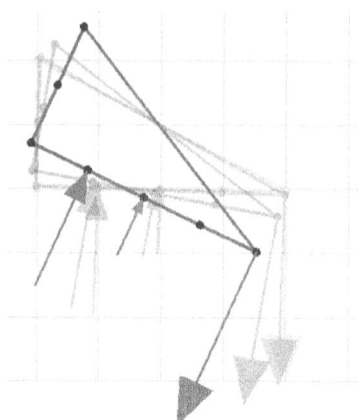

Stop-motion rendering of the simulation, showing the response of the body to the force system.

Figure 4. Body with unbalanced forces. Students must add two forces which put the body in equilibrium

Structural Frameworks Examples

Figure 5 shows an application of Arcade to a conventional truss structure. The rendering options are set so that the width of the member indicates the magnitude of the force, and the color indicates the sense of the force, with red indicating compression and blue tension.

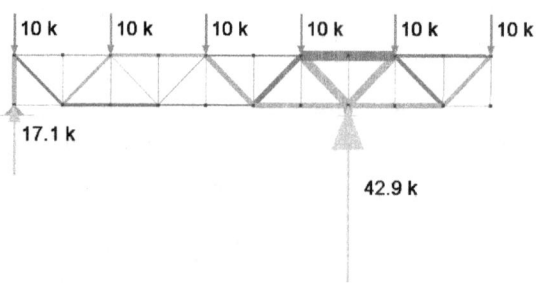

Figure 5. Truss rendered to indicate force magnitudes in members.

This rendering supports discussion of the overall patterns of forces and how the truss is working. It also shows clearly that some member have near zero force, which raises the traditional topic of zero force members, covered in most introductory texts on structures and statics. Traditionally, texts teach that in a system of three forces with two in-line, equilibrium requires the third force to be zero. This fact of statics is used to explain zero force members, and it is usually mentioned that the zero force members are necessary for secondary bracing.

Arcade allows the topic of zero force members to be cast in a new light, with its "Element disable tool" (more commonly known as the "bomb tool.")

When this tool is clicked on an element during a simulation, the element is removed from the model immediately and the structure responds accordingly. Figure 6 shows a stop-motion rendering of the truss after one of the "zero force" members is removed.

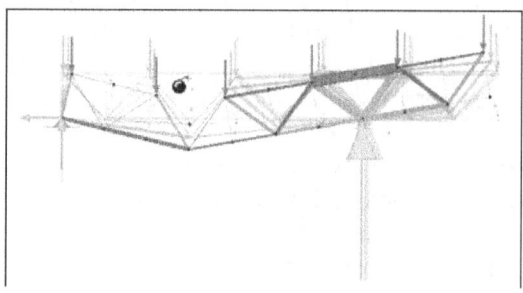

Figure 6. Stop-motion rendering of truss after a "zero force" member is removed.

During a lecture presentation, the bomb tool is used to remove different zero force members, and it becomes clear that removing some members causes collapse, while removing others does not. The class is asked to explain why that is. Before long, an astute student will note that in the case where the zero force member meets two in-line compression members, the structure collapses, but when the in-line members are in tension, the truss does not collapse.

This observation allows the traditional textbook explanation to be elaborated as follows:

> While it is true that for three forces with two in-line, equilibrium requires that the third force be zero, in a real structure, nothing is exactly in line, because the structure deforms under load, and probably wasn't built precisely in line to begin with. When the off-line "zero force" member is removed, compression in the remaining two will make them fold together, leading to collapse, while tension will make the members straighten out and stabilize.

This interpretation gives deeper insight into truss behavior than the traditional treatment of zero force members, and underscores the importance of small members that brace major compression members.

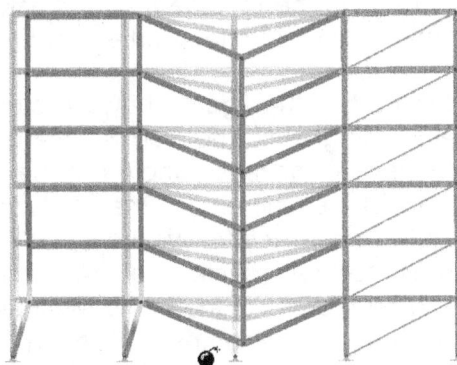

Figure 7. Stop-motion rendering a frame after a column is removed.

The bomb tool is also useful for illustrating broad aspects of frame behavior. Figure 7 shows a stop-motion rendering of a conventional building frame after a first-story column is removed with the bomb tool. The lecture presentation goes on to compare the behavior of this frame of that with more redundant frame configurations that can withstand the sudden removal of a first-story column

Brief Design Exercise

Ultimately, the reason for teaching structures to architecture students is to instill the ability to make informed decisions that recognize the interactions between structural form and behavior. Such teaching requires generative exercises, where students create original solutions in a design context with objectives and constraints. Despite the importance of generative exercises, the demands of studio projects on student time often make it difficult to include them in a structures course.

The following discussion outlines a brief (90-minute) computer-based exercise done in a computer lab setting where students generate a structural form using a highly simplified design context, objectives, and constraints. The outline of this project was published as an essay in the *Connector* newsletter in 2001. At that time, the RISA program was used for analysis [RISA 2006], and it could be carried out with that or other commercial software. The presentation here includes new aspects of the project that have emerged with the use of Arcade.

Figure 8 shows an abridged version of the problem statement. Students work in pairs at their own pace while the instructor and teaching assistants roam the room, assisting pairs that ask for help. Figure 9 shows a photograph of the lab room while the exercise is underway, and figure 10 shows a photograph of a student pair at work. During the exercise, there is a buzz of conversation in the room as pairs discuss their work.

Working in teams of two people at one computer, consider the conceptual design of a structure to suspend a platform from a cliff face, according to the geometry shown below.

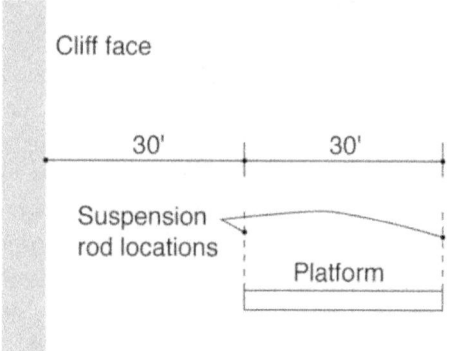

The platform is to be supported by suspension rods that attach to the structure you will design. Assume each hanger rod exerts a downward force of 20 kips.

CRITERIA

Use Arcade to design the structure using the following highly simplified criteria.

- *The maximum downward deflection of the structure should not exceed 2 inches.*
- *No single horizontal reaction should exceed 60 kips.*
- *No single vertical reaction should exceed 30 kips.*
- *All members should be steel, with a cross area of 20 in^2, and a moment of inertia of 700 in^4.*

You should try to minimize the weight of your structure while meeting the performance criteria.

Figure 8. Abridged version of problem statement for design exercise.

Figure 9. Brief design exercise in progress

Figure 10. A student pair discusses design decisions.

One of the key features of this problem is that it does not involve member sizing, which is completely unrealistic, but forces students to focus on the relationship between form and behavior, where the consideration of behavior is artificially and deliberately limited to reactions and displacement.

One common trend in this exercise is that students begin with structures that have far more members than are required for the narrowly defined problem. As the instructor and teaching assistants talk with pairs, they can ask whether there are any members can be eliminated, and then use the bomb tool to remove the members and check the response. Figure 11 shows an example.

The left part of the figure shows a student model in progress. The vertical members are ineffective because they are have a support at each end, the horizontal members appear ineffective because there is no horizontal reaction at the middle support. Four clicks of the bomb tool quickly reveal that the members are in fact unnecessary. Removing the members makes clear the primary behavior of the structure, which in the case of figure 11 is effectively two independent chevron-shaped structures, one for each load.

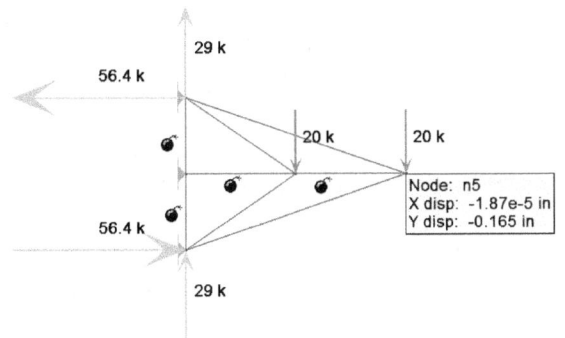
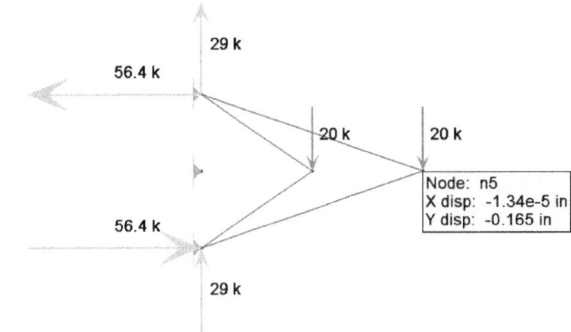

A student design with ineffective members, indicated with the bomb tool icon.

The structure after the members are removed with the bomb tool, the reactions and displacement are still acceptable.

Figure 11. Illustrating the use of the bomb tool to identify ineffective members in a framework.

Exercise Follow-up

An essential part of the exercise is a follow-up session, done as part of a lecture during the following week. In this session, the following points are projected on the screen and discussed:

The problem highlighted some important aspects of design
- *Design is a process of search within a constrained space.*
- *Design is iterative and cyclic, not linear and direct.*
- *Some things just don't work.*

The problem had good and bad points:
- ***Good***: *Allows broad exploration of design space, focusing on behavior rather than calculation details.*
- ***Bad***: *The problem was pure model manipulation without any sense of a real structure and how it would be detailed for construction, braced in three dimensions, or how the structure would look in an architectural context. It was a "stress invaders" video game.*
- ***Good***: *The problem allowed you to discover why trusses are used, and how to look carefully at the assumptions and constraints of a problem.*
- ***Bad***: *The constraints were very incomplete, since they did not include checking the strength of the members, particularly buckling.*
- ***Good***: *The problem offers an opportunity to show the value of back-of-an-envelope calculations to make decisions about overall form.*

The purpose of this review is to make sure that students understand the significant limitations of the exercise.

The follow-up session also includes a review of some of the typical design approaches in order to learn more general lessons. Figure 12 shows a few such examples, organized in a progression from worst adapted to best. Example a) shows a common approach in design practice: take a conventional structural configuration, and then modify it (in this case by adding a diagonal braces) so that it meets the criteria, resulting in an inefficient design. Example b) is slightly better than a), with example c) illustrating a good solution.

The lecture then derives the moment diagram for the load and span condition and notes that the overall profile of solutions such as that in figure 12c) is similar to the shape of the moment diagram in that its depth varies as the moment diagram varies, although the structure has both legs sloped, which is necessary to keep the individual vertical reactions within the constraints.

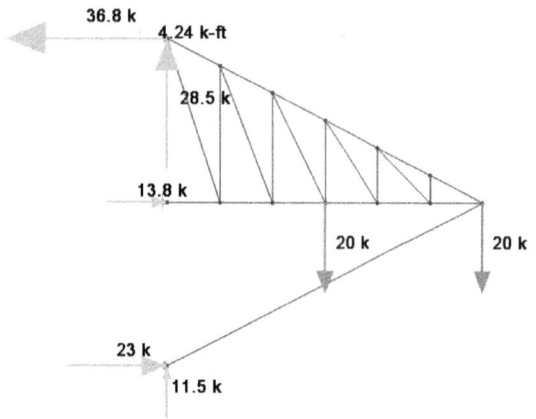

a) An ineffective design that adapts a conventional solution. Self weight 26 kips

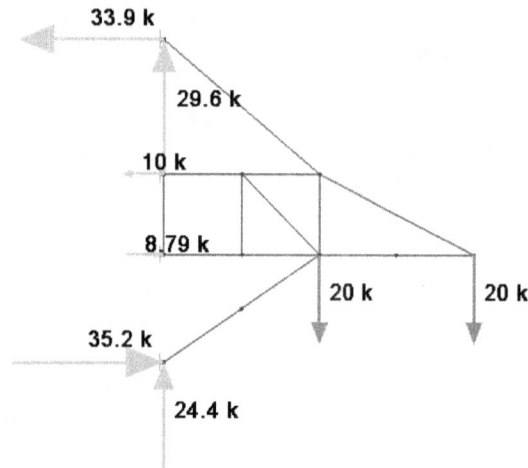

b) A design that is somewhat better adapted to the problem condition. Self weight 18 kips

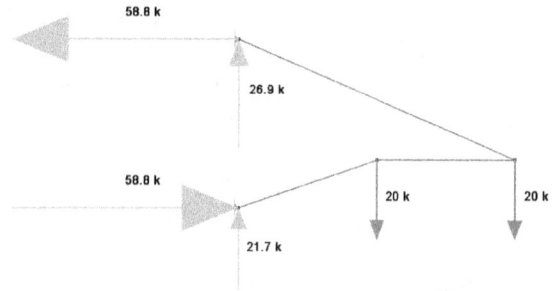

c) A design that adapts well to the constraints and objectives of the problem. Self weight 8.6 kips

Figure 12. Sample results from the brief design exercise.

The moment diagram can also be used to calculate the required depth of the structure at the supports. That depth times the maximum allowable horizontal reaction should equal the maximum moment for the cantilever. This calculation is an example of a back-of-the-envelope calculation that an experienced engineer would do, interpreting the global statics of the situation to estimate bounds and overall form.

Of course, the primary benefits of this exercise do not rely on the special features of Arcade, and can be achieved with conventional structural analysis software. Arcade brings two primary advantages:

1. **Familiarity**: Students begin using Arcade from the earliest stages of the course (e.g. statics of a particle), and those initial assignments serve as introductory tutorials so that students become familiar with the program without needing a special tutorial session to learn to operate the program.

2. **Interaction**: As discussed above, the ability to remove members and immediately and see the resulting effects is highly effective in illustrating the load-carrying action of a framework. This is a key benefit of Arcade's game-like interaction.

Limitations of Arcade

The limitations of the Arcade program in teaching include the following:

- **2 Dimensions**: The program is limited to 2-dimensional analysis; this is not a limitation of the computation method, but of Arcade's current implementation of it. A 3-dimensional version is planned.

- **Small problems**: Because the analysis runs in real time, it is computationally demanding, so that the program is limited to small scale problems (typically something less than 100 nodes, depending on the mass and stiffness properties of the structure). This is a significant limitation for commercial application, but is less of a limitation for teaching.

- **No section library or code check**: The program does not include common commercial features such as standard section libraries and code checks. Code checking would not be appropriate for Arcade, since the focus of the program is realistic behavior, but section libraries would be a useful addition.

In general, Arcade is designed toward supporting the work of teachers and students in a classroom rather than the work of an engineer at a desk, since there is already a wide range of high-quality software to support working engineers. Arcade is not intended to supplant the useful role that commercial programs can play in teaching, but rather to complement that role with capabilities that are not easily accessible with commercial programs.

Conclusions

The application of non-linear dynamic analysis in teaching elementary statics challenges two long-standing teaching assumptions for both architecture and engineering students. The first assumption is that students should learn statics before they learn computer-based structural analysis. Experience with Arcade has demonstrated that computer-based analysis can be an effective tool in teaching the most fundamental concepts of statics.

The second assumption is that when students do begin learning computer-based structural analysis, they should begin with linear elastic static analysis, and then progressively work toward mathematically more complex methods. Experience with Arcade demonstrates that its non-linear dynamic analysis method can be an appropriate entry point for learning structural behavior and analysis.

The key is that although non-linear dynamic analysis is mathematically more complex, it is physically more intuitive. Physical phenomena in real life are not linear, they are not ideally elastic, and they are not strictly static. The real-time interaction of Arcade's non-linear models is closer to student's physical experience than the more stark abstractions used in conventional analysis methods. The greater mathematical complexity of non-linear dynamic analysis combined with real-time interaction is exactly what makes its results more accessible to novice students.

The development of Arcade is ongoing, and the program can be freely downloaded from the project web site [Martini 2006].

Acknowledgement

This material is based upon work supported in part by the National Science Foundation under Grant No. 0230573. That support is gratefully acknowledged. Any opinions, findings and conclusions or recommendations expressed in this material are those of the author and do not necessarily reflect the views of the National Science Foundation.

References:

Black, R G and Duff, S 1994. *A model for teaching structures: finite element analysis in architectural education*. Journal of Architectural Education 48(1): 38-55.

Hecker, Chris. 1996. "Physics, The Next Frontier." *Game Developer,* October/November, *12-20*.

Martini, Kirk. 2005. "Teaching Structural Behavior with a Physics Engine." *American Society of Civil Engineers Structural Congress 2005*, New York, CD-ROM publication. Also available from http://www.arch.virginia.edu/arcade/pubs/arcade-asce-2005.pdf

Martini, Kirk. 2006. *Arcade: Interactive Non-linear Structural Analysis and Animation;* [cited July 9, 2006] Available from http://www.arch.virginia.edu/arcade

Formation Design Systems. 2006. *Multiframe Integrated Structural Engineering Software.* [cited July 9, 2006] Available from http://www.formsys.com/multiframe

RISA Technologies. 2006. *Structural Engineering Software*; [cited July 7, 2006] Available from http://www.risatech.com.

Witkin, Andrew. 1997. *Physically Based Modeling: Principles and Practice: Particle System Dynamics* [cited July 9, 2006] Available from http://www.cs.cmu.edu/afs/cs/user/baraff/www/sigcourse/notesc.pdf

Haptic Structures: The Roll of Kinesthetic Experience in Structures Education

Deborah Oakley
University of Maryland

Introduction

As predominantly visual thinkers, many architectural students find courses in structural technology distant and abstract, especially when presented as mere "watered-down" versions of comparable courses taken by their peers in civil or mechanical engineering. While they may learn to do the mathematics with some proficiency, complaints can also be heard simultaneously that they have no idea what it all really means, or that they don't see the connection to actual built structures in the stick diagrams of beams and so on that they learn in class. This is both a shame and a missed opportunity, because of all of the allied engineering disciplines, structures is at once the most immediate (i.e., no structure means no architecture), as well as potentially the most form-shaping of all.

It is my contention that everyone to a greater or lesser degree possesses some amount of structural "instinct" or "gut sense," simply because our very own bodies are physical structures subject to the forces of gravity and wind, among others. The basic act of walking, for example, is an incredibly complex feat of balance and motion that young children of a certain age nonetheless perform subconsciously with ease. And yet for all our advanced technology, even today's most sophisticated robotic devices have yet to truly master this task. While conscious awareness of this structural gut instinct varies widely among individuals, it can nonetheless be stimulated and leveraged as an aid to conceptual structural understanding, as well as itself strengthened through reflection and practice. Furthermore, it is possible to draw upon this sense in connection to the mathematical calculations associated with the discipline to aid in making sense of what could otherwise be perceived as abstract notions.

What's Haptic-ning?

I've always liked the sound of the word "haptic." These days It's all the buzz in virtual reality circles, with devices that are enabling users to interact with computer systems by using resistive joysticks, sensing gloves, and a host other mechanisms in development. These devices can provide tactile feedback in a virtual computer simulation of the world much as one would experience resistance in actual direct contact in the physical world. The word itself derives from the Greek *haptesthai, which means* to touch. We gather information about the world though our senses, and the sense of touch is the most fundamental of all.

Accordingly, encountering resistance in a material is inherently different from merely reading about the same property in a textbook. It is this feedback loop of material contact that is capitalized upon when we incorporate hands-on experiences into coursework. More than 150 years ago American naturist/ philosopher Henry David Thoreau made similar observations of students in his own day when he wrote "*Which would have advanced the most at the end of a month,—the boy who had made his own jackknife from the ore which he had dug and smelted, reading as much as would be nec-*

essary for this,—or the boy who had attended the lectures on metallurgy at the Institute in the mean while, and had received a Rogers' penknife from his father? Which would be most likely to cut his fingers?" (Walden 65)

The use of physical models in education is, of course, nothing new and is a time-honored tradition to teaching in the sciences, such as in physics classes. In carrying on this tradition, then, there are a variety of simple lab exercises, classroom demonstrations and experiences I introduce to beginning structures students periodically throughout each of our two-semester sequence. Some of these are full-fledged lab experiments with a more formal rigor, while others are designed to illustrate concepts that are often difficult for new students to grasp, such as moment of inertia or restrained column buckling. Not only do they aid in conceptual understanding, but students who find technical courses challenging often excel at the hands-on experiences, and furthermore the perceived dryness and drudgery of structures as a discipline can be lessened. In addition, design can be allowed to enter in and an element of playfulness added.

Nowadays, "active learning" is the term used to describe an educational environment that encourages the participatory involvement of students in the their own learning experience. So now, a century and a half after Thoreau, academia has finally caught up with his forward thinking and active learning is itself a domain of pedagogic scholarship.

Hands-on lab classes thus form an important active-learning component to my structures classes. Typically, I try to create conditions of failure that can be analyzed and discussed to better understand how to create safe structures. This paper briefly describes several of the types of experiences that been used over the years in conjunction with the more traditional lecture period. Each type of project uses simple and readily available materials to keep costs down, while at the same time not cutting short the educational value. The lab assignments normally require a brief write-up to ensure both accountability and to facilitate retention, not to mention serving also as a checkpoint on student attendance.

Elasticity Lab: The Power of Plastic

The elasticity lab capitalizes on the properties of ordinary plastic bags to simulate a material tension test with results that very closely mimic those of structural steel.[1] You don't need a massive and expensive Tinius-Olson test machine to reinforce the basic concepts of elasticity when common trash bags will do the trick just as well.

This lab evolved out of an observation I made many years ago of certain types of plastic bags. I found that when cut into strips and stretched, they would exhibit a mild amount of elastic behavior and would return to their original shape when the force was released. With continued increase in force, however, I noticed a decided yield point where permanent deformation would set in beyond a certain level of stress. Furthermore, I noted that with continued force application the yielding would continue throughout the length of the strip until the entire length was yielded (with a surprising amount of elongation). After this point, the material entered a strain-hardened phase whereupon the "stretchiness" became con-

Figure 1. Elasticity lab using strips from plastic bags

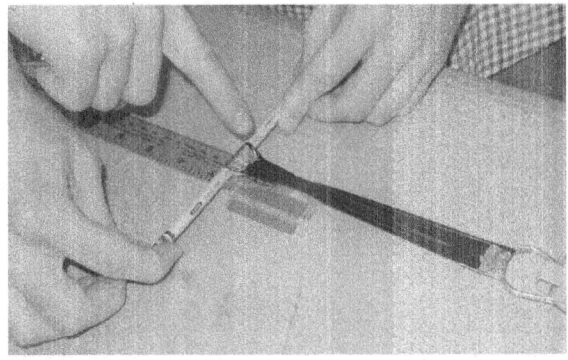

Figure 2. Moment of yielding in plastic strip

siderably less and the material noticeably tougher, with a significant increase in force capacity. Further increase of tension on the plastic, though, eventually resulted in a very sudden rupture of the strip with a strong "snap!"

This at first was a random observation that worked on various materials like bread bags, shopping bags and so on., but definitely not all. Finally after considerable experimentation the ideal material for my purposes was determined to be heavyweight industrial-strength black plastic trash can liners. It was obvious that its force/ deformation behavior mimicked structural steel to such an extent that it would be worthwhile formulating in a lab fashion. Furthermore, this material has the very nice characteristic of changing to a light shade of grey (almost translucent, in fact) that makes recognition of the yield point very obvious. It also turned out to be an extremely affordable learning experience as well. Besides using a material that from its very inception is destined for a landfill, the only additional supplies needed were a linear spring scale, a yard or meter stick, and duct tape. *(Figure 1)*

In conducting this as an in-class lab experiment (and even knowing that the characteristics of this material were so similar to structural steel) the outcome was surprising even to me. As can be seen in Figure 3, the resulting force/deformation graph for the plastic is strikingly similar to a typical stress/strain graph for mild structural steel found in any elementary text on structures.[2]

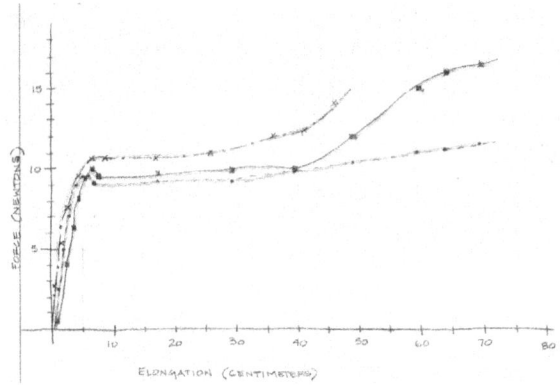

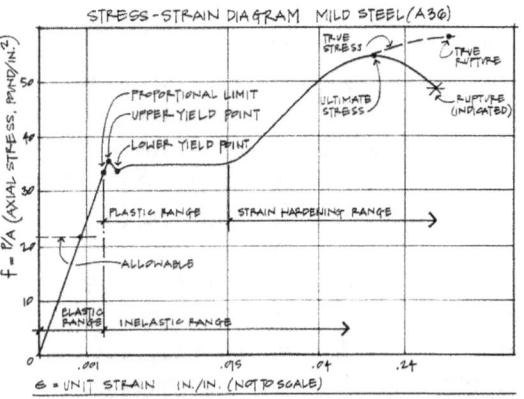

Figure 3. Comparison between lab class graph results (upper image) and stress-strain diagram for mild structural steel (lower image).

By having students take the force/deformation measurements and create this graph, related discussions of material elasticity and stress/strain diagrams take on an added dimension beyond a cursory reading; students begin to develop a *feel* for a common building material that would not otherwise be possible, simply because of the magnitude of force needed for similar experiments in steel. Nevertheless, as important as this outcome is, I don't stop with just creating the graph. Many additional valuable lessons can come from this simple experiment.

Having completed the experiment and logged all measurements, students are next required to compute the approximate structural properties of the plastic material. Knowing the amount of force at the yield point and the cross-sectional area of the plastic strip (they are simply given the bag thickness as being 4 mils), the stress level at yield may be calculated. Having measured the amount of deformation at yield relative to its original undeformed length, the strain be computed. Now, having calculated these two values, the approximate elastic modulus for the plastic can be determined as stress divided by strain. Normally, I will also give some of this information in mixed units (e.g. the plastic thickness and width in inches and the force and deformation in SI) to reinforce the process of dimensional analysis in calculations.

After computing the yield stress and elastic modulus for the plastic, the next step is to make comparative calculations with the material they've been replicating, structural steel. In calculating the ratio of stress and elastic modulus of structural steel to that of plastic, students learn that while steel is close to 100 times the *strength* of the plastic, it is on the order of tens of thousands of times *stiffer* than plastic. And so the significance of, and the distinction between, strength and stiffness is facilitated by this exercise—a common struggle for many new students to otherwise understand when presented in the abstract.

In addition to all of the above, there are yet more lessons to be wrung from this experiment. From here we may proceed to discuss other important related phenomenon in a conceptual manner. First, many of the strips will (despite taking care in cutting) end up with irregularities that result in premature failure before the entire length has yielded. The concept of stress concentration then becomes vividly significant.

Second, discussion of the concept of isotropic versus anisotropic materials is also possible. Although it seems natural to assume that, since the plastic is apparently uniform and homogeneous, it will respond to stress the same in all directions. In a related (and accidental) discovery about this material, though, I noted that the clear yielding behavior is true only in one direction (crosswise to the length of the bag)[3] There is effectively a "grain" to the plastic even though it appears uniform. Demonstrating this in

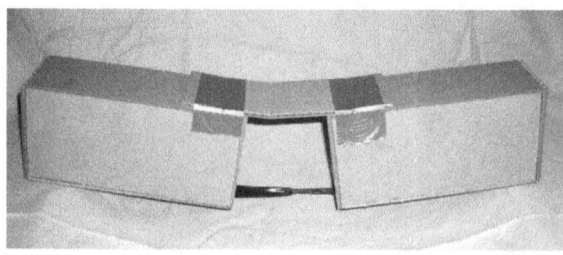

Figure 4. Pseudo "concrete" beam of cardboard using plastic bag strips as bottom tensile reinforcement. Ductile failure of under-reinforced beam (upper image) versus brittle crushing behavior of over-reinforced beam (lower image)

front of class with strips that appear identical (I use a video display projector to show them more clearly to a larger class) makes it obvious that there can be surprising differences in a material's response to force application depending on how it is oriented.

Lastly, during the initial lab experiment as the tensile forces become higher, often the tape holding the plastic will come loose. This can be discussed to illustrate the importance of secure connections, or in the case of steel reinforcement, the idea of bond and development length.

So, as can be seen, from this one simple and inexpensive experiment all of these vitally important concepts of structural materials can be not just talked about, but viscerally *experienced* by students. Through this activity, a lasting experience is possible that makes the abstract idea of elastic modulus and other material properties very real.

Before ending this discussion about the elasticity of plastic bags, it is very much worth noting another related demonstration. In this case the plastic strips can be used to describe the behavior of reinforced concrete. Here, the composite action of steel and concrete is replicated by using the plastic as "tension steel" in a cutaway beam section (I use a simple box beam of corrugated cardboard), with a strip of corrugated cardboard as the "concrete" in compression. By varying the amount of plastic used as reinforcement, the concept of under- reinforcing a beam versus over-reinforcement is made dramatically clear. Students learn vividly why the notion of "if a little steel is good, then more must be better," is a mistaken one.

With a small amount of the "plastic steel" in place at the bottom of the beam and pressing down with one's hands, a very ductile and flexible member is developed, one that exhibits a sizable amount of deflection under load. But in replacing the small amount of plastic with a much larger amount, the beam becomes stiff, rigid and unyielding. The failure is shifted from that of a gentle, ductile stretching of the plastic to a sudden almost violent crushing of the cardboard. Few students have trouble understanding why "under-reinforcing" a concrete beam is actually a desirable and good thing after that.

Although performed only as a demonstration and not yet developed into a lab experiment, this could easily be done. One of the lessons beyond the over- under- reinforcement concept could possibly include computation of the internal couple moment in resisting a measured applied load and corresponding external moment. And as described above with the elasticity lab itself, the importance of proper bond of the reinforcement c an be illustrated through varying the length of duct tape used to attach the plastic strips to the beam. If the tape comes loose before either the plastic yields or the cardboard crushes, then clearly a bond failure has occurred and a longer length of tape is needed!

K'NEX...or, "Did Somebody Say Triangulation?"

K'NEX are a children's toy based on a kit of parts that are most fundamentally a set of rods and connectors. An absolute trove of ancillary parts including decorations, small battery-operated motors, tiny doll-people, roller coaster carts and so on are also available. But for the structures class, however, the elements of greatest interest are the rods and connectors. The K'NEX corporation has been a wonderful supporter of education in the past, and has graciously provided donations of materials from production overruns, irregularities, demonstrations, and so on for use in my classes.

If you are not already familiar with this popular toy, the concept is quite simple. The rods

Figure 5 Bottom chord tension failure of K'NEX truss loaded with approximately 120 pounds of bricks.

(which snap into place with the plastic connectors in a tab-and-socket fashion) are of

Figure 6. K'NEX beam loaded by cantilever arm with sand bucket filled from upper bucket. Lateral-torsional buckling clearly evident as failure mode (lower image).

Figure 7. Top chord compression failure of K'NEX rod

advancing by the square root of two. Thus a right triangle is formed by two rods of the same size on two sides, plus one rod of the next size up on the third. Approximately a half dozen sizes of triangulation are possible through this scheme. The connectors range from straight in-line, to 45° to 360° around and all angles between at 45° increments. Furthermore, although the basic connectors are planar, there are certain types that connect to one another orthogonally thereby making spatial triangulation possible. It's simplicity and flexibility is truly genius.

Students enjoy working with these because they are quick and easy to manipulate and construction can be readily modified. I have used these as the "Magic Bullet" (to use Ed Allen's term) of my first structures class to have students build truss bridges with very little direction beyond giving them the pieces and having them span a given distance to carry the most load with the lightest structure possible. Loaded with steel weights, they learn not just the significance of triangulation in a spanning element, but many other important considerations.

Since the trusses are to be free-spanning between the ends (a 30 inch span is about right), a very common failure mode is lateral-torsional buckling. They see that proportionally lower and wider cross-sections are far less prone to this failure than taller-narrower approaches. Nevertheless, they also learn that there is a limit to how flat one can build as the depth of the truss is seen to correlate to the absolute load it can carry.

Joint separation is the most common failure mechanism and is really the greatest weakness of the system in a tensile load. I do, however, make them aware of this weakness beforehand and challenge them to find a workaround for it. *(Figure 5)* Students can be very ingenious with their solutions, which range from overlapping parts much as one would overlap wood in a laminate, to simply altering the direction of the connector.

A much more rare occurrence that really happens only in the members which successfully address the lateral-torsional buckling and connector issues, is when one of the compression rods will actually buckle under load. *(Figure 7)* Each of the aforementioned failure modes becomes an opportunity for discussion in relation to their significance in horizontally-spanning truss members.

I have gone through a number of variants on this particular exercise. As noted, one has been as the "magic bullet" first class exercise, and it has proven to be very successful in that manner, especially when I "close the loop" and provide feedback on the designs to the class as a whole. The "winner" of this project is the one that demonstrates the greatest load capacity to self-weight ratio, with runners-up being those of ingenious design or possessing other unique attributes.

I have also used this project is as an end of the semester competition where the truss is designed to be free-standing across the span, and once as part of a "Rube Goldberg device." In this elaborate scheme, not only did the students create the trusses, but the loading was done through a lever arm with a bucket of sand attached. The twist here was that the sand bucket was filled from above by another bucket that initially is plugged by a rod. *(See figure 6)* This rod was knocked out (starting the sand flow) as the end action of the "Rube Goldberg contraption." The device itself was left open to the imagination of the students and some were truly ingenious.

In place of horizontal trusses, I have had students perform compression tests of K'NEX columns as well. *(Figure 8)* The failures of these projects are typically less dramatic than the trusses; however, it is really quite surprising how much load they can be made to carry. Load capacity to self weight is here again the criterion, but the discussion of a variety of failure modes becomes possible, including overall buckling

Figure 8. K'NEX column load test. Note Buckling of various rod members.

versus localized buckling, torsion, and accidental load eccentricity and the P-Delta effect.

In other applications of this very flexible educational device, they can be used in conjunction with discussions of lateral loading. Clearly, as triangulated members the application as vertical trussing in a building frame is a natural one. But a simple horizontal two-bay box structure can be used in conjunction with a linear spring scale pulled by hand at the upper center joint to demonstrate progressively: A flexible roof diaphragm with horizontal or lateral trussing (it is effectively a semi-moment resisting frame); a braced frame with flexible diaphragm by trussing each side but not the top; and a rigid diaphragm with braced frame by trussing both the sides and the top. *(Figure 9)* Progressing through this sequence and measuring the amount of force the frame will take, one moves from a rather flexible to an absolutely rigid structure, with

Figure 9. Lateral forces lab. Measuring horizontal deflection of two-bay braced truss frame

a corresponding increase in capacity for lateral resistance and decrease in the amount of horizontal deflection (drift).

Continuing the demonstration (or lab) above, if only one side is braced, the structure with a load at the center will experience a clear torsional rotation, thereby illustrating the importance of symmetric bracing. If the top diaphragm bracing is removed, the amount of torsion is reduced considerably, showing that flexible diaphragm systems can be safely designed by ignoring any effects of torsional loading.

Lastly, the horizontally braced top diaphragm with one vertical side brace can be again modified, this time with an orthogonal *pair* of truss members on the sides perpendicular to the loading. The amount of torsion is again reduced to nearly zero, thus illustrating the concept that a structure with bracing located eccentrically from the centerline of loading will not experience torsion if at least two orthogonal walls are present. Remove one of these trusses and most of the torsion will return, thus reinforcing this understanding. If calculations are introduced, one can compute the magnitude of the resisting couple forces by simply measuring the moment due to the measured applied force and the distance away from the parallel braced wall, and dividing by the space between the couple walls.

These are just a few of the many ways this versatile child's toy can be employed as a kinesthetic sensory experience of structural behavior. Taken as a whole with all the variants possible, K'NEX is one of the mainstay devices I use for physically modeling structural behavior in my classes at all levels.

The Impossible Cube

As with many who teach building technology or structures, I find that the work of Santiago Calatrava provides for a fount of exemplary material in contemporary design. We drawn upon this for illustrative examples in projects that unite and express engineering principles clearly as an intrinsic part of architecture. Lesser known, however are Calatrava's sculptural works, many of which push the boundaries of structural potentialities and seem to defy gravity. I use these both as examples and, in once case, as an inspiration for a particular student project based on his many "cube" sculptural studies. *(Figure 10)*

I began having students make these "impossible" cubes a number of years ago in small-scale models as a way to bring a sense of art and design into structures

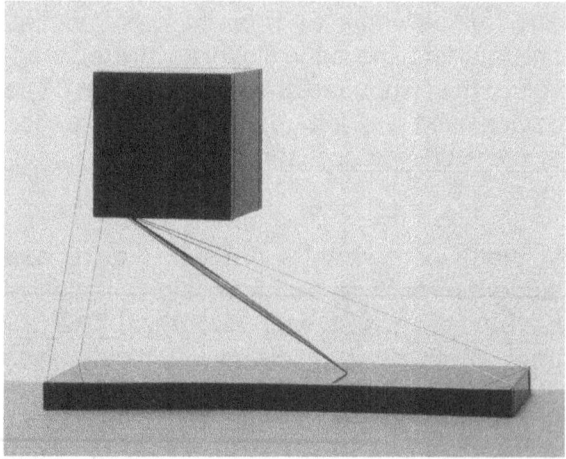

Figure 10. "Head XIB" Cable and single strut-supported ebony cube by Santiago Calatrava[1]

class. Although the project does not involve calculations (the three-dimensional statics are a little too involved for an introductory class), it nevertheless draws once again on the haptic principle of getting a real "feel" for balance and stability, plus it's just a fun project in and of itself.

The assignment is basically simple. Students are asked to provide a support for a cube of solid wood 4 inches on a side in a non-redundant manner, such that the removal of any one element will lead to a failure of the entire object. *(Figure 11a)* The primary restriction is that the supporting members cannot have end fixity...stability is to be achieved by the use of tension cables only.

It is important that the cube of wood be solid so that its mass will be distinctly activated by gravity. In the past some students have made them hollow and, while they may look nice and appear to address the project statement, at a small scale it is easy to "fake" the support and have it stand up merely by friction or stiffness. It is definitely acceptable (and I tell them desirable) if the cube sculpture is stable only in one configuration such that if, for example, the sculpture is turned upside-down it will fall apart. The goal is to find the absolute minimum members that will achieve both vertical and lateral stability, and to search for the underlying structural elegance in that minimalism.

Some students really fly with this problem and come up with some truly inventive designs, but any serious attempt provides for a meaningful learning experience. Most fundamentally they are learning the necessity of spatial triangulation involving one strut and two cables in a pyramid formation. Such a configuration can provide for both vertical as well as horizontal load resistance, and even in its simplicity a huge number of variations are possible. Another understanding is of learning just how difficult it is to construct something that appears so simple...it becomes evident to all that hav-

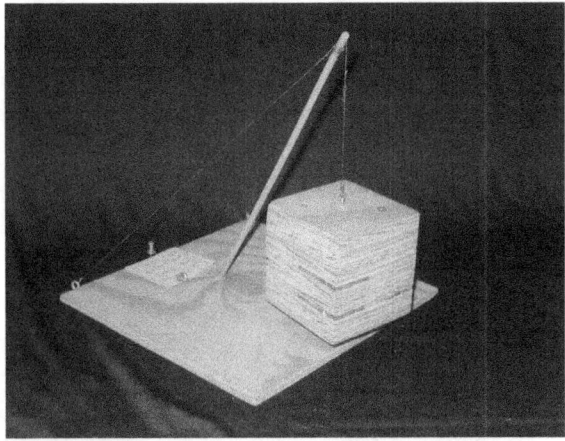

Figures 11a & b. Cube project at desktop model scale and full-scale erection.

ing several extra hands would be very helpful in the construction of these models!

While this project has been done most often at a desktop scale, one year I ramped this up to the large size with cubes three feet on a side. *(Figure 11b)* For this class it was done in a two-stage group process. Teams of seven or eight students broke down into several smaller groups, each of which created their own design. These models were reviewed and discussed in the same manner as I had done in previous years. From here, though, each of the overall teams then chose amongst themselves which of the several models they most wanted to build at a large scale.

On their own and outside of class period, each team then worked as a whole to produce the components of the large-scale model. To reduce the weight and alleviate excessive lateral force due to wind loading, the solid "cubes" at the large scale became hollow frames with mesh or screening to give the appearance of being solid. One class period was set aside for the erection of the cubes with each team working together, and the new challenges posed in constructing at the large scale became evident to many of the teams. Some who thought they had figured out the stability of their small-scale model, for example, learned that when gravity *really* came into play, they had in fact overlooked something and some quick field adjustments were necessary. Other groups encountered situations they had never thought of, such as the unpredictable response of soft soil to a large lateral thrust from a strut. In the end, though, all of the teams had a successful installation of their projects. These large-scale "impossible" cube sculptures were then on display for the entire school and University to enjoy for about two weeks afterward.

Seismic Shaker Table

One of the more important considerations that I spend a sizable portion of the second semester on is stressing the importance of designing structures for lateral forces. Although our school location on the east coast means that for most of our graduates the significant lateral force they will be confronted with is hurricane wind load, I spend a reasonable amount of time introducing the principles of seismic loading and proper design to mitigate undesirable effects such as torsion or poor design choices such as soft stories. With increasingly stringent seismic design requirements of the IBC, more and more projects on the east coast must also be checked for earthquake loads in areas that in years past had no such requirement.

As a supplemental learning exercise to this, study, I have introduced a small seismic shaker table consisting of a platform attached to a bearing supported frame that has eight centering springs (two on each side) connected to an outer frame. By applying force to the platform in any direction, the centering springs will always move it back to the initial position. The platform can be moved simply by hand, or I have also an eccentric arm that connects to an ordinary cordless drill to act as a constant shaking force. By varying the speed of the drill, it is possible to get harmonic motions in tower models (for example, those made of K'NEX or basswood).

As an end-of-semester project one year, I had students create what I called (with tongue firmly in cheek), the "Im-Pastable" tower, which was made of ordinary spaghetti and hot melt glue. *(Figure 12)* The 18" high towers were locked to the table with hold down plates and a brick affixed to the top. Varying speeds of drill-induced oscillations were then used until the towers were shaken to destruction. The criteria this time was not really how much load the

Figure 12. Soft story failure of pasta tower in shaker table test

tower could carry, but rather for how long it would carry the load under shaking. Each pair of students in a team was given an ordinary one pound box of spaghetti to work with, and as usual the design criteria was to make the least weight structure possible. Surprisingly, though, the hot melt glue imparts a considerable ductility to the otherwise fragile spaghetti and some of the students made towers from that were strong enough to actually stand on! Needless to say, it was not possible to break these on the shaker table, and thus not really possible to ascertain the true strengths and weaknesses of a the design. In future offerings of this exercise, I have learned that a much smaller amount of material will perform well for this task to ensure that the tower can in fact be broken by the shaking alone.

The Structures Journal

Although there are other projects and demonstrations I do with my classes (for example, see Figures 14-16) I will close this discussion with another valuable experience, although it is not a lab-type experiment such as previously described. This exercise I call the "Structures Journal," and serves as a vehicle for helping students become more aware of structures they have seen all around for their whole life but have never taken notice of. As an engineering student, one remarkable professor I had for fluid mechanics introduced me to this exercise and it has left a memorable impression on me ever since. The guidelines of the experience were remarkably simple: "Keep a log/journal of fluidic phenomena in the world around you." In performing this weekly exercise I suddenly found myself looking at all kinds of things like the way water drained in a tub, the wafting of smoke in the air, or the ever changing patterns of rolling and billowing clouds—all familiar phenomena now seen in a new light. Inasmuch as the calculations we learned required quite a bit of high level integral calculus, I found the journal to be a welcome reprieve from this density and

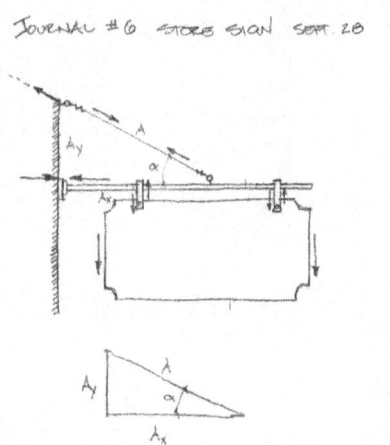

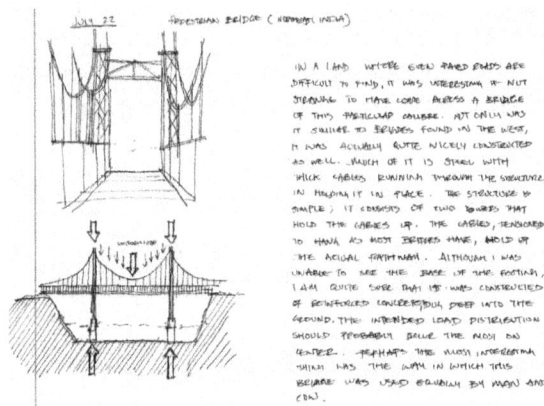

Figure 13. Example structures journal entries

struggle, and helped bring to life the more abstract mathematical formulae.

And so in this spirit I have introduced this project to my own students, though this time oriented to structures. *(Figure 13)* Since one of the important notions I try to impart is the ubiquity of structures in the world, in their once weekly journal entry, I ask that they make five entries from structures they observe in the natural world (plants, animals, etc.), five from the object scale (tools,

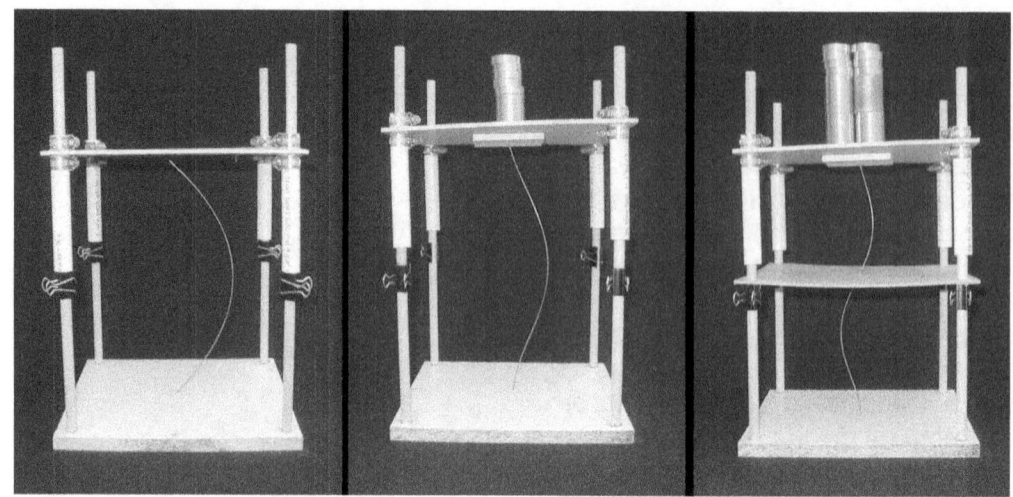

Figure 14. Substantial increase of column buckling load capacity illustrated by progressive alteration to end fixity and intermediate bracing conditions on 1/8" diameter piano wire.

household articles and so on), and five from the architectural scale (buildings and bridges). As we go through the semester, I ask that students try to relate their observations to material we are currently studying. For instance, if we are covering moments and rotational equilibrium, to look at this phenomena in specific. *(See figure 13)*

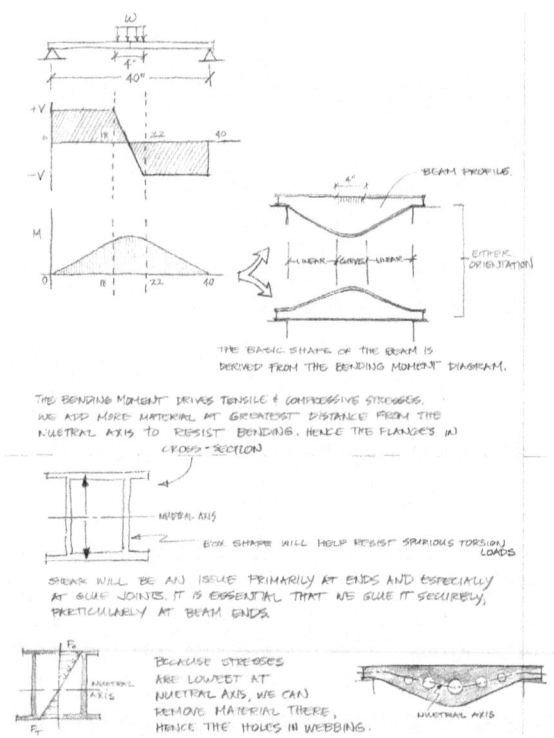

Figure 15. Student design of cardboard beam tested in lab class

Conclusion

Structures classes for architectural students have a fundamentally different role than comparable courses for students of engineering. For the most part architects will not be designing actual structures aside from perhaps smaller-scale projects, and even there the role is normally quite limited. Yet the realm of architecture encompasses the holistic perspective of buildings in their entirety, including learning to properly plan and proportion their structural systems. If a building structure is properly conceived at the schematic level, then when actual engineering design *is* undertaken, it will be much more likely that wise choices have been made such that the engineer is not fighting against the forces of nature for sake of a structurally ill-informed architect's dream. While I personally have a penchant for structures that unite architecture and engineering as an inseparable whole (my heroes being the likes of Kahn, Nervi, Foster, Candela, Calatrava and so on), I also accept that my students may not share this value. Nevertheless we live in an era of rapidly growing awareness of the limitations and scarcity of our natural resources, and it is increasingly unconscionable that architects end up causing engineers to "force" a structural system to work by virtue of inap-

Figure 16. Test loading of cantilevered corrugated cardboard beam

propriate or inefficient designs at the most basic conceptual level. "Making" a structural system work, while almost always in some way possible, is rarely if ever economical of means, or conservative of resources.

The above hands-on exercises may in some cases be short on numeric calculation, but are nonetheless long on conceptual import and are designed to facilitate the development of what has sometimes referred to as "structural intuition." Interspersed with the traditional calculations in this type of class, they can become an important aspect in the way structures classes are taught, and serve to reinforce and clarify the analytical components.

So, in the end, what do students think they get out of the exercises? Sometimes the results are clear in the enthusiasm and energy they display. At other times the reactions are harder to judge with results that are frustratingly mixed. Quite frequently I receive many positive comments about these experiences as being excellent reinforcements to other aspects of the class that also address variations in learning styles. Yet some other students have remarked that they are nothing more than superfluous busywork. One student for instance commented that the full-sized cube structures seemed to be nothing more than "for show." Or take for example the case of the structures journal described above. The results of this exercise have produced some truly outstanding observation records by a number of students that clearly reveal a deep level of engagement with the material. Surprisingly, though, when polling the class anonymously, the exercise received a resounding thumbs down.[4] In looking at the journal entries, though, it seems that although ostensibly unpopular, many students do not really realize just how much they are learning through the process.

Nevertheless, despite the lack of universal student acclaim, I am a firm believer in the importance of these exercises and will continue to employ them. I will, however, continue the search for an optimal balance between the kinesthetic experiences and computational aspects of the classes. In this quest, I welcome feedback from others on this approach taken to making structures both more engaging as well as a more rich learning experience, one that leaves a lasting memory and positively influences the understanding of fundamental structural behavior.

References:

Levin, Michael. Santiago Calatrava—The Art Works: A Laboratory of Ideas, Forms and Structures, Basel, Switzerland, Birkhäuser, 2003.

Oakley, Deborah. Technology in a Trash Bag, *Connector,* Vol. XV. No. 1, Summer 2006.

Onouye, Barry & Kane, Kevin. Statics and Strength of Materials for Architecture and Building Construction, 2nd Ed., Upper Saddle River, NJ, Prentice Hall, 2001.

Thoreau, Henry David, Walden: Or Life In The Woods. Mineola, NY: Courier Dover Publications, 2002 (From the original 1854 edition by Tichnor & Fields, Boston).

Notes

[1] For a complete description of the lab including directions on how to set it up and record measurements, see "Technology in a Trash Bag" in the Summer 2006 *Connector* newsletter.

[2] The purist will argue that there are certain inaccuracies in the process, the most significant being that the measured deformation is not simply that of the plastic, but also that of the spring in the scale. But in the overall scope of things, I believe this to be of minor consequence, and that getting overly technical and detailed in the process would only obfuscate the underlying concept. Such refinements could perhaps be the topic of more advanced lessons.

[3] Not being a materials scientist I can only speculate that this is due to a linear alignment of polymer chains in the "up and down" direction of the bag as it would normally be placed in the trash can. Close inspection of the material in bright light revels subtle but definite and perfectly straight parallel striations along the length of the bag. I theorize that by tensioning *across* these polymer chains, one is effectively "opening them up" and the clear yielding behavior is happening by separation of the molecules. When stressed *along* the length of the polymer chains, one is merely elongating or uncoiling them without separation. I welcome clarification or correction of this speculation by any knowledgeable chemist!

[4] By way of personal response devices ("clickers"), an anonymous poll was conducted at the end of the spring 2006 semester. The question was posed as follows: "The structures journal has been a useful tool for reflection on material being studied in class." 37% of students disagreed and 45% of students strongly disagreed with this statement, indicating that some 92% of the class considered this exercise to be essentially without value. For a full description of personal response systems in lecture classes, please see my paper "Two Way Structures" elsewhere in these proceedings.

Two-Way Structures: Enhancing Lecture-Based Structures Courses with Interactive Personal Response Devices

Deborah Oakley
University of Maryland

Introduction

When we hear the term "two-way structure" in an architectural context, we typically understand this to mean a constructive system designed to distribute load (normally gravity loads on a floor slab) simultaneously in orthogonal directions to the supporting framework, in contrast to one-way structures that transfer them in a linear manner. As a pedagogic concept, in an analogous manner the term is used here to describe a mechanism to facilatate to the interchange and dialog between teacher and student in an otherwise conventional lecture format class.

As the number of students in class grows beyond a certain size, it becomes increasingly challenging to make connections with students at a more personal level. Who that has taught in a lecture class has not at one time or another been confounded by the silence of passive students too timid to speak up even when directly questioned? Studies have demonstrated that, for many students, the traditional classroom lecture is an ineffective means to learning and engagement with subject matter. This is not only a concern in architecture, but other allied disciplines such as civil engineering also face similar, if not identical challenges (see for example Bernold 67).

Active learning techniques have been shown to be an effective approach to breaking down the barrier of distance and passivity in the classroom. The essential notion is to engage students in the learning process and thereby increase understanding and retention while adding participation and interest.[1] Active learning is the third of the seven principles outlined in the seminal *Seven Principles for Good Practice in Undergraduate Education* (Chickering & Gamson).

As an active learning strategy, one of the most effective means of teaching structural concepts to students of architecture is arguably through a studio-type course. Considerable one-on-one dialog can take place in such a setting and basic structural concepts can be applied to hypothetical design projects in a more holistic manner with a great deal of instructional feedback provided. The reality for most schools, however (and particularly at the larger state-funded institutions), is that the relative luxury of teaching structures and related classes in such a resource intensive manner is not financially possible, however desirable it might be pedagogically.

In most cases, then, the lecture format is likely to be the predominate mode of in-

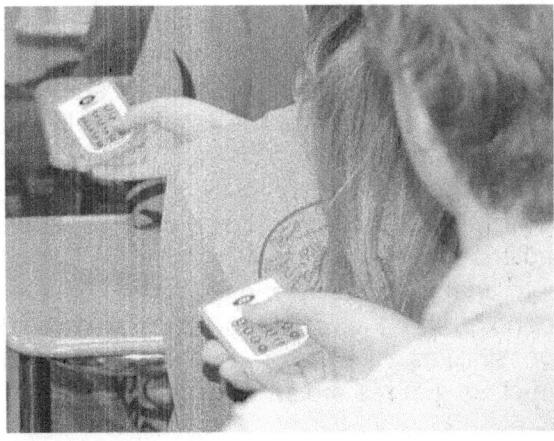

Figure 1 Typical Personal Response Devices in Use (Photo Courtesy Turning Technologies, LLC)

structional delivery. Yet despite their proven successes, the possible range of active learning techniques is more limited in larger lecture class settings, and even more so in rooms with fixed seating. So with class sizes of 75, 100 or more being not uncommon, we remain confronted with the dilemma of how to connect with and engage a larger body of students. However, at a growing number of institutions around the world a quiet revolution has been taking place over the past decade in the way large format lectures are being conducted, one that at least in part addresses this challenge through modern technology.

Known variously as "personal response devices," "'audience (or classroom) response systems'"—or simply as *clickers* or *keypads* in the vernacular, as the systems will be referred to herein—these small handheld devices offer a technological means to stimulate active learning environments. When properly employed, clickers can generate more enthusiastic student participation by creating an immediately responsive two-way learning experience, one not easily attained through other active learning approaches in larger class settings.[2]

Clicker implementation essentially consists of a receiver connected to a computer at the professor's end and a remote keypad used by students to provide responses to questions and situations shown in a Microsoft PowerPoint-type of presentation. Class response results can be instantly tallied giving students and professor alike an immediate feedback to the level of understanding on the question. With such systems it is possible, for example, to know whether students are "getting it" during the lecture itself, not merely later on during an exam, and adjust lecture content dynamically as needed. Carefully crafted questions can generate polarized responses that can then be turned into peer discussion/learning exercises. Depending on the software used, additional possibilities such as group competition and in-class quizzes are also possibilities.

Originating in the sciences first in the mid 1990s, the use of clickers is becoming increasingly widespread in a number of disciplines. At my university, as a part of a pilot study being made campus wide,[3] I spearheaded the use of clickers in the structures curriculum for architecture students for the first time in the spring semester, 2006. The remainder of this paper will illustrate how they have been used in the introductory structures class, some of the results of this usage, what has been learned so far, and how they are envisioned to be employed in future course offerings. Although a number of such response systems are available (each with their own particular strengths and weaknesses), experiences cited herein are based on the standard system being adopted at the University of Maryland, known as "TurningPoint," marketed by Turning Technologies, LLC.

Enabling Technology

On the popular TV game show "Who Wants to be a Millionaire?" when confronted with uncertainty in their answer to a question, one option contestants are given is to "poll the audience." In so doing, audience members provide what they believe to be the correct answer using a keypad at their seat. The results are immediately tallied by computer and provided in a graph as an aid in the contestant's decision-making. This is essentially how clickers operate in a classroom setting as well. But not being game show hosts, what exactly are the types of things that we can do with clickers in the lecture hall?

It should first off be realized that the clickers are a tool that needs to be properly applied, and that in and of itself cannot make bad teaching good. But, well employed, clickers can be used to facilitate a review of key concepts after a lecture presentation for example, or to conduct class assessments such as obtaining demographic or other background information, to get baseline understanding of a topic, or take polls on sensitive topics that many students might be disinclined from responding to in a non-anonymous manner. If the software is set up to record the student answers explicitly versus anonymously, then scored 'mini-quizzes' and tests are possible, as well as keeping track of attendance simply by checking if the student answered the questions given that day. In addition, depending on the software used, it is possible to do more advanced functions such as conducting in-class competitions. But perhaps most importantly, they can be used to facilitate peer learning experiences and student-to-student engagement through questions designed to provoke discussion. In whatever manner they are used, the responses are immediately displayed for all to see, and therein lies the power of the instrument.

Data generated from the clicker polling is also not static to the one slide being shown, but all questions and responses in a given presentation are stored in a computer document that the software can then use to create reports in Microsoft Word or Excel. I have personally found the MS Excel reports to be most useful. A log is kept of each day's questions and answers from each student in a cumulative spreadsheet with a separate tab for each class period. By inspecting these reports, it is possible to obtain a clear performance picture for each individual student through the course of the semester. Attendance information is logged into another spreadsheet used for grading.

Framing Questions to Elicit Dialog

Figure 2 illustrates a typical PowerPoint slide that includes both a question as well as student responses after being tallied by the computer. Initially any given slide has just the question with possible answers, and remains with no tallying until either an automatic countdown timer (if so set on the slide) reaches zero, or the instructor terminates the response period.

This question was asked during the next class day following an in-class exercise designed to help develop a physical feel for the relationship of rope tension to inclination. In the exercise, pairs of student volunteers were asked to pull on each end of a rope with a 25-pound weight suspended in the middle in order to lift it from the ground. This was done several times with progressively flatter angles to the horizontal, where clearly an ever-increasing force was needed to lift the weight from the floor. At very low angles, even the strongest men in class were barely able to lift the weight!

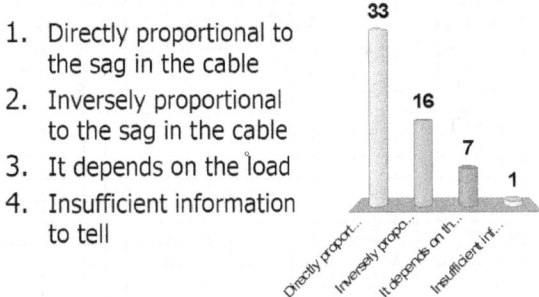

In a cable spanning a distance carrying a load, the magnitude of the force in the cable will be:

1. Directly proportional to the sag in the cable
2. Inversely proportional to the sag in the cable
3. It depends on the load
4. Insufficient information to tell

Figure 2. Typical PowerPoint slide with question and tallied student responses.

As can be seen in this case, a common misconception that force in a cable is directly proportional to its sag (versus the correct answer of inversely proportional) was held by 33 of the 57 students responding (these numbers can also be set to display in percentage). So in this instance more than half of the class either did not correctly understand the concept or otherwise misinterpreted the answer, despite the in-class rope demonstration the previous day. The concept was then reiterated and discussed once more to ensure that a broader understanding was achieved, and that students would become more aware of subtleties in their thought processes.

One of the best learning events that can occur with clickers, though, is when a question is posed such that it will elicit polarized responses…that is to say when roughly half of the class chooses one answer, and roughly half select another. Take for example the

"What are the correct senses for the unknown vectors in the system below?"

1) A-Comp., B-Tension
2) A-Tension, B-Comp.
3) A-Tension, B-Tension
4) A-Comp., B-Comp.
5) Impossible to tell

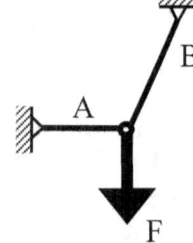

Figure 3. Clicker question on vector equilibrium

qualitative question posed in Figure 3 with regard to vector equilibrium. Here students were asked to mentally reason out the correct sense (tension or compression) of the two members supporting a force "F". The initial responses to the question are summarized in Table 1:

	(Percent)	(Count)
A-Comp., B-Tension	45.3%	24
A-Tension, B-Comp.	3.8%	2
A-Tension, B-Tension	49.1%	26
A-Comp., B-Comp.	0.0%	0
Impossible to tell	1.9%	1
	100%	53

Table 1. Initial responses to question posed in Figure 3

It is evident that roughly equal numbers of students were divided between member "A" being either a tension member or a compression member. But now rather than simply *explaining* the correct answer to the class, this polarization can then become a teachable moment for an active learning exercise of peer engagement, where students can be asked to speak with one another. At this point typically I will say, "Okay, whatever answer you chose, take two minutes to talk with your neighbor and convince them of why you think you are correct."

After the two minutes are up, the same question is re-polled. In this case the results are summarized in Table 2. As can be seen, there was a substantial shift of the majority of the class to the correct answer of both members "A" and "B" being in tension. At this point with the class engaged and more alert from an active participation exercise, a further discussion can ensue explaining how one can mentally (or with a quick sketch) break down the vectors into their components and do a quick non-numeric equilibrium analysis.

	(Percent)	(Count)
A-Comp., B-Tension	17.0%	9
A-Tension, B-Comp.	0.0%	0
A-Tension, B-Tension	83.0%	44
A-Comp., B-Comp.	0.0%	0
Impossible to tell	0.0%	0
	100%	53

Table 2. Responses to question posed in Figure 3 after peer discussion

In another example, a true-false question about moment was posed following the previous class where the concept of moment was introduced: "The sense of a moment is either positive or negative" (Table 3).

	(Percent)	(Count)
True	67.3%	37
False	32.7%	18
	100.0%	55

Table 3. Responses to question about moment sense

Although not equally polarized, enough students did not grasp the notion that moment is described as clockwise/counterclockwise versus positive and negative that it was clear further elaboration was needed. A similar period of peer discussion then ensued, followed immediately by another re-polling of the question. Data in Table 4 illustrates a substantial shift in understanding after the peer discussion period.

	(Percent)	(Count)
True	34.5%	19
False	65.5%	36
	100.0%	55

Table 4. Re-polling responses to question about moment sense

In addition to using clickers to stimulate discussion, following suggestions in the literature, periodic and typically unannounced "clicker quizzes" were given throughout the semester (Duncan 39). These questions were essentially similar to others, however they were given a value of two points for a correct answer and one point for an incorrect answer. Counting overall for 5% of their final grade, this was done to provide an incentive for students to attend class, and to act as token rewards. Generally the questions were kept simple and any calculations were of a very basic nature (For example as in Figure 4). The point values are low enough so that even if a student incorrectly answered every question for the entire semester (unlikely) the worst it could hurt the grade is by 2.5% of the final total in a 600 point class, or 15 points. Additionally, students were informed that the lowest four clicker grades would be dropped so as to alleviate concern for missing a class or perhaps forgetting or losing their keypad.

Clicker Quiz:
What are the X & Y components of this vector?

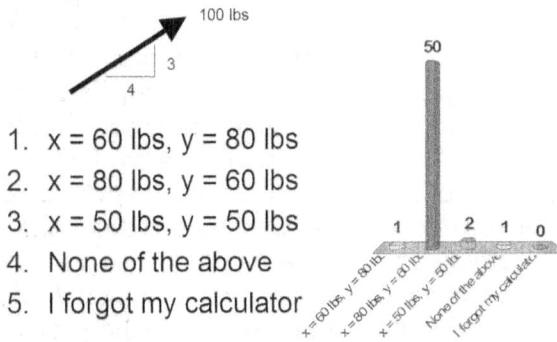

1. x = 60 lbs, y = 80 lbs
2. x = 80 lbs, y = 60 lbs
3. x = 50 lbs, y = 50 lbs
4. None of the above
5. I forgot my calculator

Figure 4. Typical "Clicker Quiz"

Back 'atcha

In the spirit of the two-way structures class, the learning experience is not just on the part of the student, but also for the instructor as well. One of the things I have learned from the student responses, for example, is that sometimes wording I took for granted was at times the source of confusion. For instance, in one clicker quiz, I asked students a question I pose every year in the entry-level structures class regarding the influence of span direction of decking and the resulting load shape on the supporting member. This question read "Decking framing perpendicular to a member produces a load on this member that is:" (the possible answers being 'uniformly distributed,' 'concentrated,' uniformly varying,' and 'insufficient information to tell.'

In the past I had implicitly taken the use of the word "framing" as a verb when used in this context. But I learned here that some students were confused by the question ("we don't understand what you're asking") because they had taken "framing" as a noun. Even though I had used this very question on quizzes and exams many times before and most students did in fact answer it correctly, I had never previously received feedback that the wording itself was a source of confusion for a certain number of students.

In another situation, when discussing buckling behavior a recurrent struggle with some students is in developing a correct understanding for the influence of cross sectional shape. Which axis is the 'major' and which is 'minor' seems to typically be problematic for about one third of any given class. Though I go to great lengths to make very clear the distinction of "major axis" versus "minor axis," it was only after posing a clicker question that read "Identify the strong axis of a column with the cross-sectional shape below" did I come to learn that some students were interpreting "strong axis" to mean the *direction* in which the column is most resistant to buckling. Since bucking occurs *about* an axis, if we say that the larger moment of inertia is about the x-axis, it will be most resistant to buckling movement in the *direction* of the y-axis...and thus some students interpret this to mean that the strong axis is the y-axis because it is not inclined to move in that direction. This is a very subtle distinction, one that I had heretofore not picked up on but which I will be certain to be clear about with future classes.

Problems in Paradise

Despite the promise, at present all is not golden and there are hidden 'costs' and challenges that go along with the technology. To paraphrase a saying, it is seldom that a solution to one problem does not itself breed new problems. As with any new technology there are bound to be unforeseen difficulties with its early implementation, both in terms of the learning curve for the user as well as in maturity of the software itself. It is therefore important when adopting a new device such as clickers that one be careful to not overdo things or hold initial expectations too high.

With regard to the learning curve, despite the glitzy show of the corporate presentations touting its ease of use, I found that even with a fairly strong background of computer usage it took a substantial time investment in the early part of the semester in learning to use this tool. Of course in being a part of the pilot program on campus I'm at the "bleeding edge," as it were. A well-developed training program for users has yet to emerge, which in time will alleviate the struggles of learning its use on one's own.

Operationally (at least with the version of TurningPoint we used) I found that PowerPoint itself ran more sluggishly and took noticeably longer to start up. In addition, undocumented characteristics, poorly documented features and specific operational quirks were frustrating. At times I could sense irritation in some students with occasional system problems and things not always going according to plan in class. I discovered, for example, that unless one is using a dual computer/projector setup, one cannot easily embed many photo images with clicker questions in the same presentation. Doing so creates difficulties in terms of generating excessively large response data file sizes and file save times that strain computing resources. For now, my work-around is to either not include or otherwise greatly limit the use of images in presentations with clicker questions. This operational encumbrance significantly limits the flexibility in usage of the system at present.

Nevertheless, these issues should be taken as growing pains attributable to early adoption, and some are likely unique to this particular software package. It does, however, underscore that one should expect the unexpected. Feedback has been delivered to the software vendor that hopefully will result in corrections to these and other limitations. Furthermore, as with anything else, effective and efficient use also comes with user experience. The literature indicates that with continued usage, the favorable response from students about the use of clickers increases.

Finally there can also be the cost factor assumed by the student. Although some publishers are bundling clickers with textbooks, this only works with compatible software systems. Some schools may also purchase clickers that stay with the room and students only use them in that class, but this limits the student-specific information that can be gathered. At the University of Maryland, students are required to purchase the keypads for $48. Although to a student this cost is not trivial, they may sell them back to the bookstore at half cost, or sell them to an upcoming student the next year, so the expense is mitigated and can be thought of more akin to a 'rental' fee. Since the system is being adopted here campus-wide, it is anticipated that incoming freshman students will purchase the keypads and retain them throughout their college career and use them in multiple classes.

Some Initial Outcomes and Surprising Findings

In the final class for the semester, an anonymous survey using clickers was taken to assess the impact and effectiveness of their use. Questions related to clicker usage in specific are shown at the end of this document. Other questions related to specific course activities were also asked but have been omitted as being out of context in this presentation. Some questions of a similar nature were asked more than once where there was something I was very specifically interested in knowing, such as how much students felt clickers helped their learning experience.

The results of this initial implementation, while very encouraging, are also not overwhelmingly positive and indicate that there is ample room for improvement in the effectiveness of this new tool. But considering that this is the first time the system has been employed and that the learning curve was at times steep, this is not surprising. And in point of fact approximately one half of the students polled either 'agreed' or 'strongly agreed' that clickers made the class material more engaging.

There was a fairly even polarization of opinion whether clicker questions should have point values in the form of "clicker quizzes," with 20 students either 'agreeing' or 'strongly agreeing,' and 19 either 'disagreeing' or 'strongly disagreeing,' and the remainder being 'neutral.' For the most part, students were no more inclined to come to class when they otherwise would not have because of the clickers.

A few results were quite astonishing. For one, I learned that over two-thirds of the class either seldom or never read or consulted the class textbook (*Structures*, by Daniel Schodek). Even more surprising was that 6% seldom and 92% never used the CD-ROM that comes with the text which contains sample problems and excellent step-by-step presentations—this despite showing the CD in class on a number of occasions. I continue to ponder the meaning of this and how to address it, with one possibility being the use of clicker quizzes immediately following assigned reading.

Looking to the Future

Having now worked with clickers for one semester, many of the system 'bugs' are now worked out. The learning curve has leveled and I have become comfortable with most all features of their use. The initial results are encouraging enough to indicate that with continued practice, clickers will have a useful place in the teaching of this and other similar lecture classes. In specific, I plan to implement the following changes in the fall semester:

- Using clickers in connection with in-class demonstrations (e.g., "what do you think will be the behavior or this element?" etc.)
- Clicker quizzes right after lecture presentations to reinforce the key ideas. Students who frequently don't take notes may find more incentive to do so.
- Outcome assessments immediately after a lab session or project
- More repetition of principle ideas and questions on basic concepts

Conclusion

That clickers are a useful means of engaging students in the classroom has been demonstrated repeatedly through careful studies in a variety of disciplines. The evidence strongly supports that this technology facilitates active learning environments in large lecture settings, increases student interest and enthusiasm, and helps provide feedback to their level of understanding. In the context of teaching structures to architectural students, this is potentially an important technology to combat the "snooze factor" commonly encountered. Structures class need not be so dryly abstract that it drives out the desire to learn it from our students. But technical competence at some level is expected and clickers represent one more tool in our belt to help develop the best critical thinking skills in the future generations of young professionals.

Appendix: Representative Exit Survey Question Results

The semester exit survey was given with the clickers in an anonymous mode, controllable by the software, to help ensure sincerity of response. Representative questions from this survey and the response rates are shown below. There were several students absent that day, as well as another few who forgot their clickers or had problems, so the sample is less than the full class size of 58.

The numbers at the far right of each table represent the number of responses to each question choice, and the corresponding percentage of those who responded. Note that not all students responded to all questions. This at times is due to functional problems with the keypad device (not pushing the button properly) and, I believe, a certain amount of apathy among those students who feel the clickers are not a useful tool. Perhaps another question could be added to this reading something like "If you did not respond to each question, please indicate your reason."

The use of clickers has made this course material more engaging

Strongly Agree	8.3%	4
Agree	41.7%	20
Neutral	29.2%	14
Disagree	12.5%	6
Strongly Disagree	8.3%	4
	100.0%	48

Clicker questions helped me to know how well I was learning the material

Strongly Agree	4.1%	2
Agree	36.7%	18
Neutral	22.4%	11
Disagree	24.5%	12
Strongly Disagree	12.2%	6
	100.0%	49

By using clickers in this class, I got feedback on my understanding of class material

Strongly Agree	8.0%	4
Agree	42.0%	21
Neutral	26.0%	13
Disagree	16.0%	8
Strongly Disagree	8.0%	4
	100.0%	50

For me, earning "clicker points" motivates me to come to class

Strongly Agree	4.0%	2
Agree	28.0%	14
Neutral	26.0%	13
Disagree	18.0%	9
Strongly Disagree	24.0%	12
	100.0%	50

I chose my answer to each clicker question carefully

Strongly Agree	25.0%	12
Agree	37.5%	18
Neutral	22.9%	11
Disagree	12.5%	6
Strongly Disagree	2.1%	1
	100.0%	48

Clicker questions should periodically have point values ("clicker quizzes")

Strongly Agree	8.3%	4
Agree	33.3%	16
Neutral	18.8%	9
Disagree	20.8%	10
Strongly Disagree	18.8%	9
	100.0%	48

I attended class when I otherwise would not have because of the clickers

Strongly Agree	8.5%	4
Agree	12.8%	6
Neutral	17.0%	8
Disagree	25.5%	12
Strongly Disagree	36.2%	17
	100.0%	47

I read and consulted my textbook:

Frequently	2.1%	1
Fairly often	4.2%	2
On occasion	25.0%	12
Seldom	41.7%	20
Never	27.1%	13
	100.0%	48

When planning an architectural space in my studio projects, I see structural principles as influential in my decision-making:

Strongly Agree	14.3%	7
Agree	40.8%	20
Neutral	22.4%	11
Disagree	18.4%	9
Strongly Disagree	4.1%	2
	100.0%	49

When looking at the natural environment, I now see structural forces and patterns that were always right in front of me that I never took note of before:

Strongly Agree	2.4%	1
Agree	65.9%	27
Neutral	22.5%	9
Disagree	7.3%	3
Strongly Disagree	2.4%	1
	100.0%	25

I used the course web site:

Frequently	12.5%	6
Fairly often	31.3%	15
On occasion	43.8%	21
Seldom	10.4%	5
Never	2.1%	1
	100.0%	48

I consulted the book-supplied CD:

Frequently	2.0%	1
Fairly often	0.0%	0
On occasion	0.0%	0
Seldom	6.1%	3
Never	91.8%	45
	100.0%	49

As supplementary learning experiences to the more calculation-based material, the hands-on projects (in-class and assigned) were:

Very helpful	12.0%	6
Somewhat helpful	56.0%	28
Neutral	20.0%	10
Not very helpful	10.0%	5
Useless	2.0%	1
	100.0%	50

How many hours per week did you typically spend on this class outside of lecture?

More than 12	2.2%	1
10-12	6.5%	3
8-10	6.5%	3
6-8	39.1%	18
Less than 6	45.7%	21
	100.0%	46

References:

Banks, David A., Editor. Audience Response Systems in Higher Education. Hershey, Pennsylvania: Information Science Publishing, 2006.

Bernold, L.E., "Typical Lectures Fail Students." Engineering News-Record vol. 244, no. 23 (2000): p. 67.

Bransford, John, Ann L Brown, and Rodney R. Cocking, Editors. How People Learn: Brain, Mind, Experience, and School: Expanded Edition. Washington, D.C.: National Academies Press, 2000.

Chickering, Arthur W., and Zelda F. Gamson, "Applying the Seven Principles for Good Practice in Undergraduate Education," New Directions for Teaching and Learning Vol. 47 (1991), San Francisco: Jossey-Bass Inc., Publishers.

Duncan, Douglas, Clickers in the Classroom: Pearson Education, Inc., 2005

Prince, Michael, "Does Active Learning Work? A Review of the Research," Journal of Engineering Education, 93 (3), 1-9, (2004)

Silberman, Mel. Active Learning: 101 Strategies to Teach any Subject. Needam Heights, Massachusetts: Allyn & Bacon, 1996.

Shmueli, Galit, Ross Malaga, Interactive Student Response System: Pilot Project: Report to the faculty in fulfillment of an STI grant: Robert H Smith School of Business, University of Maryland, 2005. Retrieved from <http://www.smith.umd.edu/faculty/gshmueli/HomePage/Clicker%20Pilot%20Study%20Report%20Jan_2005.pdf>, June 2006.

The Active Learning Site, Dr. Charles Bonwell, Active Learning Workshops 18 June, 2006 <http://www.acive-learning-site.com>

Wood, William B, Clickers: A Teaching Gimmick that Works: Cell Press, 2004

Notes:

[1] The literature available on Active Learning has grown to staggering proportions in recent years, and active learning theory falls outside the scope of this paper. The reader is directed to publications including books such as Silberman's *Active Learning: 101 Strategies* for very practical techniques, and to Internet recourses such as the *Active Learning Site,* which provides links to scores of publications in a wide array of disciplines.

[2] For an in-depth scholarly study of the research available on classroom response devices, the reader is directed to Banks (2004), which contains more than two dozen papers by authors in a wide array of disciplines.

[3] A study made by the University of Maryland Robert H. Smith School of Business (Shmueli and Malaga) determined that the TuningPoint system by Turning Technologies offered the greatest benefit over competing vendors, largely due to the integration with Microsoft PowerPoint and a more fully-developed software at the time of the study. Following a later separately conducted campus-wide study that took into consideration a favorable pricing structure offered by Turning Technologies, TurningPoint has been established as the new University Standard. An ongoing pilot program jointly run by the Center for Teaching Excellence and the Office of Information Technology is now underway in departments throughout campus, including my structures class in the School of Architecture, Planning and Preservation.

Designing Building Failures

Jonathan Ochshorn
Cornell University

Introduction

The discipline of structural engineering is quite explicit about the probabilities, causes, and prevention of structural failure. In reinforced concrete design, for example, the probabilities of overloading (about 1:1000) and of inadequate strength (about 1:100) result in a structural failure probability of about 1:100,000, or 0.001 percent.[1] But what of other "building technology" failures that occur primarily within the architect's purview? It is commonly acknowledged that a much greater percentage of buildings experience non-structural failure, in particular failures of the building envelope: one study conservatively estimates that such failures occur at a rate of 3 to 5 per cent.[2] What are the causes of non-structural failure and what strategies could reduce their occurrence? This paper proposes to investigate one aspect of these questions by looking at the relationship between building envelope failure and attitudes towards design. A concluding section examines the implications for pedagogy and practice.

Traditional construction

Failure in traditional, pre-modern, building typically results from the misuse of materials or methods of construction, whether from ignorance of correct practice or willful disregard of such practice to save time, money, or both.[3] A variation on these failure modes can be seen in the attempt to extend technology, correct at a conventional scale of operation, beyond the point at which it remains viable—for example, through an inappropriate increase in size without a corresponding increase in strength or stiffness.[4]

Figure 1. Construction of brick walls from Alberti's Ten Books on Architecture (1485)

Almost all guidance for avoiding building failure in traditional construction involves the proper selection, preparation, and arrangement of materials of construction; the proper spacing and thickness of walls, columns, arches, and beams; the proper orientation and siting of buildings; and proper maintenance. In general, this advice is based on accumulated experience, combined with a primitive building science which at times seems remarkably "modern" in its sensitivity to issues of climate, orientation, and so on, but at other times seems riddled with superstition. Yet if good practice is followed, even when its underlying rationale is mystified and misunderstood, buildings may survive for hundreds of years. Roofs are sloped adequately; walls are thick enough to absorb and then release any accumulated water; foundations are set on firm strata; ventilation is provided to prevent the accumulation of excess humidity. The lack of a consistent and rigorous building science is counterbalanced by an empirical base of successes and failures from which standards of building practice are derived.

Problems can still certainly develop—the detailed instructions for the preparation and use of building materials from Vitruvius onward indicate the extent to which reliable building required then, as it does now, serious attention to technical matters—but such problems are caused, in general, by the same types of errors described by modern critics of building failure: ignorance, carelessness, negligence and greed.[5]

It should also be emphasized that traditional buildings, even when well-constructed, still rely on periodic maintenance, repair, and replacement. At the extreme, whitewashing of mud-brick walls needs to be renewed annually. Yet even durable materials require periodic attention. Stonemasons not only build new structures but also work to repair the existing infrastructure of masonry buildings. Carpenters replace wooden rafters and beams that no longer function adequately.[6]

The nineteenth century was a transitional era during which the science of structures and materials advanced considerably, while the construction of buildings remained caught between traditional modes of building described by Vitruvius and Alberti, and the potentials opened up by new discoveries in material science and the emerging requirements of industrial capitalism. Joseph Gwilt, the English author of one of last great encyclopedic works on architecture published in the nineteenth century, still refers to both Vitruvius and Alberti as sources of certain construction practices, but on the other hand he makes clear the qualitative difference in the scientific knowledge available to the nineteenth-century architect. He notes, for example, that Vitruvius "does not allude to the assistance which may be afforded in the construction of edifices by a knowledge of the resolution of forces."[7] Viollet-le-Duc, writing in 1872, points out the increasing complexity of modern construction: "While the Egyptians, in erecting a temple with blocks of limestone, placed in juxtaposition, had but few observations to make on the effects displayed in their structure, the architect who builds a house in Paris, in which stone, brick, mortar, wood, wrought and cast iron, lead, zinc, slate, and plaster are simultaneously employed, must necessarily accumulate a considerable number of practical observations." He then adds, with more than a slight hint of sarcasm: "It is singular that there should be a desire to imitate with this considerable variety of materials edifices that were built with only one."[8]

The point here is not to dwell on instances of traditional building failure, but rather to draw the following conclusion from such failures and their causes: whether due to ignorance, carelessness, negligence or greed, they were not directly influenced by concerns of an aesthetic nature; that is, the *architectural* content of the building, however that may be conceptualized, was not complicit in the mode of failure. In fact, what is striking about traditional texts including those of Vitruvius, Alberti, and even Rondelet and Gwilt, is the extent to which the art and science of architecture are reconciled within them. Even in the *Lectures* of Viollet-de-Duc, the alleged "failure" of nineteenth-century architectural practice refers not so much to a literal failure of construction systems, but to a moral failure to properly reconcile the technological potential of the modern age with its appearance.[9] This is in stark contrast with texts from the twentieth century, in which the art and science of architecture seem to finally and irrevocably diverge.

Modern construction

The causes of building failure characteristic of traditional construction continue into the twentieth century, but new attitudes also surface. In particular, early modernism brings a qualitatively more radical attitude towards formal abstraction into building design which, in the absence of a correspondingly rigorous building science, leads to a new category of building failure. It is not so much that architectural abstraction per se is new or intrinsically antithetical to proper construction practices; rather it is the extent to which formal design becomes *abstracted from its technological basis* that creates a crisis in modern building technology.

This separation of design ideas from building science in the twentieth century manifests itself both in a lack of technical theory within design manifestos, and in a lack of design theory within construction handbooks; but the roots of this division between "art" and "science" are ancient. While traditional architectural texts represent architectural aesthetic and technological concerns in a relatively unified manner, there is nevertheless an emerging tendency in which abstract design and material reality are seen as increasingly independent. For Vitruvius, beauty ("delight") is certainly considered a distinct aspect of architecture, but it comes about through proper ordering, arrangement, eurythmy, symmetry, and propriety of actual elements of construction, not as a result of abstract formal ideas imposed upon, and independent of, construction. In fact, there are numerous passages where it is impossible to disentangle "aesthetic" from "practical" advice.[10]

With Alberti, the distinction between aesthetics and practical matters becomes more pronounced, though they are still often conflated. Convenience, beauty, and strength remain, as they are for Vitruvius, the necessary conditions for architecture, but Vitruvian beauty, obtained through the proper arrangement and proportion of otherwise necessary elements of construction, is now explicitly defined as being independent of physical "matter." In addition, Alberti defines ornament as something that can make the bad acceptable and the good even better; that can improve deficient works "by painting and concealing any thing that was deformed, and trimming and polishing what was handsome." Unlike beauty, ornament is "somewhat added or fastened on, rather than proper and innate."[11]

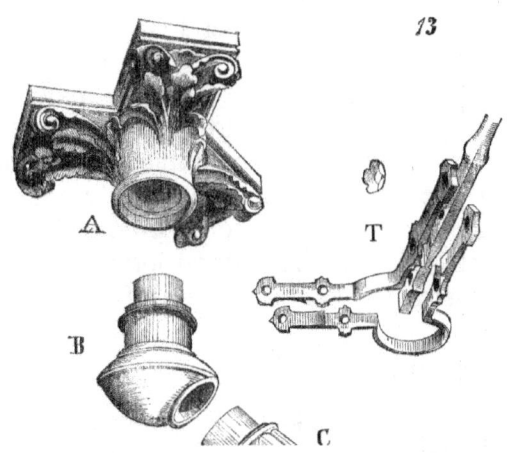

Figure 2. Viollet-le-Duc's ornamental embellishment of cast iron struts and capitals (1872)

Yet this liberal attitude towards ornament would not survive. Nineteenth-century writers as different as Ruskin, Semper, and Viollet-le-Duc all tended to value "honesty" and "truth" in the deployment of ornament, albeit in their own ways; and by the twentieth-century, theorists generally rejected as unsustainable the entire premise of an honest ornament, and instead searched for honesty in unadorned structure and cladding. What was not rejected was the Vitruvian idea of *delight* and the Albertian valuation of *design* as an abstract exercise independent from material construction.

Abstraction, which for Ruskin is an operation specified for ornamental features, now has a wider field of application. While there are numerous competing tendencies, each of which employs abstraction in different ways (e.g., Art Nouveau, or stripped-down classicism), it is early twentieth-century European modernism, drawing upon contemporary experiments in painting and sculpture, that most radically threatens conventions of building construction. For the first time, architectural forms not based on abstractions of, or ornamental elaborations over, conventional building elements (e.g., walls, columns, vaults, domes, windows, roofs) begin to be built. Abstract compositions appear whose points of departure are visual experiments with line, surface, solid, and void analogous to those occurring in the fine arts. The simultaneous appearance of new materials and systems of construction (steel and reinforced concrete in particular), rather than providing a countervailing model of construction based on pragmatic or objective factors, is instead integrated into the abstract system of mass-surface-void.

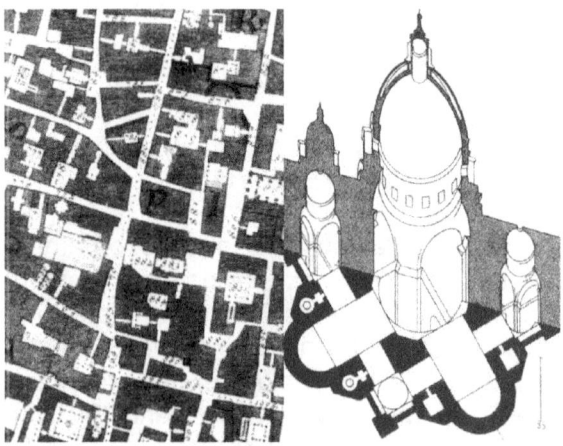

Figure 3. Nolli's map of Rome (1748) contrasted with Choisy's cut-away axonometric (1899)

Signs of this tendency to view structure and other aspects of construction primarily as diagrams pointing to opportunities for formal development can be seen at the end of the nineteenth century in Choisy's influential *Histoire de l'Architecture*, whose characteristic cut-away axonometrics use the same precise, yet abstract, graphic techniques found 150 years earlier in Giambattista Nolli's map of Rome, except extended into the third dimension.[12] While techniques and details of traditional structure and construction are abstracted from the diagrammatic drawings by Choisy, they are available elsewhere, and empirically validated. Modern design, on the other hand, is inherently incompatible with such empirically-based rules of construction: new structural forms and materials, new methods of enclosure, and new environmental control systems that emerge alongside the development of industrial society provide a range of choice and a degree of complexity that can no longer be adequately captured by existing empirically-based rules. Instead, what is required is the development of new techniques of design and analysis derived from the various branches of building science. In the case of structure, advances in the theory of structural analysis and the development of an autonomous discipline of structural engineering compensate for the loss of an empirical basis. Similarly, technological advances, and corresponding engineering disciplines, emerge in the area of environmental systems.

In the case of enclosure, however, the obsolescence of traditional wall systems brought about by new structural frameworks and new technologies of environmental control leaves more of a void: neither an adequate "science of construction" nor a class of "constructional engineers" emerges to design correspondingly rational enclosure systems. Instead, what characterizes architecture in the twentieth century is an abstract conception of enclosure in which formal values overwhelm technical considerations. "The expression of the wall as a thin sheathing, of no more structural importance than the window, is a manifestation of modern constructional methods. The function of the wall has changed; it is a thin skin, hung on a framework instead of standing on a foundation... and we see that where the modern purpose of the wall is appreciated by the architect there is something of a revolution in the design of the façade. The wall surface is regarded, aesthetically, as a continuous plane; as a skin enveloping and expressing the surface of a volume."[13]

This type of abstraction, in and of itself, is not the cause of building failure; rather it is the *interaction* of several factors relating to the use of abstraction in modern architecture—not all of which are necessarily present in any given instance—that creates problems.

Abstraction precedes function. Abstract ideas tend to precede, rather than evolve from, considerations of a technical or functional nature. This is partly a result of a misplaced confidence in the power of science to compensate for any a priori design decisions, and partly a result of an education in construction derived from empirically-based rules that provide neither the theory to grasp, nor even the vocabulary to define, the issues that were to become relevant in the design of enclosure systems. As a result, abstract "volumes brought together in light" often experience problems when they are also, invariably, brought together in rain, wind, and snow; and subject to unanticipated environmental pressures.

Enclosure is architecture. Whereas a steel or concrete structural framework (or an environmental control system) can be conceptually and physically separated from the rest of the building, permitting a specialized process of engineering design that supports the architectural concept, it is difficult to see how the enclosure of a building can be dealt with in an analogous manner without reducing the architect's role to a purely schematic one: from the standpoint of both traditional and modern architecture, the enclosure, to a great extent, *is* the architecture. Delegating the detailed design of enclosure to others (aside from loss of prestige and remuneration) opens up the risk of compromising the abstract basis of the design. Vertical surfaces may terminate in unwanted copings; what was conceived as abstract void may appear as conventional window; and the precise articulation of formal elements, based on subtleties of alignment and proportion, may suffer.[14]

Technology as threat to freedom. The architect, while maintaining control over the building's external surfaces, tends to resist serious application of "engineering" criteria to the design of building envelopes. Within the design studio as well as in practice, such criteria are perceived as threats to the freedom of formal invention characteristic of modernist abstraction. In the words of Piet Mondrian: "If one takes technique, utilitarian requirements, etc., as the point of departure, there is a risk of losing every chance of success, for intuition is then troubled by intelligence."[15]

Risk of failure not appreciated. The risk of enclosure failure is neither as obvious, immediate, nor usually as catastrophic, as is the case with structural failure, so there is less pressure to develop the necessary theoretical or empirical basis. Details often seem reasonable when initially conceived and executed, as their intrinsic defects may be far from obvious. In fact, "obvious" or "common-sense" solutions are sometimes problematic: for example, the popularity of non-redundant barrier walls "may result from a common-sense approach to the problem of rain exclusion—when it is raining, we wear a mackintosh, so why not treat our buildings likewise?"[16] Additionally, many non-structural failures take years to manifest themselves. Even "short-term or accelerated tests may give misleading indications. A tentative judgment only may be possible, based on technical knowledge and subject to confirmation in due course by observation."[17] Cracking and bowing of marble cladding panels on the Standard Oil Company Headquarters in Chicago were first noticed almost seven years after initial construction, became increasingly prevalent only within thirteen years of construction, and finally led to complete replacement after nineteen years.[18] Such non-structural failures are often costly, inconvenient, and dangerous, but they are rarely catastrophic.

We don't know what we don't know. Because the traditional means of dealing with enclosure is primarily based on empirical rather than on scientific knowledge, modern architects do not necessarily *know* what they don't know about the subject, and are thus more inclined to either extrapolate inappropriately from prior experience, or simply invent constructional details based on a superficial understanding (i.e., a misunderstanding) of the complex forces at work. In other words, the empirical basis for much prior construction success, having little basis in a theory of building science, is discarded without the modern architect knowing exactly (or even approximately) what is being lost. If a 24"-thick load-bearing masonry wall seems to work well at keeping water out, it may not be clear why 8"-thick cladding supported on a structural frame wouldn't keep water out just as well. The process of abstraction, unmediated by any serious building science, reduces the complex behavior of specific wall-types to formal ideas: the "wall" becomes a "plane," a "surface," or a constituent part of a "volume" or "mass." Even the origin and purpose of the pitched roof, understood traditionally as a culturally-specific response to environmental conditions, is dismissed by R.S. Yorke, architect and author of *The Modern House*, as a structural anachronism made obsolete by the employment of "frame construction and concrete slabs."[19]

Heroic status of structure and cladding. In the modern conception of construction, visible and "heroic" elements of building are seen either as purely formal elements (enclosure) or as abstract manifestations of "structure," while the subtle realities of material behavior and their relationship to the construction of buildings are often ignored. As a more rigorous building science develops, these attitudes become increasingly untenable.[20]

Inventions based on wishful thinking. With neither a working knowledge of building science, nor empirically-based standards for reliable detailing, it is not surprising that the modern architect may be incapable of inventing reliable strategies for enclosing buildings. Yet it is still common for architects to creatively "invent" construction details. Some of the reasons for this have already been given: the risk of failure is not fully appreciated; the lack of theory associated with an empirically-based construction practice makes it difficult to know what one doesn't know; and the state of building science itself may be relatively undeveloped. Additionally, an attitude of heroic contempt for the conventional may be present: *The Architects' Journal* wonders in 1975 whether the cause of misguided architectural invention lies "in a disdain for the 'standard solution' or the principle, perhaps, that any designer worth his salt should be able to work everything out from first principles?"[21]

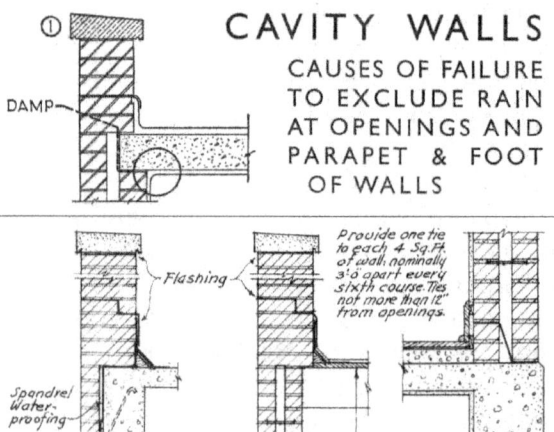

Figure 4. Causes of failure shown in Principles of Modern Building, 1959 (top) are recommended in Architectural Graphic Standards, 1956 (bottom).

Durability, maintenance, and greed. There is also a tendency to overestimate the durability of many modern systems and materials; as "modern" becomes identified in popular culture with overcoming traditional labor-intensive practices, habits of maintenance characteristic of traditional building practice (continual repair, replacement, pointing, painting, etc.) are loosened from their bearings. While expectations of permanence, toughness, and resiliency become part of the culture, if not the reality, of modern materials, two other factors make decisions regarding durability more difficult for the architect.

First, it is not easy to obtain definitive information on the performance characteristics of complex components, equipment, and systems.[22] Knowledge is limited because those who have it tend to view it in a proprietary manner, and are reluctant to share it. Competing manufacturers vying for market share may not always be inclined to objectively compare their products with others. Second, the desire to extract the maximum profit from investments in commercial building tends to encourage both marginal construction practices and deferred maintenance.[23]

Graphic standards. Many twentieth-century texts on construction practice lack both a coherent theory of building science as well as a base of empirical knowledge corresponding to the new architectural forms, materials, and systems that are emerging.[24] Charles Ramsey and Harold Sleeper describe a situation in which "facts are so deeply buried in the body of technical literature that they only come to light in the course of research..." Their *Architectural Graphic Standards*, first published in 1932, is intended to overcome the "pressure of time [that] often forces the making of assumptions and trusting to luck."[25] But there are at least two problems with these assertions. First, it is not clear that the "research" referred to is yet capable of dealing with the complexity of modern materials and systems. For example, effective utilization of insulating material, vapor retarders, and air barriers is still, after more than 80 years of discussion and research, subject to uncertainty and inconsistent practice.[26] Second, it is not clear that available "state-of-the-art" research is being incorporated consistently into the graphic details. Research into the relationships among insulation, vapor migration, and condensation, already available in 1923, does not begin to appear in *Architectural Graphic Standards* until 1951.[27] Even when such research conclusions finally appear, they are not consistently applied to the details; for example, generic advice on condensation doesn't prevent the continued reprinting of numerous details that contradict the theory.

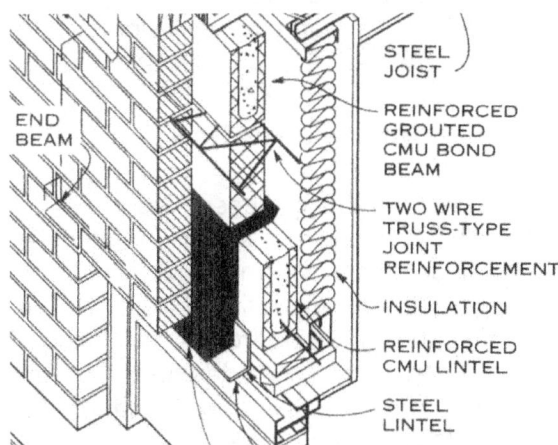

Figure 5. Detail from 2000 Architectural Graphic Standards (student edition) omits vapor barrier and air barrier.

Publishing graphically-oriented material with little explicit theoretical grounding also makes the underlying premise—that of providing a "core of skeleton data useful for further development, design, or improvement"—a dangerous proposition. For how can one modify or extrapolate from a detailed drawing if the underlying logic is not known?[28] Details supplied by manufacturers of specific systems are also often difficult to incorporate properly into an overall building design, but for a different reason. Perhaps to avoid liability for providing information about elements over which they have no control, many manufacturers avoid showing precisely how their systems connect to adjacent construction.[29]

Untested combinations. Even where familiar materials are used, many problems in modern construction arise from the untested interactions among those materials. Viollet-le-Duc refers to this potential, already manifested in nineteenth-century construction, as being proportional to the variation in component materials.[30] Twentieth-century practice, with its proliferation of new materials, makes the problem worse. Even familiar materials may cause problems when used in new contexts.[31] Not only individual materials may interact to cause failure, but individual factors, each by itself perhaps acting below the threshold of damage, can combine to trigger failure.[32]

Postmodern construction

Postmodern building—used here as a catch-all for numerous stylistic tendencies that critique "classical" modernism—has its own characteristic modes of building failure, in some cases resulting from a prioritizing of abstract and formal considerations that are evocative precisely because, and to the extent that, they specifically eschew rationality and common sense. Looked at from the point of view of design attitudes, certain postmodern building failures seem to arise from a "perfect storm" of conditions characteristic of our epoch.

Rejection of conventional technology. A disdain for conventional applications of technology may seem somewhat paradoxical, in light of modernism's invocation of precisely this technology in its manifestos opposing traditional modes of building. But several factors are at play. There is, first, a growing distrust of, and backlash against, technical solutions within postmodern culture, and this general phenomenon lends support to architectural forms that express these feelings by literally distorting that which appears as logical within modernist practice.[33] Second, with the victory of modernism over traditional construction practices, what was "heroic" and "radical" in the deployment of steel and reinforced concrete frames becomes conventional. Given the cyclic movement of fashion, it is inevitable that an avant-garde style, once integrated and accepted within popular culture, must give way to something new—the negation of the logic embedded within modernist conventions becomes the stylistic path of least resistance.[34] Third, technology is still expressed, even fetishized, in its irrational manifestations. Glass is re-imagined, no longer merely as the "void" in modernist abstraction, but as the visible and universal boundary between inside and outside; cladding is similarly abstracted as universal surface; structure is bent, angled, cantilevered, hyper-articulated, and so on, using techniques based on distortion or other forms of defamiliarization.

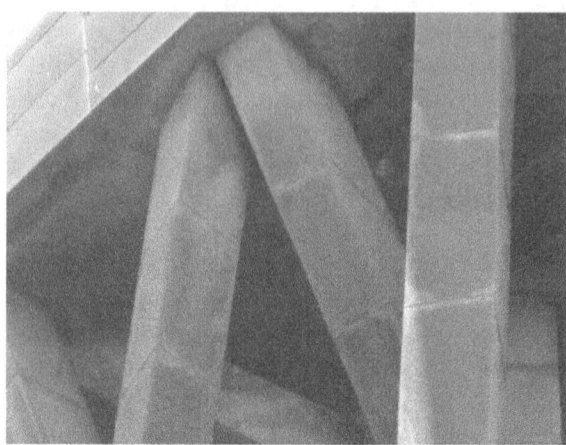

Figure 6. Frank O. Gehry's angled columns at 340 Main St., Venice, California (1991). Photo by author.

Still heroic. Modern attitudes to construction tend to focus on structure and cladding as "heroic" materials through which the ideas of the designer are made visible. In the postmodern reaction to modernism, such attitudes survive largely intact: critiques of modernist idealism still rely on structure and cladding as expressive formal elements. Yet as building science evolves, the failure to acknowledge an emerging paradigm shift in the *actual* requirements of building—from the use of relatively unsophisticated enclosure strategies characteristic of modernism to the more subtle application of non-heroic systems based on air-vapor barriers and insulation, and incorporating issues of sustainability—is increasingly problematic.[35]

Magic pill. At the same time, even as the *expression* of technology as a manifestation of rationality is subjected to formal critique, technology itself is not actually rejected, but in fact assumes an almost mystical aura. If the engineer of modernism, "inspired by the law of Economy and governed by mathematical calculation, puts us in accord with universal law [and] achieves harmony," the postmodern engineer rejects the constraints of economy, values ambiguity over harmony, and relies on complex numerical methods programmed within the "black box" of sophisticated analytical software to transcend the limitations of traditional mathematical calculation. "Structure need not be comprehensible and explicit. There is no creed or absolute...It can be subtle and more revealing. It is a richer experience...if a puzzle is set or a layer of ambiguity lies over the reading of 'structure.'"[36]

Technology in this context is thought to possess almost limitless power to overcome problems originating in any predetermined form, no matter how arbitrary and illogical. Form, in other words, can be abstracted from virtually all considerations of a technical nature; and technology, much like the digital "improvements" common in photography, music, and film, can compensate for what might have been a hopelessly misconceived or inadequate "performance."[37] The problem with this attitude is twofold. First, such technical "solutions," focusing only on internal criteria of success, may lose sight of other criteria external to the immediate problem. For example, a "solution" to a problem of environmental control may require excessive energy use. Second, such an attitude is unrealistic. Unlike structural frameworks or other relatively straight-forward technical systems within buildings, the reliability of the building envelope is threatened by thousands of highly complex, and often unpredictable, interactions among building materials and systems subjected to differential movement, chemical reactions, environmental agents, construction and maintenance operations, and so on. Architectural form based upon empirically-validated principles of building science—form that *minimizes the collisions* among these countless variables—has a greater probability of success than does architectural form that either willfully distorts these principles or operates as if such principles can be applied after the fact.

Conclusion: Pedagogy and practice

Practice. Building envelopes consist of numerous sub-systems, each of which is put together using hundreds, or even thousands, of separate pieces. Failure within these systems may occur in literally hundreds of modes, yet typical design practice does not make use of an explicitly probabilistic design strategy to realistically assess the reliability of the building envelope.[38]

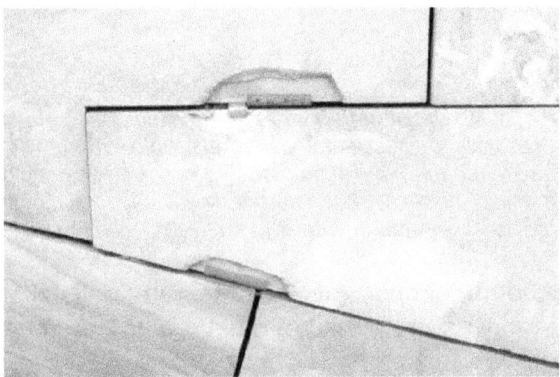

Figure 7. Failure of stone veneer, James Stirling's Schwartz Center for the Performing Arts at Cornell University (1989). Photo by author.

Reliability theory, developed during and after Word War II in response to concerns about the reliability of weapon systems, provides a probabilistic framework for the design of products and systems. It offers insight into the types of questions architects should be asking, and strategies for reducing the risk of failure. For example, the multiplicity of elements within buildings might be usefully organized within three categories: *components* (which are not repairable); *equipment* (often an assemblage of components); and *systems* (combinations of components and equipment).[39] Within that framework, the idea that certain elements require periodic maintenance (repair or replacement), while others are expected to last for the life of the building, can be made more explicit.[40]

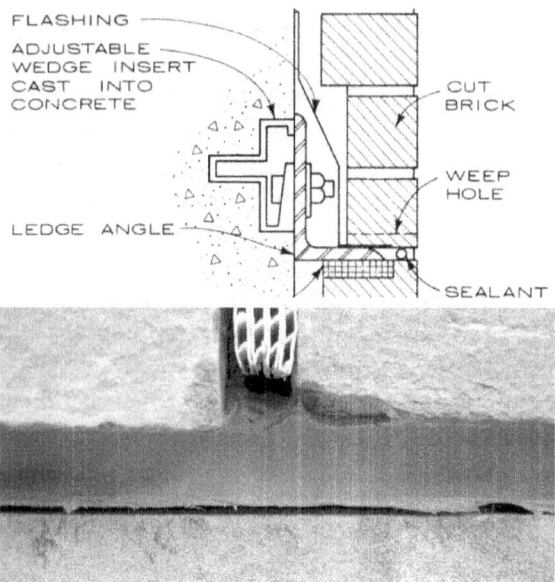

Figure 8. Detail (top) from 1981 Architectural Graphic Standards invites water penetration into wall cavity; photo (bottom) by author shows drip edge flashing detailed correctly but improperly installed, similarly providing a path for water into the wall cavity

Another important insight from reliability theory is that failure must be understood probabilistically. Current practice, based on building codes and referenced standards, requires a "weather resistant exterior wall envelope," but does not provide a methodology for assessing the probability that such a condition will actually be met.[41] Even tests for water penetration (ASTM E-331) or structural performance (ASTM E-330) may not provide adequate guidance, since the actual exterior wall has a much higher probability of failure than does a small, carefully built, sample.

In general, it is the *connections* between or within those building elements that are intended to behave as continuous systems, rather than the elements themselves, that are most likely to fail. Metal flashing and coping details are notorious in this regard, often behaving more like horizontal gutters directing water *into* the building. The practice of cutting two-dimensional sectional views through such continuous systems at locations *between* joints and connections tends to obscure, rather than illuminate, this problem.[42]

To control the incidence of non-structural failure, three general principles could be more systematically applied to the building envelope. First, develop performance criteria, design methodologies, and prescriptive details based on a *probabilistic assessment of reliability and maintainability*. For building envelopes, manufacturers should be encouraged to provide specific guidelines indicating how their products can reliably connect to other materials, including information on maintenance and replacement schedules. In other words, what is needed is a *matrix of connection standards*, in addition to detailed specifications for isolated products. Second, develop reliable means for implementing what is designed. This has two parts: creating "constructible" and "maintainable" details corresponding to actual conditions in the field; and providing for testing or inspection in cases where conformance to specifications may be uncertain.[43] Third, establish professional certification for expertise in envelope design.

Pedagogy. Reliability theory requires that an "intended function" be articulated, yet even this basic concept is subject to dispute within architectural pedagogy. Is the "function" of architecture defined from the subjective standpoint of aesthetics; or by the multiplicity of objective "performance mandates" relating to spatial and environmental conditions?[44] The apparent symmetry of this question encourages the notion that, within schools of architecture, integration of design and technology can proceed from either starting point. That is, design ideas can evolve from (or be superimposed on) a technologically-rigorous base; or an abstract design process can be taken to "another level of development" through interactions with technical consultants and exposure to issues of building science.[45]

Traditional design (i.e., the subtle compositional arrangement of otherwise necessary elements to which "layers" of ornamental embellishment are added) consistently adopts the former strategy: that is, it takes the prevailing technology of construction as a fixed point of departure. Only with the onset of early twentieth-century modernism, emboldened by the apparent obsolescence of traditional construction systems and the seemingly unlimited potential of new materials and systems, is the latter strategy—in which design is abstracted from issues of technology—commonly employed. Yet from the standpoint of reliability theory, this latter strategy is more likely to result in failure precisely because it rejects a priori the *formal* consequences of technological principles. Perhaps, then, adding "architecture" to "building" (as Ruskin suggested), rather than initiating design purely on the basis of formal expression, should be reexamined as a starting point for the teaching and practice of architecture.[46]

Notes

[1] Nilson, Arthur, David Darwin, and Charles Dolan. Design of Concrete Structures, 13th edition. Boston: McGraw-Hill, 2004, p.18.

[2] Marshall, Robert R. "2001 Building Failures Study." CMHC Technical Series 01-140 (2001): 1-4. Conceptual Reference Database for Building Envelope Research. <http://alcor.concordia.ca/~raojw/crd/referen ce/reference002296.html>

[3] "We proceed wilfully—we are perfectly cognisant of the methods employed by the ancient builders,—we do not sin through ignorance." Viollet-le-Duc, Eugène-Emmanuel. Lectures on Architecture Vol. II. New York: Dover Publications, 1987, Lecture XI, p.13.

[4] "Sometimes ignorance is evidenced when we, without sufficient basis, extrapolate from limited experience and knowledge into a wide and large field." Kaminetzky, Dov. Design and Construction Failures. New York, McGraw-Hill: 1991, p.166. See also Petroski, Henry. Design Paradigms: Case Histories of Error and Judgment in Engineering. Cambridge: Cambridge University Press,1994, pp.29-35.

[5] "There are three basic types of human error: 1. Errors of knowledge (ignorance); 2. Errors of performance (carelessness and negligence); 3. Errors of intent (greed)." Kaminetzky, Dov. Design and Construction Failures. New York, McGraw-Hill: 1991, pp.5-8.

[6] Descriptions of stone masonry maintenance and deterioration of wood rafters can be found, for example, in Thomas Hardy's Jude the Obscure and Gustave Flaubert's Madame Bovary.

[7] Gwilt, Joseph. The Encyclopedia of Architecture: Historical, Theoretical, and Practical. New York: Crown Publishers, 1982 (1867 edition), p. 354. Rondelet similarly shows an appreciation of both theory and traditional (empirical) knowledge: "...theoretical results must be considered as conditional solutions, always subordinated to the material circumstances of the construction...In the art of building, much can be known only by experiment" (translated by the author). Rondelet, Jean. Traité Théorique et Pratique de L'art de Bâtir. Septième Edition, Tome Premier, Paris: Librairie de Firmin Didot Frères, Fils et Cie, 1864.p.2.

[8] Viollet-le-Duc, Eugène-Emmanuel. Lectures on Architecture Vol. II. New York: Dover Publications, 1987, Lecture XI, p.3.

[9] Greek architecture served as a model for the correspondence of structure and appearance: "The architectural orders invented by the Greeks composed the structure itself; that is to say, in the architecture that accorded with these orders there was only one mode of structure; therefore the structure of the Greek edifices and their appearance were essentially

united." Viollet-le-Duc, Eugène-Emmanuel. Discourses on Architecture Vol. I. New York: Grove Press, Inc, 1959, Lecture VI, p.210.

[10] For example, proportions of columns and intercolumniation are alternatively defended on the basis of convenience, beauty, and strength. Pollio, Marcus Vitruvius. The Ten Books on Architecture. New York: Dover Publications, 1960. p.80.

[11] Alberti, Leone Battista. Ten Books on Architecture. London: Alec Tiranti, 1965 (original Latin text published 1485), p.1 on the independence of "design" and "matter"; pp.112-113 on beauty and ornament.

[12] Several of Choisy's three-dimensional drawings are reproduced in Le Corbusier. Towards a New Architecture. New York: Praeger Publishers, 1970 (first published in 1923 as Vers Une Architecture). Le Corbusier's own Maison Domino perspective similarly treats structure as an abstract diagram: see pp.212, 216.

[13] Yorke, R.S. The Modern House. London: The Architectural Press, 1934, pp.46-47.

[14] Describing the renovation of his House VI, Peter Eisenman writes: "It is clear that two different restorations...have changed the nature of the house as it was originally designed. If baseball is a game of inches, this house was a game of fractions." Frank, Suzanne. Peter Eisenman's House VI: The Client's Response. New York: Whitney Library of Design, 1994, p.109 ("Afterword" by Peter Eisenman).

[15] Mondrian, Piet. L'Architecture Vivante (Autumn, 1925), p.11; quoted in Collins, Peter. Concrete: The Vision of a New Architecture, 2nd edition. Montreal: McGill-Queen's University Press, 2004, p.281.

[16] [Fitzmaurice, R.]. Principles of Modern Building Vol. 1, 3rd edition. London: Dept. of Scientific and Industrial Research (Building Research Station), Her Majesty's Stationary Office, 1959, p.198.

[17] [Fitzmaurice, R.]. Principles of Modern Building Vol. 1, 3rd edition. London: Dept. of Scientific and Industrial Research (Building Research Station), Her Majesty's Stationary Office, 1959. p.81.

[18] Snoonian, Deborah. "Sleuthing out Building Failure." Architectural Record. 188.8 (August 2000), p.168. See also Brock, Linda. Designing the Exterior Wall: An Architectural Guide to the Vertical Envelope. Hoboken, NJ: John Wiley & Sons, 2005. 264-265.

[19] Yorke, R.S. The Modern House. London: The Architectural Press, 1934. p.55.

[20] This paradigm shift becomes even more evident in the latter part of the twentieth century. See note 35.

[21] "Building Failure Patterns and Their Implications." The Architects' Journal. 161.6 (Feb. 5, 1975), p.308.

[22] Dorris, Virginia Kent. "How Long Should Buildings Last?" Architectural Record. 185.12 (December 1997). p.136. Even when knowledge exists to prevent failure, it may not be disseminated widely. See Petroski, Henry. Design Paradigms: Case Histories of Error and Judgment in Engineering. Cambridge, New York, Cambridge University Press: 1994, p.7.

[23] See, for example: Templin, Neal. "Leaks Cause Buckets of Woes." Wall Street Journal (Nov. 12, 1997).

[24] In contrast, examples of three recent texts that more systematically integrate details with building science include: Allen, Edward, Architectural Detailing: Function, Constructibility, Aesthetics. New York: John Wiley & Sons, 1993; Brand, Ronald, Architectural Details for Insulated Buildings. New York: Van Nostrand Reinhold, 1990; and Brock, Linda, Designing the Exterior

Wall: An Architectural Guide to the Vertical Envelope. Hoboken, NJ: John Wiley & Sons, 2005.

[25] Ramsey, Charles and Harold Sleeper. "Preface." Architectural Graphic Standards (1932 facsimile edition). New York: John Wiley & Sons, 1990).

[26] See, for example: Lawton, Mark D. and William C. Brown, "Considering the Use of Polyethylene Vapour Barriers in Temperate Climates." Proceedings of the Ninth Canadian Conference on Building Science and Technology (Design and Construction of Durable Building Envelopes). Vancouver: February, 2003; also online at <http://www.buildingenvelopeforum.com>.

[27] Rose, William B. "Moisture Control in the Modern Building Envelope: History of the Vapor Barrier in the U.S., 1923-52," APT Bulletin. 28.4 (1997). 13-19.

[28] Ramsey, Charles and Harold Sleeper. "Preface." Architectural Graphic Standards (1932 facsimile edition). New York: John Wiley & Sons, 1990). An example in which extrapolation proved disastrous is described in Harris, Samuel P. Building Pathology: Deterioration, Diagnostics, and Intervention. New York: John Wiley & Sons, 2001, pp.440-443. Excessive leakage occurred when a standard 2-5/8" high brick veneer detail was modified by use of an 8" high brick; vertical mortar joints reacted in an unexpected manner to the reduction in the frequency of horizontal joints.

[29] As an example, "...the trade literature is disturbingly deficient on good frame-to-wall construction." Allen, William. Envelope Design for Buildings. Oxford: Butterworth-Heinemann, 1997. p.177

[30] Viollet-le-Duc, Eugène-Emmanuel. Lectures on Architecture Vol. II. New York: Dover Publications, 1987, Lecture XI. 2-3.

[31] "Experience of previous behaviour can be a most unreliable guide when a material is used in a novel manner; many disastrous failures have resulted from the supposition than an unfamiliar combination of familiar materials can be used with complete freedom." [Fitzmaurice, R.]. Principles of Modern Building Vol. 1, 3rd edition. London: Dept. of Scientific and Industrial Research (Building Research Station), Her Majesty's Stationary Office, 1959, p.82.

[32] An example describing the interaction of three factors—loss of memory, aesthetic bias, and greed—that together cause problems with wood windows can be found in Allen, William. Envelope Design for Buildings. Oxford: Architectural Press, Butterworth-Heinemann, 1997. p. 167.

[33] For examples of distrust, or critique, of large-scale technology see, for example, Schumacher, E.F. Small is Beautiful: Economics as if People Mattered. New York: Harper & Row, 1973; or Heidegger, Martin. The Question Concerning Technology, and Other Essays. New York: Harper & Row, 1977.

[34] "A fashion dies when it becomes completely accepted and stereotyped." Warke, Val K. "'In' Architecture: Observing the Mechanisms of Fashion," Architecture: In Fashion. Ed. Deborah Fausch, et.al., New York: Princeton Architectural Press, 1994. p.140.

[35] "Specifically the problems of support (structure) and enclosure have been redefined as problems of creep and deflection, heat loss, air infiltration, permeance to vapor, condensation and exposure of the building interstices to water. At the same time, the traditional materials of construction are being transformed into products and systems whose material content is often obscure." Ochshorn, Jonathan. "Disembodied Technology and Design." Body, Technology, and Design. Washington, DC: ACSA Press, 1993; online at <http://www.people.cornell.edu/pages/jo24/comments/disembodied.html>.

[36] The two quotes are from, respectively, Le Corbusier. Towards a New Architecture. New York: Praeger Publishers, 1970. p.16; Balmond, Cecil with Jannuzzi Smith. Informal. Munich: Prestel, 2002. p.64.

[37] Ben Folds analyzes and comments on this phenomenon within the field of music: "I'm rockin' the suburbs/ I take the cheques and face the facts/ that some producer with computers fixes all my shitty tracks." Folds, Ben, "Rockin' the Suburbs." Rockin' the Suburbs. Audio CD, Sony, 2001.

[38] "Reliability is defined as: The probability that a device will operate for a specified period of time under specified conditions." Moss, T.R. The Reliability Data Handbook. New York: ASME Press, 2005. p.9.

[39] Moss, T.R. The Reliability Data Handbook. New York: ASME Press, 2005. pp.13-21. Research into this type of categorization in Canada resulted in four proposed "service-life tiers" ranging from the building shell (primary tier) to furniture. Dorris, Virginia Kent. "How Long Should Buildings Last?" Architectural Record. 185.12 (December 1997). p.137.

[40] Blischke, Wallace R. and D.N. Prabhakar Murthy, Eds. Case Studies in Reliability and Maintenance. Hoboken, NJ: John Wiley & Sons, 2003. p.1

[41] International Code Council. "Chapter 14 Exterior Walls." International Building Code. 2000.

[42] On metal coping: "Your chances of making it watertight are nil, so put a waterproof membrane underneath;" any metal counterflashing below the coping "would be merely a decorative sun screen that some idiot will nail through the membrane." Annotated details in: Brand, Ronald. Architectural Details for Insulated Buildings. New York: Van Nostrand Reinhold, 1990. p.17. "The unsealed lap joint between segments of flashing is a common oversight brought on, we suspect, because such details are drawn in section... If the designer called the detail a gutter, and not a flashing, he or she would know immediately what to do with the water." Harris, Samuel P. Building Pathology: Deterioration, Diagnostics, and Intervention. New York: John Wiley & Sons, 2001. p.453.

[43] See sections on "constructibility" in Allen, Edward, Architectural Detailing: Function, Constructibility, Aesthetics. New York: John Wiley & Sons, 1993. 127-168.

[44] For example, the "function of walls, floors, and roofs is to enclose space in such a way that some or all of the physical environmental conditions... can be regulated within acceptable limits." Hutcheon, Neil B. and Gustav O.P. Handegord, Building Science for a Cold Climate. New Brunswick: Construction Technology Centre Atlantic Inc., 1983, p.7. Alternatively, six "building performance mandates" are identified in Rush, Richard, Ed. The Building Systems Integration Handbook. Boston: Butterworth-Heinemann, 1986. p.233. Mondrian, representing the other extreme, has already been quoted (see note 15).

[45] For a discussion of the latter pedagogical model, see Mostafavi, Mohsen interviewed by Seng Kuan and Angela Pang. "Education in Process: New Directions at Cornell." Architecture and Urbanism. 428 (May 2006), p.18.

[46] On Ruskin's attitude toward building versus architecture, see: Ruskin, John. The Seven Lamps of Architecture. New York: The Noonday Press, 1974 (originally published 1848). 15-16.

Seismic Web Site

G G Schierle, PhD, FAIA
University of Southern California

Abstract

Given the increased complexity of seismic design, it is mostly the domain of structural engineers. However, during schematic design architects often make design decisions that are very important for seismic safety. The seismic web site was developed to visualize and streamline seismic design for architects and architectural education. The site features Seismic Design and Seismic Failure. Seismic Design is based on the International Building Code, IBC 03, adapted from LRFD to ASD design methods to be compatible with IBC table 2606.4.1 of ASD shear wall capacities. Seismic Failures are Northridge Earthquake failures. The web features PDF files of interactive Power Point lectures presented at two AIA National Conventions. Two file types include: color displays and printable handouts. The web site also includes recent seismic papers and excerpts of *Structures in Architecture* by the author. The following screen samples are color displays for Seismic Design and printable handouts for Seismic Failure.

Introduction

While seismic design in the past was based on seismic zones, IBC requires seismic design to be based on local site conditions. The seismic web has a link to a USGS web site that provides Spectral Response Accelerations (SA) S_S and S_1 for low-rise and high-rise structures, respectively. Seismic Design Graphs on the web provide numeric values and visualize the respective seismic design values C_S, S_{DS}, and S_{D1} based on the USGS parameters and local soil conditions. The seismic parameters S_S and S_1 are also available on a CD from USGS and IBC. The CD and USGS web site require site coordinates (global latitude and longitude). The seismic web has a link to a web site for latitude and longitude based on street address or zip code. Seismic Design includes an overview of seismic events, critical design issues, and seismic base shear with Seismic Design Graphs.

Base shear is computed as follows:

$$V = C_S W$$

C_S = seismic coefficient
V = seismic base shear (lateral force at building base)
W = building mass (dead load + 25% storage live load + 20% flat roof snow load > 30 psf)

Based on USGS Spectral Accelerations the author developed three graphs for seismic design:

C_S Graph for low-rise light wood shear wall structures

S_{DS} Graph for other low-rise, $T<T_S$, usually < 5 stories

$$C_S = I\, S_{DS} / R$$

S_{D1} Graph for high-rise, $T>T_S$, usually > 8 stories

$$C_S = I\, S_{D1} / (TR)$$

I = Importance factor (IBC table 1604.5)
I = 1.5 for essential facilities
  (Hospitals, police and fire stations)
I = 1.25 for large occupancy
I = 1 for other structures
R = Response factor (IBC table 1617.6.2)
T = Building period of vibration
T ~ 0.1 second per story height
$T_S = S_{DS} / S_{D1}$
(See Design Response Spectrum below)

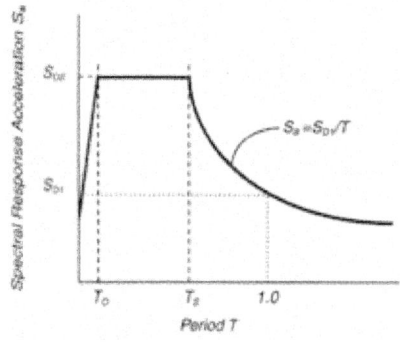

References:

ACSE: *ACSE 7*,
   American Cociety of Civil Engineers, 2002
ICC: International Building Code,
   International Code Council, 2003
Schierle, G G: Structures in Architecture, USC, 2006
   Posted at: https://www.usc.edu/structures

Seismic Web Site https://www.usc.edu/seismic

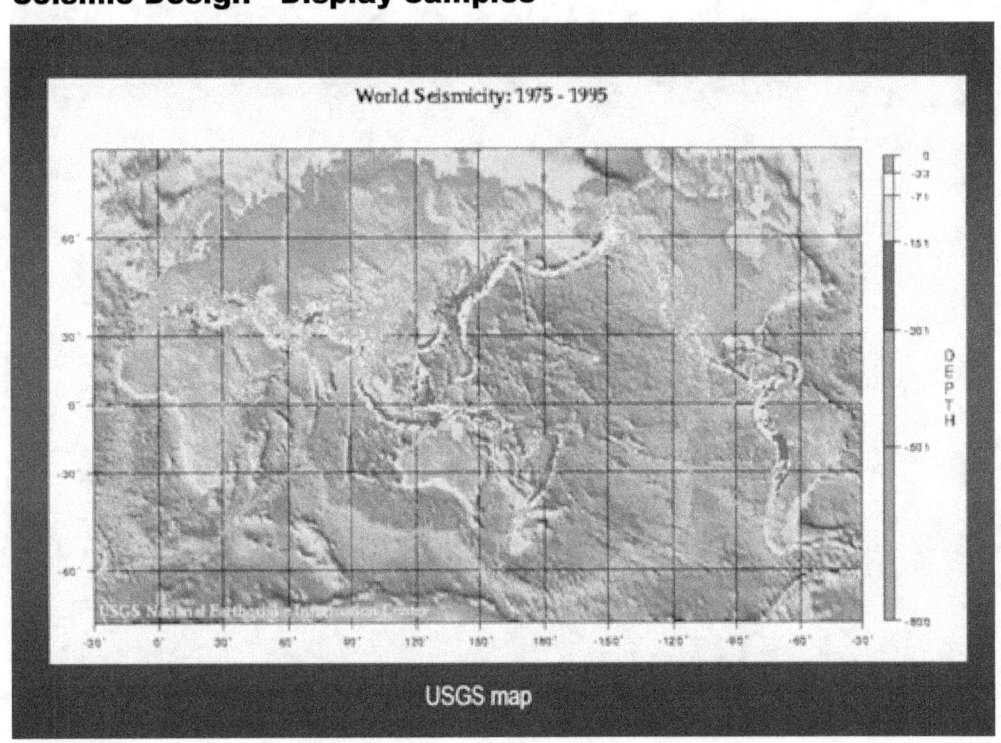

Design for Earthquake Safety
G G Schierle, PhD, FAIA
SD-Graphs

based on IBC-03
Equivalent Lateral Force Analysis
for Allowable Stress Design (ASD)
(ASD = LRFD / 1.4)

Light framing with wood panels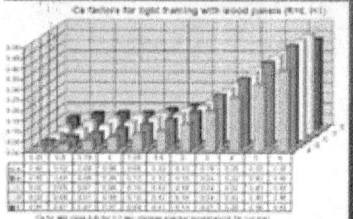

Other low-rise structures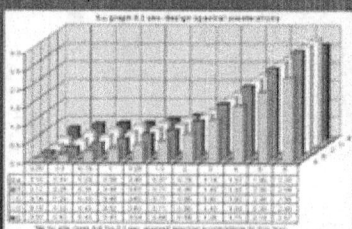

High-rise structures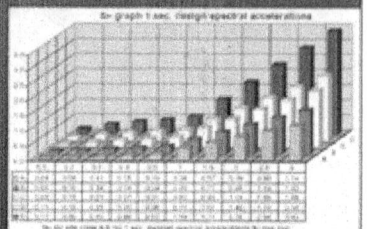

OUTLINE

- Earthquake background
    - Plate Tectonics
    - Largest quakes since 1900
    - Seismic Waves & Epicenter
    - Richter Scale
    - Earthquake cause and effect
- Seismic design background
- Base shear
- Seismic design parameters
- C_S graph for wood panel structures
- S_{DS} graph for low-rise structures
- S_{D1} graph for high-rise structures
- Vertical force and shear distribution
- Example wood residences
- Horizontal diaphragms
    - Flexible diaphragm
    - Rigid diaphragm
- Seismic design issues
    - Hill site design
    - Eccentricity
    - Hazard configurations
    - Critical wood-frame items
    - Moment frames
    - Eccentric bracing
    - Visco-elastic bracing
    - Base isolators
- Earthquake fatalities 1970–99
- Light-weight structures

Portions of this document reproduce sections from the 2003 International Building Code, International Code Council, Falls Church, Virginia. Reproduced with permission. All rights reserved. USGS data, courtesy US Geological Survey.

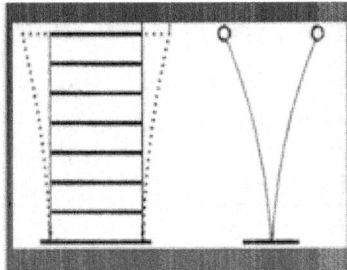

Seismic force = mass x acceleration / R

Mass = building dead weight; R = reduction factor

Acceleration = **Spectral acceleration** = a mass on a rod of equal period as a structure of equal height

Acceleration spectra (Seed, 1976) define interaction of structures with 4 soil types

(basis of **Equivalent Lateral Force Analysis**)

IBC Design Response Spectrum

$T < T_s$ governs low-rise structures of short periods

$T > T_s$ **governs tall structures of long periods**

T structure period, T ~ 1/10 sec per story

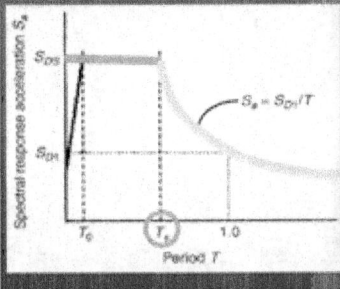

Base shear V (lateral force at base of building)
$V = C_S W$

C_S = seismic coefficient (see graphs)
W = Dead load (+ 25% storage live load)
C_S varies with spectral acceleration S_S & S_1 and type of structure
(defined on the following pages)
C_S example in seismic areas:
C_S ~ 3 % for tall steel frame structures
C_S ~ 15 % for low-rise wood structures
C_S ~ 30 % for masonry wall structures

W = w A (w = DL {psf}, A = floor area)
w varies with type of construction – for example:
w ~ 15 to 25 psf for wood structures
w ~ 70 to 100 psf for steel structures
w ~ 150 to 200 psf for concrete structures

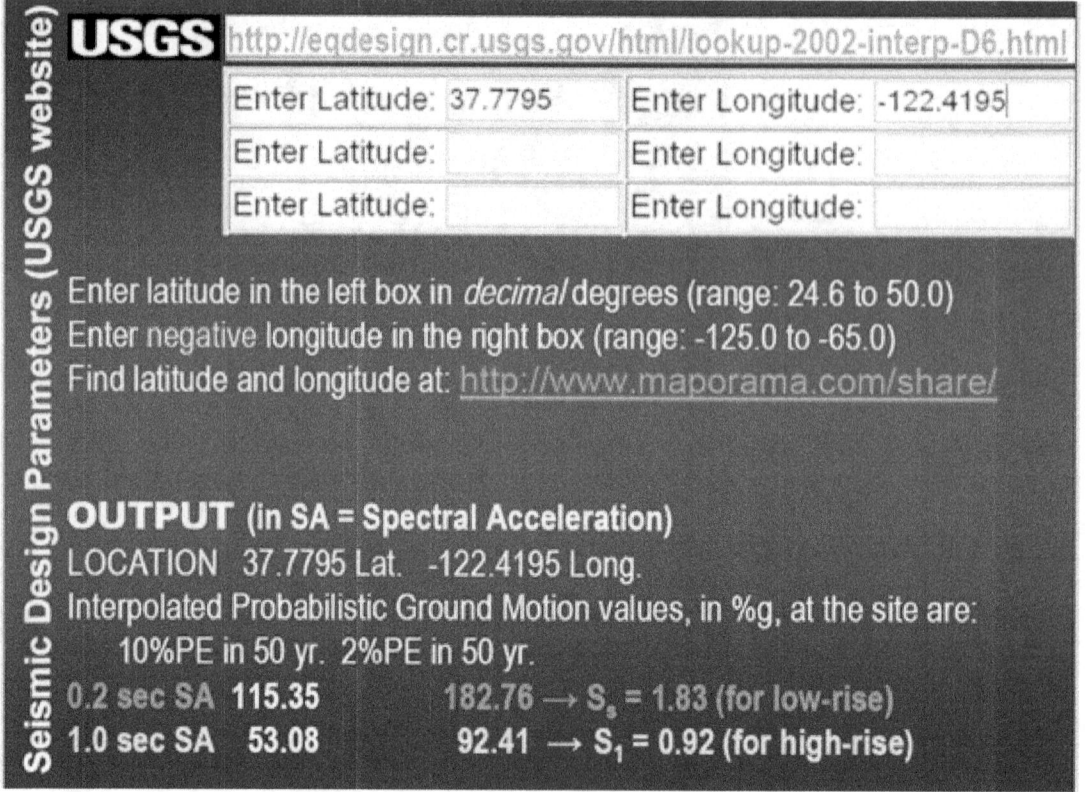

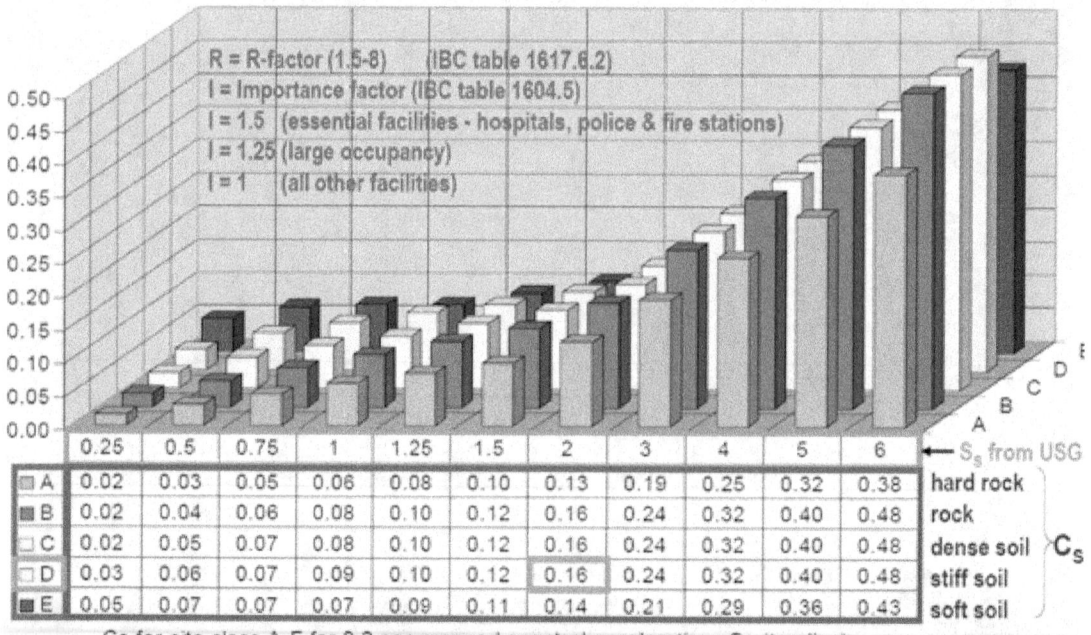

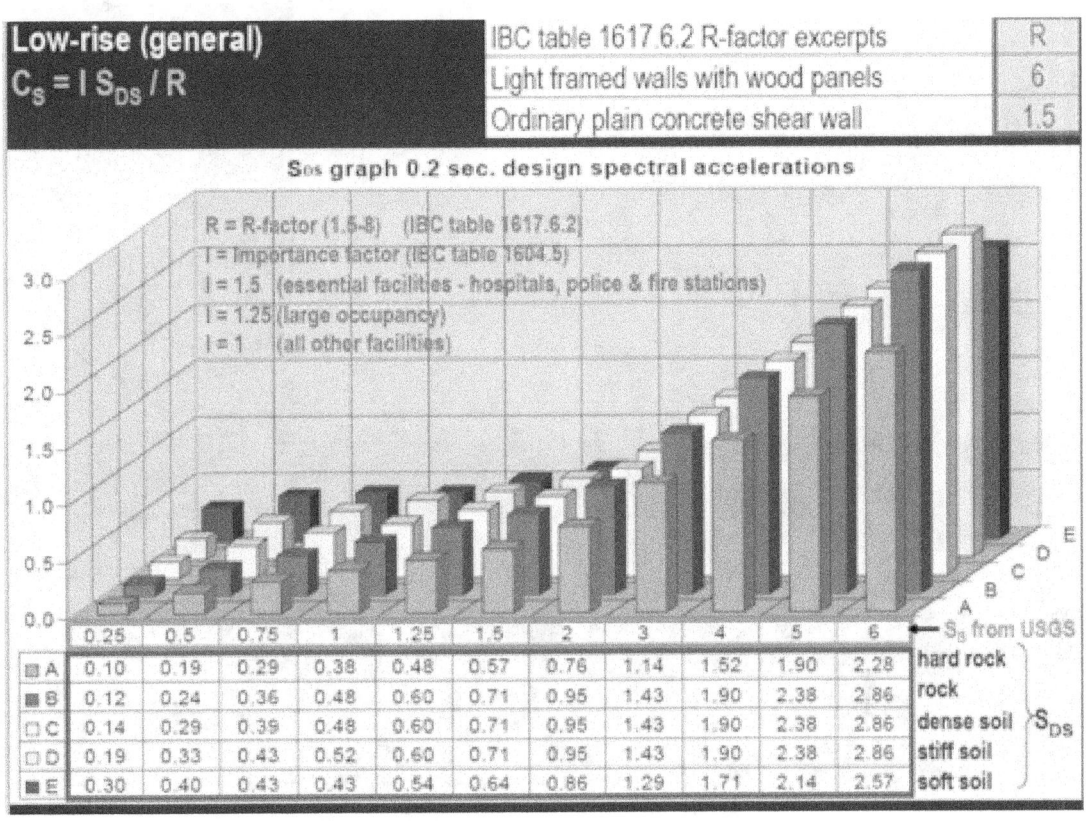

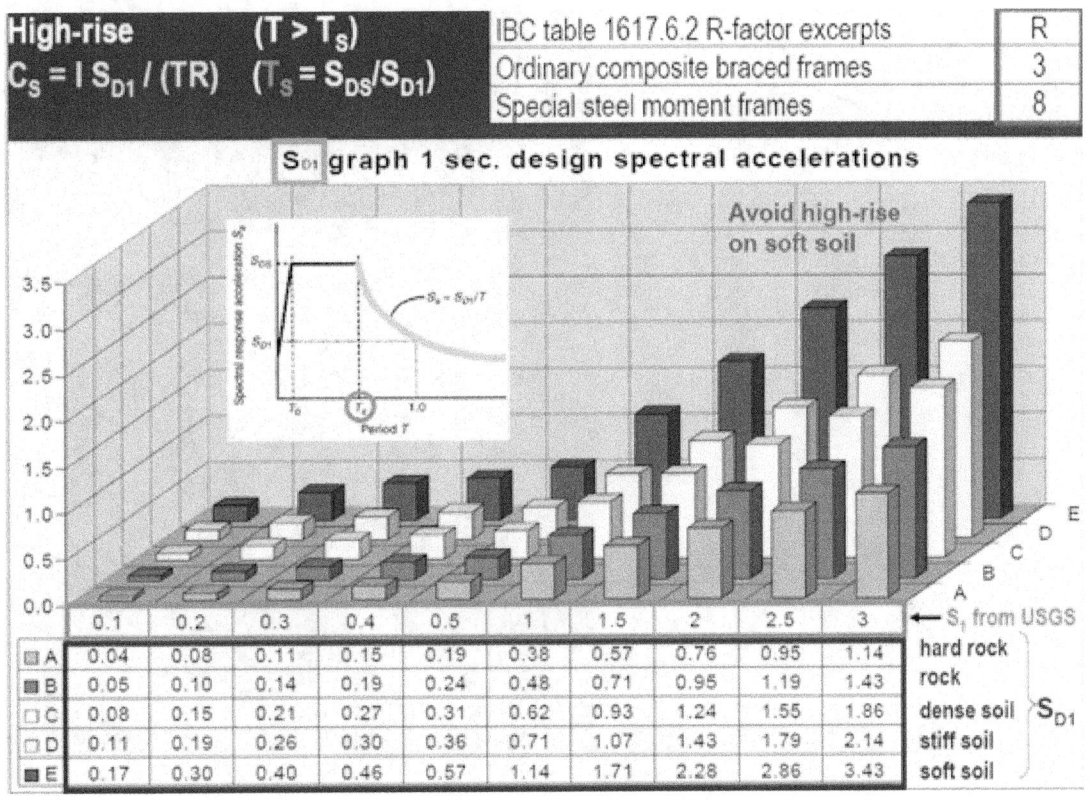

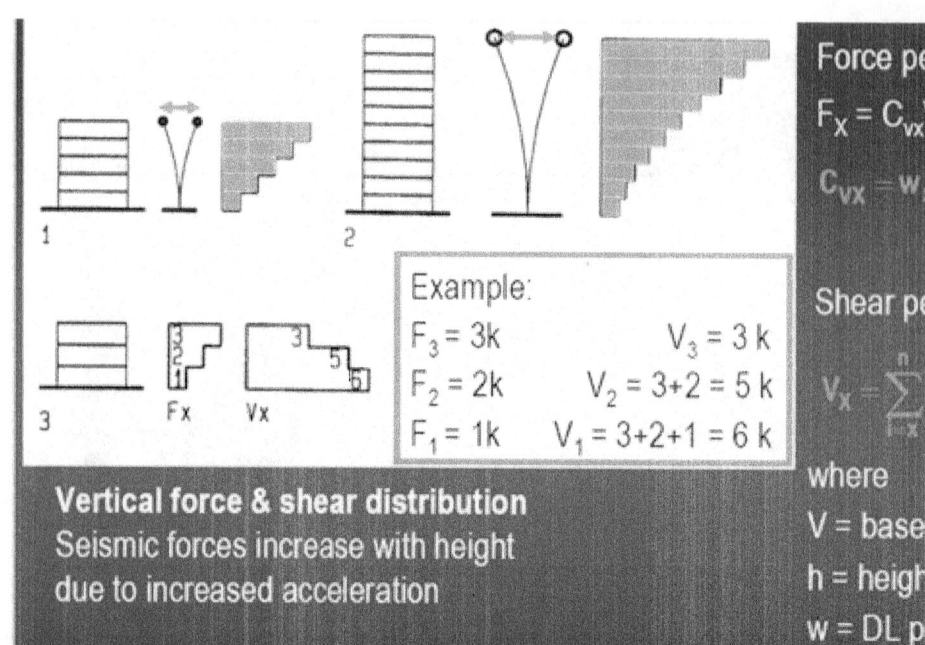

Force per level x

$$F_X = C_{vx}V$$

$$C_{vx} = w_x h_x^k / \sum_{i=1}^{n} w_i h_i^k$$

Shear per level x

$$V_x = \sum_{i=x}^{n} F_i$$

where
V = base shear
h = height of level
w = DL per level
k = 1 for T < 0.5 sec
k = 2 for T ≥ 2.5 sec
interpolate @ 0.5-2.5

Example:
$F_3 = 3k \qquad V_3 = 3\ k$
$F_2 = 2k \qquad V_2 = 3+2 = 5\ k$
$F_1 = 1k \qquad V_1 = 3+2+1 = 6\ k$

Vertical force & shear distribution
Seismic forces increase with height due to increased acceleration

1 Linear low-rise force increase
2 Non-linear high-rise force increase
3 Three-story example

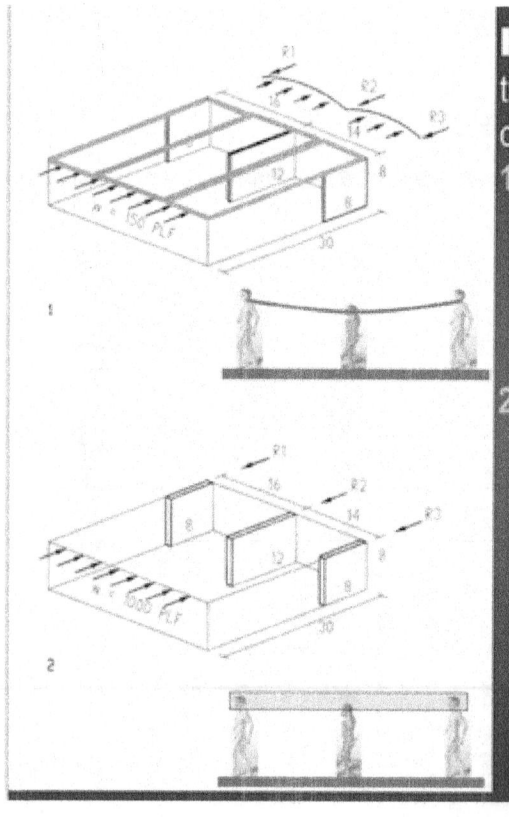

Horizontal Diaphragms
transfer lateral load to shear walls and other elements two ways
1 **Flexible diaphragm** (wood)
  transfers in proportion to tributary area.
  Wall reactions are:
  R = w (tributary area supported by wall)
  w = uniform load
2 **Rigid diaphragm** (concrete & steel)
  transfers in proportion to wall stiffness.
  Reactions for walls of equal material:
  $R1 = WL1^3 / \Sigma L^3 \qquad (\Sigma L^3 = L1^3 + L2^3 + L3^3)$
  $R2 = WL2^3 / \Sigma L^3$
  $R3 = WL3^3 / \Sigma L^3$
  where
  L = Lengths of walls
  W = Total load supported by all walls

Base Shear (from last page) $V = 5,280\ \#$

Shear walls required - use 3/8 panels, 8d nails at 6" $q = 230\ plf$

$L' = V / q = 5,280 / 230 = 23'$ (total length each way)

Wall A: $L = 23' / 2 = 11.5'$ (~ symmetry)   use 12' walls

Wall B: $L = 23' \times 20' / (10+20) = 15.3'$ use 16' wall

Wall C: $L = 23' \times 10' / (10+20) = 7.7'$ use 8' wall

Walls B & C are inversely proportional to distance from centroid of mass

IBC table 2306.4.1 excerpts
Allowable shear for wood panels with Douglas-Fir-Large or Southern Pine

Panel grade	Panel thickness	Nail penetration	Nail size	Nail spacing at panel edge (inches)			
				6	4	3	2*
				Allowable shear (lbs / foot)			
Structural I sheathing	5/16 in	1 1/4 in	6d	200	300	390	510
	3/8 in	1 3/8 in	8d	230	360	460	610
	7/16 in	1 3/8 in	8d	255	395	505	670
	15/32 in	1 3/8 in	8d	280	430	550	730
		1 1/2 in	10d	340	510	665	870

* Requires 3 x framing and staggered nailing

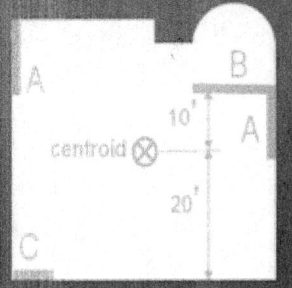

Example: Two-story wood residence

$DL = 24\ psf$ (floor+walls), $13.5\ psf$ (roof+walls) $C_S = 0.16$

Dead load (DL)

Roof $DL = W = 13.5\ psf \times 40' \times 50' / 1000\ \#$ $W = 27\ k$

Floor $DL = W = 24\ psf \times 40' \times 50' / 1000\ \#$ $W = 48\ k$

Base shear

$V = W\ C_S = (27+48)\ 0.16$ $V = 12\ k$

Vertical distribution $(0.53 = 540 / 1,020)$

$F_x = V\ w_x h_x / \sum (w_i h_i)$ $(0.47 = 480 / 1,020)$

Level: w_x h_x $= w_x h_x$ V F_x V_x

Roof: $27\ k \times 20' = 540\ k'$ $0.53 \times 12\ k = 6.4\ k$ $6.4\ k$

Floor: $48\ k \times 10' = 480\ k'$ $0.47 \times 12\ k = 5.6\ k$ $12.0\ k$

$\sum w_i h_i = 1,020\ k'$ $V = 12.0\ k$

Shear wall: use 5/16" plywood, 6d @ 4", $q = 300\ plf$

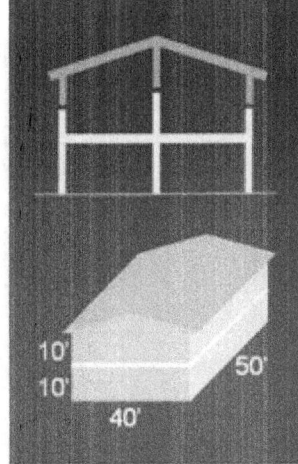

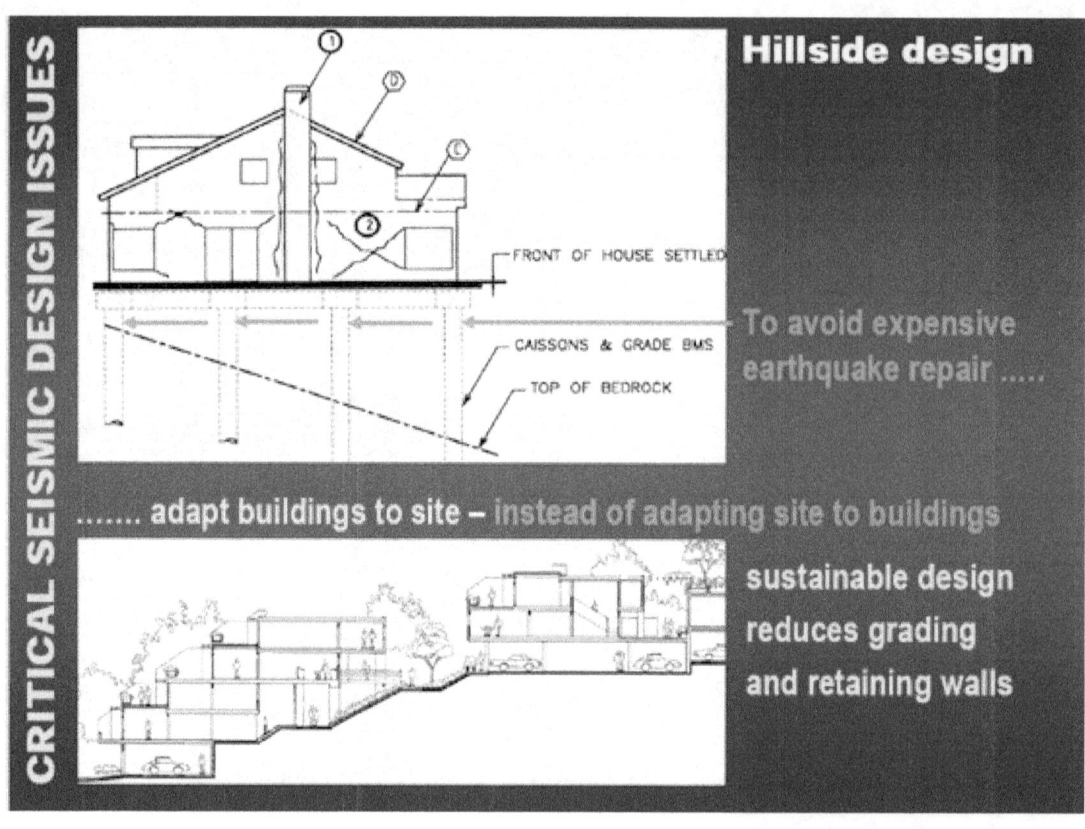
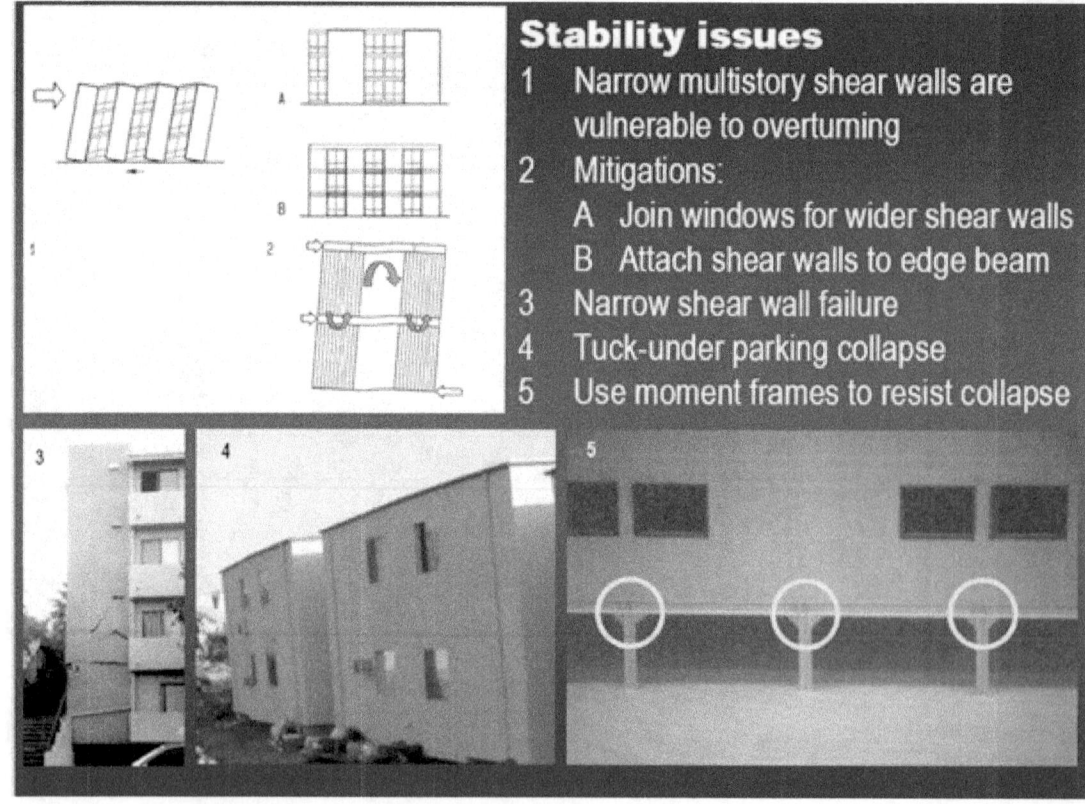

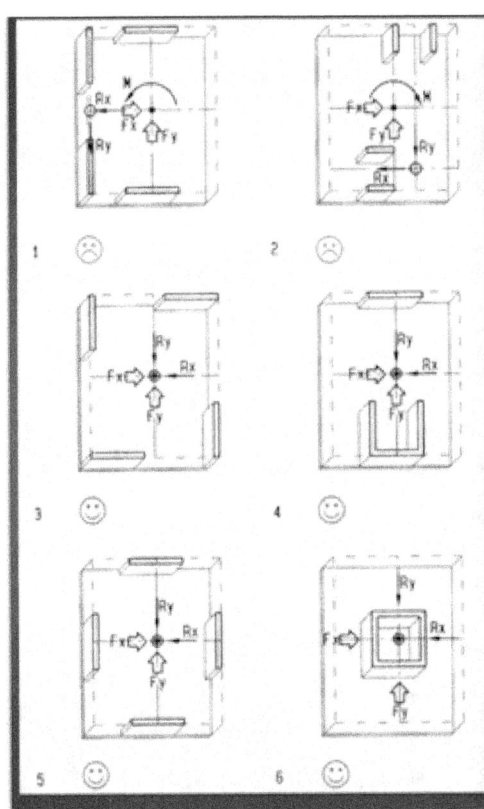

Eccentricity issues (avoid it)

1. X-direction concentric
   Y-direction eccentric

2. X-direction eccentric
   Y-direction eccentric

3. X-direction concentric
   Y-direction concentric

4. X-direction concentric
   Y-direction concentric

5. X-direction concentric
   Y-direction concentric

6. X-direction concentric
   Y-direction concentric

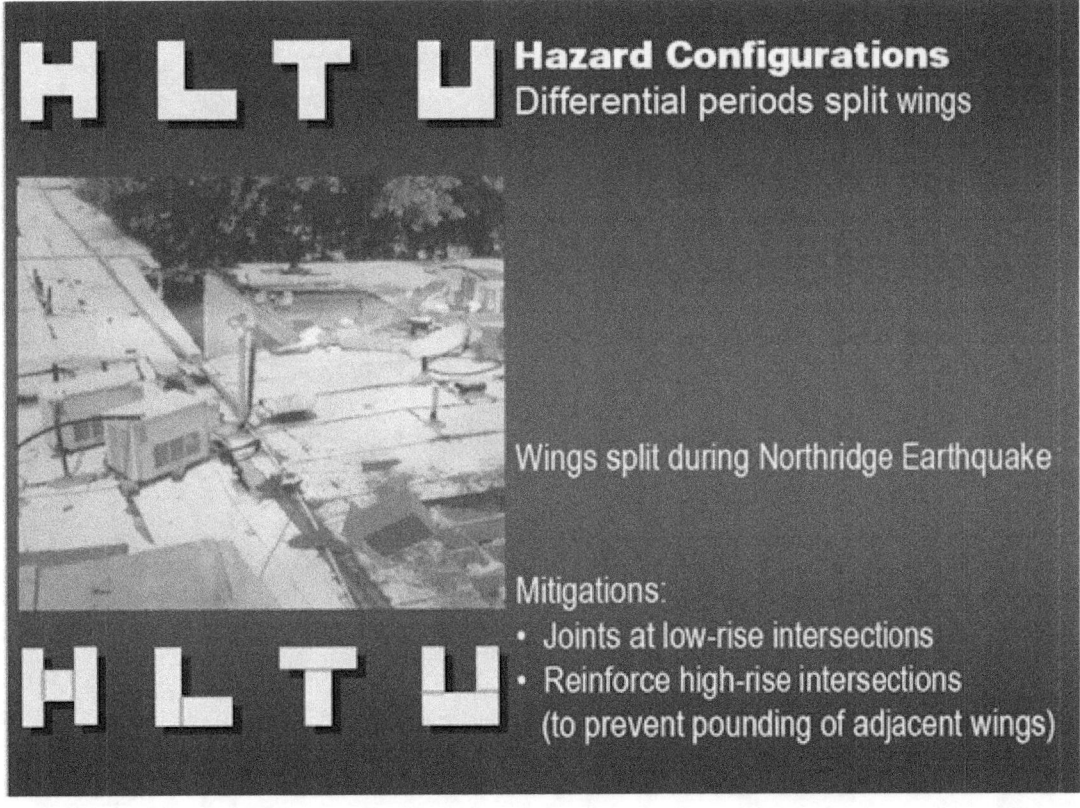

Hazard Configurations
Differential periods split wings

Wings split during Northridge Earthquake

Mitigations:
- Joints at low-rise intersections
- Reinforce high-rise intersections
  (to prevent pounding of adjacent wings)

SEISMIC DESIGN ITEMS

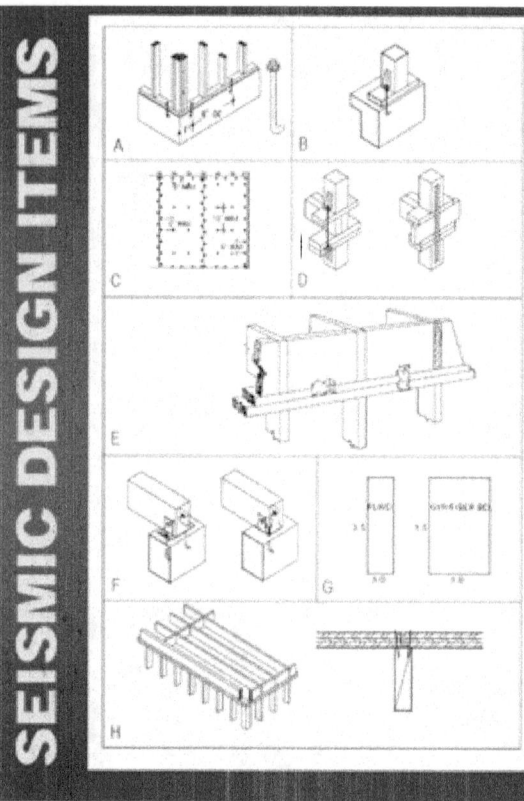

Critical woodframe items
A Shear wall anchor bolts
   Resist wall slippage
B Hold-down
   Resist shear wall overturning
C Shear wall nailing
   Attaches panels to framing
D Wall-to-wall hold-down
   Resist shear wall overturning
E Framing anchor clips
   Transfer shear from floor to floor
F Beam connection
   Resist beam slippage
G Shear wall width/height ratio
   Minimum 1 : 3.5 for stability
H Joist blocking
   Transfers shear at panel edges

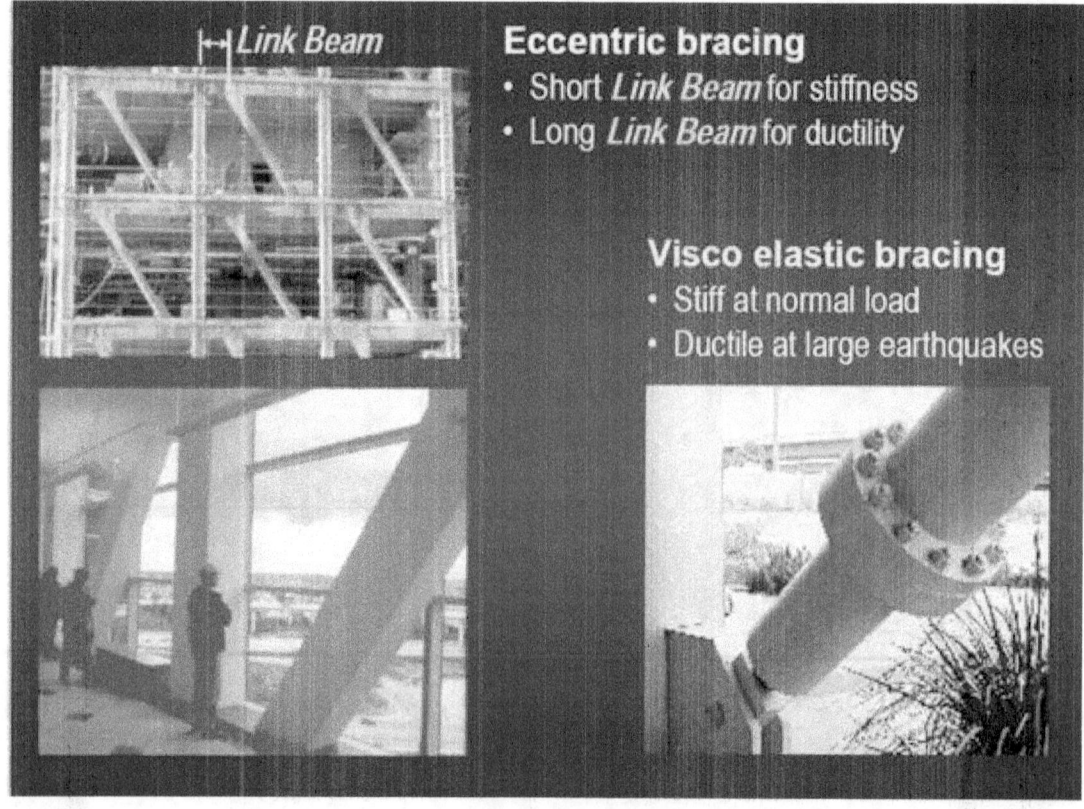

Eccentric bracing
- Short *Link Beam* for stiffness
- Long *Link Beam* for ductility

Visco elastic bracing
- Stiff at normal load
- Ductile at large earthquakes

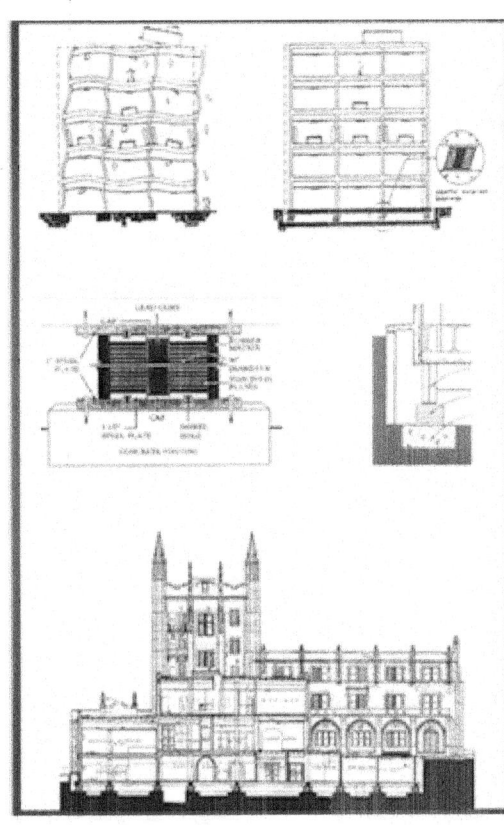

Base Isolators
- Dampen seismic load and reduce drift
- Good for low-rise
- Not good for high-rise

Base isolators consist of
- Rubber sheets and steel plates
- Joined by a bolt and lead cylinder
- Isolate building from ground

UCLA Kerckhoff Hall base isolators
Courtesy WWCOT Architects

Light-weight structures minimize seismic forces

$$V = C_s W$$

Saddle shape Wave shape Arch shape Point shape

Seismic Failure – Handout Samples

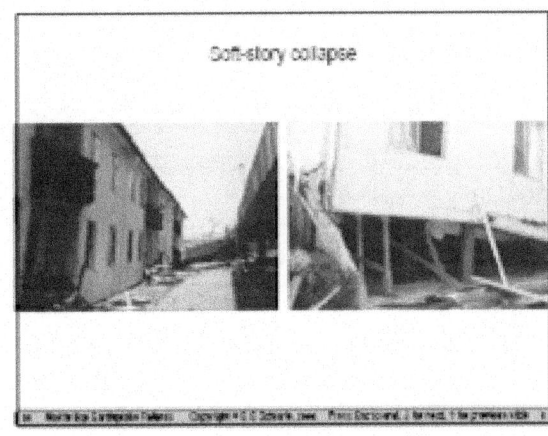

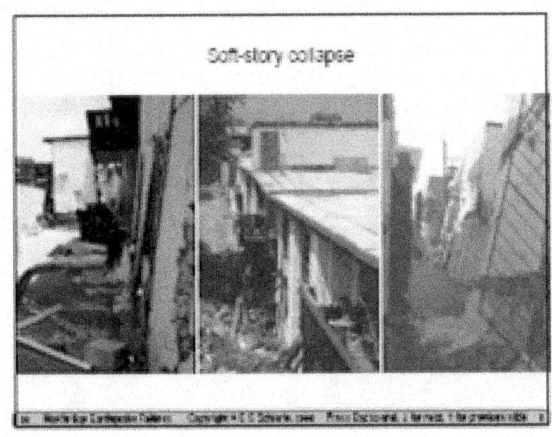

The Art of Structure – The Structure of Art

Edgar Stach & Douglas Smith
University of Tennessee

Abstract

The paper will explore the connections between the practice of sculpture and architecture through design and construction of lightweight structures. Students from the College of Architecture and Design and The School of Art[1] at the University of Tennessee developed and build kinetic art[2] projects by investigating and introduce to design determinants such as lightweight structures, deployable structures, kinetic structures, smart structures etc. with a focus on the primary categories of frame, skin, and kinetic systems.

The projects were investigating the construction of the sculpture, how to monitor stimuli, development of algorithms, and how to have the sculpture respond; dealing with both the design and technical issues. Thy incorporate the viewers and alter the sculptural according to those viewers.

---

[1] Responsible faculty member was Assistant Professor Jason Brown
[2] Kinetic art, term referring to sculptured works that include motion as a significant dimension. The form was pioneered by Marcel Duchamp, Naum Gabo, and Alexander Calder. Kinetic art is either nonmechanical, e.g., Calder's mobiles, or mechanical, e.g., works by Gabo, László Moholy-Nagy, and Jean Tinguely. The latter sort of kineticism developed in response to an increasingly technological culture. The Columbia Electronic Encyclopedia, 6th ed.

Figure 1. Buck Fuller: Geodesic Domes

Figure 2. Buck Fuller

The creation of a well defined and innovative structure or sculpture was the goal. Use of computerization in the kinetics is needed to create movement that is not random but many appear that way. Thoughts in actuality the movements are based off of preset stimuli and the reactions to those stimuli. The course was organized to design and fabricate structures that demonstrate these principles of the overall kinetic structure.

1. Introduction

The turn of the 20th century brought an increased scientific interest in components and structure, which combine to form a whole. An understanding of a form requires an understanding of its structure; of the separate parts joining to be comprehended as something entirely different; a whole. That search for knowledge greatly influenced not only the world of science, but that of art, as well. Artists began to approach artwork differently than the previous Impressionists. Art was an innovative exploration, a scientific study into how a viewer perceived a piece of work.[3]

The word kinetic means relating to motion. Kinetic art is art that depends on motion for its effects. Since the early twentieth century artists have been incorporating movement into art. This has been partly to explore the possibilities of movement, partly to introduce the element of time, partly to reflect the importance of the machine and technology in the modern world, partly to explore the nature of vision. Movement has either been produced mechanically by motors or by exploiting the natural movement of air in a space.

2. Frame, Skin, and Kinetic Systems

2.1. Deployable Structures

The limits and potentials of deployable structures demand that they be lightweight, kinetic, and idealized for environment and use. As there are many options available to the designer, distinction between particular strategies or systems is beneficial and frequently required. The initial investigation explored the potentials of integrated surfaces, framing systems, and structural principles.

In general the research centered on:
1. Analysis of lightweight structure
2. Relationship between structure and construction
3. Understanding the kinetics / mechanics Representation of such analysis through three dimensional diagrams

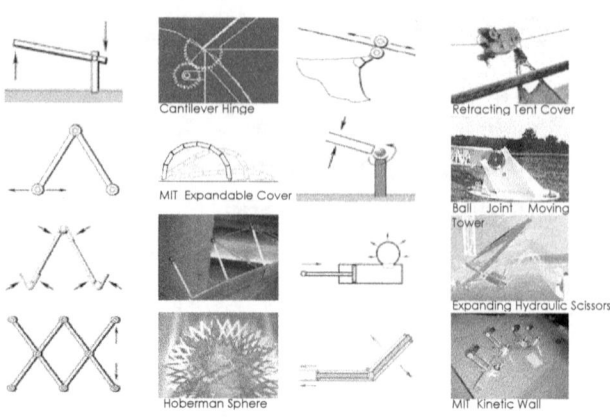

Figure 3. Kinetic systems:
http://kdg.mit.edu/Matrix/matrix

2.2 In general kinetic systems can be categorized into:

- Tensegrity
- Telescope systems
- Tensile, Membranes and Pneumatics Structures
- Umbrella Principles
- Scissors principles
- Coilable Structures
- Foldable systems, Origami, miura-ori shape and others

Tensegrity

Tensegrity is a balanced system composed of two main forces, a constant pull balanced by a discontinuous push. When the two forces are at equilibrium with each other, the system reaches its maximum strength. The structure is made of struts, cables, and pins. The cables provide the constant pull; the struts give a discontinuous push and the pins allow these two forces to become one. A poetic way of explaining tensegrity is "islands of compression floating in a sea of tension." This metaphor proved to be the metaphor from which Buckminister Fuller began his brainstorming on geodesic domes.

---

[3] By Emily Atwood, Princeton

Figure 4. Snelson: Needle Tower,
Figure 5. Buck Fuller: Geodesic Domes

Tensile, Membranes and Pneumatics Structures

Smart Pneumatic Structures in Architecture
An example for a smart pneumatic structure in architecture is the pneumatic exhibition building that was developed by Festo (Fig. 7/8) reacts to environmental influences like a living organism. 330 single air-inflated chambers and a computer create a self-controlled system which checks the pressure of each chamber at regular intervals and controls it in accordance with a weather station. Pneumatic muscles (elastic tension elements) are contractile hoses which - with the help of air pressure - are able to generate tension forces that can be controlled exactly.

Figure 7. The pneumatic exhibition building © Festo AG Esslingen, Germany

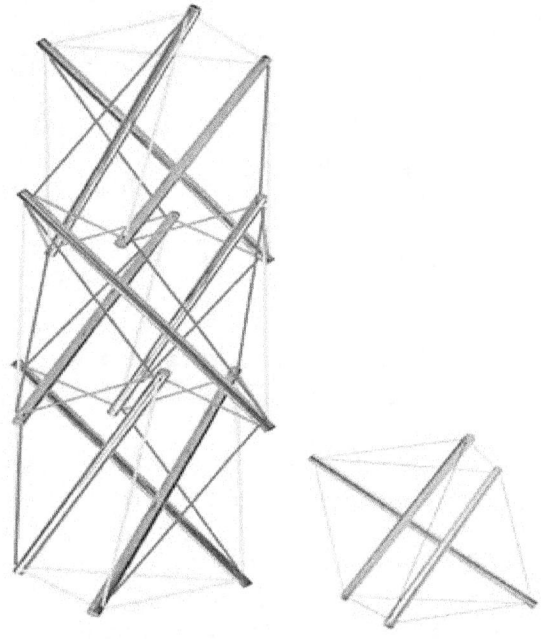

Figure 6. T3, 3 struts, 6 nodes, 9 tensioning cables

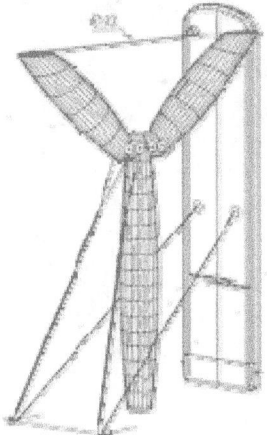

Figure 8. Y-shaped column connected to a wall component and the pneumatic muscles (elastic tension elements).

Umbrella Principles

The umbrella principle can be found in simple system or application but also ranges into highly complex applications such as surgical implements or large scale space structures. The integrated surface system is the source for these design solutions.

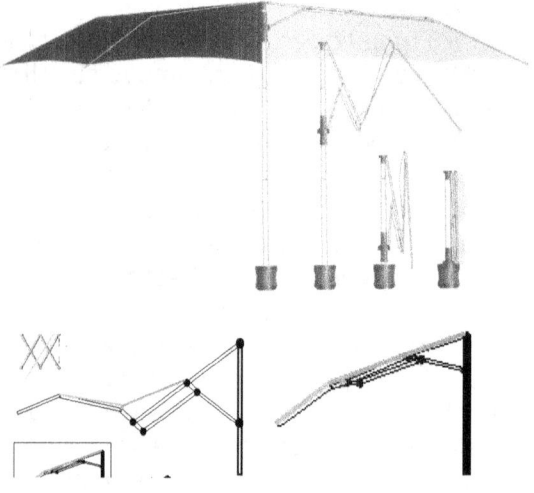

Figure 9. Collapsible Umbrella

The Umbrella principle is defined as a lightweight system which is both enclosure and structure. The frame is integral to surface, just as the surface is integral to frame. Both frame and surface are need for the statics and kinetics of the piece to work. This dynamic homeostasis is achieved between the interplay of tension and compression.

Figure 10. Deployable space structures

Scissor Principles

Figure 11. Hoberman Sphere: Japan

Figure 12. Deployable space Truss 12. MIT Deployable Space Masts

Deployable space structures based on the scissors principle

When one applies these structural units vertically they become a foldable tower. These triangles create great structural ability. While the scissors allow for the structure to be easily deployed and retracted. The umbrella principle allows these frames to contain or incorporate skins.

Figure 13/14. A triangular mast consists of six rods that form three pairs which are connected by means of tension cables. The cables then act in pure tension and cause the structure to have great structural capabilities.

Coilable boom antenna4

Coilable Masts still utilize the cable for deployment and retraction but they work differently than the triangular mast. They are lattice structures with a triangle cross section and are designed specifically for elastic folding.

Figure 15. Able Deployable Articulated Mast

---

[4] ATK-Able Engineering Company, Inc. www.aec-able.com see also www.atake-sdl.com, www.ilcdover.com

The diagonal members priestess the bay by being made shorter than their nominal length. By doing this the structure becomes in a permanent state of compression.

ADAM- Able Deployable Articulated Mast was developed by AEC. It was designed to support a 792 pound antenna structure and carry 400 pounds of stranded copper, coaxial fiber optic cable, and thruster gas lines along it's length. When retracted, it can fit into a space that is 56 inches wide. It takes the structure only 20 minutes to become fully deployed at the length of 200 feet. The horizontal batten and the vertical members are made of carbon fiber that is reinforced in plastic and ball joints and tension cross members are made of stainless steel and titanium.

Foldable systems, origami, miura-ori shape and others collapsing membranes

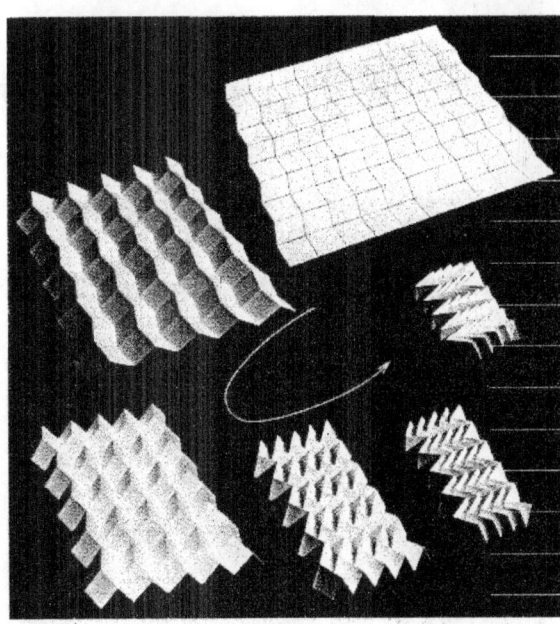

Figure 15. Leaf, Figure 16/17. Miura-ori module.

Tree leaves are a good example of skins that contract. The pattern which allows the young leaves to fit inside the small buds allows for this compaction. Hornbeam and beech leaves have a particularly simple and regular corrugation pattern. Maple leaves have a more complex pattern, involving seven elements of corrugation, each connected to its neighbor. The fold lines in a corrugated leaf model. Solid lines indicate crest folds and dashed lines indicate valley folds. The angle between the midrib and the side veins, is the vein angle. There are nine stages in the deployment of the leaf-folding pattern as the surface extends simultaneously in two directions.

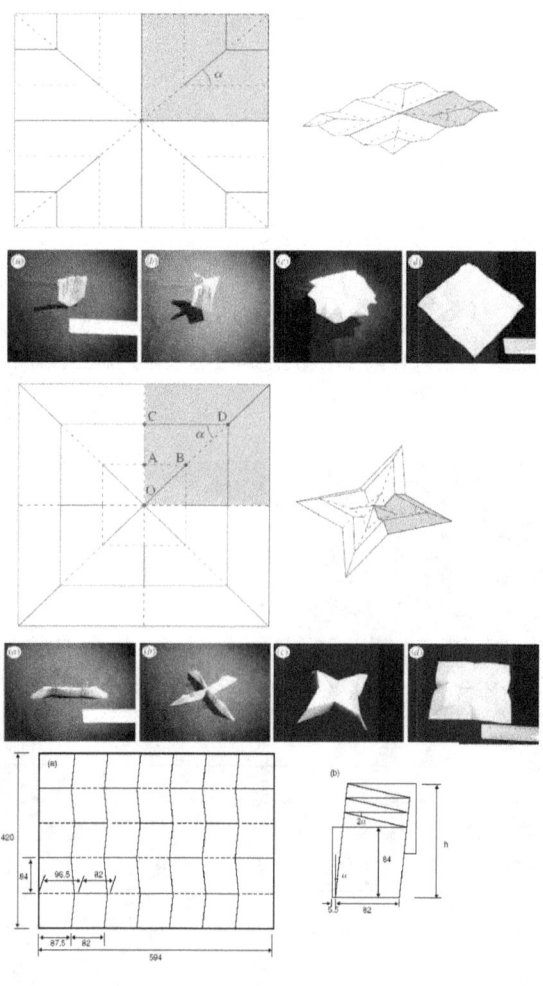

18. Origami Folding Studies. Biaxial shortening of a plane into a developable double-corrugation surface (unfolding of sheet folded according to Miura-ori).

4. Kinetic and Computational Systems

For condoling the kinetic aspects of the structure microcontroller (Basic Stamp) and a wide range of sensors were used.

The project had to address the following questions:
- types of devices that generate environmental readings.
- how these devices are connected to a computer.
- the material aspects of the sculpture; membrane design.
- how to write computer programs which activate other devices to move the sculpture.
- how to get input from the Internet.
- how to display the sculpture in real time on theInternet.
- the mechanical and electrical components required to make a sculpture move.
- development of the algorithms that will take the environmental readings and convert them to interesting responses; orderly or randomly generated.
- In addition to movement in the sculpture, can it make sound, or control lighting.
- the lighting of the sculpture, as prototyped, are the shadows produced as interesting a design as the moving parts.
- review of the area of kinetic sculpture.
- review of the current design of the sculpture.

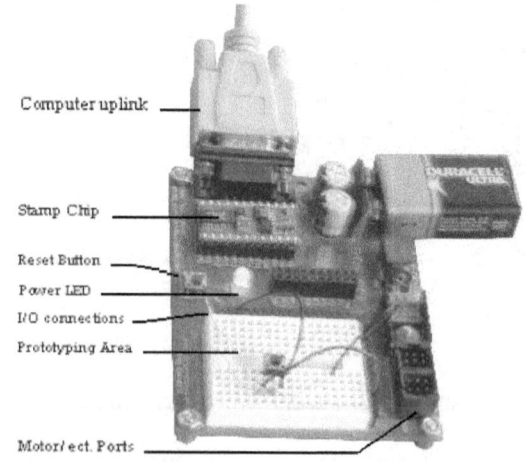

Figure 19. Basic Stamp

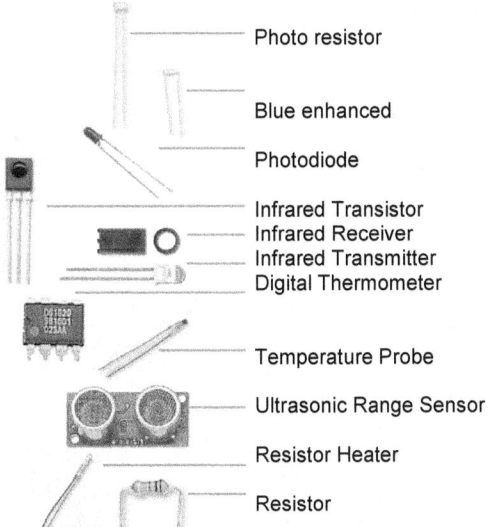

Figure 20. Sensors and Resistors www.Parallax.com

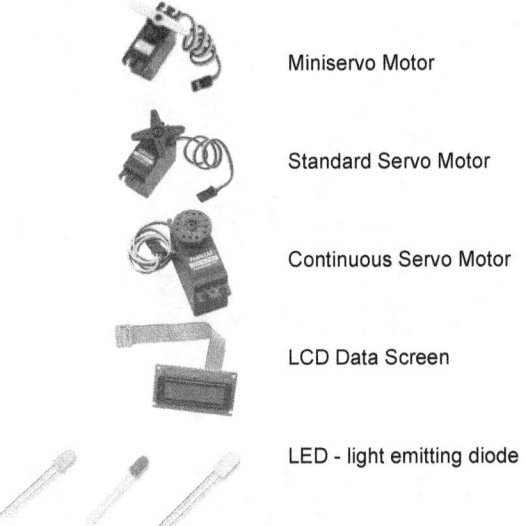

Figure 21. Motors and Output www.Parallax.com

Questions regarding the Programming Movement:
- Figure number of motors or actuators needed for movement in structure.
- Decide if other reactions or output are needed: lights, sound, ect.
- Decide on external stimuli for structures movement and type of input devices.

5. Design project

This projects attempts to use a piece of kinetic sculpture as a response device to demonstrate smart building type systems. The design project is focusing on different kinetic systems that are available today, how they work, and how they can be used to make decisions and actually respond physically. For example, a project could be developed to analyze the data collected over time to look for patterns. Depending on the installation the project would encompass a single wall or a room.

The focus of this project was to investigate the ability of architecture to respond to its environment. Goal was to develop a prototype /sculpture which can react to temperature, light, sound, occupant presence, image recognition, movement, touch, Web requests, or direct commands. These stimuli will generate a response based on interesting mathematical relationships or functions.

The projects investigated the construction of the sculpture, how to monitor stimuli, development of algorithms, and how to have the sculpture respond; dealing with both the design and technical issues.

The Emphasis was on:
    analysis of lightweight structures
    relationship between structure and construction
    understanding kinetics / mechanics
    represent analysis through three dimensional diagrams
    investigate buildings ability to respond to their environment
    demonstrate smart building systems
    investigate construction techniques, systems
    how to monitor stimuli
    development of algorithms
    production of computer programming to mechanize sculpture

5.1. Kinetic Light Tube

The initial concept was to create a hanging kinetic sculpture in the atrium space of the Art and Architecture Building. The object will be activated by a motion sensor which controls the up and down motion of the object. Throughout the day, the structure will deploy and contract itself creating a continually changing spatial condition. The tube will be covered in materials stretched across structure.

Figure 22. Rendering Figure 23. Kinetic Model 1:5m with basic stamp controller and sensor

Transparent, translucent and opaque materials will be used to accentuate the light and reflective qualities of the form. The structure is based on the scissor principle. By connecting a series of scissored "V"s a triangular space is formed when expanded and a planer triangle when collapsed.

Figure 27. Full scale structure suspended in atrium

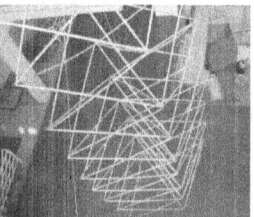

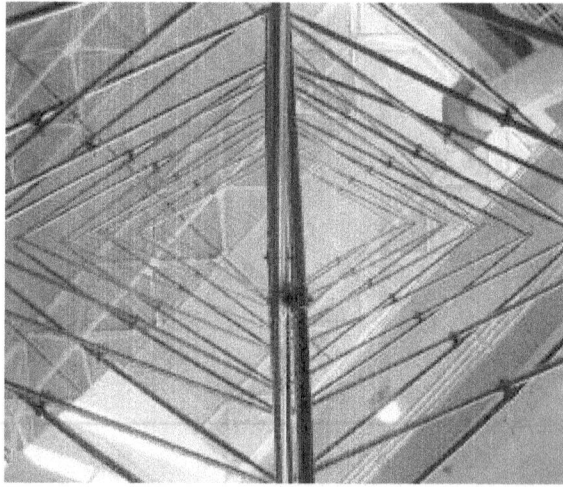

Figure 24-26. Full scale structure suspended in atrium

5.2 Expanding Space Frame

The Initial concept of the space frame was to create a modular folding structure to serve the purpose of designating spaces while providing physical interaction and manipulation of the object. The space frame can adapt to wide variety of uses and spaces. The structure itself is made of aluminum rings. A semi-elastic skin serves to refract light and create a translucent membrane above the observers. Motion is activated by infrared sensors and when one approaches the structure it begins to unfold. When the observer leaves the area, the structure retracts into its dormant state.

Figure 29. Rendering

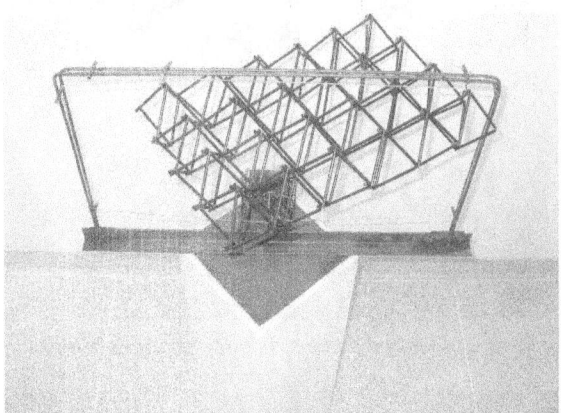

Figure 30. Kinetic Model 1:5m with basic stamp controller and sensor

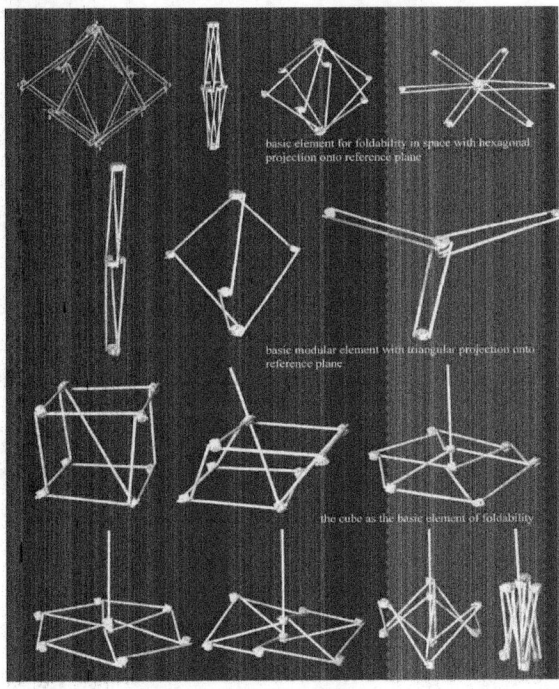

Figure 28. Diagram of one unit

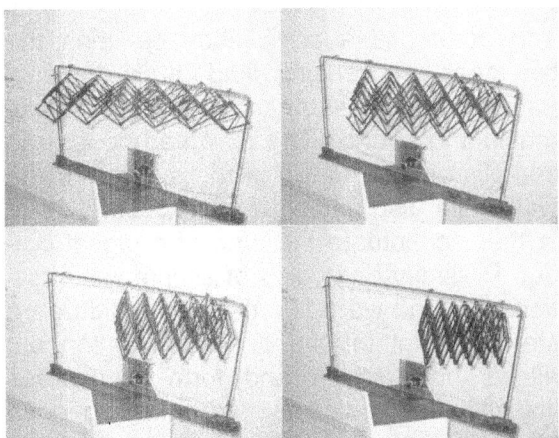

Figure 31-34. Kinetic Model 1:5m with basic stamp controller and sensor

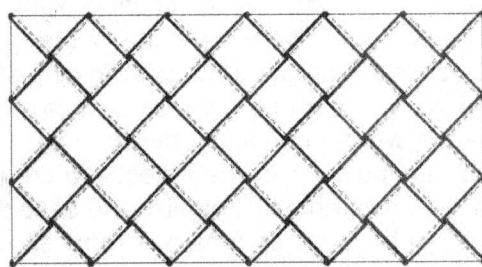

Figure 26. Top view canopy 4x6 cells

Figure 35-39. Full scale structure suspended in atrium, Figure 40. Joint and PVC Pipes

5.3 Acoustic Articulation

The project is a compilation between the two ideas of a bending, fluid form with visual transparency to show movement or flow of music and sound. The form had be able to compliment the music in the surface of the wall while also adding a second attribute to further accentuate the tune of a digital output. Preliminary studies of simple visualization of sound were first used to decide on a starting point for the design. The concept allows both speed and form to express visually the music, and accentuating each other.

The acoustic articulation project creates a canopy that is in a constant state of motion; collapsing and expanding, which defines the space it resides in by casting light and shadows. The Initial concept of the space frame was to create a modular folding structure to serve the purpose of designating spaces while providing physical interaction and manipulation of the object. To create a wall which is able to visualize the aspects of music into form; or create a form showing sound waves forms and allow digital sound outputs to be utilized, creating movement or reactions on the wall.

Thought the design of the wall, the casual observer will be afforded the opportunity to experience the visualization of sound. Panels in the wall fold and expand to creating visual difference due to music. Origami pattern were utilized to allow for panel movement and to create a pliable, structural form.

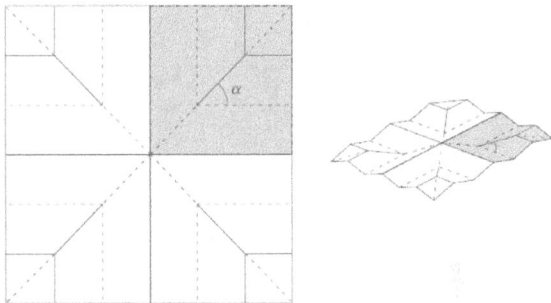

Figure 41. Rendering Acoustic Articulation Object

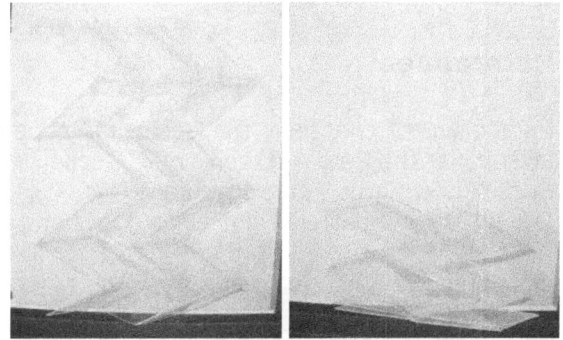

Figure 42. Kinetic Model 1:5m with basic stamp controller and sensor

Figure 43/44. Origami Folding Study
Figure 45. Kinetic Plexiglas model
Figure 46. Full scale structure suspended in atrium

47. Show at the Knoxville Museum of Art

References:

Per Mollerup, Collapsible: The Genius of Space-Saving Design
Inventions: The Patented Works of R. Buckminster Fuller
Buckminster Fuller: Anthology for the New Millennium, First Edition
Oliver Herwig, Featherweight: Light Mobile and Floating

http://bryantyeh.net/byeh_abs.html
http://kdg.mit.edu
http://archnet.org/library/
http://www.n55.dk/Index.html
http://www.jcdainc.com/
http://www.odesco.net/
http://www.atake-sdl.com, Expanding Space Truss
http://www.aec-able.com
http://archnet.org/library/
http://math.serenevy.net/?page=Origami-ApplicationLinks
http://new.idsa.org/webmodules/articles/articlefiles/ed_conference02/41.pdf
http://www.u3p.net/fold/pliage_a.htm
http://www.britishorigami.org.uk/theory/miura.htm
http://www.britishorigami.org.uk/theory/theory.htm
http://www.llnl.gov/nif/lst/diffractive-optics/newtecheye.html
http://www.nature.com/nsu/020218/020218-1.html
http://news.bbc.co.uk/2/hi/technology/3301947.stm
http://cio-today.newsfactor.com/perl/story/16379.html
http://www.space.com/businesstechnology/technology/origami_design_020220-1.html
http://www.spacedaily.com/news/mars-mers-04r.html
http://www.nagata.co.jp/news/news0212-e.htm

Designing Structures: Four Exercises Integrating Fundamental Structural Issues Into Students' Design Processes

Andrea Swartz
Ball State University

Abstract

Too often, as an educator in both the architectural design studio and the lecture hall, I've shared the common lament that "support" course content, technology in particular, is inconsistently synthesized into the architectural student's design process. In the introductory structures course I teach for undergraduate architecture students, I have experimented with various methods of developing pedagogical links between the lecture course and the design studio throughout the past several years. This presentation and paper will elaborate on a series of four sequential "hands-on" exercises given this past year that were intended to address this issue of students seeing structure as a design opportunity. In doing so, these exercises created links between technological knowledge and the architectural design process, ideally resulting in an appreciation of how architecture can be enhanced by structural issues during design.

In order to initiate the bridging between these two knowledge bases (architectural structures and design) and corresponding two learning environments (lecture hall and studio), the initial exercises were designed to engage the students' "design minds" in structures while the final exercise was designed to engage the student's awareness of forces and stability in studio. The assignments required hands-on consideration of fundamental structural issues being addressed abstractly in the numbers-based lecture environment. The first three assignments were topic based: "column support," "spanning the gap" and "system/stability." Each of these explorations was initiated with a lecture on the general structural issues for consideration (for example, for "column," this included the discussion of slenderness, end conditions, cross-sectional shape), followed by a series of short student experiments meant to manifest these issues, and finally with built designs made out of cardstock that were tested in class. The final, more synthetic exercise was a structural model of their concurrent design studio project, intended to extend the prior considerations (column, beam and system) holistically into their design process.

This theme of heuristic experimentation in combination with the more conventional lecture delivery, gave students a greater appreciation of opportunities for the qualitative consideration of structures in their design processes. This paper describes the four assignments, from introductory lectures to student results. Also, the pedagogical context for this course (including brief descriptions of our architecture department's curricular organization as it pertains to technology education) and the course's primary pedagogical objectives and organization, will also be discussed. Methods, successes and failures will be shared as opportunities for improving the conventional technology lecture course, thereby facilitating students' stronger embrace of technology in the exploration of architecture.

A Question of Relevance

For the past twelve years I have taught introductory structures as well as design studio. Educated as an architect, initial teaching assignments included teaching the introductory architectural structures classes; an assignment I've enjoyed. However, as a design studio instructor, I've often noted the students' lack of technology synthesis with their design processes: average design solutions do not pursue technological issues such as the identification of a structural system, address of passive environmental strategies, consideration of material nuances, and detailed connection explorations.

Given the amount of technology instruction in our school (seven required courses), it is a perplexing shortcoming. Somehow, this typical curriculum of lecture classes covering the three technology "streams" (building technology, structures and environmental systems) apparently does not facilitate integration. Specific to structures, there is little evidence that students see the connection between the "math" problems covered in the morning lectures and the making of architecture in the afternoon. Furthermore, from my own experiences as an architect, I've observed that practicing architects rarely engage in the types of number crunching exercises discussed in the lecture hall to figure out structural solutions. Rather, it is primarily a conceptual awareness of structural issues that informs architects' design processes.

In noting the seemingly minimal student conceptual awareness of structures as a design opportunity, and the actual use of structural knowledge by professional architects, I constantly wonder how architectural structures courses can be taught better. More specifically, how can instruction in architectural structures more effectively facilitate architecture students developing a structural "intuition" and interest; a mind-set that is fostered by a qualitative understanding of how building performance can be enhanced by issues of structural and material technologies? How can this instruction more effectively prepare them for how structures will be integrated into their professional practice of architecture? How can this structural education become more relevant?

Pedagogic Context

While pursuing answers to these questions, I also question how to balance their pursuit while fulfilling my role in the pedagogic context of teaching structures in our current curriculum: a program still in the process of transitioning from a five year Bachelors of Architecture program to a 4+2 masters program (our last B.Arch. students graduated last spring and our first Masters of Architecture class will receive their first professional degree in two years). The introductory structures course is taken by second year undergraduate students and has the following catalogue description:

> ***Structural Systems 1:*** *Basic introduction to the mathematical foundations of statics: equilibrium, balance, centroids, neutral axis - with primary focus on developing a basic understanding of concepts and conditions of equilibrium and force systems.*

This course description emphasizes a calculation-based understanding of structural issues, while at the same time alluding to a conceptual understanding of the material. The first theme (mathematical calculation as the basis for learning) is picked up holistically in the subsequent structures courses in the sequence of three structures courses.

There are merits in this approach of a numerical, problem solving language to convey issues: lecturing on analytical problem solving is a delivery method which is package-able in fifty minute sound bites; lecturing is the most economic delivery method for the large number of students required to take the class (typically three to four sections of up to thirty-five students); teaching the numeric calculation of issues such as maximum internal bending moment or shear provides an easy and objective way to evaluate student performance; and, the mathematical delivery of information (while abstract in its conceptual relevance to architecture) is ironically tangible to the more math inclined students. Having taught introductory structures, I am the first to admit to the seductive influence of numbers in my lectures.

However, the problems with this delivery method are important to note as well. A lecture delivery creates a fundamentally different learning environment from the design studio. Ideas, generally discussed through numbers and calculations, lead to the pursuit of "right" answers. The conventional structures course, mathematically focused, delineates a precise methodology, which if replicated, will result in the correct answer. This pursuit is the antithesis of the design studio where "right" answers are initially shunned; it is only through the design process of trial and error that correct solutions slowly emerge. Good design solutions are pursued through a spiraling, reiterative process of posed solutions, analysis of successes/failures, and subsequently improved iterations. The linear pursuit of finite answers in the technology classroom does not work in studio.

These different methods of teaching and learning enhance the divide between studio and technology courses. As a result, while most students are generally successful in understanding the mathematical delivery of information and replicating calculation procedures to determine resulting values, they understandably struggle with the applicability and integration of mathematically based knowledge into their creative design process. For instance, knowing what the maximum internal shear or bending stress in the beam is and where it is located, rarely translates into a design exploration of beam shape in their studios.

To address this schism, it seems realistic that if technology educators embrace (to some degree) the experiential, heuristic approach that is a fundamental part of the design studio, integration of the technological subject matter into their design process will be less alien to architecture students. If they are using the same methods in both classes to explore ideas, the boundaries between subject materials will diminish. It is also likely that learning through physical experimentation will increase their interest and curiosity about the structural issues being discussed. Experiential learning is effective in this regard as it "can be not only motivating, but very effective in developing exploration and experimentation," an atmosphere consistent with the pulse of the design studio.[1]

Acknowledging the potential of hands-on experimentation as a teaching tool, I've conducted an on-going series of trial-run assignments to bridge the gap between structures and studio. In previous years (under an earlier curriculum of four structures courses and consequently more time), fellow instructors and I used "lab" assignments. These included case studies of noteworthy examples of architectural

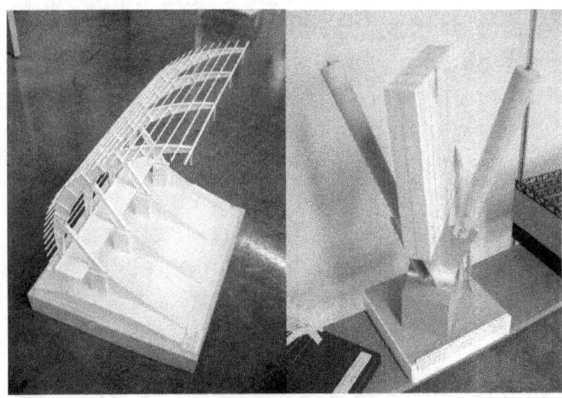

Figure 1: Case study models

structures (research, analysis, presentations, write-ups, detail models, system models); the design, fabrication and testing of a small-scale truss to support a specific load (demonstrating truss behavior); and a design process structural model depicting the structural system of the student's own, concurrent, design project. When I also taught the second semester of structures (strength of materials) in the previous, four-semester curricular sequence, the labs also included stretching hung wire in the school's atrium (axial stress/strain); and assignments for the design and fabrication of a concrete tile and wooden stool (material qualities, axial stress).

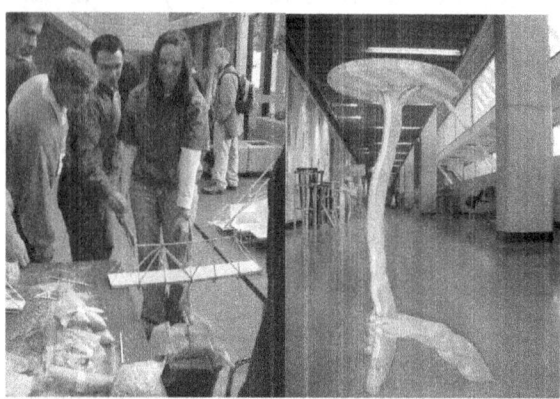

Figure 2: Truss testing and Stool fabrication labs

These projects had various successes and failures. The material fabrications such as the stool reinforced the tenet of material craftsmanship in good design. The truss experiment was effective in generating student excitement because of the competitive testing at the end of the project. The precedent studies generated student interest in the architectural relevance of structures, however their analysis of what was happening structurally was minimal. The design process structural model has consistently been an effective example of showing the exciting opportunities for integrating structural concerns into studio at a conceptual level.

Now teaching just the first, introductory semester of structures, I revisit this ongoing pursuit for a relevant structural education. Coordinating lessons in the lecture hall and studio can enhance the communication of even the most fundamental aspects of architectural structures. Topics of concurrent and non-concurrent force systems, equilibrium and centroids can be made physical, and thereby more meaningful. At the same time, balance must be achieved between the hands-on experimentation and the "mathematical foundations of statics" conveyed in the course description. The quantitative delivery of structural issues must be covered (in our current curriculum) as the second and third semesters of structures build on this quantitative pedagogy.[2]

Experiment objectives, definition and student results

Pedagogically, the intentions of the experiments described in this paper are a continuation of the efforts previously described. Experimental design and fabrication projects were used to enhance the learning of these basic structural ideas. At a fundamental level, the introductory structures content in the course can be reduced to two primary discussion areas:

1. concurrent force system behavior with discussions of axial force (extended into truss analysis via method of joint) occurring in force systems in equilibrium.
2. non-concurrent force system behavior introducing the idea of moment (a force's tendency to cause rotation). This most easily is demonstrated by discussions of beam behavior: equilibrium as well as shear and moment diagrams to describe the internal force in beams.

A third issue, not specifically identified in the course description, also was an important objective for these beginning architecture students:

3. introducing different types of structural systems to promote their awareness of how their architectural ideas can be conceived of structurally.

These three issues defined the scope of the three exercises, with the overall objective of these three and the final exercise specifically being the integration of structural thinking in the students' design process.

The delivery of each exercise followed a consistent pattern: a slide presentation on the fundamental issues addressed by the assignment (immediately posted on Blackboard to facilitate subsequent review by the students); experimentation that made

Figure 3. Wohlen High School, Calatrava

the primary issues visible (done by students outside of class); design/fabrication; and final testing. Class time devoted to these four experiments was one class for the issues and assignment presentation and questions; and one class for the discussion/testing of the final product. The first two experiments each took about two weeks, while the latter two were each four weeks. These sequential experiments were designed to reference back to ideas covered in each prior assignment (i.e., "spanning the gap" builds on ideas introduced in the column design, system stability builds on ideas introduced in the consideration of columns and spanning methods, the structural model builds on all). Reiteration was therefore built into the flow of these projects, allowing continued reconsideration of the ideas discussed.

Experiment #1, "Column Support," builds off of ideas of concurrent force systems and cross-sectional properties being discussed analytically in class. These ideas are applied to the description of column behavior which, when ideally loaded, exemplifies a concurrent (collinear) force system. It is also a component of architecture that students can readily identify in their consideration of architecture. The slide presentation discussed *issues* of column behavior through pictorial examples of built architecture (see Figure 3). Slenderness, end conditions and cross-sectional shape were talked about through reference to these architectural examples.

The assignment then required teams of two students to conduct and record their observations of small experiments articulated to demonstrate the behavior of compressive structural members (issues of slenderness, end conditions, buckling, bracing, cross-sectional shape) on their own. This led to the final requirement: an

Figure 4: Buckling test / final column design

18" tall card-stock support, responsible for supporting a minimum load of several books (see Figure 4). The design emphasis was for them to consider the issues discussed and explored through the experiments (end conditions, the cross-sectional shape, and the "elevational" shape), while applying them to their own column design. These were tested in class, after the team's column design strategy was articulated. Noteworthy was that only a few of the submitted designs failed under the required load (many were so over-designed they could even support a student).

The second experiment, "Spanning the Gap," builds off of ideas of non-concurrent force systems as exemplified by beam behavior. Again, the slide presentation used architectural examples where spanning members were conceived as design opportunities. The pre-test assignments encouraged consideration of the spanning member's cross-sectional shape (testing the spanning capacity of accordion folded paper versus plain paper, wide flange shaped sections versus "box" beams) and funicular or "elevational"

Figure 5: Span testing in studio

shaping. The final requirement asked the teams of two to span 20" with a cardstock fabricated spanning member. To address the over-design in the column experiment and invite the potential of learning through failure, additional emphasis was placed on considering how the design would fail after supporting the required load (two books), but before the load was tripled (six books). During the in-class testing, the teams were asked to articulate their design objectives prior to testing their structure, and explain how the structure might fail.

The third experiment tried to stitch together the two prior explorations, with an emphasis on "system." The primary objective of the assignment was to provide an overview of different types of structural systems used in architecture. The "testing" aspect of the experiments encouraged the consideration of lateral stability by requiring the students'

Figure 6: Span testing in class

models to resist a horizontal shearing force (applied by hand); this requirement provided

a good way to focus the exploration of the different types of structural systems. The slide presentation identified structural strategies such as post and beam frame, bearing wall, slab, trusses, suspension, arch/vault/dome, responded to lateral loads. Materials for the models to be tested in class included cardstock, pins, wood, string/thread and cardboard. During the class review of these models, students needed to describe the structural system and discuss/demonstrate how lateral stability was achieved.

The final iterative evolution of these three analytical experiments was the final lab requiring each student to holistically integrate the consideration of a building's structural system in their own architectural design process. The emphasis was placed on consideration of how identifying a structural system could impact the organization of the design, as well as exploring how the structure (and structural elements such as columns and beams) could enhance the communication of architectural ideas. Accurate

Figure 7: Stable System model

sizing of the structural members was not as important (beyond the generalities extracted from experiments #1, #2 and #3 such as that horizontally spanning structural members have a more difficult job, therefore should be dimensionally greater than the vertical support members). The PowerPoint for Experiment #3 on different types of systems as well as different reference sheets for structural system rules-of-thumb were referenced and available on Blackboard for student review. Textbooks, including Ed Allen's <u>The Architect's Studio Companion</u>, <u>Understanding Structures</u> by Fuller Moore and <u>Structure and Architectural Design</u> by Corkill, Puderbaugh and Sawyers were placed on reserve in the library for reference.

The review process for this assignment was two-fold. Most importantly there was a pin-up submission of each student's in-process structural design ideas. These were handled as efficiently as possible with each student required to attend a twenty-minute pin-up session with two other students (requiring about six hours of time outside of class to look at the work of approximately sixty-four students). Students were asked to come prepared to quickly articulate their general design objectives and how these were furthered by the structural system selection. These pin-ups demonstrated that structures can be talked about in a 'design' sense, that structural considerations can be used to

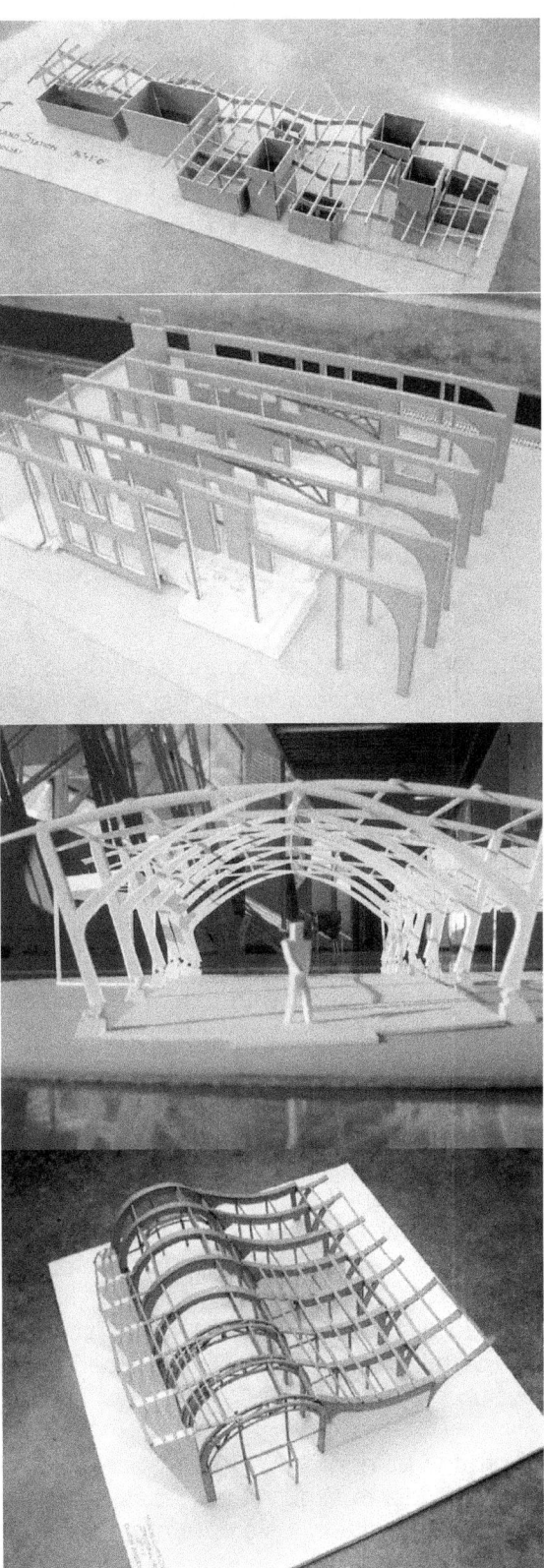

Figure 8: Structural model examples

generate good design, and that structures is not purely an analytical pursuit. Final reviews of the student's structural solutions were addressed in the students' final studio review. In the final discussion of these structural models in our class, a few were selected for discussion with the whole class. These were projects that demonstrated an understandable, organizationally influential structural system, explored the schematic design of some of the structural members (trusses, columns, beams, connections, etc.), as well as designs where the structural model was truly influential in the project's evolutionary process. (See Figure 8 for structural model examples.)

Conclusions

This series of experiments set out to encourage the exploration of design opportunities in technology with the ultimate intention of encouraging the further embrace of technology in the holistic design process. Learning through experimentation and fabrication, making the abstract physical, has been demonstrated over the years as an effective method in the communication of structural ideas.[3] The success of this approach was apparent during the semester as the students explored innovative solutions to the problems posed. From semester-end feedback, they articulated their appreciation in seeing the application of the abstract ideas presented in class. Also, the competitive spirit of the testing at the end of each project also served to excite the students about exploring the ideas each project addressed. To succeed, students had to pursue avenues of interest while attending to the different aspects of the experiment's set-up.

From my point of view, I appreciated listening to students explain their ideas and demonstrate how their design performed. I found this required more student accountability and involvement than the passive lecture environment. By comparison, in the lecture portion of the course students seem to passively soak up the information being discussed, accepting on faith that a particular line of inquiry is valid and important without having any participation or experience in reaching that conclusion. In this environment of blind faith, students' are less interested in exploring their own curiosities about the subject material.[4] These experiments, by contrast, tapped into this curiosity.

Another lesson from this effort was to emphasize *failure* more next time. Often, the designs were over-built to the point of obfuscating how the structure was actually working. The next iteration of these projects will embrace failure as part of the learning process by somehow rewarding failure (as attempted in the 'spanning' experiment #2). Having students explain the principles behind how their structure failed will (potentially) make the issue more memorable. From my own experiences in making, it is through failure that the most poignant lessons are conveyed. The importance of shear walls becomes more convincing when the model collapses to the side with a sideways push. Also, "students need to see that it is acceptable to make mistakes as long as they can apply what they learned from the process and try to solve the problem again. This mirrors the real world more accurately."[5] Failure encourages reflection; success is often a forgotten checkmark.

Beyond the pedagogical benefits of hands-on learning, the other successes of these projects include information technology resources and aspects of the project set-up. Having the PowerPoint lectures for each assignment permanently accessible through the use of Blackboard (or other web-based class communication systems) allows students to revisit the ideas and images presented as often as needed to stimulate and focus their design ideas. Having the students to do specific issues-based experiments on their own time, prior to their final design (and documenting this process) was helpful. Digital documentation of these early experiments and the written reflections on the lessons learned allowed me to share in their efforts without sacrificing class time. Also, limiting the primary material that was used for the design explorations to inexpensive cardstock eliminated the preciousness of each proposal, thereby encouraging more attempts. Finally, in the last project, the importance of the initial pin-up is significant; seeing a 'structures' professor actively engaged with their architectural interests, albeit through a structural eye, connects them to the potential of this issue in their architecture.

Finally, the experiments were most effective when coordinated with the lecture material. This was evident particularly in the first two projects of 'column support' (concurrent force system example, cross-sectional properties) and 'spanning the gap' (non-concurrent force system, cross-sectional properties). The exercise in span would have been even more informative if done in tandem with shear and moment diagrams (which occurred later in the semester). For the latter two projects (system stability and structural model), the disconnect between the project content and the lecture content was apparent and (when the projects are revisited) poses an opportunity for improvement. It seems that subsequent, more advanced structures courses beyond statics would have even more opportunity for the discussion of structural systems.[6]

Therein I return to my ongoing question regarding the instruction of structures for architecture students. What would ultimately benefit architects the most in terms of the inclusion of structural issues in their design? Is a mathematical foundation a helpful language to establish, even though it is rarely applied in the practice of architecture? Does an early mathematical emphasis serve well to introduce the issues, from which more creative investigations can stem? What is fundamentally relevant in the structural education of architects? While considering these questions, I'll continue to pursue an effective balance between heuristic experiences for the students, as epitomized by these projects, and the conventional communication, with a quantitative emphasis, of course material.

References/Notes

[1] Stephen Yurkiw, Learning with Confidence: Encouraging Risk and Failure in Learning, http://www.elearnspace.org/Articles/valueoffailure.htm

[2] This approach presumably leads to success on the registration exam, perhaps one measure of pedagogical effectiveness, but also a debatable one as our curriculum transitions to a 4+2 program. Do undergraduate students *majoring* in architecture benefit from such a quantitative emphasis?

[3] The work of Mario Salvadori and Richard E. Kellogg are most notable in this respect.

[4] Yurkiw

[5] Yurkiw

[6] I would welcome the opportunity to revisit the articulation of the quantitative emphasis of all courses, however it would need to be discussed in the context of the registration exam and the practice of architecture.

Bibliography

Foug, Carolyn Ann and Joyce, Sharon, *Perspecta 31: Reading Structures*, MIT Press, 2000.

Kellogg, Richard, *Demonstrating Structural Behavior With Simple Models*, 1997.

Smith, Ryan E., "Bridging Structures, Construction and Studio," Connector 13 (Spring 2004): 1-3

Swann, Joanna, "What Doesn't Happen in Teaching and Learning?," Oxford Review of Education 24 (1998): 211-223.

Swartz, Andrea, "Learning By Doing: A Qualitative Approach to Teaching Architectural Technology," Ball State University Creative Teaching Grant Application (2004)

Yurkiw, Stephen, "Learning with Confidence: Encouraging Risk and Failure in Learning," http://www.elearnspace.org/Articles/valueoffailure.htm

Seismic Design Education in U.S. Schools of Architecture

Christine Theodoropoulos
University of Oregon

Abstract

Currently, no comprehensive or coordinated information exists on seismic design education for architects and architecture students in the United States. This subject deserves attention, particularly in view of recent trends toward the nationalization and globalization of architectural practice. Many architects, educated and based in areas of infrequent seismicity, find themselves more and more frequently required to design in regions of the U.S. or abroad where the seismic hazard is more serious. Unfortunately, this has not been adequately reflected in architectural education. Architects assume a pivotal role in seismic resistant design and are responsible for communicating seismic resistant strategies to building owners and community leaders. It is important that seismic design educators and practitioners understand how seismic design is currently taught in schools of architecture in order to identify new avenues for seismic design education and disseminate best teaching practices.

This paper reports on findings from: a survey of professors who teach structures in the U.S. schools accredited by the National Architectural Accrediting Board (NAAB); a review of school catalog materials; and an examination of school performance related to relevant student performance criteria used in the accreditation process. It includes a review of the seismic design content of architecture programs and the methods used to teach seismic design in an effort to chart how students learn seismic design concepts at various institutions. Findings include information about regional influences and the professional profile of instructors as well as faculty assessment of currently available teaching materials and identification of future teaching materials needs. Most significant is evidence suggesting that although most schools of architecture address the concepts central to seismic design across the curriculum in a variety of courses, there are barriers that may prevent students from learning how to incorporate seismic design lessons into the architectural design process.

Background

In the past two decades the National Science Foundation (NSF) and the Federal Emergency Management Agency (FEMA) have funded several projects directed to architectural education. Recently, the Earthquake Engineering Research Institute (EERI), with the support of FEMA, completed *Designing for Earthquakes*, a manual for practicing architects that was developed in response to the need for a text that consolidated information needed by architects preparing for practice in earthquake country.

In 2000, the Building Science Safety Council (BSSC), with the support of FEMA, funded the development of a number of modules of a slide show directed to architects, predominantly related to the FEMA publications on the *NEHRP Provisions for New Buildings* and the publication on the *Seismic Rehabilitation of Existing Buildings*. These presentations have been given to a number of AIA continuing education classes but have had limited reach into the required curricula in schools of architecture.

In 1995, following the great Hanshin-Awaji Earthquake, NSF funded a team from the American Institute of Architects (AIA), in co-operation with the Japan Institute of Architects (JIA), to visit Kobe to focus on architecture and planning issues of reconstruction. Subsequently, in 1996 a joint AIA/JIA workshop was held in Washington, DC and a set of proceedings was published entitled "Architectural and Planning Lessons from the Great Hanshin-Awaji Earthquake.

Prior to this work a number of seminars for architects were developed and presented through support by FEMA to the AIA and the Association of Collegiate Schools of Architecture (ACSA) through the AIA/ACSA Council on Research. Later, derived from these seminars, a self-study course was developed that includes a short textbook and a videotape: this course was aimed at the AIA Continuing Education program. However, the work was not followed up, the course is no longer available, and the AIA/ACSA Council on Research was disbanded and reconstituted into the Institute for Architectural Research (IAR), which ceased to be active in 2003. Unfortunately in the process, past initiatives related to seismic design education for architects have been disregarded and resources are becoming out-of-date and out-of-print.

In addition to the seminars, two institutes on seismic design education involved architectural faculty members teaching general building design. This activity culminated in a *charrette*--a three-day, hands-on design course-- held in Los Angeles in 1997. In this course, faculty/student teams from a number of Los Angeles architectural schools participated in a Rapid Visual Screening exercise in Pasadena, California, designed information kiosks for use at FEMA disaster sites, and finally, constructed full size prototypes of the kiosks using wood frame construction and requiring some seismic calculations and construction detailing. In 1998 the AIA/ACSA team organized a national student design competition for the design of seismically resistant housing on a site in Hollywood, California.

These projects gave researchers some experience in the possibilities and constraints involved in teaching seismic design, both to students and practitioners. In addition researchers gained understanding of the state of seismic design education at architectural schools that enabled them to develop a list of faculty members involved in teaching, using a variety of approaches. This experience provided a valuable foundation upon which to develop a more systematic and extensive survey of seismic design education.

Project Approach

Information about the seismic design education of architects in the United States was gathered using the following methods:

1) A review of recent studies of building technology education in U.S. schools of architecture.

2) Analysis of data provided by the National Architectural Accrediting Board (NAAB).

3) A survey of faculty members most familiar with the seismic design curriculum at schools of architecture accredited by NAAB.

4) An examination of architecture school catalogs and course information available on the internet. (This method was used to assist the survey process and augment information gathered in the survey.)

Based on this information the project team developed recommendations for approaches to improving seismic design education in schools of architecture.

NAAB Accredited Programs

The NAAB accredits professional programs offering the Bachelor of Architecture (B.Arch.), Master of Architecture (M.Arch.)

and Doctor of Architecture (D.Arch.) degrees. Most state architectural licensure boards identify completion of an accredited degree as the minimum educational requirement to qualify for architectural licensure. There are currently 114 accredited architecture programs in the United States. Their distribution in relation to the United States Geological Survey (USGS) ranking of states according to earthquake activity is shown in the table 1.

Only 4,500 or 18% of architecture students enrolled in accredited degree programs in the United States are studying at schools located within the top ten most seismically active states where public awareness of seismic design is highest and the local community of practicing architects is more experienced with seismic design.

USGS GROUPING OF STATES BY EARTHQUAKE ACTIVITY	SCHOOLS	APPROXIMATE NO. OF STUDENTS ENROLLED	B.ARCH	M.ARCH	D.ARCH
Top ten: Alaska, California, Hawaii, Nevada, Washington, Idaho, Wyoming, Montana, Utah, Oregon	17	4,500	9	12	1
Second Ten: New Mexico, Arkansas, Arizona, Colorado, Tennessee, Missouri, Texas, Illinois, Oklahoma, Maine	21	4,200	10	18	0
At least one Magnitude 3.5 and greater earthquake in 30 years: New York, Alabama, Kentucky, South Carolina, South Dakota, Virginia, Nebraska, Ohio, Georgia, Indiana, New Hampshire, Pennsylvania, Kansas, North Carolina, Massachusetts, Michigan, Minnesota, Mississippi, New Jersey, Louisiana, Rhode Island, West Virginia	59	14,100	39	40	0
0 Magnitude 3.5 and greater earthquake in 30 years: Connecticut, Delaware, Florida, Iowa, Maryland, North Dakota, Vermont, Wisconsin (Washington D. C. and Puerto Rico included)	17	2,600	7	11	0

Table 1. Distribution of Architecture Schools and Students by Earthquake Activity in U.S. States

NAAB Student Performance Criteria Related to Seismic Design

The 1998 criteria (revised in 2002) for student performance identified 37 subject areas that must be included in accredited programs. A new version of this document with 34 criteria was adopted in 2004. Although student performance criteria that specifically address structural systems are most likely to address earthquake resistant design directly, other subject areas address issues relevant to the practice of seismic design. The Criteria, with changes adopted from the 2004 document, include:

Structural Systems: Understanding of the principles of structural behavior in withstanding gravity and lateral forces, and the evolution, range, and appropriate applications of contemporary structural systems

Building Systems Integration: Ability to assess, select, and conceptually integrate structural systems, building envelope systems, environmental systems, life-safety systems, and building service systems into building design

Comprehensive Design: Ability to produce a comprehensive architectural project based on a building program and site that includes development of programmed spaces demonstrating an understanding of structural and environmental systems, life safety provisions, wall sections, and building assemblies, and the principles of sustainability.

Site Conditions: Ability to respond to natural and built site characteristics in the development of a program and design of a project.

Code Compliance: Understanding of the codes, regulations and standards applicable to a given site and building design, including occupancy classifications, allowable building heights and areas, allowable construction types, separation requirements, occupancy requirements, means of egress, fire protection, and structure. (This criterion was eliminated by NAAB in 2004)

Legal Responsibilities: Understanding of the architect's responsibility as determined by registration law, building codes and regulations, professional service contracts, zoning and subdivision ordinances, environmental regulation, historic preservation laws and accessibility laws.

There is also a student performance criterion called "Life Safety." However NAAB evaluation of this criterion focuses primarily on design for egress. None of the 34 criteria for student performance include a specific mention of seismic design or design in response to natural hazards. The most closely related topic is the mention of lateral loads in the "Structural Systems" criterion.

School Performance on Criteria Pertinent to Seismic Design Education

As part of a self-study NAAB recorded the results of visiting team assessment of student performance criteria for the years 1999, 2000, 2002, and 2003. During these years 92 schools, 80 % of the accredited schools in the U.S., were visited. Table 2 below shows percent of schools that failed to meet student performance criteria related to seismic design.

Structural Systems	0 %
Building Systems Integration	29.3 %
Comprehensive Design	33.7 %
Site Conditions	4.3 %
Legal Responsibilities	6.5 %
Building Code Compliance (eliminated in 2004)	14.1 %

Table 2. Failure rates for student performance criteria

Although all schools reviewed during this period met the student performance criterion for structural systems, and most schools met the criteria for site conditions and legal responsibilities of architects, approximately one third did not meet the performance criteria associated with comprehensive design and nearly 30% did not meet the criteria associated with building systems integration. These results suggest that accredited architecture programs provide students with a basic understanding of subjects needed to understand seismic design concepts but may not consistently prepare students to integrate technical systems into the architectural design process effectively.

Survey of Educators

The research team designed the survey of seismic design educators to gather information about the following aspects of seismic design education:

curricular context within which seismic design subjects are taught;

degree to which various seismic design topics are addressed in the required curriculum;

presence of elective and extra-curricular opportunities for students and continuing education opportunities for design professionals;

instructional methods used to present seismic design topics;

instructors' views about the appropriateness of design-based learning methods for teaching seismic design topics;

instructors' educational backgrounds, appointment types and teaching experience;

publications and other materials used to teach seismic design.

instructors' views about adequacy of currently available teaching materials and resources needed for teaching seismic design;

relative difficulty of the seismic design curriculum and its effectiveness at preparing students for the seismic design portion of the Architectural Registration Examination (ARE);

Survey Administration

114 schools accredited by the National Architectural Accrediting Board were invited to participate in the survey by an email sent to school administrators and through an article published in *Connector,* a newsletter distributed to building technology educators in schools of architecture. Through this process the research team identified professors who oversee the structures curriculum at 82 schools and contacted these individuals by email, phone or letter.

54 professors familiar with the seismic design curriculum at 54 schools completed the survey; 50 by phone and 4 by email. Data from 11 additional schools was gathered from university catalogs and course descriptions available on the internet. Data gathered in this study represents 57% of NAAB accredited schools and the response rate for individuals contacted was 66%.

Data analysis included both quantitative sorting of responses to questions seeking specific information about curriculum and compilations of professors' comments to open ended questions related to their views and experiences.

Survey Findings

Architecture students learn most about structural aspects of seismic design and least about the seismic design of non-structural systems and components or the seismic design considerations relevant to site and regional planning. Some of the most important aspects of seismic design for architects—areas for which architects have primary responsibility are not included in required curricula. In most schools, seismic design is taught solely within structures courses.

Seismic design education focuses primarily on new buildings. Architecture students have relatively little exposure to concepts related to the evaluation of existing buildings, retrofit design or approaches to protecting historic structures.

Although computer aided design methods are used extensively in schools of architecture, fewer than half of the faculty teaching seismic design ask students to use computer models of building performance in their study of structural concepts.

The majority of faculty members teaching seismic design in schools of architecture are structural engineers. 70% of the instructors surveyed reported that their highest degree was in engineering. 30% have degrees in architecture.

Interdisciplinary seismic design learning experiences that combine architecture and engineering students are uncommon and faculty crossover tends to be one-way with engineers actively teaching engineering principles to architecture students but architects rarely teaching architectural principles to engineering students.

The majority of respondents (67%) agreed that building design projects were an appropriate vehicle for teaching seismic design, however many identified obstacles to teaching seismic design concepts in the design studio. These include the need for students to acquire more theoretical background prior to beginning design, lack of willingness of studio faculty to prioritize seismic design issues and inadequate time available to teach this subject. Faculty members who advocated for a design-based learning approach identified the studio as an effective format for learning how to place principles into practice. The centrality of the design studio and the priority students and faculty place on the studio component of their academic programs was also seen as a good way to promote interest in the subject.

The majority of respondents (57%) believe that materials currently available for teaching seismic design concepts to architecture students were inadequate. When asked about their preferences for new teaching materials the most common requests were: case study examples, design based exercises or handbooks containing rules of thumb for the design studio, graphic presentations of qualitative seismic design concepts and comprehensive chapters on seismic design in general structures textbooks developed for architecture students. Only a few faculty members indicated that their students were required to read material in textbooks on seismic design and many acknowledged that the limited time available to cover the subject made it unrealistic to expect students to engage in in-depth readings or extensive projects dedicated to seismic study.

The extent and content of seismic design education in schools of architecture is greatly influenced by the seismicity of the region where schools are located. Most schools located in high-wind regions reported that their coursework emphasized wind-resistant design with significantly less time spent on seismic design. Respondents also observed that studio design projects are sited primarily within the region where the schools are located so that students in less seismically active areas are unlikely to develop a design for an earthquake prone site. Several respondents in areas of low seismicity reported that their school's curriculum did not address seismic design specifically although general concepts related to lateral load resistance of structural systems were covered.

The educational background and professional experience of the instructor can have a significant impact on the content of the seismic design curriculum. Faculty members with particular knowledge in seismic design tended to spend more time teaching seismic design content.

The seismic design component of the structures curriculum is less challenging for students than the general structures curriculum but may be sufficient to prepare students for the architects' registration examination. Many instructors reported that they presented the seismic design portion of the structures curriculum qualitatively rather than quantitatively and that seismic study was perceived by students as being less difficult than other areas of their structures curriculum. Very few instructors reported using quantitative analysis, fieldwork and the construction of digital or physical models--teaching methods that require more hours of student engagement. However, the majority of respondents (66%) predicted that students who completed their schools' structures curriculum were likely to be able to pass the lateral loads portion of the ARE without additional preparation because of the qualitative and conceptual emphasis of the exam content.

Prior Studies of Building Technology Education in Schools of Architecture

In 2005, David J. Thaddeus at the University of North Carolina conducted a survey on technology education for the ACSA. The project was sponsored by the American Institute of Steel Construction (AISC) for the purpose of gathering information about structural steel education in schools of architecture. The survey also included other questions of interest to the ACSA. 92 faculty members teaching building technology subjects in accredited architecture programs in the US and Canada responded to questions about architectural education concerning school profiles; faculty qualifications and teaching assignments, curricular content and teaching materials. Only 8% of respondents said the subject of seismic structures was covered explicitly in the required curriculum. 6% responded that seismic design was addressed in advanced elective courses. A question concerning the need for teaching materials showed faculty requests for case studies (12%), design rules of thumb (11%) and visualizations of structural behavior (11%).

In 1994, Daniel L. Faoro at the University of North Dakota surveyed faculty members teaching structures in schools of architecture. Surveys were sent to 117 schools and 58 responses were received. Over 60% of the respondents had graduate degrees in engineering, approximately one quarter of them had professional degrees in architecture. 10% of respondents reported that seismic design was their primary research area. Many different structures textbooks were in use; no book on seismic design was mentioned as a required or recommended text for structures courses. 28% reported having elective seminars on specialized structures topics; but only one school reported offering a seminar on seismic design. 11% reported that the studio curriculum at their schools included special topics studios in structures. When asked to rank the emphasis placed in the structures curriculum of various topical areas, most respondents ranked quantitative analysis and qualitative understanding of structural behavior above design applications. The lowest ranked subject areas were history of structural development and use of computer simulations. 74% of respondents agreed that closer integration of technical courses and studio instruction is needed.

Conclusions and Recommendations

All of the sources consulted in this study: the NAAB, the surveys of seismic design educators and prior surveys on building technology education confirm that architectural educators and professional evaluators of architecture programs believe that architecture schools can do a better job at teaching students how to integrate technical aspects of building design into the architectural design process. The failure to integrate seismic study into the design curriculum in schools of architecture appears to be due to the compartmentalization of seismic design education into a relatively small portion of structures coursework usually taught by individuals who are not qualified to teach architectural design studio. Many instructors responsible for the seismic design portion of their school's curriculum expressed frustration at the lack of time available to teach the subject and the lack of follow through in design studios which are the focus of students' design experience and occupy the center of schools' curricula. Architecture students who do study seismic design tend to do so in the context of learning about structural systems—an aspect of design that is primarily the responsibility of engineers and do not study aspects of seismic design, related to non-structural systems or site planning-- areas that are primarily the responsibility of architects. Even though the professional practice of architecture increasingly crosses national and international borders, regionalism prevails at schools of architecture, particularly in the design studio component of student experience. Most students do not have the opportunity to undertake a design project that address natural hazards that are not prevalent in their region.

The need for curricular development in the area of seismic design is clear, however structural changes to curricula in schools of architecture can be difficult to implement. It is unlikely that schools will have the financial or time resources available to add or expand courses or hire specialized faculty members to teach seismic design. Given these constraints, future seismic design initiatives in architectural education should emphasize faculty development programs that engage instructors who teach design studio, professional practice and other coursework in subject areas other than structures. The primary audience for past initiatives in seismic design education aimed at architecture faculty has been structures instructors. This is partly due to self-selection—structures instructors are interested in the subject and volunteer to participate; and partly due to choices made by school administrators who tend to forward calls for seismic design opportunities to structures faculty. Although there has been some involvement of design studio instructors from California schools, past initiatives in seismic design education have not reached faculty responsible for teaching architectural design studio.

For faculty development programs to be successful they must be relevant to the teaching and research interests of the faculty and provide incentives for faculty participation. Addressing seismic design in a way that connects to subject areas across the curriculum where faculty members have teaching responsibility can increase relevance. Incentives can include stipends to assist in covering the cost of participation, but longer-term results may be achieved if professional development programs assist junior faculty in attaining promotion and tenure through competitive grant awards, peer reviewed publication, national recognition of teaching achievement and opportunities to contribute to research projects.

There is a pressing need for new and revised teaching materials that support the integration of seismic design into the broader contexts of architectural design. The available literature on seismic design is inadequate because it does not provide architecture students with information that is at an appropriately rigorous level in a visual format. Seismic design information in standard textbooks that are required for building technology courses lacks rigor. Architecture students respond best to information presented graphically because graphic inquiry is central to the architectural design process. Case studies were among the most frequently requested materials. Some respondents recommended that emphasis be placed on case studies that are recognized for overall architectural excellence. The examination of case studies and learning from precedents is a standard practice across the curriculum in architectural education. Teaching materials projects that address the insertion of seismic design information into case studies that are already used in other subject areas may be an effective strategy to raise student and faculty awareness of seismic design and provide convincing illustrations of the integration of seismic design into the broader context of architectural design.

Demonstration projects that build upon existing frameworks in architectural education can be used to promote broader understandings of the architect's role in seismic design. Data from this study confirms that every school of architecture is unique. Missions of the schools and the stakeholders schools serve shape diverse approaches to architectural education. Although all accredited schools must meet the student performance criteria established by the NAAB, coursework in schools of architecture is not standardized. Faculty members develop courses in response to the school's context and instruction is tailored to the specific needs and interests of the students and faculty members at a particular school. A review of course syllabi collected as part of the faculty survey suggest that there are few, if any, examples of best practices in seismic design education that are readily transferable to a majority of architecture programs. Most depend on the ability of uniquely qualified faculty or access to regional professional resources in areas of high seismicity. The development of demonstration projects that are carefully designed for transferability could help schools address seismic design efficiently and effectively. These projects could examine ways to access expertise from outside of an architecture department and test ways to equip faculty members who are generalists rather than specialists. Motivation of student interest in seismic design is a key factor in advancing learning outcomes. Projects that demonstrate ways to engage students studying in regions of lower levels of seismicity in designing for earthquake country would be particularly valuable.

Earthquake community partnerships with national organizations that support excellence in architectural education could promote seismic design education. The two national organizations with the most direct links to the greatest number of architecture faculty members are the ACSA and the AIA. Both organizations undertake initiatives related to architectural education through committee work conducted by members and through research and service projects related to architectural education. Partnerships between architecture faculty and student organizations with organizations that support academic and professional interests has been very effective within the green design community and there are many lessons to be learned from examining the shift that has taken place in the area of sustainable design from an activity driven by specialists to one driven by generalists. Vehicles to consider are: the committees of the AIA, especially the AIA's Knowledge Communities with interests in building performance and in education; programs administered by the ACSA, particularly the association's student competition and curriculum development projects; and the national and regional meetings of the ACSA, the AIA and the American Institute of Architecture Students (AIAS).

Finally, it is clear from an analysis of the NAAB student performance criteria that schools of architecture and accreditation review teams do not receive a specific directive to address seismic design or disaster resistant design in the curricula of architecture schools. The development of a white paper containing proposals for revisions to the NAAB student performance criteria would be an effective strategy for moving disaster resistant design onto the agenda of a national dialog that involves the ACSA, the AIA, the AIAS and the National Council of Architectural Registration Boards (NCARB), the five collaterals that comprise NAAB.

References:

American Institute of Architects. Architectural and Planning Lessons from the Great Hanshin–Awaji Earthquake, *1995*, Washington, DC. 1996.

American Institute of Architects/Association of Collegiate Schools of Architecture. Buildings at Risk, Washington, DC. 1994.

Building Seismic Safety Council, Presentations for the Architectural Community, Washington, DC. 2000.

Faoro, Daniel, L., Structures Curriculum Survey, a report of the Department of Architecture, North Dakota State University, Fargo, North Dakota, 1994.

The Earthquake Engineering Research Institute (EERI), Designing for Earthquakes: a Manual for Practicing Architects, The Federal Emergency Management Agency, Washington, DC. (publication scheduled for 2006)

The National Architectural Accrediting Board, NAAB Conditions for Accreditation for Professional Degree Programs in Architecture, 2004 edition, Washington, DC. 2006.

The National Architectural Accrediting Board, NAAB Conditions for Accreditation for Professional Degree Programs in Architecture, 2002 edition, Washington, DC., 2003.

The National Architectural Accrediting Board, NAAB Conditions for Accreditation for Professional Degree Programs in Architecture, 1998 edition, Washington, DC., 1999.

The National Architectural Accrediting Board. *NAAB* Statistics Report 2004, Washington, DC., 2005

Building Literacy: The Integration of Building Technology and Design in an Architecture Curriculum

Shahin Vassigh & Kenneth MacKay
University at Buffalo, The State University of New York

Introduction

The *Building Literacy* project is developing a learning environment that improves building technology education for the architecture curriculum through the use of advanced digital media. A prototype is in production through a seed grant from University at Buffalo. The project is developing a pedagogy and instructional tools to more effectively teach building technology concepts and assist students to better apply building technology within the design process.

Back ground

The practice of architecture requires an applied understanding of the technical issues of structures, construction and environmental systems (lighting/electrical, plumbing, heating/cooling/ventilation), and construction. Over the last decade, extensive examination of the preparation for architectural practice has revealed an almost universal agreement that the nation's universities are producing graduates who are not adequately prepared for the professional practice of architecture (Commission on Engineering and Technical Systems 51).

A number of factors contribute to this problem. First, courses in structures, building services and construction technology are rarely, if ever, fully integrated into the broader architecture program and design studios. Architectural design studios are the backbone of most architectural curricula, where students apply concepts learned

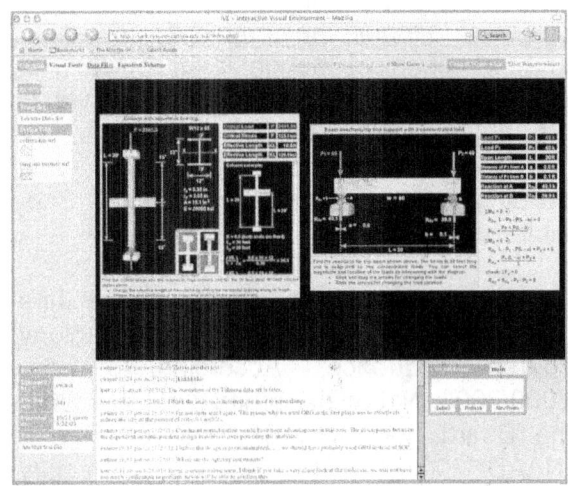

Figure1. Screen shots of the proposed project interface

elsewhere in the program. Students are poorly served when technological aspects of building design are absent in the studio environment. Thus, valuable opportunities to reinforce and apply the learned concepts of technology courses are squandered, the pivotal importance of technology as a design tool is overlooked, and the development of an integrated conceptual and technical design strategy is not encouraged.

Second, building technology curriculum, teaching methods, and instructional tools are frequently developed outside of the architectural discipline, usually borrowed from engineering programs with little modification. Instruction is highly quantitative, using abstract mathematical models and nomenclature. Since architecture students have neither the disposition nor the mathematical skills required to understand this method of teaching, they quickly become frustrated or intimidated by the building technology curriculum. The consequence is that many architecture students fail to master basic concepts as well as the more demanding aspects of innovative building technology design.

According to T.F. Peters in an ongoing experiment published in the Journal of Architectural Education, architects primarily react visually to their environment. Unfortunately, technical subjects are often taught simplistically and non-visually, reinforcing the difficulties of teaching the complexity and ambiguity of technical thought and choice (Peters 14). Unlike many engineers, architects are taught to think spatially and need to understand how architecture, structure, and building services are integrated into three-dimensional space.

Finally, many architecture programs hire adjunct faculty to teach the technology course sequence. According to the 2000/2001 National Architectural Accrediting Board, Inc. (NAAB) Statistics Report [NAAB 2002], nearly 58% of all faculty members in the 113 NAAB architecture schools in the United States are part-time. Although most adjunct faulty bring significant practice experience to the classroom, their commitment to the educational institutions is very limited, as a result course material development and use of innovative teaching methods suffer.

Although there has been significant effort among various faculty across the nation to address poor technical preparation in architecture, it still lacks concrete, proven solutions. To address this educational weakness, the National Architectural Accrediting Board (NAAB) introduced a curriculum requirement mandating the integration of design and technology in 1998. This NAAB defines comprehensive design as the ability to produce an architectural project informed by a comprehensive program, from schematic design through the detailed development of programmatic spaces, structural

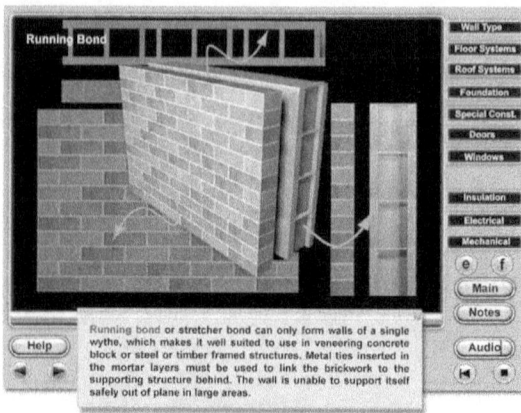

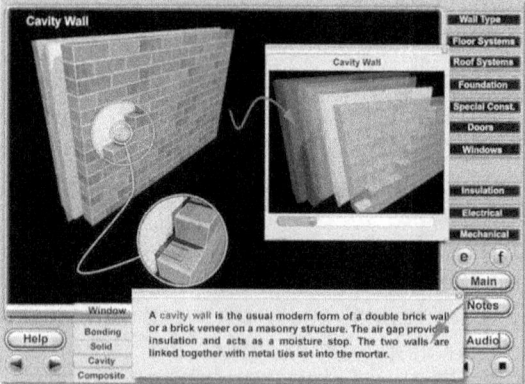

Figures 2 & 3. screen shots of the Building and Construction Module

and environmental systems, life safety provisions, and building systems integration.

Although the NAAB requirements are implemented in all accredited programs, the learning environments that facilitate the integration of design and technology are not fully developed. *Building Literacy* project aims to produce educational materials that are designed for use in comprehensive design studios.

Learning Theories & Architecture Pedagogy

In the past two decades educational theory has focused on the role of student participation in the learning process, and a paradigm shift from the teacher centered classroom or "instructional paradigm" to student centered learning environments. The basis of this theory is that the passive lecture format where the teacher lectures and the students listen is not the best setting for learning.

Carl Raschke, who has written extensively on the topic, explains the premise of active learning as the following "...it implies that learning, or teaching for that matter, is optimized whenever the inquiring mind is turned loose on a set of tasks or aims, rather than simply loading the brain with a carload of prefabricated materials" (Raschke, 28).

In a learner centered environment, the teacher bases leadership, curriculum, and instructional modes directly on the needs, interests, and goals of each learner. The learning structure is holistic, approaching the subject from broad issues to individual parts, rather than looking at components prior to the whole. This mode of teaching uses a variety of means including problem-based inquiry, collaborative group learning, individual research and individual mentorship to allow "self-directed" learning.

In architecture education, the design studio offers a suitable set up for creating a learner centered environment. As varied as they are, the design studios tend to keep students active in the learning process. The support studio activities such as field trips, site studies, and hands-on construction are all designed to engage students in producing knowledge and gathering information, rather than just receiving it. The *Building Literacy* project aims to produce educational materials that fit within this process.

Computer-Mediated Teaching

Digital tools are rapidly improving and the possibility of creating entirely virtual environments for teaching is becoming a reality. Digital modeling combined with advanced computer graphic applications constitute powerful tools to create interactive environments appropriate for self-directed learning. In addition, this new media facilitates realistic visualization which has not been possible in the past.

Since architects are trained to think spatially, and need to develop skills for understanding how building systems are integrated into three-dimensional space, instruction utilizing sophisticated visualization can be extremely productive. For example, in teaching structural analysis, virtual environments can be designed and manipulated to emphasize or de-emphasize certain structural or material properties. Material behavior that is not visible by the naked eye can be exaggerated to convey certain principles. In teaching lighting principles, providing access to a "building component database" can enable students to change various building parameters such as windows, ceilings or light shelves to visualize the effects on light distribution within a space and examine each condition in relation to heat flow and its impact on the structural components. Building mechanical systems can be examined by digitally deconstructing a building layer by layer to expose the positioning and performance of each system such as plumbing or HVAC in relation to others.

Building Literacy Project

The fundamental objectives of the Building Literacy project are: 1) produce a pedagogy that better integrates building technology with the architecture comprehensive design studio and; 2) produce an innovative learning environment which takes advantage of the interactive capabilities of state-of-the-art computing technology. The completed project will include four modules: 1) Building and Construction Technology; 2) Environmental Systems; 3) Structures and; 4) Virtual Case Studies.

The Building and Construction Technology module surveys current building materials, construction systems and processes including building envelope enclosure systems. The Environmental Systems module provides an overview of two types of environmental systems heating, ventilation and air conditioning (HVAC), and lighting, including both artificial and natural light. The Structures module[i] is a complete reference to structural concepts, analysis and design, and the Virtual Case Studies module that is a compendium of building technology principles demonstrated through the study of recently completed significant works of architecture that exemplify the most effective integration of architecture, structure, services, building envelope, and construction.

Project Prototype

The project prototype is designed to addresses the issues of architectural lighting in relation to other building systems such as structure, heating, ventilation and air conditioning. In this module students can input architectural features such as windows, ceilings and light shelves, with the capacity to be moved, and varied in size in order to visualize the resulted lighting conditions. In addition external conditions such as sky conditions and urban barriers could also be accounted for. Figure 4, shows a screen shot of the prototype that demonstrates how changing the barrier height transforms the lighting condition within the space. Figure 5 shows a heat flow diagram associated with each window opening size, thus enabling students to look at lighting quality as well as energy issues within the space and evaluate tradeoffs. The prototype is in the process of completion and will be tested and evaluated in the comprehensive studio at university at Buffalo in the near future.

Closing Remarks

Improving the teaching of technology in architecture programs is essential for the practice of architecture. The central principle underlying development of the project is to provide a learning environment designed to accommodate the thinking, strengths and interests of architecture students. Building Literacy will utilize digital graphics and animations to provide a visual and direct means of communicating concepts, grounding them in a real-world context.

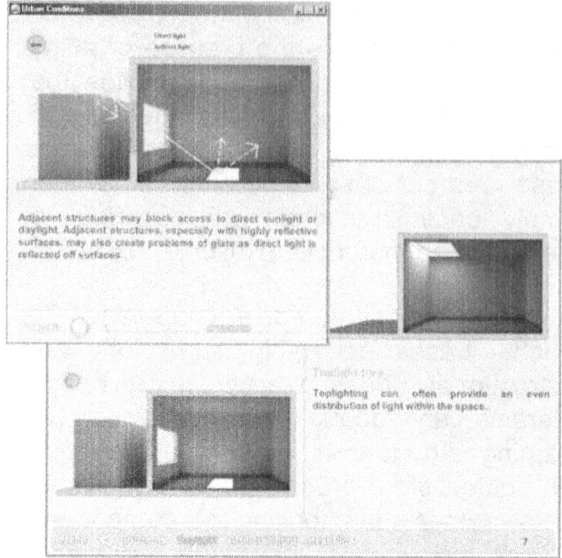

Figure 4. Screen shot of the project prototype showing the impact of urban barriers

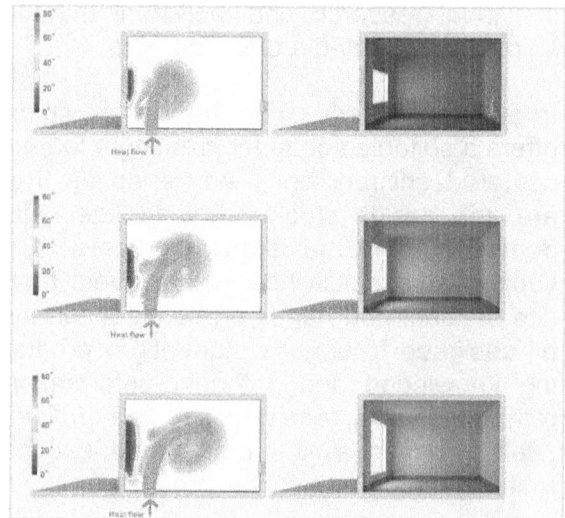

Figure 5. Screen shot showing heat flow diagrams associated with each window opening

References

Commission Engineering and Technical Systems (1995), Education of Architects and Engineers for Careers in Facility Design & Construction, The National Academies Press.

National Architectural Accrediting Board Inc., http://www.naab.org/usr_doc/2000-2001_Stat_Synposis.doc, accessed June 2003.

Peters, Tom. Report of an Ongoing Experiment: Case Studies in Construction as Examples of Theoretical Approaches to Teaching Technology in Architecture
Journal of Architectural Education *(1986)* Vol. 39, No. 4

Rachke, Carl. (2003), The digital revolution and the coming of postmodernist University, Routlege Falmer, London

Notes

[1] The structures module was completed through funding by the U.S. Department of Education, the Fund for the Improvement of Postsecondary Education (FIPSE). The project has produced a multimedia software "Interactive Structures: Visualizing Structural Behavior Using Advanced Media". The software is currently being distributed by John Wiley and Sons Inc.

Empathic Vectors

Fredrick H. Zal
Atelier Z: an.architecture and industrial design studio

This paper delineates a methodology, which endeavors to rationalize qualitative perceptions of space into quantifiable and constructive form through implementing a range of two-dimensional, three-dimensional, calculation and interactive physical modeling tools at varying scales. The presentation format of the paper cycles through a series of paired 'design intent' and 'process' elements. The purpose of this 'why' / 'how' pairing is to keep the focus of the dialogue connected with the empathic intent of design, and to not stray to less important tangents during the formulation processes. This methodology of weaving empathic vectors into and amongst the fields of force that create our inhabited world is currently in an experimental process of formation and is open to critical dialogue.

Introduction

Design gives shape to an environment where human activities are made possible, and has a responsibility to imaginatively speculate upon the ongoing drama of human existence, narrative, emotions and memories. Architectural technology must engage the mundane detail of everyday life at the same time that it addresses the sometimes vague and difficult questions of who and what we are as individuals and as communities. Architecture and Engineering is unique in this charge amongst the fine and applied arts to create spaces that engage the psyche by embodying our sociocultural conditions. We must create specific active and passive spaces that allow both individuals and groups to engage their environment.

To speculate upon methodologies, which harmonize both active and passive verb-based spatial design to evoke humanistic feeling; my students, clients and I have speculated upon the fundamental and poetic concepts of sight, sound, touch, movement, and time in symbiotic relationships. I have been using this methodology in both my academic teaching at design institutes across the Pacific Northwest, and in my professional practice as an architect, sculptor and industrial designer. By developing this process, we have developed a strong foundation to our design work, which may fluidly respond to the morphological needs of a project

whether a path of travel, moment of contemplation or a place for work. The process enables us to survey the existing conditions of a site, speculate upon appropriate inter-

Figure 1.1: Empathy [Fredrick H. Zal, 2006.]

ventions, test these ideas, reiterative the process as required, refine them based upon building requirements, and then verify their manifestation of the original empathic design intentions.

Design Intent: Empathy

Empathy can be understood to be the projection of one's emotional state upon a space or object, or the vicarious experience of a situation through identification, understanding and the internalization of such feelings about the space or object. Empathy spans the quantitative and qualitative aspects of how our world is perceived and translated by the human psyche to create degrees of passionate and visceral response. Respecting both the romantic and pragmatic implications of our design intentions, we can refine an idea to align with or challenge socio-cultural perceptions, as many of these cultural memories are tied to physiological roots. Body positioning in juxtaposition to mass and/or void evoke memories that trigger emotional reactions.

By imaging what your feelings would be in differing physical settings, you can illustrate the principles behind empathy theory. If one is alone in a vacuum, with no external stimuli, they would feel a certain amount of unrest. To then have a simple plane in space near them, a sense of relativity can anchor us to feel a bit more comfort. As this plane folds or curves to create a concavity, we begin to feel a sense of directionality. There is an area in front / behind and inside / outside as space is defined. Then, as this concavity builds up overhead to envelope us, a sense of stability is reached and we are sheltered within its form. Knowing of a place within and without, we can make choices to our placement in space dependant upon our emotional desires and needs for environmental protection.

Process: Experimenting

To initiate this process, let us begin with the most simple of our primordial tasks as designers; the act of sheltering. Key to human existence, it is considered to be one of our three minimal needs; along with eating and wearing protective clothes. It is important to understand that the root of our work is not the static noun form of 'shelter' espoused by Abbé Marc-Antoine Laugier since 1755, but rather to provide a sense of shelter, a perceptual verb / action base for spatial design.

Depending upon the local climate, the way in which this space shelters will differ. Be it an element to screen, shield, block or guard; the interior must foster a sense of protection from the external environment. It is this perceived sense, the design, definition and creation of this feeling which is important, and it does not matter what the element is built from, or which platonic geometry it echoes. This protective gesture of "sheltering" could be perceived under a single blade of grass, the wisp of a feather, the web of a spider, or the mass of an overhanging rock. In each case there is a complex balance between the dualities of solid / void, light / shadow, and inside / outside. The mind interprets the gradation between dualities to form a perception of the space, and in turn is what makes us feel 'comfortable', 'vulnerable', 'suffocated' or 'empowered'.

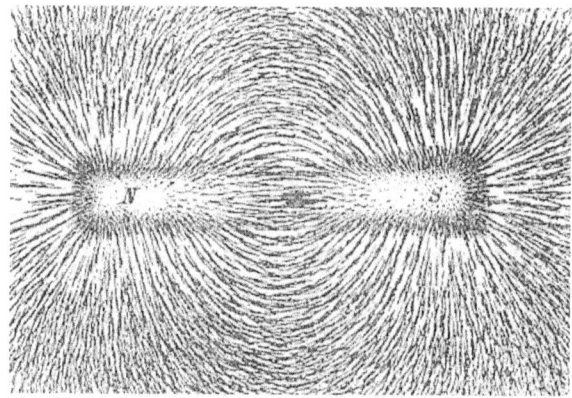

Figure 2.1: Magnetic Phenomena [Michael Faraday, 1831.]

Design Intent: Embodying

These dualities create metaphysical fields of force in our perception of space much like the positive / negative flows of geomagnetics, which is a commonly accepted example of metaphysical forces interpreted visually. These metaphysical lines of force were illustrated by Michael Faraday in 1831 by scattering metal shavings around dipole bar magnets. The metal shavings follow the lines of force and create a series of discrete arcs radiating from each end of the magnet. Faraday believed that these lines of forces fill the space in which we live, which would otherwise be a perceptual vacuum. The lines of force are not just metaphysical, but have a physical sense, just as we now understand how light can behave like a particle. But, popular science of the time rejected his qualitative metaphysics in preference for the quantifiable mathematical theorems of William Thomson and James Clerk Maxwell. Society was transforming from a legacy of spirituality to the age of rational thought, and therefore rejected all propositions that could not be labeled and quantified. In our current age of optimism, these and other principles are being rediscovered. The principles of physical / metaphysical hybrids hold true and may allow us to better understand the multiphasic world in which we live and design.

Process: Forming

Our orientation in space, and relationship to mass and void through our bodies is the key to understanding the empathic forces and forming appropriate inter-relationships between orders of scale and sequences of spaces. When the body is moving through space, standing still, gazing about, sitting down or laying at rest there are different physiological needs. Our need for a sense of comfort will unconsciously orient us toward the sun's warmth or place the protective mass of a rock behind us much like the needle on a geomancer's compass. Distances between floor and ceiling or opposing walls will augment a sense of comfort or oppression. Angling or modulation of these elements in reference to the binocular field of vision will further enhance the sense of movement. Creating spaces that are specific to body positioning or paths of movement are quintessential to this tact of design and is what makes empathic design most profound. After all, a space designed for working is certainly not the same physical and phenomenological space needed for quietly contemplating or traveling.

To converse in the complex sensory per-

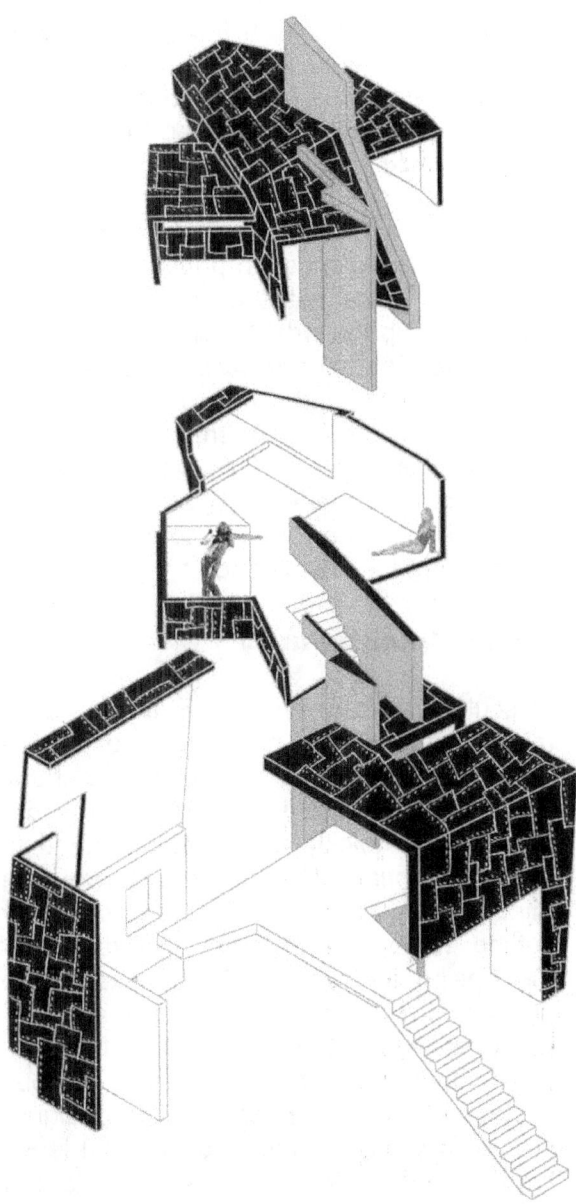

Figure 3.1: Honme Dwelling [Atelier Z, 2004.]

ceptions tied to physiology, we may engage

the field of ergonomics. Ergonomics is the study of interactions between the human body, space and objects for the optimization of comfort and performance. The Honme Dwelling [2004] was designed through a reiterative process that integrated careful ergonomic studies of the clients' body dimensions, range of motion and comfort preferences. This existing residential structure will be augmented with a number of pre-fabricated shards. The largest shard is a tower on the Northwest corner that parasitically springs up from the ground plane. Its form is derived from the integration of two separate paths of travel. One path being of speed and verticality, so that the shy partner could flee the cacophony of company when needed. The other is extroverted, and allows for a sense of grand entry, promenade and even pontification when desired. As the paths converge into one, they reach up towards the sky and sunlight. The upper chamber is divided into a place for sleep, work and study directly proportional to the bodily engagement required for the action or inaction. The ergonomics are mediated by a vertical support, protective skin and solar filters, which combine to create a sumptuous experience.

Design Intent: Purity

In sculpting the desired form, it should remain pure, and must not become over analyzed or self-referential. To ensure that this purity remains, it is important that the designer work quickly and does not need to have tangential tasks that would sway the mind's focus, such as precise measuring or cutting, while creating a physical version of the design intentions. As we move into physical space formation, there is a potential to misinterpret or loose some of the purity understood from our enteric nervous system or gut. If possible, the designer should fully engage this intuition, and leave the logical left side of the brain in a state of calm meditation. The paradox being that anything physical by definition eschews being ephemeral, let alone phenomenological. Further, as inventors of physical artifacts, we of course need to design and propose ideas that may be constructed. But for now, these aspects need to step aside, and patiently wait for an appropriate point in the evolution of the design process for their implementation.

Frank Lloyd Wright tried to clarify one of the primary lessons espoused by his mentor Louis Henry Sullivan, that "form ever follows function" as it is still misunderstood by the majority of the professional and lay public. Wright clarified that "form and function should be one, joined in a spiritual union". This speaks to an understanding of the inter-relationship between physics and metaphysics in architectural space. It is important to further understand that the "function", to which they both refer, is speaking about the passive or active verb engagement of the space, and not the banality of economics or industrial standardization. Both of these Architects worked closely with craftspeople to create unique and customized designs for their clients. Sullivan's intention was not that we should design based upon the geometry of a plywood sheet, 2x4, brick, or any symbolic nomenclature, but that we should harness the power in both the practical and phenomenological. The function of the space must remain true to the intended use of the space at all cost, even if new methods of construction or calculation must be invented to satiate these needs.

Process: Tools

Today we could design using the zero-volume of Non-uniform Rational B-splines [NuRBs] in digital space that can be fluidly

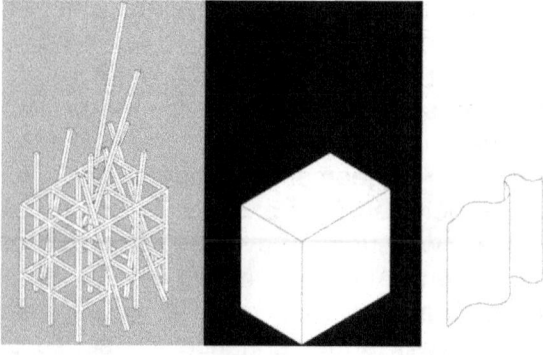

Figure 4.1: Frame / Mass / Skin Language [Fredrick H. Zal, 2002.]

sculpted and later quantified with Building Information Modeling [BIM]. But, such technology still has a few limitations due to secondary interfaces and output devises, and is not readily available to all demographics. As it is the mind and the design idea that needs to be forefront, and not the tool; I have been searching for other primitive and humble design methods that share the same potential.

Many have worked with a kit of parts arranged in Cartesian space. But their predictable nature leads to a repetition of exactly what we want to transcend. The rectilinear spaces, though seemingly provocative, were no more suited as space for working then they were for sitting, standing, sleeping, gazing, or running. The process was predestined for failure with the given materials, and needed to find another tool with greater potential. As a drop of ink on mylar can transform into anything that the author desires to render in two-dimensional media, we needed to devise an interactive three-dimensional form that would have the same degrees of freedom. Building a detailed digital topography for the Armadillo Zen House [2002], I was fascinated by how all complex forms were rationalized through a series of triangulated facets. This concept of rendering organic form started with the study of Crystallography by Giovanni Struver in 1888, and was later brought to the fine arts by Michael Heizer's "Chaotic Geometrics" in 1987. The language of organic abstraction continues today in the work of Coop Himmelb[l]au and Daniel Liebeskind, amongst others. While as the designed forms are not geometrically pure, the design premise is both descriptive and constructible from standardized sheet goods. It seems like a strong compromise between the logic needs of the left brain and the holistic narrative of the right.

To experiment with these ideas, hundreds of random-sized triangles are tossed upon the table. Then, as the designer envisions a gestural response, pieces are quickly hot-glued in place. Like a wave breaking upon the ocean, a global form is envisioned. Each particle of water is pulled towards the force of the wave's motion, but does not need to follow the geometry of the crest exactly. This form of modeling was a partial success, as the elements were able to describe the intended holistic narrative of the space without getting hung-up on precision of the parts. The designs balanced between the vague and the specific to allow the mind to interpret perceptions laden with phenomena. But, the balance was still a touch off, since these design iterations share a fractured and angular aesthetic; which was keeping with the misunderstanding of Sullivan, but not the pure purpose of design. The module of design was wrong and their geometrical bias caused them to be labeled critically.

Figure 5.1: Wall of Amir [Atelier Z, 2002.]

Figures 6.1, 6.2, + 6.3: Viellet Loft [Atelier Z, 1999.]

Alvar Aalto would emphasize that to use any constructive module larger then one millimeter will cause us to limit the potential of our design. This is because every unit of of the brain. So that every time we start designing with a quantitative system of measurement; whether it is the modular, golden section, cubit, ken 間, foot, or meter, we loose grasp of the pure intent of our design. Therefore, we needed an element, which could geometrically describe point, line, plane and curve equally well. We needed a physical version of a NuRB, something pure and without any associated measurement or physical module has an implicit geometry and prescribed set of defining conditions that engage the left side

labels. Then one day, the simplest of things occurred to me. A plane is defined by the intersection of a line with a point. Hyperbola are described through a series of lines, much like the sculptures of Naum Gabo. And a line, when viewed from its end, transforms into a point. The solution therefore was to build out of pure lines. To physically construct gestural line drawings full of raw energy!

Figure 7.1: Shade Catcher [Fredrick H. Zal, 2005.]

This breakthrough has been extremely successful! Empathic stick vectors may be easily experimented with by building from toothpicks, straws, dowels, rebar, galvanized conduit, timber bamboo, pine 2x2's, or any other linear element appropriate to the scale of the interactive modeling.

The first professional application of these empathic stick vectors was the Jean-Pierre Viellet Artist Loft [1999]. This remodel of an industrial warehouse space into a mix of artist studio, fabrication shop and personal living space needed to have a clear demarcation between the differing uses. A path of travel and light was determined, against which forces were exerted by the individual needs of the spaces. These forces instigated the creation of a translucent mediating skin of polycarbonate over metal frames that welcomed clients, showcased the artists' aesthetic and filtered light and dust respectively.

To increase my intuitive knowledge of the spaces created through this process, I have been sculpting temporary installations of empathic stick vectors at an occupiable human scale. This has allowed me to experiment with how the body may engage space and how such speculative spaces will be perceived in real life. In the Summer of 2005, the Shade Catcher was erected to challenge the preconceptions of how we interact with known spaces in our environment. It was created upon the tabula rasa of the desert and focused upon how acts of cooking, resting, gazing and storing of materials may respectfully engage each other. Each discrete space was formed upon the minimal dimensions and kinematic requirements of the bodies that would inhabit it for just over one week. Filters between public extroversion and privacy were enhanced through a series of diffusing elements and gestural forms. The space was not only greatly appreciated by hundreds, but also demonstrated that great structural strength is possible through redundancy of low-tech slender elements.

Design Intent: Translating

To engage our understanding of personal body space into the larger context of urban or rural scale, it is instructive to create drawings that interpret them into a visual language we can discuss. The process begins with looking at the external conditions of a site to be able to map, translate and derive contextual form from the physical and phenomenological nature of the context into a shared language. The site is considered a

Figures 8.1, 8.2 + 8.3: Analytiques [Leben, Elliott, and Medina, 2003.]

Figures 9.1 + 9.2: para[SITE] [Fredrick H. Zal, 2005.]

hybrid landscape, where both formal and phenomenological elements of the past, present and future are merged, putting forth a character that is simultaneously, both familiar and unfamiliar, vague and specific, qualitative and quantitative, etc. By harnessing the physical and metaphysical power of these forces we can design space that resonates with the pure conditions of the human psyche, and therefore design with a language inherent to architectural space, which will enhance and maintain the psychological and cultural nature of our society.

This is a part of the process which is much more familiar to design pedagogies, since contrary to all other arts, the field of architecture has been primarily developing from the outside inwards for the last four hundred years in both academia and the profession. These external pressures are certainly quintessential to the forces exerted upon a design, but they need to act symbiotically with those, which are coming from the internal experience and the sense of movement in, amongst and between the two.

Process: Integrating

An interwoven composite of the analytiques are then used as the impetus for the construction of a three-dimensional site investigation at varying scales of engagement with morphological layers that mediate between exterior and interior conditions. It is important to balance the two vantage points of inside – outside with outside – inside into a symbiotic whole. The figure / ground of context and design must work together harmoniously! This physical speculation is hence constructed from the pure phenomena and formalistic qualities that compose the nature of the site itself.

A method that we have been employing is the creation of plan and section psychographic analytiques. These figure-ground ink drawings represent metaphysical conditions perceived by the mind, much like the dark ferrous shavings accumulated on Faraday's clear sheets of glass. The analysis looks beyond simply the formal aspects of the site, and questions how other elements can be explored to construct and communicate the totality of our cerebral perception of the place. The series of analytical plan gestures are inspired from a multitude of potential elements, such as: public / private layers, fear / tranquility, thresholds, transformations, day / night, sound, enclosure, textures, natural / artificial light, use, solid / void, historic relativity, etc. The medium of ink drawings was selected due to the inherent freedom that ink has in application by brush, pen, hand or air. Plus, as ink has the potential of rendering very specific language, it is possible for a designer to experiment with effectively translating qualitative phenomena into quantitative terms. To communicate the third and fourth dimensional relationships within the experience of place, the gestures incorporate varying lineweights, tones and figure-ground hierarchies. Their intention is to capture emotions, history or other sensations in as pure and gestural of a state as possible. Representation and analysis of an existing context in this form develops an awareness and understanding of the various elements that define the experience of a specific environment for both the designer and inhabitants.

Design Intent: Intervening

The city or countryside has rhythms and patterns that will beg to be followed. Areas of entry, transition, occupation and egress will naturally occur. Each space's need for volume and direction will demand to be heard. Linkages between the spaces will flow dependent upon their sequence. The natural elements, topography and movement will advise orientations and weaving of layers. Just as Faraday's metal shaving moved along the magnetic lines of force, architectural elements should naturally find a place along the phenomenological fields of force.

Another installation in 2005, entitled para[SITE], was commissioned by the Urban Art Network to specifically engage how fire code defines movement from the interior space of their headquarters to the exterior City along a path of egress. Without any threat to public safety, empathic stick vectors hovered and flowed with the directional forces of tenants' movements along the path and out to the surrounding context.

The forgotten nature of their movement along this path of travel was reinterpreted to allow users to take pause and reflect upon their daily movements through time and space.

Process: Mediating

To create designs that are respectful of the pressures exerted by both interior / exterior conditions and needs or the transition from differing spaces along a path of travel, I have been working with the concept of a zone of zero-thickness that exists between the discrete conditions to form connective tissue. This connective tissue I have termed "zero-space" in my Land|Form an.Architecture dialectic.

By applying forces upon the surface of the zero-space skins and folding them into new forms that are derivative of the empathic and phenomenological needs of space; we begin to form the artifice, which we call architecture. The geomorphic terrain of the zero-space folds around the body and thicken as required to create a place to sit, lie, or stand. The body's needs carve apertures from both within and without. The body reaches out to exert pressure and creates surfaces that enhance their emotional and physical needs for inhabitation of this new space. As the body moves through this evolving space, juxtapositions of positive and negative space are instigated that provide cadence for walking and climbing. It is a holistic space still visceral and exciting; full of the kinematics of pure empathy.

As multiple Land|Form spaces evolve around multiple bodies, complex dialogues

Figure 10.1: Land|Form [Fredrick H. Zal, 2003.]

interlock these mediating zero-space skins like a complex puzzle. The idea of these mediating Land|Form skins takes the concept of poché, structural mass between spaces, activates it to a higher level by interlocking not just the physical elements in plan and section, but also their narrative. This concept can be visualized as the acrobatic tension between two capoeira dancers or viscous fluids rolling across each other, but never quite touching. The sensuous nature of this interaction will become entwined in the final composition to enhance each unique space's sensorial state upon the body, echoing throughout the spaces to foreshadow spatial sequences.

As the applied forces continue to evolve, the skin itself becomes not just a mediator of inside / outside, but actual form, distinct from its previous non-dimensional relation. The mediating zone is neither inside nor outside, neither solid nor void; it is the zero-space. The empathic and phenomenological qualities, which derived the forms, call out for specific material properties. Differentiation between opacity and translucence, the sound of hard against soft, tactility of smooth in relation to rough; these are the properties which allow us to define material constructions and detail their intersections.

The deRidder Farmhouse has allowed this methodology to engage a project that is scheduled for construction in 2006. Looking at the contextual tensions between occupant needs, zoning code, topography, vague programmatic volumes and solar orientation; a sculptural composition of vectors solidified into an appropriate form. The design was further developed through exerting the internal forces from places to sleep, converse, create and circulate within the overall form. Areas with gravitational concentration were solidified into masonry mass. Gestures towards or to protect from the sun evolved into cantilevers of zinc. Juxtapositions of internal divisions allow for a balance between open communication and the needs for private personal space in a growing family.

Design Intent: Rationalizing

Building with lines is much like watching a spider construct a web. The first lines are

Figures 11.1 + 11.2: deRidder Farmhouse [Atelier Z, 2004-2006.]

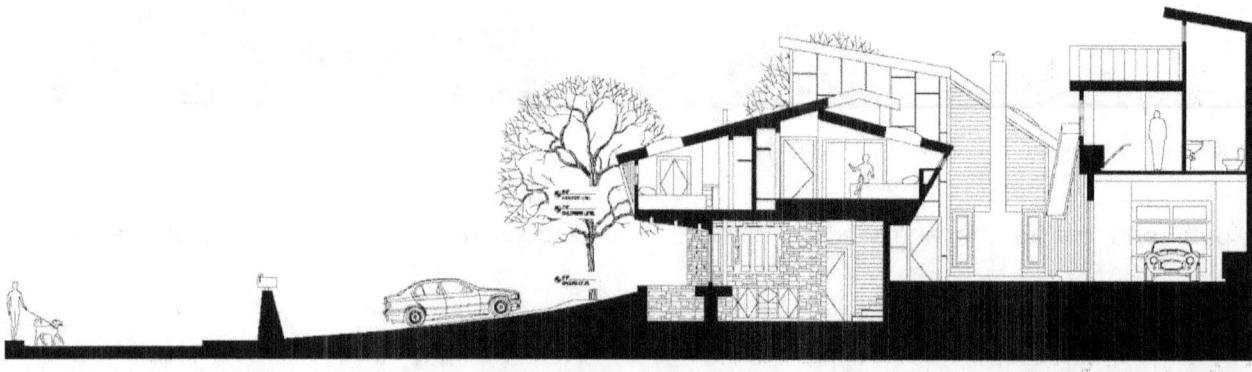

parasitic, as they latch onto the surrounding context for structural support. But, as the design grows and begins to find a balance between the interior and exterior forces shaping it, non-essential elements may be removed or clipped so that only the essential connections with the context remain. This redundancy of elements allows for no single element to bear the structural weight of the entire composition. There are no given load paths, primary members or material definitions; so the design remains pure, informal and open to interpretation. The important focus is actually not even the vectors themselves, but the nodes of intersection that like a hologram may work together to describe an infinite number of design options.

Cecil Balmond has been working with the concepts of: scatter, cloud, and zone in contrast to grid, axis, or line as a new language for design rationalization. The belief is that each design, no matter how seemingly chaotic, has its own internal rhythms and patterns, much like the politics of a complex urban culture. Working with this intrinsic pattern allows the design intentions to flourish into a rationalized beauty that is pure. This is the new form of architecture that le-Corbusier had called for with "Vers une architecture" in 1923. Structure, skin and space integrated to form a beautiful and logical whole.

Process: Constructing

This informal language can be seen in many contemporary projects. Of particular note, and illustrative of this informal structural language are Villa dall'Ava [1991] by Rem Koolhaas in St Cloud, Paris, France and the Olympic Archery Training Range [1990] by Enric Miralles and Carme Pinós in Barce-

Figure 12.1: Villa dall'Ava [Office of Metropolitan Architecture, Rem Koolhaas, 1991.]

lona, Spain. Both projects endeavor to create a sense of lightness and hovering by having a redundancy of slender members that support their physical and psychological loads in tandem. No single member is predominant and could easily be removed or translated through space to have a different orientation for a greater perceptual impact. The mind is forced to accept the composition of space in its totality, and cannot parse it down into predetermined static systems.

The Villa dall'Ava makes use of a series of slender columns to hold-up the second apartment on the southwest corner of its composition. Making use of perspectival

Figure 12.2: Olympic Archery Training Range [Enric Miralles + Carme Pinós, 1990.]

parallax, Rem Koolhaas purposely obscured the ability for the mind to define the structural system in 'civilized' terms. Albeit a simple trick of Gestalt psychology that abuses the left-brain's logic center, this allows the mind to enjoy the composition in a more organic manner, like a grove of bamboo holding up a massive canopy of leaves or as the legs of a giraffe that lend to its grace. By freeing the effects of structural preconception to create a seeming perception of anti-gravity, the project effectively employs the concepts within leCorbusier's "five points".

The Olympic Archery Training Range designed for the Barcelona Olympics employ a similar strategy. The inspiration for the design was the trajectories created by the raw force of an archer's arrows interacting with the turbulent flow of air through space. The roof, a series of opposing planes, creates a sense of fluid undulation skewered by apertures of light to the locker rooms below. Then an assortment of simple shafts are cast into the sand as dropped from an archer's sheath, and gracefully support the flow of the roof above. Again it is this seemingly 'random' nature of the supportive columns that obfuscate their structural nature and allow the roof above to maintain its sense of airborne freedom. But in reality, it is precisely the seemingly random angles of the columns that allows for a most efficient transfer of loads in a relatively perpendicular direction from the ever-changing roof geometry down to the ground.

In both examples, the array of elements conjures empathic fields of force vectors that we can feel with our mind and body. Through photographic representation, the array can be input as vectors along two-force elements into a digital model, or analyzed using graphic statics and free-body diagrams. These methods of analysis take a form, which is pure in its design intent, determines the direction and quantity of load paths so that one can assign structural properties to them. Tensile elements can be replaced with cables to create tensegral clouds, planar nodes can be consolidated into shear panel skins, and consolidated compressive elements can be molded to create a minimal section modulus or allow for the transfer of moment.

Validating and Reiteration

Before 'finalizing' the design, one should review the original design requirements of site, program, emotions, budget, etc. Are the physical, psychological and capital requirements met? May the design solution have a refined palette of systems that eloquently address the problem efficiently and effectively? The term 'efficiency' is complex and should not be defined only by the economic use of members or sheets of required calculation, but by ease of meeting design intentions. If done intelligently, this not only efficiently responds to the flow of forces through it, but also communicates an intuitive structural language of materials and space that has life-cycle benefits.

Through reiteration of the process, one may ensure that all of the qualitative stimuli now embodied in a quantifiable form are still adhering to the originally intended design sensations. It can be painful to scrap a design, start over, or feel like one is going 'backwards' in the process. But, to repeat the process after working through it one or more times, the designer has a greater understanding of the pathways. They can avoid pitfalls, preconceptions, or other earlier errors to create something stronger. As no problem has an unique solution, reiteration will remove the egotistical fetishization of a singular solution, style or artifact and place it amongst the multitude of possibilities from a diversity of cultural and sociological perspectives.

Conclusion

This drawing, modeling and calculation process has infused my academic and professional career with a raw energy that I highly recommend. Collaborations with students, performance artists, and consulting engineers remain fluid while simultaneously focused upon both 'reality' and the true empathic intent of professional design work.

I look forward to continuing a dialogue about this process as you experiment with ways to apply it within your established or evolving curricula and professional practices.

Fredrick H. Zal, NCARB, is a sculptor and the principal architect of Atelier Z: an.architecture and industrial design studio, which advocates dialogue in the fine + applied arts. By striking a balance between praxis and theoros, Atelier Z passionately engages works with a focus upon theoretical morphology, materiality and empathy theory. As a professor of design and active practitioner, Fredrick's work is published, exhibited and lectured upon nationally.
Website: http://www.fhzal.com   E-mail: fzal@fhzal.com   Phone: 503.236.4855

Figures:

Figure 1.1: Empathy [Fredrick H. Zal, 2006.] These images show a base series of spatial conditions: void, plane, concavity, and enclosure. Imagine yourself there and vicariously experience what it would feel like in each of these spaces.

Figure 2.1: Magnetic Phenomena [Michael Faraday, 1831.] Reference: Friedel, Robert D. "Lines and Waves Exhibition", Institute of Electrical and Electronics Engineers History Center, 1981.

Figure 3.1: Honme Dwelling [Atelier Z, 2004.] The unfolding form of this dwelling is based upon a series of incredible discussions between the client and architect about space, form, sociology, aesthetics, the delicate warm light found in the film "La Double Vie de Véronique" by Krzysztof Kieslowski, the morphological systems of 1850's crystallography by Struver, concepts of materiality as it pertains to both contemporary Japanese minimalism and also Ned Ludd's theories of a luddite society experienced in the films "Brazil", "12 Monkeys", "City of Lost Children", and "Matrix". The pre-fabricated shards are being constructed of Structural Insulated Panels [SIPs] and clad with riveted zinc by Blazer Industries inc.

Figure 4.1: Frame / Mass / Skin Language [Fredrick H. Zal, 2002.] The phonetics here are based upon the conceptual design work of Bernard Tschumi's "Decomposition of Cube" and "Recombination". His studies led to a matrix of the potential permutations of recombined platonic forms. These additive forms subsequently defined the constructed designs for the follies at the Parc de la Villette. The lineage of this work can also be seen in the Stockholm Exhibition [1930]. Original Publication: Zal, Fredrick H., ACSA West Proceedings: Imagined Realms | Remaking Worlds "Gestalt of deFamiliarized Urbanism", November 2002, p.257-262.

Figure 5.1: Wall of Amir [Atelier Z, 2002.] This remodel of a historic school house room at Portland State University sprang from the architectural theory taught by the faculty. It is a physical manifestation of the phenomenological rhetoric that guides the students' pedagogy. The single office was divided into two. The first being a solid mass of fractured darkness, and the other being transcendental and composed by a simple plane of light and text. The shared entry area allows for a student conference table with a light fixture cantilevering out as a fractured shard from the mass beyond.

Figures 6.1, 6.2, + 6.3: Viellet Loft [Atelier Z, 1999.] This S.E. Portland loft is designed to be both the home for two independent designers and as their office / shop. The WWII era poured-in-place concrete building currently houses an automotive racing engine shop, and overlooks the Brooklyn rail yards. The designed fractured translucent wall filters light from the uninsulated south-facing windows as it transitioned into the wood / metal shop. The entry space dramatically cascade into their office / living space. The design not only creates an incredible space for living, it also creates a venue to exhibit their skilled craftmenship and design. The images depicted show the evolution from an original gestural plan sketch, through empathic stick forming, to the rationalization into a framework of metal studs clad in 3/8-inch translucent double-wall Polygal polycarbonate sheet.

Figures 7.1: Shade Catcher [Fredrick H. Zal, 2005.] With temperatures pushing over 120ºF on the desert floor of Gerlach, Nevada, survival requires a place to catch shade and rest. Weaving around a series of static elements, this sculptural space was created using fifty bamboo stalks. To create the strength needed to withstand gusting winds and dust storms, they were lashed together and triangulated, with an element of redundancy. This redundancy not only provided stiffness, but it also allows for very small members to support great weight in a mysterious manner that the mind cannot easily track. At the end of the 8-day event, all elements were burnt; so as to allow the entropic nature of creation to come full-circle. The image shows the embodied construction of empathic forces for cooking, eating, storing, resting and gazing.

Figures 8.1, 8.2 + 8.3: Analytiques [Erin Leben, Allison Elliott and Carlos Medina, Portland State University, Architecture Design Studio 281: "Design Fundamentals Studio II, Place Response", 2003.] These student analytiques of 'isolation', 'fear', 'order', etc. became the impetus for construction of expressive three-dimensional designs inspired by the formal characteristics and less tangible phenomena experienced in an actual cultural context.

Figures 9.1 + 9.2: para[SITE] [Fredrick H. Zal, 2005.] This spatial installation is based upon a long and complex history of sculptural and architectural parasitic / symbiotic works that respond specifically to their environment. The intention of this piece was to work within the building and fire-safety allowance for contemporary architectural space, while allowing for a freedom of design often ameliorated by lethargic and standardized practices. By enveloping the spaces of this egress staircase and ADA ramp, while still allowing for legal clearance requirements, the occupants of this building were able to perceive a space, which they pass through daily, in a new manner. Many tenants appreciated the intervention, as it gave them pause to reflect upon the inherent possibilities in the everyday object and/or spaces around us. Pictured is local architect Richard Potestio after leaving a long day at the office. The installation was commissioned by Peyto Yellin and Jennifer Kapnek of the Urban Art Network and existing only momentarily; for three hours. The work was 43-feet by 22-feet by 16-feet tall and composed of 100 sticks of 3/4-inch galvanized EMT conduit, typically used by electrical contractors. All of my empathic vector installation sculptures have always been 'recycled' to the full physical and theoretical extent of entropic design. I have been fascinated for years by found objects, detritus, spent elements of our post-industrial culture; as these objects have an embodied narrative in them. They were nibbled upon, hewn, welded, pounded, ridden, tossed about, or just left idle in a corner for decades. They have stories within their molecular structure that they long to share. Embodied wisdom in the potent material enters the sculptural dialogue to inform its future artistic incarnation. Then, going beyond the "post consumer waste" in dumpsters, salvage yards and rail lines, these sculptures embody the concept of "pre-consumer waste-not". This is when prior to an element being used in it's pre-conceived consumerist manner; be it clothes hanger rod, wood 2x2, electrical conduit, etc; it is given a subterfuge life. They are like a Goth diva having to pull herself into work at the crack of dawn to sit in a banal cubicle, but she can smile wryly knowing of the vampish secrets still whispering in her mind from the night prior.

Figure 10.1: Land|Form [Fredrick H. Zal, 2003.] Imagine a line that mediates between the Earth and the Sky. As this is a dimensional situation, the line transforms into a zero-plane, a skin of no thickness that is draped between the undulations of the Earth/Sky, stretching out beyond the quantification of our perceived horizon. It is quintessential to my philosophy that anything we create is merely a modification of this relationship, and not a purely creative act; similar to the geotectonic forces that from time to time shall swell up and spew stone up towards the heavens; leaving chasms into its belly. We do not create space, we only transform relationships between matter and air for the purposes of our emotive intents. Original Publication: Zal, Fredrick H., <u>NCBD 19 Proceedings</u>: "Land|Form an.Architecture", April 2003.

Figures 11.1 + 11.2: deRidder Farmhouse [Atelier Z, 2004-2006.] The inspiration for this beautiful home comes from the original Peterkort barn, which is now the clients' home. The Peterkort farm has been divided up over the last few decades to become what is now known as Beaverton, Oregon. Over the years, the building has had a number of lives: barn, school house, labrador kennels, etc. With each segment of time, the structure has grown, shrunk, been sliced, adapted and tweaked to the specific needs of the owners. The deRidders have paid close attention to this historic narrative implicit to the Cedar Mills area, and are looking forward to finely crafting their new home with traditional labor and materials.

Figure 12.1: Villa dall'Ava [Office for Metropolitan Architecture, Rem Koolhaas, 1991.] Photography: Hans Werlemann.

Figure 12.2: Olympic Archery Training Range [Enric Miralles + Carme Pinós, 1990.]

Further Exploration:

Aalto, Alvar. <u>RIBA Annual Discourse</u>: "The Architects Struggle", vol.64, May 1957.
Balmond, Cecil. "Informal". Prestel Publishing, 2002.
Berliner, Anna. "Lectures on Visual Psychology", The Professional Press, 1948.
Friedel, Robert D. "Lines and Waves Exhibition", Institute of Electrical and Electronics Engineers, 1981.
Jarzombek, Mark. "De-Scribing the Language of Looking: Wölflin and the History of Aesthetic Experientialism", <u>Assemblage</u>. #23, v.28, 1994.
Koolhaas, Rem. "S,M,L, XL: Villa dall'Ava, St Cloud, Paris, France". Monacelli Press, 1995. p.132-193.
Mallgrave, Harry Francis + Ikonomou, Eleftherios. "Empathy, Form, and Space: Problems in German Aesthetics, 1873-1893". University of Chicago Press, 1994.
Mark, Robert. "Architectural Technology up to the Scientific Revolution", MIT Press, 1993.
Merleau-Ponty, Maurice. "Phenomenology of Perception". Routledge, 2002.
Miralles, Enric + Pinós, Carme. "The Architecture of Enric Miralles and Carme Pinós". Lumen Books, 1990. p.43-47.
Prix, Wolf + Swiczinsky, Helmut. "The Power of the City". Verlag Press, 1988.
Shelden, Dennis R. "Digital Surface Representation and the Constructibility of Gehry's Architecture", MIT, 2002.
Snelson, Kenneth. "Sculpture". Hirshhorn Museum, Smithsonian Institution, 1982.
Struver, Giovanni (1842-1915), mineralogist, University of Rome, Italy.
Williams, Blake. "Armadillo Zen", <u>Seattle Case Study Homes: a plan book of modern home designs</u>. 2002, p.10.
Woods, Lebbeus. "System Wien". Hatje Cantz Publishers, 2006.
Zalewski, Waclaw + Allen, Edward. "Shaping Structures : Statics". Wiley, 1997.

www.ingramcontent.com/pod-product-compliance
Lightning Source LLC
Chambersburg PA
CBHW060308240426

43661CB00059B/2699